March 14–18, 2015
Vancouver, BC, Canada

Association for Computing Machinery

Advancing Computing as a Science & Profession

L@S 2015

The Second ACM Conference on Learning @ Scale

Sponsored by:

ACM

Supported by:

Google, Pearson, edX, Coursera, and gradescope

Association for
Computing Machinery

Advancing Computing as a Science & Profession

The Association for Computing Machinery
2 Penn Plaza, Suite 701
New York, New York 10121-0701

Notice to Past Authors of ACM-Published Articles
ACM intends to create a complete electronic archive of all articles and/or other material previously published by ACM. If you have written a work that has been previously published by ACM in any journal or conference proceedings prior to 1978, or any SIG Newsletter at any time, and you do NOT want this work to appear in the ACM Digital Library, please inform permissions@acm.org, stating the title of the work, the author(s), and where and when published.

ISBN: 978-1-4503-3411-2 (Digital)

ISBN: 978-1-4503-3513-3 (Print)

Additional copies may be ordered prepaid from:

ACM Order Department
PO Box 30777
New York, NY 10087-0777, USA

Phone: 1-800-342-6626 (USA and Canada)
+1-212-626-0500 (Global)
Fax: +1-212-944-1318
E-mail: acmhelp@acm.org
Hours of Operation: 8:30 am – 4:30 pm ET

Printed in the USA

Learning at Scale 2015: Chairs' Welcome

It is our great pleasure to welcome you to ACM conference *Learning at Scale 2015*. In this, the second year of the conference, we have seen a significant growth in the number of submissions to the conference and an overall improvement in the quality of the contributions. This year's conference continues the tradition of being the premier forum for presentation of research results and inside stories about what makes online educational systems operate at scale.

The call for papers attracted submissions from all over the world, covering a broad range of topics from the theoretical to the pragmatic.

The program committee reviewed and accepted the following:

Venue or Track	*Reviewed*	*Accepted*	
Full Technical Papers	90	23	25%
Short Technical Papers	12	5	41%
Work in Progress Papers	54	47	80%

Since the conference is still in its formative years, we accepted a large fraction of all the Works in Progress because we found the experience of reading through them to be so valuable. We are still a nascent field, and learning about the very latest work reflects the rapidly changing nature of what we know to be true.

We encourage attendees to attend both keynotes. These valuable and insightful talks can and will guide us to a better understanding of the future of our field:

- *Achieving 96% mastery at national scale through inspired learning and generative adaptivity,* Zoran Popovic (University of Washington)
- *Machine Learning for Learning at Scale,* Peter Norvig (Google)

Putting together *Learning at Scale 2015* was truly a team effort. We first thank the authors for providing the content of the program, and we are grateful to the program committee and all the reviewers who worked very hard assessing the papers and providing feedback for authors. We also want to thank the ACM for their fantastic support. A special thank you goes to our generous corporate supporters: Google, edX, Coursera, and Pearson.

We hope that you will find this program interesting and thought-provoking. We trust that the conference will provide you with many valuable opportunities to share ideas with other researchers and practitioners from institutions around the world.

Gregor Kiczales
General Chair
University of British Columbia, Vancouver, Canada

Daniel M. Russell
Program Co-Chair
Google
Mountain View, CA, USA

Beverly Woolf
Program Co-Chair
University of Massachusetts
Amherst, MA, USA

Table of Contents

Session 4: Learning

Session 5: Grading

Session 6: Design

Closing Keynote

Works in Progress (Posters)

Learning at Scale 2015 Conference Organization

General Chair: Gregor Kiczales *(University of British Columbia)*

Program Chairs: Daniel M Russell *(Google)*
Beverly Woolf *(University of Massachusets, Amherst)*

Proceedings Chair: Daniel M Russell *(Google)*

Communications Chair: Ido Roll *(University of British Columbia)*

Treasurer & Registration Chair: Yan Timanovsky *(ACM Staff Liaison)*

Steering Committee Chair: Ravi Sandhu *(George Mason Institute and NSD Security)*

Steering Committee: Ryan Baker *(Teachers' College, Columbia University)*
Armando Fox *(University of California, Berkeley)*
Marti Hearst *(University of California, Berkeley)*
Scott Klemmer *(University of California, San Diego)*
Ken Koedinger *(Carnegie Mellon University)*
John Mitchell *(Stanford University)*
Carolyn Penstein Rosé *(Carnegie Mellon University)*
Jeremy Roschelle *(SRI)*
Mehran Sahami *(Stanford University/ex officio ACM Ed Board)*
Karen Swan *(University of Illinois, Springfield)*
Yan Timanovsky *(ACM Staff Liaison)*

Program Committee: Alan Lesgold *(University of Pittsburgh)*
Andrew Bernat *(Computing Research Association)*
Ben Bederson *(University of Maryland)*
Björn Hartmann *(University of California, Berkeley)*
Candace Thille *(Stanford University)*
Carolyn Rosé *(Carnegie Mellon University)*
Chinmay Kulkarni *(Stanford University)*
Cindy Hmelo-Silver *(Indiana University)*
Colleen Lewis *(Harvey Mudd College)*
Dan Garcia *(University of California, Berkeley)*
Dave Pritchard *(Massachusetts Institute of Technology)*
David Karger *(Massachusetts Institute of Technology)*

Program Committee (continued):

Doug Fisher *(Vanderbilt)*
Emma Brunskill *(Carnegie Mellon University)*
Gautam Biswas *(Vanderbilt)*
Irene Greif *(IBM)*
Janet Kolodner *(Regents' Professor Emerita, Georgia Institute of Technology)*
Jeremy Roschelle *(SRI)*
John Mitchell *(Stanford University)*
Joseph Beck *(Worcester Polytechnic Institute)*
Juho Kim *(Massachusetts Institute of Technology)*
Karen Brennan *(Harvard)*
Ken Koedinger *(Carnegie Mellon University)*
Lee Giles *(Penn State)*
Marie Bienkowski *(SRI)*
Marti Hearst *(University of California, Berkeley)*
Mehran Sahami *(Stanford University)*
Philip Guo *(University of Rochester)*
Rene Kizilcec *(Stanford University)*
Ryan Baker *(Teachers' College, Columbia University)*
Scott Klemmer *(University of California, San Diego)*
Sidney D'Mello *(Notre Dame)*
Sumit Basu *(Microsoft Research)*
Tiffany Barnes *(North Carolina State University)*
Vincent Aleven *(Carnegie Mellon University)*

Learning at Scale 2015: Sponsor & Supporters

Sponsor: acm Association for Computing Machinery

Platinum Supporter: Google

Gold Supporter: PEARSON

Bronze Supporters: edX

coursera education for everyone

gradescope

Achieving 96% Mastery at National Scale through Inspired Learning and Generative Adaptivity

Zoran Popovic
Professor and Director the Center for Game Science, University of Washington
Founder and Chief Scientist, Enlearn

Abstract: Most of the current research on improving learning outcomes focuses on a small subset of variables of an immensely multi-dimensional space of the learning ecosystem. Most digital learning tools primarily focus on individual students, other research focuses only on teacher professional development, or only on curriculum improvement. In this talk I will describe our efforts on how to discover optimal parameters of the entire ecosystem that considers student factors (engagement and mastery), classroom factors (blended learning variations and group learning variations), curriculum factors (multidimensional variation of existing curricula), and teacher factors (in-class tools that mitigate weaknesses, and promote teacher development). I will describe our work on algorithms to discover optimal learning pathways in this high-dimensional space. I will conclude with the outcomes of deploying a portion of our platform on algebra challenges conducted on two US states and the country of Norway.

Bio: Zoran Popovic is a Director of Center for Game Science at University of Washington and founder of Enlearn. Trained as a computer scientist his research focus is on creating interactive engaging environments for learning and scientific discovery. His laboratory created Foldit, a biochemistry game that produced three Nature publications in just two years, an award-winning math learning games played by over five million learners worldwide. He is currently focusing on engaging methods that can rapidly develop experts in arbitrary domains with particular focus on revolutionizing K-12 math education.

His Algebra Challenges conducted in Washington, Minnesota, and Norway, have shown that 96% of children even in elementary school can learn key algebra concepts in 1.5 hours. He has recently founded Enlearn to apply his work on generative adaptation to any curricula towards the goal of achieving full mastery by 95% of students. His contributions to the field of interactive computer graphics have been recognized by a number of awards including the NSF CAREER Award, Alfred P. Sloan Fellowship and ACM SIGGRAPH Significant New Researcher Award.

L@S 2015, March 14–18, 2015, Vancouver, BC, Canada.
ACM 978-1-4503-3411-2/15/03
http://dx.doi.org/10.1145/2724660.2724684

Effective Sampling for Large-Scale Automated Writing Evaluation Systems

Nicholas Dronen
University of Colorado & Pearson
Boulder, CO, USA 80301
dronen@colorado.edu

Peter W. Foltz
Pearson & University of Colorado
Boulder, CO, USA 80301
peter.foltz@pearson.com

Kyle Habermehl
Pearson
Boulder, CO, USA 80301
kyle.habermehl@pearson.com

ABSTRACT
Automated writing evaluation (AWE) has been shown to be an effective mechanism for quickly providing feedback to students. It has already seen wide adoption in enterprise-scale applications and is starting to be adopted in large-scale contexts. Training an AWE model has historically required a single batch of several hundred writing examples and human scores for each of them. This requirement limits large-scale adoption of AWE since human-scoring essays is costly. Here we evaluate algorithms for ensuring that AWE models are consistently trained using the most informative essays. Our results show how to minimize training set sizes while maximizing predictive performance, thereby reducing cost without unduly sacrificing accuracy. We conclude with a discussion of how to integrate this approach into large-scale AWE systems.

ACM Classification Keywords
I.2.7. Natural Language Processing: Text analysis; G.3. Probability and Statistics: Multivariate statistics

INTRODUCTION
Automated writing evalution (AWE) is the use of natural language processing and statistical modeling to score samples of writing. The first model for automatically scoring essays was created on punch cards in the 1960s [17]. At present there are several commercial automated essay scoring operations [19, 15, 1]. They are often used as the sole scorer in formative applications [25, 7] and increasingly in summative assessments (e.g. Pearson Test of English Academic). Even wider adoption of automated writing evaluation appears to be underway. Recently, for example, the Hewlett Foundation sponsored open competitions for essay-length and short answer AWE modeling on Kaggle.com to help foster greater adoption of the technology [12, 13]. The edX platform for massive open online classes (MOOCs) contains a system for automated writing evaluation [6, 3, 5].

L@S 2015, March 14 - 18, 2015, Vancouver, BC

ACM 978-1-4503-3411-2/15/03$15.00
http://dx.doi.org/10.1145/2724660.2724661

Typically, an AWE model is trained using supervised learning and performs best when it has been trained for a specific prompt and scoring trait [9]. Training an AWE model starts with a batch of essays and one or more human scores for each essay. In the usual training procedure, the essays are preprocessed by a natural language processing pipeline, which results in a feature vector for each essay. The feature vectors and scores are then input to a learning algorithm that learns a model mapping feature vectors to scores. When the feature vector of a previously unseen essay is presented to the model, it can immediately provide a score.

Historically, the process of training an AWE model has required at least several hundred human-scored essays. The purpose of this requirement is twofold: to reduce sampling noise in the training set and to ensure that the model performs about as well as one trained with many more essays. In an online setting, however, a system for collecting essays and human scores can cause an AWE model to be trained whenever a new human score is entered into the system. For example, the edX AWE system allows models to be trained with as few as ten essays [4]. If the training set is sampled randomly, then training with so few essays will – with high probability – yield an AWE model that performs poorly.

The challenge of adopting AWE in large-scale contexts is that the best way to use the technology – with a customized scoring model for each prompt – is also quite expensive. In an enterprise environment, the human cost of scoring ranges from $3-6 USD per essay. Assuming 500 essays for a training set and 250 for test, the human cost per prompt is $2250-4500. In this paper we show how to overcome this key barrier to the widespread adoption of AWE in large-scale contexts. The method we use minimizes the number of essays that need to be scored and maximizes the information that each training example provides. This can also enable an online data collection system to intelligently choose which essays to be scored by humans. We conclude by discussing how to effectively integrate this method into AWE systems.

There are two bodies of literature about effective methods for choosing samples for training a supervised model. The older is *optimal experimental design* [8], a subfield of statistics that originated with the work of Kirstine Smith in the early 20th century [21]. The paradigmatic supervised learning algorithm for this literature is linear regression. In machine learning, *active learning* occupies much the same space as optimal design, although the literature tends to focus more on classification than regression [20].

The usual scenario for optimal experimental design is when samples are expensive to obtain, as with clinical trials or gathering samples during field studies in remote areas. An optimal design algorithm chooses samples from a pre-specified set of feature vectors in such a way as to minimize the variance in the supervised model. In active learning the assumption is usually that one begins with a set of *unlabeled* samples and wishes to obtain labels for them. For example, unlabeled samples can be HTML documents obtained by crawling the web and the desired labels can be the topics of the documents. Papers about regression in the active learning literature often cite the optimal design work of Valerii Fedorov (e.g. [16, 23, 2]).

When using an algorithm to choose samples prior to training a supervised learning algorithm, obtaining good results requires that the assumptions of the sampling algorithm match the assumptions of the learning algorithm. Here we use parametric linear regression and we employ an algorithm from the optimal experimental design literature [8] that is derived from the same foundations as linear regression.

Since we start with essays and ask which ones should be graded, ours is really the classic active learning scenario. We, however, stick mostly to the terminology from the optimal design literature throughout this paper.

DATA SETS

An AWE data set consists of some number of written responses and a set of scores for each response. In our experiments we use the industry track data from the Automated Student Assessment Prize (ASAP) Automated Essay Scoring (AES) competition sponsored by the Hewlett Foundation held in 2012 [12]. It contains training and test sets numbered 1 through 8. Key parts of the rubric of each set are summarized in Table 1.

In sets 1 and 2, a student is asked to write persuasively. Essay set 1 has the student take a position on the effects of computers on society and write a letter to the editor of a newspaper arguing for this position. Sets 3-6 are *response to source* prompts; they have the student read and analyze some source text and provide evidence from the text to support their analysis. The source of essay set 5 is a passage about the son of Cuban immigrants growing up in New Jersey. The student must describe the mood of the text. The narrative task tends to be more open ended. In essay set 8, the task is to write about an experience in which laughter was an important element.

The target variable of the data sets is the score or sum of scores that an essay was given by one or more human raters. The range of the target variable for each essay set is shown in Table 1. Essay set 2 has two target variables, which we identify as $2a$ and $2b$ depending on which target variable the model was trained to predict. For all essay sets the target variable includes all integers between the minimum and maximum scores. The target variable for essay set 7, for example, is the integers 2, 3, ..., 30.

The size of the training and test sets are shown in Table 2. While relatively small, these test sets are nonetheless sufficient to ensure that the performance we report in the results section approaches the performance one might expect on a much larger sample. The same table shows the rounded average number of words in each essay set. A peculiarity of these sets is that in some cases the average length is quite low. This is true for all of the response-to-source sets, suggesting that students write less when performing a more focused task.

Before using an algorithm to select which essays raters should score, we compute the feature vector for each essay. In our experiments we use a subset of twenty-eight features – related to mechanics, grammar, lexical sophistication, and style – from the Intelligent Essay Assessor [9].

Table 1: ASAP AES rubric

Set	Task	Grade	Range
1	Persuasive	8	2-12
2a	Persuasive	10	1-6
2b	Persuasive	10	1-4
3	Source	10	0-3
4	Source	10	0-3
5	Source	8	0-4
6	Source	10	0-4
7	Narrative	7	2-30
8	Narrative	10	0-60

Table 2: ASAP AES data summary

Set	Train n	Test n	Avg. Words
1	1785	589	372
2a	1799	600	386
2b	1799	600	386
3	1699	568	110
4	1763	586	96
5	1805	601	124
6	1800	600	154
7	1469	495	174
8	917	304	636

REGRESSION MODELING

The target variable for automated essay scoring tasks is the student's score on an essay. It is typically an integer in a relatively narrow range determined by the scoring rubric. The ordering inherent in the target variable implies that essay scoring data are best modeled using a regression algorithm. Here we describe the approach we take to regression modeling in our experiments.

When the length of feature vectors in a design matrix ξ exceeds the number of feature vectors, the ordinary least squares solution is ill-posed. In this paper we allow m, the number of feature vectors to be as small as ten. Since p, the number of features, is twenty-eight, the ordinary least squares solution would be suboptimal for some of the models we train. Thus we use regularized regression instead of ordinary least squares. The regularized linear regression solution for β is the solution for ordinary least squares augmented with a penalty function $J(\beta;\lambda)$,

$$\hat{\beta}(\lambda) = \arg\min_{\beta} [RSS(\beta) + J(\beta;\lambda)],$$

where λ is the regularization coefficient and is usually selected empirically (e.g. by cross validation).

We use ridge regression [10], which imposes a penalty on the L_2 norm of β, as in:

$$J(\beta;\lambda) = \lambda \sum_i \beta_i^2$$

This penalty constrains the coefficients such that irrelevant ones shrink towards zero without being eliminated from the model altogether.

Since the predictions of a linear model trained in such a way are real values, not integers, the predictions have to be mapped back onto the integer-valued score range. One method for determining the integer-valued score for a real-valued prediction $\hat{y}$ that lies between adjacent scores z_1 and z_2 is to apply thresholds as follows:

$$Score(\hat{y}, z_1, z_2) = \begin{cases} z_1 & \text{if } \hat{y} \leq \frac{z_1+z_2}{2}; \\ z_2 & \text{otherwise.} \end{cases} \quad (1)$$

Other reasonable approaches to the problem are to use ordinal logistic regression or to choose the thresholds based on performance on a validation set. Here we use Equation 1.

OPTIMAL DESIGN ALGORITHMS

In our experiments, we start with a set of n candidate essays. We wish to sample a subset of m of these essays that will give us a reasonably accurate predictive model after a human scores them.

More formally, let $\mathbf{X} \in \mathbb{R}^{n \times p}$ be the n length-p feature vectors of the essays. Call this the *feature space*. The ith row of $\mathbf{X}$ is x_i and the jth column is x_j^T. Assume we lack the *target variable* $\mathbf{Y} \in \mathbb{R}^{n \times 1}$. Also let Ξ be the set of all subsets of rows of $\mathbf{X}$; this is the *design space*. A *design* ξ is an m-row member of Ξ. The goal of the algorithms described in this section is to find ξ such that, when it is agumented with $\mathbf{Y}_\xi$ – the $m \times 1$ matrix containing the target for the feature vectors in ξ – a supervised model that learns $P(\mathbf{Y}_\xi|\xi)$ has better predictive performance on unseen feature vectors than one would expect if ξ were chosen at random.

In our case the model $P(\mathbf{Y}_\xi|\xi)$ is linear regression. Consider a regression with feature x and target y. If we only allow an algorithm to choose two (in this case, unidimensional) feature vectors, which choices might result in a better regression model? The consequences of different choices are illustrated in Figure 1, where one can see that the greater the distance between the x values, the greater the probability that the model will perform almost as well as one trained with all of the data. This is the basic concept behind effective sampling of feature vectors for regression models. It motivates our selection of the algorithms we discuss in this section. The choices they make constitute a spectrum from choosing maximally distant feature vectors to choosing uniformly distant ones.

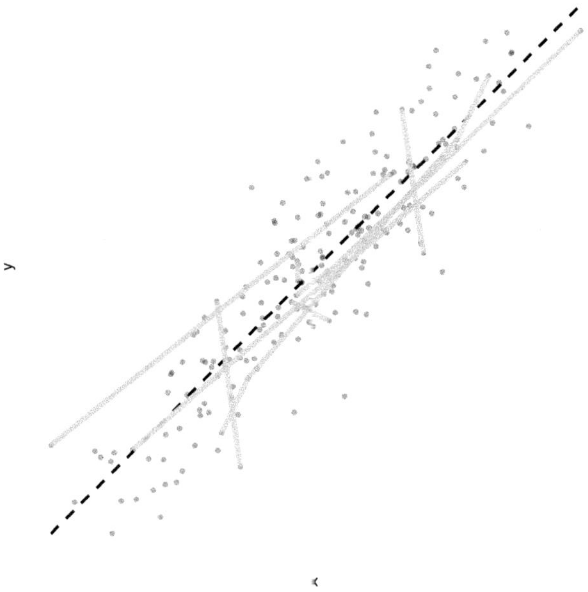

Figure 1: When fitting a regression line on a subset of the data, using distant points increases the probability that the fit will be close to the best fit. The regression line for all of the data is the dashed line. For contrast, lines connecting near and distant points are shown in different colors. The data are two hundred simulated points, with x drawn from a random normal distribution and $y = 1.5x + \epsilon$.

The R statistical language [18] has implementations of the algorithms we discuss in this section. The implementation of the Fedorov algorithm we used is in the AlgDesign package [24]. The prospectr package [22] contains implementations of Kennard-Stone and k-means sampling.

Fedorov exchange algorithm (with D-optimality)

The Fedorov exchange algorithm [8] is a greedy stepwise algorithm for finding ξ. Its purpose is to optimize various optimal design criteria – D-optimality, A-optimality, I-optimality, or others [11]. Most criteria are some function of the information matrix of ξ, defined as $M(\xi) = \frac{1}{m}\xi^T\xi$. D-optimality, for instance, searches for the ξ that maximizes the determinant $det\ M(\xi)$. In experiments with internal data sets, we didn't see major differences among D-optimality, A-optimality, or I-optimality, but the D-optimality criterion did tend to perform somewhat better, so for simplicity of exposition we limit ourselves to D-optimality in the experiments we conduct with the ASAP essay scoring data.

The first step of the Fedorov algorithm is to randomly initialize ξ with m rows from X. Subsequent steps replace a row in ξ with a row from X that is not already in ξ. The swapped rows are chosen greedily to optimize the design criterion. The algorithm can get stuck in a local optimum, depending on the initial choice of ξ. The remedy for this is to run the algorithm several times with different initial states and to choose the best one. The resulting design ξ consists of feature vectors

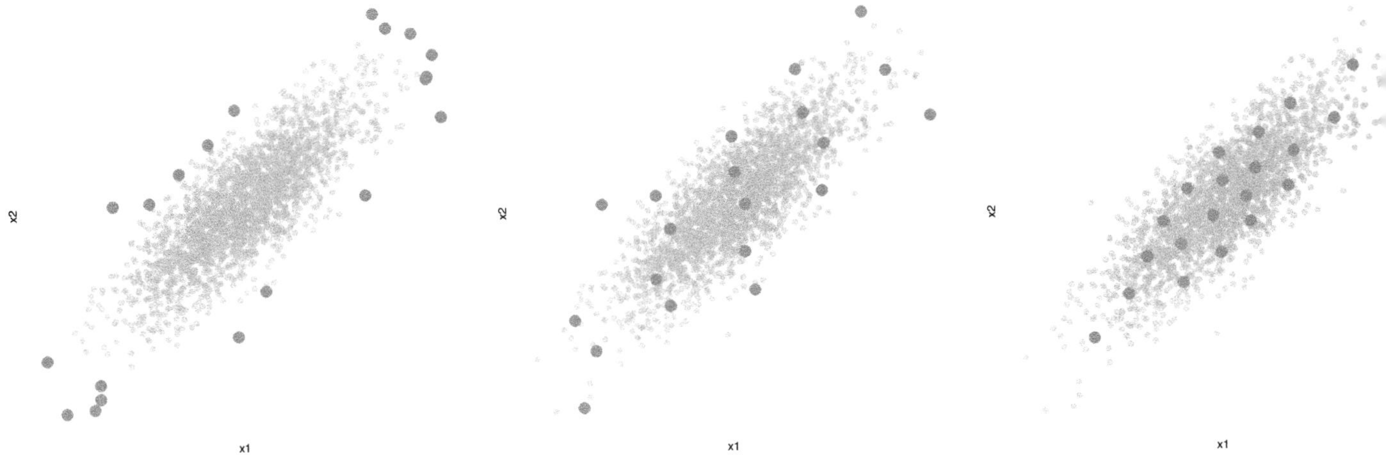

(a) Fedorov with D-optimality (b) Kennard-Stone (c) K-means

Figure 2: The points chosen by algorithms are distributed differently in the feature space. Here the larger points are twenty points selected by an algorithm. The data are simulated. In each figure, a point is one out of a thousand samples drawn at random from a two-dimensional multivariate normal distribution.

that are maximally distant from the centroid of the feature space, as can be seen in Figure 2a.

Kennard-Stone algorithm

The initialization step of the Kennard-Stone algorithm [14] is similar to D-optimality in that it chooses two feature vectors at the periphery of the feature space. Thereafter, however, it chooses feature vectors so as to distribute them uniformly. More precisely, let $d(u, v)$ be the distance between u and v. The first step of the Kennard-Stone algorithm is to choose indices i, j such that

$$\arg\max_{i,j \in 1 \dots n} d(x_i, x_j),$$

then to initialize ξ with x_i, x_j and set $I_\xi = \{i, j\}$. Define

$$\Delta_{x_j}(\xi) = \min_{i \in I_\xi} d(x_j, \xi_i).$$

On each subsequent step the index j is added to I_ξ and x_j is added to ξ:

$$\arg\max_{j \notin I_\xi} \Delta_{x_j}(\xi).$$

After initialization, the point that is furthest from the point in the existing design are added at each step. The distances can be computed in any metric space. Here they are computed in Mahalanobis space. Figure 2b shows that a few of the feature vectors n the design are maximially distant from the centroid of the feature space and the rest are maximally distant from one another.

k-means sampling algorithm

This is simply the k-means clustering algorithm with an extra step at the end: after determining the final centroids, the design is determined by choosing the observation closest to each of the k centroids. Thus when searching for a design of size m, we set $k = m$.

Here the design is approximately uniformly distributed throughout the feature space in Figure 2c. This design does not include feature vectors at the periphery of the feature space, because the centroid of a cluster to which a peripheral point belongs will almost always be closer to some other point that is not peripheral. The uniformity on display here is in part an artifact of the simulated data. In real data the feature vectors would be distributed less than smoothly, so the centroids of the final clusters would be distributed less than uniformly.

Persistence of selections

An important question is the degree to which the feature vectors selected by these algorithms persist across sequential values of m. If the design ξ at $m - 1$ is always included in ξ at m, its selections persist perfectly. The degree of persistence can be measured as

$$Persistence = \frac{|\xi_m \cap \xi_{m+1}|}{|m|}. \tag{2}$$

The persistence of selections for increasing values of m is shown in Figure 3. Kennard-Stone starts with the same two maximally distant feature vectors and adds further ones sequentially according to a deterministic procedure, so its selections are perfectly persistent. The Fedorov algorithm runs several times with different starting points in order to avoid getting stuck in local optima. This results in some loss of persistence, which appears to improve as m increases. In the range $150 < m < 175$, however, the Fedorov algorithm's persistence is erratic, suggesting the existence of multiple local optima that are nearly indistinguishable according to the optimality criterion. The k-means algorithm exhibits the lowest persistence of the three algorithms. This is expected, as the final centroids will change as k, the number of clusters, increases.

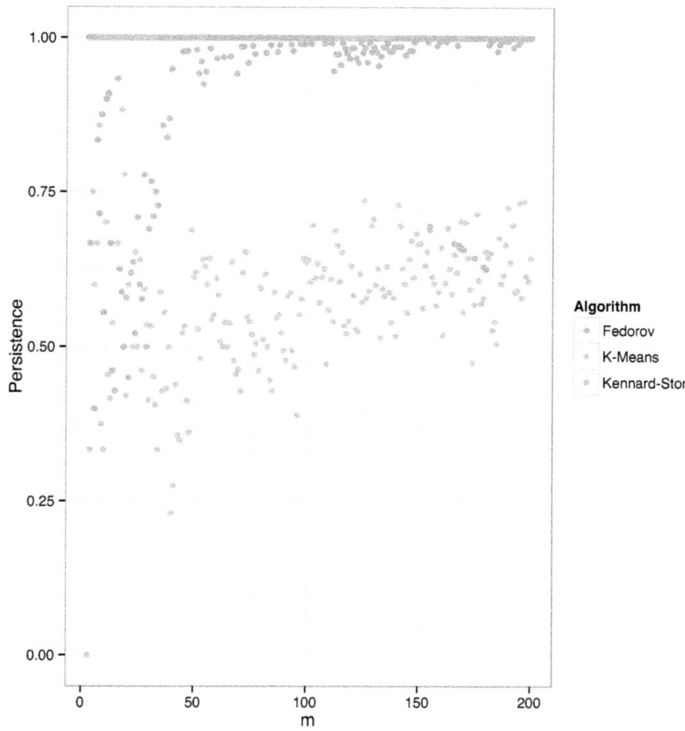

Figure 3: The persistence of selections from ASAP AES essay set 1. The Kennard-Stone algorithm's persistence is 1 everywhere.

EVALUATION

To evaluate the performance of the algorithms, the ideal would be to have access both to an effectively infinite number of unscored essays and to an oracle that could provide scores upon request. Since we have finite data, we simulate a much larger amount of data by repeatedly sampling half of the entire training set (without replacement) before choosing feature vectors to be scored by humans. Of course, since we already have the scores, the human-scoring step of our evaluation doesn't actually occur. The algorithms don't look at the scores, however, so no information leaks unfairly into the process.

We let the desired training set size m range from 10 to 100 in increments of 10. This allows us to simulate an operational environment where new essays arrive over time. After fixing m and sampling half of the entire training set, we use each algorithm to choose a subset of m feature vectors, pretend to have the corresponding essays scored by humans, and train one regression model with each algorithm's chosen subset. A model's performance on the test set is the evaluation criterion – specifically, the Pearson correlation coefficient of its rounded predictions with the scores of the human raters. Since test set essays are the same for all models, the performance of each model is comparable regardless of the size of the training set. To provide smoothed estimates, we averaged the correlations for each of the 300 models trained using a particular combination of training set, sampling algorithm, and size m.

The baseline design algorithm is random sampling without replacement. For a given design size m, the baseline algorithm selects a design ξ_m of unique feature vectors from X at random. Models trained using a design chosen by an optimal design algorithm are expected to perform better than ones trained using this baseline. Assuming an algorithm performs better than the baseline, the key question is how its performance over the baseline changes as m increases. The hallmark of an effective optimal design algorithm is that it prefers to choose the essays that are most informative to the model; this should manifest itself as a *larger* margin above the baseline when m is small. As $m \to n$ (where n is the number of feature vectors from which to choose), the margin should go to 0.

RESULTS

Table 3 shows the percent change of the average of each algorithm's models over the baseline. To test for significance, we transform the correlations using the Fisher Z-transform before applying the two-sample t-test at the 0.001 level. The test is an approximation, as the normality assumption of the t-test does not hold, but the correlation coefficients are unimodal and the sample sizes are relatively large, so we assume that the approximation is quite good. For interpretability, the percent change is calculated using the Pearson correlation. The means of Fedorov and Kennard-Stone results are significantly different from the baseline for most ASAP AES essay sets and training set sizes Fedorov and Kennard-Stone, with the exception of the anomalous essay set 4. The k-means results are more often indistinguishable from the baseline.

To achieve parity with the baseline at $m = 100$, the Fedorov algorithm typically needs to select only about 50 essays. With essay set 1, for instance, it only needs to select 10 essays, as can be seen in Figure 4.

With respect to average performance, the Kennard-Stone algorithm tends to perform well on the same sets as the Fedorov algorithm. The confidence intervals in Figure 4 aren't prominent enough to illustrate a notable difference. The standard deviations of the Kennard-Stone models tend to be greater, and for some test sets are even worse than the baseline, as can be seen in Figure 5. This suggests that the Fedorov algorithm is the most robust: models trained with the essays it selects have the best average performance and the least variance. It also supports the notion – illustrated in for 1-d data in Figure 1 – that the periphery of the feature space is the most effective region from which to choose feature vectors.

We should expect the Fedorov algorithm to perform best when the underlying process that generates the data is best fit using a linear model. Overall, the ranking of optimal design algorithms – from best to worst – conforms to this expectation: Fedorov, Kennard-Stone, and k-means. The only anomaly is essay set 4, where the k-means models perform best for $10 < m < 60$, with respect both to the mean of the Pearson correlation coefficient and its standard deviation. Two possible explanations of this are noise introduced by

Set	m									
	10	20	30	40	50	60	70	80	90	100
1	42	18	10	7	5	4	3	2	2	2
2a	86	69	47	37	26	26	22	18	18	15
2b	94	68	48	39	32	27	26	23	18	17
3	26	18	16	10	8	8	5	5	4	4
4	25	7	**4**	**3**	5	4	**3**	**3**	**4**	**2**
5	25	12	7	4	3	2	1	1	1	1
6	59	30	17	12	8	7	5	4	3	3
7	54	29	16	10	6	5	4	2	2	2
8	106	84	62	93	80	65	74	84	50	63

(a) Fedorov

Set	m									
	10	20	30	40	50	60	70	80	90	100
1	36	15	9	6	5	4	3	2	2	2
2a	62	70	48	36	26	26	21	18	18	15
2b	70	67	45	36	30	25	25	22	17	17
3	25	13	13	9	7	9	6	5	5	4
4	-33	**-2**	**-1**	**0**	**1**	**2**	**1**	**2**	**2**	**1**
5	**-5**	11	7	5	4	3	2	1	1	1
6	52	28	17	11	8	6	4	4	2	3
7	25	22	11	8	5	4	3	2	3	2
8	52	66	45	54	73	53	69	85	53	62

(b) Kennard-Stone

Set	m									
	10	20	30	40	50	60	70	80	90	100
1	-8	**-1**	**1**	**0**	**1**	**0**	**0**	**0**	**0**	**0**
2a	30	42	32	23	17	19	16	13	14	12
2b	53	40	32	28	23	19	20	18	14	14
3	**-4**	**0**	5	**3**	**1**	3	1	1	1	1
4	13	14	13	7	8	6	4	4	**3**	**0**
5	**4**	9	5	4	3	2	1	1	1	1
6	15	8	10	9	7	6	5	4	3	3
7	**0**	7	8	6	4	4	3	2	2	2
8	46	52	45	41	40	33	40	43	**22**	25

(c) K-means

Table 3: Percent change over baseline of the mean performance of models trained with essays selected by optimal design algorithms. Statistically insignificant differences are shown in bold. Significance is determined by a two-sample t-test of means of z-transformed correlations with a 0.001 significance level.

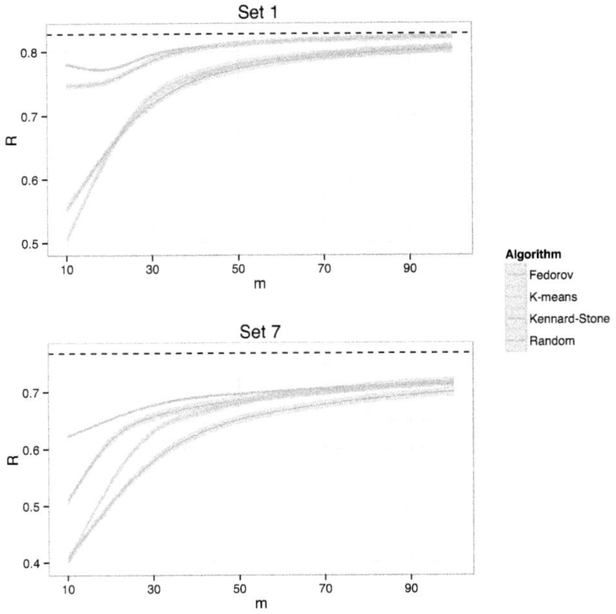

Figure 4: The performance of each algorithm on two test sets. Lines are the smoothed average of 300 models with 95% confidence intervals of the mean. The X axis, m, is the number of essays selected. The Y axis, R, is the Pearson correlation between the model and human raters on the test set. The dashed horizontal line is the mean test set performance when training with all of the data available *in an iteration*.

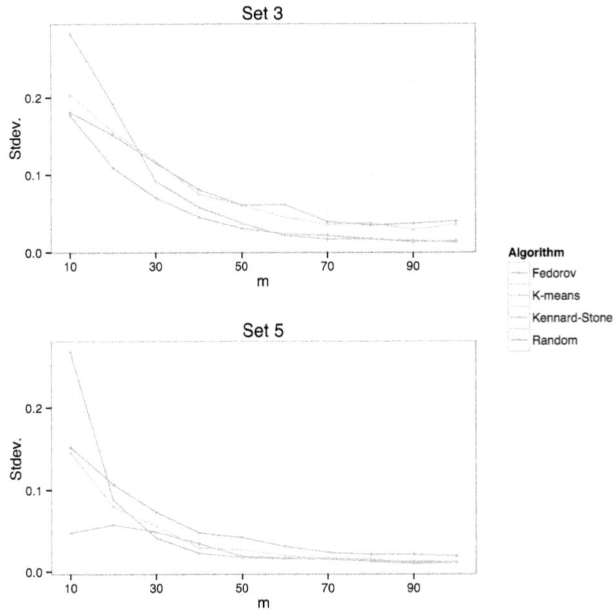

Figure 5: Standard deviations of each algorithm's performance on two test sets. The Y axis is the standard deviation of the Pearson correlation coefficients of 300 models trained with essays selected by an algorithm. The X axis, m, is the number of essays selected.

human raters or an insufficient set of features in the feature space.

Based on the relative performances of the three optimal design algorithms, we strongly favor the use of the Fedorov algorithm with D optimality. The Kennard-Stone algorithm's performance is a close second, but the models trained with the essays it selects tend to have greater variance and when m is small it doesn't approach the impressive performance of the Fedorov algorithm.

CONCLUSION

Effective sampling disciplines the unruly process of obtaining training sets for AWE models. Our simulations show that models trained using a relatively small number of intelligently-chosen essays tend to perform well on out-of-sample essays, at times almost as well as a model trained on an entire training set. In several of the data sets, training with 30-50 essays yields approximately the same performance as a model trained with hundreds of essays. The key implication is that it is possible to minimize the number of human scores necessary for training an AWE model without unduly sacrificing accuracy.

These results also have implications for designing systems that allow rapid integration of new AWE scoring prompts into large-scale systems. One such approach is to train models incrementally. For example, in a large MOOC, a professor may post a new writing prompt for the students. After the first few hundred students submit their essay, the optimal design algorithm selects a subset for the professor or teaching assistant to score. Using this initial training set, a scoring model can quickly be built that will start automatically scoring student essays, so that students can receive feedback on their writing. As more essays are received from students, the optimal design algorithm can select additional essays for human scoring that will be most informative to help refine the accuracy of the scoring model. The model can then be automatically retrained with even greater accuracy of scoring.

When a model is retrained as scores arrive into a data collection system, using optimal design to select the essays from a large pool will ensure that the initial training set consists only of essays that are likely to result in a reasonable model. It will also both ensure that subsequently-added essays are maximally informative and minimize the duplication of the effort of human raters.

Optimal design is necessary but not sufficient for making incremental training of AWE models effective and accurate. While it minimizes the sampling noise in a training set, it doesn't guarantee a minimum level of performance. To ensure that models are not deployed prematurely, a validation set of essays should first be selected from the pool and scored by humans. Measuring model performance with a validation set will ensure that the model performs well enough before it is deployed. Each time a new human score enters the data collection system, the model can be retrained, and its performance on the validation set can be computed. If the model doesn't perform well enough to be deployed to a production environment, additional essays can be selected to be scored. This process should repeat until the model reaches an acceptable level of performance.

In experiments with internal data sets, we noticed that when a model trained on the entire training set performed to our satisfaction, optimal design performed well too. The conditions that caused a model trained on the entire training set to perform poorly also caused the performance of optimal design to degrade. The most common cause of not meeting the conditions for good model performance is noise due either to poor agreement among human raters or model misspecification. An example of model misspecification is when the feature set does not capture textual semantics and the rubric instructs the human raters to give a higher score to an essay if it covers some set of topics[1]. Our recommended solution to avoiding model misspecification, which we don't evaluate here, is to be generous with one's feature set and to let a regularizer shrink uninformative features. We expect the results we report here to generalize to other tasks and populations as long as the conditions are right for a model trained on the entire training set to perform satisfactorily.

While these results are promising for the scoring of essays, we expect that it will be less effective with short answer data sets. Short answer data sets are often modeled using a learning algorithm that employs a set of decision trees, such as random forest. The feature vectors are often different, too, because such models perform well when they know exactly which words a student used. Consequently, it is common for the feature vectors to be rows of a *document-term matrix* – an occurrence matrix with terms as columns and documents as rows – constructed from the training set responses. In that representation, the feature vectors are sparse and relatively long. Optimal design and active learning work best when the assumptions of the sampling algorithm agree with the assumptions of the subsequent supervised learning algorithm. Thus, using the Fedorov algorithm to select a subset of short responses to be scored by humans when the supervised model is random forest trained with a document-term matrix is not guaranteed to yield the best results.

The use of optimal design for AWE training sets can be seen as a form of manufacturing process control in which the amount of information provided by a human score is maximized and its variance minimized. From this perspective, the goal of our use of optimal design is primarily to make the output of the human scoring process – that is, the quantity of information in a single human score – more predictable. The effect of this is to enable safe and reliable incremental training of AWE models. Overall, the approach solves a barrier to the adoption of AWE into large-scale formative and summative systems, allowing the computer to minimize the amount of human effort needed to collect and score essays by choosing effectively which essays humans need to score.

[1]There has been some recent work on active learning for misspecified models [23, 2], but their thrust has been primarily theoretical and do not appear to be immediately helpful for this problem.

REFERENCES

1. Attali, Y., and Burstein, J. Automated essay scoring with e-rater v. 2. *The Journal of Technology, Learning and Assessment 4*, 3 (2006).
2. Bach, F. R. Active learning for misspecied generalized linear models. *Adv. Neural Inf. Process. Syst.* (2007).
3. `https://github.com/edx/discern`. Accessed: 2013-10-7.
4. `https://github.com/edx/discern/blob/master/ml_grading/ml_model_creation.py`. Accessed: 2013-10-7.
5. `https://github.com/edx/ease`. Accessed: 2013-10-7.
6. `http://edx.org`. Accessed: 2013-10-7.
7. `https://criterion.ets.org`. Accessed: 2013-10-13.
8. Fedorov, V. V. *Theory Of Optimal Experiments*. Probability and mathematical statistics. Elsevier Science, 1972.
9. Foltz, P. W., Streeter, L., Lochbaum, K. E., and Landauer, T. K. Implementation and applications of the intelligent essay assessor. In *Handbook of Automated Essay Evaluation: Current Applications and New Directions*, M. D. Shermis and J. Burstein, Eds. Taylor & Francis, 2013, 68–88.
10. Hoerl, A. E., and Kennard, R. W. Ridge regression: Biased estimation for nonorthogonal problems. *Technometrics 12*, 1 (1 Feb. 1970), 55–67.
11. John, R. C. S., and Draper, N. R. D-Optimality for regression designs: A review. *Technometrics 17*, 1 (1975), 15–23.
12. The hewlett foundation: Automated essay scoring — kaggle. `http://www.kaggle.com/c/ASAP-AES`. Accessed: 2013-10-7.
13. The hewlett foundation: Short answer scoring — kaggle. `http://www.kaggle.com/c/ASAP-SAS`. Accessed: 2013-10-7.
14. Kennard, R. W., and Stone, L. A. Computer aided design of experiments. *Technometrics 11*, 1 (1 Feb. 1969), 137–148.
15. Landauer, T. K., Laham, D., and Foltz, P. W. Automatic essay assessment. *Assessment in Education: Principles, Policy and Practice 10*, 3 (2003), 295–308.
16. MacKay, D. Information-Based objective functions for active data selection. *Neural Computation 4*, 4 (July 1992), 590–604.
17. Page, E., and Paulus, D. The analysis of essays by computer. final report.
18. R Core Team. *R: A Language and Environment for Statistical Computing*. R Foundation for Statistical Computing, Vienna, Austria, 2014.
19. Rudner, L. M., Garcia, V., and Welch, C. An evaluation of IntelliMetric essay scoring system. *The Journal of Technology, Learning and Assessment 4*, 4 (2006).
20. Settles, B. Active learning literature survey. *University of Wisconsin, Madison* (2010).
21. Smith, K. On the standard deviations of adjusted and interpolated values of an observed polynomial function and its constants and the guidance they give towards a proper choice of the distribution of observations. *Biometrika 12*, 1/2 (1 Nov. 1918), 1–85.
22. Stevens, A., and Ramirez-Lopez, L. *An introduction to the prospectr package*, 2013. R package version 0.1.3.
23. Sugiyama, M. Active learning for misspecified models. *Adv. Neural Inf. Process. Syst.* (2005).
24. Wheeler, B. *AlgDesign: Algorithmic Experimental Design*, 2014. R package version 1.1-7.2.
25. `http://writetolearn.net`. Accessed: 2013-10-13.

Improving Student Modeling Through Partial Credit and Problem Difficulty

Korinn Ostrow, Christopher Donnelly, Seth Adjei, Neil Heffernan
Worcester Polytechnic Institute
100 Institute Road
Worcester, MA 01609
{ksostrow, cdonnelly, saadjei, nth}@wpi.edu

ABSTRACT

Student modeling within intelligent tutoring systems is a task largely driven by binary models that predict student knowledge or next problem correctness (i.e., Knowledge Tracing (KT)). However, using a binary construct for student assessment often causes researchers to overlook the feedback innate to these platforms. The present study considers a novel method of tabling an algorithmically determined partial credit score and problem difficulty bin for each student's current problem to predict both binary and partial next problem correctness. This study was conducted using log files from ASSISTments, an adaptive mathematics tutor, from the 2012-2013 school year. The dataset consisted of 338,297 problem logs linked to 15,253 unique student identification numbers. Findings suggest that an efficiently tabled model considering partial credit and problem difficulty performs about as well as KT on binary predictions of next problem correctness. This method provides the groundwork for modifying KT in an attempt to optimize student modeling.

Author Keywords

Student modeling; tabling method; partial credit; problem difficulty; next problem correctness; knowledge tracing

ACM Classification Keywords

K.3.1 Computer Uses in Education, I.2.6 Learning, I.6.4. Model Validation and Analysis

INTRODUCTION

Modeling student learning within an intelligent tutoring system can be a daunting task. In order to make predictions about a student's knowledge or their next problem correctness, models must decipher noisy input and isolate only those features that define the probability of knowledge or learning. As such, designers of intelligent tutoring systems have largely relied on Knowledge Tracing (KT), as presented by Corbett & Anderson [2], to model the probability of student learning at real time within popular systems such as Cognitive Tutor [5]. Other methods, such Performance Factors Analysis, seek to model learning when considering overlapping knowledge components (i.e., skills) and individualized student metrics [11], offering an alternative to KT in certain circumstances.

Despite the popularity of KT and PFA, the standard models rely on binary input to establish predictions of students' knowledge state or performance, failing to consider continuous metrics that would better individualize the model across students or skills. Expansion in the field educational data mining has since lead to a number of alternative or supplementary learning models. For instance, researchers have attempted to impart individualized prior knowledge nodes for each student [8], to supplement KT with a flexible metric for item difficulty [9], to ensemble various methods of binning student performance (i.e., partial credit) with standard KT models [12], and to consider the sequence of a student's actions within the tutor to help predict next problem correctness [3].

Without modifying KT or PFA directly, adding parameters to student learning models can be a limited approach. Tabling methods that quickly establish maximum likelihood probabilities have previously been used by Wang & Heffernan [12, 13] to test and optimize various potential adaptations to KT. Following in this process, the present study uses a tabling method to lay the groundwork for future modifications to KT that will allow for predictions of next problem correctness using the partial credit score and difficulty estimate of the current item. While previous work has shown the benefit of ensembling tabling methods with KT, we hope to use the findings presented herein to modify KT directly, as it has previously been suggested that ensembling can be a rather sensitive approach [4].

Perhaps standard learning models rely on binary correctness as measured by a student's first response at each skill opportunity (i.e., a sequence of correct and incorrect responses based on a student's first action within each problem) due to the complexity of accurately and universally defining an algorithm that validates partial credit scores within intelligent tutoring systems. Within the

L@S 2015, March 14–18, 2015, Vancouver, BC, Canada.

.http://dx.doi.org/10.1145/2724660.2724667

majority of current learning models, a student would be penalized with a score of zero for taking advantage of the tutoring that plays an integral role in these platforms. Yet the primary goal of most intelligent tutoring systems is not solely to assess student knowledge, but to simultaneously promote student learning through adaptive feedback, making binary correctness a stale concept. Students often require multiple attempts to solve a problem or request system feedback for guidance, thus assigning value to the concept of partial credit. Attali and Powers [1] suggested the benefits of considering partial credit when predicting learning outcomes in adaptive environments, as evidenced by the modification of standardized tests to allow partial credit when predicting GRE scores.

Within ASSISTments, an adaptive mathematics tutor, a naïve model of partial credit scoring was previously established by Wang and Heffernan [12], termed the "Assistance" Model. This method calculated maximum likelihood probabilities for next problem correctness using a twelve-parameter table built from binning students' hint usage and attempt count. In this manner, the authors used system features to indirectly gauge a partial credit metric that would help predict binary performance.

The present study provides methodological evidence that student modeling can be enhanced through the use of algorithmically derived partial credit scores and a binned metric of problem difficulty. We first use tabling method (a probabilistic approach employing maximum likelihood estimations) that considers the partial credit score of the current problem to predict both binary and partial next problem correctness. We also establish a more complex prediction table that considers both partial credit and problem difficulty. Through this novel concept, we hope to show that students can ultimately gain knowledge from a problem even if they fail to earn full credit. Our findings argue for the design of a modified KT model that is sensitive to a continuous measure of partial credit rather than binary input, and that isolates a known level of problem difficulty for each question. We seek to answer the following research questions:

1. Does an algorithmically determined partial credit score outperform binary metrics when used to predict next problem correctness?
2. Does a binned metric of current problem difficulty (e.g., Low, Medium, or High difficulty) provide a valid prediction of next problem correctness?
3. Can current problem difficulty supplement partial credit score to outperform similar modeling techniques?

DATASET

The dataset used for this analysis was compiled from problem logs from the ASSISTments platform during the 2012-2013 school year. The original file included roughly 1.5 million rows of problem level data (i.e., each row detailed all logged actions for one problem for one student). For this study, we chose to analyze only the top ten most densely populated knowledge components. Attributes of these skills are further explained in Table 1. The dataset examined here has been made publicly available at [7].

In order to properly calculate partial credit, approximately 5,000 rows were removed due to a lack of logged end time, meaning that these problems had never been properly completed. Using the platform's current grading method, which is based on the students' first response, these logs carry binary correctness scores. However, as the problem was ultimately considered incomplete, partial credit could not be determined with certainty and the logs were therefore excluded from analysis. Further, the analysis presented herein reports only on main problems. Scaffolding problems, a feedback style within the ASSISTments platform typically used to break a problem down into steps or to provide worked examples, were excluded from the final dataset. The decision to work with main problems was based in part on the justification made by Pardos & Heffernan [9] when using a similar dataset from the ASSISTments platform. As scaffolding problems are guided, they offer a less accurate view of skill knowledge and skew performance data within an opportunity based analysis. An analysis of the remaining dataset revealed that only 0.3% of first actions were scaffold requests, further supporting the intuition that the removal of scaffolding data was appropriate.

Due to the time constraints involved in running multiple models with five fold cross-validation (explained further in the Compared Models and Model Testing and Training sections), we chose to restrict the dataset to a maximum of 15 opportunities per student per skill. This reduced the dataset by 46,680 rows, primarily removing students who were excessively struggling and those gaming the system; the majority of students were unaffected by this refinement.

The resulting dataset consisted of 338,297 problem logs representative of 15,253 unique student identification numbers. On average, each student identifier linked to approximately 3.3 skills. Further exploration of this dataset revealed that it was comprised of 7,363 unique problems. A total of 3,787 unique assignments were made by 417 teachers spanning 231 schools. The skill content ranged from grades 6-8 as shown in Table 1. The majority of logged problems (over 90%) were completed by students who 'mastered' or finished the full assignment from which the problem originated.

Three types of questions were represented in the dataset. The majority of problems logged, 84.3%, were 'mathematical expressions,' a problem type that accepts any answer that is mathematically equivalent to the correct answer (i.e., answers of 1/2 and 0.5 are both accurate). In contrast, 12.5% of problems logged were 'fill-in,' a problem type that requires the student to input an *exact* string matching the preset correct response (i.e., if 1/2 was the preset answer, 0.5 would be incorrect). The remaining 3.2% of problems logged in the dataset were 'multiple choice,' featuring two or more answers available for selection.

Skill ID	Definition	Grade Level	# Logs (Rows)	% Resulting Dataset
277	Addition and Subtraction of Integers	7	44,731	13.2
311	Equation Solving with Two or Fewer Steps	7	44,005	13.0
280	Addition and Subtraction of Fractions	6	42,550	12.6
276	Multiplication and Division of Positive Decimals	6	37,033	10.9
47	Conversion of Fractions, Decimals, and Percentages	6	32,741	9.7
67	Multiplication of Fractions	6	31,716	9.4
61	Division of Fractions	6	28,809	8.5
278	Addition and Subtraction of Positive Decimals	6	27,301	8.1
310	Order of Operations	8	25,132	7.4
79	Proportions	7	24,279	7.2

Table 1. Skill details and distribution in resulting dataset

Further assessment of students' responses provided insight into their first actions, attempt counts, and hint usage. For 95.5% of logged problems, the student's first action was to make an answer attempt. Using ASSISTments' current scoring scheme, these attempts would receive binary scores of either correct (1) or incorrect (0). Within this subgroup of logged problems, 24% of the problems were marked as incorrect while 76% were marked as correct. This suggests that a partial credit metric could provide benefit for approximately one quarter of attempted questions. Of the remaining logged problems, 4.2% represented first action hint requests, and 0.3% represented first action scaffolding requests.

Given that partial credit scores for the present study are algorithmically derived from an assessment of the student's attempt count and hint usage for each logged problem, these variables were examined thoroughly. Analysis of attempt counts across logged problems revealed a minimum of 0 and a maximum of 496, with a mean of 1.47 and a standard deviation of 2.23. For logs that were marked as incorrect based on first action, mean attempts rose to 2.70 with a standard deviation of 3.99. Within the full dataset, students made a total of 496,533 attempts.

Hint counts were also analyzed across logged problems and compared to the total number of hints available for each problem. Each problem had at least one hint, usually serving as the bottom out hint (i.e., it provided the answer). The average number of hints available per problem was 3.38, with a standard deviation of 0.88. The majority of problems had three hints (38.9%) or four hints (33.4%), with the maximum number of hints available in any problem topping off at seven. Across all logged problems, a total of 1,090,225 hints were available. Of the available hints, students only used a total of 167,371, or roughly 15.4%. The average number of hints used was 0.49 with a standard deviation of 1.20. For problem logs in which students answered incorrectly on their first attempt, 55.8% of available hints were utilized. Information particular to the bottom out hint showed that within problems initially answered incorrectly, only 14.5% of students proceeded to the bottom out hint. Thus, when struggling, the majority of students used the adaptive feedback inherent to the tutoring system in an appropriate manner. This provides further evidence for consideration of valid partial credit metrics.

Figure 1 provides a screenshot of a typical problem within the ASSISTments tutor. Specifically, this problem is a representation of the second most densely populated skill in the 2012-2013 ASSISTments log file: "Equation Solving with Two or Fewer Steps." This skill is exemplified, rather than highlighting the top skill, "Addition and Subtraction of Integers," as the problem provides a more robust example of the system's tutoring feedback. As shown in Figure 1, the student is presented with the equation and asked to solve for the missing variable. He or she can make an attempt to solve the problem, or may ask for the first of three hints. The hints increase in specificity, in an attempt to guide the student without providing excess assistance. The first hint shown in Figure 1 provides a worked example of a similar problem solving for the missing variable, x. If the student is unable to proceed using only the worked example, he or she can request the second and third hints as needed. The third hint in Figure 1 is the bottom out hint; it provides the correct answer ("-24") in an attempt to keep the student from getting stuck in the assignment, as it is not possible to skip problems and return at a later point as one can with traditional bookwork.

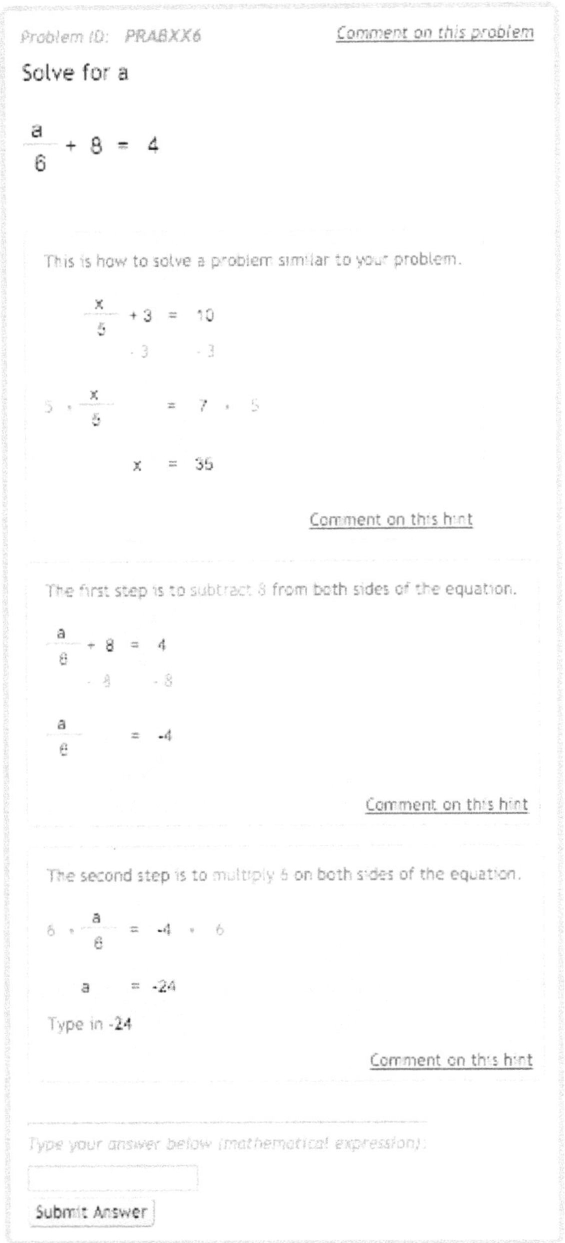

Figure 1. An example problem featuring three hints for the skill "Equation Solving with Two or Fewer Steps"

COMPARED MODELS

The following subsections explain the design and brief history (when appropriate) of the five models compared in the current study. All five models are primarily designed to predict binary next problem correctness. For permitting models, we present predictions of partial credit next problem correctness using continuous probabilities for additional consideration.

Partial Credit Predicting Next Problem Correctness

A naïve partial credit algorithm was derived by the ASSISTments design team in hopes of providing the system with partial credit scoring capabilities based on students' attempt count and feedback usage. Scores were determined subjectively based on teacher input and a conceptual understanding of how students typically behave within the tutoring platform. For this study, the algorithm was altered slightly to consider multiple problem types and to account for the students' first action. For instance, if a student asked for tutoring feedback without making an attempt to solve the problem, we felt that a larger penalty was merited.

The resulting algorithm used to define partial credit scores is depicted in Figure 2. Rather than establishing a deduction method on a per hint or per attempt basis as shown in previous work [12], the algorithm presented in Figure 2 places each logged problem into one of five partial credit bins (0, .03, 0.6, 0.7, 0.8, 1.0) by considering the logged data pertaining to first response type (attempt = 0, hint request = 1, scaffold request = 2), attempt count, and hint count.

For example, if a student makes only one attempt and is correct without requiring feedback, they earn full credit (a score of 1). This is similar to the notion of binary correctness on first response that ASSISTments currently employs. However, in the current method, all other first actions equate to an incorrect answer (i.e., requesting a hint or scaffold, or making a first attempt that is incorrect would both earn the student a score of 0).

As shown in Figure 2, after ruling out a 'correct' response, the partial credit algorithm considers whether the student requested a scaffold before even making an attempt. This behavior would suggest that either the student was not actually trying to answer the problem, or that he or she was struggling conceptually. Thus, rather than earning no credit, the student is only discounted to a score of 0.6.

```
IF type = algebra OR type = fill_in
   IF attempt = 1 AND correct = 1 AND hint_count = 0
      THEN 1
   ELSIF first_action = 2
      THEN .6
   ELSIF attempt < 3 AND hint_count = 0
      THEN .8
   ELSIF (attempt <= 3 AND hint=0)
      OR (hint_count = 1 AND bottom_hint != 1)
      THEN .7
   ELSIF (attempt < 5 AND bottom_hint != 1)
      OR (hint_count > 1 AND bottom_hint != 1)
      THEN .3
   ELSE 0

IF type = multiple_choice
   IF correct = 1
      THEN 1
   ELSE 0
```

Figure 2. Algorithm used to determine Partial Credit score based on first response, attempt count, and hint usage

Regardless of the student's first action, if he or she uses less than three attempts and does not request any hints, they earn slightly more, with a score of 0.8. The next bin is marked by students who have three or fewer attempts and have not used a hint, or those who have asked for only one hint and were not provided the answer (i.e., if a student's first action is to request a hint that is not the bottom out hint, they would fall into this bin). These students earn a score of 0.7. If the student can solve the problem within 5 attempts without seeing the bottom out hint, or if he or she uses multiple hints without ultimately reaching the bottom out hint, their partial credit score is 0.3. Finally, for students who use five or more attempts, or for those that see the answer, the problem is marked incorrect (a score of 0).

For multiple-choice questions the algorithm reverts to binary correctness because this type of problem does not usually provide feedback and guessing can be far more prevalent and consequential. Thus, if a student fails to get the correct answer on their first attempt, he or she receives a score of 0. This method was employed to keep the problem type from gaining an unfair advantage within the dataset. For instance, using the algorithm applied to other problem types, a student guessing through a multiple-choice problem with only four responses would still receive a score of 0.3.

The full algorithm was run across the dataset and partial credit scores were obtained for each logged problem. These partial credit scores were then used to define a pivot table to predict averages for both binary and partial next problem correctness, using maximum likelihood estimation. Results are presented in Table 2. For all parameter Tables, the number of logged problems falling into respective bins is depicted by sample size, *n*. The distribution of the data suggests that slight improvements could be made to the partial credit algorithm as few students fell into the 0.6 bin. Of all available 'next problem' data, only 14.7% of logs had partial credit values between 0 and 1. Thus, 85.3% of students would be insured by the platform's current method of binary correctness. This suggests that any significant finding among the models considered in the present study would be quite intriguing, as only a small portion of the sample is actually receiving the 'partial credit' treatment.

Partial Credit	n	Binary	Partial
0	45,735	0.5062	0.5634
0.3	6,471	0.5902	0.7438
0.6	940	0.3660	0.7948
0.7	12,077	0.6921	0.8396
0.8	22,797	0.7085	0.8668
1	200,287	0.8050	0.8785

Table 2. Parameters for predicting Binary and Partial Next Problem Correctness from current problem Partial Credit

It should be noted that a potential problem inherent to this tabling method (apparent in all tabled models in the present study) is the inability to predict correctness on a student's first opportunity within a skill, as there is no preceding problem data. This essentially causes the loss of 49,990 rows of data representing first problem predictions. Thus, sample sizes in Tables 2, 3, and 4 total 288,307 logs rather than 338,297.

Problem Difficulty Predicting Next Problem Correctness

A continuous metric of problem difficulty was calculated by retrieving data from all problems logged in the platform that were created before August 2012 (i.e., prior to the first timestamp in the modeling dataset). For each unique problem, all existing logs were averaged and a percentage of correct responses were determined. The resulting value offers an inverse metric of the problem's difficulty level. For instance, a problem on which students averaged 80% on all previous opportunities would not be considered very difficult. This metric was then binned into Low, Medium, and High difficulties by defining Medium difficulty as scores falling within +/- 0.5 standard deviations from the mean. Considering the inverse nature of the metric, High difficulty problems therefore had continuous values *below* this cut off, and Low difficulty problems had continuous values *above* this cutoff.

The bins for current problem difficulty were used in a maximum likelihood probability table to predict averages for both binary and partial scores for next problem correctness. Resulting parameters are presented in Table 3.

Difficulty	n	Binary	Partial
Low	91,712	0.7764	0.8465
Medium	107,901	0.7452	0.8297
High	88,694	0.6928	0.7895

Table 3. Parameters predicting Binary and Partial Next Problem Correctness from current problem Difficulty

Partial Credit and Problem Difficulty Predicting Next Problem Correctness

Based on the definitions of partial credit and problem difficulty defined in the singular models above, our goal was to create a novel model that used a tabling approach to consider partial credit together with problem difficulty to make predictions about next problem correctness. For each logged problem, partial credit score and problem difficulty were referenced to determine parameters for both binary and partial credit next problem correctness. Resulting probabilities are presented in Table 4.

	High			Medium			Low		
Partial Credit	n	Binary	Partial	n	Binary	Partial	n	Binary	Partial
0	8,357	0.5130	0.5621	16,307	0.5027	0.5622	21,071	0.5062	0.5650
0.3	1,107	0.6035	0.7401	2,332	0.6017	0.7548	3,032	0.5766	0.7367
0.6	29	0.5902	0.8508	236	0.3388	0.7897	675	0.3661	0.7943
0.7	2,829	0.6971	0.8288	4,888	0.6987	0.8463	4,360	0.6816	0.8391
0.8	5,094	0.7770	0.8753	8,342	0.7354	0.8712	9,361	0.6473	0.8581
1	74,296	0.8116	0.8787	75,796	0.8072	0.8841	50,195	0.7921	0.8697

Table 4. Parameters predicting Binary and Partial Next Problem Correctness from Partial Credit and Problem Difficulty

Knowledge Tracing

Knowledge Tracing (KT) is perhaps the most common method for modeling student performance. The standard KT model [2] has successfully proven itself as the basis for modeling student knowledge within intelligent tutoring systems [5] and thereby serves as a stable comparison for new work.

As shown in Figure 3, the standard model of KT is a Bayesian Network comprised of four learned parameters. Two parameters represent student knowledge (*prior knowledge* and *learn rate*) and two parameters represent student performance (*guess rate* and *slip rate*). The standard KT model is binary in that skills can only be in a 'learned' or 'unlearned' state, and questions can only be 'correct' or 'incorrect.' The model is updated with each skill opportunity based on the student's performance by using the following equation as defined by Corbett & Anderson [2]:

$$p(L_n) = p(L_{n-1}|evidence) + (1 - p(L_{n-1}|evidence)) * p(T)$$

Standard KT Model

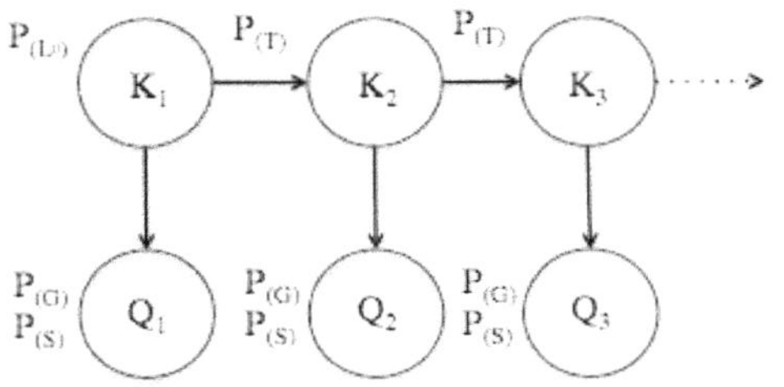

$P_{(L_0)}$ = Prior Knowledge $P_{(T)}$ = Learn Rate
$P_{(G)}$ = Guess Rate $P_{(S)}$ = Slip Rate

Knowledge nodes (K_n) & Question nodes (Q_n) have binary states (0 or 1)

Figure 3. The standard Knowledge Tracing model with all learned parameters and nodes explained

Forgetting does not factor into the standard KT model when observing individual skills, as *guess* and *slip* parameters are thought to account for incorrect answers within the students' sequence of opportunities. For further information regarding the details of KT, refer to [2].

For this study, KT analysis was performed using the Bayes Net Toolbox (BNT), a popular open-source code for fitting directed graphical models within MATLAB [6].

Performance Factors Analysis

Performance Factors Analysis (PFA) was proposed as an alternative to KT by Pavlik, Cen, and Koedinger [11]. The method can model problems with multiple skills and has been shown to accurately model and select practice within adaptive systems. PFA was derived from Learning Factors Analysis (LFA), an approach that considers a parameter for student ability, a parameter for the skill's difficulty, and a learning rate for each skill. While PFA still considers skill difficulty, β, the model improves upon LFA by considering the frequency of both correct and incorrect answers in a student's response pattern, rather than simply assessing the frequency of skill practice. Thus, PFA predictions are updated with each skill opportunity based on a cumulative history of the student's successes (weighted by γ) and failures (weighted by ρ), as depicted in the following equation defined by Pavlik, Cen, and Koedinger [11]:

$$m(i, j \in KCs, s, f) = \sum_{j \in KCs} (\beta_j + \gamma_j s_{i,j} + \rho_j f_{i,j})$$

The log-likelihood (m) attained through this equation can then be passed through an exponential function to find the probability that the student will get the item correct. This model suggests that learning is defined by more than just skill practice, and that performance is strongly tied to skill acquisition.

For this study, PFA was performed using unpublished code within MATLAB. With properly formatted data, the analysis can also be performed using logistic regression in common statistical packages like IBM's SPSS.

MODEL TRAINING AND TESTING

Five-fold cross validation was used to train and test each model. In order to perform five-fold cross validation within our tabled models, the dataset was divided using a modulo operation on each student's unique identification number. Thus, for every student in the file, student id mod 5 was called, returning a remainder falling into bins from 0 to 4, thereby assigning students to folds. The distribution of the resulting folds was roughly equivalent, as shown in Table 5. With 15,253 unique student identification numbers in the dataset, the largest fold had 3,082 student ids and the smallest fold had 2,996 student ids, leaving a range of 86 and a standard deviation of 33.7.

Within each iteration of the cross-validation process, the model was trained on approximately 80% of the data and tested on the 20% that had been held out. Thus, when trained on folds 1, 2, 3, and 4 (80% of the data) the model would impart predictions on fold 0 (the held out 20%). In this manner, for each tabling method described in Section 3, table parameters were learned using four training folds and predictions were made on the held out fold. The process was repeated for all folds, thus resulting in five probability tables for each prediction type (i.e., five 'training' tables for partial credit predicting binary next problem correctness). Using an extensive formula in Microsoft Excel, the predicted averages were then applied back to each logged problem respective of test fold. For predictions of binary next problem correctness, rather than arbitrarily selecting a cutoff point for classifying binary correctness (e.g., simply using values greater than 0.5 to convey '1'), we instead subtracted the prediction directly from the actual binary result. Thus, when predicting next problem correctness using partial credit alone, if the next problem is actually correct using binary standard, the resulting residual is calculated as: 1.0000 - 0.7085 = 0.2915. In this manner, residuals were calculated for each log entry in each test fold that contained data for next problem correctness.

A similar method of five fold cross-validation was coded into the KT and PFA analyses within MATLAB. Without modification, KT and PFA are not intended to accurately predict partial credit next question correctness, and as such we have saved these analyses for future work.

Fold	Unique Students	# Logs	% Dataset
0	3074	67,715	20.0
1	3046	68,081	20.1
2	3082	68,739	20.3
3	3054	67,996	20.1
4	2996	65,766	19.4

Table 5. Distribution of data across five folds

To compare our tabled models with KT and PFA, slight modifications were made to the standard modeling procedures. Unlike tabling, these models carry the benefit of being able to predict performance on a student's first opportunity within a skill. Based on a 'prior knowledge' parameter, KT is able to predict the student's initial knowledge state, K_1, and therefore their performance on the first question, Q_1. Similarly, the equation for PFA defaults a prediction of the skill's difficulty parameter, β, as the student's initial state. These values essentially define a baseline for the student's knowledge, prior to any practice. Thus, in order to provide a fair comparison to tabled models, these first opportunity predictions were removed by shifting predictions to align with our 'next problem' analysis. Within KT, all subsequent skill opportunities were predicted using Expectation Maximization, a standard method for parameter learning within KT. The model was supplied the following initial parameters as 'ground truths' to begin the hill climbing process: *prior knowledge* = 0.30, *learn rate* = 0.20, *forget rate* = 0.00, *guess rate* = 0.20, and *slip rate* = 0.08. Within PFA, all subsequent skill opportunities were predicted by updating the equation presented in the previous section. These modifications resulted in the same number of data points for each model, providing grounds for fair comparison of the models.

Further, as noted briefly in the Dataset section, all models were restricted to 15 predicted opportunities per student per skill. This method was chosen largely to reduce the computation time required to fit KT using five-fold cross validation on such an extensive dataset. By capping the opportunity count, analysis time was reduced to approximately 20 hours. Other models were far less time intensive, all taking under three hours to arrive at predictions. Setting this restriction also served to reduce potential skewing in student level analyses by removing outliers with extensive opportunity counts.

RESULTS

All models were compared using the fit statistics of RMSE, R^2, AUC, and model accuracy. As the tabled models were not restricted to binary input, fit statistics were also found for consideration of modeling partial credit next problem correctness.

For each model, these statistics were found at the problem log level, the skill level, and the student level where merited. These statistics were then averaged across the level of analysis, resulting in the findings presented in Table 6, Table 7, and Table 8 respectively. Thus, at the problem log level, fit statistics were determined overall for the 288,307 predictions, without consideration of student or skill before being averaged across all problems. At the skill level, ten sets of fit statistics were determined (one set for each skill), which were then averaged across skills. At the student level, 15,253 sets of fit statistics were determined (one set for each student), which were then averaged across students. The latter two procedures were intended to

Model	Binary NPC				Partial NPC			
	RMSE	*R^2*	*AUC*	*Accuracy*	*RMSE*	*R^2*	*AUC*	*Accuracy*
Partial Credit + Problem Difficulty	0.4241	0.0674	0.6365	0.7310	0.3326	0.1062	0.5395	0.7298
Partial Credit	0.4244	0.0660	0.6309	0.7309	0.3327	0.1060	0.5351	0.7298
Problem Difficulty	0.4379	0.0057	0.5464	0.7300	0.3511	0.0043	0.3953	0.7298
Knowledge Tracing	0.4240	0.0680	0.6621	0.7298	--	--	--	--
Performance Factors Analysis	0.4227	0.0738	0.6644	0.7485	--	--	--	--

Table 6. Problem Level Average RMSE, R^2, AUC, and Accuracy for Models Predicting Next Problem Correctness (NPC)

Model	Binary NPC				Partial NPC			
	RMSE	*R^2*	*AUC*	*Accuracy*	*RMSE*	*R^2*	*AUC*	*Accuracy*
Partial Credit + Problem Difficulty	0.4224	0.0670	0.6300	0.7414	0.3284	0.1032	0.5130	0.7399
Partial Credit	0.4229	0.0656	0.6290	0.7414	0.3284	0.1031	0.5103	0.7399
Problem Difficulty	0.4364	0.0046	0.5323	0.7402	0.3473	0.0037	0.3560	0.7399
Knowledge Tracing	0.4225	0.0602	0.6500	0.7466	--	--	--	--
Performance Factors Analysis	0.4212	0.0664	0.6506	0.7499	--	--	--	--

Table 7. Skill Level Average RMSE, R^2, AUC, and Accuracy for Models Predicting Next Problem Correctness (NPC)

Model	Binary NPC				Partial NPC			
	*RMSE**	*R^2*	*AUC*	*Accuracy*	*RMSE**	*R^2*	*AUC*	*Accuracy*
Partial Credit + Problem Difficulty	0.3864	0.1027	0.5431	0.7684	0.2702	0.1108	0.3593	0.7674
Partial Credit	0.3866	0.0994	0.5392	0.7683	0.2701	0.1057	0.3619	0.7674
Problem Difficulty	0.4064	0.0829	0.5219	0.7676	0.2941	0.0851	0.3145	0.7674
Knowledge Tracing	0.3897	0.1057	0.4425	0.7729	--	--	--	--
Performance Factors Analysis	0.3882	0.0970	0.5003	0.7754	--	--	--	--

*R^2, AUC, and Accuracy are reported with less data than RMSE due to the nature of student level data.

Table 8. Student Level Average RMSE, R^2, AUC, and Accuracy for Models Predicting Next Problem Correctness (NPC)

properly weight skill and students based on their contribution to the dataset, thereby improving measures of model fit.

Student level statistics of RMSE were calculated based on all predictions. However, it should be noted that measures of R^2, AUC, and model accuracy could not be calculated for students with less than three skill opportunities. This discrepancy should affect all models equally, and thus we provide these measures for comparison in Table 8 with the caveat that they should not be directly compared to measures of student level RMSE.

DISCUSSION

The fit statistics for both the problem log and skill level generalizations paint very similar pictures of the relative success of our tabling method. The combined Partial Credit and Problem Difficulty model performs about as well as KT at both levels of analysis. At these levels, PFA appears to be the 'best' model for predicting binary next problem correctness, showing the lowest RMSE and highest AUC and model accuracy. However, we feel that a simple tabling method that can be performed with extreme efficiency yet still meets the standards of KT is well worth discussion.

Our first research question, "Does an algorithmically determined partial credit score outperform binary metrics when used to predict next problem correctness?" was answered with mixed results for binary predictions. Considering problem log level analysis, while KT and PFA attained fit statistics relative to those accepted in the field, our tabling method for partial credit considered alone only slightly underperformed these standards (RMSE = 0.4244, R^2 = 0.0660, AUC = 0.6309, Accuracy = 0.7309). However, when considering student level analysis, our partial credit tabling method outperformed both KT and PFA in terms of RMSE and AUC. To confirm that these findings were significantly different, we used a two-tailed paired samples t-test for RMSE comparison at both the student level and skill level. RMSEs obtained using our tabling method with partial credit alone were significantly different from those found using KT at the student level, t = 5.65, p < .001, but were not significantly different at the skill level, t = -1.65, p = 0.133. Thus, it is difficult to tell if this finding is truly significant.

Our second research question, "Does a binned metric of current problem difficulty (e.g., Low, Medium, or High difficulty) provide a valid prediction of next problem correctness?" was answered by assessing the "Problem Difficulty" model. When taken alone, problem difficulty is not very helpful in predicting next problem correctness. This was the worst performing model across all granularities of analysis. A paired samples t-test was again used to compare student level and skill level RMSEs to those observed using the KT model. RMSEs obtained using our tabling method for Problem Difficulty were significantly worse than those found using KT at the student level, t = -41.27, p < .001, as well as those found using KT at the skill level, t = -9.93, p < .001. Of the tabled models, this model was also the lowest performing model when considering predictions of partial next credit correctness, drastically underperforming models that considered current problem partial credit score. Thus, we argue that problem difficulty alone is a poor metric for modeling student performance.

Our final research question, "Can current problem difficulty supplement partial credit score to outperform similar modeling techniques?" was answered by assessing the fit statistics for the combined "Partial Credit + Problem Difficulty" model. At the student level, this model outperformed both KT and PFA on predictions of binary next problem correctness as measured by RMSE (0.3864) and AUC (0.5431). This finding was significant using a two-tailed paired samples t-test comparing student level RMSEs, t = 6.50, p < .001, but was not significant when considering skill level RMSEs, t = -1.34, p = 0.214. Despite the low performance of the Problem Difficulty model, this combined model consistently outperformed partial credit when modeled alone, suggesting possible mediation effects. Using a paired t-test comparison, this difference was significant at the student level, t = -4.55, p < .001, but was not significantly reliable at the skill level, t = -1.03, p = .310. As such, it is difficult to quantify the potentially negative impact of considering problem difficulty when using partial credit to model next problem correctness.

Model fit indices for the prediction of partial credit scores for next problem correctness are provided for further consideration, but do not specifically link to our research questions. Drastic improvements in model fit suggest that intelligent tutoring systems should incorporate partial credit scoring as it has the potential to enhance the precision of student modeling. In the current study, these findings cannot be compared to standard KT and PFA models that utilize binary input and essentially predict binary performance. Future research will incorporate modifying these models to predict continuous partial credit metrics, thus allowing for further comparison.

CONTRIBUTION

The results from the present study suggest that considering partial credit for each skill opportunity can enhance the accuracy of student modeling. While the concept of using a tabling method to establish partial credit metrics that predict binary correctness is not novel [12], tabling a model based on algorithmically determined partial credit is, to the best of our awareness, a unique approach. This method was shown to perform about as well as KT when predicting binary next problem correctness. We feel that this finding still provides a significant contribution to the field, as KT is far more computationally expensive. Our KT analysis took approximately 20 hours to run, while all tabling methods were conducted by hand in less than three hours. While this is impressive in and of itself, the second author was then able to implement the tabling method presented here within the ASSISTments test database, arriving at a replication of our predictions in less than two minutes. If automated in such a manner, our Partial Credit + Problem Difficulty model could predict next problem performance on par with KT in approximately one 600th of the time. This increase in efficiency could prove essential for intelligent tutoring systems that currently incorporate KT models to adaptively control student skill practice.

Further, the partial credit model was novel in its ability to predict partial credit scores for next problem correctness, thereby enhancing model fit even further. In future research, we hope to modify the standard KT and PFA models to allow for the prediction of continuous variables for comparison. We also anticipate directly comparing our partial credit model to the "Assistance" Model established in previous research [12]. The "Assistance" Model cited a clear cut, albeit subjective, method for the provision of partial credit scores. As the tabling technique employed made predictions on a continuous scale rather than by binning partial credit as we have shown in the present study, comparison was not presently possible without ensembling our findings with standard KT measures [12]. However, as alternating ensembling techniques lead to inconsistent results [4], we argue for direct modifications within KT that will allow the model to learn partial credit scores at each opportunity and to gauge a student's knowledge state on a continuum. A similar model was previously suggested by Pardos & Heffernan [10], but to our knowledge has never been implemented. Thus, the present study lays the groundwork for future research in modifying KT.

The assessment of models considering problem difficulty also provides a contribution to the modeling literature. It seems intuitive that problem difficulty should influence a students' ability to answer the current problem correctly, and that it likely influences their knowledge state and next problem correctness. The findings here suggest that problem difficulty alone, when binned into generic groups of Low, Medium, and High difficulty, does not provide accurate models of next problem correctness. However, problem difficulty appeared to enhance modeling when coupled with partial credit in comparison to partial credit modeled alone, although this difference was not shown to be significant. Still, we believe that some measure of problem difficulty is important to consider when modeling student learning. Future research should investigate using a continuous metric or designing an alternative binning approach for this feature. Future work should also consider devising an approach to remedy the issue of being unable to predict a student's first opportunity within a skill when using tabled models. Possible solutions include per student estimates of prior knowledge based on performance on other skills within the tutor, or simply implementing problem difficulty as a measure of likelihood for accuracy.

Despite the impressive performance of our partial credit model, we retain skepticism in regards to the subjective nature of our partial credit algorithm. As multiple arbitrary partial credit models have now been designed to assess log data from the ASSISTments platform [12], we argue for the design of a data driven algorithm that considers and compares a myriad of logged features. Future work will examine a grid search of possible hint and attempt penalties to examine the sensitivity of the approach described herein. The data files of intelligent tutoring system are rich with information pertaining to students' actions, including the time required for first response, their sequence of actions within each problem, and the specific misconceptions that are driving incorrect responses. These features may provide critical information for the scoring of partial credit. When considering the approach used in the present study, using an algorithm to establish partial credit scores prior to tabling provides the leeway for tabled models to consider these additional features. Future research could easily replicate similar models, combining partial credit with novel features for additional exploration of the observed effect.

ACKNOWLEDGMENTS

We acknowledge funding from NSF (grant #'s 1316736, 1252297, 1109483, 1031398, 0742503), ONR's "STEM Grand Challenges," and IES (grant #'s R305A120125, R305C100024). Thanks to S.O. & L.P.B.O.

REFERENCES

1. Attali, Y. & Powers, D. (2010). Immediate feedback and opportunity to revise answers to open-end questions. *Educational and Psychological Measures*, 70 (1), 22-35.
2. Corbett, A.T., Anderson, J.R. (1995). Knowledge Tracing: Modeling the Acquisition of Procedural Knowledge. *User Modeling and User-Adapted Interaction*, 4: 253-278.
3. Duong, H.D., Zhu, L., Wang, Y., & Heffernan, N.T. (2013). A Prediction Model Uses the Sequence of Attempts and Hints to Better Predict Knowledge: Better to Attempt the Problem First, Rather Than Ask for a Hint. In S. D'Mello, R. Calvo, & A. Olney (Eds.) Proceedings of the 6th International Conference on Educational Data Mining. Memphis, TN. 316-317.
4. Gowda, S.M., Baker, R.S.J.D, Pardos, Z., & Heffernan, N.T. (2011). The Sum is Greater than the Parts: Ensembling Student Knowledge Models in ASSISTments. Proceedings of the KDD 2011 Workshop on KDD in Educational Data.
5. Koedinger, K.R. & Corbett, A.T. (2006). Cognitive tutors: Technology bringing learning science to the classroom. In K. Sawyer (Ed.), *The Cambridge handbook of the learning sciences* (61-78). New York: Cambridge University Press.
6. Murphy, K. (2001). The Bayes Net Toolbox for MATLAB. Computing Science and Statistics, 33(2), 1024-1034.
7. Author1. (2014). L@S 2015 Submission: Dataset. Retrieved 10/14/14, http://tiny.cc/LaS2015Submission
8. Pardos, Z.A. & Heffernan, N.T. (2010). Modeling Individualization in a Bayesian Networks Implementation of Knowledge Tracing. In Proceedings of the 18th International Conference on User Modeling, Adaptation and Personalization. 255-266.
9. Pardos, Z.A., & Heffernan, N.T. (2011). KT-IDEM: Introducing Item Difficulty to the Knowledge Tracing Model. In Joseph A. Konstan et al. (Eds.): UMAP 2011, LNCS 6787, 243-254.
10. Pardos, Z.A. & Heffernan, N.T. (2012). Tutor Modeling vs. Student Modeling. Proceedings of the Twenty-Fifth International Florida Artificial Intelligence Research Society Conference, 420-425.
11. Pavlik, P.I., Cen, H., Koedinger, K.R. (2009). Performance Factors Analysis - A New Alternative to Knowledge Tracing. In: Proceedings of the 14th International Conference on Artificial Intelligence in Education, Brighton, UK, 531-538.
12. Wang, Y. & Heffernan, N.T. (2011). The "Assistance" Model: Leveraging How Many Hints and Attempts a Student Needs. The 24th International FLAIRS Conference.
13. Wang, Y. & Heffernan, N. (2013). Extending Knowledge Tracing to Allow Partial Credit: Using Continuous versus Binary Nodes. In K. Yacef et al. (Eds.) AIED 2013, LNAI 7926, 181-188.

Addressing Common Analytic Challenges to Randomized Experiments in MOOCs: Attrition and Zero-Inflation

Anne Lamb
Harvard University
anne_lamb@mail.harvard.edu

Jascha Smilack
Harvard University
smilack@fas.harvard.edu

Andrew Ho
Harvard University
andrew_ho@gse.harvard.edu

Justin Reich
Harvard University
justin_reich@harvard.edu

ABSTRACT
Massive open online course (MOOC) platforms increasingly allow easily implemented randomized experiments. The heterogeneity of MOOC students, however, leads to two methodological obstacles in analyzing interventions to increase engagement. (1) Many MOOC participation metrics have distributions with substantial positive skew from highly active users as well as zero-inflation from high attrition. (2) High attrition means that in some experimental designs, most users assigned to the treatment never receive it; analyses that do not consider attrition result in "intent-to-treat" (ITT) estimates that underestimate the true effects of interventions. We address these challenges in analyzing an intervention to improve forum participation in the 2014 JusticeX course offered on the edX MOOC platform. We compare the results of four ITT models (OLS, logistic, quantile, and zero-inflated negative binomial regressions) and three "treatment-on-treated" (TOT) models (Wald estimator, 2SLS with a second stage logistic model, and instrumental variables quantile regression). A combination of logistic, quantile, and zero-inflated negative binomial regressions provide the most comprehensive description of the ITT effects. TOT methods then adjust the ITT underestimates. Substantively, we demonstrate that self-assessment questions about forum participation encourage more students to engage in forums and increases the participation of already active students.

Author Keywords
MOOCs; A/B testing; randomized controlled trials; attrition; zero-inflation; treatment-on-treated; engagement

ACM Classification Keywords
K.3.1 Distance Learning.

INTRODUCTION
While the first years of massive open online course (MOOC) research have been characterized by post-hoc analysis of observational data [5, 7], MOOC platforms are beginning to fulfill their promise of enabling easily implemented randomized experiments [2, 9]. Researchers and course developers can randomly assign students to encounter different course materials or questions. Because MOOCs generate detailed data from thousands of users around the world, the effects of these interventions can be evaluated on a wide variety of outcome measures, including student performance, persistence, and participation. Along with the benefits of these abundant data, experiments conducted in MOOCs present researchers with analytic challenges not often encountered in traditional education settings or even other online venues.

Student heterogeneity is a distinctive feature of MOOCs. Some students register for MOOCs to browse the materials, while others fully commit to completing all course activities [14]. Many students cease participation soon after registration, while a small number of students are extremely active [7]. This variation in student behavior produces distinct empirical features in MOOC data. First, many distributions of student outcome measures stray far from normal distributions. Measures of student participation and engagement are often operationalized as counts of activities, such as page views or problem attempts. These counts are zero-inflated by the many browsers who stop out early and right-skewed by the activity of the most devoted students. Conventional statistical tests cannot necessarily provide the appropriate inferences about interventions when facing such unusual distributions.

Additionally, high levels of attrition lead to complexities in determining differences between the effect on the assigned treatment group versus those who actually received the treatment. Social scientists often distinguish between analyses of the intent-to-treat (ITT) and treatment-on-treated (TOT) [3]. The former analyzes differences between persons *assigned* to control or experimental conditions, while the latter analyzes differences between persons who *experience* a treatment and those in the control condition. Since attrition from MOOCs is high, particularly at the beginning of a course, many assigned to a treatment group may attrite before experiencing an intervention. Additional analytic effort is necessary to estimate the differences between ITT effects and TOT effects, differences which can be substantial in MOOC contexts.

We explore these two issues—analyzing zero-inflated, skewed participation metrics and estimating treatment-on-

L@S 2015, March 14–18, 2015, Vancouver, BC, Canada.

ACM 978-1-4503-3411-2/15/03…$15.00.
http://dx.doi.org/10.1145/2724660.2724669

treated effects—in the context of an experimental intervention to increase discussion forum participation in an edX MOOC, JusticeX.

BACKGROUND ON JUSTICEX

Michael Sandel's Justice course at Harvard University introduces students to theories of justice, and encourages them to critically examine their own views on moral and political controversies. One of Harvard's most popular residential courses for undergraduates, it was offered as a HarvardX course for the first time in 2013 [15].

JusticeX (the online version of Justice) includes 24 content chapters, each of which consists of key readings and a 20-30 minute lecture video. After the readings and video, participants encounter a discussion prompt that poses a challenging moral dilemma without a clear answer. Example prompts include: *Would it be right, as a last resort, for the police to use torture to extract information from a suspected terrorist about the location of a bomb? How involved should government be in legislating morality?* Participants are invited to view arguments for both sides and then discuss these issues in the forums.

Fostering debate and dialogue among participants is critical to achieving the goals of the course. As is typical of MOOC courses, however, only a small proportion of all enrollees ever participate in the forums [10]. In the 2013 version of JusticeX, 16% of registrants posted at least once to the discussion forum. Although this was one of the highest levels of forum participation across Harvard and MIT MOOCs at the time, one of the main goals of the 2014 run of the course was to improve rates of forum participation.

Interventions to Improve Forum Participation

To encourage increased dialogue and engagement among participants, the instructional team implemented three interventions in the Spring 2014 version of JusticeX. The first treatment consisted of a *self-test participation check.* Following each of the 24 lectures, participants could complete a three-question, non-credit quiz. In the first six lectures, those who were assigned to the first treatment received an additional question: "Have you participated in the discussion forum?" The participants could select "No" or "Yes, I've upvoted 2 or more good comments and posted at least 1 response." This non-credit question served as a reminder for students and set norms for desired levels of participation.

The second treatment consisted of *discussion priming*, where students could access discussion summaries from the 2013 course. For the third treatment, the JusticeX team sent *discussion preview emails*, which previewed the course content for the coming week and summarized the topics that would be addressed in the discussion forums.

After comprehensive analysis of all three treatments, we found evidence that only the first intervention led to increased participation in the forum discussions. To simplify our discussion of how to address common methodological challenges, in the remainder of this paper, we limit our focus to the first treatment, the participation check. We mention the other treatments for transparency.

Random Assignment

By default, the A/B testing framework in edX dynamically assigns users to experimental groups whenever the system "needs to know" their group identity. Assignment can happen when students load a page or navigate to a sub-section that includes randomized content, or when faculty generate a course grade report that is dependent upon a randomized problem. Thus, students can be assigned to a treatment condition *without encountering the treatment.*

In the case of these JusticeX experiments, since at least one of the interventions (preview emails) was not embedded within the platform, a "trick" was used to assign all students as early as possible. A blank, or "hidden," HTML unit was embedded at the bottom of the first course page that nearly every student would encounter. Upon navigating to this page, the platform assigned students to the experimental or control group for each of the three interventions.

The disadvantage of assigning students to a treatment group as early as possible was that many soon quit participating in the course. Assigning students early, in a context with high attrition, increases the likelihood that students never experience the treatment and that resulting distributions are zero-inflated. As expected, students were assigned in approximately equal numbers to treatment and control conditions in all three treatments. To avoid possible treatment contamination, we focus only on the "control" subgroup that received no treatments, and on the subgroup that received only the self-test participation check. There were 2,399 students assigned to the control condition. Of these students, 44% were female, the mean age was 33, and 64% had a BA or higher. The treatment group with 2,378 students was statistically indistinguishable from the control group on demographic characteristics.

Operationalizing Engagement as "Forum Actions"

Like many indirect measures of engagement in online environments, we operationalize forum participation as a count variable. We count the number of times students conduct any of four forum actions: creating a new post, replying to an existing post, editing a post or reply, and upvoting a comment. Upvoting allows users to "like" or agree with what another user has written, and all users can see how many votes a certain discussion post has received. We call the primary outcome of interest the number of "forum actions," an indicator of student participation. From this measure, we can infer whether experimental interventions increased student participation in the forums.

Ideally, the outcome measures for these experiments would also measure student learning, such as an assessment of student's moral reasoning ability. Since such complex

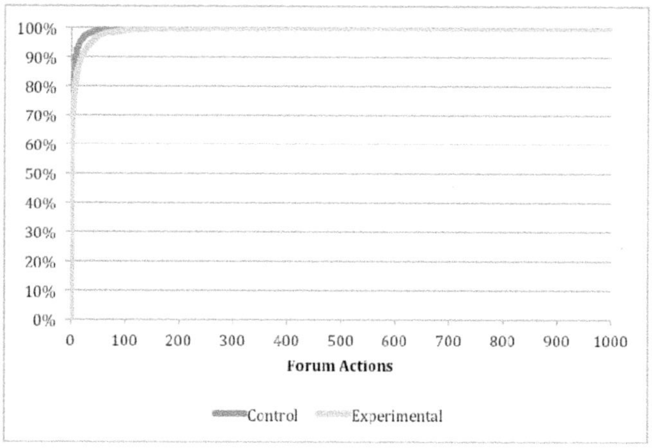

Figure 1: Cumulative distributions of forum actions for control (*n*= 2399) and treatment (*n*=2378) groups in 2014 JusticeX.

domains are difficult to assess at scale, we are limited to examining how the intervention affected users' quantity of forum participation.

CHALLENGE #1: MODELING ZERO-INFLATED, SKEWED COUNT OUTCOMES

In this section, we compare a variety of approaches for estimating the effect of the self-test discussion check on forum actions, and we suggest advantages and disadvantages for each approach.

A visual inspection of the CDFs of forum actions in the experimental and control conditions, shown in Figure 1, highlights the analytic challenges with our outcome variable. Due to a combination of high attrition and low overall forum participation, forum activity is zero-inflated relative to characteristic count distributions such as Poisson or negative binomial distributions. Moreover, right-hand (positive) skew in these distributions results from the relatively small proportion of extremely active users in the course [8].

In typical social science experiments, researchers expect an intervention to induce a shift in the mean outcome among those receiving an intervention. Therefore, the effect of an intervention is often summarized by a simple difference in means. We, too, begin by comparing the difference in mean forum actions using OLS. However, means of distributions can be misleading indicators of the effect of an intervention in cases of zero-inflation or extreme values. Unlike in a Gaussian distribution, the mean does not represent a peak or any visually interpretable feature of the distribution.

Instead of relying only on a difference in means to quantify the effect of this intervention, we also consider a variety of other ways to summarize the effect. While OLS suggests that the intervention increased forum actions among those in the treatment group, the nature of the distributional shift is unclear. Did it reduce the number of people with zero posts, without affecting the activity of frequent posters? Did it only engage the most active posters, without shifting the behavior of non-posters? Did it evenly shift the distribution to the right? In this section, we present four different analytic approaches to address these questions: OLS, logistic regression, quantile regression, and count regression. In these analyses, we include all those assigned to the experimental condition regardless of actual exposure to the treatment, an intent-to-treat analysis.

Ordinary Least Squares

Ordinary Least Squares (OLS) regression is familiar to many analysts, simple to conduct, and an appropriate exploratory step in analyzing MOOC participation metrics. In the case of this intervention, absent of including any covariates, OLS provides simple summary statistics of the mean number of forum actions However, the risk of OLS in the MOOC context, either when analyzing non-experimental results or when including covariates, is that it assumes the residuals will be normally distributed. While we can expect OLS to give a good linear approximation of the average treatment effect given our large sample size [3], a difference in means is not an ideal summary of treatment effects with a skewed distribution. Furthermore, the common interpretation of parameter estimates—that the effect of the intervention is of a similar magnitude at all levels of the outcome—is incorrect here. Finally, statistical inferences about the difference in means in the population will be incorrect, although this is generally not problematic when sample sizes are as large as they are MOOCs.

One common approach to dealing with non-normal distributions in an OLS framework is to transform them, although this typically does not work with count variables [12]. We briefly demonstrate the futility of transformation in this context. We take a series of transformations, including a log transformation, square and cubic roots, and a variety of inverse transformations. While the log and cubic root transformations (shown in Figure 2) succeeded in stretching out the values, the resulting distributions still appear far from normal.

Despite the violation of normality, OLS estimates are likely to be consistent given our large sample size. We perform a simple bivariate regression of the number of forum actions on a dichotomous indicator of whether the individual was assigned to the treatment. From this simple model, we obtain our first estimate of the average treatment effect: on average, users assigned to the treatment group had about 4.2 more forum actions relative to those in the control group (p<.001). Participants in the control condition have an average of 3.1 forum actions and those assigned to treatment have an average of 7.3 actions. In the two-sample case, the model will always recover the means exactly, and indeed we find that the OLS estimates are identical to the conditional means of the sample. Although the means are not the most interpretable indicator of central tendency in the outcomes, and the statistical inferences about the

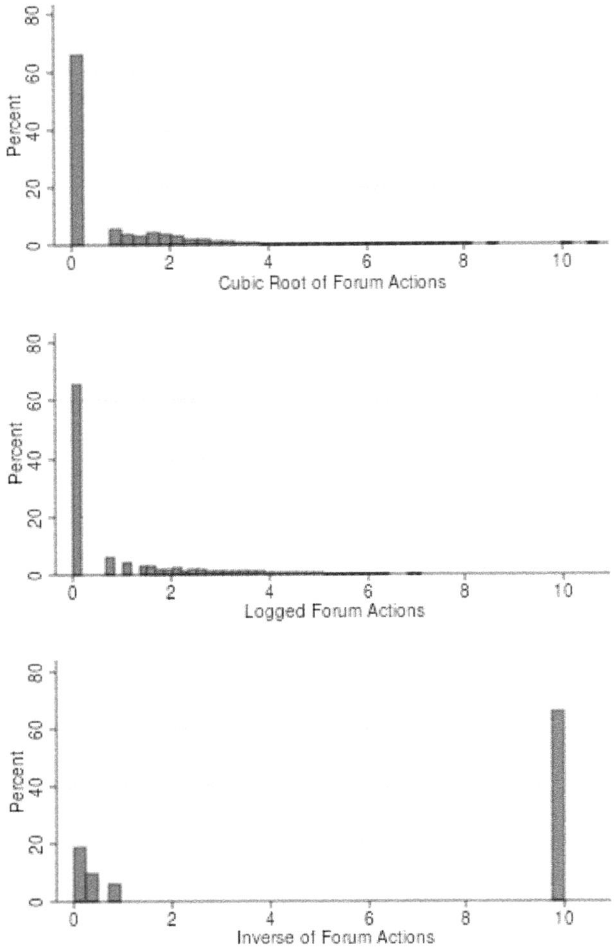

Figure 2: Cubic root, log, and inverse trasformations of forum actions

population are suspect, the model accurately summarizes the mean treatment effect.

Logistic Regression

As an alternative expression of the effect of the treatment, we dichotomize the dependent variable, distinguishing only between zero actions and one or more actions. We can then fit the dichotomous outcome data using a logistic regression model. Dichotomization sacrifices all distinctions between nonzero counts of actions, however, if the purpose of the treatment is merely to increase the likelihood of any action, and there is no interest in distinctions between one action and thousands of actions, logistic regression on the dichotomous outcome is appropriate. Due to the dichotomization, this approach cannot estimate the additional effect of the treatment among those who already had at least one action.

The logit model estimates the log-odds of having had one or more forum actions conditional on assignment to treatment.

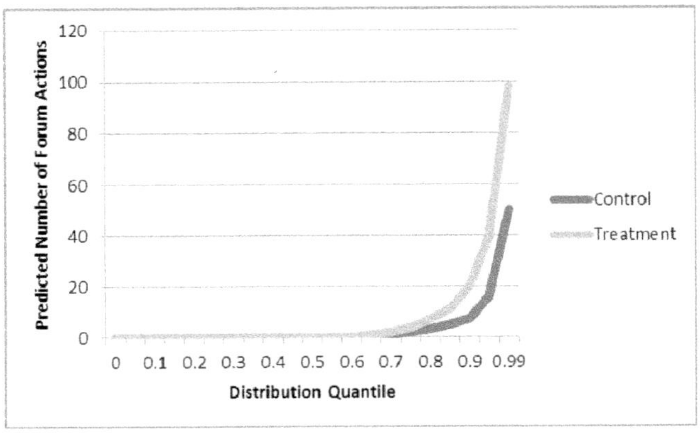

Figure 3. Predicted number of forum actions by quantile of forum action by experimental condition.

On average, being assigned to the treatment group increases the log-odds of having a forum action by 0.284 (p<.001). We estimate that students in the control condition have a 31.8 percent probability of having at least one forum action, and students in the treatment condition have a 38.2 percent probability of having one action, a difference of 6.4 percentage points. Again, the two-sample setup ensures that the model recovers the observed logits and corresponding probabilities exactly. The p-values are slightly different than OLS given the loss of information in the outcome and the alternative model specification, however, the sample size is sufficiently large to render the difference moot.

Quantile Regression

We use quantile regression to begin to explore the distribution effects of the treatment. Quantile regression allows us to determine how an intervention changes the shape of an entire distribution – whether it spreads out or is compressed, or whether it shifts upward or downward. We use the conditional quantile function, $Q_t(Y_i|X_i)$, to describe the relationship between our predictor, assignment to treatment, and the outcome at different points along the conditional distribution of forum actions. At a specified quantile, the estimator works by asymmetrically weighting over- and under-predictions [3].

The single dichotomous predictor again allows observed conditional quantiles to be fit perfectly by the model at each quantile (Figure 3). At the median, users in both groups have zero forum actions. The number of forum actions diverges by the 65th percentile, when those in the treatment group have 1 forum action relative to the control group that has 0 actions. This discrepancy diverges even more substantially beyond the 75th percentile. At the 80th percentile, those in the treatment have approximately 4 more forum actions, close to the average treatment effect. By the 90th percentile, those in the treatment have 13 more forum actions, and by the 99th percentile, they have almost 50 more forum actions. From the 65th percentile and onward, those assigned to treatment have nearly double the number of forum actions as those in the control group.

	(1a) Forum Actions	(1b) Structural Zero
Treatment	0.826***	-0.103
	(0.1281)	(0.1927)
Constant	1.425***	-1.113
	(0.1469)	(0.5790)
Ln Alpha	1.775***	
	(0.2114)	
Observations	4,937	4,937

Robust standard errors in parentheses
*** p<0.001, ** p<0.01, * p<0.05

Table 1: Zero-inflated negative binomial regression of the number of forum actions on assignment to treatment.

Zero-Inflated Negative Binomial

Thus far, we have contrasted OLS (which expresses the average treatment effect), logistic regression (which fits differences in probabilities of having at least one forum activity), and quantile regression (which captures the effect of the intervention on the different quantiles of the distribution). In this section, we fit a model that seems appropriate for the non-normal shape of the outcome distribution. To do so, we turn to the family of regression models for count data. We choose a zero-inflated negative binomial (ZINB) model, because over half of the observations in our sample have zero values and the data are over-dispersed [13]. In the absence of zero-inflation, we could use an ordinary negative binomial.

The ZINB models zero-inflated, over-dispersed count data using two separate processes. First, it assumes the existence of "structural" zeros, and models the probability, for the entire sample, of having such a zero. A structural zero exists when it is not possible for the user to have a value other than zero. For instance, approximately 35% of users attrite before encountering either the discussion forum or the first self-assessment: they could not experience treatment or have an outcome.

(Although we can observe users who have an actual zero value, the model does not allow us to distinguish between those with structural zeros and those with zero counts.) The ZINB then uses a negative binomial regression to model the count data among those without structural zeros. These processes together produce two estimates: the probability of having a structural zero and the predicted count of forum actions. We show the results of this model in Table 1. In column 1b, we estimate that the differences in structural zeros are not statistically significant. In column 1A, we estimate that the treatment causes a .0826 increase in the log of the counts. When we exponentiate this estimate, we obtain an incidence rate ratio of 2.3. Counts can be thought of as resulting from a process with a rate of activity, in this case the rate at which a student completes forum actions over the duration of the course. We can interpret the incidence rate ratio as indicating that the participation self-check intervention increases the rate of forum activity by a factor of 2.3.

We display the predicted probabilities of structural zeros and the mean predicted counts resulting from the ZINB model in Table 2. In the first column, we show the predicted probability of structural zeros, though the difference is not statistically significant. Of those without structural zeros, users in the treatment have, on average, about 4.2 more forum actions than those in the treatment, recovering the sample means consistently with OLS results. We also compare differences in the predicted probabilities of counts along the distribution. Users in the treatment have higher fitted probabilities of having each corresponding count than those in the control, consistent with our findings that the treatment yields distribution effects not captured by the average effect. If the data are indeed generated by the ZINB process, this approach would be more parsimonious than quantile regression, where the latter would be encourage interpretation of chance differences between quantiles of the treatment and control distributions.

	Probability of Structural Zero	Predicted Mean Forum Actions	Pr ($Y \geq 3$) 75th Pct.	Pr ($Y \geq 7$) 90th Pct.	Pr ($Y \geq 50$) 99th Pct.
Control	25%	3.1	25%	13%	1%
Treatment	23%	7.3	32%	20%	4%

Table 2: Predicted probability of a degenerate zero, predicted mean forum actions, and predicted probabilities of the number of forum actions greater than or equal to the 75th, 90th, and 99th percentile of the distribution of forum actions for the control group, by treatment status, based on the ZINB model results.

Key Outcome Estimate	Interpretation	Advantages	Disadvantages
OLS			
β_{OLS}=4.2	The mean number of forum actions was 4.2 actions higher for the treatment group versus the control.	• Simple • Unbiased and consistent estimator of the average treatment effect	• Normality assumption violated • May be misinterpreted as estimated effect for all treated individuals
Logistic Regression			
Pr(Y|T=1) = 38.2% PR(Y|T=0) = 31.8%	Students in the treatment group have a 6.4 percentage-point higher probability of having at least one forum action compared to the control group	• Assumptions of the model are met	• Dichotomizing the outcome leads to a loss of information • Cannot estimate distribution effects
Quantile Regression			
$Q_Y(.75\|T=1) = 2$ $Q_Y(.95\|T=1) = 23$ $Q_Y(.99\|T=1) = 48$	At the 75th percentile, those assigned to treatment have 2 additional forum actions compared to those in the control. Above the 65th percentile, users in the treatment group in each quantile had at least double the forum actions as users in the control group.	• More comprehensive summary of distributional treatment effects • Appealing visualization of differences across the distribution	• No single summary statistics • Can only describe difference in each quantile
Zero-Inflated Negative Binomial			
β_{NB}=0.826 IRR= 2.3	No differences in structural zeros between treatment and control. The log of the counts of forum actions is 0.826 higher for users assigned to the treatment group relative to the control group. Being assigned to the treatment increases the rate of forum activity by a factor of 2.3.	• Designed to address zero-inflated, skewed distributions of count variables • Provides multiple avenues by which the intervention influences the outcome	• More complicated to fit and test • Less familiar to many researchers and practitioners • Parameter estimates more difficult to interpret and explain

Table 3: Summary of modeling strategies for the effect of assignment to treatment on forum actions in JusticeX

Summary of Intent-to-Treat Results

In Table 3, we summarize the pros and cons of the four methods we use for analyzing the intent-to-treat effects. OLS is simple to use and interpret, but suffers from a poor fit. Moreover, the average treatment effect fails to capture the full impact of the treatment. Dichotomizing the outcome and employing a logistic regression addresses issues with model fit, but again, provides only a limited explanation of the treatment effects. The quantile regression provides a more comprehensive picture of the distributional effects, showing that among those who actually use the forum, the treatment increases activity. However, as a series of separate regression models, it resists a simple summary statistic. Finally, the ZINB provides insight into both average effects and distribution effects. It shows that the treatment increases the rate of posting among those who do visit the forum discussion.

We find the combination of these estimates critical for accurately summarizing the ITT effects. Assignment to treatment for the participation checks increased forum actions. On average, users assigned to the treatment had 4.2 more forum actions than users in the control group. We predict a 6.4 percentage point increase in in the probability of having any forum activity for those assigned to the treatment group over the control group. Additionally, assignment to treatment increases forum activity for those at the upper end of the distribution. Beginning at the 65th percentile of the outcome distribution, in which the control group had 0 actions relative to 1 action among the treatment students, students in the experimental condition had at least twice the forum actions at each respective quantile. We estimate that assignment to treatment increases the rate of forum actions by a factor of 2.3.

CHALLENGE #2: IDENTIFYING AND MODELING TREATMENT ON TREATED

In the previous section, we compared all students assigned to the self-test participation check treatment with an equivalent control group randomly assigned to no intervention. Since we know that many students attrite from MOOCs before engaging with any of the course content [7], we harbor an intuition that our intent-to-treat analyses underestimates the effect of the intervention on students who *actually encountered the intervention*.

The edX data stores provide a simple database of all those assigned to a treatment condition, but identifying students who actually received the intervention proves more complicated. It requires at least two steps: operationalizing the definition of "receiving the treatment" and then extracting evidence of receiving treatment from the tracking logs. For the self-test participation check intervention, we could operationalize receipt of treatment in several possible ways: simply viewing the page with the self-test questions, answering at least one question on the page, or answering the actual discussion self-check question. The first two options are more capacious, and potentially include students who navigated to the page but did not actually see the self-check question. The latter operationalization addresses this problem, but potentially omits students who saw the question and chose not to answer it, perhaps because they had not yet participated in the forum. Nevertheless, we chose this latter option, defining receipt of treatment as answering the self-check question. We acknowledge that alternative definitions may be defensible, and they could provide helpful sensitivity analyses.

We can further complicate the issue of treatment-on-treated by considering the "dosage" of the treatment. The self-test discussion check appeared after each of the first six lectures, so students could have been exposed to the treatment as many as six separate times. Of those assigned to the treatment group, 36% answered at least one discussion self-check, 10% answered at least three, and 1% answered all six. Thus, we could define receipt of treatment broadly as having encountered at least one discussion self-check, or we can identify the linear effect of multiple treatments by measuring different "doses" of treatment.

With these decisions in mind, we demonstrate three approaches for adjusting the intent-to-treat effects to estimate the treatment-on-treated (TOT) effects. All approaches attempt to correct the underestimation of treatment effects inherent in the intent-to-treat analyses presented in the prior section. First, we present a simple Wald estimate of the TOT, by dosage of treatment received. Doing so adjusts the average treatment effects from the intent-to-treat analysis. Second, we perform a manual two-stage least-squares estimate where we use a logistic regression in the second stage. Finally, we attempt to quantify the distribution effects of the TOT using an instrumental variables quantile regression.

	Some (Answered 1 or More Prompts)	Half (Answered 3 or More Prompts)	All (Answered 6 or More Prompts)
Wald Estimator	11.7	42.7	312.9
Conditional Sample Means	14.2	27.3	37.4

Table 4: Wald estimate of treatment on treated using the primary outcome, number of forum actions.

One strategy we cannot use is simply restricting our comparison to those who received the treatment and those who were assigned to the control group. Those who receive the treatment (our "compliers") likely differ along key unobservable characteristics related to our outcome relative to those who do not comply. If we made this naïve comparison, our treatment effects would be biased, thus eliminating the benefit of randomization. Because of this, unlike our intent-to-treat estimates, our TOT estimates are not so easily compared to observational sample data.

Wald Estimator

The Wald estimator provides the simplest approach to average TOT estimates in the case of one predictor variable and one instrument. The Wald estimator is simply a ratio of the difference in mean forum actions between the control and assignment to treatment groups to the difference in proportion of users receiving the treatment (which in this case equals the proportion of those receiving the treatment from the assignment to treatment group). It rescales the OLS estimate of the average treatment effect by the proportion of those who actually received the treatment. In Table 4, we present the Wald estimator corresponding to the three different "dosages" of treatment received compared to the conditional sample means. While the Wald estimator for those receiving *some* of the treatment seems plausible, the estimator does not appear realistic for those receiving *half* or *all* of the treatment. The Wald estimator becomes less reliable when compliance rates are so low.

Two-Stage Least Squares Logistic Regression

In two-stage least squares (2SLS), the first stage regresses an endogenous predictor variable on an exogenous instrumental variable. The predicted values are then substituted into the structural equation of the second stage in order to predict the relationship between that endogenous variable and the outcome of interest using only the variation in the endogenous variable induced by the exogenous instrument. While typical 2SLS uses linear regression in both stages, we modify this approach to use a second stage logistic regression. By doing so, we aim to adjust our ITT estimates from the logistic regression in order to identify the effects on users receiving the treatment. Essentially, our approach amounts to using the probability of receiving

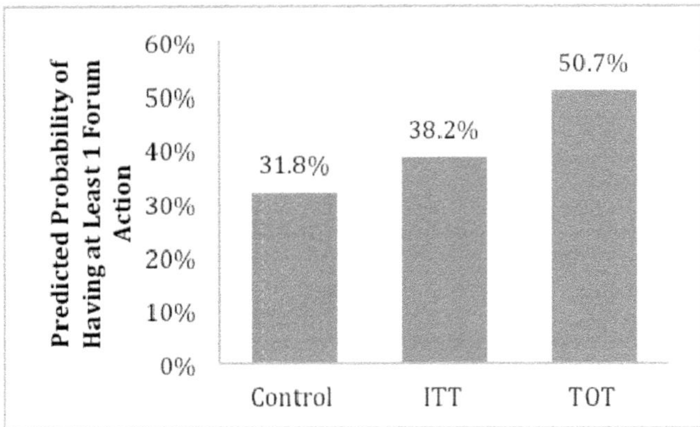

Figure 4: Predicted probabilities of having at least one forum action.

treatment as the predictor of having had at least one forum action in the logistic regression.

The results of this modified 2SLS approach reveal that, as expected, the predicted probability of having at least one forum action is higher for those induced to receive the treatment compared to the general sample of those assigned to treatment. In Figure 4, we compare the ITT and TOT estimates of the predicted probability of having forum activity. Those who actually answer the self-check question have a nearly 51% probability of having at least one forum action, which is almost 20 percentage-points higher than the probability for the control group. It is also substantially higher than the original ITT estimate. In fact, when comparing this final estimate to the conditional mean from the sample, it seems on target. Of individuals who answered the self-check, two-thirds had at least one forum action.

Instrumental Variable Quantile Regression

We first used quantile regression to determine how the distribution of forum actions changed as a result of assignment to treatment. Here, we employ an instrumental variables quantile regression to adjust the distribution effects relative to those who actually received the treatment. The instrumental variables approach allows us to incorporate a binary endogenous regressor indicating exposure to treatment into the quantile regression model [1]. Since, as with regular instrumental variables estimates, the IV quantile regression gives us the estimates for the compliers only, we expect the estimates to increase relative to the intent-to-treat estimates.

The results of the IV quantile regression confirm that those who receive the treatment are more active on the forum than those in the control. The effects of the treatment-on-treated begin to show by the 40th percentile, and the difference in predicted forum actions between the treated and the control group grows rapidly toward the higher end of the distribution. At the median, the compliers have, on average, 3 more forum actions than the control group. By the 80th percentile, the difference in forum actions has risen to 15, by the 95th percentile, the compliers have about 43

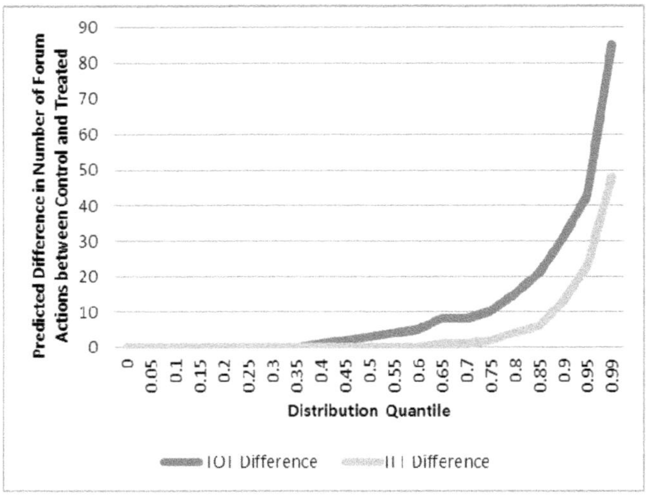

Figure 5: Difference between treatment and control conditions in the number of forum actions by quantile.

more actions than the control group, and at the 99th percentile the difference is 85 actions.

For the sake of comparison, in Figure 5 we plot the difference in predicted number of forum posts by quantile for (1) those assigned to treatment (ITT) versus the control, and (2) those induced to receive treatment (TOT) versus the control. As expected, the intent-to-treat effects underestimated the true effects of the treatment-on-the-treated. The entire curve shifts upward when correcting for the bias of the ITT estimates. While the ITT estimates indicated no difference in forum participation by participants all the way to the 60th percentile, the TOT estimates imply that users in the 40th percentile and greater have increased forum activity.

Summary of Treatment-on-Treated Results

Many JusticeX participants, due to attrition, our narrow definition of "receipt of treatment," or preferences for non-linear course progression, did not encounter the self-check question prompt intervention. While our intent-to-treat analyses provided strong evidence that assignment to treatment did have an effect on forum activity, we were also interested in quantifying the additional effect the intervention may have had on those users who actually received the treatment. Therefore, we used three methods to adjust our ITT estimates to uncover the impact of TOT.

The Wald estimator adjusted the average treatment effect by dividing the OLS estimate by the proportion of compliers. This simple adjustment implies that the ITT estimate should be increased by approximately a factor of 3 to uncover the effect of the intervention on those who received the treatment, or that those who received the treatment had, on average, approximately 12 more forum actions than those in the control. We were less certain of our Wald estimates when assessing higher doses of the treatment. Our manual 2SLS with a logistic second stage regression allowed us to adjust our original logistic results, again testing whether the intervention encouraged additional students to become active on the forum. We find that while approximately one-third of users in the control are predicted to have at least one forum action, over half of those who receive treatment are predicted to do so. Finally, by employing the IV quantile regression, we notice that the trend predicted by the ITT estimate is magnified among the compliers; the treatment shifts the curve even higher for those who receive the treatment.

CONCLUSION

In analyzing the results of a randomized experiment in the MOOC JusticeX, we encountered two issues that will likely impact other researchers analyzing MOOC experiments. First, because our outcome of interest was a participation metric—fundamentally a count variable—its distribution had substantial right-hand skew and zero-inflation. Second, due to high rates of attrition at the beginning of the course, many students assigned to treatment stopped out before encountering the intervention. Precisely estimating the intervention's effects requires accounting for this "non-compliance."

To address the first issue, we use four approaches to estimate both the average treatment effects and the distribution effects of the participation self-check. While the naïve OLS estimates appear to adequately estimate the difference in means between the control group and those assigned to treatment, on the whole, the average treatment effect is an unsatisfactory statistic for quantifying the breadth of the treatment effects. Rather, we prefer to describe the effect of the treatment using a variety of summary statistics. Logistic regression with a dichotomized outcome variable uncovers the effect of assignment to treatment on getting students to participate at least once. We estimate that assignment to treatment increases the probability of participating in the forums by six percentage-points. We also found value in using an approach that could model distributional effects, in this case, the ZINB and quantile regressions. The former allows us to summarize the effect of the treatment on those who did participate in the forum: we estimate that the treatment increased the rate of student forum actions by a factor of 2.3. As a substantive conclusion, it appears that including self-assessment questions about forum participation is a low-cost, low-burden, and effective way of getting more students to participate more often in course discussion forums.

In addressing the second challenge of estimating treatment-on-treated effects, adjusting the treatment effects for compliance proves important given the high rates of attrition and inactivity. A simple Wald estimator provides an easy to implement adjustment, but may not work for situations with very low compliance, and we interpret the estimator with caution. Still, we believe that a simple intent-to-treat OLS analysis may substantially underestimate the effect of the treatment on those who actually answered the discussion prompt. With the Wald, we estimate that, on average, students who received treatment had 12 more forum actions than students in the control group. Again, this should not be interpreted as an average effect at any point in the distribution.

Our 2SLS logistic regression further emphasizes the importance of estimating TOT effects. We estimate that those who received the intervention had a 20 percentage-point higher probability of having a forum action than the control group. The IV quantile regression confirms the initial distribution effects, and shows that among those induced to receive treatment by random assignment, the magnitude of effects increase at each quantile along the distribution, though the IV quantile regression resists a simple summary statistic. In interpreting the TOT effects, our estimates likely represent an "upper bound," since we narrowly define receipt of treatment. These findings further reinforce the substantive conclusion that participation self-checks could be a valuable tool for increasing engagement.

One method that we would have liked to use to estimate the treatment-on-treated effects is an IV ZINB. Theoretically, this would be similar to running a two-stage least-squares model with the zero-inflated negative binomial as the second stage. Currently, an analogous program exists for doing this with a Poisson model [11] but has not yet been modified for use with the ZINB. Software innovations in this regard would be a useful contribution, as manual implementation will produce inaccurate standard errors.

We have elided two other important challenges to analyzing MOOC experiments in this paper. First, it may be possible for students skipping back and forth [6] through a course to encounter an opportunity to generate an outcome variable before exposure to treatment. For instance, some JusticeX students may have participated in the forums before experiencing the treatment intervention. This would indicate that we have overestimated the effect of treatment. Given our early treatment assignment and use of an aggregate outcome metric, we think the risk is small here, but it could be significant in other studies. Another important challenge that we did not address in this paper is dealing with multiple factor experiments and interactions. We limited our samples to only those exposed to one of three treatments and a true control group exposed to no treatments, but we could analyze students exposed to multiple treatments to explore possible interactions. When factorial designs intersect with issues of treatment compliance and complex outcome distributions, the analytical challenges multiply. Yet, as the online learning environment appears poised to host many different studies simultaneously, addressing interactions among MOOC experiments is a critical frontier for research.

Zero-inflated and skewed outcomes, high attrition after assignment to treatment groups, difficulty in defining and measuring exposure to treatment, difficulty in defining dosage of treatment, unclear timing between outcome and treatment, and factorial experimental designs all conspire to make the analysis of MOOC experiments more complicated—in most circumstances—than running a simple t-test.

Our work to address a few common methodological challenges – zero-inflated, skewed outcome distributions and identification of treatment-on-treated effects—gives rise to a number of implications for MOOC designers who wish to implement randomized trials. First, researchers should consider tradeoffs when they assign students to treatment conditions [4]. Assigning all students immediately to treatment groups upon course entry allows for simple intent-to-treat analysis, but complicates treatment-on-treated analysis. Dynamically assigning students to treatment groups upon encountering a possible treatment condition might simplify treatment-on-treated analysis, but could complicate defining intent-to-treat analyses and lead to exposure to treatment after the outcome of interest. Researchers should also be careful in their analysis of experiments where actual treatment is difficult to measure, such as email-based experiments. These experiments allow flexible interactions with participants outside the confines of a platform, but it can be difficult to measure compliance with treatments, since many platforms mask whether a person receives or opens an email. When designing experimental interventions, researchers should also carefully consider how exposure to treatment will be defined. In our situation, having users actually answer the self-assessment problem provided one clear way, but not the only way. We encourage researchers to perform sensitivity analyses to better understand how defining this concept affects the results.

The introduction of easily implemented A/B tests in MOOC platforms greatly expands the possibility of conducting causal research in online spaces. Researchers using these platforms must be attentive to the peculiarity of MOOC outcomes and consider carefully how best to analyze experiments and present results in ways that will be accessible to both researchers and course developers.

REFERENCES

[1] Abadie, A., Angrist, J. and Imbens, G. Instrumental variables estimates of the effect of subsidized training on the quantiles of trainee earnings. *Econometrica*, 70, 1 (2002), 91-117. DOI=10.1111/1468-0262.00270.

[2] Anderson, A., Huttenlocher, D., Kleinberg, J. and Leskovec, J. Engaging with Massive Online Courses. in *Proceedings of the 2014 International World Wide Web Conference*, (2014), 687-698.

[3] Angrist, J. D. *Mostly harmless econometrics: An empiricist's companion.* Princeton: Princeton University Press, Princeton, 2009.

[4] Bakshy, E., Eckles, D. and Bernstein, M. S. Designing and deploying online field experiments. in *Proceedings of the 23rd international conference on World wide web.* (2014), 283-292.

[5] Breslow, L., Pritchard, D. E., DeBoer, J., Stump, G. S., Ho, A. D. and Seaton, D. Studying learning in the worldwide classroom: Research into edX's first MOOC. *Research & Practice in Assessment*, 8(2013), 13-25.

[6] Guo, P. J. and Reinecke, K. Demographic differences in how students navigate through MOOCs. in *Proceedings of the First ACM Conference on Learning@Scale Conference.* (Atlanta, USA, 2014). ACM, 21-30.

[7] Ho, A. D., Reich, J., Nesterko, S. O., Seaton, D. T., Mullaney, T., Waldo, J. and Chuang, I. *HarvardX and MITx: The First Year of Open Online Courses, Fall 2012-Summer 2013.* HarvardX & MITx Working Paper No. 1. , 2014.

[8] Huang, J., Dasgupta, A., Ghosh, A., Manning, J. and Sanders, M. Superposter behavior in MOOC forums. in *Proceedings of the First ACM Conference on Learning@Scale Conference.* (Atlanta, USA, 2014). ACM, 117-126.

[9] Kizilcec, R. F., Schneider, E., Cohen, G. and McFarland, D. Encouraging forum participation in online courses with collectivist, individualist, and neutral motivational framings. *eLearning Papers*, 37(2014), 13-22.

[10] Manning, J. and Sanders, M. How widely used are MOOC forums? A first look. *Signals: Thoughts on Online Learning*, (2013).

[11] Nichols, A. IVPOIS: Stata module to estimate an instrumental variables Poisson regression via GMM. *Statistical Software Components*, (2008).

[12] O'Hara, R. B. and Kotze, D. J. Do not log-transform count data. Methods in Ecology and Evolution, 1, 2 (2010), 118-122. DOI=10.1111/j.2041-210X.2010.00021.x.

[13] Rabe-Hesketh, S., Skrondal, A. and Stata Corporation. *Multilevel and longitudinal modeling using Stata.* Stata Press Publication, College Station, Tex., 2008.

[14] Reich, J. MOOC Completion and retention in the context of student intent. *EDUCAUSE Review Online*, (2014).

[15] Reich, J., Nesterko, S. O., Seaton, D. T., Mullaney, T., Waldo, J., Chuang, I. and Ho, A. D. *JusticeX: Spring 2013 Course Report.* HarvardX Working Paper No. 4, 2014.

Structure and Messaging Techniques for Online Peer Learning Systems that Increase Stickiness

Yasmine Kotturi[1], Chinmay Kulkarni[2]
Michael S. Bernstein[2], Scott Klemmer[1]
[1]University of California, San Diego, [2]Stanford University
{ykotturi, srk}@ucsd.edu, {chinmay, msb}@cs.stanford.edu

ABSTRACT
When students work with peers, they learn more actively, build richer knowledge structures, and connect material to their lives. However, not every peer learning experience online sees successful adoption. This paper articulates and addresses three adoption challenges for global-scale peer learning. First, peer interactions struggle to bootstrap critical mass. However, class incentives can signal importance and spur initial usage. Second, online classes have limited peer visibility and awareness, so students often feel alone even when surrounded by peers. We find that highlighting interdependence and strengthening norms can mitigate this issue. Third, teachers can readily access "big" aggregate data but not "thick" contextual data that helps build intuitions, so software should guide teachers' scaffolding of peer interactions. We illustrate these challenges through studying 8,500 students' usage of two peer learning platforms, Talkabout and PeerStudio. This paper measures efficacy through sign-up and participation rates and the structure and duration of student interactions.

Author Keywords
Peer learning; online education; social learning.

PEER LEARNING: VALUABLE YET UNDERUSED
Many online classes use video lectures and individual student exercises to instruct and assess students. While vast numbers of students log on to these classes individually, many of the educationally valuable social interactions of brick-and-mortar classes are lost: online learners are "alone together" [30].

Social interactions amongst peers improves conceptual understanding and engagement, in turn increasing course performance and completion rates [11, 20, 22, 26, 28]. Benefits aren't limited to the present: when peers construct knowledge together, they acquire critical-thinking skills crucial for life after school [3]. Common social learning strategies include discussing course materials, asking each other questions, and reviewing each other's work [2].

However, most peer learning techniques are designed for small classes with an instructor co-present to facilitate, coordinate, and troubleshoot the activity. These peer activities rely on instructors to enforce learning scripts that enable students to learn from the interaction [25].

How might software enable peer benefits in online environments, where massive scale prevents instructors from personally structuring and guiding peer interactions? Recent work has introduced peer interactions for summative assessment [23]. How might peer interactions power more pedagogical processes online? In particular, how might software facilitate social coordination?

Three impediments to adoption... and remedies
Educational peer platforms connect students in massive online classes in order to discuss course topics, reflect on others' ideas, and build esprit de corps [5, 23]. Over the last two years, three challenges have consistently recurred as we have introduced peer learning into massive online classes.

First, many courses falsely assume that students will naturally populate the peer learning systems in their classes: "build it and they will come". This assumption often seems natural; after all, students naturally engage with social networks such as Facebook and Twitter. However, students don't yet know why or how they should take advantage of peer learning opportunities. Peer learning platforms sit not in a social setting, but in an educational setting, which has its own logic of incentives: both carrots and sticks are required to keep the commons vibrant.

Participation in educational settings has a different incentive structure than a socialization setting. In particular, the benefits of participation are not immediately apparent. For instance, many American college graduates retrospectively credit their dorms as having played a key role in their social development [12]. Yet, universities often have to require that freshmen live in the dorms to ensure the joint experience. We encourage instructors to take a similar reinforcing approach online: integrating peer-learning systems into the core curriculum and making them a required or extra-credit granting part of the course, rather than optional "hang-out" rooms.

L@S 2015, March 14–18, 2015, Vancouver, BC, Canada.

ACM 978-1-4503-3411-2/15/03...$15.00.
http://dx.doi.org/10.1145/2724660.2724676

The second challenge is that students in online classes lack the ambient social encouragement that brick-and-mortar settings provide [14]. The physical and social configurations of in-person schools (especially residential ones) offer many opportunities for social encouragement [11, 22]. For example, during finals week, everyone else is studying too. However, other students' activity is typically invisible online, so students do not receive the tacit encouragement of seeing others attend classes and study [13, 15]. We hypothesize that in the minimal social context online, software and courses must work especially hard to keep students engaged through highlighting codependence and strengthening positive norms.

The third challenge we have encountered is that instructors can, at best, observe peer interactions through a telescope clouded by big data exhaust: there are few visible signals beyond engagement (e.g. course forum posts and dashboards) and demographics. Student information is limited online [29], and knowing how to leverage what demographics instructors do know is non-obvious. In-person, instructors use a lot of information about people to structure interactions [27]. For example, instructors can observe and adapt to student reactions while facilitating peer interactions. The lack of information in online classes creates both pedagogical and design challenges [21]. For instance, in an online discussion, do students completely ignore the course-related discussion prompts and, instead, talk about current events or pop culture? To address such questions, teachers must have the tools to enable them to learn how to scaffold peer interactions from behind their computers.

This paper addresses these three logistical and pedagogical challenges to global-scale peer learning (Figure 1). We suggest socio-technical remedies that draw on our experience with two social learning platforms – Talkabout and PeerStudio–and with our experience using peer learning in the classroom.

We report on these challenges with both quantitative and qualitative data. Quantitative measures of efficacy include sign-up and follow-through rates, course participation and activity, and participation structure and duration. Qualitative data includes students' and instructors' comments in surveys and interviews. We describe how peer learning behavior varies with changing student practices, teacher practices, and course materials.

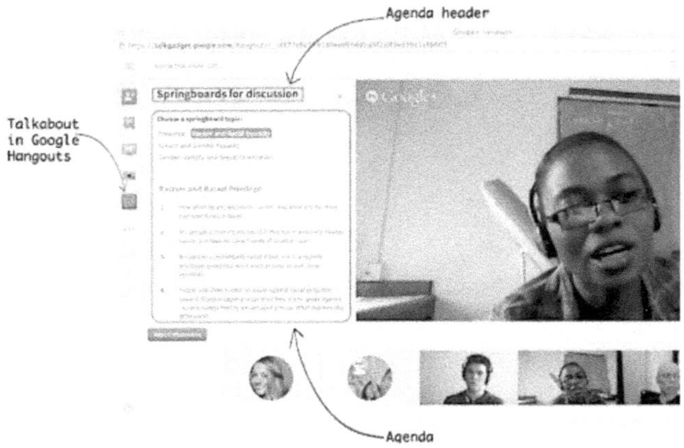

Figure 2: Our experiences developing and deploying Talkabout, a tool that brings students in massive courses together, helps guide our discussion in this paper.

How students use two peer learning platforms

Over the last two years, we have developed and deployed two large-scale peer-learning platforms. The first, Talkabout (Figure 2), brings students in MOOCs together to discuss course materials in small groups of four to six students over Google Hangouts [5]. Currently, over 4,500 students from 134 countries have used Talkabout in 18 different online classes through the Coursera and Open edX platforms. These classes covered diverse topics: Women's Rights, Social Psychology, Philanthropy, Organizational Analysis, and Behavioral Economics. Students join a discussion timeslot based on their availability, and upon arriving to the discussion, are placed in a discussion group; on average there are four countries represented per discussion group. We have seen that students in discussions with peers from diverse regions outperformed students in discussions with more homogenous peers, in terms of retention and exam score [22]. We hypothesize that geographically diverse discussions catalyze more active thinking and reflection.

The second platform, PeerStudio (Figure 3), provides fast feedback on in-progress open-ended work, such as essays [23]. PeerStudio has been used by over 4,000 students in

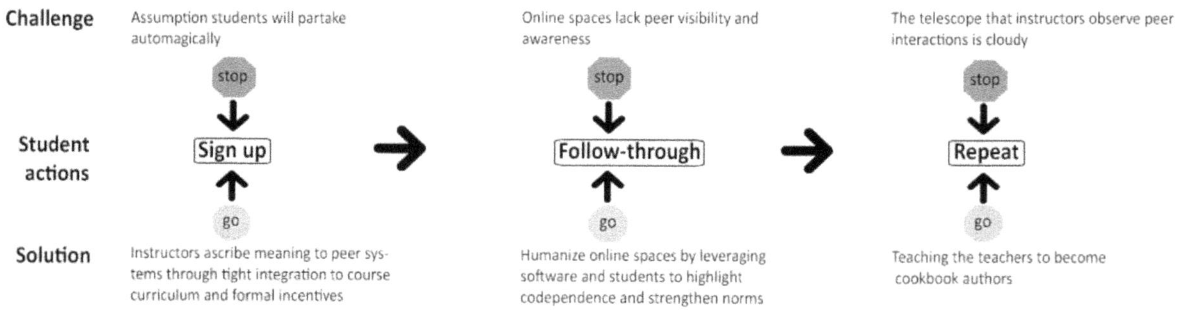

Figure 1: The challenges and remedies of adoption of peer learning systems presented in this paper.

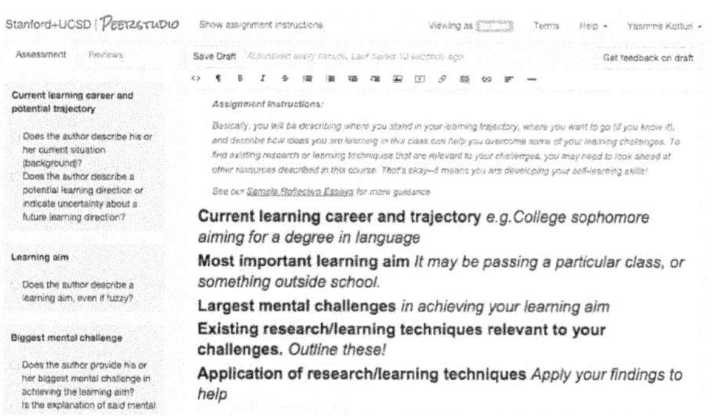

Figure 3: We also draw from our experience developing and implementing PeerStudio, a peer assessment tool that gives students rapid feedback on in-progress open-ended work.

two courses on Coursera and OpenedX. Students submit a draft, an essay for example, and are then prompted to review two other drafts. After completing two reviews, they can access the feedback on their essay. With PeerStudio, students can receive formative feedback on their draft work within hours. A randomized controlled experiment showed students created better revisions when they have rapid feedback from their peers, on average 20 minutes in our deployments at scale.

SOCIAL CAPABILITIES DO NOT GUARANTEE SOCIAL USE

Peer learning systems share many attributes with collaborative software more generally [16]. However, the additional features of the educational setting change users' calculus. Throughout the deployments of our platforms, we've observed different approaches that instructors take when using our peer systems with their material.

Often, instructors dropped a platform into their class, then left it alone and assumed that students would populate it. For example, one course using Talkabout only mentioned it once in course announcements. Across four weeks, the sign-up rate was just 0.4%, compared to a more successful sign-up rate of 6.6% in another course; sign-up rate being the number of students who signed up to participate in the peer system out of the number of active students (students who watched a lecture video) in the course. Low percentages represent conservative estimates as the denominator represents students with minimal activity. When this theme recurred in other Talkabout courses, it was accompanied with the same outcome: social interactions languished. Why would instructors who put in significant effort developing discussion prompts introduce a peer learning system, but immediately abandon it?

Through discussions, we noticed that instructors assumed that a peer system would behave like an already-popular social networking service like Facebook where people come en masse at their own will. This point of view resonates with a common assumption that MOOC students are extremely self-motivated, and that such motivation shapes their behavior [4,17]. In particular, instructors were *not* treating the systems like novel learning technology, but rather as bolted-on social technology. The assumption seemed to be that building a social space will cause students to just populate it and learn from each other.

However, peer learning systems may need more active integration. The value of educational experiences is not immediately apparent to students, and those that are worthwhile need to be signaled as important in order to achieve adoption.

Chat rooms underscored a similar point of the importance of pedagogical integration. Early chat room implementations were easily accessible (embedded in-page near video lectures) but had little pedagogical scaffolding [9]. Later, more successful variants that strongly enforced a pedagogical structure were better received [10].

Peer software as learning spaces

Even the best-designed peer learning activities have little value unless students overcome initial reluctance to use them. Course credit helps even students to commit, and those who have committed, to participate. Consider follow-though rates: the fraction of students who attend the discussion out of the students signed up for it. In an international women's rights course, before extra credit was offered, Talkabout follow-through rate was 31%. After offering extra credit, follow-through rate increased to 52%. In other classes, we've seen formal incentives raise follow-through rates up to 64%.

Faculty can signal to students what matters by using scarce resources like grade composition and announcements. We hypothesize that these signals of academic importance and meaning increase student usage. For example, in a course where the instructors just repeatedly announced Talkabout in the beginning, 6.6% of active students signed up, a large increase from the 0.4% sign-up rate when there was only one mention of Talkabout.

We saw similar effects with PeerStudio. When participation comprises even a small fraction of a student's grade, usage increases substantially. In one class where PeerStudio was optional, the sign-up rate was 0.8%. The fraction of users was six times higher in another class where use of PeerStudio contributed to their grade: the sign-up rate was 4.9%. To maintain consistency with insights from Talkabout, sign-up rates for PeerStudio also represents the number of students who signed up to participate out of the number of active students (students in the course who watched a lecture video).

Students look up to their instructors, creating a unique opportunity to get and keep students involved. One indicator of student interest is if they visited the Talkabout website. Figure 4 shows Talkabout page views after instructors posted on the course site discussing Talkabout, and a decrease in page views when no announcement is made. Talkabout traffic was dwindling towards the end of the course, so the instructor decided to offer extra credit for the last round of Talkabout discussions. During the extra-credit granting Talkabout discussions, page views increase around twofold the previous four rounds.

To understand how pedagogical integration and incentives, and follow-through rate interact, we divided 12 Talkabout courses into three categories, based on how well Talkabout was incentivized and integrated pedagogically (see Figure 5). Courses that never mentioned Talkabout or mentioned it only at the start of the course are labeled "Low integration". Such courses considered Talkabout a primarily social opportunity, similar to a Facebook group. Few students signed up, and even fewer actually participated: the average follow-through rate was 10%. The next category, "Medium integration," was well integrated but poorly incentivized, classes. These classes referred to Talkabout frequently in announcements, encouraged students to participate, and had well-structured discussion prompts, but they had no formal incentive. Such classes had an average follow-through rate of 35%. Well-incentivized and integrated classes, "High integration," offered course extra credit for participation and continuously discussed Talkabout in course announcements, and averaged 50% follow-through rate. This visualization highlights the pattern that the more integrated the peer learning platform is, the higher the follow-through rate is. We have found that offering even minimal course credit powerfully spurs initial participation, and that many interventions neglect to do this. As one student noted in a post-discussion survey, "I probably wouldn't have done it [a Talkabout session] were it not for the 5 extra credit points but I found it very interesting and glad I did do it!"

The Talkabout course with the highest follow-through rate not only offered Talkabout for extra credit, but also offered technical support, including a course-specific Talkabout FAQ (Talkabout has an FAQ but it is not course specific). Looking at the forums, the role of the FAQ became apparent: many students posted questions about their technological difficulties and the community TAs and even other students would direct students to this FAQ–loaded with pictures and step by step instructions to help these students understand what Talkabout is and how it's related to them. Moreover, the course support team answered any questions that could not be answered by the

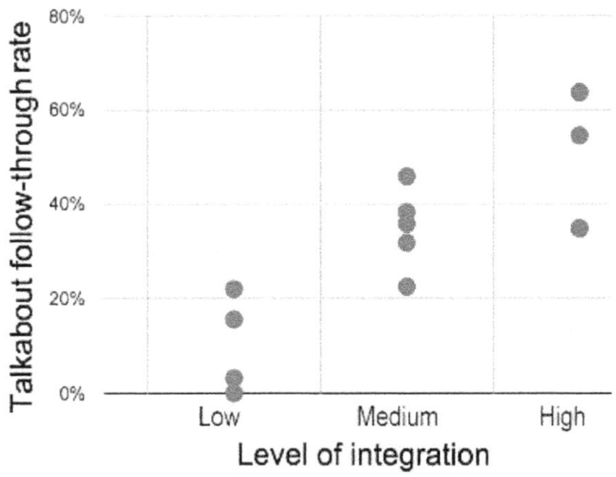

Figure 5: Follow-through rate from 12 Talkabout courses increases as integration increases.

FAQ, ensuring that anyone who was interested in using the peer learning platform got the chance to do so.

However, online classes must also accommodate students with differing constraints from around the world. For instance, Talkabout is not available to some students whose country (like Iran) blocks access to Google Hangouts. Other students may simply lack sufficient reliable Internet bandwidth. One course offered small-group discussions for credit that were held either online (with Talkabout) or in-person in order to combat this challenge. When the strongest incentives are impractical, courses can still improve social visibility to encourage participation.

SOCIAL TRANSLUSCENCE IS LIMITED ONLINE

Online students are "hungry for social interaction" [17]. Especially in early MOOCs, discussion forums featured self-introductions from around the world, and students banded together for in-person meet-ups. Yet, when peer-learning opportunities are provided, students don't always participate in pro-social ways; they may neglect to review their peers' work, or fail to attend a discussion session that they signed up for.

We asked 100 students who missed a Talkabout why they did so. 18 out of 31 responses said something else came

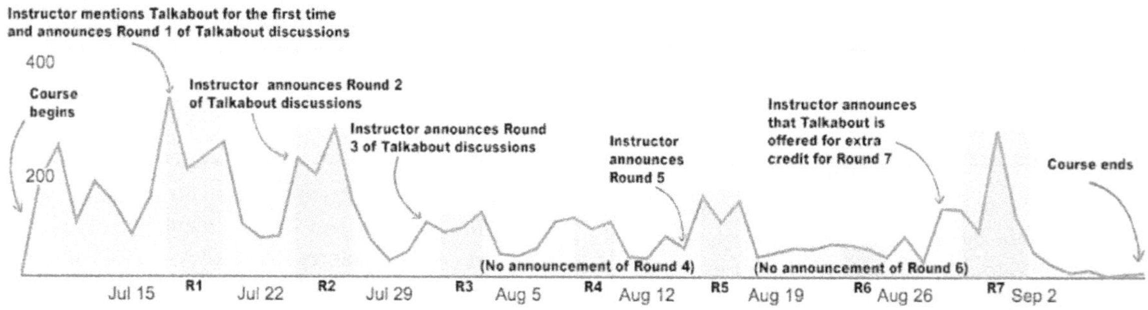

Figure 4: When instructors highlight peer learning software, students use it. Talkabout pageviews of a women's right course. Instructor announcements are followed by the largest amount of Talkabout pageviews throughout the course. R1 represents Round 1 of Talkabout discussions, and so on, with orange rectangles framing the duration of each round. When instructor does not mention Round 4 and 6, pageviews are at their lowest.

up or they forgot. While many respondents apologized to us as the system designers, none mentioned how they may have let down their classmates who were counting on their participation. This observation suggests that social loafing may be endemic to large-scale social learning systems. If a student doesn't feel responsible to a small set of colleagues and the instructor instead diffuses that responsibility across a massive set of peers, individuals will feel less compunction to follow through on social commitments.

To combat social loafing, we must reverse the diffusion of responsibility by transforming it onto a smaller human scale. Systems that highlight co-dependence may be more successful at encouraging pro-social behavior [8]. In a peer environment, students are dependent on each other to do their part for the system to work. Encouraging commitment and contribution can help students understand the importance of their participation, and create successful peer learning environments [21].

Norm-setting in online social interaction

Norms have an enormous impact on people's behavior. In-person, teachers can act as strong role models and have institutional authority, leading to many opportunities to shape behavior and strengthen and set norms. Online, while these opportunities diminish with limited social visibility, other opportunities appear, such as shaping norms through system design. Platform designers, software and teachers can encourage peer empathy and mutually beneficial behavior by fostering pro-social norms.

Software can illuminate social norms online. For instance, when PeerStudio notices that a student has provided scores without written feedback, it reminds them of the reciprocal nature of the peer assessment process (see Figure 6). As a different example, students that are late to a Talkabout discussion are told they won't be allowed to

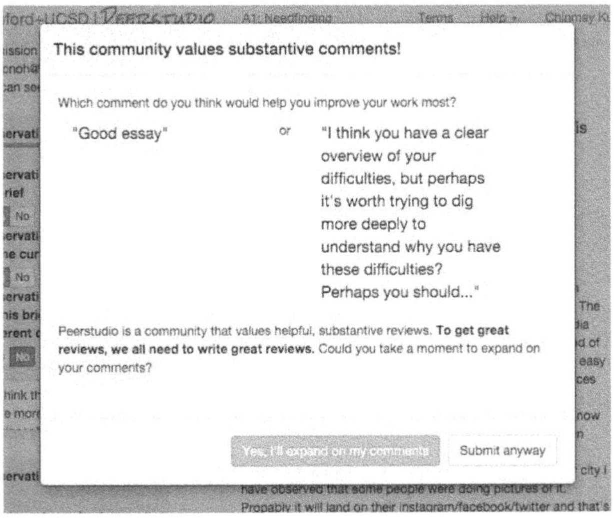

Figure 6: When PeerStudio detects a review without comments, it asks the reviewer if they would like to go back and improve their review by adding comments.

join the discussion, just as they'd not like to have a discussion interrupted by a late classmate. Instead, the system provides them an option to reschedule. Systems need not wait until things go wrong to set norms. From prior work, we know students are highly motivated when they feel that their contribution matters [2, 24]. As an experiment, we emailed students in two separate Talkabout courses before their discussion saying that their peers were counting on them to show up to the discussion (see Figure 7). Without a reminder email, only 21% of students who signed up for a discussion slot actually showed up. With a reminder email, this follow-through rate increased to 62%.

How can we leverage software and students to highlight codependence and ascribe meaning?

PeerStudio recruits reviewers by sending out emails to students. Initially, this email featured a generic request to review. As an experiment, we *humanized* the request by featuring the custom request a student had made. For example, the generic boilerplate request became the personalized request that the student had written before submitting his draft. Immediately after making this change, review length increased from an average of 17 words to 24 words.

Humanized software is not the only influencer: forum posts from students sharing their peer learning experiences can help validate the system and encourage others to give it a try. For example, one student posted: "I can't say how much I love discussions…and that's why I have gone through 11-12 Talkabout sessions just to know, discuss and interact with people from all over the world." Although unpredictable [7], this word-of-mouth technique can be highly effective for increasing stickiness [1]. When students shared Talkabout experiences in the course discussion forums (2000 posts out of 64,000 mentioned Talkabout, 3%), the sign-up rate was 6% (2037 students), and the follow-through rate was 63%. However, the same course offered a year later, did not see similar student behavior (260 posts out of 80,000 mentioned Talkabout, 0.3%). The sign-up rate was 5% (930 students) and follow-through rate was 55%. Although influenced by external factors, this suggests that social validation of the systems is important.

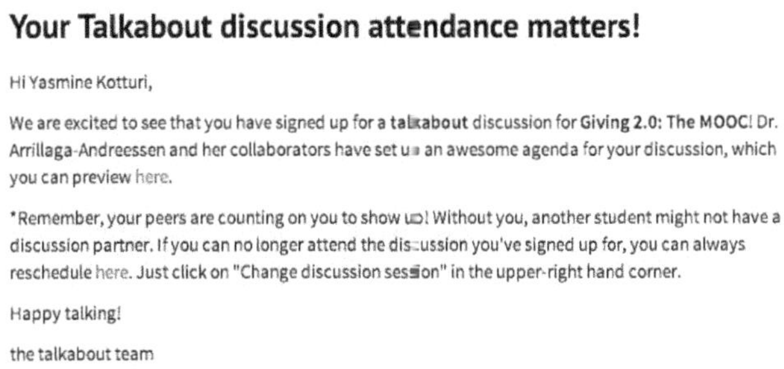

Figure 7: An email sent to students prior to their discussion, reminding them of the importance of their attendance, increases follow-through rate 41%.

Leveraging students' desire to connect globally

Increasing social translucence has one final benefit: it allows students to act on their desire for persistent connections with their global classmates. For example, incorporating networking opportunities in the discussion agenda allocates times for students to mingle: "Spend five minutes taking turns introducing yourselves and discussing your background." However, we note that this is not a "one-size-fits-all" solution: certain course topics might inspire more socializing than others. For instance, in an international women's rights course, 93% of students using Talkabout shared their contact information with each other (e.g. LinkedIn profiles, email addresses), but in a course on effective learning, only 18% did.

DESIGNING & HOSTING INTERACTION FROM AFAR

Like a cook watching a stew come to a boil and adjusting the temperature as needed, an instructor guiding peer interactions in-person can modulate her behavior in response to student reactions. Observing how students do in-class exercises and assimilating non-verbal cues (*e.g.*, enthusiasm, boredom, confusion) helps teachers tailor their instruction, often even subconsciously [18].

By contrast, the indirection of teaching online causes multiple challenges for instructors. First, with rare exceptions [6], online teachers can't see much about student behavior interactively. Second, because of the large-scale and asynchronous nature of most online classes, teachers can't directly coach peer interactions. To extend–and possibly butcher–the cooking metaphor, teaching online shifts the instructor from the in-the-kitchen chef to the cookbook author. Their recipes need to be sufficiently stand-alone and clear that students around the globe can cook up a delicious peer interaction themselves. However, most instructors lack the tools to write recipes that can be handed off and reused without any interactive guidance on the instructor's part.

Guidelines for writing recipes: scaffolding peer interactions from behind a computer

Most early users of Talkabout provided both too little student motivation and discussion scaffolding. Consequently, usage was minimal [22]. Unstructured discussion did not increase students' academic achievement or sense of community [9]. To succeed, we needed to specifically target opportunities for self-referencing, highlight viewpoint differences using boundary objects, and leverage students as mediators [22]. To understand this range of structure, we looked the discussions from 12 different courses and compared agenda character length and discussion duration. We split discussions into two categories: long and short discussion agendas, with 250 words as the threshold, and compared credit-granting and no credit discussions (see Figure 8). Average discussion duration was

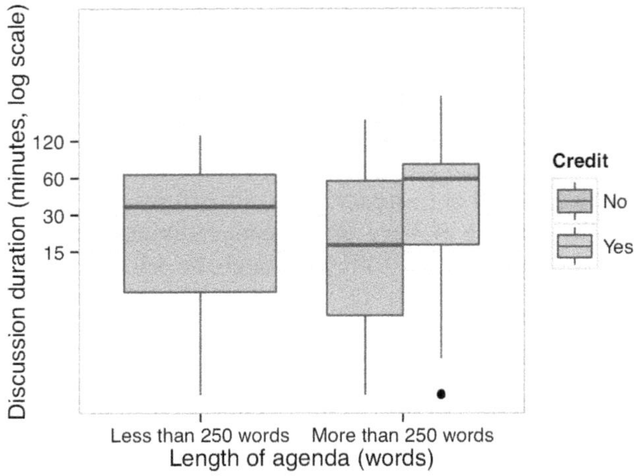

Figure 8. Longer discussion agendas incentivize students to discuss longer; but only when they are accompanied by course credit for participation.

31 minutes for short agendas. However, only those long agendas that awarded credit successfully incentivized students to discuss longer: the average discussion with credit was 49 minutes, and without was 30 minutes. All agendas asked students to discuss for 30 minutes; students were staying the extra time voluntarily.

We worried that over-structuring an interaction with lengthy and tiresome agendas would leave no space for informal bond-building. However, even with sufficient structure, students can easily veer from the schedule and socialize, exchange social networking information, and offer career advice.

Software systems, platforms, and data-driven suggestions each play a more active role in helping teachers create effective recipes. While most early Talkabout instructors provided too little discussion scaffolding, our data showed instincts led early Talkabout instructors to worry too much about scheduling. For example, time zones are a recurring thorn in the side of many types of global collaboration, and peer learning is no exception. Every Talkabout instructor was concerned about discussion session times and frequency, as this a major issue with in-person sections. Instructors often asked if particular times were good for students around the world. Some debated: would 9pm Eastern Time be better than 8pm Eastern Time, as more students would have finished dinner? Or would it be worse for students elsewhere? Other instructors were unsure of how many discussions timeslots to offer. One instructor offered a timeslot every hour for 24 hours because she wanted to ensure that there were enough scheduling options. However, an unforeseen consequence of this was that the participants were too spread out over the 24 discussions, and thus some students were left alone.

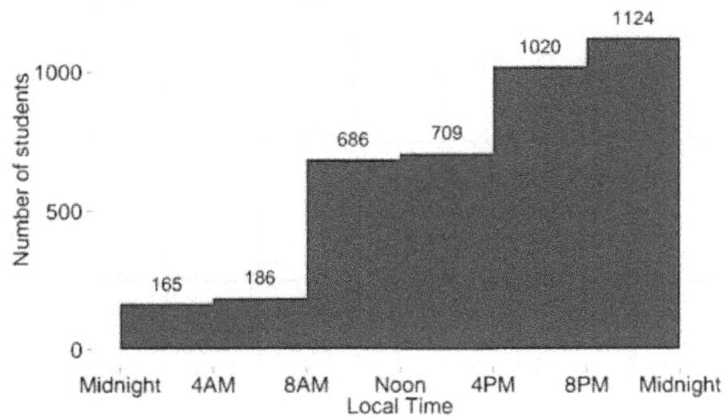

Figure 9. Data from nine classes and 3400 students shows that most students discuss in the evening, but there are students that will discuss at all 24 hours.

Analyzing when students participate in discussions taught us that most students prefer evenings for discussions. Yet, different students prefer different times, with every day of time being preferred by someone (Figure 9). This data suggests that it is unimportant for instructors to find a particular scheduling "sweet spot," and instead their time is better utilized elsewhere: creating the discussion agendas, for example. In summary, these examples illustrated where intuitions can lead teachers and system designers astray. Data-driven suggestions are important to transform expert cooks into cookbook authors.

TEACHING TEACHERS BY EXAMPLE

Even fantastic pedagogical innovation can be hamstrung when there is a mismatch between curricular materials and platform functionality. When curricula did not match to the needs of the setting, the learning platforms languished. We emphasize the importance of *teaching by example*: creating designs and introductory experiences that nudge instructors toward the right intuitions. While always true with educational innovation, the online education revolution is a particularly dramatic change of setting, and instructor scaffolding is particularly important.

One of the most robust techniques we have found for guiding instructors is to provide successful examples of how other teachers have used the learning platform. In many domains, from design to writing research papers, a common and effective strategy for creating new work is to template off similar work that has a related goal [19]. During interviews with Talkabout instructors, a common situation recurred: the instructor was having a hard time conceptualizing the student experience. Therefore, to help instructors navigate the interface and create effective discussion prompts, we added an annotated example of a Talkabout discussion (see Figure 2). Still, we observed that many instructors had difficulty creating effective discussion agendas, e.g. they were very short and did not leverage the geographic diversity Talkabout discussions offer. As an experiment, we walked an instructor through Talkabout – in a Talkabout – and showed an excellent ex-

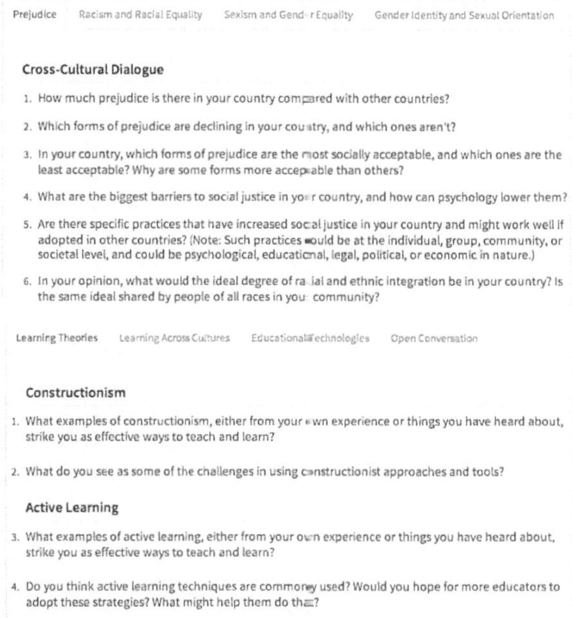

Prejudice | Racism and Racial Equality | Sexism and Gender Equality | Gender Identity and Sexual Orientation

Cross-Cultural Dialogue

1. How much prejudice is there in your country compared with other countries?
2. Which forms of prejudice are declining in your country, and which ones aren't?
3. In your country, which forms of prejudice are the most socially acceptable, and which ones are the least acceptable? Why are some forms more acceptable than others?
4. What are the biggest barriers to social justice in your country, and how can psychology lower them?
5. Are there specific practices that have increased social justice in your country and might work well if adopted in other countries? (Note: Such practices could be at the individual, group, community, or societal level, and could be psychological, educational, legal, political, or economic in nature.)
6. In your opinion, what would the ideal degree of racial and ethnic integration be in your country? Is the same ideal shared by people of all races in your community?

Learning Theories | Learning Across Cultures | Educational Technologies | Open Conversation

Constructionism

1. What examples of constructionism, either from your own experience or things you have heard about, strike you as effective ways to teach and learn?
2. What do you see as some of the challenges in using constructionist approaches and tools?

Active Learning

3. What examples of active learning, either from your own experience or things you have heard about, strike you as effective ways to teach and learn?
4. Do you think active learning techniques are commonly used? Would you hope for more educators to adopt these strategies? What might help them do that?

Figure 10. Two discussions prompts: top used as a template to show a new Talkabout instructor an excellent example. Bottom prompt generated based off the example.

ample agenda from another class. This helped onboard the new instructor to working with Talkabout: she was able to use the example as a framework that she could fill in with her own content (see Figure 10). Next, we showed example course announcements that described Talkabout using layman's terms and offering pictures of the Talkabout discussion. Since course announcements are viewed by most online students, it is important to describe peer learning platforms in basic terms to convey a straight forward message.

The next step was to help instructors gain an understanding of what occurs during student discussions. To do this, we showed an instructor a video clip of a Talkabout discussion along with a full discussion summary. In response, the instructor said, "The most interesting point was around the amount of time each student spoke. In this case, one student spoke for more than half of the Talkabout. This informs us to be more explicit with time allocations for questions and that we should emphasize that we want students to more evenly speak." By helping her visualize the interactions, she was able to restructure her discussion prompts in order to achieve her desired discussion goal; in this case, encouraging all students to have equally share their thoughts.

CONCLUSION

This paper provided evidence for three challenges to global-scale adoption of peer learning, and offered three corresponding socio-technical remedies. We reflect on our experience from developing, designing and deploying our social learning platforms: Talkabout and PeerStudio, as well as our experience as teachers in physical and online classes. We looked at student practices, teacher practices and material design, and assessed the relationship between those and peer learning adoption. When peer systems and curricula are well integrated, the social context is illuminated, and teachers' and system designers' intuitions for scaffolding are guided by software, students do adopt these systems.

ACKNOWLEDGEMENTS

We are grateful to Scott Plous, Ed Hutchins and all instructors who used Talkabout and PeerStudio for their thought-provoking discussions and feedback; Coursera and Open EdX teams for their help integrating the platforms; the many students who interacted with their peers and shared their stories with us. This research was funded in part through NSF grants #1351131 and #1444865 and the Hasso Plattner Design Thinking Program. This research was conducted under the Stanford IRB protocols #30319 and #30324.

REFERENCES

1. Bakshy, E., Karrer, B., and Adamic, L.A. Social influence and the diffusion of user-created content. *Proceedings of the 10th ACM conference on Electronic commerce*, (2009), 325–334.
2. Bransford, J., Brown, A., and Cocking, R. *How People Learn.* 2000.
3. Bransford, J. and Schwartz, D.L. Rethinking Transfer: A Simple Proposal with Multiple Implications. *Review of Research in Education 24*, (1999), 61–100.
4. Breslow, L., Pritchard, D., DeBoer, J., Stump, G., Ho, A., and Seaton, D. *Studying learning in the worldwide classroom: Research into edX's first MOOC.* 2013.
5. Cambre, J., Kulkarni, C., Bernstein, M.S., and Klemmer, S.R. Talkabout: Small-group Discussions in Massive Global Classes. *Learning@Scale*, (2014).
6. Chen, M. Design of a virtual auditorium. *MULTIMEDIA '01 Proceedings of the ninth ACM international conference on Multimedia*, (2001), 19–28.
7. Cheng, J., Adamic, L., Dow, P., Kleinberg, J., and Leskovec, J. Can cascades be predicted? *Proceedings of the 23rd international conference on World wide web*, (2014), 925–936.
8. Cialdini, R. and Goldstein, N. Social influence: Compliance and conformity. *Annual review of psychology 55*, (2004), 591–621.
9. Coetzee, D., Fox, A., Hearst, M.A., and Hartmann, B. Chatrooms in MOOCs: all talk and no action. *Proc. of the ACM conference on Learning @ scale*, ACM Press (2014), 127–136.
10. Coetzee, D., Lim, S., Fox, A., Hartmann, B., and Hearst, M.A. Structuring Interactions for Large-Scale Synchronous Peer Learning. *CSCW: ACM Conference on Computer Supported Collaborative Work*, (2015).
11. Crouch, C.H. and Mazur, E. Peer Instruction: Ten years of experience and results. *American Journal of Physics 69*, 9 (2001), 970.
12. Dourish, P. and Bell, G. The infrastructure of experience and the experience of infrastructure: meaning and structure in everyday encounters with space. *Environment and Planning B Planning and Design 34*, 3 (2007), 414.
13. Dourish, P. and Bellotti, V. Awareness and coordination in shared workspaces. *Proceeding CSCW '92 Proceedings of the 1992 ACM conference on Computer-supported cooperative work*, (1992), 107–114.
14. Erickson, T. and Kellogg, W. Social translucence: an approach to designing systems that support social processes. *ACM Transactions on Computer-Human Interaction (TOCHI) - Special issue on human-computer interaction in the new millennium, Part 1 7*, 1 (2000), 59–83.
15. Greenberg, S. Embedding a design studio course in a conventional computer science program. In *Creativity and HCI: From Experience to Design in Education.* Springer, 2009, 23–41.
16. Grudin, J. Groupware and social dynamics: eight challenges for developers. *Communications of the ACM 37*, 1 (1994), 92–105.
17. Kizilcec, R.F. and Schneider, E. Motivation as a Lens to Understand Online Learners: Towards Data-Driven Design with the OLEI Scale. .
18. Klemmer, S.R., Hartmann, B., and Takayama, L. How bodies matter: five themes for interaction design. *Proceedings of the 6th conference on Designing Interactive systems*, (2006), 140–149.
19. Klemmer, S.R. *Katayanagi Lecture at CMU: The Power of Examples.* .
20. Konstan, J.A., Walker, J.D., Brooks, D.C., Brown, K., and Ekstrand, M.D. Teaching recommender systems at large scale. *Proc of the ACM conference on Learning @ scale conference*, ACM Press (2014).
21. Kraut, R.E., Resnick, P., Kiesler, S., Burke, M., Chen, Y., Kittur, N., Konstan, J., Ren, Y., and Riedl, J. *Building Successful Online Communities: Evidence-Based Social Design (Google eBook).* MIT Press, 2012.
22. Kulkarni, C., Cambre, J., Kotturi, Y., Bernstein, M., and Klemmer, S. Talkabout: Making distance matter with small groups in massive classes. *CSCW: ACM Conference on Computer Supported Collaborative Work*, (2015).
23. Kulkarni, C., Wei, K.P., Le, H., Chia, D., Papadopoulos, K., Cheng, J., Koller, D., and Klemmer, S.R. Peer and self assessment in massive online classes. *ACM Transactions on Computer-Human Interaction (TOCHI) 20*, 6 (2013), 33.
24. Ling, K. and Beenen, G. Using Social Psychology to Motivate Contributions to Online Communities. *Journal of Computer-Mediated Communication 10*, 4 (2005), 00.
25. O'Donnell, A.M. and Dansereau, D.F. Scripted cooperation in student dyads: A method for analyzing and enhancing academic learning and performance. In *Interaction in cooperative groups: The theoretical anatomy of group learning.* Cambridge University Press, Cambridge, UK, 1995, 120–141.
26. Porter, L., Lee, C.B., and Simon, B. Halving fail rates using peer instruction: a study of four computer science courses. *Proceeding SIGCSE '13 Proceeding of the 44th ACM technical symposium on Computer science education*, (2013), 177–182.
27. Rosenberg, J., Lorenzo, M., and Mazur, E. Peer instruction: Making science engaging. *Handbook of college science teaching*, (2006), 77–85.
28. Smith, M., Wood, W., Adams, W., Wieman, C., Knight, J., Guild, N., and Su, T. Why Peer Discussion Improves Student Performance on In-Class Concept Questions. *Science 323*, 5910 (2009), 122–124.
29. Stephens-Martinez, K., Hearst, M.A., and Fox, A. Monitoring MOOCs: which information sources do instructors value? *Proceedings of the first ACM conference on Learning @ scale conference*, (2014), 79–88.
30. Turkle, S. *Alone Together: Why We Expect More from Technology and Less from Each Other.* Basic Books, 2011.

The Prediction of Student First Response Using Prerequisite Skills

Anthony Botelho
Worcester Polytechnic Institute
abotelho@wpi.edu

Hao Wan
Worcester Polytechnic Institute
hale@wpi.edu

Neil Heffernan
Worcester Polytechnic Institute
nth@wpi.edu

ABSTRACT

A large amount of research in the field of educational data analytics has focused primarily on student next problem correctness. Although the prediction of such information is useful in assessing current student performance, it is better for teachers and instructors to place attention on student knowledge over a longer period of time. Several researchers have articulated that it is important to predict aspects that are more meaningful, inspiring our work here to utilize the large amounts of student data available to derive more substantial predictions over student knowledge. Our goal in this paper is to utilize prerequisite information to better predict student knowledge quantitatively as a subsequent skill is begun. Learning systems like ASSISTments and Khan Academy already record such prerequisite information, and can therefore be used to construct a method of prediction as described in this paper. Using these inter-skill relationships, our method estimates students' initial knowledge based on performance on each prerequisite skill. We compare our method with the standard Knowledge Tracing (KT) model and majority class in terms of the predictive accuracy of students' first responses on subsequent skills. Our results support our method as a viable means of representing student prerequisite knowledge in a subsequent skill, leading to results that outperform the majority class and that are comparably superior to KT by providing more definitive student knowledge estimates without sacrificing predictive accuracy.

Author Keywords

predicting student knowledge; mastery speed; initial knowledge; prerequisite; subsequent skills; first response prediction; Knowledge Tracing

INTRODUCTION

A large amount of research in the field of educational data analytics has focused primarily on student next problem correctness. Events such as the Knowledge Discover and Data Mining Competition held in 2010 (*www.kdd.org*), more commonly referred to as the KDD Cup, directs the attention of the field to the prediction of next problem correctness; while perhaps useful in performance evaluation, the ability to predict next problem correctness has certain limitations in regards to utility especially when assessing student knowledge over larger periods of time. Others in the field have begun raising other meaningful questions[3] [8][10], realizing the importance of predicting or observing aspects that are much more substantial. Intelligent tutoring systems (ITS) provide a wealth of student data from which more meaningful predictions and observations can be derived. Our work here aims to utilize this data to provide more significant information pertaining to student knowledge to teachers and instructors.

For our research, we emphasize constructing a more precise prediction on students' initial knowledge approaching a new skill. In the general case, students move gradually from an initial state of knowledge toward mastery, and student models should capture this change. Thus, a more accurate estimation of this initial knowledge could lead to a better understanding of a student's knowledge state at any observable time, and consequently, we could use the model's results to develop more precise predictions of future performance.

In this paper, we utilize prerequisite information to predict student initial knowledge on subsequent skills. If a skill 'A', is a prerequisite of skill 'B,' students should have mastered 'A' before proceeding to 'B.' The prerequisite relationships used in this work are defined by domain experts. Due to human effect, some skill relationships might be overestimated, or they may not exist in other applications. As such, we are seeking to answer the following two questions in this paper:

1. Does prerequisite information really help to improve the estimation of initial knowledge on subsequent skills?

2. Are all prerequisite relationships reliable?

We address these questions through three experiments to first observe trends of distribution across our proposed binning method, and then to compare the predictive accuracy of that method to that of KT and majority class across all skills and at an individual skill level.

The next section will introduce a background of our comparative model, KT, after which we will described the dataset used in our trials. The following section will discuss our proposed binning methodology before illustrating the results of

L@S 2015, March 14–18, 2015, Vancouver, BC, Canada.

http://dx.doi.org/10.1145/2724660.2724675

our experiments, and, finally, we state our contributions, conclusions and intended future work in this field of research.

BACKGROUND

The knowledge tracing (KT) model [4] developed by Corbett and Anderson has long been successful in the field of student assessment. Its implementation and use in tutoring systems and use in performance analysis systems exemplifies its practical applications, scalability, and appropriation across many fields of study. The KT model is widely used in these tutoring systems and the field of educational data analytics due to its accuracy in predicting student correctness by utilizing only a small amount of data.

The KT model gains its accuracy through the training of four parameters representing students' prior knowledge, learning rate, probability of guessing, or answering correctly while not knowing a skill, and chance of slipping, or answering incorrectly while in a supposed "learned" state. Knowledge tracing relies heavily on the successful training of these parameters to properly model a student beginning a new skill, and then to build upon that model at a student level given a sequence of responses. For this reason, each student beginning a particular skill receives the same base model. Therefore, each student within a skill will be given the same prediction for the first response. The model could be greatly improved if another prediction procedure, such as the method described in this work, could use a more intelligent approach to predict first response.

In the standard KT model, initial knowledge is represented by a parameter $P(L_0)$, the probability of mastering the skill [4]. As such, KT is often used to estimate each student's initial knowledge [8]. In the standard KT model, the parameter $P(L_0)$ is trained on all students' records in the a training set, and assumes that all students have the same initial state of knowledge. However, this assumption is too strong to use the model to predict each individual student's first response. To overcome this drawback, Pardos and Heffernan use three heuristic functions to model individualization in KT [9], and find that the method, setting initial individualized knowledge based on individual students' performance over all skills, yields superior results. This approach, however, overestimates the relationships between skills. If learning a skill does not promote, or even hinder [5], learning another skill, then it is not appropriate to use knowledge in one skill to estimate another.

Baker et al. uses another method [6] that compares a student's overall performance and all other students' performance on a skill to build an individualized model. Like the standard KT model, this method suffers two major problems: falling into local maxima and the existence of multiple global maxima[2]. Thus, we cannot know if the value of $P(L_0)$ obtained by the model represents true student initial knowledge.

Knowledge Tracing's many strengths have made it a kind of comparative model in many works and is used again here as such. Knowledge Tracing builds upon the performance history of each student to calculate a probability that the student will answer the next problem correct. For this reason, it often fails to accurately predict students' first responses as there is less information for KT to accurately calculate a prediction. The method of prediction proposed in this work focuses entirely on first responses of students undertaking a new skill by observing student performance in prerequisite skills. Using knowledge tracing as a comparative model, our method of prediction aims to outperform KT in terms of accuracy in regard to students' first responses while providing a more definitive measure of initial knowledge.

DATASET

The dataset used in our work is comprised of real-world algebra and geometry-based student data from the 2009-2010 academic year taken from the ASSISTments tutoring system. This system is administered by teachers to students through assigned problem sets that track student performance in addition to many other features to be used for better assessing each student's knowledge and understanding of each topic, or skill. It is intended that each student completes problems pertaining to the assigned skill until a status of mastery is reached, which by default is defined as three consecutive correct answers. Each problem, or opportunity as it will be referred to in this work, is recorded by the system and is used to evaluate that student's overall performance.

Within ASSISTments, skills are arranged in an intended prerequisite-to-subsequent skill structure defined by domain experts as a recommended sequence of topics for instructors. It is the teacher's choice which skills and problems to assign as well as the order in which to assign them. As will be discussed later, the relationships between skills in this predefined prerequisite structure is worth further inspection, but are trusted for our initial experiments.

It was found that of the 230 skills listed as subsequent skills in our ASSISTments dataset, 28 contained usable prerequisite data; we define student data as usable if the sequence in which students complete skills matches the prerequisite structure defined within the system. The usable dataset consisted of 983 unique students across all skills, providing 3466 rows of response data. We acknowledge that our results may provide more reliable conclusions with a larger dataset, but our work here is intended to be used as initial work from which further research may expand upon and is therefore viewed as sufficient for this paper.

From the student performance, we also calculate each student's individual speed of mastery, defined as the number of opportunities, or individual problems, completed in order to gain mastery status as described above. We use this mastery speed as a measure of student knowledge and aptitude across skills and is used to calculate predicted responses as described in the next section. For this work, only problem correctness, expressed as binary values in the system, is used to calculate mastery speed and overall student performance, neglecting other features such as time between problems and skills and also partial credit evaluations. Other methods of determining mastery, discussed briefly in a later section, may lead to improved accuracy in our method, but are not the focus of this work; we use the simple "three right in a row" method of determining mastery for all of our experiments.

Student	Prerequisite	Mastery Speed	Skill	First Response Correctness
Tom	Adding	4	Division	Correct
Tom	Mult.	8	Division	
Bill	Adding	3	Division	Incorrect
Bill	Mult.	6	Division	
Joe	Adding	3	Division	Correct
Joe	Mult.n	3	Division	
Sue	Adding	5 LPC	Division	Incorrect
Sue	Mult.	DNF LPC	Division	

⇓

Attempts	Prediction	Number of Students
3-4 incl.	1.0	1
4-8 excl.	0.5	2
8+	0.0	0
DNF High % Cor.	0.0	0
DNF Low % Cor.	0.0	1

Figure 1. The hypothetical students and data shown, fabricated to show our methodology, exemplifies the table creation process. Using a training set, a probability table is created for each skill by categorizing students with similar performance history

Methodology

The method described in this work attempts to better predict student first problem correctness on a subsequent skill by categorizing, or binning, students with similar mastery speed in a prerequisite skill; for purpose of clarification, the terms bin and category will be used interchangeably throughout this paper. Such a method has shown success in the past [12] when making other predictions such as next problem correctness using different features from a similar dataset. This method, labeled as "Prerequisite Binning" (PB), involves categorizing students based on a set of features, such as mastery speed, and inferring a relationship between them. For example, we binned students with similar ranges of mastery speed in order to create a prediction for any student that also could be placed in the same bin. If successfully identified, certain trends may appear within the bins, which are addressed in a later section.

The method of binning, as mentioned, groups students based on prerequisite mastery speed. For this, we used a 5 fold cross-validation on our dataset, using 80% as a training set to predict performance on the remaining 20%. The training set was used to construct the bins, which splits students based, again, on the number of opportunities needed to master each prerequisite skill. An average mastery speed across all prerequisite skills was calculated, placing students into one of five bins. The first bin contains those who averaged three to four opportunities inclusively ($3 \leq x \leq 4$) to master all prerequisite skills; as three opportunities is the lowest possible mastery speed and four opportunities indicates an incorrect response on only the first problem, this bin presumably represents the highest knowledge students. The second bin, following the first in terms of mastery range, contains students who require, on average, between four and eight opportunities exclusively ($4 < x < 8$). The third bin encompasses students with an average mastery speed of eight or more ($8 \leq x$) across all prerequisite skills. Following this categorizing strategy, a fourth bin would contain those students that did not reach mastery status on prerequisite skills before proceeding to the subsequent skill. However, our dataset shows that a large percentage of students fall into this category, many of which respond to only a small number of problems; the reason for neglecting to finish a particular skill could be explained by boredom, simple negligence, poor time management, or a lack of knowledge. For these reasons, the "did not finish" (DNF) category, describing students that did not master all prerequisite skills, is represented by two bins. Our fourth bin contains students that did not master at least one of the prerequisite skills with a high percent correctness (HPC) across those skills (greater than or equal to 66.67% correctness), while the fifth and final bin contains such students with a low percent correctness (LPC) across all prerequisite skills (less than 66.67% correctness). The fourth and fifth bins handle the case where a student began a prerequisite skill, but did not reach mastery status; this means that at least one problem was attempted, but the student either completed less than three or failed to answer correctly on three consecutive opportunities. Bin four is therefore meant to represent students that failed to complete the prerequisite skills for reasons other than lack of knowledge, while the fifth contains students genuinely struggling and are perhaps experiencing wheel spinning[1].

With students from the training set categorized based on performance in prerequisite skills, a prediction value was calculated for each bin by finding the percentage of students in each category to respond correctly on the first opportunity of the subsequent skill. The reasoning for this method of binning, again, stems from the theory that particular trends exist for students in each bin and will extend to other students that also fall into that category. Therefore, it was expected that the prediction value of each bin constructed by the training set would apply to similar students in the test set.

Bin	Num. of Students	Num. of Students with First Response Correctness	Bin Prediction
1	29	24	0.828
2	53	26	0.491
3	3	0	0.000
4	2	1	0.500
5	3	0	0.000

Table 1. The bin student distribution and prediction values calculated for Fold 1 of Skill 47 of our dataset.

Figure 1 exemplifies the bin creation process using a set of hypothetical students (the names and values do not reflect any real person/dataset and are purely exemplary). In that example, prerequisite information from four students is used to construct the five bins. As Tom averaged a mastery speed of 6 opportunities across all his prerequisite skills, he is placed into the second bin with Bill, who averaged a mastery speed of 4.5 opportunities. Since Tom answered correctly on the first problem of the subsequent skill and Bill did not, the prediction for the second bin becomes 0.5, as half of the students in that bin answered the first problem of the subsequent skill correctly. Joe mastered each prerequisite skill with the minimum three attempts and is therefore placed into the first bin. That bin is given a probabilistic prediction of 1.0 due to the fact that all students in that bin answered correctly on the first question of the subsequent skill. Sue is placed into the fifth bin, as she did not master one of the prerequisite skills, and had a low percent correctness (less than 66.67%) across both prerequisites. She did not answer the first problem correct on the subsequent skill, leading to a prediction of 0.0, as no student in that bin answered correctly on the first question of the subsequent skill.

The values depicted in Table 1 were generated from our actual dataset. This table illustrates the prediction calculation methodology using skill 47 of our dataset corresponding in the ASSISTments tutoring system to the Conversion of Fraction Decimals Percents. As described in the earlier example, students in a training set are placed into each bin based on estimated student knowledge. Using this categorization, a prediction is calculated by observing the number of students in each bin to answer the first problem of the subsequent skill correctly.

RESULTS

The results of our work are exemplified through several metrics. Before comparing the predictive accuracy of our binning method to any other model, we must verify that each bin represents the intended level of knowledge within our dataset. Our method is able to illustrate this representation by observing the percentage of students within each bin to answer correctly on the first problem of a subsequent skill.

Bin	Number of Students	Percent Correct on First Response
1	806	61.79%
2	1170	60.00%
3	172	54.65%
4	732	52.59%
5	586	50.51%

Table 2. The overall percent correctness on the first response of all subsequent skills for each of the five bins.

Table 2 shows the distribution of knowledge within each bin across all skills in the observed dataset. The values show a distribution of higher knowledge students in the lower bins and lower knowledge students in the higher bins. This result supports the claim that our method is properly representing the intended level of knowledge.

The distribution of the number of students in each bin, particularly the fourth and fifth bin, indicates that our dataset contains a large percentage of students that did not complete prerequisites before attempting a subsequent skill. This was the reasoning behind splitting this "DNF" bin into a high knowledge and low knowledge bin based on percent correct in the prerequisite skills. Further splitting these bins may lead to better predictive accuracy of our method, but is sufficient for our work in its current state and avoids over-complicating what is meant to be a simple categorization method.

Comparison of Overall Performance

The results of our method, entitled "Prerequisite Binning" in Table 3, was compared to knowledge tracing as well as a majority class (MC) prediction to act as a control in our experiment. We chose knowledge tracing as it is widely used and studied in the field of educational data analytics and attempts to learn student initial knowledge for use in its calculation. Through this experiment we are first observing the effectiveness of our model by comparing it to the majority class, a prediction made for all students using the average correctness of the dataset, and then observing the differences in error between our method and KT; results illustrating a comparable error between the two methods supports the use of our binning method over KT, as it provides more definitive estimates of student knowledge without sacrificing predictive accuracy. Knowledge tracing was run using Kevin Murphy's Bayes Net Toolbox for MATLAB [7] with initial parameters of 0.30, 0.14, 0.20, and 0.08 for prior, learn, guess, and slip respectively. For our experiment we ran a five fold cross validation on our dataset, using 80% of the data from each skill as a training set to predict the remaining 20%. The results in Table 3 represent the averages of all folds for each method.

Each of the three prediction methods are compared using RMSE and AUC two common measurements of error. A low RMSE indicates a more accurate prediction method while a larger AUC indicates higher accuracy. As observed in Table 3, the prerequisite binning method outperforms the majority class in both metrics indicating that it is a successful prediction method. When compared to knowledge tracing, however, the results show nearly the same RMSE value, but a superior AUC value.

While the binning method may not outperform knowledge tracing in all metrics, the predictive accuracy is comparable. The purpose of this work, again, is not to provide a method that outperforms KT, but rather to construct a modeling method that can provide teachers with more meaningful information regarding student knowledge. Unlike KT, where the learned parameters such as prior/initial knowledge are unusable metrics in describing true student knowledge due to the identifiability problem [2], our binning method provides an initial knowledge estimate based on previously observed performance; this initial knowledge estimate, represented as the probabilistic prediction calculated for each bin, is shown to be just as reliable as KT in predictive accuracy, while also providing a more definitive metric to describe a bin-wide initial knowledge that avoids problems of identifiability.

	RMSE	AUC
Majority Class	.496	.570
KT	.472	.626
Prerequisite Binning	.473	.651

Table 3. Results of our trials over all skills

Based on the results of our trial, we can conclude that prerequisite information can be used to predict student performance on subsequent skills in regards to first response. This supports our argument that knowledge and learning can be observed between prerequisite and subsequent skills.

Comparison Over Individual Skills

We also compare our method with KT on each individual skill. Figure 2 shows the difference of RMSE for these two models, that is: RMSE(KT) − RMSE(Bin); each positive difference value, therefore, indicates that our binning method outperforms KT in that skill, while negative difference values indicate KT outperforms binning in that particular skill. Each bar in the figure has an accompanying p-value above. This p-value is computed by applying a statistical T-test on the five-fold cross validation results. From this figure, we observe that our method outperforms KT in 14 of the 28 observed skills. Looking at the T-test results, there is a significant difference (p-value ≤ 0.05) between the two models on only 3 skills. This statistic further supports the comparability of the two models in terms of accuracy.

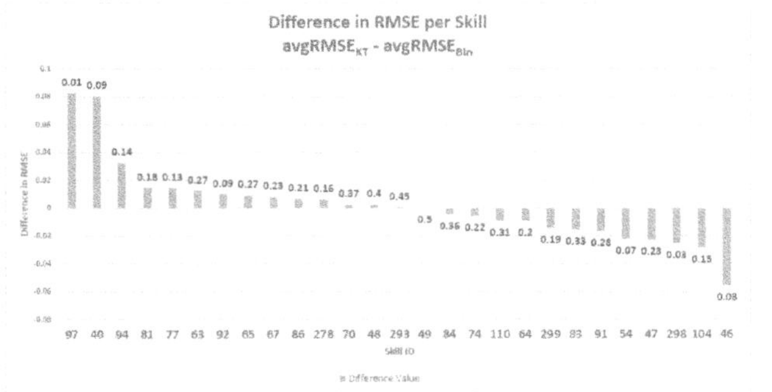

Figure 2. The difference of RMSE per skill when comparing our method of binning to standard knowledge tracing, ordered from highest to lowest difference. The number above each skill indicates the p-value of the difference.

A similar histogram illustrating the difference of RMSE for the majority class and our binning method, RMSE(MC) − RMSE(Bin), can be seen in Figure 3. The majority class represents a prediction for each student that is equal to the percent correctness of the training set of students. Again, as we used a five fold cross validation, 80% of the data from each skill is used as a training set to predict the remaining 20%. Comparing our binning method to the majority class should provide results that take into account the difficulty of each skill, defined by the average correctness calculated in majority class predictions.

This result attempts to answer the second question in introduction pertaining to the reliability of the prerequisite skill relationships. In accordance with our initial thoughts, the stronger the relationship between a prerequisite and subsequent skill, the better we can predict the performance of the subsequent skill from the knowledge of the prerequisite skill. Using Figure 3, we can observe significant differences (p-value ≤ 0.05) in terms of RMSE on a total of 5 individual skills. Therefore, at least on skills 97 and 49, the skills with better statistically significant results, we have strong confidence that the prerequisite relationships are reliable. For those skills with significantly lower results, skills 54, 298, and 46, the causal relation of the prerequisite skills may not be strong as expected by domain experts. All other skills, however, do not illustrate results significant enough to make a claim. These particular inconclusive results may be explained by inspecting our dataset. As indicated in our first observations pertaining to the distribution of students in each bin, a large percentage of students are categorized into bins four and five. Many of those students, as indicated by our dataset, attempt less than three problems, preventing mastery and also making it more difficult to properly estimate knowledge.

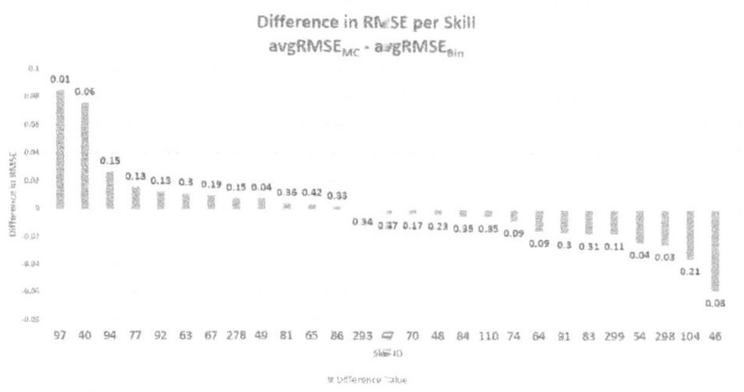

Figure 3. The difference of RMSE per skill when comparing our method of binning to majority class predictions, ordered from highest to lowest difference. The number above each skill indicates the p-value of the difference.

There may be two reasons for this occurrence. First, the prerequisite skills may too hard for the students to master. This may result from the teacher's decision not to assign particular prerequisite skills, or the skill relationship graph is incomplete. A second possibility may allude to a case where a teacher does not assign enough questions for students to master the prerequisite skills. As a teacher has control over the administering of skill problems, a number of such scenarios could lead to such results. In summary, these findings potentially indicate a need to further inspect the causal relationships defined by domain experts as they appear in the observed systems.

CONTRIBUTION

Our goal in this paper was to utilize the prerequisite information that many systems record to infer aspects of the students in our data. The current predominantly used knowledge tracing model employed in many learning systems assumes that all the skills are independent of each other. In this work, however, prerequisite information is used to better understand the relationship between the prerequisite and subsequent skills. The added consideration of this relationship in a model can be used to make better statements and inferences about not only the students, but also in the manner that such skills are presented to students.

We have shown here, to our knowledge, the first model that attempts to use the relationships between prerequisite skills to predict subsequent knowledge. This is on its way to make a larger contribution to better personalizing and individualizing student models by acknowledging and utilizing more of the data. We will make note that there are many other researchers that have used aggregate information, but have not paid attention to the prerequisite structure. Many psychometricians have found, for instance, that if students who do well on a topic A tend to do well on a topic B, that information can be used to better predict performance on topic B. In this context, however, we prefer to view such information differently. Our ultimate goal is to be able to make statements to teachers regarding information that is more causally related, and we do not want to influence predictions of future performance for unrelated tasks where there is little knowledge overlap. By imposing this constraint upon us, it will reduce our ability to make predictions, but will increase the significance of our statements to teachers.

The goal of this paper extends beyond the intent to develop a more accurate prediction methodology. We wish to look at the causal effects from which our results derive. It is more of a question of why using this data from prerequisite skills produces the accurate predictions across some skills and not in others. Our findings support the intuitive claim that certain skills are related, while others are not. Our trials provide a means of visualizing aspects of such skills to show that, as in Figure 3, prerequisite information does not have the same effect for all subsequent skills. Observing little difference in some skills between a method utilizing prerequisite information and a method, such as KT or majority class, that does not use such information may point to several issues in either our dataset or the prerequisite graph of the system. It is an interesting observation that some skills, while listed as a prerequisite, may not have as strong a relationship to a subsequent skill, which is vitally important information to teachers who need to consider a sequence to introduce new skills.

CONCLUSION AND FUTURE WORKS

The results and observations presented in this paper open new research opportunities in student assessment. Through our results we have observed several factors that help to better model student knowledge and aptitude across skills. The trials of this paper certainly raise some curiosities as to the extent subsequent skills are affected by prerequisite performance. In this paper, we focus exclusively on first responses of subsequent skills and, as the results were successful, we can now look beyond the first response to observe trends in prerequisite influence over an entire subsequent skill response sequence.

With these findings, our method can be adapted and/or appropriated to benefit other models like KT. Implementing our method into a modified KT model could lead to more accurate representations of student initial knowledge. As the method we propose here requires little in terms of processing time while providing more definitive student knowledge estimates than other models like KT, we aim to, through similar methods, represent other aspects of student learning such as aptitude and knowledge retention.

The accuracy of this method of binning is largely impacted by the reliability of the method of determining mastery. In our experiments, as it is in ASSISTments, mastery is defined simply as a student answering correctly on three consecutive opportunities; this method, while simple, may not be the best means of representing such a status universally for all students. Further work in exploring more precise methods of determining mastery speed may prove to benefit our method; such a method may include the individualization of mastery speed requirements for each bin, as it is likely that not all student levels of knowledge can be confidently labeled as having mastered a skill with the same number of sequential correct responses.

In this work, we concern ourselves with and direct our attention to the concept of student growth and knowledge over time. We believe that such information identifies aspects of the student more definitively than next problem correctness. In the future, we hope to continue similar work, looking into the influences that prerequisite skills exhibit in the other student models, like the wheel spinning model [1]. We would also like to make further observations and inferences on prerequisite skills, such as their impact on the student learning process itself, or the retention performance [11] of this prior.

ACKNOWLEDGMENT

We acknowledge funding from NSF (grant #'s 1316736, 1252297, 1109483, 1031398, 0742503), ONR's STEM Grand Challenges, and IES (grant #'s R305A120125, R305C100024).

REFERENCES

1. Beck, J., and Rodrigo, M. M. T. Understanding wheel spinning in the context of affective factors. In *Intelligent Tutoring Systems*, Springer International Publishing (2014), 162–167.

2. Beck, J. E., and min Chang, K. Identifiability: A fundamental problem of student modeling. In *User Modeling 2007*, Springer Berlin Heidelberg (2007), 137–146.

3. Beck, J. E., min Chang, K., Mostow, J., and Corbett, A. Does help help? introducing the bayesian evaluation and assessment methodology. In *Intelligent Tutoring Systems*, Springer Berlin Heidelberg (2008), 383–394.

4. Corbett, A., and Anderson, J. Knowledge Tracing: Modeling the Acquisition of Procedural Knowledge. *User Modeling and User-Adapted Interaction 4*, 4 (1994), 253–278.

5. Cree, V. E., and Macaulay, C., Eds. *Transfer of Learning in Professional & Vocational Education*.

6. d. Baker, R. S. J., Corbett, A. T., Gowda, S. M., Wagner, A. Z., MacLaren, B. A., Kauffman, L. R., Mitchell, A. P., and Giguere, S. Contextual slip and prediction of student performance after use of an intelligent tutor. In *User Modeling, Adaptation, and Personalization*, Springer Berlin Heidelberg (2010), 52–63.

7. Murphy, K. Bayes net toolbox for matlab. `https://github.com/bayesnet/bnt/`.

8. Pardos, Z. A., and Heffernan, N. T. Navigating the parameter space of bayesian knowledge tracing models:

Visualizations of the convergence of the expectation maximization algorithm.

9. Pardos, Z. A., and Heffernan, N. T. Modeling individualization in a bayesian networks implementation of knowledge tracing. In *User Modeling, Adaptation, and Personalization*, Springer Berlin Heidelberg (2010), 255–266.

10. Wang, Y., and Heffernan, N. Extending knowledge tracing to allow partial credit: Using continuous versus binary nodes. In *Artificial Intelligence in Education*, Springer Berlin Heidelberg (2013), 181–188.

11. Xiong, X., Beck, J., and Li, S. Class distinctions: Leveraging class-level features to predict student retention performance. In *Artificial Intelligence in Education*, H. Lane, K. Yacef, J. Mostow, and P. Pavlik, Eds., vol. 7926 of *Lecture Notes in Computer Science*. Springer Berlin Heidelberg, 2013, 820–823.

12. Xiong, X., Li, S., and Beck, J. E. Will you get it right next week: Predict delayed performance in enhanced its mastery cycle. In *FLAIRS Conference* (2013).

Blended Learning in Indian Colleges with Massively Empowered Classroom

Edward Cutrell[1], Jacki O'Neill[1], Srinath Bala[1], B. Nitish[1], Andrew Cross[1], Nakull Gupta[1], Viraj Kumar[2], William Thies[1]

[1]Microsoft Research [2]PES University, Bangalore

ABSTRACT
Students in the developing world are frequently cited as being among the most important beneficiaries of online education initiatives such as massive open online courses (MOOCs). While some predict that online classrooms will replace physical classrooms, our experience suggests that blending online and in-person instruction is more likely to succeed in developing regions. However, very little research has actually been done on the effects of online education or blended learning in these environments. In this paper we describe a blended learning initiative that combines videos from a large online course with peer-led sessions for undergraduate technical education in India. We performed a randomized controlled trial (RCT) that indicates our intervention was associated with a small but significant improvement in performance on a summative exam. We discuss the results of the RCT and an ethnographic study of the intervention to make recommendations for future, scalable blended learning initiatives for places such as India.

Author Keywords
Massive open online course; MOOC; India; Blended learning; RCT; Online education.

ACM Classification Keywords
K.3.1 Computers and Education

INTRODUCTION
A common claim made by supporters of online educational systems such as MOOCs is that they offer a revolutionary opportunity for global parity in the availability of education. The same high-quality education provided to those lucky enough to attend Stanford or MIT can be had by anyone with an internet connection, whether they live in Miami, Monrovia or Mumbai [16]. And while most MOOCs are still almost exclusively in English, more and more material is available in other languages: Khan Academy is working to translate much of its content to Spanish [11], Coursera and edX are working to extend the MOOCs to Chinese [9, 14] and the Queen Rania Foundation and edX recently announced *Edraak*, a partnership to provide MOOCs with Arabic content [15].

L@S 2015, March 14 - 18, 2015, Vancouver, BC, Canada.

ACM 978-1-4503-3411-2/15/03…$15.00.
http://dx.doi.org/10.1145/2724660.2724666

Despite the hype and fevered activity, very little research has explored the real and potential impact of online education in the developing world. In order to understand how advances in online education might benefit undergraduate education in India, we built and deployed Massively Empowered Classroom (MEC), an experimental system designed to support MOOC-like functionality and blended learning for Indian colleges. While many users of MOOC platforms are adult learners, we are particularly interested in how to engage existing students that are currently enrolled in traditional educational systems. Our pilot is focused on undergraduate technical education (specifically computer science). MEC currently offers four courses in partnership with more than ten large technical universities in India, serving educational content to more than 27,000 students.

In this paper we review the context of technical education in India and how online education is currently employed with a focus on existing students. With this as a backdrop, we describe a small scale randomized controlled trial (RCT) that we performed with a blended learning intervention based on MEC. We found that our blended learning intervention led to a small but significant improvement in learning as measured by a final exam. By combining this result with data from an ethnographic study of the intervention and the data collected from student satisfaction surveys, we make some recommendations for the effective use of blended learning interventions and directions for future research.

RELATED WORK

MOOCs and the developing world
While much has been made of the potential impact of MOOCs and online education initiatives for learning in developing regions such as Africa, Asia and Latin America [24, 37], there is little evidence so far of successes in these regions to match the hopeful claims. Most scholarly work to date on MOOCs in the Global South comprises either general overviews of MOOCs and the issues they may be expected to run into or solve [27, 11, 5] or program proposals tuned for the context of the Global South [38, 26].

Aside from our own work with MEC discussed in this paper, several other initiatives are now underway in India, Jordan, Rwanda, Francophone Africa, and several other countries [22]. For example, in May of 2014, IIT Bombay announced the launch of three courses on the edX platform and there have been several government and private initiatives to introduce online teaching to Indian students [39]. As these programs are implemented, we hope to see some studies emerge describing how they fare.

Studies of blended learning

Online educational tools are used in a wide range of contexts for many different goals, but there is an increasing focus on blended learning, where online tools are combined with classroom activities and instruction to provide an overall improvement in educational outcomes [18, 4]. While descriptions and discussions around blended learning go back almost 40 years [e.g., 19, 40], the recent surge of activity surrounding MOOCs has provided a renewed interest in different ways to marry online learning with the classroom. For example, a proposal by Dr. Phatak from IIT Bombay advocates a blended learning model with MOOCs for technical colleges in India [38].

Along with this activity, there have been a variety of studies that have attempted to explore whether blended learning actually improves learning outcomes. One study that has received much attention was an experiment in San Jose State University where a course was supplemented with the MIT edX course on circuits [20]. They found that 91% of the students in the new blended learning format passed the course, compared with 59% of students in the traditional course offered the previous year, and that midterm and final exam scores were 10-12% higher than the previous year. These are very impressive results, though it should be noted that this intervention came at a substantial cost of time and effort by the teacher and students [23]. However, work by Lovett, Meyer & Thille showed large learning benefits with evidence that students were not working more outside of class [29].

A recent meta-analysis of 45 studies suggested that students in blended learning environments perform modestly better than those in face-to-face classes [31]. However, the authors note that most of these studies tend to confound additional learning time, instructional resources, and other course elements that may have contributed to the positive outcomes. We should note that some of these aspects seem less confounds than fundamental to the nature of blended learning pedagogy.

Other studies of blended learning have reported essentially no differences in outcomes [26, 5, 21]. Of particular note are two randomized controlled trials (RCTs) carried out by Ithaka S+R [5, 21]. In these studies, researchers conducted a number of trials with American universities to explore whether MOOCs could be hybridized with more traditional formats to improve outcomes and/or reduce costs for students enrolled in traditional institutions. They found that students taking courses in hybrid formats did as well or slightly better than students in traditional sections in terms of pass rates, exam scores and grades with less average class time from faculty.

There have also been efforts to understand the potential of blended learning for primary education in India. A project called Digital Study Hall has reached many students in rural schools, but has proven difficult to evaluate quantitatively [2]. A short-term study of multimedia teaching aids in peri-urban Bangalore found learning benefits in English but not in science [33].

However, to our knowledge there have not been any studies that evaluate the impact of blended learning in the context of higher education in developing regions such as India. While tertiary institutions often have better infrastructure than rural primary schools, they still have many constraints and are in urgent need of improved technical education. Considering the number of aspiring students in these regions, the potential benefit of new educational models is immense. In this paper we demonstrate some initial evidence suggesting that blended learning models can improve learning outcomes in engineering education in India.

We should note that our study of blended learning in the context of undergraduate engineering education in India is well-defined (as described below), and therefore repeatable. Although the possibility of blending online videos (such as the corpus created by the National Programme on Technology Enhanced Learning, NPTEL) with traditional curriculum delivery has been suggested [34], directives issued by the concerned educational agencies in this regard do not formulate clear implementation guidelines [31].

TECHNICAL EDUCATION IN INDIA

The context of technical education in India is very different from that in the Global North. In order to understand how online tools might be used to improve technical education in India, a brief summary of the scale, organization and constraints may be helpful. Engineering education in India is a huge enterprise and is very heterogeneous. In 2014, there were more than 3400 engineering institutes in India, teaching approximately 4 million students, and the rate of increase in enrollment is enormous: between 2009 and 2014, the intake of engineering colleges grew from 1.1 to 1.6 million students [1]. Outside of India, many people are familiar with elite institutes such as the Indian Institutes of Technology (IIT), National Institutes of Technology (NIT), Birla Institutes of Technology and Science (BITS), and others. However, these teach only a small fraction of all the engineering students in India (e.g., the total number of new seats for all 16 IITs in 2014 was ~10,000 [25]). The vast majority of engineering students enroll in a variety of other institutes across the country. Some of these are autonomous "deemed" or private universities, and a large proportion are colleges affiliated with state universities.

State universities are run by the governments of each of the states and territories of India and can be very large. For example, Visvesvaraya Technological University (VTU) in the state of Karnataka comprises 201 affiliated colleges, teaching more than 67,000 undergraduate students [43], and

Anna University in the state of Tamil Nadu comprises 520 affiliated colleges, with more than 120,000 engineering students [3]. All affiliated colleges in a university share a single, synced curriculum for every course. Textbooks, syllabus, and order of presentation of material are all prescribed by a central university authority, and for each course there is a single shared final examination taken by every student in the university.

A web of difficulties

These so-called "second-tier institutes" face a number of serious challenges. First, there is a critical shortage of qualified teachers. Every year, the number of students in engineering increases and there are not enough instructors to meet the demand. Some first-time teachers told us that they never intended to become teachers, but only did so because they could not find a job in industry and leave if they find an industry job. This leads to enormous inequality between institutions, with a few high-performing schools and a long tail of institutions with under-qualified staff. Because of high turnover and limited experience, teachers are given very little autonomy and must follow a rigid curriculum. In addition, they are given very little latitude in grading, with the majority of a student's grade coming from standard final exams set by the university. In turn, colleges are often evaluated by their graduation rate, and thus have an incentive to evaluate students favorably. Therefore, most exams test rote knowledge instead of deeper understanding. High marks are given to students who memorize textbook responses rather than learn subject material, and the best students have little opportunity to distinguish themselves.

A lack of well-trained teachers and the limited relevance of classroom performance leads to uninspired students with little interest in subject mastery. In many instances, students spend their time optimizing for short term goals (e.g., memorizing questions from test banks) rather than learning the material. Naturally, this creates a feedback loop in which many teachers have little incentive to improve their skills or enhance the classroom experience for uninterested students who have no reason to pay attention.

As a result of these problems, industry has largely given up on many colleges' ability to deliver quality education. Large companies such as Infosys and TCS hire students mostly on "raw intelligence" and then train them in custom computer science curriculum for up to 6 months before putting the new hires to work [41]. In our view, this represents an enormous waste of time and energy and leads to the question: Can this situation be improved through innovations in pedagogy such as blended learning and online education?

ONLINE EDUCATION IN INDIA

MOOCs and other initiatives in online education have taken center stage in much of the public and academic discourse surrounding pedagogy in the US, Canada and Europe. However, in India these efforts are still virtually unknown outside of an elite population. While supporters cite the thousands of students from India that enroll in MOOCs, these numbers are still very small as a proportion of the student population of India (4 million undergraduates in engineering alone). Our research suggests that currently these resources are mostly used by adults for continuing education and a very small fraction of students who are driven to learn. Indeed, while students in elite institutions such as IITs are likely to be aware of these kinds of online resources, it seems that those who could benefit most from better quality teaching are the least aware of MOOCs.

Starting in 2012, our research group began a systematic exploration of how online education is currently used in India, what factors were holding it back, and how these tools might best be used to improve educational practice in undergraduate technical education. Much more detail is available in a separate report [10], but one finding stood out: on the whole, very few of the students or faculty we spoke with had ever heard of MOOCs (edX, Coursera, Khan Academy, etc.), and still fewer had actually participated in a course—and these were only top students at the better-resourced colleges. Many teachers were aware of NPTEL (a government-sponsored archive of online lectures by IIT professors) [42], though again, very few students or teachers regularly used this as a learning resource.

From these discussions we distilled four main reasons that we believe MOOCs and other online resources have had limited success in Indian undergraduate education so far:

1) The syllabi of online courses differ from university courses, and the level/speed of teaching is often too fast for students at regional colleges. In some ways this echoes the experience of other recent attempts to mix MOOCs with courses in other institutes [7]. A corollary of differing syllabi is that online materials are not directly relevant for exams. Students optimize virtually all their effort around cracking exams (see below). Even if online material relates directly to concepts taught in class, if it won't directly improve exam scores then students aren't interested. At the end of the day, it all comes down to employment and currently students do not feel that online content will improve their prospects.
2) Language and accent is a serious concern. While English is the official medium of instruction for undergraduate technical education in India, in practice many students from less affluent areas have only limited competency in English. Furthermore, many MOOC teachers have an American accent that can be particularly difficult for Indian students.
3) There remain serious network bandwidth constraints for most colleges and students. In every college we visited, video streaming was difficult, if not impossible. Outside of colleges, students see huge variability in bandwidth availability and cost. However, most online courses assume the constant availability of high-bandwidth connectivity to support video streaming and other interactive content.

4) Finally, but perhaps most significantly, these tools have not been embraced by college administrations. Teaching practice in India is extremely conservative (particularly at second-tier colleges) and teachers have little autonomy; students do what their teachers tell them to do, and teachers do precisely what their administration tells them to do (and little more). Unless a pedagogical technique such as using MOOCs for blended learning is dictated from the top, it is unlikely to be incorporated into any classrooms. Simply put, in the current university structure there are no real incentives for teachers and students to use MOOCs beyond intrinsic motivation, which is why it has had limited uptake.

These concerns motivated and informed our design of MEC.

Massively Empowered Classroom

We built Massively Empowered Classroom (MEC) to explore how online educational content and techniques in blended learning might be used for teaching computer science at state technical universities in India. Because online education is virtually unknown in these colleges, our research goals for MEC were broad and exploratory. However, beyond research, the primary goal was to provide students access to high-quality teaching for the curriculum that they were already enrolled in. We wanted to provide an environment in which students could learn everything they need to know for the subject they were studying.

To facilitate our exploration, we built our own platform. While at the time of this writing (late 2014) there are a few potential platforms that we might be able to use (e.g., [36]), when we began this investigation in 2012 these options were not available. Building our own platform gave us the flexibility to explore features and experiment with different ideas, as well as access to data and statistics about usage. MEC was designed to incorporate several features of MOOCs that we thought would be useful for this context, as well as a number of features that are not as common for MOOCs. Much more detail about the design and features of MEC is available elsewhere [10].

The first course we prepared was Design and Analysis of Algorithms (DAA), one of the core courses in Computer Science curricula. Anyone could sign up and take the course, but it was specifically designed for students affiliated with colleges in several partner universities. Content was created by a team of three to four teachers drawn from local research institutes and colleges. These teachers worked together to ensure that the material was of good quality and matched the syllabus of each university course. In addition, they made sure that the content was pitched to the level of the students and delivered in clear Indian English.

The DAA course provided for VTU (our first partner university) had over 45 videos, each 8-15 minutes long, covering eight units from the course syllabus. In the classroom, the university allocates 52 hours of teaching to cover this material. On MEC, there were also about 10 multiple-choice "quizzes", roughly one per week (the number of videos varied somewhat for different university syllabi). Students were offered certificates at various levels to encourage participation. In the spring of 2014, we offered a "participation" certificate for scoring an aggregate of 50% or better on quizzes, a "completion" certificate for scoring 75% or better and a "distinction" certificate for passing a final exam administered in-person by the MEC team.

In addition to the standard online streaming of videos, the MEC platform attempts to manage bandwidth constraints by allowing students to download content for offline viewing on a PC and with an Android smartphone app.

A TRIAL OF PEER-LED BLENDED LEARNING

While the DAA course on MEC attempted to respond to several of the limitations with MOOCs identified above (e.g., matching syllabus, using local Indian teachers, and provision of offline and mobile viewing), MEC has largely been provided to students on a purely voluntary basis. We were also interested in seeing how MEC might be more tightly integrated into class as part of the basic course experience.

We have frequently observed that smart, motivated students take leadership roles in classes, often making up for absent or sub-par teachers. We wanted to see if a class based on MEC and led by a peer could be an effective way of improving learning for all students in a course, not just the students motivated enough to seek out MEC on their own.

To investigate this hypothesis, we performed a small RCT with several local engineering colleges. We hired a student in his 4th year of undergraduate studies in computer science from a local engineering college to facilitate weekly sessions in which videos from MEC were played to a group of students during regularly scheduled labs or recitations. In addition to playing videos, our class facilitator answered questions related to the video and discussed various practical applications for the material. At the end of the term, we conducted an exam to measure any potential differences in learning outcomes compared to a set of control colleges.

In addition to the exam, we collected both qualitative and quantitative data about the MEC sessions and the students' perspectives on this approach.

METHODS

Selection of colleges for intervention

We restricted our experiment to colleges affiliated with Visvesvaraya Technological University (VTU). VTU comprises more than 200 technical colleges spread across Karnataka, with a high concentration of schools in the Bangalore area. All VTU colleges follow the same syllabus for each course, and students are evaluated with a single (identical) final exam across all colleges at the end of the term. By focusing on VTU, we hoped to reduce some of the variability across colleges due to curriculum and timing. To identify colleges for our study, we worked with the administration of VTU to obtain a list of anonymized exam scores of all students enrolled in the previous two years of

College	2013 Class Size	2013 Exam (StdDev)	2014 Class size
1 Ctrl	235	57.6 (15.3)	233
1 Intvn	298	57.6 (13.1)	281
2 Ctrl	205	55.1 (13.1)	204
2 Intvn	216	54.0 (13.1)	207
3 Ctrl	199	53.6 (12.3)	217
3 Intvn	187	53.9 (14.8)	174
4 Ctrl	292	53.2 (13.9)	272
4 Intvn	260	53.1 (16.2)	234
5 Ctrl	119	48.8 (13.1)	109
5 Intvn	124	50.5 (14.4)	117
Total Ctrl	1050	54.1 (13.9)	1035
Total Intvn	1085	54.4 (14.5)	1013

Table 1. Class sizes and exam scores for control (Ctrl) and intervention (Intvn) colleges.

VTU's Design and Analysis of Algorithms (DAA) course in all VTU colleges. From this list, we selected five pairs of colleges from the Bangalore area where each pair was roughly matched on class size and exam scores from previous years (a loose proxy for quality of students and instruction). The five pairs of colleges ranged from more exclusive schools (known for competitive enrollment and higher exam scores) to less competitive colleges with lower exam scores. Other eligibility criteria for colleges included:

- More than 100 students enrolled in DAA in 2013
- Fewer than 10 students enrolled in MEC in 2013
- Not an outlying high or low performer

From each pair, we randomly assigned one college to the intervention and the other as a control. See Table 1 for population and exam details for each college pair.

We then contacted the administrators and teachers for each intervention college to seek permission to work with their DAA classes for the spring term of 2014. We arranged for our research assistant to visit each college once a week, usually during lab or recitation, to conduct sessions featuring videos from the MEC DAA course. As an incentive and token of thanks, each college was promised a plaque indicating their participation with our organization in the initiative.

The intervention

At the beginning of the term, our peer mediator (PM) visited each intervention college and encouraged all the students enrolled in DAA that term to create an account on MEC. At this first meeting, he described how the system worked (how to login, watch videos, use the forum, etc.), and played the introductory video to the group. Then for the next seven weeks, the PM visited each college for a session with MEC, for a total of 8 sessions. The PM was explicitly instructed not to go beyond the material shown in videos and was very careful to limit his discussion only to those concepts he played in each session. In three colleges, students from classes in Information Science and Engineering (ISE) and Computer Science and Engineering (CSE) participated. Because of the large numbers of students in these colleges, sessions were divided up into multiple sections in a day (see Table 2 for details). Note that in some colleges we were only able to hold sessions for a subset of students. Due to a variety of scheduling conflicts and administrative issues, we were only able to hold 3 sessions for one college (#5) and had to drop them from the intervention. On average, the PM taught approximately 22 sections per week for about 180 total sections.

Note that for both intervention and control colleges, students spent the same total amount of time in class. At the intervention colleges, students spent an hour each week with the PM viewing and talking about MEC videos, while in control colleges students spent this time in their regularly scheduled labs/recitations.

It is also useful to note that while the PM was certainly a very good student who was passionate about CS, he did not have a particular interest in algorithms and was not considered a "topper" in his own DAA class when he took it. He estimates he was in the top 50% of his DAA class, though he was particularly good at implementation vs. theory. While the PM had no experience teaching, he did have some experience speaking to student groups as an evangelist for OpenStack.

Learning outcomes—terminal review exam

At the end of the term, we conducted a final exam for students in both intervention and matched control colleges. The exam was described to students as a "review exam" covering material from the full range of topics covered by the VTU syllabus for DAA. At the end of the exam, a member of our team went over each question and walked through the solution. The exam was designed by two of the authors; one was a professor at a local college and familiar with the VTU syllabus. The test comprised ten multiple-choice questions (the last two were connected and graded as a two-point unit), for a total maximum score of 10. A time limit of 40 minutes was set for the exam. The exam can be viewed at http://research.microsoft.com/~cutrell/DAAex.pdf

The teachers and administrators at these colleges were keen to host our review session, and made attendance mandatory for all students enrolled in DAA. At each college we recognized the top five scorers on our exam and gave them some small awards (t-shirts and gift cards).

As noted above, we were unable to conduct regular sessions with college #5 and had to drop it from the experiment. Also, due to scheduling problems we were unable to perform the exam for either college #4 or their control. Ultimately, a total of six colleges—intervention colleges #1-3 and their controls – took the exam.

Intervention college	Sections CSE	Sections ISE	Sessions Conducted (per section)
1	5	3	8
2	3	1	8
3	4	2	8
4	2	-	8
5*	2	-	3

Table 2. Sessions conducted for each intervention college. Note that we were unable to complete the intervention for college 5.

Field study and satisfaction surveys

To understand how students experienced our intervention, we conducted an ethnographic study of some of the MEC sessions. An ethnographer accompanied the facilitator to conduct observations of the sessions and in situ interviews with students and teachers. The ethnographer attended 78 sessions, visiting all five intervention colleges at least twice (for a total of around 16 days of observation). In the first session for each section the ethnographer introduced herself and got permission to record and take photographs. After that she typically sat at the back of the class observing and taking notes. Data was collected through detailed field notes, audio recordings, short video recordings and photographs. The analytic approach to the material was broadly ethnomethodological [17], an approach which reveals how social order is achieved in settings such as offices [35] and schools [29].

Finally, in the last of the MEC sessions, the PM conducted a student satisfaction survey consisting of a mixture of ratings (using a 5 point Likert scale) and free text response to establish how the students felt about various aspects of the MEC sessions, from their opinions about the facilitator to whether the sessions helped them understand the practical applications of algorithms.

RESULTS

MEC usage beyond the classroom

We examined the usage logs from MEC to look at how students used MEC individually outside of class. Overall, MEC was not extensively used by many students outside of the classroom sessions. While 308 students in intervention colleges (about 30% of those enrolled in DAA) watched at least part of one video, 206 of those students never opened more than three videos. The median total time of video watched for these 308 students was just 10 minutes, and only 50 students watched more than an hour of total video. This was moderately disappointing, as we hoped that the classroom sessions would increase independent usage outside of class much more than it did.

Of course, individual use of MEC in the control colleges was even less: only 39 students watched at least one video (about 4% of students enrolled in DAA), but about the same proportion (66%) never opened more than three videos. We expected the number of users in control colleges to be less since they would have only heard about MEC through word-of-mouth or general announcements across VTU (versus the active promotion in intervention colleges).

Observations of blended learning in practice

To put the results of the RCT in context it is useful to understand some details about what went on in the intervention and how students responded. Overall, MEC sessions were fairly consistent; the PM would typically repeat the same topic across colleges and sections, and the same topic looked similar in each session. Variations typically stemmed from the engagement and academic level of students (e.g., responsiveness to questions, ability to arrive at the right answer). For the purposes of this paper it suffices to give a general overview of the sorts of activities the PM and the class engaged in.

Classes were highly interactive from the beginning. The PM would start off by asking the group what they had covered already in class in relation to the day's topic. For example, "What are the different algorithms for sorting?" or "What have you learned about greedy algorithms?" Questions were answered by the group or individually and served to make the content relevant to the students' learning, to engage them and to give the PM an idea of level of learning. The PM would then play that day's MEC video. On most occasions, he would play a few minutes of video (1-2 minutes) and then pause to discuss. In a very few observed sessions he played longer segments of video (e.g., 7-10 minutes); although students initially attended to the video, the visible attention level in the classes rapidly dropped. To address this the PM interspersed video and interaction, pausing the video to do several activities:

1) *Soliciting a solution to a problem posed in a video before the answer is revealed.* The PM would ask the class to solve the problem – typically getting some class members to come to the front and write the solution on the board before continuing the video. For the most part this was an engaging and well-received strategy (confirmed by interviews with students). However it was a notable failure in at least two cases, where the PM failed to get any engagement on one particular problem, seemingly because it was too hard for the given section.
2) *Priming the video by asking about concepts before they are introduced.* At one point the PM paused the video, wrote 'encryption' on the board, and asked "what does this term mean?" The resulting interaction was a set of student responses which he probed further. When restarting the video, it would typically repeat some of what had just been covered before moving on.
3) *Pausing the video to emphasize a point,* e.g., making it relevant to the student's experience.

These interludes between the video clips typically lasted between a few seconds and several minutes. While we cannot say that the PM did not discuss anything at all that was not on the video, by and large he did not add content. Rather he made the session more interactive, encouraging group responses and competition for solving problems and pushing quieter members of the class to answer questions. In this way a 10-15 minute video could occupy an hour class and sometimes he did not even finish playing the video. At the end the PM wrapped up by summarizing what they had learned and often giving them a small task they could go and try themselves.

One challenge to the typical pattern occurred when there were power cuts. In about four of the observed classes the PM could not play video for the entire section. Nonetheless, these classes followed the same topics as the other sessions, as by that stage the PM seemed to know the material by rote.

Although purely subjective on this matter[1], the impression of the ethnographer was that classes combining video and facilitation resulted in the best engagement.

Student feedback

In the short interviews with students conducted just after the sessions or in the college corridors, students said that they appreciated the interactivity of the classroom sessions and learning about the practical applications of algorithms. They compared it favorably to the standard teaching they received, which they described as largely involving the teacher writing on the board while they took notes. Some even said that labs took a similar shape (the teacher wrote the code on the board and they typed it into the computer).

Student satisfaction forms were distributed to the students at four colleges (excluding college 5) during the final session and 326 were returned completed. A majority (60%) rated the overall MEC sessions good or excellent (4 and 5 on the scale), 7% poor or fair (1 and 2 on the scale) and 32% satisfactory. Most (69%) also agreed (or strongly agreed) that the sessions "improved my understanding of algorithms", with only 5% disagreeing and 27% neutral. We also asked the students to rate the "outreach MEC lecturer" (the PM) and the "videos played in class" to see if one appeared more influential than the other in the students perception of MEC classes. About 63% rated the PM as good/excellent, whereas 50% rated the videos as good/excellent. Students' ratings of the PM were significantly higher than MEC videos, Wald $\chi^2(1) = 9.21, p<0.002$.

Students were able to provide free text comments for each question and a majority of students did so. Around a third of the comments about the overall MEC sessions praised the sessions for being interactive, interesting, practical or just plain different from their normal classes. This backs up the interviews, indicating that students appreciate this different pedagogy to the usual "chalk and talk." Almost half the comments mentioned personal factors about the PM, mentioning things such as communication skills, accent, enthusiasm and teaching style; about two-thirds were positive, and the rest were negative. In terms of the videos, 40% did not find them interactive or practical enough, however nearly 80% of students who commented on their clarity of explanation and depth were positive. Finally, 11% noted that the 'playback quality' in class made it hard to engage (due to sound, screen size, etc.). In some sessions, videos were played on a desktop computer monitor for 20 students, so this is not surprising.

Review exam

A total of 935 students from six colleges participated in our review exam. In five of the six colleges, students from both CSE and ISE departments participated (in one college the ISE students were unable to attend). According to school records, there were 1316 students enrolled in DAA at these

[1] While it is relatively easy to judge visible engagement on a minute by minute basis, it is another matter to judge engagement over a whole class period.

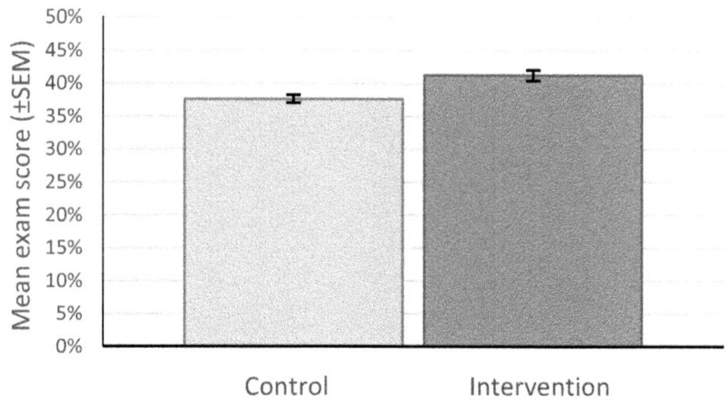

Figure 1. Mean scores on cumulative review exam for control and intervention colleges.

six colleges, so ~70% of enrolled students participated. Note, however, that some enrolled students were in neither CSE nor ISE departments, and are not included in our analysis.

Our hypothesis was that the MEC intervention would improve performance on tests of understanding basic concepts in DAA. In addition we were curious whether the intervention might have a differential impact on ISE students. CSE departments are typically more competitive than ISE, and ISE students usually do not do as well as those in CSE. As our intervention was a substantial departure from typical Indian pedagogy, we wondered if there would be any difference in how students performed.

We performed our statistical analysis on log-transformed data to overcome the mildly skewed distributions of exam scores and to normalize variances between conditions. However, we performed a 2 (Intervention) x 2 (Department) between-subjects ANOVA on log-transformed exam scores[2]. We found a small but significant effect for Intervention, $F(1,930) = 14.54$, $p<<0.01$, $\eta 2 = 0.02$, with our intervention colleges scoring on average about 3.6 percentage points better than the controls (see Figure 1). There was a borderline effect for Department, $F(1,930) = 3.37$, $p<0.07$, where CSE students scored about 1.9 percentage points better than ISE overall. Finally, there was also a small borderline interaction effect between Intervention and Department, $F(1,930) = 3.46$, $p<0.06$. To test for possible moderation effects of Department on Intervention, follow-up simple effects show that there was a significant effect for Department in the Control group, $F(1,930) = 8.15$, $p<0.004$, $\eta 2 = 0.01$, with CSE students scoring on average 3.5 percentage points better than ISE in control colleges and only 0.4 percentage points better in intervention colleges (see Figure 2). That is, ISE students performed almost as well as CSE students in intervention colleges.

[2] A potentially more rigorous analysis is to regress scores on our exam against the previous year's final exam scores. This actually led to a slightly larger effect, as intervention schools performed worse than control schools in the prior year (in the three matched pairs that took our exam). However, for simplicity of presentation, we chose to present the ANOVA.

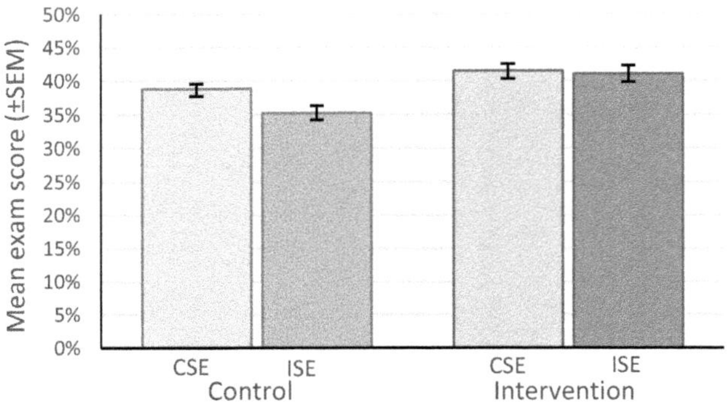

Figure 2. Mean scores on cumulative review exam for control and intervention colleges broken down by department.

A detailed exploration of performance on each question indicated that two questions seemed to account for most of the difference in exam scores between control and intervention colleges. Figure 3 plots the difference between the percentage of intervention and control students that were correct for each question. Note that while most questions are close to zero, questions one and five stand out: more students in the intervention answered Q1 and Q5 correctly, by 17 percentage points and 9 percentage points, respectively.

We performed a chi-square test of independence between intervention and performance on the first eight questions. To control for multiple comparisons, a Bonferroni correction was used to set $\alpha = 0.006$. Only questions one and five were significant. For Q1, $\chi^2(1, N{=}934) = 24.7, p{<<}0.001, \varphi = 0.16$, and for Q5, $\chi^2(1, N{=}934) = 9.5, p{<}0.002, \varphi = 0.10$.

While we are not certain why the two groups performed differently on these two questions, we speculate that it may be because these were the only two questions on the exam that required students to work through a piece of pseudo-code. We discuss this in more detail below.

DISCUSSION

To our knowledge, this is the first study to show improved learning outcomes for a blended learning intervention in India. We found that a relatively small number of group sessions with video content led by a student facilitator

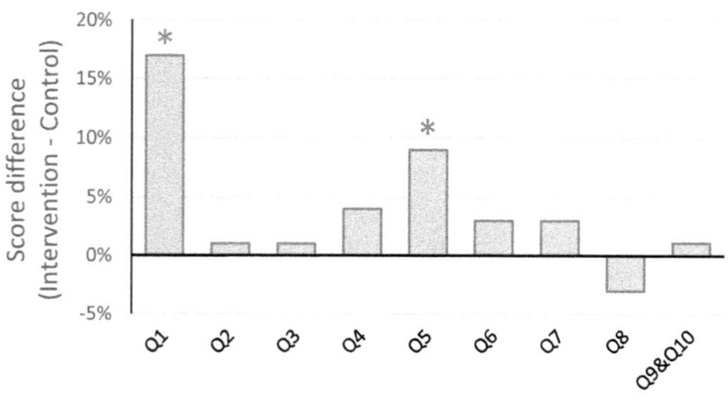

Figure 3. Score difference (% correct) between intervention and control for each exam question. Differences for Q1 and Q5 are significant at $p < 0.006$.

resulted in an overall improvement in a cumulative exam at the end of the course relative to a control. Even though the size of the effect is relatively small (an average of about 3.6 percentage points improvement), it is statistically reliable.

While this difference in exam scores is very encouraging, there are a number of factors in our intervention that may have contributed to this effect. Though one might argue that many are integral to the blended learning initiative itself, it is worth pointing them out here. Several of these factors are similar to the "confounds" noted in the meta-analysis by Means, et al. [32]. While hardly exhaustive, we discuss some of the factors that one might argue contributed to the improvement in learning performance:

1) *Novel pedagogy*. Unlike the standard "chalk and talk" teaching style typical of Indian classroom instruction (where the teacher writes on the board and students copy into their books), MEC sessions with the PM were very interactive. Video watching was frequently interspersed (typically every few minutes) with classroom interaction—completing problems, answering questions and emphasizing points. This served to keep the class engaged, except where problems or topics seemed too difficult for the class level. By making these sessions highly interactive, the PM capitalized on the full classroom experience of blended learning, including elements of competition, peer learning, humor and so on—all of which served to make the classroom experience more engaging. While more investigation is needed it seems likely that this is one of the most important factors and is consistent with prior work [29].
2) *Novelty*. Rather than the standard recitations and labs that students were used to, MEC sessions with the PM were a break in the routine. It is possible that this basic novelty was sufficient to cause students to pay a bit more attention than they otherwise would have. The difference between these sessions and normal lectures was a positive theme reported in the satisfaction survey.
3) *Quality video material*. The MEC videos were simply effective at communicating the content to students.
4) *Personality of facilitator*. The PM is a very outgoing and energetic person. His dynamism may have been enough to cause students to pay attention when they otherwise would have been drifting.
5) *Peer effect*. Instead of their normal professor, a peer (fellow student) discussed the material with them.
6) *Company branding and certification*. Our organization is very well known and an association with the company is likely to be very motivating for students.
7) *Independent use of MEC*. We actively evangelized the use of MEC outside of class and more students in the intervention colleges did use MEC on their own than in control colleges. It's possible that this use by the 50 or so students in the intervention colleges is what carried the difference in the exam, though we think this is unlikely.
8) *Use of code in teaching*. In most colleges we partnered with, the use of code (or pseudo-code) is rarely if ever

used when teaching DAA. In contrast, this is fairly common in MEC videos. The performance boost associated with the two questions on our exam containing code fragments suggests that this might be important.

One fascinating observation in our study was the potential differential effect of the intervention for ISE students. We are not certain why ISE students in the intervention colleges performed so much better than those in the control colleges. Since the exam scores that we received from VTU in Table 1 did not separate out ISE and CSE students, we were not able to explicitly control for the strength of departments. It is possible that the ISE departments in the interventions schools were simply stronger than those in the controls. However, if ISE students in intervention colleges were similar to those in the controls, it is possible that the MEC sessions were particularly effective for the weaker students in ISE. This finding would be consistent with observations by Cima and Ghadiri, et al. [8, 20] that online learning is particularly beneficial for lower performers. While we would like to believe this is true, we cannot conclude from this data why we saw this.

A few notes about peer-led blended learning

While any (or all) of the factors above may have contributed to the learning gains, it seems likely that the novel pedagogy played a very important role in at least keeping students engaged. In particular, the combination of the videos and the student facilitator seemed to be important. While the content of the videos was generally good, it is unlikely to be the main factor. The videos certainly didn't get universal approval, and there were mixed opinions around how interesting they were. Furthermore, playing 4 or 5 minutes of video resulted in a noticeable drop in attention. However, the PM organized his sessions entirely around the videos; while he was indeed an enthusiastic and passionate person with a strong interest in practical aspects of computing he was by no means an expert teacher. For example, he had difficulty tailoring his explanations to the different levels of understanding found in various colleges and sessions, even when classes completely failed to solve set problems. This was the case despite the video content including easier examples which might have been used with these students.

It seems likely that the success of the blended learning initiative comes not so much by forcing students to consume video content but by combining video content with engaging classroom interaction. Some interesting points arise from this observation: 1) Videos which *enable classroom activities*, such as problem solving, seem to be particularly appropriate for blended learning scenarios. This suggests that online lectures intended for blended learning might be specifically designed to incorporate these kinds of strategies. 2) *One size does not fit all*, even when the content has been designed for the relevant syllabus. How could online courses help to guide less experienced facilitators to adapt their sessions to the level of the class? It would be interesting to consider how blended learning material might be designed to support this as in [29]. 3) *Blended learning doesn't make teaching easy*. While it seems that an experienced teacher is not needed to run a successful blended learning class, it is still no easy thing to do. Despite his efforts to make algorithms practical, the PM often had to work extremely hard to stir up any sort of engagement or interest. Even as we design materials to maximize the potential of non-experts and peers as teachers, these teachers will still need to have some grounding in the subject they teach as well as passion and enthusiasm; it seems unlikely that technology will substitute for these human factors any time soon.

CONCLUSION

We found that offering a peer-led blended learning session once a week for eight weeks in the place of a normal recitation or lab led to a small but significant improvement in learning outcomes as measured in an RCT in Indian technical colleges. A concurrent ethnographic study of the intervention suggests that much of the success of the intervention had to do with the way in which the combination of video and peer facilitation drove student engagement. We believe that interventions such as this could help to ease some of the serious constraints in higher education in India and other developing regions where the demand for education far outstrips the supply of trained teachers. Our research suggests that an interactive combination of video teaching by local professors and an energetic peer facilitator can be effective in "second-tier" technical colleges.

ACKNOWLEDGMENTS

This work would not have been possible without the assistance of many people. In particular we want to thank the many people at Microsoft Research India who helped keep MEC running and our partner colleges who worked with us on the interventions. Finally, we would like to thank the reviewers for their very helpful comments on this paper.

REFERENCES

1. All India Counsel for Technical Education "AICTE." http://www.aicte-india.org/
2. Anderson, R., Robertson, C., Nab., E., Sahni, U., and Setia, T. (2012). Facilitated video instruction in low resource schools. *ICTD 2012*.
3. ANNA University. http://www.annauniv.edu/cai13b/Options.html
4. Aycock, A., Garnham, C., & Kaleta, R. (2002). Lessons learned from the hybrid course project. *Teaching with Technology Today*, 8(6).
5. Boga, S., & McGreal, R. (2014). Introducing MOOCs to Africa. Whitepaper from *Commonwealth of Learning*. Retrieved from: http://www.col.org/PublicationDocuments/MOOCs_in_Africa_2014_Boga-McGreal.pdf
6. Bowen, W. G. Chingos, M. M., Lack, K. A. & Nygren, T. I. (2012). Interactive Learning Online at Public Universities: Evidence from Randomized Trials. Ithaka S+R. Retrieved from: http://www.sr.ithaka.org/sites/ default/files/reports/sr-ithaka-interactive-learning-online-at-public-universities.pdf
7. Bruff, D. O., Fisher, D. H., McEwen, K. E., & Smith, B. E. (2013). Wrapping a MOOC: Student perceptions of an

experiment in blended learning. *MERLOT Journal of Online Learning and Teaching*, 9(2), 187-199.

8. Cima, M.J. (2013). My experience teaching 3.091x. *MIT Faculty Newsletter*, 26(1), 15-17.
9. Coursera Zone (2013) http://blog.coursera.org/post/63406806112/a-new-partnership-to-bring-coursera-to-the-hundreds-of
10. Cutrell, E., Bala, S., Bansal, C., Cross, A., Datha, N. John, A., Kumar, R., Parthasarathy, M., Prakash, S., Rajamani, S. & Thies, W (2013). Massively Empowered Classroom: Enhancing technical education in India. *Microsoft Research Technical Report*, no. MSR-TR-2013-127.
11. Czerniewicz, L., Deacon, A., Small, J., & Walji, S. (2014). Developing world MOOCs: A curriculum view of the MOOC landscape. *JOGLTEP*, *2*(3).
12. Donlan, K.A. Carlos Slim's foundation puts its weight behind Khan Academy. *Forbes* (Jan 14, 2013).
13. edX Code. http://code.edx.org/
14. edX (2013). Open Source Platform Chosen to Power China's New Online Education Portal. *PR Newswire,* Oct. 10, 2013.
15. edX (2013). Queen Rania Foundation Partners with edX to Create First MOOC Portal for the Arab World. https://www.edx.org/press/queen-rania-foundation-partners-edx
16. Friedman, T. Come the revolution. *New York Times* (May 15, 2012).
17. Garfinkel, H., *Studies in ethnomethodology.* Englewood Cliffs, N.J.: Prentice-Hall, (1967)
18. Garrison, D. R., & Kanuka, H. (2004). Blended learning: Uncovering its transformative potential in higher education. *The internet and higher education*, 7(2), 95-105.
19. Gibbons, J. F. (1977). Tutored videotape instruction. *Conference on Educational Applications of Satellites*, Arlington, VA.
20. Ghadiri, K., Qayoumi, M.H., Junn, E., Hsu, P., & Sujitparapitaya, S. (2013). The transformative potential of blended learning using MIT edX's 6.002x online MOOC content combined with student team-based learning in class. *JUCE Journal*, No.3.
21. Griffiths, R., Chingos, M. Mulhern, C & Spies, R. (2014). Interactive Online Learning on Campus: Testing MOOCs and Other Platforms in Hybrid Formats in the University System of Maryland. Ithaka S+R. Retrieved from: http://www.sr.ithaka.org/sites/default/files/ reports/S-R_Interactive_Online_Learning_Campus_ 20140716.pdf
22. Haggard, S. (2013). The Maturing of the MOOC. *BIS Research Paper Number 130.* Department for Business and Innovation Skills, Government of the UK
23. Hollands, F.M. & Tirthali, D. (2014). MOOCs: Expectations and reality. Full report. Center for Benefit-Cost Studies of Education, Columbia University, NY. Retrieve from: http://www.academicpartnerships.com/sites/default/files/MOOCs_Expectations_and_Reality.pdf
24. Hyman, P. (2012). In the year of disruptive education. *Communications of the ACM*, **55**(12), 20-22.
25. JEE Brochure. http://www.jee.iitb.ac.in/#
26. Joseph, A. M., & Nath, B. A. Integration of Massive Open Online Education (MOOC) System with in-Classroom Interaction and Assessment and Accreditation: An extensive report from a pilot study. WORLDCOMP '13.
27. Kamat, R., Keleher, P., Patil, A., & Pujar, S. M. (2013). Promulgation of Higher Education in India: From University to Meta University via Massive Open Online Courses (MOOCs). *Proc. IETEC '13 Conference*, Ho Chi Minh City.
28. Lim, D. H., Morris, M. L., & Kupritz, V. W. (2014). Online vs. blended learning: Differences in instructional outcomes and learner satisfaction. *Journal of Asynchronous Learning Networks*, 2007 (11).
29. Lovett, M, Meyer, O. & Thille, C. (2008). The open learning initiative: Measuring the effectiveness of the OLI statistics course in accelerating student learning. *Journal of Interactive Media in Education*, 2008(1).
30. Macbeth, D. H. (1990). Classroom Order as Practical Action: the making and un-making of a quiet reproach. *British J. of Sociology of Education*, *11*(2), 189-214.
31. Mantha, S. S. (2013). Adoption of blended learning mode by technical institution in the State -- Emphasis on popularization of courses through e-content. Retrieved from: http://dteap.nic.in/Downloads/Downloads479.pdf
32. Means, B., Toyama, Y., Murphy, R.F., & Baki, M. (2013). The effectiveness of online and blended learning: A meta-analysis of the empirical literature. Teachers College Record, 115(3), 1-47.
33. Nixon, L., Roy, J., Latha, H., Rao, S., Rangachar, B., & Thies, W. (2014). Measuring the Learning Benefits of Electronic Teaching Aids in Low-Resource Classrooms. *DEV 2014*
34. NPTEL. http://nptel.iitm.ac.in/, http://nptel.ac.in/faq.php#3
35. O'Neill, J., Martin, D., Colombino, T., & Grasso, A. (2011). When a little knowledge isn't a dangerous thing. CHI 2011.
36. Open EdX http://code.edx.org/
37. Pappano, L. (2012). The Year of the MOOC. *The New York Times*, 2(12).
38. Phatak, D. B. (2014). Adopting MOOCs for quality engineering education in India. Invited paper, *ICTIEE 2014.*
39. Saraswathy, M. & Pathak, K. (2014). Online education gains traction, *Business Standard* (Oct. 3, 2014).
40. Singh, H., & Reed, C. (2001). A white paper: Achieving success with blended learning. *Centra software, 1.*
41. TCS Brochure for new hires. http://www.tcs.com/SiteCollectionDocuments/Brochures/TCS_Software_Engineer_Profile.pdf
42. Venkataraman, B. (2013). MOOC in developing countries: a case study from India. PCF7, Seventh Pan-Commonwealth Forum on Open Learning.
43. Visvesvaraya Technological University. http://vtu.ac.in/index.php/about-us/about-vtu.html

Attrition and Achievement Gaps in Online Learning

René F. Kizilcec
Department of Communication
Stanford University
kizilcec@stanford.edu

Sherif Halawa
Department of Electrical Engineering
Stanford University
halawa@stanford.edu

ABSTRACT
Attrition in online learning is generally higher than in traditional settings, especially in large-scale online learning environments. A systematic analysis of individual differences in attrition and performance in 20 massive open online courses ($N > 67,000$) revealed a geographic achievement gap and a gender achievement gap. Online learners in Africa, Asia, and Latin America scored substantially lower grades and were only half as likely to persist than those in Europe, Oceania, and Northern America. Women also exhibited lower persistence and performance than men. Yet more persistent learners were only marginally more satisfied with their achievement. The primary obstacle for most learners was finding time for the course, which was partly related to low levels of volitional control. Self-ascribed successful learners reported higher levels of goal striving, growth mindset, and feelings of social belonging than unsuccessful ones. Insights into why learners leave online courses inform models of attrition and targeted interventions to support learners achieve their goals.

Author Keywords
Online education; massive open online course; MOOC; persistence; dropout; individual differences; self-regulation; volition; social belonging; growth mindset; goal striving

ACM Classification Keywords
K.3.1. Computers and Education: Computer Uses in Education; H.5.m. Information Interfaces and Presentation (e.g. HCI): Miscellaneous

INTRODUCTION
Educational environments have become increasingly diverse in format. Traditional schools and universities have a characteristically rigid structure, including instructor-defined syllabi, fixed time schedules, entry requirements, and material costs to enter and exit. Novel institutional structures have been developed to overcome particular constraints. Community colleges, for instance, were created in an attempt to democratize education by offering instruction at a lower cost, with lower admission criteria, and with more flexible schedules to accommodate those who cannot afford to be full-time students [8]. Distance learning programs have delivered education to remote parts of the world and to people who simply could not attend in-person classes. Course materials, including assessments, were delivered through mail (correspondence education), radio, television, and eventually the Internet, thereby addressing geographical and time related constraints of traditional instruction [15].

The latest generation of online learning environments, characterized by massive open online courses (MOOCs), has pushed the boundary on the scale of education [26]. By design, MOOCs provide course materials to millions of people worldwide. This scale could be achieved by pre-recording lectures, designing assessments that can be graded automatically, and by leveraging the momentum of the number of people involved (e.g., to facilitate peer learning or peer assessment). Maybe by virtue of their large scale, their prominent instructors, or their adherence to contemporary interface designs, MOOCs rapidly became an online media phenomenon. People would sign up weeks in advance of the course launch date, many of whom would never even enter the course site. And among those who enroll and enter the site, a large proportion would only "sample" some content and leave again [12]. Many of the prototypical behaviors observed in MOOCs resemble those on online media platforms [12, 3]. This trend is also reflected in the large spectrum of learners' motivations for enrolling in MOOCs [13].

Shortly after the first wave of courses had finished, extensive media coverage led to MOOCs becoming associated with high attrition rates [14, 18]. Early MOOC research cautioned against dichotomizing learners into successes and failures based on course completion [12, 20]. Instead, more nuanced categorizations based on learner behavior [12, 4], motivations [13], or intentions [29] have been suggested. Perspectives on attrition in open online courses ultimately depend on how these courses are viewed. For instance, MOOCs can be viewed as bridging two worlds: one is governed by the user-centric norms of online media, where everyone is encouraged to be as active as they wish; the other adheres to the "grammar of schooling" [25], which presupposes instructor-defined goals that students strive to achieve [13]. This view of MOOC participation clearly adds complexity to interpretations of attrition. The present work extends the empirical base of research on attrition to inform the theoretical discourse and pave the path for novel practices.

This paper presents a systematic investigation of attrition in online learning based on self-report and behavioral data collected from over 100,000 learners in 21 courses in total. Iden-

L@S 2015, March 14–18, 2015, Vancouver, BC, Canada.

ACM 978-1-4503-3411-2/15/03$15.00
http://dx.doi.org/10.1145/2724660.2724680

tifying characteristics associated with attrition and reasons for disengaging can facilitate earlier recognition of learners struggling to achieve their learning goals. These learners could benefit from changes to the course or targeted interventions. We briefly review the large literature on attrition in educational environments, with a focus on key developments in understanding the causes of attrition. Building on this review, Study 1 offers insights into reasons for disengaging from MOOCs, learners' satisfaction, and individual differences in attrition and performance. For Study 2, we invited around 6,053 learners who were predicted to have disengaged from a MOOC to provide feedback. We examined differences in psychological factors between subjectively successful and unsuccessful learners, and investigated the role of volitional control for those who reported having not enough time. Learners' open responses about challenges they faced while taking the course were iteratively coded to develop an empirically-grounded list of reasons for attrition.

RELATED WORK

Research and theory on attrition has a rich history in education. This review focuses on how conceptions of attrition have evolved over the last decades. As this review is intended to serve as a foundation to build on with the current research, we concurrently develop hypotheses and research questions to investigate.

In-person Education

The majority of early work on attrition centered around theoretical models of students' decision to persist or drop out of a traditional higher education setting. The literature on attrition in higher education is largely concerned with students disengaging from a course of study rather than a single course. An early model suggested that students' persistence is largely driven by their prior behavior, attitudes, and norms [7]. The psychological processes involved in turning an intent to learn into the decision to persist were thought to be mediated by volition, the extent to which the student engages in goal-directed behavior in the face of distraction [5]. Motivation alone is necessary but not sufficient for persistence, because students may fail to sustain efforts in the absence of strong self-regulatory skills.

H1 Successful learners exhibit higher levels of goal striving than unsuccessful learners.

The next generation of psychological models, which were highly influential in the literature, emphasized the critical role of students' "fit" in the institution. Tinto's [24] student integration model posited that college students' decision to persist is a function of individual students' characteristics, prior experiences, and experiences during college. While prior experiences and characteristics are fixed, schools can influence the college experience, including the degree of social and academic integration. Tinto operationalized academic and social integration by GPA scores and the frequency of positive interactions with peers and instructors, respectively. This resonates with recent work highlighting the critical role of students' feelings of social belonging in achievement-oriented environments (e.g. [27]).

RQ1 How are learners' characteristics (demographics, geographic location, intentions, prior experience) related to their persistence and performance in the course?

H2 Successful learners exhibit a greater sense of social belonging than unsuccessful learners.

Tinto's work, which specifically targets traditional college students, prompted universities to be proactive in establishing environments that support student integration. Research on attrition in community college settings reiterates the importance of academic and social integration, but points out that non-persistence could indicate success depending on students' intent—students may leave after accomplishing their goal [2]. Nevertheless, a brief psychological intervention that taught community college students an incremental theory of intelligence (instilling a growth mindset [6]) was found to halve attrition rates and increase academic achievement [19]. This highlights the critical role of mindset and cautions against overinterpreting non-persistence as an indicator of goal achievement.

RQ2 How is learners' satisfaction related to their persistence in the course?

H3 Successful learners have a stronger growth mindset than unsuccessful learners.

Distance Education and e-Learning

Distance education, relative to traditional in-person education, tends to attract a more mature student demographic and provide fewer opportunities for social integration. Students in distance learning programs are more likely to lead social lives outside of school, maybe working part-time and living with their partner. Building on Tinto's model, Bean and Metzner [1] proposed a conceptual model of persistence that would be more applicable to nontraditional students. Persistence is thought to be a function of background characteristics (demographics, etc.), academic and environmental variables (study habits, financial resources, work and family obligations, etc.), and academic and psychological outcomes (GPA, satisfaction, etc.). The significant change from Tinto's original model was the inclusion of environmental variables to account for the added complexity of nontraditional students' lives.

Rovai [21], combining Tinto's and Bean and Metzner's models with factors specific to online learning and pedagogical styles, proposed a composite persistence model specifically for students in online distance education programs. Among other novel factors, Rovai's model acknowledges the critical role of computer literacy in online learning. And yet, these increasingly complex theoretical models were difficult to apply to real-world settings, and hence, the empirical evidence to support them remained sparse. An exploratory study of reasons for attrition of over 1,000 online students found eight relevant factors: academic and technical skills, learner motivation, time and support for studies, cost and access to the Internet, and technical problems [17]. An analysis of student behavior on an online education platform showed that 31% of variation in achievement could be accounted for by a small set of participation measures [16].

Table 1. Summary statistics for 20 massive open online courses

			Survey Responses							Videos Watched		
	Topic Area	Enrolled	Initial	Feedback	Both	Female	Age[1]	Education[2]	Dropout[3]	> 30%	> 50%	> 80%
C1	Business	61,233	8,618	1,796	1,282	47%	36 (28,43)	94%	11%	11%	9%	6%
C2	Business	45,202	5,951	789	631	43%	36 (27,42)	90%	10%	11%	8%	6%
C3	Computer Science	28,086	5,918	2,815	2,295	36%	33 (23,40)	63%	3%	15%	11%	8%
C4	Computer Science	56,314	2,686	749	352	14%	33 (25,39)	79%	21%	13%	10%	8%
C5	Computer Science	79,273	7,319	1,740	1,236	16%	31 (24,36)	81%	11%	15%	11%	8%
C6	Education	40,214	24,192	5,174	4,969	56%	28 (15,40)	n.a.	5%	17%	13%	8%
C7	Education	5,325	2,429	624	615	80%	43 (35,50)	99%	2%	24%	17%	12%
C8	Engineering	11,958	2,341	262	196	16%	35 (26,43)	84%	16%	14%	9%	6%
C9	Engineering	5,701	5,652	396	347	16%	33 (24,38)	73%	16%	18%	11%	7%
C10	Engineering	7,139	1,250	197	168	17%	31 (22,36)	72%	7%	11%	8%	6%
C11	Humanities	7,656	2,512	142	131	89%	33 (24,38)	82%	9%	14%	9%	6%
C12	Humanities	4,949	2,921	292	270	91%	33 (25,38)	83%	17%	15%	10%	7%
C13	Mathematics	49,509	3,031	836	510	35%	37 (26,47)	76%	32%	12%	9%	6%
C14	Mathematics	13,310	2,861	346	298	10%	31 (25,34)	93%	15%	15%	10%	6%
C15	Natural Sciences	9,918	3,957	1,351	1,223	51%	37 (26,47)	78%	4%	19%	15%	11%
C16	Natural Sciences	543	163	79	50	47%	34 (26,39)	98%	18%	27%	20%	12%
C17	Physics	6,452	1,069	269	269	14%	36 (25,46)	82%	11%	15%	10%	6%
C18	Statistics	11,733	11,465	1,837	1,569	22%	36 (28,41)	96%	9%	34%	25%	15%
C19	Statistics	13,161	3,495	819	627	n.a.	n.a.	n.a.	6%	13%	9%	7%
C20	Writing	35,374	12,514	2,877	2,876	n.a.	n.a.	n.a.	8%	23%	14%	8%

[1] mean (upper, lower quartile) [2] bachelor's or higher degree [3] self-reported in the feedback survey

MOOCs

A survey of over a hundred learners who dropped out of a MOOC showed that the majority indicated having too little time due to work responsibilities, not enough social support inside and outside of the course, and insufficient academic and technical support from the course [9]. A qualitative analysis of public records, especially forum posts, from 42 MOOCs suggested the following reasons for attrition: lack of time, learner motivation, feelings of isolation, lack of interactivity, insufficient prior knowledge or skills, and hidden costs [11]. A survival analysis of close to 800 learners who had posted on a MOOC discussion forum suggested that the likelihood of dropout was lower for those who i. actively participated in the first week of the course; ii. served as an authority figure in the community on the forum, and iii. did not engage in a particular subcommunity on the forum [30]. In addition, a number of machine learning approaches yielded promising results for early dropout prediction (e.g. [23, 10]), but fell short of offering insights into why a given learner would leave the course.

RQ3a What reasons do learners report for disengaging from a course?

RQ3b How do reasons for disengaging vary by learner characteristics?

STUDY 1: INDIVIDUAL DIFFERENCES, SATISFACTION, & REASONS FOR ATTRITION

The present study extends the existing literature on attrition with a large-scale quantitative treatment of attrition in MOOCs. We address the research questions developed in the previous section with the larger objective of informing our understanding of attrition in online courses to better support learners. This could be achieved through general changes to the course content or presentation; or, using targeted interventions that support particular groups of struggling learners.

Methods

Twenty MOOCs on topics in a variety of disciplines were selected for investigation. Table 1 provides summary statistics for enrollment, survey response rates, demographics, self-reported dropout, and a subset of behavioral indicators for each course. For each course, we combined data from an initial course survey (distributed in the first weeks of the course), a feedback survey (distributed in the last weeks of the course), and behavioral data collected in the learning environment. On the initial course survey, learners reported their gender, age, education, prior experience with the topic and MOOCs, and how many hours per week they intended to spend on the course. On the feedback survey, learners reported their satisfaction with the course (5-item index, possible range from 0 to 5.2, $M = 3.95, SD = 0.81, \alpha = .81$), and whether they 'stopped participating in the course before it ended' or 'remained active until the end'. Those who indicated that they stopped participating also reported 'what influenced their decision to stop participating' using a grid of 14 binary-choice items (cf. Figure 2).[1] Geographic location was determined by IP address and aggregated by continental region. Behavioral indicators were chosen to represent course milestones: watching (or downloading) over 30%, 50%, 80% of lecture videos, attempting over 30%, 50%, 80% of assessments, and achieving a grade above the 60th, 80th percentile.

To analyze individual differences, we fit a logistic mixed-effects (hierarchical) model predicting binary persistence and performance milestones using learner characteristics, including demographic and geographic features. The analysis included 67,333 learners who completed the initial course survey, but excluded 381 learners who left all questions unan-

[1] Instead of a select-all-that-apply question, this question style encouraged learners to consider each reason separately. The response options were "Did influence my decision to stop" and "Did NOT influence my decision to stop" to reduce acquiescence bias relative to a Yes/No or Agree/Disagree scale.

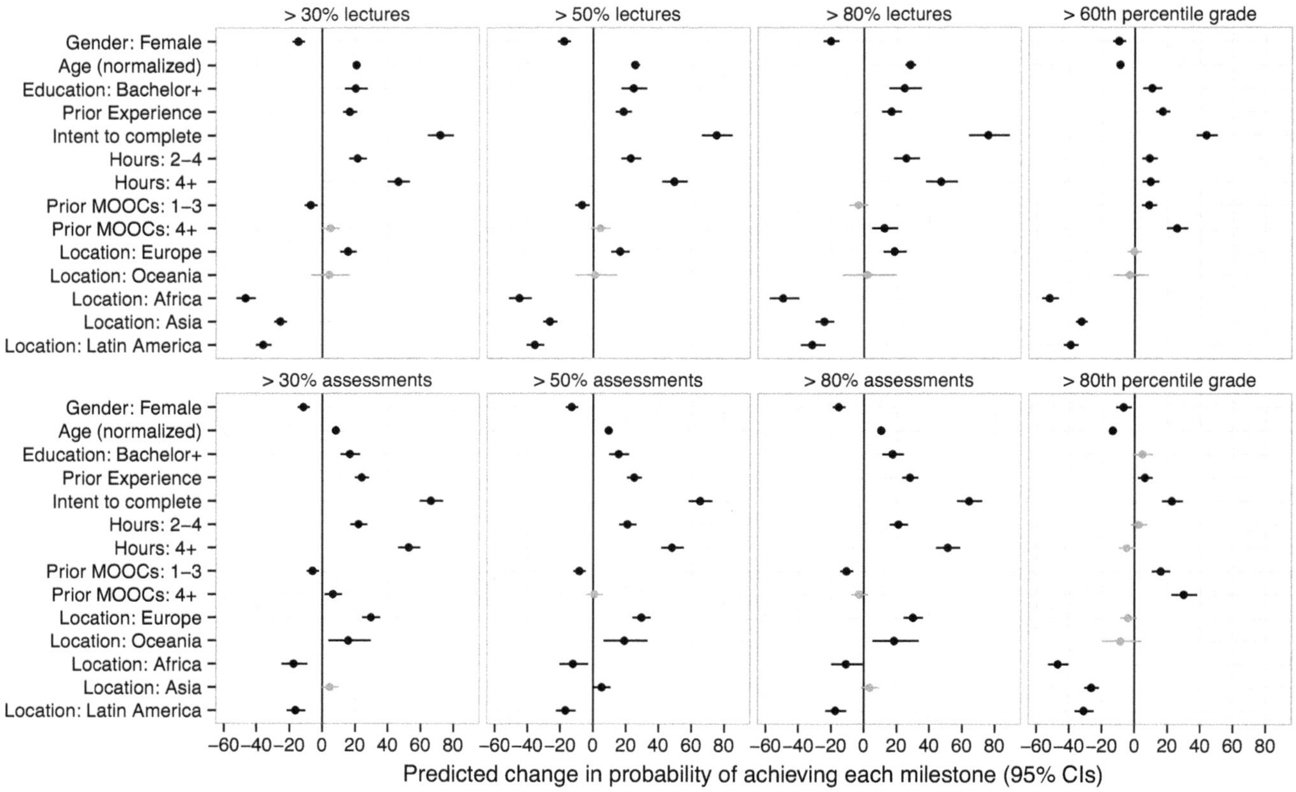

Figure 1. Individual differnces in persistence and course grades showing substantial achievement gaps. An estimate of -10 indicates a 10% lower chance of achieving a milestone.

swered and learners in courses C6, C7, C19, C20 due to missing survey items. Any remaining missing survey responses were multiply imputed using other survey responses. We report pooled estimates that account for added uncertainty.[2] Correlations between predictors were low ($|r| < 0.15$), except for age and education ($r = 0.27$), which were each significant predictors if the other was excluded. Courses were modeled as a random effect (instead of including dummy variables) to generalize to a larger population of similar MOOCs.

Results and Discussion

We address the posed research questions in three parts: first, a regression analysis of differential attrition and performance ($RQ1$); second, a comparison of satisfaction levels across learner subgroups ($RQ2$), and third, a descriptive analysis of reported reasons for disengaging from the course ($RQ3$).

Individual Differences in Attrition and Performance

Individual differences in attrition and performance are illustrated in Figure 1 as transformed regression coefficients with 95% confidence intervals for each milestone. The estimates represent changes in the likelihood of achieving a milestone relative to an arbitrary baseline population. The regression intercept corresponds to the following baseline group that derives from the coding of regressors: average-aged male learners in Northern America[3] without a bachelor's degree, without prior experience with the topic or other MOOCs, prepared to spend up to 2 hours/week on the course, and not intending to complete it. This choice notably corresponds to the dominant power structure narrative, but is solely statistically motivated. The baseline probability for each milestone was as follows: lectures watched (20% above 30%, 11% above 50%, 4% above 80%), assessments attempted (37% above 30%, 25% above 50%, 18% above 80%), and grades (30% above the 60th, 22% above the 80th percentile).

A number of significant and substantial individual differences emerged. Women were 12 to 20% less likely than men to persist with lectures and assessments. Women, who constituted 34% of learners in the sample, were also 10% (7%) less likely than men to score a grade above the 60th (80th) percentile. Moreover, learners in Africa ($N = 2,458$), Asia ($N = 13,280$), and Latin America ($N = 5,344$) were 24 to 50% less likely to persist with lectures and 31 to 52% less likely to achieve grade milestones than learners in Northern America ($N = 26,651$). In contrast, learners in Europe ($N = 17,988$) exhibited 16 to 30% higher persistence with lectures and assessments than learners in Northern America. While learners in Asia exhibited lower persistence with

[2]Multiple imputation ($m = 10$) using the R mice package.

[3]Learners in the United States, Canada, Bermuda, Greenland.

videos, they were at least as likely to attempt assessments as learners in North America. Learners in Oceania ($N = 1,612$) performed similarly to those in Northern America and Europe. Besides gender and geography, older learner were more likely to persist with lectures and assessments, but achieved lower grades than younger learners. More educated learners, those with a bachelor's or higher degree, were 15 to 25% more likely to persist and 10% more likely to score above the 60th percentile. Not surprisingly, prior experience, intending to learn about all topics in the course, and being prepared to spend more hours in the course were strong predictors of persistence. Learners who participated in prior MOOCs had mixed persistence patterns, but achieved higher grades.

Leveraging the large scale of MOOCs, this study has revealed a global achievement gap and a gender achievement gap in online learning. Performance and persistence in the course was substantially lower for women and learners in Africa, Asia, and Latin America than men and learners in Europe, Oceania, and Northern America. There was a good representation from each geographic region in the dataset and the courses under consideration were on diverse topics, including some in the humanities and business with high female participation rates. The strength and significance of these relationships is remarkable, in particular with several additional demographic, geographic, and preference measures in the model. The first generation of large-scale online learning, characterized by MOOCs, is apparently not immune to inequalities that have pervaded traditional educational settings. The present work presents evidence for the existence of these gaps, but cannot explain why they occur. Of course there exists no innate feature of women or people in certain locations that is responsible for these gaps. The achievement gaps could plausibly result from differences in Internet access, language barriers, or from feelings of psychological threat, such as fears of confirming a negative stereotype [22] or not belonging in the course [27]. A geographical categorization to compare countries with a high and low propensity of English speakers could be misleading, due to confounding with psychological barriers that are less likely to hinder learners in English-speaking countries. More work is needed to identify potential causal mechanisms underlying these gaps.

Satisfaction

Attrition can be a sign of success if a learner has achieved their personal learning objectives. We investigated how satisfied learners were with their achievements for those who reported to have stopped participating and those who persisted to different extents ($RQ2$). Satisfaction ratings were compared using mixed-effects regression with multiple imputation of missing values ($N = 23,390$). Learners who reported that they stopped participating were 12% less satisfied than those who reported not to have stopped ($t_{453} = 21, p < .001$). Moreover, we examined if persistent learners, those who watched more lectures, were also more satisfied. The proportion of videos significantly predicted higher satisfaction ($t_{101} = 20, p < .001$), such that those who watched over 75% of videos were 8% more satisfied than those who watched under 25% ($M_{<25\%} = 3.80, M_{>75\%} = 4.09$). As levels of self-reported satisfaction were generally high, it remains unclear if the estimated differences in satisfaction are consequential. Learners who disengaged early were only somewhat less satisfied than those who persisted in the course, which suggests that some learners arrived with modest course goals and achieved them. The following analysis of reasons for attrition can shed more light on this hypothesis.

Reasons for Attrition

A fraction of learners who completed the course feedback survey reported having left the course early and indicated reasons for disengaging on a predefined list ($RQ3a$). This list may not be collectively exhaustive, which is addressed in Study 2, but responses were collected from 1,698 learners in 20 different courses. Figure 2 illustrates how frequently each reason was selected across courses. Around half of the respondents indicated two time-related reasons as influencing their decision to stop participating. In a typical course (median proportion), 66% faced issues keeping up with deadlines and for 46% the course demanded too much time. According to expectancy-value theory [28], the learner is a rational agent who allocates time to different activities to maximize subjective gains. The shortage of time could be due to an abundance of higher-priority tasks, as enrolling in a MOOC neither guarantees that a learner can nor intends to allocate enough time to complete the course. Alternatively, a low capacity for volitional control [5] could lead learners to misallocate time to lower-priority activities that promise nearer gratification, instead of allocating it to the next highest priority task. Learners' general time issues may be a product of high-priority obligations as well as a result of a low capacity for volitional control. We investigate this hypothesis in Study 2.

Other reasons for attrition were less prevalent, but still reported by around 10 to 25% of respondents. Notably, 17% of respondents in a typical course stopped participating because they had learned all they intended to learn. This finding resonates with some prior work on attrition in community colleges, where attrition has been interpreted as a sign of success. It also supports the conclusion that progress in the course and satisfaction were only weakly related. We investigated the underlying factor structure of the reported reasons for disengaging using an exploratory factor analysis. The optimal number of factors was determined by the parallel analysis criterion and corresponding scree plot. The following four-factor solution emerged: first, *general time issues* (course requires too much time; can't keep up with deadlines); second, *difficulty* (too advanced, exam too difficult); third, *format & content* (didn't enjoy online format confusing videos, materials not explained well, not what I'm looking for, technical difficulties), and fourth, *goals & expectations* (only exploring, learned all I wanted, not challenging, credential not valuable). The 'late start' item failed to load onto any factor. General time issues and difficulty are very interpretable factors, while the other two factors comprise a complex set of reasons that should probably be further separated.

Reasons for disengaging from a course are likely to vary by learner characteristics ($RQ3b$). To explore if the substantial

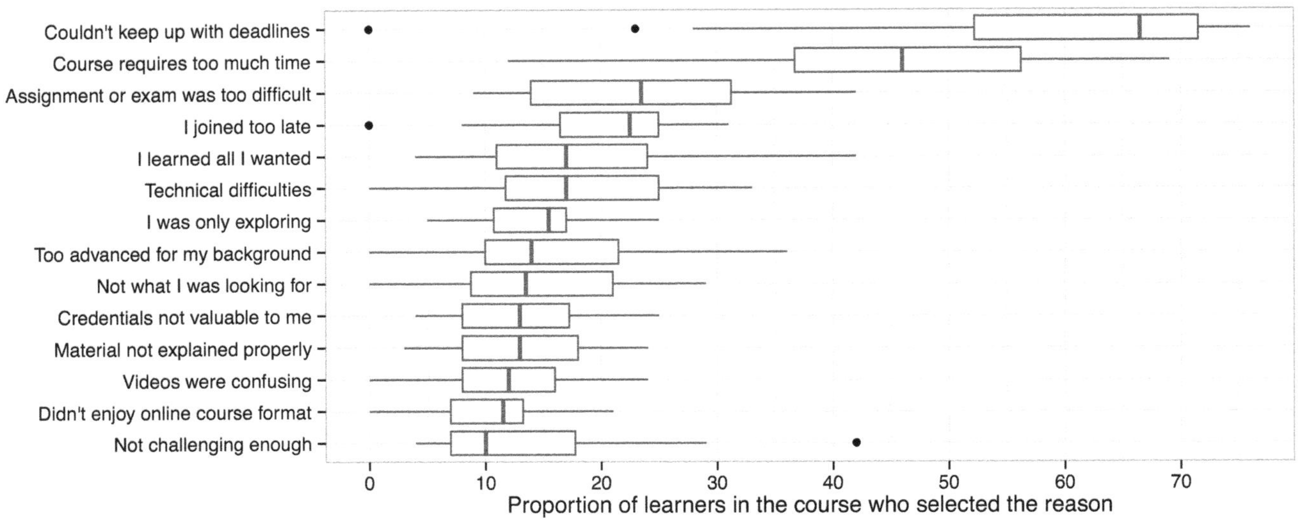

Figure 2. Distribution of self-reported reasons for attrition across 20 MOOCs.

individual differences in attrition identified above could be associated with different reasons for disengaging, we investigated variation by geographic region ($N = 1,698$) and gender ($N = 1,039$ due to missing gender information). Learners in Africa, Asia, and Latin America were more likely to disengage due to technical difficulties (61% more likely), too demanding deadlines, and starting late ($ps < .03$), while learners in Europe, Oceania, and Northern America were more likely to disengage because the course was not a good fit for them ($p = .02$). Women were more likely than men to report disengaging due to technical difficulties and because the course required too much time ($p < .01$). Technical difficulties were a critical individual difference that could be a source of the observed achievement gaps. The pre-defined list of reasons for attrition unfortunately did not include an item on language difficulties, which could be another plausible source of the global achievement gap.

STUDY 2: PSYCHOLOGICAL FACTORS IN ATTRITION

To gain a better understanding of the attrition patterns identified in Study 1, we designed a smaller, more focused follow-up study. This study investigates reasons for attrition based on psychological measures and learners' own descriptions of the challenges they faced. We collected feedback from learners who were likely to have stopped following the course. They were identified with a predictive model and invited to complete a survey. The survey included self-report measures of psychological constructs to test hypotheses $H1, H2$, and $H3$ on the role of goal striving, social belonging, and growth mindset in the success of online learners. Moreover, in Study 1, most learners indicated that they disengaged due to a shortage of time. A variety of factors could influence the amount of time learners have at their disposal. Higher priority obligations, such as professional, academic, and personal commitments are presumably large contributors. Another critical factor, especially in the context of MOOCs as largely unguided learning environments, is a learner's volitional control to engage in self-regulated learning [5]. Low volitional control could reduce learners' ability to allocate time for the course in the presence of potential distractors of subjectively lower importance than taking the course (watching TV, etc.). In contrast to attrition due to important obligations, there exist techniques to help learners become more self-regulated, which could boost their persistence. We constructed the following hypotheses about the role of volition in time-related attrition:

H4a Learners who report having 'not enough time' can be grouped into those with higher priority obligations (professional, academic, and personal) and those with low volitional control.

H4b Learners who do not report specific higher-priority obligations tend to exhibit lower volitional control than those who specify particular obligations.

Methods

The particular MOOC under observation was an undergraduate-level course on an advanced topic in computer science. It was offered in 2014 through Coursera. There were 20,048 enrolled learners; 10,510 watched at least one video, and 5,912 attempted at least one assignment. The following subsections describe how disengaging learners were identified, which measures were included in the feedback survey, and how open responses were iteratively coded.

Predicting Disengagement

We constructed an 'early warning' prediction model to flag learners who had disengaged from the course or were about to disengage. The following three criteria were chosen as benchmarks to evaluate the practical and theoretical value of our prediction model.

Prediction accuracy: Prediction recall (fraction of correctly predicted disengaged learners) should be high to deliver the survey to as many disengaged learners as possible. The false positive rate (fraction of active learners who are incorrectly predicted as disengaged) should be low to avoid sending surveys to learners who do not experience challenges in the course.

Prediction lag: The period between a learner's last site activity and the time they are flagged as disengaged should be short. A shorter prediction lag improves the likelihood of successfully intervening to help learners resume the course.

Transferability: Whether or not a learner disengages from the course cannot be determined before the end of the course. We thus trained the prediction model using data from previous courses. The performance of the prediction model should be good in courses other than those on which it was trained.

The training set was composed of learners' interaction data (predictors) and disengagement states (outcome) from 20 MOOCs. The large number of courses should improve model transferability by favoring features that are strongly predictive across different courses. Five hundred learners from each MOOC were included in the training set ($train$), and 500 other learners from the same MOOCs were selected for the first test set ($test_1$). A second test set of similar size was composed from 20 other MOOCs ($test_2$). Features extracted from the interaction data included different aspects of learners' video, assignment, and forum activity; their pace of viewing videos relative to the course pace, as well as various aspects of engagement time, such as the last time the learner interacted with the course (cf. [10], for additional information on the prediction model).

To control the length of the prediction lag, the model was only provided with learners' activity data until they were absent for 14 consecutive days. In the training phase, if the learner disengaged but the model did not detect it within 14 days of their last activity, the case was counted as a false negative. This construction results in a model with features that all fall within the defined prediction lag period. The model was fit by logistic regression with two-fold learner-level and course-level cross-validation. Prediction performance measured by the area under the ROC curve (AUC) very high (0.931 for $train$, 0.929 for $test_1$, 0.922 for $test_2$). Two of the predictors in the fitted model are highly influential. The first is the number of days since the learner has last been active. The likelihood that the learner drops out increases substantially if the learner disengages for 14 days or more. However, the likelihood of such a learner re-engaging increases with the fraction of released videos the learner has viewed prior to the absence; this is the second most influential feature in the model. The fact that almost identical results were obtained for $test_1$ and $test_2$ suggest good transferability of the model. A learner was flagged if their dropout probability exceeded 50%. Out of the 20,048 enrolled learners in the course, only those 10,510 were considered who watched at least one lecture video, and 6,074 of them were flagged as likely to drop out. The survey was sent out to 6,053 learners (excluding 21 learners with invalid email addresses or duplicate accounts).

Feedback Survey

Every learner who was predicted to disengage from the course was sent an email kindly requesting their help: "You are enrolled in [course name], but you've been less active recently. Could you help us understand why?" A low response rate was expected for this subpopulation that was defined by low engagement. And yet, 756 out of 6,053 learners started the survey (12.5% response rate), and 459 completed it (61% completion rate). Missing values were multiply imputed by predictive mean matching using responses to all survey questions. All estimates were pooled across ten imputations, with standard errors adjusted for added variance. The majority of respondents were male (85%), 35.6 years old on average ($SD = 12.5$), and 80% had achieved a bachelor's or more advanced degree.

Learners were asked to report how satisfied they were with their progress in the course, and whether they were using the course materials more, less or exactly as much as they would have liked. These items served as measures of personal success. They were then asked to openly report "what challenges, inside or outside of the course, [they] experienced while [they were] taking this course, if any?" The instructions encouraged them to list all challenges they could think of. This question was asked prior to any survey questions that could suggest particular reasons for disengaging.

Two research assistants independently developed codebooks for the resulting 448 non-empty open responses. Their codebooks were consolidated and applied on Amazon Mechanical Turk (AMT) in three iterations. The codebook was updated in each iteration to reliably fit the open response data. Specific updates to the initial codebook were informed by code frequency, code correlations, and inter-coder agreement. In the first iteration, 250 randomly selected responses were each coded by four 'classification experts,' which is an AMT-specific qualification. In the second iteration, the remaining responses were coded in the same way. In the final iteration, all responses were coded by two classification experts (ties were resolved by two researchers). The iterative coding yielded 399 relevant coded responses, which were analyzed in combination with the remaining survey data.

Learners self-reported social belonging (17 items on their sense of social and academic fit [27], $M = 4.66, SD = 0.71, \alpha = 0.86$); mindset (4 items on the stability of intelligence and talent[4]; $M = 4.44, SD = 0.92, \alpha = 0.77$), goal striving (4 items on motivation, perceived importance, committment, and confidence; $M = 3.12, SD = 0.95, \alpha = 0.82$), and the degree of volitional control they exerted (one item on the extent to which lower-priority distractions have hindered the learner's course progress; $M = 2.73, SD = 1.29$).

Results and Discussion

First, we tested hypotheses about the role of psychological factors in the self-ascribed success of online learners. In a second set of analyses, we further investigated reasons for leaving a course ($RQ3a$) and the role of volition ($H4$).

Psychological Factors

Hypotheses $H1$, $H2$, and $H3$ about goal striving, perceived social belonging, and mindset, respectively, were tested by

[4]Adapted from http://mindsetonline.com/testyourmindset

Table 2. Descriptive and inferential statistics for psychological measures by self-ascribed success

	N	Goal Striving ($H1$)	Social Belonging ($H2$)	Growth Mindset ($H3$)
Relative Progress				
Successful	241	3.46 ($SD = 0.91$)	4.70 ($SD = 0.74$)	4.58 ($SD = 0.99$)
Unsuccessful	515	2.96 ($SD = 0.93$)	4.63 ($SD = 0.70$)	4.38 ($SD = 0.87$)
		$t_{201} = 6.3, p < .001, d = 0.55$	$t_{60} = 1.0, p > .25, d = .09$	$t_{152} = 2.4, p = .017, d = 0.21$
Satisfaction				
Successful	325	3.43 ($SD = 0.83$)	4.76 ($SD = 0.70$)	4.47 ($SD = 0.93$)
Unsuccessful	431	2.88 ($SD = 0.97$)	4.58 ($SD = 0.71$)	4.42 ($SD = 0.91$)
		$t_{166} = 7.2, p < .001, d = 0.59$	$t_{158} = 3.1, p = .002, d = .26$	$t_{175} = 0.6, p > .25, d = .05$

comparing self-ascribed successful with unsuccessful learners. Self-ascribed success was measured by relative progress and satisfaction with progress: 68% of respondents reported using the course materials less than they would have wanted, and 57% reported not being satisfied with their progress in the course (18% were very or extremely dissatisfied). The two measures of success were correlated, $r = .35, t_{754} = 10, p < .001$; satisfied respondents were, however, equally likely to be successful or unsuccessful in terms of their progress. Table 2 provides summary statistics for each psychological measure by these two self-ascribed success metrics. Successful learners exhibited higher levels of goal striving in general. Social belonging was significantly higher only for learners who were also more satisfied. The pattern was reversed for growth mindset, which was stronger only for learners who were successful in terms of progress. This pattern reflects differences in the underlying process by which these psychological factors shape learner behavior and perception. Social belonging relates to feeling comfortable and connected in the learning environment, whereas mindset relates to one's ability to master demanding materials. The observed differences would presumably be larger in the full population of learners than in this homogeneous sample of at-risk learners.

Personal success in a MOOC was associated with three established psychological factors: goal striving, social belonging, and growth mindset. Prior work in more traditional achievement-oriented environments found reduced levels of these psychological factors to result in lower persistence and performance. The current observational findings highlight the critical role of these factors in an online learning environment. Learners with higher levels of goal striving, social belonging, and growth mindset reported greater personal success ($H1, H2, H3$). An online learner with, for instance, a strong sense of social belonging may derive greater satisfaction from the course and persist for longer than one with a weak sense of belonging. These psychological factors tend to vary across people based on prior experiences and they can change as a result of contextual cues. Psychological factors could thereby, at least partially, account for the individual differences in persistence and performance observed in Study 1.

The methodology used in this study can be extended to deliver timely and targeted interventions. The predictive model was successful in identifying a large number of learners who were facing challenges with taking the course. The majority of them were unsuccessful in their own terms. All three psychological factors under investigation were found to distinguish self-ascribed successful from unsuccessful learners. Recent work on psychological interventions showed lasting positive effects of brief interventions involving reading and writing tasks (e.g., [27]). Cultivating a growth mindset was found to help community college students persist in prior work, and our findings provide correlational evidence that subjectively successful learners hold a more fluid notion of intelligence than their less successful peers. Struggling learners can be identified by leveraging predictive models of persistence. However, it requires explanatory models to decide which type of intervention should be delivered to support learners who face particular challenges, such as low goal striving, a fixed mindset, or perceived threat to their sense of belonging in the course. More research is needed to construct such explanatory models.

Reasons for Dropout

The majority of survey respondents (550 of 756; 73%) reported being at most 'somewhat satisfied' with their progress in the course. While many of them (66%) were substantially held back by other commitments that took up time they had planned to spend on the course, only one in four (25%) indicated being hindered by distractions of lower priority than the course (a sign of lower volitional control). These two time-related measures, which only differ in the assigned level of priority, were not significantly correlated ($r = .05, t_{548} = 1.3, p = .21$). Reasons for learner attrition were measured using iteratively coded open responses. Table 3 provides each coded reason and percentage of open responses that indicated it. This list of reasons maps partially onto the factors identified in Study 1 (general time issues, difficulty, format & content, and goals & expectations). A number of significant correlations between these challenges stood out: having not enough time was negatively associated with disliking the format or teaching style ($r = -.52$), needing additional course materials ($r = -.26$), finding the course uninteresting or not valuable ($r = -.45$), and facing technical difficulties ($r = -.29$). Hence, if a learner had not enough time, this tended to be the primary challenge.

To test hypotheses $H4ab$, we examined the 336 open responses that indicated having too little time. It revealed that no particular commitment was specified in about half of them (53%). This distinction was a salient feature in the initial codebooks, but could not be coded with sufficient reliability across coders. Coders would have required additional training to avoid reading specific reasons into unspecific responses. We thus operationalized the distinction by string matching to capture professional, academic, and personal rea-

Table 3. Iteratively-Coded Reasons for Attrition ($n = 399$)

What challenges have you experienced while taking this course?	%
Not enough time for the course	84
The course format or teaching style is not a good fit	18
The level of the course is too advanced	10
The course is not interesting or valuable enough	7
Additional course materials needed to learn the topic	4
Technical difficulties	2
Language barrier	1

sons for having not enough time.[5] While the list of reasons is certainly not collectively exhaustive, it was based on frequently mentioned terms in the open responses. Relative to those who specified a reason, learners who indicated too little time without specifying a reason also reported significantly lower levels of volitional control, i.e. their progress was more severely hindered by lower-priority distractions ($t_{331} = 2.9, p = .003, d = .32$). However, the two groups did not significantly differ in how much they were held back by commitments that took up time they had planned to spend on the course ($t_{333} = -.75, p = .45$). These findings lend strong support to hypotheses $H4ab$: that is, while the large group of learners who reported having not enough time generally faced higher-priority obligations, a substantial proportion appeared to be hindered by low volitional control—and reporting no specific reasons for having not enough time was indicative thereof.

The majority of learners indicated that they had not enough time: some struggled due to higher priority obligations that took up too much time, while others were hindered by low levels of volitional control ($H4a$). A learner needs to be highly self-regulated to be successful in open learning environment that provide little guidance, such as MOOCs. Very few learners explicitly indicated issues with self-regulation in their open responses. They may not possess the metacognitive skills to consciously notice the issue or they preferred not to admit to this undesirable trait. Learners who reported a shortage of time without providing specific reasons were more likely to admit getting distracted by lower-priority tasks, hinting at insufficient volitional control ($H4b$). This could be a useful proxy for identifying issues of self-regulation in future work. Overall, the results suggest that additional support and guidance to build stronger self-regulatory skills could help many learners persist in the course for longer.

GENERAL DISCUSSION

This study of over 100,000 online learners in 21 courses, combining behavioral and survey data, extends the empirical base of research on attrition in online learning environments. The three major findings are, *first*, the presence of substantial gaps in persistence and performance between learners of different gender and learners from different geographic locations; *second*, the relation between self-ascribed success in online learning and higher levels of goal-striving, social belonging, and growth mindset, and *third*, the challenges faced by online learners, most importantly having not enough time, which appeared frequently related to low levels of volitional control. Moreover, we developed a survey item for measuring reasons for disengaging from a course (cf. Table 3), which should be tested and potentially extended based on more empirical evidence from additional courses.

In addressing research questions and testing hypotheses which emerged from a review of the literature, we sought to advance theory on attrition and provide empirical evidence. In line with early models of attrition that emphasized the importance of goal-directed behavior, we found goal striving to be higher in subjectively successful than unsuccessful learners. Moreover, volitional control was identified as a major contributor to reported time-related challenges with taking a MOOC. Tinto's [24] classic model of attrition emphasizes the role of academic and social integration, and incorporates individual learner characteristics as contributors to learners' decision to persist in a course of study. The current work provides evidence for the critical role of individual characteristics, such as gender, age, intentions, prior experiences, and geographic location. Social integration also remains an important factor, but in terms of perceived social belonging [27]. In contrast to Tinto's concept of social and academic integration, which characterizes a general state in an institution, social belonging is a subjective experience based on perceptions and interpretations of environmental cues. Yet, this subjective experience is typically shared by individuals with a common identity, such as female learners in male-dominated fields. Models of attrition should be updated to account for the potential impact of psychological barriers, which can cause achievement gaps that would otherwise remain unnoticed or be misinterpreted.

Among a number of practical implications of this work, it provides new evidence for the need and feasibility of targeted interventions in online learning environments. While the current work does not provide explanations for the presence of substantial achievement gaps, we can speculate that similar psychological processes as in traditional educational environments are involved. Brief and scalable online interventions (mindset, social belonging, goal striving, etc.) could potentially narrow existing achievement gaps in online learning. Advances in this area require more research on explanatory models to both identify struggling learners and predict what challenges they may face. The increasing digitization of education provides new opportunities to make learning environments more adaptive. It is time to abandon the one-size-fits-all model for education and focus on supporting individual learners achieve their goals.

ACKNOWLEDGMENTS

We thank Candace Thille, Octavia Zahrt, Emily Schneider, and Andreas Paepcke for their helpful feedback, and Elise Ogle and Ruth Bram for their assistance developing a codebook. The authors contributed equally to this work.

REFERENCES

1. Bean, J. P., and Metzner, B. S. A conceptual model of nontraditional undergraduate student attrition. *Review of Educational Research 55*, 4 (1985), 485–540.

[5]Pattern: *work|job|school|university|college|family|kids|health*

2. Bers, T. H., and Smith, K. E. Persistence of community college students: The influence of student intent and academic and social integration. *Research in Higher Education 32*, 5 (1991), 539–556.

3. Breslow, L., Pritchard, D. E., DeBoer, J., Stump, G. S., Ho, A. D., and Seaton, D. Studying learning in the worldwide classroom: Research into edxs first mooc. *Research & Practice in Assessment 8* (2013), 13–25.

4. Clow, D. Moocs and the funnel of participation. In *Proceedings of the Third International Conference on Learning Analytics and Knowledge*, ACM (2013), 185–189.

5. Corno, L. Volitional aspects of self-regulated learning. In *Self-regulated learning and academic achievement: Theoretical perspectives*, D. H. S. Barry J. Zimmerman, Ed. Routledge, 2001, ch. 6, 191–225.

6. Dweck, C. *Mindset: The new psychology of success*. Random House LLC, 2006.

7. Fishbein, M., and Ajzen, I. *Belief, attitude, intention and behavior: An introduction to theory and research*. Addison-Wesley Publishing Company, 1975.

8. Goldrick-Rab, S. Challenges and opportunities for improving community college student success. *Review of Educational Research 80*, 3 (2010), 437–469.

9. Gütl, C., Rizzardini, R. H., Chang, V., and Morales, M. Attrition in mooc: Lessons learned from drop-out students. In *Learning Technology for Education in Cloud. MOOC and Big Data*. Springer, 2014, 37–48.

10. Halawa, S., Greene, D., and Mitchell, J. Dropout prediction in moocs using learner activity features. *eLearning Papers* (2014), 1–10.

11. Khalil, H., and Ebner, M. Moocs completion rates and possible methods to improve retention-a literature review. In *World Conference on Educational Multimedia, Hypermedia and Telecommunications*, vol. 2014 (2014), 1305–1313.

12. Kizilcec, R. F., Piech, C., and Schneider, E. Deconstructing disengagement: Analyzing learner subpopulations in massive open online courses. In *Proceedings of the third international conference on learning analytics and knowledge*, ACM (2013), 170–179.

13. Kizilcec, R. F., and Schneider, E. Motivation as a lens to understand online learners: Towards data-driven design with the olei scale. *ACM Transactions on Computer-Human Interaction (TOCHI) 22*, 2 (in press), 24.

14. Lewin, T. After setbacks, online courses are rethought. *New York Times* (2013, December).

15. Moore, M. G., and Kearsley, G. *Distance education: A systems view*. Wadsworth Publishing Company, 1966.

16. Morris, L. V., Finnegan, C., and Wu, S.-S. Tracking student behavior, persistence, and achievement in online courses. *The Internet and Higher Education 8*, 3 (2005), 221–231.

17. Muilenburg, L. Y., and Berge, Z. L. Student barriers to online learning: A factor analytic study. *Distance Education 26*, 1 (2005), 29–48.

18. Parr, C. Mooc completion rates 'below 7%'. *Times Higher Education* (2013, May).

19. Paunesku, D., Yeager, D., Romero, C., and Walton, G. A brief growth mindset intervention improves academic outcomes of community college students enrolled in developmental mathematics courses. *Unpublished manuscript, Stanford University, Stanford, CA* (2012).

20. Rivard, R. Measuring the mooc dropout rate. *Inside Higher Ed 8* (2013).

21. Rovai, A. P. In search of higher persistence rates in distance education online programs. *The Internet and Higher Education 6*, 1 (2003), 1–16.

22. Spencer, S. J., Steele, C. M., and Quinn, D. M. Stereotype threat and women's math performance. *Journal of experimental social psychology 35*, 1 (1999), 4–28.

23. Taylor, C., Veeramachaneni, K., and O'Reilly, U.-M. Likely to stop? predicting stopout in massive open online courses. *arXiv preprint arXiv:1408.3382* (2014).

24. Tinto, V. Dropout from higher education: A theoretical synthesis of recent research. *Review of Educational Research* (1975), 89–125.

25. Tyack, D., and Tobin, W. The "grammar" of schooling: Why has it been so hard to change? *American Educational Research Journal 31*, 3 (1994), 453–479.

26. Waldrop, M. Online learning: Campus 2.0. *Nature 495*, 7440 (2013), 160–163.

27. Walton, G. M., and Cohen, G. L. A question of belonging: race, social fit, and achievement. *Journal of personality and social psychology 92*, 1 (2007), 82.

28. Wigfield, A., and Eccles, J. S. Expectancy–value theory of achievement motivation. *Contemporary educational psychology 25*, 1 (2000), 68–81.

29. Wilkowski, J., Deutsch, A., and Russell, D. M. Student skill and goal achievement in the mapping with google mooc. In *Proceedings of the first ACM conference on Learning@ scale conference*, ACM (2014), 3–10.

30. Yang, D., Sinha, T., Adamson, D., and Rosé, C. P. Turn on, tune in, drop out: Anticipating student dropouts in massive open online courses. In *Proceedings of the 2013 NIPS Data-Driven Education Workshop* (2013).

Towards Detecting Wheel-Spinning: Future Failure in Mastery Learning

Yue Gong
Facebook
yuegong@fb.com

Joseph E. Beck
Worcester Polytechnic Institute
josephbeck@wpi.edu

ABSTRACT

Wheel-spinning refers to a phenomenon in which a student has spent a considerable amount of time practicing a skill, yet displays little or no progress towards mastery. Wheel-spinning has been shown to be a common problem affecting a significant number of students in different tutoring systems and is negatively associated with learning. In this study, we construct a model of wheel-spinning, using generic features easily calculated from most tutoring systems. We show that for two different systems' data, the model generalizes to future students very well and can detect wheel-spinning in an early stage with high accuracy. We also refine the scope of the wheel-spinning problem in two systems using the model's predictions.

Keywords

Student modeling; mastery learning; wheel-spinning; behavioral detector; prediction;

INTRODUCTION

Mastery learning has been implemented and applied in intelligent tutoring systems (ITS) in a variety of contexts. One common foundation builds on the ACT-R theory, which assumes that procedural knowledge of a skill can be acquired through problem solving of what is initially declarative knowledge [1]. The rationale of mastery learning is also well supported by the theory of "learning-by-doing," which refers to the capability of learners to improve their efficiency by regularly repeating the same type of action via practice [2]. The use of mastery learning is driven by the desire to provide students efficient practice, by avoiding giving too many problems to solve, which could waste valuable learning time [3] and possibly jeopardize student motivation to learn, but simultaneously ensuring there are not too few practice problems, which might leave students poorly prepared for learning future content [4] due to the lack of mastery.

L@S 2015, March 14–18, 2015, Vancouver, BC, Canada.
Copyright is held by the owner/author(s). Publication rights licensed to ACM.
ACM 978-1-4503-3411-2/15/03…$15.00
http://dx.doi.org/10.1145/2724660.2724673

An application of mastery learning is that students are presented as many problems as needed to master the skill. Consequently, the system keeps giving the student more problems to practice in the hope that he might utilize these new opportunities to master the skill. The student however could keep failing to learn the skill, which triggers the system to present even more problems to the student. Thus, the student can possibly become trapped in the mastery learning cycle if he fails to achieve mastery. We term this phenomenon "wheel-spinning", analogous to a car stuck in mud or snow; its wheels are spinning rapidly, but it is not going anywhere. Similarly, students are being presented many problems, but they are not making progress towards mastery.

PRIOR WORK: THE SCOPE OF WHEEL-SPINNING

In our prior work [5], we investigated the scope of the wheel-spinning problem for two tutoring systems: the Cognitive Algebra Tutor (the CAT) and ASSISTments, a math tutor. To provide a background for this work, we briefly describe what we have found previously.

We defined mastery of a skill by a student correctly responding to three consecutive questions on the skill on his first attempt. This criterion is a lower bar for determining mastery compared to what was used in some system (e.g., [6]). We purposefully used a weaker mastery criterion as we did not want to artificially amplify the wheel-spinning problem by picking an overly strict criterion of mastery which is hard to achieve by students. We used real data to examine student progression to mastery. For the CAT, there are 146,479 problems done by 575 students for 111 algebra skills, forming 23,517 student-skill instances (i.e., a student working on a skill). For ASSISTments, there are 220,539 problems done by 5,997 students for 190 Math skills, forming 45,787 student-skill instances.

In Figure 1, the x-axis represents the number of problems and the y-axis represents the percent of student-skill instances that have demonstrated mastery. As we define wheel spinning as problem solving without making progress towards mastery, we set a limit of 15 practice attempts in the CAT and 10 practice attempts in ASSISTments before declaring wheel spinning. Similar to mastery, wheel-spinning exists in a context of students and skills, meaning it is only meaningful to say a student masters or wheel-spins on a skill. In addition to mastering a skill or wheel spinning, there is a third possible outcome:

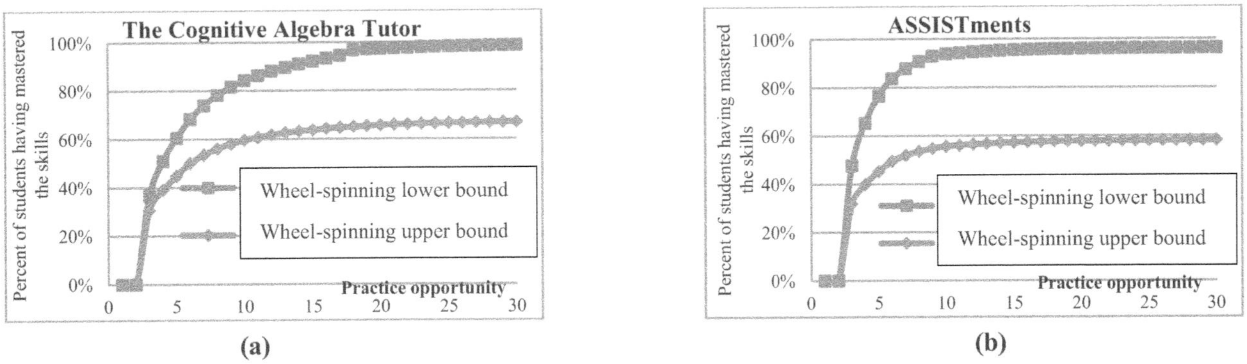

Figure 1 Wheel-spinning's lower bound and upper bound for the CAT (a) and ASSISTments (b).

what if a student who only practices a small number of problems on a skill? Consider a student using the CAT who solves 4 problems, but fails to master the skill – how should we categorize this student's performance? We call this third performance type "indeterminate," as we are unable to categorize it as either wheel spinning or mastery.

We leveraged indeterminate instances to estimate the scope of the wheel-spinning problem. We consider both an optimistic view that assumes all indeterminate instances would end with the student mastering the skill, and a pessimistic view that assumes that students would instead wheel spin in these instances. These two views establish an estimate of the scope of the wheel-spinning problem.

In Figure 1 (a) and (b), the top curves correspond to the optimistic view of mastery. It includes both direct observations of mastery, and imputed mastery from assuming all indeterminate cases would result in mastery. Since mastery and wheel-spinning are complementary, these curves also represent the lower bound of the wheel-spinning problem, which is the least severe case. Namely, that wheel spinning occurs approximately 16% of the time in the CAT and 6% of the time in ASSISTments. The bottom curves represent the pessimistic view of mastery, including observed wheel-spinning instances and imputing indeterminate instances as leading to wheel spinning. These curves represent the upper bound of the wheel-spinning problem, the worst case of wheel-spinning, which is about 40% in the CAT and 44% in ASSISTments. The difference between the upper and lower estimates of wheel spinning (16% to 40% and 6% to 44%) are large, and warrant further analysis to refine the scope the wheel spinning problem. At minimum, 16% and 6% rates of wheel spinning are substantial, and suggest wheel spinning should be investigated and addressed in computer tutors.

A GENERIC MODEL OF WHEEL-SPINNING

We wanted to understand whether wheel-spinning occurs randomly or it is associated with some factors that allow us to model it, and hopefully detect it at an early stage. Early detection would enable early intervention so as to not waste a learner's time. Our goal in this study is to build a generic model. Here, we are not over-claiming generalizability that one set of coefficient estimates can work for data from various systems. Rather, we want to find one set of features, which are computable based on data commonly stored by most ITSs, and by using this set of features, wheel-spinning can be modeled well in those ITSs.

We used the same criterion to determine mastery and wheel-spinning as in prior work. Three correct responses in consecutive questions of a skill is used as the mastery criterion. We chose 15 practice opportunities for the CAT and 10 for ASSISTments as the wheel-spinning determination checkpoints. A student could wheel-spin on one skill, while mastering another. Thus, the unit of declaring wheel-spinning is a student-skill pair.

Feature Engineering

Feature engineering is crucial in student modeling. Since learning and problem-solving are complex cognitive and affective processes, many student models succeed due to using extracted features (e.g. [4], [7]). We selected features to model wheel-spinning from three aspects: student in-tutor performance, the seriousness of the learner, and general factors.

Student In-tutor performance (on this skill)

Intuitively, whether a student is able to master a skill has much to do with how well the student understands the skill. We constructed five features to represent student in-tutor performance. These features are specific to the skill. Observations associated with other skills will not affect the calculations of feature values associated with this skill.

"Correct_Response_Count" - The prior number of problems solved correctly by the student on his first attempt. This feature is used in the Performance Factors Analysis model (PFA) [8], and found very useful in prediction [9].

"Correct_Response_In_A_Row_Count" - The current streak of correct responses on the first attempt. Since we define mastery as 3 correct responses in a row, the student's current streak is important. For example, if the student has got two problems right in a row, for the third problem, the value of this feature is 2. If his or her answer to the third problem happens to be incorrect, for the fourth problem, the value of this feature is reset to 0.

"Exp_Mean_Response_Time_Z-Score" - This feature is derived based on response times of prior questions of the same skill. Response time is the length of time spent by the student after being presented a problem and before taking the first action. Anderson et al. reported that according to ACT-R, fast speed of responding to a question often comes after high accuracy [10]. In practice, the winner of the KDD cup 2010 also applied this feature [7]. Instead of using an absolute value of time, we used exponential mean of the z-scores of response times as follows. For each problem, we collected all response times across all students to that problem. Then, we calculated the mean and standard deviation of the response times and used those to compute z-scores for all of the response times. Next, we aggregated all prior problems done by the student for the skill together and organized them in chronological order. On this series of z-scores, we used the following formula to calculate the exponential mean, γ * *prior_average* + *(1- γ)* * *new_observation*, with $\gamma = 0.7$. The exponential mean is a method of summarizing sequential data, but provides lesser weight to older observations, as prior observations are decayed by γ at each time step.

"Prior_Problem_Count_With_Hint_Request" - The number of prior problems on which the student requested a hint.

"Prior_Problem_Count_With_At_Least_5_Hint_Requests" - The number of prior problems of the skill for which the student requested 5 or more hints.

Many computer tutors provide multiple hints, with the final, or "bottom out" hint providing students the answer. Bottom-out hinting has a wide usage in student modeling as a predictor of student performance [11-13]. We were unable to compute from the provided log files whether CAT hints were bottom-out, so resorted to using two measures of hint usage as a proxy.

The Seriousness of the Learner (across skills)

Given the rich literatures on the connection between learning and the seriousness of the learner (e.g., [12-14]), we think of the seriousness of the learner as another type of factor possibly related to wheel-spinning. We found two aspects which seem reasonable to reflect the seriousness of the learner's attitude: the speed of responding to a problem and asking for hints in consecutive problems. Similar features capturing these two aspects were used in gaming detectors (e.g., [12-14]).

We designed 6 features reflecting response speed, and 2 features for consecutive hinting. Since these features are intended to represent the seriousness of the learner, they are calculated *across all* (in contrast to the student in-tutor performance features) skills, as we assume student attitude tends to be temporally stable across skills. The 6 features reflecting response speed are based on Z-score data described previously. This approach is appropriate as 25 seconds might be a fast response for a complex problem, but a slow response for a simple one. As we did not have access to all the details of the content presented, we relied on population statistics for that item to define relatively fast and slow responses. Fast responses were response times more than 1 standard deviation below the mean for that item. Slow responses were more than 1 standard deviation above the mean for that item, while normal responses were within 1 standard deviation of the mean for that item.

"Prior_Problem_Count_Fast_Correct" - the number of prior problems the student solved correctly and more than 1 standard deviation faster than the mean response time for that item.

"Prior_Problem_Count_Normal_Correct" - the number of prior problems the student solved correctly and within 1 standard deviation of the mean response time for that item.

"Prior_Problem_Count_Slow_Correct" - the number of prior problems the student solved correctly and more than 1 standard deviation more than the mean response time for that item.

"Prior_Problem_Count_Fast_Incorrect",
"Prior_Problem_Count_Normal_Incorrect",
"Prior_Problem_Count_Slow_Incorrect" – these three features are similar as the above three, yet for problems solved incorrectly.

We also computed 2 features based on hint usage. We used the same feature definition as we used for student in-tutor performance, with the tweak that rather than just looking at student performance on the skill being practiced, we look at performance across all skills. As a rationale, consider a student who asks for considerable help on just one skill. The likely explanation is the student is struggling with that skill. In contrast, a student who asks for considerable help on every skill is either confused about every skill, or is bored with the homework and is trying to get through the problems with minimal effort. The latter category is what we are trying to model with features capturing the seriousness of the learner.

"Prior_Problem_Count_With_Hint_Request_In_a_Row" - The number of consecutive prior problems across skills for each of which the student requested at least 1 hint.

"Prior_Problem_Count_With_At_Least_5_Hint_Requests_In_a_Row" - The number of consecutive prior problems across skills for each of which the student requested at least 5 hints.

General Features

We used two independent variables to track general information.

"Prior_Problem_Count" - The number of prior problems that have been practiced by the student for this skill. This feature is used in the Learning Factors Analysis model (LFA) [15]. We treated this feature as a factor as we did not see a strong reason to assume that there is a linear relationship between this variable and our target, wheel-spinning. Therefore, for each possible value (0 to 14 for the CAT and 0 to 9 for ASSISTments) our model estimates a unique value, indicating the effect to wheel-spinning given that many practices opportunities have passed.

"Skill_ID" - skill identification. This feature reflects skills may have different effects on wheel-spinning. It is treated as factor, and the parameter estimate for each skill could conceptually be interpreted as how difficult the skill is. Skill difficulty is a widely used feature in almost all types of student models. Research found that skill difficulty is very useful [16] in predicting student performance.

MODEL EVALUATION

Data

We applied three rules of data pre-processing. First, we removed indeterminate problems, as the wheel-spinning status is not certain and thus the value of the dependent variable is missing. Second, we removed student practice after reaching mastery on a skill, as in this case the status this student-skill pair was already determined. Third, for the similar reason, we removed all problems for a student after he reached the wheel-spinning cutoff (10 problems for ASSISTments and 15 for the CAT).

After data pre-processing, the CAT data set contains 96,919 problems done by 567 students. There are 76,684 mastery problems and 20,235 wheel-spinning problems. The ratio of the two classes is 3.8: 1. The ASSISTments data set contains 133,061 problems done by 5,103 students. There are 104,961 mastery problems and 28,100 wheel-spinning problems. The ratio of the two classes is 3.7: 1.

There are three types of predictions in student modeling [17]. In this paper, we examined type 1 prediction, how unknown students will perform on the observed problems. We conducted a three-fold cross-validation at the student level. As data were split at the student level, in each fold, students in the test data set have no intersection with those in the training data set. Therefore, to the model, these students serve as future, unseen, students, and the task for the model is to predict whether the student will master a problem or wheel-spin on it. All results are from averaging performance across all three folds.

Model Fitting

We trained separate logistic regression models to fit the CAT and ASSISTments data. The dependent variable is represented by a binary value, indicating mastery or wheel-spinning. We found that two sets of coefficient estimates are highly correlated to each other, suggesting that most features' effects on predicting wheel-spinning are consistent across the two systems. We do not include the estimates due to limited space. The interpretations below apply to the two models.

Among the features reflecting student in-tutor performance, "Correct_Response_In_A_Row_Count" is the most important feature and is negatively associated with wheel-spinning. The two features representing hinting are positively associated with wheel-spinning. Both of these results are in the expected direction.

In the features for the seriousness of the learner, in general, more prior incorrect responses is positively associated with wheel-spinning, which is worsened when combined with too fast responses. The two features representing "consecutive bottom-out hinting" are estimated as being positively associated with wheel-spinning.

In the general factors, we found that there is a clear, yet unexpected, linear trend that the more problems a student has attempted on a skill without mastery, the more likely he is to wheel-spin.

Model accuracy

We evaluated our wheel-spinning model on the training and test data sets for the CAT and ASSISTments. We present results in Table 1. We used three metrics, percent correct, AUC and R^2 to measure model accuracy.

Percent Correct is simply the percent of correct model predictions, interpreting model predictions above 0.5 as indicating wheel spinning and below 0.5 as indicating mastery. AUC is area under curve of the ROC. AUC measures how well the model is able to classify an instance of a binary category. The possible range of this metric is from 0.5 to 1. 0.5 means a random classification, and 1 means a perfect classification. Both Percent Correct and AUC show high performance on both the training and test sets. So we have confidence that our model generalizes to unseen students, and are able to interpret our parameter estimates as there is no evidence of overfitting.

Table 1 Model performance on the training and test data sets of the CAT and ASSISTments

	The CAT		ASSISTments	
	Training	Test	Training	Test
Percent Correct	86%	85%	87%	86%
AUC	0.89	0.88	0.89	0.88
R^2	0.40	0.38	0.42	0.40

The R^2 values are slightly more complicated, and are calculated based on the residuals between the actual value of the dependent variable, a binary categorical value of 0 or 1, and the predicted value of wheel-spinning, a decimal value ranging from 0 to 1. This metric, compared to the above two metrics, focuses less on classification ability, but more on the magnitude difference between the predicted values and true values. The R^2 value ranges between 0 and with 1 indicating a perfect fit. The measurements are around 0.4 for the training data and slightly lower for the test data. The values of this metric appear to be less satisfying than AUC at the first glance. However, given that the general performances of other major behavioral models, where the measurements of this metric is normally around

0.1 on test data [18, 19], our wheel-spinning model shows good performance, especially in its strong ability to generalize.

Model misclassifications

Typically, it is necessary to examine a classifier's misclassifications for each class of the dependent variable. This is particularly important for data where one class is of more interest than the others, or with imbalanced classes, one or more classes dominate the data set. In our context, we are particularly interested in investigating how the model performs for the wheel-spinning instances, as the ultimate goal is to address the question whether we can rely on the classifier to detect wheel-spinning and drive tutor interventions to prevent it. The two data sets also have imbalanced class distributions with many more instances of mastery than wheel spinning. The accuracy measure, which is used to compare classifiers, may not be well suited for evaluating models derived from imbalanced data sets. Therefore, we present the confusion matrices in Table 2 and Table 3 to help evaluate the models. The correct classifications are in the left top cell and the bottom right cell. The misclassifications are in the right top cell and the left bottom cell. We highlighted the numbers of misclassifications in italic. We also show the percent of each category in parentheses.

Table 2 Confusion matrix for test data on the CAT

		Predicted Category	
		Mastery	Wheel-spinning
Actual Category	Mastery	24,128 (74.7%)	*1,433 (4.4%)*
	Wheel-spinning	*3,172 (9.8%)*	3,572 (11.0%)

Table 3 Confusion matrix for test data on ASSISTments

		Predicted Category	
		Mastery	Wheel-spinning
Actual Category	Mastery	33,469 (75.5%)	*1,518 (3.4%)*
	Wheel-spinning	*4,390 (9.9 %)*	4976 (11.2%)

Table 2 and Table 3 have similar trends: more correct classifications on mastery than on wheel-spinning Most misclassifications occurred as false negatives (bottom left cell), while false positives (top right cell) is a minor problem. That is, the classifier is more likely to overlook a wheel spinning case than incorrectly assert wheel spinning when a student goes on to master a skill.

To focus on wheel-spinning, we used two additional metrics, precision and recall, which are useful when one of the classes is considered more important. Precision determines the fraction of instances that are actually wheel-spinning problems and the classifier has declared as a wheel-spinning problem. Recall measures the fraction of wheel-spinning instances correctly detected by the The precisions and recall results in Table 4 show moderate abilities of our models for the minority category: wheel-spinning. The precision rates are good, showing that over 70% declared wheel-spinning instances are accurately classified. The recall rates are lower in both models. The numbers are slightly above 50%, indicating that the model's ability to distinguish the wheel-spinning problems out of mastery problems is weaker. Thus, our model overlooks nearly half of the wheel spinning cases.

Table 4 Precision and recall on wheel-spinning on test data of the CAT and ASSISTments models

	Precision	**Recall**
The CAT	71.1%	52.7%
ASSISTments	76.6%	53.1%

Typically, there is a trade-off between precision and recall. We argue that compared to precision, a low recall rate is more acceptable. It is better to miss some students who will wheel spin than to incorrectly trigger interventions for students who will not struggle. This point is especially true as one of the first interventions we plan on attempting is informing the actual teacher that a student is likely to struggle on a particular skill. Given the limits on a teacher's time, allocating that effort efficiently is key.

Speed at detecting wheel-spinning

Unlike most behavioral detectors aimed at detecting a student's current behavior, a wheel-spinning detector is meant to detect something that happens over a longer period of time. Although wheel spinning is not flagged until problem 10 or 15, a student starts to struggle on a skill from the outset. Therefore, an important characteristic of this kind of detectors is its ability to detect the construct of interest quickly. We did fine-grained measures of detector performance at each practice opportunity, and plotted the evolutions in Figure 2. The x-axis is practice opportunity (PO). The y-axis represents both precision and recall.

It is particularly worth pointing out that due to the way we did data pre-processing, both the size and balance of the data change with PO. Removing excessive problems after mastery causes the data sets to shrink at each PO with fewer mastery instances left. For example, suppose we used 10 problems as the threshold to determine wheel-spinning. There are only two students, Ann and Mary, and one skill in the data set. Ann mastered the skill after practicing 4 problems. Mary practiced 12 problems in total without mastery, so she was wheel-spinning. We formed 10 sub data sets with each corresponding to a PO. In each of the sub data sets corresponding to PO1-PO4, there were 2 problems. One is from Ann, and the other is from Mary. The size and balance of the sub data sets of PO1-PO4 remain the same: the size is 2 and the ratio of mastery vs. wheel-spinning is 1:1.

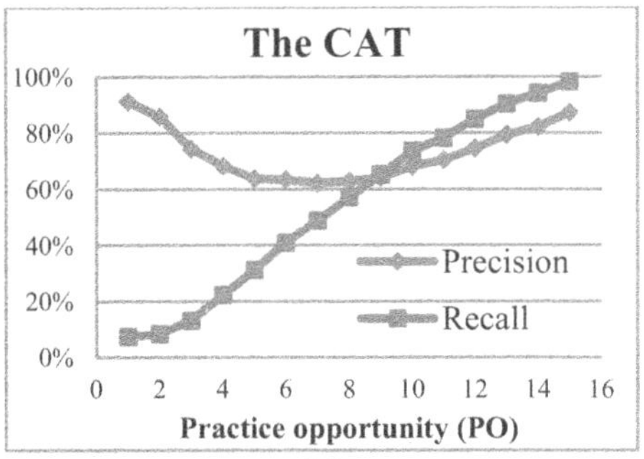

(a)

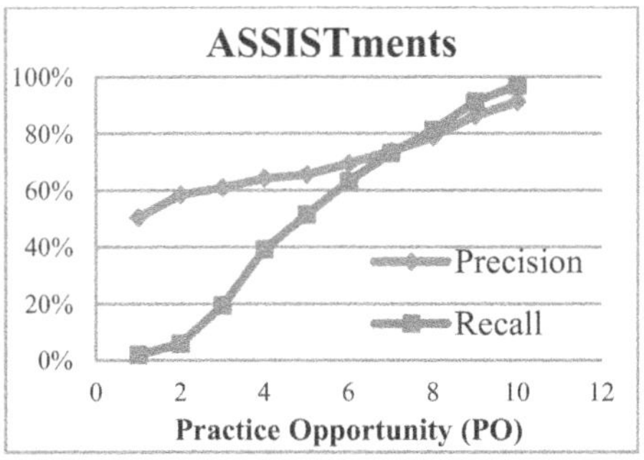

(b)

Figure 2 Precision and recall on wheel-spinning, broken down by practice opportunity for the CAT (a) and ASSISTments (b)

Starting from PO5, every sub data sets contains only 1 problem, which is done by Mary, as Ann has mastered the skill and no more problems of hers are in the original data set. The size of the sub data sets from PO5 to the last PO is 1, and the ratio of mastery vs. wheel-spinning is 0:1. Therefore, mastery becomes rarer over POs and wheel-spinning remains constant during the entire time.

Based on the quantitative relationship between mastery and wheel-spinning, we categorize POs into three chronological phases. Phase 1 [PO1-PO3] is the initiation phase in which the number of mastery student-skill pairs remains constant, so the ratio of mastery to wheel spinning is constant too. The ratio is quite high (10:1 for the CAT and 8:1 for ASSISTments). Phase 2 [PO4-PO10] for the CAT and [PO4-PO7] for ASSISTments, is the evolution phase in which the ratio of master to wheel spinning gradually decreases to roughly 1. Phase 3 is the termination phase, in which mastery becomes the minority class.

Figure 2 shows precision and recall for the CAT and ASSISTments on wheel-spinning by PO. The cold start problem is obvious and hurts recall badly. In the initiation phase, data balance at this time is poor as described above. Consequently, for PO1, the detectors have a near-zero recall rate. However, the detector is able to adapt quickly. At the end of the initiation phase, at PO3, when the detectors gathered information from only two prior problems, the recall rate of the CAT model increases to around 15%, and the recall rate of the ASSISTments model increases to 20%. Note that during this phase, neither data size nor balance changes; therefore the model should be credited for the improvements. In the following two phases, the recall rate rises gradually.

Precision looks very surprising to us. First, it is not hurt as badly as recall by the cold start problem. For ASSISTments, the initial measurement of precision is around 50%. This could be explained by the fact that the model is also informed by features across skills, and despite the first problem for the student-skill pair, the model has collected information from prior problems of other skills solved by the student.

More surprisingly, precision is around 90% at PO1 for the CAT model. It has a decreasing trend in the initiation phase and the first half of the evolution phase. We found this divergence is due to a dominant skill in the CAT through fine examinations.

Specifically, features representing student in-tutor performance have no effect at PO1, as their values at this point are 0. Then, we found no clear difference between the CAT and ASSISTments models in model estimates of the across-skills features. For the first general feature, Prior_Problem_Count, the parameter estimates of the two models at PO1 are both biases towards predicting mastery instead of wheel-spinning. Therefore, the only feature that could possibly be responsible for this divergence in the CAT vs. ASSISTments is "Skill_id".

We found that in the ASSISTments data set, among all declared wheel-spinning problems at PO1, the skills are distributed randomly. On the other hand, in the CAT data set, at PO1, 79% declared wheel-spinning problems are associated with one skill. For some reason, many students failed that skill, resulting in wheel-spinning. The model captures this point, yielding an estimate for the skill representing a very low probability of mastering the skill. 79% declared wheel-spinning problems are associated with this skill, and they are correctly classified. This results in a high precision at PO1. The proportion of the declared wheel-spinning problems associated with this particular skill decreases over POs. With the lost of domination, precision drops after PO1 until PO7.

Both precision and recall continue to improve after the middle of the evolution phase. When the detectors enter the termination phase, at PO10 for the CAT and PO7 for ASSISTments, we see reliable performances. Both precision and recall are close to or above 70%. Note that at this point, the data sets have a good balance where two classes have roughly equal instances. There are still a couple of POs left before the wheel-spinning is certified, which means we can still accurately capture a good number of students and intervene to possibly prevent wheel-spinning.

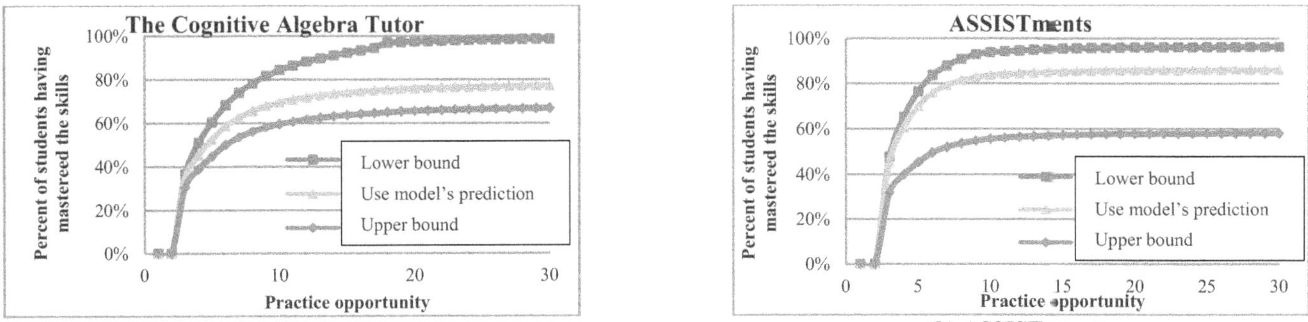

(a) The CAT (b) ASSISTments

Figure 3 The bounding and estimated curves (a) of the CAT (b) of ASSISTments

REFINING THE SCOPE OF WHEEL-SPINNING

In our prior work, we noted the difference in the upper- and lower-bounds warranted a closer investigation. We now utilize the wheel-spinning model we trained to estimate the true extent of the wheel-spinning problem. We elaborate the approach by using a concrete example. Suppose there are only two student-skill pairs in a data set, Ann-Addition and Mary-Subtraction. Ann did 5 problems for Addition and mastered the skill at the 5th PO. Mary did 5 problems for Subtraction and did not master the skill. We use 10 problems as the wheel-spinning checkpoint. Ann-Addition is a determinate instance, as mastery has been achieved. Mary-Subtraction is an indeterminate instance due to insufficient observations to determine wheel-spinning. The pessimistic upper bound on wheel spinning is computed by assuming Mary-Subtraction remains unmastered. The optimistic lower bound on wheel spinning is computed by assuming Mary-Subtraction is mastered. We now discuss how we use our model to estimate the true amount of wheel spinning within this envelope.

To impute indeterminate cases, we used our model's prediction for the last problem in the student-skill sequence. Using the above example, we would use the model's prediction for Mary-Subtraction after observing the fifth completed problem. We use the last datapoint since the model's accuracy will be highest. Suppose the prediction of the last problem of Mary-Subtraction is 0.3, meaning a 30% chance to demonstrate mastery. We would therefore split this case between mastered and unmastered, allocating 0.3 units towards the number of mastered cases and 0.7 units towards the wheel spinning cases. By fractionally allocating cases as mastery or wheel spinning according to our model's predictions, we can get a more accurate estimate of the rate of wheel spinning.

Figure 3 demonstrates how students make progress towards mastery as a function of PO. These graphs are identical to Figure 1, except the indeterminate cases are allocated according to our model's predictions as represented by the middle curve in both graphs. In Figure 3 (a), we see that the middle curve is closer to the bottom curve, the upper bound of the wheel-spinning problem. At PO 15, the wheel-spinning cutoff, the model's estimate of wheel spinning reaches about 75%. Thus, for the CAT, the wheel-spinning problem is estimated to affect approximately 25% of student-skill pairs. In Figure 3 (b), the wheel-spinning problem seems less severe in ASSISTments, as at PO10 (the wheel-spinning checkpoint) the estimate climbs up to around 82%, leaving 18% of the student-skill pairs wheel-spinning.

There are two points that we want to make in particular. First, 25% and 18% of student-skill pairs is a large number of lessons from which the learner gains nothing, but wasting learning time, and it could lead to frustration. Second, we speculate that wheel-spinning is underestimated by our model. Indeterminate student-skill instances have relatively few problems, which end at early POs. Take the ASSISTments model as example, at PO 3 in Figure 2, precision is around 60% and recall is around 20%; therefore, the true number of wheel-spinning problems is $3n$, three times of the problems having been declared wheel-spinning. This systematic undercount of wheel spinning biases the model in favor of predicting mastery.

CONTRIBUTIONS, FUTURE WORK AND CONCLUSIONS

We made several contributions in this work. First, we deepened the understanding of the wheel-spinning problem by finding that it is not random. Instead, we showed that a set of features, computable from typically stored data by most ITSs, have consistent and robust associations with wheel-spinning across different learning environments and student populations. In student modeling, models often depend on detailed information specific to the system [4, 12, 13], which may expose the work to the issue of "most published research findings are false" due to barriers to replicate a study [20]. Building a generic model is important from a scientific point of view, as it makes replicating our results easier in other tutoring systems.

Second, we built a behavioral detector for wheel-spinning. We applied machine leaning techniques to generate the wheel-spinning model, which saves lots of human labor as needed in human-generated models, nor do we need human observers as in [21]. Unlike most behavioral detectors aiming to detect the student's state over a brief temporal interval [4, 12, 13], the wheel-spinning detector is designed to detect what happens over a long time period (10 - 15 problems away in the future). Furthermore, this work sheds light on research of behavioral detectors that require both high accuracy and fast speed of detection. Our detector has robust performances across different tutoring systems with over precision and recall.

Finally, we refined the scope of the wheel-spinning problem, which is important for understanding this generally-occurred problem, and showed it affected a substantial number of students using the CAT and ASSISTments. In addition, by using the model to estimate the amount of wheel-spinning, we presented an approach to evaluate the effectiveness of a tutoring system.

One interesting future work is to refine/design a wheel-spinning model by other machine learning techniques, especially for addressing the low recall problem. The most important open question is what we can do about wheel-spinning? The CAT and ASSISTments are effective tutoring systems and both have been developed to help students reach mastery. Nevertheless, wheel-spinning still hurts students in both systems. We are eager to know what interventions might be effective in reducing wheel spinning.

To sum up, in this work, we built a model with a set of generic features for wheel-spinning. We showed for the CAT and ASSISTments, the model can generalize very well to unseen students with satisfying accuracy and detection speed. Finally, we used model predictions to refine the scope of wheel-spinning, and showed that it affects a substantial proportion of students for both systems.

REFERENCES

1. Anderson, J.R., et al., Cognitive tutors: Lessons learned. The Journal of the Learning Sciences, 1995. 4: 167-207.
2. Wikipedia. Learning-by-doing (economics). http://en.wikipedia.org/wiki/Learning-by-doing_(economics).
3. Cen, H., K. Koedinger, and B. Junker. Is More Practice Necessary? - Improving Learning Efficiency with the Cognitive Tutor through Educational Data Mining. in International Conference on Artificial Intelligence in Education. 2007.
4. Baker, R.S., S. Gowda, and A. Corbett, Automatically Detecting a Students Preparation for Future Learning: Help Use is Key, in the 4th International Conference on Educational Data Mining, M. Pechenizkiy, et al., Editors. 2011. p. 179-188.
5. Gong, Y. and J.E. Beck, Wheel-spinning: An important problem with the mastery learning framework International Journal of Artificial Intelligence in Education, (in preparation).
6. Farrell, R.G., J.R. Anderson, and B.J. Reiser. An Interactive Computer-Based Tutor for LISP. in Fourth National Conference on Artificial Intelligence. 1984.
7. Yu, H.-F., et al., Feature engineering and classifier ensemble for KDD cup 2010. KDD Cup 2010: Improving Cognitive Models with Educational Data Mining, 2010.
8. Pavlik, P.I., H. Cen, and K. Koedinger, Performance Factors Analysis - A New Alternative to Knowledge Tracing, in the 14th International Conference on Artificial Intelligence in Education. 2009. p. 531-538.
9. Gong, Y. and J.E. Beck, Items, Skills, and Transfer Models: Which Really Matters for Student Modeling? , in the 4th International Conference on Educational Data Mining. 2011. p. 81-90.
10. Anderson, J.R., Rules of the mind. 1993, Hillsdale, NJ: Lawrence Erlbaum Associates.
11. Feng, M., et al. Addressing the assessment challenge in an Intelligent Tutoring System that tutors as it assesses. User Modeling and User-Adapted Interaction, 2009. 19: p. 243-266.
12. Gong, Y., et al., The impact of gaming (?) on learning at the fine-grained level. The 10th International Conf. on Intelligent Tutoring Systems. 2010. 194-203.
13. Baker, R.S.J.d., et al., Developing a Generalizable Detector of When Students Game the System. User Modeling and User-Adapted Interaction., 2008.
14. Arroyo, I. and B. Woolf, Inferring learning and attitudes from a Bayesian Network of log file data in the 12th International Conference on Artificial Intelligence in Education. 2005: Amsterdam.
15. Cen, H., K. Koedinger, and B. Junker. Learning Factors Analysis - A General Method for Cognitive Model Evaluation and Improvement. in Intelligent Tutoring Systems. 2006. Jhongli, Taiwan: Springer.
16. Gong, Y. and J.E. Beck, Looking Beyond Tranfer Models: Finding Other Sources of Power for Studnet Models, in The 19th International Conference on User Modeling, Adaptation and Personalization. 2011.
17. Chi, M., et al., Instructional Factors Analysis: A Cognitive Model For Multiple Instructional Interventions, in the 4th International Conference on Educational Data Mining, M. Pechenizkiy, et al., Editors. 2011. p. 61-70.
18. Gong, Y., J.E. Beck, and N.T. Heffernan, How to Construct More Accurate Student Models: Comparing and Optimizing Knowledge Tracing and Performance Factors Analysis. International Journal of Artificial Intelligence in Education, 2010.
19. Baker, R.S.J.d., et al., Ensembling Predictions of Student Knowledge within Intelligent Tutoring Systems, in The 19th International Conference on User Modeling, Adaptation, and Personalization. 2011. p. 13-24.
20. Ioannidis, J.P.A., Why Most Published Research Findings Are False. PLoS Med 2005. 2(8:e124).
21. Liu, Z., et al., Sequences of Frustration and Confusion, and Learning, in the 6th International Conference on Educational Data Mining, S. D'Mello, R. Calvo, and A. Olney, Editors. 2013: Memphis, TN. p. 114-120.

PeerStudio: Rapid Peer Feedback Emphasizes Revision and Improves Performance

Chinmay Kulkarni[1], Michael S. Bernstein[1], Scott Klemmer[2]
[1] Stanford University, [2] UC San Diego
{chinmay,msb}@cs.stanford.edu, srk@ucsd.edu

ABSTRACT

Rapid feedback is a core component of mastery learning, but feedback on open-ended work requires days or weeks in most classes today. This paper introduces *PeerStudio*, an assessment platform that leverages the large number of students' peers in online classes to enable rapid feedback on in-progress work. Students submit their draft, give rubric-based feedback on two peers' drafts, and then receive peer feedback. Students can integrate the feedback and repeat this process as often as they desire. In MOOC deployments, the median student received feedback in just twenty minutes. Rapid feedback on in-progress work improves course outcomes: in a controlled experiment, students' final grades improved when feedback was delivered quickly, but not if delayed by 24 hours. More than 3,600 students have used PeerStudio in eight classes, both massive and in-person. This research demonstrates how large classes can leverage their scale to encourage mastery through rapid feedback and revision.

AUTHOR KEYWORDS

MOOC; peer assessment; peer learning; mastery learning; deliberate practice

INTRODUCTION

Online learning need not be a loop of watching video lectures and then submitting assignments. To most effectively develop mastery, students must repeatedly revise based on *immediate, focused feedback* [12]. Revision is central to the method of deliberate practice as well as to mastery learning, and depends crucially on rapid formative assessment and applying corrective feedback [16]. In domains as diverse as writing, programming, and art, immediate feedback reliably improves learning; delaying feedback reduces its benefit [23].

Unfortunately, many learning experiences cannot offer tight feedback-revision loops. When courses assign open-ended work such as essays or projects, it can easily take a week after submission to receive feedback from peers or overworked instructors. Feedback is also often coupled with an unchangeable grade, and classes move to new topics faster than feedback arrives. The result is that many opportunities to develop mastery and expertise are lost, as students have few opportunities to revise work and no incentive to do so.

L@S 2015, March 14–15, 2014, Vancouver, Canada.
ACM 978-1-4503-3411-2/15/03.
http://dx.doi.org/10.1145/2724660.2724670

Could software systems enable peers in massive classes to provide rapid feedback on in-progress work? In massive classes, peer assessment already provides summative grades and critiques on final work [25], but this process takes days, and is often as slow as in-person classes. This paper instead introduces a peer learning design tailored for near-immediate peer feedback. It capitalizes on the scale of massive classes to connect students to trade structured feedback on drafts. This process can provide feedback to students within minutes of submission, and can be repeated as often as desired.

We present the *PeerStudio* system for fast feedback on in-progress open-ended work. Students submit an assignment draft whenever they want feedback and then provide rubric-based feedback on two others' drafts in order to unlock their own results. PeerStudio explicitly encourages mastery by allowing students to revise their work multiple times.

Even with the scale of massive classes, there are not always enough students online to guarantee fast feedback. Therefore, PeerStudio recruits students who are online already, and also those who have recently submitted drafts for review but are no longer online. PeerStudio uses a progressive recruitment algorithm to minimize the number of students emailed. It reaches out to more and more students, emailing a small fraction of those who recently submitted drafts each time, and stops recruiting immediately when enough (e.g., two) reviewers have been recruited.

This paper reports on PeerStudio's use in two massive online classes and two in-person classes. In a MOOC where 472 students used PeerStudio, reviewers were recruited within minutes (median wait time: seven minutes), and the first feedback was completed soon after (median wait time: 20 minutes). Students in the two, smaller, in-person classes received feedback in about an hour on average. Students took advantage of PeerStudio to submit full drafts ahead of the deadline, and paid particular attention to free-text feedback beyond the explicit rubric.

A controlled experiment measured the benefits of rapid feedback. This between-subjects experiment assigned participants in a MOOC to one of three groups. One control group saw no feedback on in-progress work. A second group received feedback on in-progress work 24 hours after submission. A final group received feedback as soon as it was available. Students who received fast in-progress feedback had higher final grades than the control group ($t(98)=2.1$, $p<0.05$). The speed of the feedback was critical: receiving slow feedback was statistically indistinguishable from receiving no feedback at all ($t(98)=1.07$, $p=0.28$).

PeerStudio demonstrates how massive online classes can be designed to provide feedback an order of magnitude faster than many in-person classes. It also shows how MOOC-inspired learning techniques can *scale down* to in-person classes. In this case, designing and testing systems iteratively in massive online classes led to techniques that worked well in offline classrooms as well; Wizard of Oz prototyping and experiments in small classes led to designs that work well at scale. Finally, parallel deployments at different scales help us refocus our efforts on creating systems that produce pedagogical benefits at any scale.

RELATED WORK

PeerStudio relies on peers to provide feedback. Prior work shows peer-based critique is effective both for in-person [8,29] and online classes [25], and can provide students accurate numeric grades and comments [13,25].

PeerStudio bases its design of peer feedback on prior work about how feedback affects learning. By *feedback*, we mean task-related information that helps students improve their performance. Feedback improves performance by changing students' locus of attention, focusing them on productive aspects of their work [21]. It can do so by making the difference between current and desired performance more salient [17], by explaining the cause of poor performance [5], or by encouraging students to use a different or higher standard to compare their work against [26].

Fast feedback improves performance by making the difference between the desired and current performance more salient [23]. When students receive feedback quickly (e.g., in an hour), they apply the concepts they learn more successfully [23]. In domains like mathematics, computers can generate feedback instantly, and combining such formative feedback with revision improves grades [18]. PeerStudio extends fast feedback to domains such as design and writing where automated feedback is limited and human judgment is necessary.

Feedback merely changes what students attend to, so not all feedback is useful, and some feedback degrades performance [21]. For instance, praise is frequently ineffective because it shifts attention *away* from the task and onto the self [1].

Therefore, feedback systems and curricular designers must match feedback to instructional goals. Large-scale meta-analyses suggest that the most effective feedback helps students set goals for future attempts, provides information about the quality of their current work, and helps them gauge whether they are moving towards a good answer [21]. Therefore, PeerStudio provides a low-cost way of specifying goals when students revise, uses a standardized rubric and free-form comments for correctness feedback, and a way to browse feedback on previous revisions for velocity.

How can peers provide the most accurate feedback? Disaggregation can be an important tool: summing individual scores for components of good writing (e.g. grammar and argumentation) can capture the overall quality of an essay more accurately than asking for a single writing score [9,24]. Therefore, PeerStudio asks for individual judgments with yes/no or scale questions, and not aggregate scores.

PeerStudio uses the large scale of the online classroom in order to quickly recruit reviewers after students submit in-progress work. In contrast, most prior work has capitalized on scale only after all assignments are submitted. For instance, DeduceIt uses the semantic similarity between student solutions to provide automatic hinting and to check solution correctness [14], while other systems cluster solutions to help teachers provide feedback quickly [6].

ENABLING FAST PEER FEEDBACK WITH PEERSTUDIO

Students can use PeerStudio to create and receive feedback on any number of drafts for every open-ended assignment. Because grades shift students' attention away from the task to the self [21], grades are withheld until the final version.

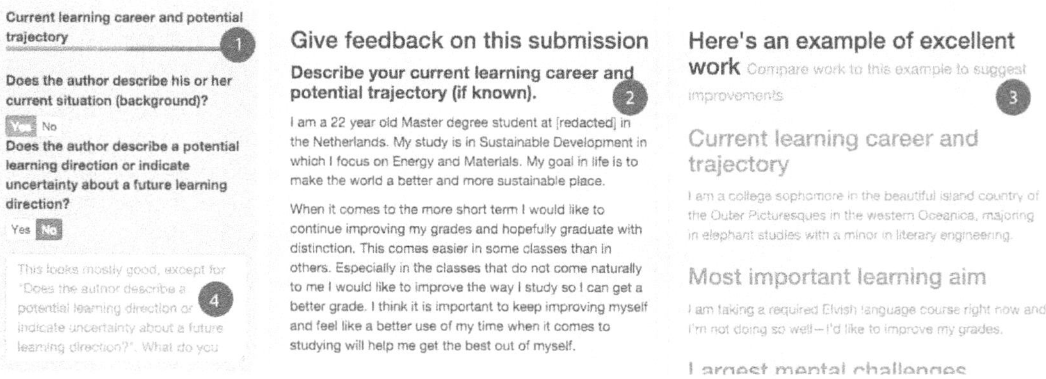

Figure 1: PeerStudio is a peer learning platform for rapid, rubric-based feedback on drafts. The reviewing interface above shows (1) the rubric, (2) the student draft, (3) an example of excellent work to compare student work against. PeerStudio scaffolds reviewers with automatically generating tips for commenting (4).

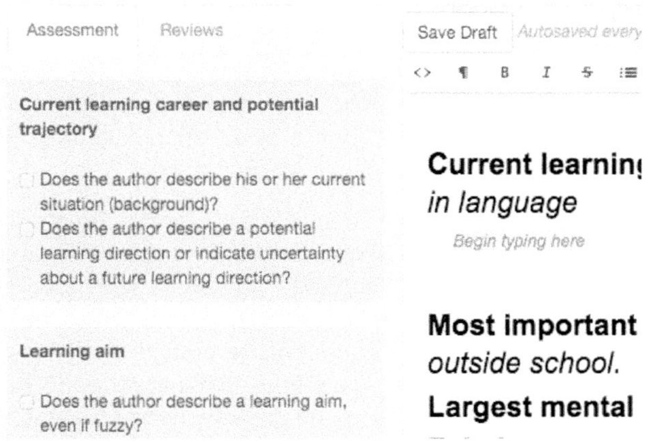

Figure 2: The drafting interface shows the assignment rubric, and a starter template. Reviews on previous versions are also available (tab, top-left).

Creating a draft, and seeking feedback

PeerStudio encourages students to seek feedback on an initial draft as early as possible. When students create their first draft for an assignment, PeerStudio shows them a minimal, instructor-provided starter template that students can modify or overwrite (Figure 2). Using a template provides a natural hint for when to seek feedback—when the template is filled out. It also provides structure to students that need it, without constraining those who don't. To keep students focused on the most important aspects of their work, students always see the instructor-provided assignment rubric in the drafting interface (Figure 2, left). Rubrics in PeerStudio comprise a number of criteria for quality along multiple dimensions.

Students can seek feedback on their current draft at any time. They can focus their reviewers' attention by leaving a note about the kind of feedback they want. When students submit their draft, PeerStudio starts finding peer reviewers. Simultaneously, it invites the student to review others' work.

Reviewing peer work

PeerStudio uses the temporal overlap between students to provide fast feedback. When a student submits their draft, PeerStudio asks them to review their peers' submissions in order to unlock their own feedback [4]. Since their own work remains strongly activated, reviewing peer work immediately encourages students to reflect [27].

Students need to review two drafts before they see feedback on their work. Reviewing is double blind. Reviewers see their peer's work, student's review request notes, the instructor-created feedback rubric, and an example of excellent work to compare against. Reviewers' primary task is to work their way down the feedback rubric, answering each question. Rubric items are all yes/no or scale responses. Each group of rubric items also contains a free-text comment box, and reviewers are encouraged to write textual comments. To help reviewers write useful comments, PeerStudio prompts them with dynamically generated suggestions.

Reading reviews and revising

PeerStudio encourages rapid revision by notifying students via email immediately after a classmate reviews their work. To enable feedback comparison, PeerStudio displays the number of reviewers agreeing on each rubric question, as well as reviewers' comments. Recall that to emphasize iterative improvement, PeerStudio does not display grades, except for final work.

After students read reviews, PeerStudio invites them to revise their draft. Since reflection and goal setting are an important part of deliberate practice, PeerStudio asks students to first explicitly write down what they learned from their reviews and what they plan to do next.

PeerStudio also uses peer assessment for final grading. Students can revise their draft any number of times before they submit a final version to be graded. The final reviewing process for graded submissions is identical to early drafts, and reviewers see the same rubric items. For the final draft, PeerStudio calculates a grade as a weighted sum of rubric items from reviews for that draft.

PeerStudio integrates with MOOC platforms through LTI, which allows students to login using MOOC credentials, and automatically returns grades to class management software. It can be also used as a stand-alone tool.

PEERSTUDIO DESIGN

PeerStudio's feedback design relies on rubrics, textual comments, and the ability to recruit reviewers quickly. We outline the design of each.

Rubrics

Rubrics effectively provide students feedback on the current state of their work for many open-ended assignments, such as writing [2,3], design [25], and art [29]. Rubrics comprise multiple dimensions, with cells describing increasing quality along each. For each dimension, reviewers select the cell that most closely describes the submission; in between values and gradations within cells are often possible. Comparing and matching descriptions encourages raters to build a mental model of each dimension that makes rating faster and cognitively more efficient [15].

When rubric cell descriptions are complex, novice raters can develop mental models that stray significantly from the rubric standard, even if it is shown prominently [24]. To mitigate the challenges of multi-attribute matching, PeerStudio asks instructors to list multiple distinct criteria of quality along each dimension (Figure 4). Raters then explicitly choose which criteria are present. Criteria can be binary *e.g.*, "did the student choose a relevant quote that logically supports their opinion?" or scales, *e.g.*, "How many people did the student interview?"

Our initial experiments and prior work suggest that given a set of criteria, raters satisfice by marking some but not all matching criteria [22]. To address this, PeerStudio displays binary questions as dichotomous choices, so students must choose either yes/no (Figure 4); and ensures that students answer scale questions by explicitly setting a value.

To calculate final grades, PeerStudio awards credit to yes/no criteria if a majority of reviewers marked it as present. To reduce the effect of outlying ratings, scale questions are given the median score of reviewers. The total assignment grade is the sum of grades across all rubric questions.

Scaffolding comments

Rubrics help students understand the current quality of their work; free-text comments from peers help them improve it. Reviews with accurate rubric scores, but without comments may provide students too little information.

To scaffold reviewers, PeerStudio shows short tips for writing comments just below the comment box. For instance, if the comment merely praises the submission and has no constructive feedback, it may remind students "Quick check: Is your feedback actionable? Are you expressing yourself succinctly?" Or it may ask reviewers to "Say more…" when they write "great job!"

To generate such feedback, PeerStudio compiles a list of relevant words from the student draft and the assignment description. For example, for a critique on a research paper, words like "contribution", "argument", "author" are relevant. PeerStudio then counts the number of relevant words a comment contains. Using this count, and the comment's total length, it suggests improvements. This simple heuristic catches a large number of low-quality comments. Similar systems have been used to judge the quality of product reviews online [19].

PeerStudio also helps students provide feedback that's most relevant to the current state of the draft, by internally calculating the reviewer's score for the submission. For a low-quality draft, it asks the reviewer, "What's the first thing you'd suggest to get started?" For middling drafts, reviewers are asked, "This looks mostly good, except for [question with a low score]. What do you suggest they try?" Together, these commenting guides result in reviewers leaving substantive comments.

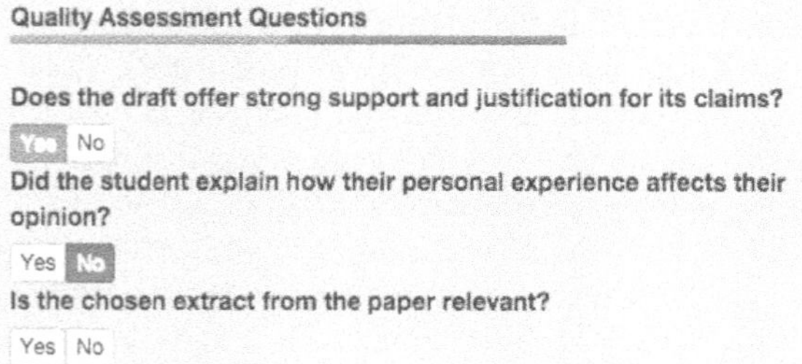

Figure 4: Example dichotomous questions in PeerStudio. The last question is not yet answered. Students must choose yes/no before they can submit the review.

Recruiting reviewers

Because students review immediately after submitting, reviewers are found quickly when there are many students submitting one after another, *e.g.*, in a popular time zone. However, students who submit at an unpopular time still need feedback quickly.

When enough reviewers are not online, PeerStudio progressively emails and enlists help from more and more students who have yet to complete their required two reviews, and enthusiastic students who have reviewed even before submitting a draft. PeerStudio emails a random selection of five such students every half hour, making sure the same student is not picked twice in a 24-hour period. PeerStudio stops emailing students when all submissions have at least one review. This enables students to quickly receive feedback from one reviewer and begin revising.

To decide which submissions to show reviewers, PeerStudio uses a priority queue. This queue prioritizes student submissions by the number of reviews (submissions with the fewest, or no, reviews have highest priority), and by the time the submission has been in the review queue. The latest submissions have the highest priority. PeerStudio seeks two reviewers per draft.

FIELD DEPLOYMENT: IN-PERSON AND AT SCALE

This paper describes PeerStudio deployments in two open online classes: *Learning How to Learn* (603 students submitting assignments), *Medical Education in the New Millennium* (103 students) on the Coursera and OpenEdX platforms respectively. We also describe deployments in two in-person classes: a senior-level class at the University of Illinois at Urbana-Champaign on *Social Visualization* (125 students), and a graduate-level class in education at Stanford University, on *Technology for Learners* (51 students).

All four classes used PeerStudio for open-ended writing assignments. In *Learning how to Learn*, for their first

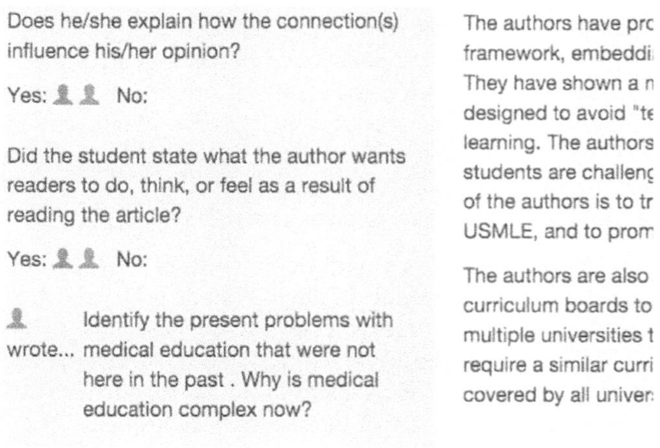

Figure 3: Students see reviews in the context of their draft (right, clipped). PeerStudio displays the number of reviewers (two here) agreeing on each rubric question and comments from each.

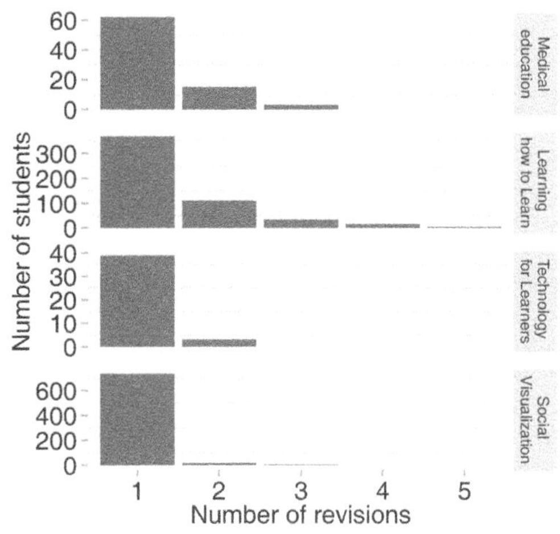

Figure 5: Most students created a single revision. Students in MOOCs revised more than students in in-person classes.

assignment students wrote an essay about a learning goal and how they planned to accomplish it using what they learned in class (*e.g.*, one student wrote about being "an older student in Northern Virginia retooling for a career in GIS after being laid off"). In the second assignment, they created a portfolio, blog or website to explain what they learned to others (*e.g.*, one wrote: "I am a professor of English as a Second Language at a community college. I have created a PowerPoint presentation for my colleagues [about spaced repetition and frequent testing]").

The Social Visualization and Medical Education classes asked students to critique research papers in the area. In Social Visualization, students also used PeerStudio for an open-ended design project on data visualization (*e.g.*, one student team designed a visualization system that used data from Twitter to show crisis needs around the US). Finally, the Technology for Learners class used PeerStudio as a way to critique a learning tool (*e.g.*, ClassDojo, a classroom discipline tool). This class requested its reviewers to sign reviews, so students could follow-up with each other for lingering questions.

Deployment observations

Throughout these deployments, we read students' drafts, feedback, and revisions. We regularly surveyed students about their experiences, and spoke to instructors about their perspectives. Several themes emerged.

Students requested feedback on full rough drafts

Rather than submit sections of drafts, students submitted full rough drafts. Drafts were often missing details (*e.g.*, lacking examples). In the Medical Education critique, one question was "did you find yourself mostly agreeing or mostly disagreeing with the content of the research paper? Why?" In initial drafts, students often pointed out only one area of disagreement, later drafts added the rest. Other drafts were poorly explained (*e.g.*, lacking justification for claims) or too rambling.

Students typically asked for four kinds of feedback: 1) On a specific aspect of their work, *e.g.*, "I guess I need help with my writing, vocabulary and grammar, since I'm not an English native-speaker"; 2) On a specific component of the assignment: *e.g.*, "Can you let me know if part 4 and 5 make sense—I feel like I am trying to say too much all in one go!" 3) As a final check before they turned in their work: *e.g.*, "This draft is actually a 'release candidate'. I would like to know if I addressed the points or if I missed something." 4) As a way to connect with classmates: *e.g.*, "I just want to hear about your opinions :)".

When students revised their draft, we asked, "Overall, did you get useful feedback on your draft?" as a binary question—80% answered 'yes'.

Students revise rarely, especially in in-person classes

Most students did not create multiple drafts (Figure 5). Students in the two MOOCs were more likely to revise than students in in-person classes ($t(1404) = 12.84$, $p < 0.001$). Overall, 30.1% of online students created multiple revisions, but only 7% of those in in-person classes did.

When we asked TAs in the in-person classes why so few students revised, they told us they did not emphasize this feature of PeerStudio in class. Furthermore, student responses in surveys indicated that many felt their schedule was too busy to revise. One wrote it was unfair to "expect us to read some forty page essays, then write the critiques and then review two other people, and then make changes on our work... twice a week." These comments underscore that merely creating software systems for iterative feedback is not enough—an iterative approach must be reflected in the pedagogy as well.

Students see comments as more useful than rubric feedback

Students could optionally rate reviews after reading them and leave comments to staff. Students rated 758 of 3,963 reviews. We looked at a random subset of 50 such comments. In their responses, students wrote that freeform comments were useful (21 responses) more often than rubric-based feedback (5 responses). Students also disagreed more with reviewers' comments (7 responses) than with their reviewers' marked rubric (3 responses). This is possibly because comments can capture useful interpretive feedback, but differences in interpretation lead to disagreement.

An undergraduate TA looked at a random subset of 150 student submissions, and rated reviewer comments on a 7-point Likert scale on how concretely they helped students revise. For example, here is a comment that was rated "very concrete (7)" on an essay about planning for learning goals:

"What do you mean by 'good schedule'? There's obviously more than one answer to that question, but the goal should be to really focus and narrow it down. Break a larger goal like "getting a good schedule" into concrete steps such as: 1) get eight hours of sleep, 2)...

We found 45% of comments were "somewhat concrete" (a rating of 5 on the scale) or better, and contained pointers to resources or specific suggestions on how to improve; the rest of the comments were praise or encouragement. Interestingly, using the same 7-point Likert scale, students rated reviews as concrete more often than the TA (55% of the time).

Students reported relying on comments for revising. For instance, the student who received the above comment wrote, "I somehow knew I wasn't being specific… The reviewer's ideas really helped there!" The lack of comments was lamented upon, "The reviewer did not comment any feedback, so I don't know what to do."

One exception to the general trend of comments being more important was students who submitted 'release candidate' drafts for a final check. Such students relied heavily on rubric feedback: "I have corrected every item that needed attention to. I now have received all yes to each question. Thanks guys. :-)"

Comments encourage students to revise
The odds of students revising their drafts increase by 1.10 if they receive any reviews with free-form comments (z=4.6, $p < 0.001$). Since fewer than half the comments contained specific improvement suggestions, this suggests that, in addition to being informational, reviewer comments also play an important motivational role.

Revisions locally add information, improve understandability
We looked at the 100 reflections that students wrote while starting the revision to understand what changes they wanted to make. A majority of students (51%) intended to add information based on their comments, *e.g.*, "The math teacher [one of the reviewers] helped me look for other sources relating to how math can be fun and creative instead of it being dull!" A smaller number (16%) wanted to change how they had expressed ideas to make them easier to understand, *e.g.*, "I did not explain clearly the three first parts… I shall be clearer in my re-submission" and, "I do need to avoid repetition. Bullets are always good." Other changes included formatting, grammar, and occasionally wanting a fresh start. The large fraction of students who wanted to add information to drafts they previously thought were complete suggests that peer feedback helps students see flaws in their work, and provides new perspectives.

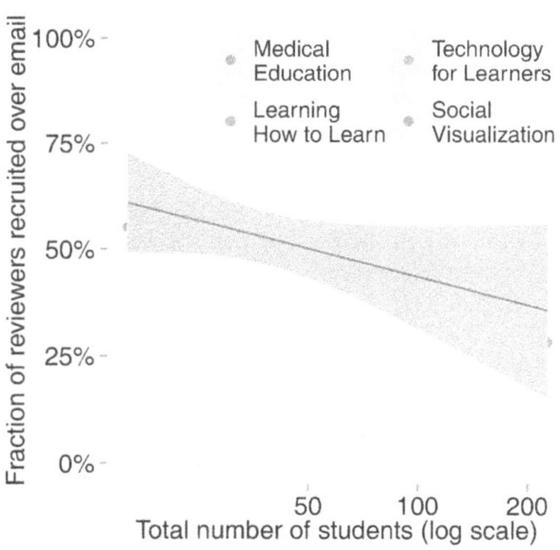

Figure 7: More students in large classes are likely to be online at the same time, so fewer reviewers were recruited by email.

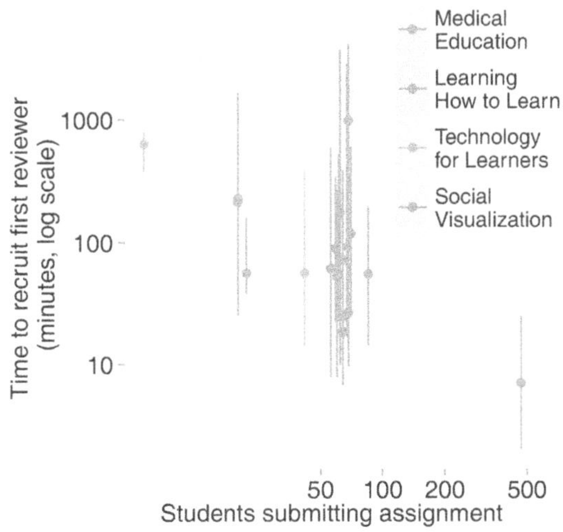

Figure 6: Reviewers are recruited faster in larger classes.

Most students reworked their drafts as planned: 44% of students made substantive changes based on feedback, 10% made substantive changes not based on the comments received, and the rest only changed spelling and formatting. Most students added information to or otherwise revised one section, while leaving the rest unchanged.

PeerStudio recruits reviewers rapidly
We looked at the PeerStudio logs to understand the platform's feedback latency. Reviewers were recruited rapidly for both in-person and online classes (see Figure 6), but the scale of online classes has a dramatic effect. With just 472 students using the system for the first assignment in Learning How to Learn, the median recruitment-time was 7 minutes and the 75th quartile was 24 minutes.

Few students have long wait times
PeerStudio uses a priority queue to seek reviews; it prioritizes newer submissions given two submissions with the same number of reviews. This reduces the wait time for the *average* student, but unlucky students have to wait longer (e.g. when they submit just before a popular time, and others keep submitting newer drafts). Still, significant delays are rare: 4.4% had no reviews in the first 8 hours; 1.8% had no reviews in 24 hours. To help students revise, staff reviewed submissions with no reviews after 24 hours.

Feedback latency is consistent even early in the assignment
Even though fewer students use the website farther from the deadline, peer review means that the workload and review labor automatically scale together. We found no statistical

difference in recruitment time (t(1191) = 0.52, p = 0.6) between the first two and last two days of the assignment, perhaps because PeerStudio uses email to recruit reviewers.

Fewer reviewers recruited over email with larger class size.
PeerStudio emails students to recruit reviewers only when enough students aren't already on the website. In the smallest class with 46 students submitting, 21% of reviews came from Web solicitation and 79% of reviews were written in response to an emailed request. In the largest, with 472 students submitting, 72% of reviews came from Web solicitation and only 28% from email (Figure 7). Overall, students responded to email requests approximately 17% of the time, independent of class size.

These results suggest that PeerStudio achieves quick reviewing in small, in-person classes by actively bringing students online via email, and that this becomes less important with increasing class size, as students have a naturally overlapping presence on site.

Reviewers spend about ten minutes per draft
PeerStudio records the time between when reviewers start a review and when they submit it. In all classes except the graduate level Technology for Learners, students spent around 10 minutes reviewing each draft (Figure 9). The median reviewer in the graduate Technology for Learners class spent 22 minutes per draft. Because all students in that class started reviewing in-class but finished later, its variance in reviewing times is also much larger.

Are reviewers accurate?
There is very strong agreement between individual raters while using the rubric. In online classes, the median pairwise agreement between reviewers on a rubric question is 74%, while for in-person classes it is 93%. However, because most drafts completed a majority of the rubric items successfully, baseline agreement is high, so Fleiss' κ is low. The median κ=0.19 for in-person classes, and 0.33 for online classes, conventionally considered "Fair agreement". In in-person classes, on average staff and students agreed on rubric questions 96% of the time.

Staff and peers write comments of similar length
Both in-person and online, the median comment was 30 words long (Figure 8). This length compares well with staff comments in the *Social Visualization* class, which had a median of 35 words. Most reviews (88%) had at least some textual comments, in addition to rubric-based feedback.

Students trade-off reviewing and revising
23% of students reviewed more than the required two drafts. Survey results indicated that many such students used reviewing as an inexpensive way to make progress on their own draft. One student wrote that in comparison to revising their own work, "being able to see what others have written by reviewing their work is a better way to get feedback." Other students reviewed peers simply because they found their work interesting. When told she had reviewed 29 more drafts than required, one student wrote, "I wouldn't have suspected that. I kept reading and reviewing because people's stories are so interesting."

Students appreciate reading others' work more than early feedback and revision
A post-class survey in *Technology For Learners* asked students what they liked most about PeerStudio (30 responses). Students most commonly mentioned (in 13 responses) interface elements such as being able to see examples and rubrics. Reading each other's work was also popular (8 responses), but the ability to revise was rarely mentioned (3 responses). This is not surprising, since few students revised work in in-person classes.

Apart from specific usability concerns, students' most frequent complaint was that PeerStudio sent them too much

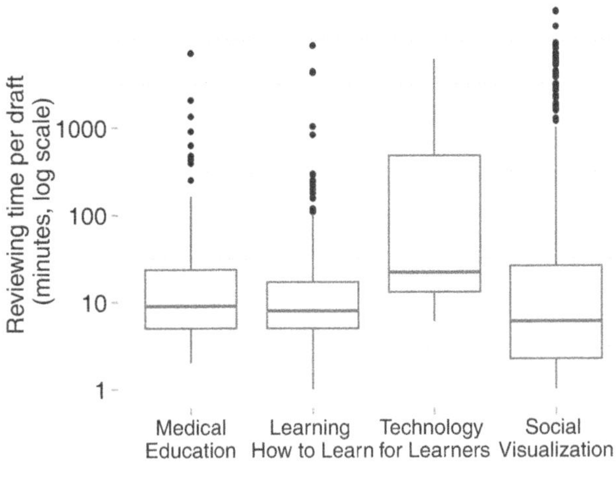

Figure 9: Reviewers spend roughly 10 minutes reviewing each draft. The graduate-level Technology for Learners class spends longer. (The larger variation is because students start reviewing in class, and finish later.)

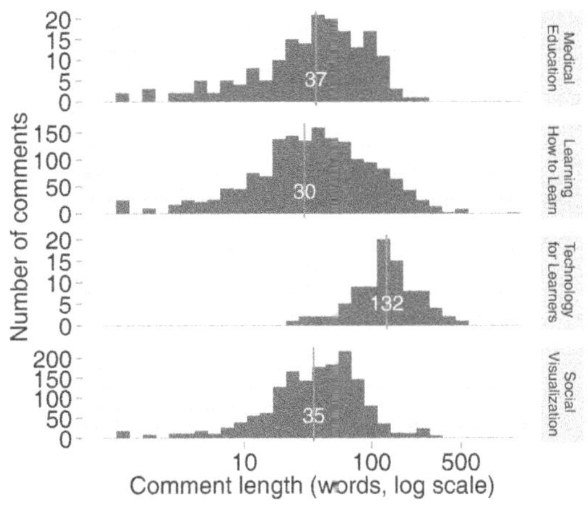

Figure 8: Students write substantive comments, both in-person and online. The graduate level Technology for Learners has longer comments, possibly because reviews were signed.

email. One wrote, "My understanding was that students would receive about three, but over the last few days, I've gotten more." Currently, PeerStudio limits how frequently it emails students; future work could also limit the total number of emails a student receives.

FIELD EXPERIMENT: DOES FAST FEEDBACK ON IN-PROGRESS WORK IMPROVE FINAL WORK?

The prior study demonstrated how students solicited feedback and revised work, and how quickly they can obtain feedback. Next, we describe a field experiment that asks two research questions: First, does feedback on in-progress work improve student performance? Second, does the speed of feedback matter? Do students perform better if they receive rapid feedback? We conducted this controlled experiment in *ANES 204: Medical Education in the New Millennium*, a MOOC on the OpenEdX platform.

Students in this class had working experience in healthcare professions, such as medical residents, nurses and doctors. In the open-ended assignment, students read and critiqued a recent research paper based on their experience in the healthcare field. For example, one critique prompt was "As you read, did you find yourself mostly agreeing or mostly disagreeing with the content? Write about three points from the article that justify your support or dissent." The class used PeerStudio to provide students both in-progress feedback and final grades.

Method

A between-subjects manipulation randomly assigned students to one of three conditions. In the *No Early Feedback* condition, students could only submit one final draft of their critique. This condition generally mimics the status quo in many classes, where students have no opportunities to revise drafts with feedback. In the *Slow Feedback* condition, students could submit any number of in-progress drafts, in addition to their final draft. Students received peer feedback on all drafts, but this feedback wasn't available until 24 hours after submission. Additionally, students were only emailed about their feedback at that time. This condition mimics a scenario where a class offers students the chance to revise, but is limited in its turnaround time due to limited staff time or office hours. Finally, in the *Fast Feedback* condition, students could submit drafts as in the slow feedback condition, but were shown reviews as soon as available, mirroring the standard PeerStudio setup.

Students in all conditions rated their peers' work anonymously; reviewers saw drafts from all conditions and rated them blind to condition. Our server introduced all delays for the Slow Feedback condition after submission. Rubrics and the interface students used for reviewing and editing were identical across conditions.

Measures

To measure performance, we used the grade on the final assignment submission as calculated by PeerStudio. Since rubrics only used dichotomous questions, each rubric question was given credit if a majority of raters marked "yes". The grade of each draft was the sum of credit across all rubric questions for that draft.

Participants

In all, 104 students participated. Of these, three students only submitted a blank essay; their results were discarded from analysis. To analyze results, we built an ordinary-least-squares regression model with the experimental condition as the predictor variable, using *No Early Feedback* as the baseline (R^2=0.02).

Manipulation check

While PeerStudio can provide students feedback quickly, this feedback is only useful if students actually read it. Therefore, we recorded the time students first read their feedback. The median participant in the *Fast Feedback* condition read their reviews 592 minutes (9.8 hours) after submission; the median for the Slow Feedback condition was 1528 minutes (26.6 hours). This suggests that the manipulation effectively delayed feedback, but the difference between conditions was more modest than planned.

Results: fast early feedback improves final grades

Students in the *Fast Feedback* condition did significantly better than those in *No Early Feedback* condition ($t(98)=2.1$, $p<0.05$). On average, students scored higher by 4.4% of the assignment's total grade: i.e., enough to boost a score from a B+ to an A-.

Slow early feedback yields no significant improvement

Surprisingly, we found that students in the *Slow Feedback* condition did not do significantly better than those in the *No Early Feedback* condition ($t(98)=1.07$, $p=0.28$). These results suggest that for early feedback to improve student performance, it must be delivered quickly.

Because of the limited sample size, it is also possible this experiment was unable to detect the (smaller) benefits of delayed early feedback.

Students with fast feedback don't revise more often

There was no significant difference between the number of revisions students created in the *Fast* and *Slow feedback* conditions ($t(77)=0.2$, $p=0.83$): students created on average 1.33 drafts; only 22% of students created multiple revisions. On average, they added 83 words to their revision, and there was no significant difference in the quantity of words changed between conditions ($t(23)=1.04$, $p=0.30$).

However, students with *Fast feedback* referred to their reviews marginally more frequently when they entered reflections and planned changes in revision ($\chi^2(1)=2.92$, $p=0.08$). This is consistent with prior findings that speed improves performance by making feedback more salient.

Even with only a small number of students revising, the overall benefits of early feedback seem sizeable. Future work that better encourages students to revise may further increase these benefits.

DISCUSSION

The field deployment and subsequent experiment demonstrate the value of helping students revise work with fast feedback. Even with a small fraction of students creating multiple revisions, the benefits of fast feedback are apparent. How could we design pedagogy to amplify these benefits?

Redesigning pedagogy to support revision and mastery

In-person classes are already using PeerStudio to change their pedagogy. These classes did not use PeerStudio as a way to reduce grading burden: both classes still had TAs grade every submission. Instead, they used PeerStudio to expose students to each other's work and to provide them feedback faster than staff could manage.

Fully exploiting this opportunity will require changes. Teachers will need to teach students about when and how to seek feedback. Currently, PeerStudio encourages students to fill out the starter template before they seek feedback. For some domains, it may be better to get feedback using an outline or sketch, so reviewers aren't distracted by superficial details [28]. In domains like design, it might be useful to get feedback on multiple alternative designs [10]. PeerStudio might explicitly allow these different kinds of submissions.

PeerStudio reduces the time to get feedback, but students still need time to work on revisions. Assignments must factor this revision time into their schedule. We find it heartening that 7% of in-person students actually revised their drafts, even when their assignment schedules were not designed to allow it. That 30% of online students revised assignments may partly be because schedules were designed around the assumption that learners with full-time jobs have limited time: consequently, online schedules often provide more time between assignment deadlines.

Finally, current practice rewards students for the final quality of their work. PeerStudio's revision process may allow other reward schemes. For instance, in domains like design where rapid iteration is prized [7,11], classes may reward students for sustained improvement.

Plagiarism

Plagiarism is a potential risk of sharing in-progress work. While plagiarism is a concern with all peer assessment, it is especially important in PeerStudio because the system shares work before assignments are due. In classes that have used PeerStudio so far, we found one instance of plagiarism: a student reviewed another's essay and then submitted it as their own. While PeerStudio does not detect plagiarism currently, it does record what work a student reviewed, as well as every revision. This record can help instructors check that the work has a supporting paper trail. Future work could automate this.

Another risk is that student reviewers may attempt to fool PeerStudio by giving the same feedback to every assignment they review (to get past the reviewing hurdle quickly so they can see feedback on their work). We observed three such instances. However, 'shortcut reviewing' is often easy to catch with techniques such as inter-rater agreement scores [20].

Bridging the in-person and at-scale worlds

While it was designed for massive classes, PeerStudio "scales down" and brings affordances such as fast feedback to smaller in-person classes. PeerStudio primarily relies on the natural overlap between student schedules at larger scales, but this overlap still exists at smaller scale and can be augmented via email recruitment.

PeerStudio also demonstrates the benefits of experimenting in different settings in parallel. Large-scale between-subjects experiments often work better online than in-person because in-person, students are more likely to contaminate manipulations by communicating outside the system. In contrast, in-person experiments can often be run earlier in software development using lower-fidelity approaches and/or greater support. Also, it can be easier to gather rich qualitative and observational data in person, or modify pilot protocols on the fly. Finally, consonant results in in-person and online deployments lend more support for the fundamentals of the manipulation (as opposed to an accidental artifact of a deployment).

Future work

Some instructors we spoke to worried about the overhead that peer assessment entails (and chose not to use PeerStudio for this reason). If reviewers spend about 10 minutes reviewing work as in our deployment, peer assessment arguably incurs a 20-minute overhead per revision. On the other hand, student survey responses indicate that they found looking at other students' work to be the most valuable part of the assessment process. Future work could quantify the benefits of assessing peer work, including inspiration, and how it affects student revisions. Future work could also reduce the reviewing burden by using early reviewer agreement to hide some rubric items from later reviewers [24].

Matching reviewers and drafts

PeerStudio enables students to receive feedback from peers at any time, but their peers may be far earlier or more advanced in their completion of the assignment. Instead, it may be helpful to have drafts reviewed by students who are similarly advanced or just starting. Furthermore, students learn best from examples (peer work) if they are approachable in quality. In future work, the system could ask or learn the rough state of the assignment, and recruit reviewers who are similar.

CONCLUSION

This paper suggests that the scale of massive online classes enables systems that drastically and reliably reduce the time to obtain feedback and creates a path to iteration, mastery and expertise. These advantages can also be scaled-down to in-person classrooms. In contrast to today's learn-and-submit model of online education, we believe that the continuous presence of peers holds the promise of a far more dynamic and iterative learning process.

ACKNOWLEDGMENTS

We are grateful to Courtney Noh for contributing to software development; Coursera and OpenEdX for platform integration and encouraging instructors to try PeerStudio; instructors of MOOCs who use PeerStudio in their classes; and the many students who taught and learned with their peers and shared their stories with us. This research was funded in part through NSF grants #1351131 and #1444865, the Hasso Plattner Design Thinking Program, and the Siebel Scholars Program. This research was conducted under Stanford IRB protocol #30324.

REFERENCES

1. Anderson, S. and Rodin, J. Is Bad News Always Bad?: Cue and Feedback Effects on Intrinsic Motivation. *Journal of Applied Social Psychology 19*, 6 (1989), 449–467.
2. Andrade, H.G. The Effects of Instructional Rubrics on Learning to Write. *Current Issues in Education 4*, 4 (2001).
3. Andrade, H.G. Teaching with rubrics: The good, the bad, and the ugly. *College Teaching 53*, 1 (2005), 27–31.
4. André, P., Bernstein, M., and Luther, K. Who gives a tweet? *Proceedings of the ACM 2012 conference on Computer Supported Cooperative Work - CSCW '12*, ACM Press (2012), 471.
5. Balcazar, F.E., Hopkins, B.L., and Suarez, Y. A critical, objective review of performance feedback. *Journal of Organizational Behavior Management 7*, 2 (1986).
6. Brooks, M., Basu, S., Jacobs, C., and Vanderwende, L. Divide and Correct: Using Clusters to Grade Short Answers at Scale. *Learning at Scale*, (2014).
7. Buxton, B. *Sketching user experiences: getting the design right and the right design.* Morgan Kaufmann, 2007.
8. Carlson, P.A. and Berry, F.C. Calibrated Peer Review and assessing learning outcomes. *Frontiers in Education Conference*, (2003).
9. Dawes, R.M. The robust beauty of improper linear models in decision making. *American psychologist 34*, 7 (1979), 571.
10. Dow, S., Fortuna, J., Schwartz, D., Altringer, B., and Klemmer, S. Prototyping dynamics: sharing multiple designs improves exploration, group rapport, and results. *Proceedings of the 2011 annual conference on Human factors in computing systems*, (2011), 2807–2816.
11. Dow, S.P., Heddleston, K., and Klemmer, S.R. The efficacy of prototyping under time constraints. *Proceeding of the ACM conference on Creativity and cognition*, ACM Press (2009), 165.
12. Ericsson, K.A., Krampe, R.T., and Tesch-Römer, C. The role of deliberate practice in the acquisition of expert performance. *Psychological review 100*, 3 (1993).
13. Falchikov, N. and Goldfinch, J. Student peer assessment in higher education: A meta-analysis comparing peer and teacher marks. *Review of educational research 70*, 3 (2000), 287–322.
14. Fast, E., Lee, C., Aiken, A., Bernstein, M.S., Koller, D., and Smith, E. Crowd-scale interactive formal reasoning and analytics. *Proceedings of the 26th annual ACM symposium on User interface software and technology*, (2013).
15. Gray, W.D. and Boehm-Davis, D.A. Milliseconds matter: an introduction to microstrategies and to their use in describing and predicting interactive behavior. *Journal of experimental psychology. Applied 6*, 4 (2000), 322–35.
16. Guskey, T.R. Closing Achievement Gaps: Revisiting Benjamin S. Bloom's "Learning for Mastery." *Journal of Advanced Academics 19*, 1 (2007), 8–31.
17. Hattie, J. and Timperley, H. The Power of Feedback. *Review of Educational Research 77*, 1 (2007), 81–112.
18. Heffernan, N., Heffernan, C., Dietz, K., Soffer, D., Pellegrino, J. W. Goldman, S.R., and Dailey, M. Improving Mathematical Learning Outcomes Through Automatic Reassessment and Relearning. *AERA*, (2012).
19. Kim, S.-M., Pantel, P., Chklovski, T., and Pennacchiotti, M. Automatically assessing review helpfulness. *Proceedings of the 2006 Conference on Empirical Methods in Natural Language Processing*, Association for Computational Linguistics (2006), 423–430.
20. Kittur, A., Chi, E.H., and Suh, B. Crowdsourcing user studies with Mechanical Turk. *Proc. of CHI*, ACM Press (2008), 453.
21. Kluger, A.N. and DeNisi, A. The effects of feedback interventions on performance: A historical review, a meta-analysis, and a preliminary feedback intervention theory. *Psychological Bulletin 119*, 2 (1996), 254–284.
22. Krosnick, J.A. Survey research. *Annual review of psychology 50*, 1 (1999), 537–567.
23. Kulik, J.A. and Kulik, C.-L.C. Timing of Feedback and Verbal Learning. *Review of Educational Research 58*, 1 (1987), 79–97.
24. Kulkarni, C., Socher, R., Bernstein, M.S., and Klemmer, S.R. Scaling Short-answer Grading by Combining Peer Assessment with Algorithmic Scoring. *ACM Conf on Learning@Scale*, (2014).
25. Kulkarni, C., Wei, K.P., Le, H., Chia, D., Papadopoulos, K., Cheng, J., Koller, D., and Klemmer, S.R. Peer and self assessment in massive online classes. *ACM Transactions on Computer-Human Interaction (TOCHI) 20*, 6 (2013), 33.
26. Latham, G.P. and Locke, E.A. Self-regulation through goal setting. *Organizational Behavior and Human Decision Processes 50*, 2 (1991), 212–247.
27. Marsh, R.L., Landau, J.D., and Hicks, J.L. How examples may (and may not) constrain creativity. *Memory & cognition 24*, 5 (1996), 669–80.
28. Sommers, N. Responding to Student Writing. *College Composition and Communication 33*, 2 (1982), 148–156.
29. Tinapple, D., Olson, L., and Sadauskas, J. CritViz: Web-Based Software Supporting Peer Critique in Large Creative Classrooms. *Bulletin of the IEEE Technical Committee on Learning Technology 15*, 1 (2013), 29.

Alumni & Tenured Participants in MOOCs: Analysis of Two Years of MOOC Discussion Channel Activity

Matti Nelimarkka
Helsinki Institute for Information Technology
Aalto University
Department of Computer Science
University of Helsinki
PO Box 15600, 00076 Aalto University
Espoo, Finland
matti.nelimarkka@hiit.fi

Arto Vihavainen
Department of Computer Science
University of Helsinki
PO Box 68, 00014 University of Helsinki
Helsinki, Finland
arto.vihavainen@cs.helsinki.fi

ABSTRACT
This study investigates chat room data from a massive open online course (MOOC) that has been organized several times since January 2012. What makes the organization unique is that the chat room has always remained the same, allowing past participants to mingle with the new course takers. Participants who have previously attended the course have started to support the novices, voluntarily taking the role of mentors, while at the same time also learning themselves. Two and a half years of chat logs and interviews show that it is possible that a community consisting of previous and current participants emerges naturally. Furthermore, there are plenty of students that unconditionally help others, even when they themselves no longer attend the course. Our observations suggest that communities of practice emerge naturally around the chat rooms of MOOCs.

ACM Classification Keywords
H.5.3 Group and Organization Interfaces: Computer-supported cooperative work; K.3.1 Computer Uses in Education: Collaborative learning

General Terms
Human Factors

Author Keywords
MOOC-alumni; tenured MOOC participant; massive open online course; community of practice; Internet Relay Chat; online community

INTRODUCTION
Social interaction and its use in supporting learning in massive online open courses (MOOCs) has received plenty of attention lately. Researchers have explored novel methods and tools to support group interaction [3, 15, 6, 5]. Social interaction research includes works that study both online [8] and offline [4] behavior. From a pedagogical perspective, social interaction has been linked to connectivist, constructivist and peer-learning approaches, which argue that knowledge is created through interaction with others [7]. These studies have stressed social interaction as an important part of any learning process. Building the community and interaction between learners takes time.

Currently contemporary MOOCs that have been organized multiple times are reset at the end of each course iteration. This makes it easier for course organizers to handle a somewhat linear course, as many of the questions in e.g. online forums are related to course assignments that typically appear in a specific order. Instructors may also choose to re-post questions from previous course instances to stimulate discussion [16]. On the other hand, having each course iteration start from a clean state effectively discourages past participants from continuing to participate in the discussions, as they may even need to re-enroll to the course.

Our viewpoint in this article is that there is plenty of benefit in encouraging students to remain participants in future courses, as they have experience that newcomers can draw upon. In this work we argue that having a community that is not reset whenever a new course iteration starts is beneficial both for the current and past members of the course.

We examine a setting where the online discussion channel of a course has been open for participants from all course iterations since January 2012. We examine how students that have chosen to remain as a part of the community after completing the course – the *alumni participants* – experience the opportunity. We acknowledge also the existence of *tenured participants* who have not completed the course, but choose to remain as a part in the discussions anyway. As both of these members are typically active, we investigate also their contributions towards the course and other participants.

This article is organized as follows. First, we outline the relevant streams of research on social interaction and learning, as well as technology-enhanced social interaction. Then, we contextualize the course under study, its existing practices, after which the data and analysis methods are discussed. Then, we provide our results and observations, and discuss the implications of our findings.

L@S 2015, March 14–18, 2015, Vancouver, BC, Canada.

ACM 978-1-4503-3411-2/15/03...$15.00
http://dx.doi.org/10.1145/2724660.2724671

RELATED WORK

Communities, learning and MOOCs

In the 1980s, social and community aspects of learning gained attention. Lave [14] argued that learning takes place in social environments and that the learners socialize themselves as part of this social environment, and learn the practices of the existing members of the social group. Wenger uses the term *communities of practice* to describe this phenomenon [26], and argues that these communities emerge around the topics that the participants experience as important. Furthermore, Wenger argues that these communities are mostly self-organizing systems where participants apply their previous skills to help others and to learn new skills. Lave continues this line of thought with her argument: "newcomers and old timers depend on each others: newcomers in order to learn, and old timers in order to carry on the community of practice" [14].

One aspect of communities of practice is tutoring and supporting other members in their learning. In formal education these practices can be used to increase the availability of assistance in exercise sessions as well as to give course alumni an opportunity to maintain a role as supporting staff and further educate themselves within the course topic (see e.g. [23, 24]). As suggested by Vikberg et al [24], a majority of these supporting TAs expect that helping other students will also increases their own skills. Even when the development of such a community is institutionally supported, it has characteristics of a community of practice.

The overall idea of communities and sharing practices is not novel in e-learning environments; for example Gray [10] and Hara [11] describe how communities are used in informal learning contexts, such as workplaces. Formal learning contexts have also noted the communicative function of learning. In her provocative article, Bruckman [2] argues that "[t]he Internet has unique affordances to support the creation of new communities of learners. Its power lies not in delivering content, but in creating a context for mutually supportive communities of learners to form". To create these communities, Bruckman proposes that learning environments must extend their reach beyond peers and teachers towards more general populations. MOOCs provide such opportunities, but for the community to emerge, the technology must support the interaction. Next, we examine technology-enhanced interaction.

Online communication for learning

Many of the currently used online course platforms provide forum functionality that allows participants to communicate: asking questions, answering them and discussing the course (e.g. [1, 8, 12]). While these online forums are asynchronous, synchronous participation can be facilitated through the use of chats. For example, Spencer & Hilz [21] introduced guided chat sessions to various course sections, including sections that were taken remotely as well as sections with face-to-face time with an instructor. Their study suggests that participants in the remote sections found the chats less useful than the participants that also had face-to-face time and the ability to continue these discussions through chats.

Recently researchers have examined how to facilitate online communication towards learning. There is research on gamification of social interaction, such as the use of reputation mechanics or badges [1, 6]. Furthermore, real-time communication may be used to improve interaction, and even to bring back some pedagogical approaches that are used in traditional classrooms, like co-operative learning where students explain their argumentation to other students [5, 15].

While research has examined these communication systems, their benefits to students are not clear. Goetzee et al's [5] study observed no improvement in course grades. Even the results on the sense of community are mixed: Gillani et al's [8] study on interaction patterns suggests that forum participants did not create a community, rather their participation was chaotic and segregated based on the participants' previous skills. However, Huang et al. [12] suggest that the active participants significantly contribute by sharing their knowledge. We view this as an indicator of interest towards the other participants, and therefore the community.

As we argue that the chosen technology plays a role in the outcomes of the participation, it is significant to understand the background of the communication tool that was used in the course in this study, Internet Relay Chat (IRC). IRC is a real-time discussion system that is used around the world, and is a textual form of computer-mediated communication where participants are identified by an alias. Chat rooms are accessed with a client application, available both as browser- and desktop-versions. The use of IRC has been studied for a few decades. To name a few examples, computer-mediated communication scholars have studied discursive mechanics, such as addressability, that supports the creation of a face-to-face -like discussion environment [27]. Also the norms and culture within IRC chat rooms [19], as well as the formation of social networks [17] have been studied.

IRC has also been used for education purposes, both to enhance communication in traditional classrooms with physically co-located lectures or other events [28] and to facilitate discussion in distance education [21]. From the MOOC perspective, especially the former case is interesting: in co-located use IRC is a supplementary channel of communication, while in distance education, it can be the primary channel of communication.

In this work we study the logs of an IRC chat room of a MOOC in programming. At the time of the study, the log covers a timespan of two and a half years, and contains the chat interactions of course participants over a number of course iterations. We specifically explore the development and change of social roles, as mediated by these discussions, and examine the social and educational uses of these chats. We observe that students stay part of the community longer than one semester as tenured or alumni participants and share insights on their contributions and experiences.

CONTEXT

The data comes from a set of Finnish introductory programming MOOCs organized by the University of Helsinki. The duration of one course is 14 weeks, and the content of the course aligns with typical CS1 courses organized around the world. During the period studied in this work, the course has been organized seven times. During each spring semester, it is offered as a paced version with deadlines, while during the rest of each year, the course is offered without deadlines once in the summer and once in the fall. Since the beginning of 2012, some 4000 students have participated in the course (calculated based on the number of students that have completed programming assignments).

The course material is offered as a blended textbook consisting of theory texts, assignments and interspersed video tutorials. The majority of the effort that the students invest into the course is spent on programming assignments that are worked within an integrated development environment that provides automatic assessment and scaffolding (details in [22]).

Peer-support is provided in an IRC chat room; the students are informed about the existence of the chat room both on a main course page, as well as within the course material. Materials also include guidance on how to join the chat room and how to ask questions in an informative way. The chat room can be accessed both using a browser-client, which makes joining the chat room a one-click process, and a client of the students' choice, such as a desktop client or a client running on a mobile phone or in the cloud. Institutional support for other forms of communication, such as forums, have not been provided for this MOOC. A handful of faculty from the University of Helsinki have been present in the IRC channel, the number of them ranging from 1 to 4 in the data.

DATA AND METHODS

Log analysis

The chat room data is publicly available on the internet[1], and the data presented here was retrieved at the end of May 2014.

In the first stage, we use this data for participant detection and examining the temporal dynamics of the community. The data was preprocessed in two steps. First, participant detection was performed, after which IRC bots and disruptive events such as join floods (bots repeatedly joining and leaving the channel) were excluded. The participant detection was performed based on both usernames and hostnames. The process started with mapping join and leaving events to hostnames that the participants originated from. Then, sessions from the same hostname were combined to form session sets, after which the usernames within session sets were grouped to form aliases that a single participant uses, and these were further used to remap stray sessions to participants. In addition, username changes within sessions were added to the aliases; some manual work was performed to discard a number of changes where participants playfully impersonated other participants.

Furthermore, the logs were analyzed based on the content. As the course was organized in Finnish, no extensive automated analysis on the nature of these chats is performed; instead we analyze word frequencies and other naive characteristics to understand the activity in this community. This allows us to examine differences between these terms on different sub-populations. To elaborate the meaning of these terms, we highlight example contexts of the common words trough sentences used by different sub-populations.

[1]`http://irc.testmycode.net/logs/`

Participant interviews

We identified participants who have been contributing members of the chat room for more than one semester from the log data. To understand their experience and motivations, semi-structured interviews with 11 participants[2] were conducted. These 11 participants were chosen randomly from a pool of 75 active tenured members, i.e. chatters who had contributed more than 50 lines per course for at least two courses.

The semi-structured interviews examined the participants' memories and experiences related to staying in the chat room, reasons and motivations for extending their stay longer than one semester, and – if not mentioned earlier – whether they remember helping other participants[3]. Applying the semi-structured interview approach, further questions were asked to clarify participants' views and to gain deeper insight; the exact framing on the questions were adapted based on the responses from participants following the list of topics presented above. These interviews were conducted trough a computer-mediated communication channel and each of them lasted about half an hour. After explicit permission from the interviewees, these interviews were recorded for analysis purposes.

To analyze these interviews we examined the major themes using an open coding approach. In this process, we identified themes present in each of the interviews and labeled them accordingly; this process was iterative – that is, the interviews were labeled twice to ensure that themes identified by the end of iteration one were also examined for all interviews in the second time. After this qualitative analysis, we proceed to synthesize the common characteristics and explain our findings in more detail [20].

Finally, to increase the reliability and validity of this approach, we present extracts from these interviews to justify our conclusions. Certain aspects were repeated in these interviews – formally said, the interviews saturated – which suggests that these responses represent similar experiences in the group. In qualitative research the saturation is considered to be an indicator that the results represent the (sub)population well [20].

OBSERVATIONS

Analysis of participants

Between January 2012 and May 2014, a total of 3,910 unique participants visited the chatroom. Together, they contributed 265,613 lines of written text. As can be seen in Table 1, the activity was higher during paced course versions (Jan-May), lower during Summer (Jun-Aug), and again higher during the Fall (Sep-Dec). As can be seen from Table 1, the average is

[2]The interview request was sent to total of 19 participants, but eight of them did not respond to our initial request.

[3]The interview protocol is provided in an appendix.

	Spring 2012	Summer 2012	Fall 2012	Spring 2013	Summer 2013	Fall 2013	Spring 2014
Number of unique chat participants	378	319	201	791	359	708	1,659
Number of chat lines	60,763	28,814	5,566	65,255	8,359	16,110	80,725
Number of lurkers	123	111	107	303	226	181	679
Average lines per participant	161	90	28	83	23	23	49
Median lines per participant	6	5	0	2	0	7	2
75 % percentile lines per participant	39	35	11	18	7	11	11

Table 1. Statistics on the chatroom use per semester. During each spring semester, the course was organized as a paced version, while during summer and fall semesters, it was provided as a version with no deadlines.

higher than both the median and the 75% of quartile of participation, indicating that the participation is highly skewed, i.e. certain participants contribute a significant number of lines to the chat.

Previous research on online communities has used different roles based on the level of participation in the community. *Lurkers* are participants who join the chat room and may follow the discussion, but do not contribute to it [18]. *Participants* are students who join the channel and contribute to the discussion casually or ask questions. Participants who contribute to the discussion significantly are called *super-participants* [9, 12]. Furthermore, many participants quit the chat room at some point, creating a fourth state in the level of engagement, the *quitters*.

As observed previously, the chat room participation is skewed; super-participants exist based on the high difference between the average and the 75% quartile of participation. For this work, we consider super-participants the top 20% of participants in terms of written lines, a more relaxed limit than those in previous studies [9, 12].

Table 2 shows the probabilities of students changing from one role to another, averaged on a monthly basis. For users that are using a desktop client, more than 60% of members stay in the chat, while those using the browser-client typically visit the chat only briefly. This is expected as the browser-client is the suggested form of support, and many visit the chat room only briefly to retrieve answers to a specific question. This can be seen by the higher number of quitters in all activity roles when they use the browser-based client.

Development of the chat room

The number of participants increases especially when a new course iteration is started. Noticeable peaks are visible during January and February, smaller peaks are observable during June and August when iterations with no deadlines are started. As can be seen in Figure 1, the number of participants has increased over time. The noticeable drops are explained by technical malfunctions, so-called net-splits, where IRC servers that host the chat room have temporarily lost connection to the internet. While the course was first offered in the "year of the MOOC", the participant numbers have been larger in the subsequent years, and an increasing trend in questions asking when the next paced version starts has been observed.

	SP	P	L	Q
Desktop client				
Super participant	57%	19%	9%	15%
Participant	12%	28%	24%	36%
Lurker	3%	12%	48%	37%
Quitter	.2%	.4%	.8%	98.6%
Browser client				
Super-participant	16%	12%	2%	70%
Participant	2%	7%	3%	88%
Lurker	.4%	1.4%	3.5%	94.7%
Quitter	.1%	.5%	.5%	98.9%

Table 2. Probabilities on role change between different user groups, averaged over monthly usage statistics and organized per client type

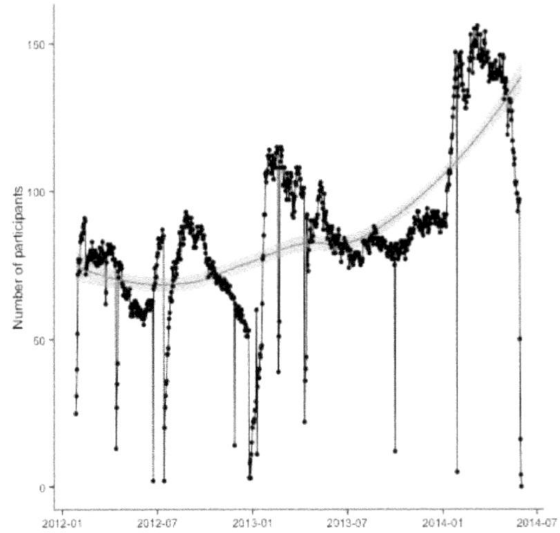

Figure 1. Number of participants in the chat room over time. The downward spikes indicate network connectivity issues.

In addition to the participant counts, we examined the time that users stayed in the chat room. As expected, the majority of browser-chat users stayed relatively short periods of time – only 1% of the web-client users spent at least 3 days on the channel, while the typical duration of a visit was less than an hour. Users that had used a desktop, mobile or cloud client stayed noticeably longer in the chat room (see Figure 2): top 20% stay in the room for at least 69 days, the top 10% for at least 178 days and the top 5% for at least 377 days.

This leads us towards understanding these participants and their reasons to stay as part of the chat room for a longer period of time. The interviews highlighted that the chat room participants that have remained in the room for a longer period than a single course can be distinguished into two groups; (1) *alumni participants* that have completed the course and remained to help newcomers and (2) *tenured participants* that

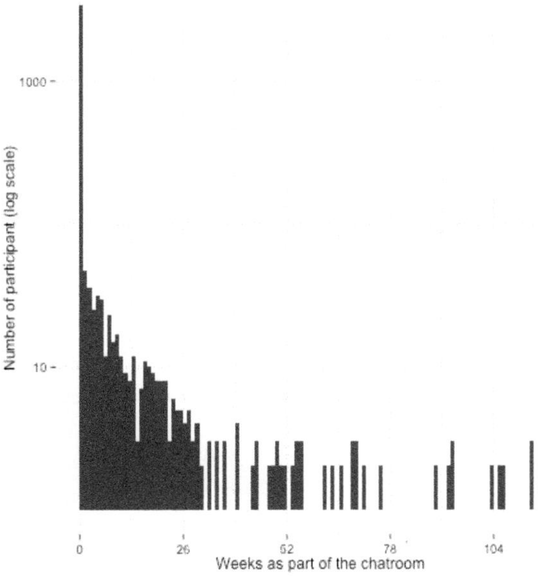

Figure 2. Number of weeks users have been members of the chat room

have joined the chat room due to general interest or being students of the organizing university.

Understanding alumni and tenured participants

The semi-structured interviews presented us with insights on the development of the community in the chatroom. The technology chosen allowed low-involvement participation to the community, which interviewers highlighted as a critical aspect of choosing to remain as a part of the community:

> A: Well, I don't actually know [why I stayed in that chat room] :D If I join a chat room and talk with other members, I don't usually leave
> A: one chatroom more makes no difference

> B: Yes, sometimes I have helped others when I've been bored
> Interviewer: Okay. Could you explain a bit more what you mean by "being bored"?
> B: If I have nothing else to do, then I check my chat rooms and typically someone just happens to ask for help at the same time [in the MOOC chat room]

> C: I haven't spoken that much recently, maybe answered someones' questions when I have a boring moment --
> C: And [bytexttt] a boring moment [I mean] when I wait for a response in another chat room

These interviews highlight the importance of using a communication channel that the participants also otherwise use, as participants engage with the MOOC chat room while chatting in other chat rooms. However, these technology enablers are not enough. There must be other factors that motivate the participants.

The interviews present how the participants experience the chat room as a community and considered serving that community, e.g. helping other participants as a valuable contribution. The community aspect is demonstrated by the participants' interest in others' performance, even after taking a part in the MOOC. The MOOC and its chat room also serves as a place to get acquainted with current and future students.

> Interviewer: We've been searching for persons who have stayed in the chat room for a longer period of time. Do you remember when you joined the chat room and why?
> B: [I joined] about same the time when the [2012] Spring MOOC started
> B: most likely to be able to follow other [participants in the MOOC] and how they are doing with the exercises

> C: I don't have any particular (or three) [unforgettable memories,] but last year I discussed things not relevant to the MOOC with some people I met later in the introduction week [at the university]
> C: It seems that some discussion of C++ was in someones' memory, as he came to greet me "are you the one who codes C++ for living?"

These responses highlight aspects usually associated with communities of practice: there is a clear domain in the chat room and participants are engaged with each others over longer periods of time, forming a community and getting to know each other. The channel also provides support for novice coders. Based on the interviews, the participants share an interest and willingness to help others, which can be interpreted as a kind of reciprocity, i.e. helping others like one has been helped.

> F: I also got help, so it's nice to share the good

> G: [...] but a few good memories related to helping someone for a longer time, and then s/he solves it

> H: [I joined the chat room] just because I was interested in the MOOC and wanted to help [the participants] with their exercises.

The interviews also highlight that the problems that novice developers experience help also the alumni and tenured members of the community. It forces them to rethink their own thinking and to examine the topic from a different perspective, i.e. the perspective of a more experienced mentor or an instructor. The interviewees say that they engage in this activity even in cases when they do not actively support the other participants and learn from the other members of the community.

> Interviewer: Could you help me understand why you have spent time helping others with their coding problems?
> B: It's a good use of leisure time and at the same time you learn from others' mistakes
> B: one sees how others think about those issues

> E: I dig following the conversations [in the chat room], it's just interesting and you can also learn new things while doing that

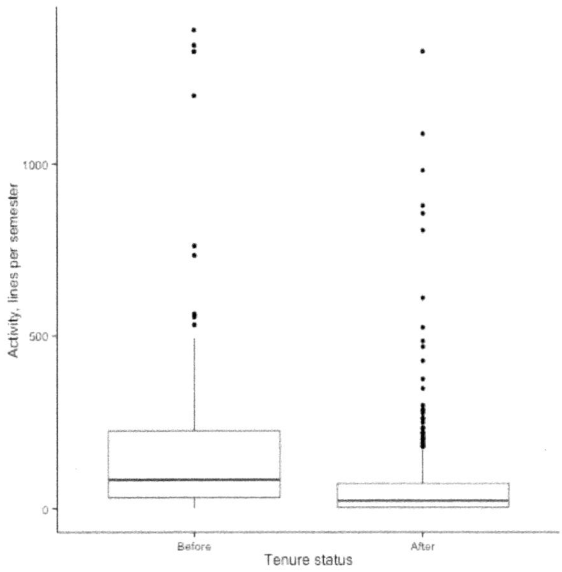

Figure 3. Activity level per semester for participants that remain longer in the chat channel.

Interviewer: What do you follow in the chat room?
D: When participants struggle with some exercises, I occasionally follow them and try to think what I would do
D: I haven't tried to help them as I don't actively practice :)
-- -- Interviewer: you don't actively practice what?
D: Coding

This practice-based peer-learning, the interest to share and to learn together, is also a criterion associated with communities of practice. These interviews therefore highlight that the members of the chat room consider the chat room to be a community of practice and their motivation for involvement even after completing the course is based on a shared interest to learn and help others to learn.

Contributions towards the community

The observation presented in these interviews on members being less active after their tenure is also supported in the log data. As shown in Figure 3, after their initial semester the members of this community become significantly less active in the community: during their first course, an average participant contributed 212 lines per month, while after the first course, the level of contribution is 77 lines per month. This difference is statistically significant ($W = 15099.5, p < 0.01$).

However, this quantitative aspect must be combined with a qualitative aspect: were the topics discussed similar before and after tenure? The difference in most used words, extracted using a naive most frequent words algorithm, indicates that before tenure more past tenses are used, where as after tenure the responses highlight less active doing and more monitoring. Following chat extracts from participants both before and after tenure demonstrate implications of these differences. Before the tenure the exercises of the course are discussed more:

1) I also got 20
2) I was struggling with one exercise for a few hours during the evening, and in the morning got it done in 10 minutes
3) I need to start doing those tomorrow

Whereas the lines from the participants that had been active in the chat for more than a single course indicate support given to other users and more general knowledge sharing:

4) that's what that error usually means
5) usually it's nice that often conducted operations are short
6) && comes before ——
7) you should try something like that before you ask, it might solve it :D
8) your printing methods don't print anything...

These examples highlight the difference in the discussion; while the participants are more active and also discuss things not related to the course as a part of getting to know each others, they transition towards a mentor role where they start helping others to succeed. We consider that these examples present the value these members bring to the community.

DISCUSSION

Our work has three contributions. First we showed that some MOOC participants are willing to stay longer in a chat room than just for the duration of a single MOOC. Semi-structured interviews were conducted to understand the motives to stay longer in the chat room. Based on interviews, two categories of participants were identified; (1) alumni that have completed the course, and (2) tenured members who have not completed the course.

As a second contribution, we identified that the behaviors of the members that choose to stay in the chat channel present many characteristics of communities of practice. We therefore argue that the chat room itself forms into a community of practice. Lastly, we showed that the participants have a lower level of contribution after their first semester and using naive textual analysis demonstrate that their focus shifts towards helping other participants, as one might expect.

Our first result highlighted the importance of the community technology. Participants who used the desktop client version of IRC were more likely to stay in the channel; where as participants on the browser-based client were more likely to quit. Our interpretation is that it is importance to tap into an existing method of communication: those using the desktop client were also likely using IRC for other communication needs. This aspect is also presented in the interviews, where the "boredom" on the communication media was said to help the MOOC chat room to gain attention from the alumni and tenured participants. We therefore suggest that MOOC communication should take advantage of the existing methods of communication and integrate with those; not to separate these channels.

Our second and third contribution suggest that alumni and tenured participants engaged in practices associated with communities of practice: they helped the junior members in a permanent online community. Similar practices have been previously presented in the education domain [24, 23]. However, to our knowledge there are no MOOCs that would have applied this long-term approach as their tutoring method. We propose that this tenure aspect could be used to help to scale individual support, which, when using using traditional TA approaches, does not scale [25]. However, to be successful, there must be some gains for the alumni and tenured members also: in our case it seems to be partly related to good-will and reciprocity, but also personal motives – most importantly learning – were present in the interviews. Future research may examine the personality characteristics as well as demographic features of these members and how they differ from those who choose not to attend the chat or who quit from the chat after the course.

Does it scale?

One may argue that the solution used in our data, a common chat room available to current, prospective, alumni and, tenured participants of the MOOC can not scale from socio-technical perspective. Said differently, there may be an upper limit on how many participants can stay in the same chat room without causing social challenges.

However, it is not necessary to have just *one* common chat room where all participants are; instead, to maintain a suitable size of community, several chatrooms can be used and community members can be distributed to each channel. To maintain familiarity, one should naturally seek to have the same participants in the same channels.

Limitations

As the course under study is computer science-related, the observations may be limited to courses with participants that are relatively familiar with computers; IRC might serve as a natural technology to distinguish course participants from main stream technologies that support (a)synchronous messaging, such as Facebook [13]. Furthermore, IRC as communication technology allows participants to stay present in the chat room even while they are away from the desktop. These characteristics have helped in the community-building aspect examined above.

This study was conducted on a dataset from a Nordic country characterized with high trust between people, rather homogeneous population and high quality of education. A majority of the discussion was held in Finnish, which means that the participants have used their native language. The shared language may contribute to the community building, and may not be directly transferred to other contexts.

As Finnish is an agglutinative language, in which words are formed by joining affix morphemes to the stem, the language is complex to analyze. The language inherently limited the amount of available natural language processing tools and libraries significantly. As a consequence, only naive methods were used for automatic analysis of the chat logs.

CONCLUSIONS

In this work we have examined an emerging online community that has developed around a MOOC in programming. As the same chat room has been used over a period of two and a half years, the data shows the emergence of participants that remain involved in helping students in the current iteration of the course. These participants included both alumni, i.e. participants who have completed a previous course instance, as well as tenured participants, who are in general interested in programming, but have not completed the course.

Based on the data, we suggest that the value of online chat in a MOOC environment should not be evaluated purely on educational standards, and that educators and MOOC facilitators can benefit immensely from not restarting the community from scratch when a new course iteration is started. Both students who are enrolled in a currently ongoing course as well as the past participants have a role in the community, and support peers that are in need of guidance.

Further, we demonstrated that the roles in the community are not static, rather there are shifts between superparticipant, lurker and regular participant roles. We interpret this as an indicator of the liveliness of the community and an ongoing evolution. The way in which these roles change is also influenced by the application used; it is also likely that the chosen tools affect the participation rates, and, depending on context, one can consider other communication methods than IRC.

The data also suggests that the emerged online community is a community of practice. This was suggested in that the participants engaged in helping junior members in their exercises, but also felt that they learned through helping these members. Therefore, we suggest that allowing participants to stay as part of the community benefits the learning process.

Acknowledgments

We thank support from the Learning Solutions Programme from the Finnish Funding Agency for Innovation for project "Learning Design – Design for Learning."

REFERENCES

1. Anderson, A., Huttenlocher, D., Kleinberg, J., and Leskovec, J. Engaging with massive online courses. *Proceedings of the 23rd international conference on World wide web - WWW '14* (2014), 687–698.
2. Bruckman, A. The future of e-learning communities. *Commun. ACM 45*, 4 (Apr. 2002), 60–63.
3. Cambre, J., Kulkarni, C., Bernstein, M. S., and Klemmer, S. R. Talkabout: Small-group Discussions in Massive Global Classes. In *Proceedings of the first ACM conference on Learning @ Scale conference 2014 - L@S '14* (2014), 161–162.
4. Chen, P.-J., and Chen, Y.-H. Facilitating MOOCs Learning Through Weekly Meet-up: A Case Study in Taiwan. In *Proceedings of the first ACM Conference on Learning @ Scale Conference*, L@S '14 (2014), 183–184.

5. Coetzee, D., Fox, A., Hearst, M. A., and Hartmann, B. Chatrooms in MOOCs. In *Proceedings of the first ACM conference on Learning @ Scale conference - L@S '14*, ACM Press (2014), 127–136.

6. Coetzee, D., Fox, A., Hearst, M. A., and Hartmann, B. Should your MOOC forum use a reputation system? In *Proceedings of the 17th ACM conference on Computer supported cooperative work & social computing - CSCW '14* (2014), 1176–1187.

7. Garrison, D., Anderson, T., and Archer, W. Critical inquiry in a text-based environment: Computer conferencing in higher education. *The Internet and Higher Education* 2, 23 (1999), 87 – 105.

8. Gillani, N., and Eynon, R. Communication patterns in massively open online courses. *The Internet and Higher Education 23* (2014), 18–26.

9. Graham, T., and Wright, S. Discursive Equality and Everyday Talk Online: The Impact of Superparticipants. *Journal of Computer-Mediated Communication 19*, 3 (2014), 625–642.

10. Gray, B. Informal learning in an online community of practice. *Journal of Distance Education 19*, 1 (2004), 20–35.

11. Hara, N., and Foon Hew, K. Knowledgesharing in an online community of healthcare professionals. *Information Technology & People 20*, 3 (2007), 235–261.

12. Huang, J., Dasgupta, A., Ghosh, A., Manning, J., and Sanders, M. Superposter behavior in MOOC forums. *Proceedings of the first ACM conference on Learning @ Scale conference - L@S '14* (2014), 117–126.

13. Lampinen, A., Lehtinen, V., and Cheshire, C. *Media Choice and Identity Work: A Case Study of Information Communication Technology Use in a Peer Community*. Emerald Group Publishing Limited, 103–130.

14. Lave, J. Situating learning in communities of practice. In *Perspectives on socially shared cognition*, L. B. Resnick, J. M. Levine, and S. D. Teasley, Eds. American Psychological Association, 1991, 63–82.

15. Lim, S., Coetzee, D., Hartmann, B., Fox, A., and Hearst, M. A. Initial experiences with small group discussions in MOOCs. In *Proceedings of the first ACM conference on Learning @ Scale conference - L@S '14* (2014), 151–152.

16. Miller, K., Zyto, S., Karger, D., and Mazur, E. Improving online class forums by seeding discussions and managing section size. In *Proceedings of the first ACM conference on Learning @ Scale conference - L@S '14* (2014), 173–174.

17. Mutton, P. Inferring and visualizing social networks on internet relay chat. In *Information Visualisation, 2004. IV 2004. Proceedings. Eighth International Conference on* (2004), 35–43.

18. Nonnecke, B., and Preece, J. Lurker demographics: Counting the silent. In *Proceedings of the SIGCHI Conference on Human Factors in Computing Systems - CHI '00* (2000), 73–80.

19. Reid, E. Electropolis: Communication and community on Internet Relay Chat. *Intertek 3*, 3 (1992), 7–15.

20. Silverman, D. *Doing Qualitative Research. A practical handbook*. SAGE Publications, London, 2000.

21. Spencer, D., and Hiltz, S. A field study of use of synchronous chat in online courses. In *Proceedings of the 36th Annual Hawaii International Conference on System Sciences - HICSS '03*, IEEE (2003).

22. Vihavainen, A., Luukkainen, M., and Kurhila, J. Multi-faceted Support for MOOC in Programming. In *Proceedings of the 13th Annual Conference on Information Technology Education - SIGITE '12* (2012), 171–176.

23. Vihavainen, A., Vikberg, T., Luukkainen, M., and Kurhila, J. Massive increase in eager tas: Experiences from extreme apprenticeship-based cs1. In *Proceedings of the 18th ACM conference on Innovation and technology in computer science education* (2013), 123–128.

24. Vikberg, T., Vihavainen, A., Luukkainen, M., and Kurhila, J. Early start in software coaching. In *Proceedings of the Agile Processes in Software Engineering and Extreme Programming - XP '13* (2013), 16–30.

25. Warren, J., Rixner, S., Greiner, J., and Wong, S. Facilitating human interaction in an online programming course. *Proceedings of the 45th ACM technical symposium on Computer science education - SIGCSE '14* (2014), 665–670.

26. Wenger, E. Communities of practice: Learning as a social system. *Systems thinker 9*, 5 (1998), 2–3.

27. Werry, C. C. Linguistic and interactional features of internet relay chat. In *Computer-mediated communication: Linguistic, social, and cross-cultural perspectives*, S. C. Herring, Ed. John Benjamins Publishing, 1996, 47–63.

28. Yardi, S. The role of the backchannel in collaborative learning environments. In *Proceedings of the 7th international conference on Learning sciences - ICLS '06* (2006), 852–858.

APPENDIX: INTERVIEW PROTOCOL

Introducing oneself as a researcher from an academic institution and explaining the scope and purpose of the research, aquiring a consent

- Have you taken part in a MOOC organized by the Department of Computer Science at the University of Helsinki? If you have, when?
- Can you recall three memorable things, discussions or memories from the course chat room?

- Base on our data you've had a long tenure on the chat room, could you describe your reasons to stay there for that long?
- [Only if not discussed above] Do you have memories of helping others? On what kind of issues? When?
- Are you still part of the chat room? [If not] What were your reasons to leave eventually the chat room?

A Playful Game Changer: Fostering Student Retention in Online Education with Social Gamification

Markus Krause
Leibniz University
Hannover, Germany

Marc Mogalle
Leibniz University
Hannover, Germany

Henning Pohl
Leibniz University
Hannover, Germany

Joseph Jay Williams
Harvard University
Cambridge, MA, USA

{markus, marc, henning}@hci.uni-hannover.de, joseph_jay_williams@harvard.edu

ABSTRACT
Many MOOCs report high drop off rates for their students. Among the factors reportedly contributing to this picture are lack of motivation, feelings of isolation, and lack of interactivity in MOOCs. This paper investigates the potential of gamification with social game elements for increasing retention and learning success. Students in our experiment showed a significant increase of 25% in retention period (videos watched) and 23% higher average scores when the course interface was gamified. Social game elements amplify this effect significantly – students in this condition showed an increase of 50% in retention period and 40% higher average test scores.

Author Keywords
Massive Open Online Courses; MOOC; Gamification; Social Engagement

ACM Classification Keywords
J.1 [Administrative Data Processing]: Education
K.3.1 [Computer Uses in Education]: Distance Learning

INTRODUCTION
Low retention rates are a widely discussed issue of learning at scale. Students of online courses report various inconveniences resulting in their dropout. Gamification is a promising method to strengthen student engagement and ease some of the disadvantages connected to online education [27]. High dropout rates are often attributed to feelings of isolation and lack of interactivity [15]—reasons directly relating to missing social engagement. Thus, we use social game elements to strengthen social engagement in students of online courses.

We conducted a controlled experiment with 213 students majoring in psychology or computer science. To discriminate the effects of gamification from effects induced through social elements, we compare three conditions: (1) a baseline condition without explicit gamification, (2) a version with game elements, but no social elements, and (3) a gamified version with social elements. We hypothesize that gamification has a stronger effect when it exhibits social elements. We found that students in our gamification condition had 23% higher average scores and an increase of 25% in retention. With social elements, the increase was almost 40% for final scores and 50% for retention period.

L@S 2015, March 14–18, 2015, Vancouver, BC, Canada.

ACM 978-1-4503-3411-2/15/03…$15.00.
http://dx.doi.org/10.1145/2724660.2724665

Figure 1. We investigate the impact of social gaming elements on student retention in online learning. Shown here is the interface of our system on a tablet. In particular, the lesson panel of the *social* game condition.

RELATED WORK
Retention remains a major challenge in MOOCs. Jordan reported that although completion rates occasionally exceed 40% the average rate is below 13% and sometimes even below 1% [13]. When analyzing retention it is important to note that student motivation is more diverse in online courses than traditional courses. The motivation also varies significantly between courses [17]. Willkowski et al. [32] asked students about their motivation to take part in the MOOC *Mapping with Google*. Only 10% of students reported that they wanted to earn a certificate. Kizilcec et. al [17] investigates this diversity in student motivation more closely. Their findings also suggest that getting a certificate is not the primary intention of students in MOOCs. Kizilcec et. al [17] further illustrate that the retention rate of students actually taking a course for a certificate are still low. According to Willkowski et. al [32] only 25% percent of those students aiming for a certificate actually achieved their goal. These results show that even students with the goal to complete the course struggle to achieve it.

There has been work on using games or game-like elements for education [1,27,30] and training [31] and explorative studies on the effects of game elements in online courses [10]. Domínguez et al. [8] investigated the effects of gamification on adult learners. Their study indicates that gamification may have an effect on students. In contrast to these explorative studies, we investigate a more specific question:

RQ1: Does gamification have a positive effect on retention?

Khalil et al. [15] investigates why students drop off from online courses and proposes strategies how to increase retention. They report that feelings of isolation and a lack of interactivity are both factors for high drop of rates in MOOCs. This indicates that social engagement is an important aspect of students' success. This is also consistent with other studies [7,17,25], which hypothesize that social engagement is a relevant factor for student retention, success, and satisfaction.

Research on social factors of learning is a well-established field [3,28,34] and there are attempts to strengthen social interactions in MOOCs [29] and various endeavors to understand social elements in online and distance education [4,18,19]. Simões et al. [25] use social elements to support younger students (K-6) in an offline environment with social game elements. Thus, there is evidence that social elements may amplify the effect of gamification. Therefore, we extend our initial research question and ask:

RQ2: Is gamification with social elements more efficient?

STUDY DESIGN

Our study follows a between subjects design with three different conditions. The first condition has no game elements (*plain* condition), while the second condition has game elements (*game* condition), and the third condition has social game elements (*social* condition). Apart from the main factor (*condition*) we also collect information on two more fixed factors: *gender* and *major*. As we required verified information of these factors, we integrated our experiment with offline courses at a university. Student retention is valuable and even more when it is correlated with learning success. Therefore, we also analyze how much students can recall from a lecture. We hypothesize that:

H1: Gamification increases retention.

H1a: Gamification increases learning success.

H2: Social game elements amplify retention gain.

H2a: Social game elements amplify learning success.

The course used for the experiment introduces *Python* as a programming language for statistical analysis and has an expected duration of four-weeks with an average workload of 4 hours per week. We organized the *course* into four *lectures,* each lecture containing 15 video *lessons* on average. No video lesson was longer than 4 minutes and videos showed either tablet drawings or code examples. Each video also features a short quiz. Quizzes are either multiple-choice questionnaires or free text input.

The online course was not required for any course of the university but lecturers of graduate and undergraduate courses in computer science (human-computer interaction) and psychology promoted the course in their lectures as a valuable addition.

PARTICIPANTS

We collected data from 71 students in the *plain* condition, 67 students in the *game* condition, and 68 students in the *social* condition. Students were studying either computer science (113) or psychology (93) for their undergraduate (87), master (116), or Ph.D. (3). Only 12 participants reported prior knowledge in python. Many students, however, had basic knowledge of statistics (85) and sometimes experience with R (56), Java (95), or C/C++ (56).

PROCEDURE

Students had to sign up for the course via an online system. As we had verified information about gender and major of students, we were able to balance condition assignment of students based on gender and major. Table 1 shows the final distribution of students in each condition:

	Gender		*Major*	
Condition	*Female*	*Male*	*Psych.*	*CS*
Plain	30	41	32	39
Game	28	39	30	37
Social	28	40	31	37

Table 1. Demographics of students in each condition.

Plain Condition

The *plain* condition does not have explicit game elements. After logging in with their university credentials students can choose one of the four lectures from a dashboard. The dashboard also provides an overview of the progress in each course and lesson. Figure 2 shows a screenshot of the dashboard. Selecting a lecture in the dashboard opens the respective lesson panel.

The lesson panel has four central elements: a video in the center, an element to navigate over the video, and a quiz panel on the left. Quizzes could take one of two forms either a multiple-choice quiz or a free text question. Students only need to type one or two words to answer free text questions.

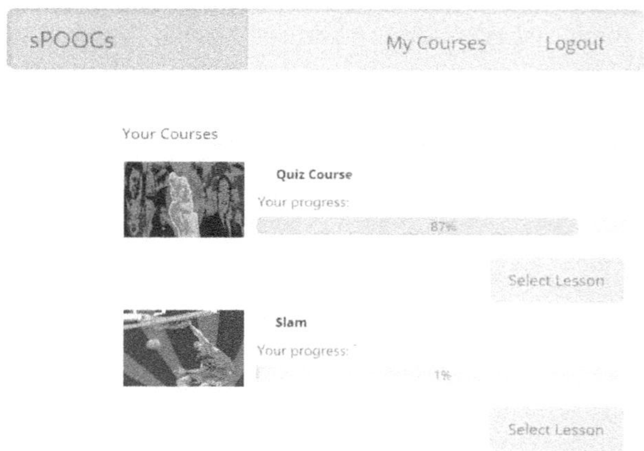

Figure 2. The dashboard of the *plain* condition. Students get an overview of their progress in courses and lessons.

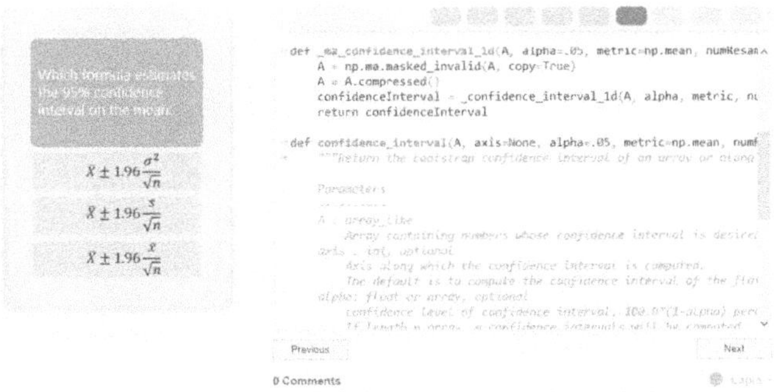

Figure 3. Main components of the lesson panel of the baseline condition (*plain*). We omitted the discussion board under the video, as it we did not change it.

The system is able to deal with common spelling errors. The lesson panel shows a discussion board below the video as seen in Figure 2.

Game Condition

We designed the *game* condition with all features of the social condition omitting only those that incorporate social elements. We only use gamification instead of more sophisticated game concepts allowing an easier interpretation of effects. We deliberately chose to leave out complex game mechanics. Complex game mechanics themselves have a learning curve and thereby introduce noise.

We restructured the dashboard. A panel on the left side shows players an overview of their achievements. This panel also contains a customizable avatar in the social condition. We show the details in Figure 5. In the *game* condition, the panel does not show this avatar but is otherwise identical. The full lesson panel is depicted in Figure 5. As the *game* condition is already very close to the *social* condition the figure shows only the final version of the panel. The lessons panels of the *game* and the *social* condition differ only in the design of their quiz elements. We show these differences in more detail in Figure 7.

For the *game* condition, we use basic gamification mechanics [33]. ***Achievements*** or ***badges*** are widespread elements in gamification. They are a representation of an accomplishment. In the *game* condition, students can acquire achievements for answering a number of quizzes correctly, taking a number of lessons, or being ranked among the top ten students of a lesson or the entire course. We award five achievements with three levels for each achievement.

Players also earn ***score points*** for each correct answer to a quiz question. We use these score points to place players in a leaderboard for each course and each lesson in a course. We are aware of the fact that ***leaderboards*** already constitute a social element and that this decision might tone down the effects between the *game* and the *social* condition.

We deliberately chose to integrate leaderboards in the game condition as they are an essential element in almost every gamification approach and do not connect players directly

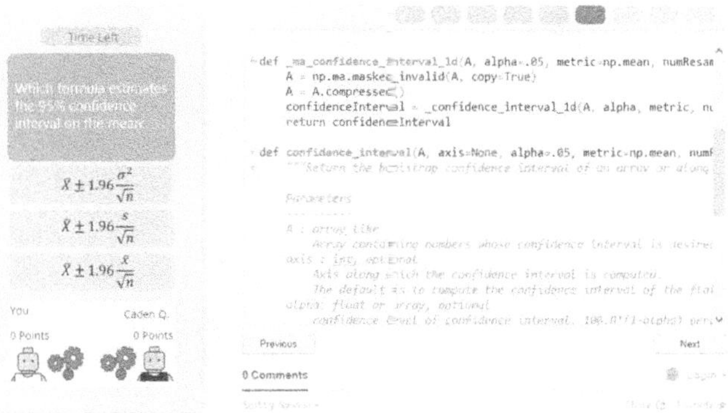

Figure 5. Main elements of the lesson panel of the *social* and *game* condition. The only differences between social and game condition is the presence of the quiz (Figure 7 shows this differences in more detail).

with one another. Aesthetics do play a relevant role in gamification using visually appealing graphics and representations one can create a sense of pleasurable satisfaction [9,14,23,24]. For the experiment, we chose a neutral comic like design. Players can design their own ***avatar***. Later during the course, students can turn in their achievements and score points to acquire different visual add-ons to place on their avatar such as hats and other items. Figure 4 shows a screenshot of the dashboard of the game condition showing an avatar and a list of achievements.

The dashboard also provides an overview of the progress in each course and lesson. Beside the integration of a customizable avatar, we overhauled the general appearance of the interface to fit the theme laid out with the avatar. Figure 6 shows the customization interface for the avatar and some of the avatars created by students during the course.

Finally, we added a countdown to each quiz in a lesson. This restricts student to a certain amount of time when solving a quiz, effectively inducing tension with this ***time limit***. To allow students to watch the video without time pressure, quizzes have to be explicitly activated via clicking. Figure 7 shows two screenshots of the quiz.

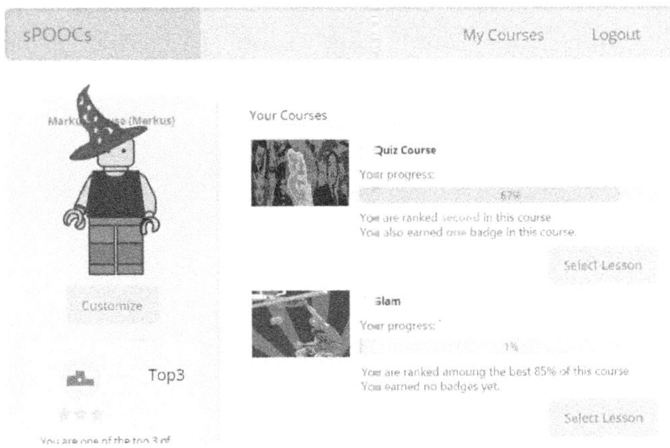

Figure 4. Dashboard of the *social* condition. Players can customize their avatar and get an overview of their progress in courses and lessons.

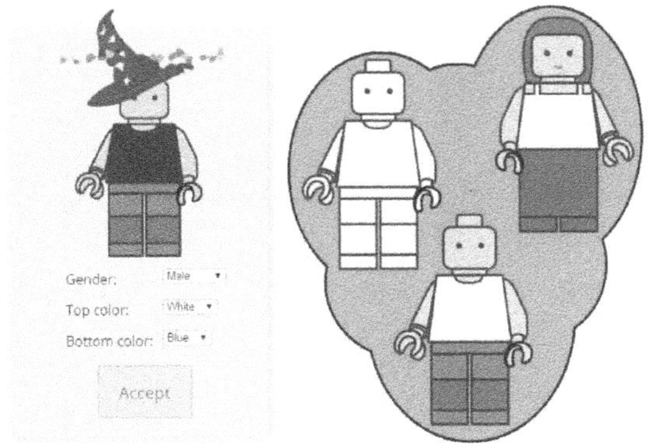

Figure 6. Students can customize their avatar. Later during the course, students can collect visual gadgets, e.g., hats or other props. Some possible avatars are shown on the right.

Social Game Condition

The *social* condition is identical to the *game* condition except for an additional set of social game elements. Prior to starting a new lecture, participants were able to choose an opponent. Students could choose a person they know from the list of participants, or play against a randomly chosen opponent. Although typical for games that highlight social aspects, we do not allow participants to invite friends via social networks or e-mail at this point. When a player starts a lesson with a random opponent, a screen illustrates the search for another player (see Figure 8).

The system does not require two players to be online at the same time. A student can play against pre-recorded actions of another student. To ensure that the system always has enough recordings we pre-recorded some sessions.

The system pairs a student with a recorded session if it cannot find another player within 30 seconds of the student choosing a random opponent. Students can also choose a specific player from a list of students currently online or with recorded play sessions. If the second student is online, the system waits until both students start the lesson. If the second

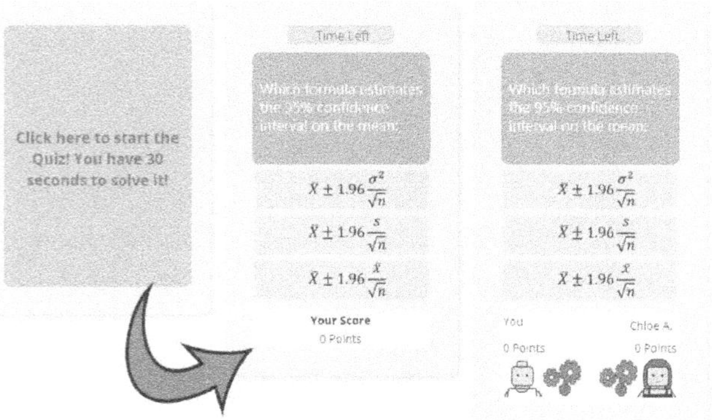

Figure 7. We changed the appearance and the behavior of the quiz from the *plain* condition. The quiz in the *game* condition (center) features a countdown (green bar) and students activate the quiz manually (left). In the *social* condition, students see the status of their opponent (right).

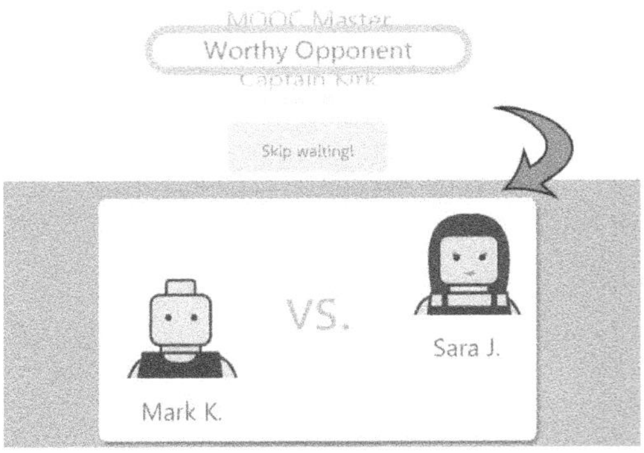

Figure 8. To highlight the social aspect we visualize the search process for a competitor (top). Students can skip this process (button in the center). The system then pairs students with a recorded session of another student. Otherwise, a notification window shows that the system found another student (lower part of the figure).

student is not online but has a recorded session for this lesson the first student plays against this recording.

To highlight the social interaction we add a status bar to the quiz panel. This bar illustrates the progress of ones opponent on the quiz as seen in Figure 7. Students get a notification if their opponent solves a quiz if they as well have an active quiz. Finally, we added a summary screen that compares the results of both students (see Figure 9).

MEASUREMENTS

To estimate student retention we measure the number of video lessons a student watches. We will refer to this measure as ***retention period***. For this experiment we consider video as watched if it played completely and the continue button was clicked afterwards. As basic knowledge of statistics and programming languages was present in our user group, we assumed that some participants skip lectures due to prior knowledge. For the experiment, we define skipping a lecture as starting the video but moving on to the next one before the video has finished. We asked participants to indicate if they skip a lecture because of prior knowledge. If a student skips a video because of prior knowledge, we still consider the video lesson as completed.

To measure learning success we conducted an exam with some of our students. We invited students that took part in our experiment to an offline test. We scheduled this test 3 month after the start of the course. 101 Students took part in

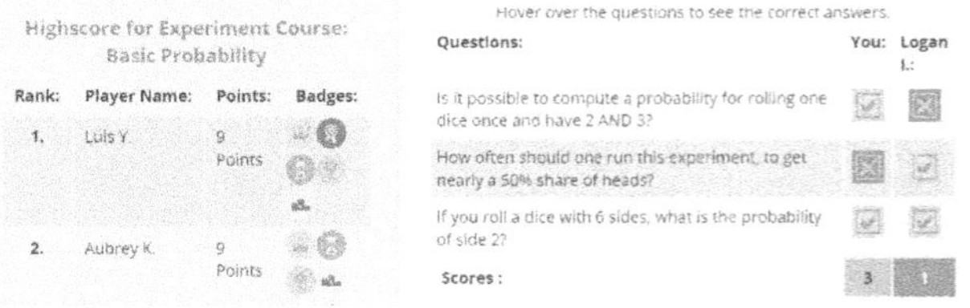

Figure 9. The resume screen of the social condition. Illustrates the player performance compared to her opponent. On the left is a leaderboard showing ranking and badges.

this test. On average, students took the test one week after the course (self-assessed). We asked students to write a python script that calculates the 95% confidence interval of the distribution of means using only standard functions.

We reviewed and graded all submissions in a blind review process. At least three different reviewers graded each submission on a range from 5 (excellent) to 1 (a lot of room for improvement). We averaged the ***test performance*** of all reviewers to measure learning success for each participant.

Besides test scores, we also use a second measure to estimate learning success. Students solve quizzes throughout the course; the average ratio of correctly solved quizzes is our last measurement: ***quiz accuracy***.

RESULTS

In accordance with Cramer and Bock [5], we performed a MANOVA on the means to help protect against inflating our Type-I error rate in the follow-up ANOVAs and post-hoc comparisons. Prior to conducting the MANOVA, we calculated a series of Pearson correlations between all dependent variables in order to test the MANOVA assumption that the dependent variables correlate. We found correlations ranging between 0.2 and 0.4 all correlations are significant at an α-level of 0.01 or lower. These values are within acceptable ranges according to Meyers et al. [26].

Additionally, the Box's M value of 16.25 was associated with a p value of 0.012, which was interpreted as non-significant in accordance with Huberty and Petoskey's (i.e., $p < .005$) [12]. Thus, the covariance matrices between the groups were assumed equal for the purpose of the MANOVA. We conducted a three-way multivariate analysis of variance (MANOVA) to test the hypothesis that there would be one or more mean differences between our conditions (*plain*, *game*, and *social*) and our measurements (*retention period*, *quiz accuracy*, and *test score*). A significant MANOVA effect was obtained, Pillais' Trace = 0.22, $F(6, 176) = 3.38$, $p = 0.003$ with an estimated multivariate effect size of 0.112.

Retention Period

We calculate the average retention period for each condition and the 95% confidence interval of the distribution of means as shown in Table 2. To estimate confidence intervals we draw 10,000 bootstrap samples from each condition using sampling with replacement.

All three conditions differ by their mean but show a slight overlap of their confidence intervals. As hypothesized the *game* and *social* conditions have a higher average retention period than the version without game elements. The *game* condition shows a 25% increase in retention period compared to the *plain* condition. The *social* condition more than doubles this effect showing an increase of the average retention period of more than 55% compared to *plain*.

Before testing our results for significance, we ensured that our data is suitable for parametric tests as hypothesized. We used an omnibus test for normality [6] for each condition and

Cond.	n	$\bar{x}$	95% CI
plain	71	11.9	[10.2, 13.5]
game	67	14.9	[12.9, 16.9]
social	68	18.5	[16.5, 20.7]

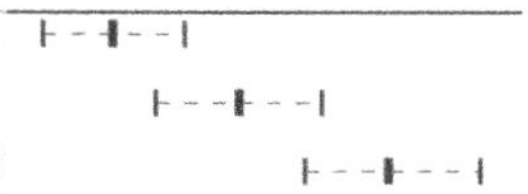

Table 2. Number of participants (n), mean retention period ($\bar{x}$), and the 95% confidence interval of the distribution of retention period means. The CI and the boxplot of means are calculated from 10,000 bootstrap samples.

did not find significant differences from a normal distribution. As we have different numbers of participants in our conditions, we also verified that our conditions have equal variance for the dependent variable prior to executing an analysis of variance (ANOVA).

As the distributions do not differ significantly from normal distributions, we use Bartlett's test for homoscedasticity (equal variance) [2]. We found, as assumed, that the variance does not differ significantly between our conditions $t(2) = 2.649$, $p = 0.265$. As our data does not hold evidence that it violates the assumptions of the ANOVA we analyze main and interaction effects with a three-way independent analysis of variance. Table 3 shows the results of this test.

Source	df	*SS*	MS	F	p
(C)ondition	2	1559.1	779.5	11.53	<0.001
(G)ender	1	194.3	194.3	3.07	0.081
(M)ajor	1	52.6	52.6	0.83	0.362
C×G	2	187.5	187.5	1.48	0.229
C×M	2	14.1	14.1	0.11	0.894
C×G×M	2	133.9	133.9	1.05	0.348
Residual	194	12270.0	63.24		

Table 3. Interaction and main effects on retention period. Abbreviations: df (degrees of freedom), SS (sum of squares), MS (mean squares).

We found that our conditions are the only significant factor in our experiment. We use post-hoc one-tailed t-tests to test for significance between individual levels of this factor and use the Holm–Bonferroni [11] method to control for family wise error rates. Figure 10 shows a violin plot of the retention periods found in our experiment. From the results we can support hypothesis *H1* as the game condition has a significantly higher average retention period ($M = 14.9$, $SD = 8.2$) than the *plain* condition ($M = 11.9$, $SD = 6.6$), with $t(137) = 2.22$, $p = 0.02$, $d = 0.38$. We can also support *H2* as the social condition has a significantly higher average retention period ($M = 18.5$, $SD = 8.7$) than the *game* condition ($M = 14.9$, $SD = 8.2$), with $t(134) = 2.48$, $p = 0.01$, $d = 0.42$. Accordingly the social condition also has a significantly higher average retention period (μ=18.5, σ=8.7) than the *plain* condition ($M = 11.9$, $SD = 6.6$), with $t(138) = 4.82$, $p<0.001$, $d = 0.79$.

Quiz Accuracy

In order to assess the influence of our conditions on students success we calculate average quiz accuracy for each condition and the 95% confidence interval of the distribution of means as shown in Table 4.

Cond.	n	$\overline{x}$	95% CI
plain	71	0.46	[0.40, 0.52]
game	67	0.52	[0.46, 0.58]
social	68	0.62	[0.55, 0.66]

Table 4. Number of participants (n), average *quiz accuracy* ($\overline{x}$), and the 95% confidence interval of the distribution of means. The CI and the boxplot are calculated from 10,000 bootstrap samples.

To estimate confidence intervals we draw 10,000 bootstrap samples from each condition using sampling with replacement. All three conditions differ by their mean and overlap in their confidence intervals. The *game* and *social* conditions have a higher average quiz accuracy than the *plain* condition. The *game* condition shows a 12.5% increase in quiz accuracy compared to the plain condition. The *social* condition again doubles this effect showing an increase of quiz accuracy of more than 31%. As for the previous measures, we conducted an omnibus test for normality and Bartlett's test for homoscedasticity. We did not find our distributions to differ significantly from the ANOVA assumptions. We therefore analyze main and interaction effects again with a three-way independent ANOVA. Table 5 shows the results of this test.

Condition is the only significant factor for quiz accuracy. Figure 11 shows a violin plot of the quiz accuracy found in our experiment. From the results we cannot entirely support hypothesis *H1a* as the difference between the *plain* (M = 0.46, SD = 0.25) and the *game* condition (M = 0.52, SD = 0.25) is not significant t(137) = 1.34, p=0.09, d = 0.23. We can however support our hypothesis *H2a* as the *social* condition has a significantly higher average quiz accuracy (M = 0.61, SD = 0.21) than the *game* condition, with t(134) = 2.19, p = 0.031, d = 0.37 and the *plain* condition, with t(138) = 3.63, p<0.001, d = 0.59.

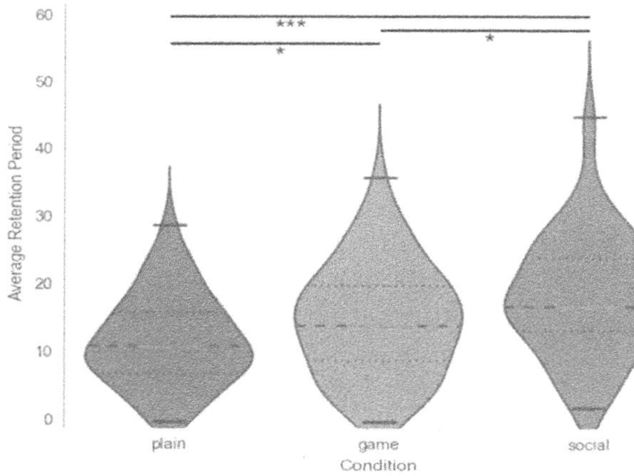

Figure 10. The *social* condition shows a significantly higher *retention period* than the *game* and *plain* conditions. The *game* condition also shows significantly higher retention rates than the plain condition. The grey lines in the violin plot indicate min and max values the grey lines on top significant differences: ∗∗∗: p < 0.001, ∗: p < 0.05.

Source	df	*SS*	MS	F	p
(C)ondition	2	76.75	76.75	6.54	0.002
(G)ender	1	5.36	5.36	0.91	0.340
(M)ajor	1	15.92	15.92	2.71	0.101
C×G	2	4.87	2.43	0.41	0.661
C×M	2	27.74	13.87	2.36	0.097
C×G×M	2	28.06	14.03	2.39	0.094
Residual	194	113.81	5.86		

Table 5. Interaction and main effects of *quiz accuracy*. Abbreviations: df (degrees of freedom), SS (sum of squares), MS (mean squares).

Final Test Performance

Our finale measurement for student success is test performance in our offline exam. We again calculate the mean and the 95% confidence interval as shown in Table 5. Again, all three conditions differ by their mean and overlap in their confidence intervals. Students in the *game* and *social* conditions have higher test scores than students in the *plain* condition. Students in the *game* condition have a 22.5% higher test performance than those in the *plain* condition. Students in the *social* condition show 40% higher scores on average.

We conducted an omnibus test for normality and Bartlett's test for homoscedasticity and analyzed main and interaction effects with a three-way ANOVA. Table 6 shows the results of this test. Condition is, as expected, the only significant factor for quiz accuracy. Figure 12 shows a violin plot of the quiz accuracies found in our experiment.

From the results we can support hypothesis *H1a* as the difference between the *plain* (M = 2.5, SD = 1.12) and the *game* condition (M = 3.06, SD = 1.10) is significant t(64) = 2.01, p = 0.049, d = 0.49. We cannot directly support our hypothesis *H2a* as the *social* condition does not show significantly higher average test scores (M = 3.50, SD = 1.12) than the *game* condition, with t(68) = 2.19, p = 0.055, d = 0.39 and the *plain* condition, with t(67) = 3.63, p < 0.01, d = 0.81.

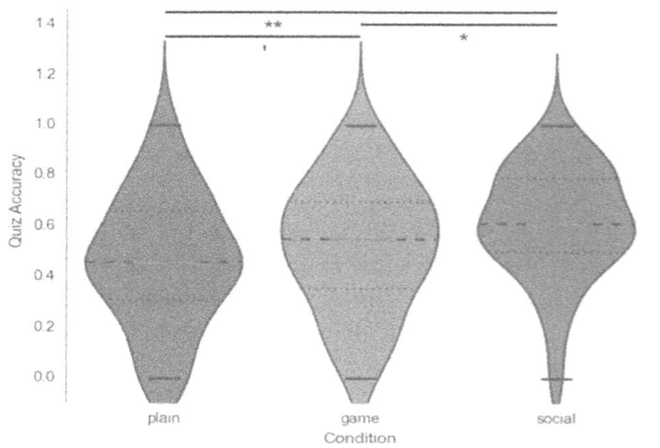

Figure 11. Student success measured with *quiz accuracy*. The grey lines in the plot indicate min and max values the grey lines on top significant differences: ∗∗: p < 0.01, ∗:p < 0.05, ':p < 0.1.

Cond.	n	$\overline{x}$	95% CI
plain	32	2.50	[2.12, 2.87]
game	33	3.06	[2.69, 3.45]
social	36	3.50	[3.13, 3.86]

Table 6. Number of participants (n), average *test score* ($\overline{x}$), and 95% confidence interval of the distribution of means (CI is estimated from 10,000 bootstrap samples).

CONCLUSION

This work presented a systematic analysis of the impact of social gamification on student retention and learning success in online courses. We posed two research questions: ***RQ1:*** does gamification support students of our online course and ***RQ2:*** do social elements amplify possible positive effects. We hypothesized that social gamification increases retention as well as strengthening learning success.

In order to assess the impact of social gamification, we analyzed three dependent variables (DVs) (*retention period*, *quiz accuracy*, and *test scores*) on three independent variables (IVs) (*condition*, *gender*, and *major*). All DVs showed a significant increase for the factor *condition* between the *plain* and *social* level. For *retention period* and *quiz accuracy*, we found two differences that were not significant on a α level of 0.05 but on a level of 0.1. However, given the p-values from both ANOVA and MANOVA a Type-I error seems unlikely in both cases. In response to our hypothesis *H1* we analyzed retention period and observed a significant increase of 25% between our *plain* and our *game* condition and a significant increase of 55% from *plain* to *social*. This lends strong support to our initial hypothesis that gamification can increase retention and that social gamification amplifies this effect.

For quiz accuracy, we found an increase of 12.5% between our *plain* and *game* conditions and an increase of 31% between *plain* and *social*, in the final test students in the *game* condition had a 22.5% higher test score compared to students in the *plain* condition. Students in the *social* condition showed an even stronger increase of almost 40% compared to students in the *plain* condition. This again lends support for our hypothesis *H2* that we can amplify beneficial effects with social gamification.

FUTURE WORK

In our experiment, social elements showed a significant impact. To control our population variables and to reduce noise

Source	df	*SS*	MS	F	p
(C)ondition	2	76.75	76.75	6.54	0.002
(G)ender	1	5.36	5.36	0.91	0.340
(M)ajor	1	15.92	15.92	2.71	0.101
C×G	2	4.87	2.43	0.41	0.661
C×M	2	27.74	13.87	2.36	0.097
C×G×M	2	28.06	14.03	2.39	0.094
Residual	194	113.81	5.86		

Table 7. Interaction and main effects of quiz accuracy. Abbreviations: df (degrees of freedom), SS (sum of squares), MS (mean squares).

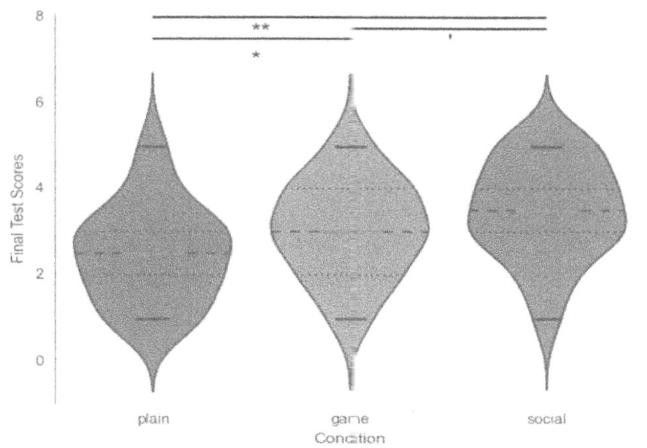

Figure 12. We measured learning success with a final offline test. In this test, students wrote a short Python script to estimate confidence intervals of means. Three independent reviewers graded each submission on a scale from 5 (excellent) to 1 (underperformed). The grey lines indicate min and max values, the grey lines on top significant differences: **: p < 0.01, *:p < 0.05, ':p < 0.1.

we restricted our experiment in terms of the user pool and the used game mechanics. Based on our findings and previous experiments we expect positive effects to be much stronger when we apply more sophisticated design concepts. Badges, achievements, and leaderboards are visually pleasing and provide a certain engagement. However, we do not expect these basic mechanics to uphold student motivation for a complete online curriculum.

In the future, we plan to investigate different social game mechanics and their impact on student success. In this paper we explored the effects of a competitive setting were students challenge each other. In the future, we also want to investigate the differences between playful elements that foster collaboration instead of competition and both methods combined. We also aim at providing sophisticated feedback to support students. However, complex game mechanics may require more advanced interaction techniques. For instance, the game could allow students who earned a certain status to add questions to the system. Thereby expanding the learning materials and allowing advanced students to compete on another level. Tools [20] and methods [16,21] that support such games already exist [22].

ACKNOWLEDGEMENTS

Many thanks to Rene Kizilcec and Gabriel Barata for sharing their research results and papers early on. Their work helped us a lot in shaping our paper.

REFERENCES

1. Barata, G., Gamma, S., Jorge, J., and Gonçalves, D. Relating Gaming Habits with Student Performance in a Gamified Learning Experience. Proc. CHI PLAY'14.
2. Bartlett, M. Properties of sufficiency and statistical tests. Proceedings of the Royal Statistical Society Series A, 160 (1937), 268–282.

3. Blumenfeld, P.C. Classroom learning and motivation: Clarifying and expanding goal theory. Journal of Educational Psychology 84, 3 (1992), 272–281.
4. Brinton, C., Chiang, M., Jain, S., Lam, H., Liu, Z., and Wong, F. Learning about social learning in MOOCs: From statistical analysis to generative model. IEEE Trans. on Learning Technologies PP, 99 (2014), 1–14.
5. Cramer, E.M. and Bock, R.D. Multivariate Analysis. Review of Educational Research 36, (1966), 604–617.
6. D'Agostino, R. and Pearson, E.S. Testing for departures from normality. Biometrika 60, (1973), 613–622.
7. Dietz-Uhler, B., Fisher, A., and Han, A. Designing online courses to promote student retention. Journal of Educational Technology Systems 36, 1 (2007), 105–112.
8. Domínguez, A., Saenz-de-Navarrete, J., De-Marcos, L., Fernández-Sanz, L., Pagés, C., and Martínez-Herráiz, J.-J. Gamifying learning experiences: Practical implications and outcomes. Computers & Education 63, (2013), 380–392.
9. De Freitas, A. a. and de Freitas, M.M. Classroom Live: a software-assisted gamification tool. Computer Science Education 23, 2 (2013), 186–206.
10. Grünewald, F., Meinel, C., Totschnig, M., and Willems, C. Designing MOOCs for the Support of Multiple Learning Styles. In Scaling up Learning for Sustained Impact. 2013, 371–382.
11. Holm, S. A simple sequentially rejective multiple test procedure. Scandinavian Journal of Statistics 6, 2 (1979), 65–70.
12. Huberty, C.J. and Petoskey, M.D. Multivariate Analysis of Variance and Covariance. In H. Tinsley and S. Brown, eds., Handbook of applied multivariate statistics and mathematical modeling. 2000.
13. Jordan, K. MOOC Completion Rates: The Data. MOOC Completion Rates: The Data, 2013. http://www.katyjordan.com/MOOCproject.html.
14. Kapp, K.M. The Gamification of Learning and Instruction: Game-based Methods and Strategies for Training and Education. Pfeiffer, 2012.
15. Khalil, H. and Ebner, M. MOOCs Completion Rates and Possible Methods to Improve Retention-A Literature Review. World Conference on Educational Multimedia, Hypermedia and Telecommunications 2014, 1236–1244.
16. Kilian, N., Krause, M., Runge, N., and Smeddinck, J. Predicting Crowd-based Translation Quality with Language-independent Feature Vectors. Proc. HComp'12, 114–115.
17. Kizilcec, R. and Al, E. Motivation as a Lens for Understanding Online Learners : Introducing and Applying the Online Learner Enrollment Intentions (OLEI) Scale. in press 0, 0 (2014).
18. Kizilcec, R.F., Piech, C., and Schneider, E. Deconstructing disengagement. Proc. LAK '13, 170.
19. Koutropoulos, A., Gallagher, M.S., Abajian, S.C., et al. Emotive Vocabulary in MOOCs: Context & Participant Retention. European Journal of Open, Distance, and E-Learning, (2012), 1–22.
20. Krause, M. and Porzel, R. It is about time. Proc. CHI EA '13, 163–168.
21. Krause, M. A behavioral biometrics based authentication method for MOOC's that is robust against imitation attempts. Proc. L@S'14 (Work in Progress), 201–202.
22. Krause, M. Homo Ludens in the Loop: Playful Human Computation Systems. tredition GmbH, Hamburg, Hamburg, Germany, 2014.
23. Liu, Y., Alexandrova, T., and Nakajima, T. Gamifying intelligent environments. Proc. Ubi-MUI'11, , 7–12.
24. Marache-francisco, C. and Brangier, E. Perception of Gamification : Between Graphical Design. (2013), 558–567.
25. Martz, W.B., Reddy, V.K., and Sangermano, K. Looking for indicators of success for distance education. In Distance learning and university effectiveness: changing education paradigms for online learning. Hershey, PA: Information Science Pub, 2004.
26. Meyers, L., Gamst, G., and Guarino, A. Applied multivariate research: Design and interpretation. Sage Publishers, Thousand Oaks, CA, USA, 2006.
27. Oblinger, D. The next generation of educational engagement. Journal of interactive media in education 8, (2004), 1–18.
28. Ryan, A.M. and Patrick, H. The Classroom Social Environment and Changes in Adolescents' Motivation and Engagement During Middle School. American Educational Research Journal 38, 2 (2001), 437–460.
29. Staubitz, T. and Renz, J. Supporting Social Interaction and Collaboration on an xMOOC Platform. Proc. EDULEARN14, 6667–6677.
30. Steinkuehler, C.A. Learning in Massively Multiplayer Online Games. Proc. ICLS '04, 521–528.
31. Stone, B., Factors, H., Defence, I., and Centre, T. Serious gaming. Education and Training, (2001), 142–144.
32. Wilkowski, J., Deutsch, A., and Russell, D. Student skill and goal achievement in the mapping with google MOOC. Proc. L@S '14, 3–9.
33. Zichermann, G. and Cunningham, C. Gamification by Design. 2011.
34. Zimmerman, B.J. A social cognitive view of self-regulated academic learning. Journal of Educational Psychology 81, 3 (1989), 329–339.

moocRP: An Open-source Analytics Platform

Zachary A. Pardos
School of Information / School of Education
UC Berkeley
zp@berkeley.edu

Kevin Kao
EECS
UC Berkeley
kkao@berkeley.edu

ABSTRACT
In this paper, we address issues of transparency, modularity, and privacy with the introduction of an open source, web-based data repository and analysis tool tailored to the Massive Open Online Course community. The tool integrates data request/authorization and distribution workflows as well as a simple analytics module upload format to enable reuse and replication of analytics results among instructors and researchers. We survey the evolving landscape of competing data models, all of which can be accommodated in the platform. Data model descriptions are provided to analytics authors who choose, much like with smartphone app stores, to write for any number of data models depending on their needs and the proliferation of the particular data model. Two case study examples of analytics and interactive visualizations are described in the paper. The result is a simple but effective approach to learning analytics immediately applicable to X consortium institutions and beyond.

Author Keywords
Open learning analytics; modularization; MOOC; dashboards; visualizations; reproducible research; edX

ACM Classification Keywords
K.3.1 Computer Uses in Education: Distance learning

INTRODUCTION
Matters of practicality and principle face the communities of educational data mining and learning analytics with both matters coming into particular relief on the topic of Massive Open Online Course data collection, management, distribution, and analytics. We introduce a new tool called moocRP, an open-source[1] analytics platform for the greater MOOC community that situates it self at the intersection of these issues.

ACM 978-1-4503-3411-2/15/03…$15.00.
http://dx.doi.org/10.1145/2724660.2724683

We will start with the issues of practicality. The non-profit higher education platform, edX, now has 36 partner universities offering or set to offer free courses online. The majority of these universities are not well prepared to handle the data they receive from edX, nor what to do with it once received. Coursera and other MOOC providers put stakeholders in a similar state of disorientation with the nuanced distinction that Coursera and others deliver data direct to the instructor of record while edX delivers data at the feet of the institution that must then co-ordinate distribution to the appropriate parties. The learning analytics community can provide much needed guidance on the cutting edge of what is actionable in the data and how it can be leveraged by instructor and student [16] towards the betterment of the learning experience. Our tool can help expand the impact of learning analytics by enabling its use among a quickly expanding new cohort of online learners and instructors. The tool also provides answers to the practical questions of how to prepare the data, grant users access to it securely, and scrutinize the data for instructionally actionable information.

Matters of principle relevant in education data analysis and distribution include a) transparency – what data is being collected, how is it being represented, and what exactly are the various technical components of moocRP doing in the background to manipulate these data behind the analytic dashboard. To address this, our tool is open source, as is the technical design of the pipeline that serves analytics to its users. New analytics and visualizations that are uploaded must also have the source viewable to all users to function on the system. In order for a data model to be imported into the system, it must describe the data elements it exposes and this description is available both to the authors and consumers of the analytics. The next principle is b) modularity – in order to foster an inclusive community of analytic contributors, analytics must be easily incorporated into the tool. We specify a simple but feature rich modular format that lowers the technical and time requirements to contribute to analytics in higher-ed. Lastly, c) privacy is of particular concern in the current climate of big data, surveillance, and ethics surrounding the beneficent use of sensitive education information [5, 17].

[1] https://github.com/CAHLR/moocRP

```
{"username": "f871051feb8eadScfk916d6N9c1L05", "host": "www.edx.org", "session": "e73339ec4477b492d7e5fbaa234bcb10", "event_source": "browser", "event_type": "play_video", "time": "2013-04-01T00:00:16.785597", "ip": "72...", "event": "{\"id\":\"i4x-BerkeleyX-CS191x-video-e824b83acd1e451e81561cb8179aec53\",\"code\":\"LFL-QLH-Z5E\",\"currentTime\":0,\"speed\":\"1.25\"}", "agent": "Mozilla/...", "page": "https://www.edx.org/courses/BerkeleyX/CS191x/2013_Spring/courseware/781b15b58ed247f4bef55587a326e915/cb2826db4a1e4de590f0d97fc422f8f0/"}

{"username": "bde1f4d184I+Udee50395/G6fffdf205i", "host": "www.edx.org", "event_source": "server", "event_type": "save_problem_check", "time": "2013-04-01T00:00:08.486659", "ip": "88...", "event": {"success": "incorrect", "correct_map": {"i4x-BerkeleyX-CS191x-problem-f3ec6a70e4584adc9416c52e8d16fafb_4_1": {"hint": "", "hintmode": null, "correctness": "incorrect", "msg": "", "npoints": 0, "queuestate": null}, ...}, "problem_id": "i4x://BerkeleyX/CS191x/problem/f3ec6a70e4584adc9416c52e8d16fafb"}, "agent": "Mozilla/...", "page": "x_module"}
```


(a) Example event logs in *raw edX event data* file

time	secs_to_next	actor	verb	object_name	object_type	result	meta	ip	event	event_type	page	agent
2013-04-01T00:00:16.785	2.678171	f8710	video_play	Week 8: Continuous quantum s	courseware		{'play	72	{"id":"	play_video	https://ww	Mozilla
2013-04-01T00:00:08.486	27.212925	bde1f	problem_check	Week 7: Quantum search and 9	courseware	incorrect		88	{u'suc	save_problem_check	x_module	Mozilla

(b) Example event logs corresponding to the ones in Figure 1(a) in *xAPI event data* format

anon_screen_name	event_type	ip_country	time	course_display_name	resource_display_name	success	... more video cols ...	goto_from	goto_dest
3fc...	book	USA	2013-11-10 06:43:10	Engineering/EE264/DSP					
6e9...	problem_check	BEL	2013-11-10 06:43:10	Engineering/Solar/2013	I-V curve				

(c) Example event logs in VPOL format

Figure 1. Examples of event logs represented in different data models

With moocRP, the analytic can be brought to the data instead of the other way around. Institutions needing to keep data close to the chest can control its distribution but still open the window to education researchers by allowing analytic module collaborations and granting researchers access to a level of acceptable transformed aggregate data or sharing the analytics results returned by the module. Similarly, individuals possessing data do not need to upload it to a centralized location to have analyses run but can instead spin up their own local instance of moocRP and import their desired analytic modules to run locally. These issues of transparency, openness, modularity, and privacy were outlined in the open learning analytics vision document [1] written by leaders of the Society for Learning Analytics Research (SOLAR).

In last year's Learning at Scale, authors suggested how modern visualization techniques could aid instructors in understanding how student activity corresponded to course success [25]. Other work categorized visualizations into groups consisting of; quantitative information (assignment grades, demographics, age) 2) qualitative information (discussions, course surveys), and 3) "real-time" visualization while the course is running. The moocRP platform allows for the visualization of all three concepts through its analytic module system. In the case studies shown in section 2.1 we discuss two proofs of concept analytics that provide interactive visualizations that are the confluence of the categories described above. These analytics, uploaded to moocRP, serve as examples of what types of modules an instructor could have access to through the usage of moocRP. With constantly growing amounts of MOOC data, visualizations and analytic modules shared among instructors and researchers can be an effective way to explore and analyze a course.

Related Work on Data Models

The pedagogical developments in online education are still changing form and function and thus the model used to represent the data coming from these new pedagogical interfaces is ever changing. In this section, we provide an overview of a few of the most visible data models currently in play in the MOOC ecosystem. All of these models are compatible with moocRP, which takes a data model agnostic approach in its design.

EdX tracking log and database model

The most primitive form of data that is obtained from edX by partner schools is the tracking and database logs [18] hosted by Amazon S3 storage service. The raw edX data consists of a set of compressed and encrypted files that contain *event data* of all courses offered by an institution. Every course is served by multiples servers. As a result, to obtain complete *event data* for one course, data must be aggregated from multiple servers. While this is getting a bit into the weeds of data wrangling, it's a reality that can be overwhelming and keep an institution and its learners from reaping the benefits of analytics. The moocRP platform has built into it data cleaning and processing scripts that manage these processes from data ingestion, decryption, through to viewing the analytics on the web.

Figure 1(a) shows an example of event logs in an event data file. One *event data* file contains all event data for all courses within one-day period in JSON format. The *database data* of a course consists of a set of SQL and mongo database files which include information about students, demographics, and survey answers provided by students, as well as grades and certification statuses.

xAPI data model

HarvardX has adopted a data format, developed by Jim Waldo [19], to package, analyze, and manipulate edX data [19]. The tool converts *edX tracking log data* into more tangible csv files based on the xAPI standard [20] (formerly Tin Can) created by Advance Distributed Learning (ADL). We call the output csv file, the *xAPI event data*. Figure 1(b) shows the same event logs as in Figure 1(a) in *xAPI event data* format.

Stanford VPOL data model

The Stanford Vice Provost Office for Online Learning (VPOL) provides MOOC data for researchers and instructors in a multi-file format [21]. It supports data derived from NovoEd, Coursera, and edX platforms. For edX data, the platform uses scripts developed by Andreas Paepcke [22] to transform *raw edX event data* and *raw edX database data* into relational tables. For example, *EventXtract* table contains event data of all courses. Figure 1(c) shows an example of an *EventXtract* table. Observe that the two logs are from different courses. Other tables such as *AcitivityGrade, Demographics,* and *Forum post* are generated from *edX database data.*

MOOCdb

The MOOCdb relational database schema [3, 23] organizes the data with respect to four different interaction modes: observing, submitting, collaborating, and feedback. Figure 2 shows the schema of the observing mode tables.

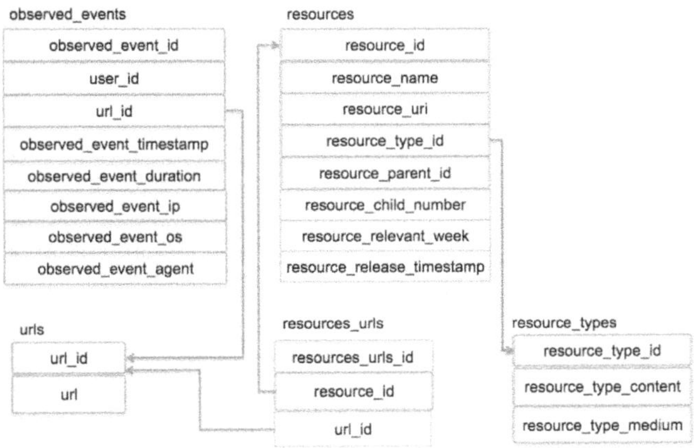

Figure 2. MOOCdb's observing mode tables

LearnLab DataShop model

In the space of data repositories, the Pittsburgh Science of Learning Center's DataShop [2] has hosted an abundance of both public and private datasets. While it has not been a MOOC repository, it is widely used in the Intelligent Tutoring Systems community, and we would be remiss to not acknowledge its impact and use in the learning community. DataShop hosts datasets as a service to the community, largely from the Cognitive Tutor [9], which was born out of the same lab, as well as from other tutoring systems such as the Andes Physics Tutor [4], the Open Learning Initiative [10] and a web-based mathematics platform, ASSISTments [7], among others. These tutoring systems are based on mastery learning [12] and the effective practice of providing immediate feedback [11] in achieving that mastery. As such, these tutoring systems are problem-solving centric, with most of the tutors breaking problems down in to a collection of steps to be answered with hints available as the primary pedagogical device. The singular data model underlying the DataShop was therefore designed to be problem centric, with each row in the data format representing an answer to a step. In MOOCs, where problem solving takes a back seat to lecture videos in student time on task [14], a wider variety of behavior and interaction is desirable to be captured. The DataShop data model was not designed to incorporate this variety of information nor social network information from the many social contexts in which learning takes place [13]. This is not to say that the DataShop model falls short of serving its purpose, or that a globally compatible data model should be sought, but rather that a single data model is not sufficient to accommodate the numerous philosophies of learning represented by various platforms of learning.

ANALYTIC MODULE CASE STUDY

In this section, we will describe some proof of concepts implementations of analytics modules[2] into the moocRP system.

Integration of analytics modules into moocRP is relatively straightforward and requires minor modifications in which the analytics source code is structured. The basic structure of an imported analytics package follows this package structure:

- `main.html`
- `/css`
- `/js`

The main display of the analytics module is placed in `main.html`, where the HTML will be rendered in a container on the analytics page of moocRP. Any script dependencies and styling dependencies must be declared in this file as well – this allows moocRP to have a single location to rewrite dependencies in a more compatible fashion. CSS files and JavaScript files are placed in the `/css` and `/js` folders, respectively.

Another minor change that needs to be made is how the data is read into the analytics module. The analytics module should access the dataset using "`<%= dataset %>`", which represents a dictionary that holds the various files associated with a data model.

To access each data model's files in an HTML file, we can use JavaScript and write the following code:

```
var dataFiles = {}
<% for (var dataFile in dataset) { %>
  <% if (dataset.hasOwnProperty(dataFile))
{ %>
    dataFiles["<%= dataFile %>"] = <%-
JSON.stringify(dataset[dataFile]) %>;
  <% } %>
<% } %>
```

Then, to access any of the data model's file contents, simply select the file using the name of the data model file as the key to the dictionary. Raw content will be stored in the dictionaries for parsing and manipulation by the analytics modules.

[2] http://www.github.com/CAHLR/moocRP_visualizations

Bayesian Network Knowledge Analysis

In this first case, the Bayesian Knowledge Tracing algorithm [4] is employed to assess student current and prior knowledge for each given problem in the course (see Figure 3). The visualization is presented along with age and level of education information so that an instructor may inspect for which demographic students lacked the requisite prior knowledge. Additional attributes can be added to this visualization including country, survey information, and outcomes for previous parts of the course.

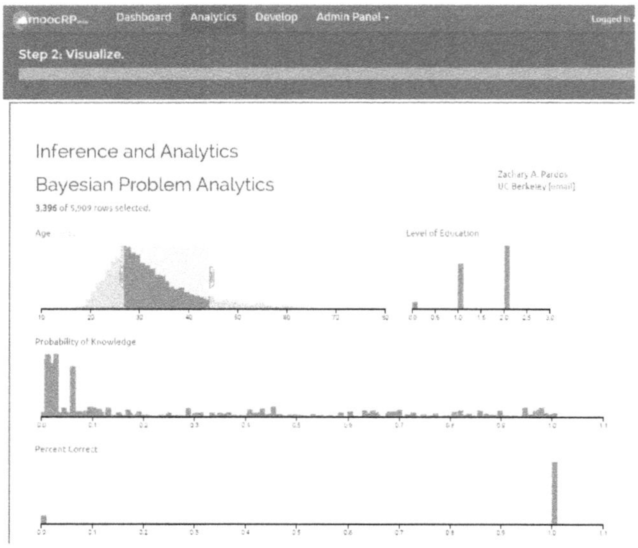

Figure 3. This analytic module is based on BNT.

To integrate this module into moocRP, we simply had to move all JavaScript and CSS dependencies that were not in the main HTML file into their respective folders as defined earlier. In the original HTML file, `d3.csv("filepath", function)` was used to read the CSV contents of a file to perform the D3 visualizations. With moocRP, instead of directly reading the file from disk using a function like `d3.csv`, we can receive the CSV file contents from the data model by including the code previously mentioned with the addition of the snippet `var data = dataFiles["output.csv"]`. Then we can use the function `d3.csv.parse` on the `data` variable, which contains the raw contents of the file. With the modifications complete, we can then zip up the `main.html` file along with the `css/` and `js/` folders and upload the archive to moocRP to be shared and applied on other datasets.

A simple example of how the data can be used with D3:

```
var raw_data = dataFiles["bnt.csv"]
                   .replace(/\\n/g, "\n");
var flights = d3.csv.parse(raw_data);
flights.forEach(function(d, i) {
    // do something to data rows
}
var flight = crossfilter(flights), ...
var chart = d3.selectAll(".chart")
    .data(charts)
    .each(function(chart) { ... });
```

Course Structure Visualizer

In the second case study, we present a module for visually inspecting the flow and course structure of a course (see Figure 4). The tree is created from parsing of the `course_structure.json` file and visualized using an expandable tree layout in D3. While this visualization shows only an interactive course tree structure, it can be used as the basis for navigating to analytics about different elements of the course, such as selecting the problem to receive the aforementioned Bayesian problem analytics for.

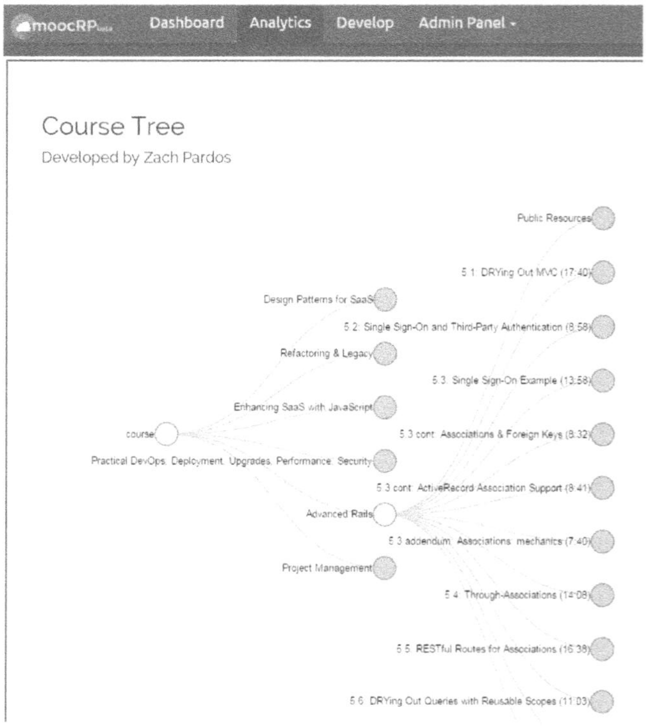

Figure 4. An analytic module used to visualize the course components of CS169 Software Engineering from BerkeleyX.

Integration of this module was similar to the first case study. This particular analytic module used the `course_structure.json` from the edX database model. moocRP can handle JSON files in an even more efficient manner, reading and passing the contents of the file as a JSON object to the HTML page instead of raw string contents. For this module then, we took out the original `d3.json("filename", function)` and simply used

```
var data =
        dataFiles["course_structure.json"]
```

to access the data, without any parsing necessary.

FUNCTIONALITY OF MOOCRP

In this section we discuss the various practical functionality of the tool, such as the data request/authorization workflow, security details, technical implementation details, and multiple data model compatibility.

Instructor-Oriented Interface

A prominent design principle kept in mind during the design of this application is the creation of an instructor-oriented dashboard.

Instructors have much to gain from inspecting various aspects of their courses through the analytics modules created by researchers and other instructors (and their GSIs), so the primary use case was that of instructors running MOOCs extracting actionable analytics.

To achieve this, we concentrated on three major areas: ease of access through an aggregated and simplistic interface, facilitation of data distribution, and security.

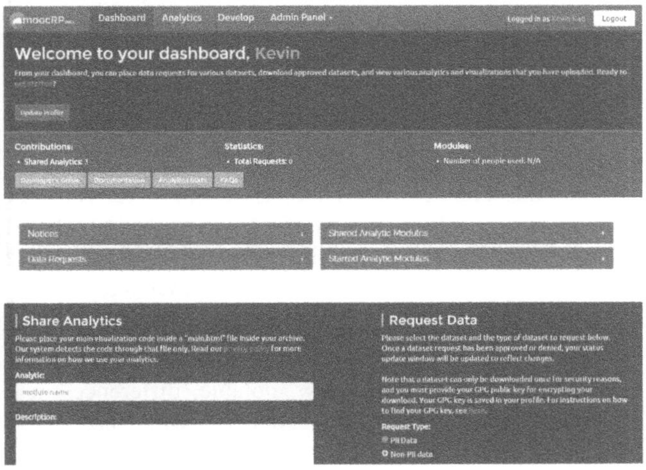

Figure 5. The main interface for moocRP, providing easy access to data requests, analytic modules, and basic stats.

Aggregated interface

moocRP provides a simple, aggregated interface to all of its basic functions. On its main page, moocRP has a series of four closed but expandable panels. The four panels provide easy access to 1) data requests, 2) data downloads, 3) shared analytics modules, and 4) starred analytics modules (see Figure 5). Below, there are two forms for requesting data and uploading analytic modules. The system for data requests and downloads are discussed further in the next section, so here, we focus on the interface for analytics. To facilitate an instructor's access to interesting modules, moocRP allows users to "star" analytic modules and visualizations, essentially creating a bookmark for quick access to the module.

The analytics page provides a paginated list of approved visualizations and analytic modules uploaded by various users of the system (see Figure 6). Each row representing a module also has a dropdown list of datasets for the module to be applied on. The datasets listed are 1) restricted to the datasets that have already been granted to the browsing user, and 2) limited to the compatible data models as specified by the uploading analytic author. For example, modules with a particular Coursera data model most likely is incompatible with an analytic module developed for a particular edX data model. A search feature is implemented in to allow instructors to quickly scout out relevant modules to their problems.

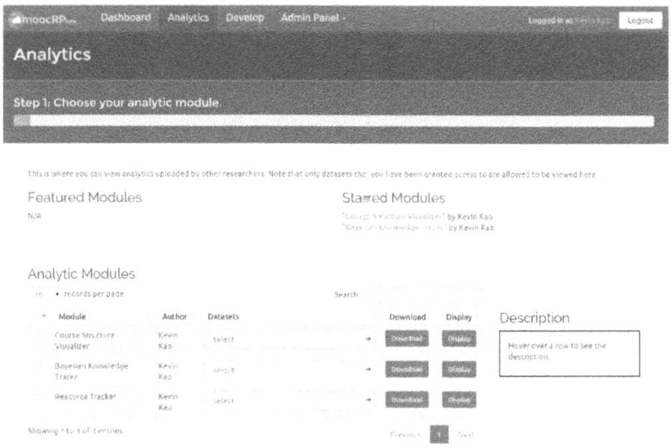

Figure 6. A two column header provides access to popular analytics modules as well as the visualizations that the user has starred. Below it is the list of available analytics modules, each with drop-down lists of compatible datasets.

A set of links is also provided for quick access to various significant moocRP developer guides, such as the documentation and data model guides for developing analytic modules.

Data distribution

A basic but essential feature of moocRP is its facilitation of data distribution. The processes to request and receive data at numerous institutions often involve a large number of email handoffs culminating in an exchange of a thumb drive with encrypted data in tow. This is just one example of a significantly inefficient process that could become more streamlined and secure. To solve this problem, moocRP provides a shorter data distribution pipeline. Upon registration, users provide a PGP public keys (step-by-step instructions on how to do so are provided on the same page). The user can then login and view the "Request Data" form, where they simply select their choice of dataset and submit the form to initiate the data request. The data scrubbing scripts packaged with moocRP can produce PII (personally identifiable information) and non-PII versions of a dataset with separate authorization for each.

After a data request is sent, any moocRP administrator can go to the administration panel and see a searchable table of data requests, which displays information about each data request (i.e. user's full name, type of dataset, dataset name, date requested). The administrator can either grant or deny the request, which would then reflect on the researcher's dashboard. The users can then easily download their approved datasets with a one-time download provided by the server.

Security

With a web application that works with sensitive datasets containing personal information, security is a major concern. This concern is reflected in the development of moocRP where security comes first at every level.

The first set of security measures comes directly from the user authentication system built into moocRP. The current release of moocRP uses the CAS protocol, otherwise known as the Central Authentication Service. Using CAS has two benefits in one: a secure way to manage users using an institution's existing CAS setup and the ability to use one set of credentials to login to multiple services. Focusing on the security aspect of CAS, we can inspect the CAS authentication process: a user logs in to moocRP, which redirects to the CAS portal of the institution, where the user enters login credentials. The moocRP back-end server waits for a response from the CAS portal that has a "ticket" – moocRP then sends this ticket back to the CAS portal for validation (to prevent access through an expired session or fabricated tickets). If validation is successful, then the user is allowed access to moocRP. CAS provides us *authentication* of the user as well as the user's identity. Future modularization of the authentication module will allow for substitutions of alternative authentication protocols into moocRP, based on each institution's needs.

The next level of security arrives directly when dealing with the datasets moocRP distributes. Upon registration, the user inputs his/her PGP public key, allowing moocRP to utilize the power of encryption to secure datasets. moocRP automates dataset encryption when a dataset is approved for download for a particular user, encrypting the dataset with 2048-bit PGP encryption using the user's public key, allowing only the original owner of the private key to decrypt the dataset.

This leads to another security measure: the entire moocRP application runs over the HTTPS protocol, with SSL built in. This secures the connection between the client and the moocRP server, preventing spoofers and eavesdroppers from gaining unauthorized access to communications. The data distribution is finally secured with CSRF protection and a one-time download link, preventing a malicious attacker from attempting to resubmit a data request form or re-download an approved dataset.

Some additional minor security features are found in the administration panel and logging. The administration panel provides features to manage users, including removal and editing of users, if needed. Uploaded analytics modules can also be removed if found to include malicious code. Logging keeps track of user actions within moocRP, which can be parsed to check for unusual activities.

The last major security measure is inherent to moocRP itself: moocRP in its present state is a relatively closed system, meaning that each moocRP instance will be used and managed by individual institutions, so only members or affiliates of the institution will be accessing moocRP. A *required level of trust* is necessary to re-inforce all of the security precautions that moocRP takes: users are only granted access to the system by each institution's administrators. Likewise, data requests and analytic modules must all go through an approval process by the administrators. PII data will not be viewable via analytics; however, many institutions have security policies around non-PII data. We believe that encryption of the data on the server and visualization of the data over SSL is a high standard of security. Data passed to analytic modules in the browser are not stored on disk and the level of risk associated with these data is not commensurate with any concern over information being resident in browser memory. While it is true that a capable user could intercept and store data passed to the analytic module, it is also the case that such an individual would also only be able to view analytics if already granted full privileges to download the data. At some point the trust bestowed to the individual must be relied upon to cover the balance of scenarios.

Technical Design

Technology stack

The choice of technologies was selected with care. During the planning phase of moocRP development, there were two obvious choices of technologies: Ruby on Rails or Node.js with a backend MVC framework. Note that Node.js should not be directly compared to Rails, since Node.js is a web server while Rails is a framework.

Rails has been on the rise, since before 2010. Node.js, on the other hand, has quickly been gaining popularity in the last couple of years. A few notable differences and considerations when using Node.js with an MVC framework versus using Rails:

- Rails is built on Ruby. Node.js is built on JavaScript, which (often times) has comparable or faster benchmark times than Ruby due to the V8 Engine[3].
- Rails is an opinionated framework, forcing a developer to adhere to its culture and stigmas. Node.js is the opposite, more allowing for a step-by-step build of various components.
- Rails has a steep learning curve with numerous Ruby intricacies to consider. Learning JavaScript is rather quick with experience in any major language like Java or C.

With these observations in mind, we can weigh some advantages and disadvantages of each. For the purposes of moocRP, we heavily favored speed and customization, so we chose Node.js. To make up for what Rails provides out of the box, we used a popular Node.js MVC framework: Sails.js. This allowed us to quickly develop a web application with basic functionality in a Rails manner while still maintaining the ability to customize the application as we desired. Since our work began, moocRP has developed greater support for web sockets, better support of databases, and will soon extend integration of AngularJS, which will allow for a smoother presentation and transfer of data to the client.

Analytics pipeline

The analytics pipeline for sharing and visualizing modules created by users is centric to moocRP. There are a few notable components of the analytics pipeline to discuss: the

[3]http://benchmarksgame.alioth.debian.org/u32/compare.php?lang=v8&lang2=yarv

file watch, the syncing of datasets to clients, and the scaffolding of uploaded analytic modules.

Essentially, moocRP simply keeps a file watch on specific folders in the base directory of moocRP for datasets. These folders are associated with the datasets of each data model in moocRP. The folders are created when an administrator creates a new data model in the moocRP admin panel.For example, a sample structure of the data directories used for analytics modules. When a new folder is detected inside these directories, moocRP will add new data models and datasets to be available for requesting by users. When a user's request is granted, the user will also be allowed to select the dataset for relevant analytic modules.

The other component of the analytics pipeline involves the uploaded modules. As mentioned in the case studies, the analytic modules is a package consisting of one HTML file, CSS files, and JS files. moocRP extracts these files into a temp folder and moves them into the correct directories to be served. The CSS and JS files are moved into the assets folder, while the HTML file is moved to a view folder used by the framework Sails.js to serve pages with additional features, e.g. template variables between the client and server. Once placed in the correct folders, moocRP will display them on the analytics page.

Support for Multiple Data Models

The moocRP tool allows an administrator to add a new data model easily. The process of adding a new data model consists of only a few steps. The administrator can navigate to the "Data Models" tab in the administration panel. The administrator then fills out a form that asks for only the user-friendly name of the new data model and a system-friendly name for the data model (see Figure 7). The system-friendly name is a name that the moocRP can use to automatically create the appropriate directories on the server. Then, the administrator only needs to configure the tools necessary for transforming the data into the new data model formats in a way such that the tools output the datasets in the directories that moocRP created. Therefore, once a new data model is added in the administration panel, moocRP will be able to recognize the new data model and be able to provide support for it for analytics modules and for data distribution.

edX data scrubbing

On the administrator's side, moocRP includes an edX data scrubbing tool out of the box that helps the administrator

- download edX data from the Amazon servers
- decrypt the downloaded data
- organize event data logs across multiple servers into one event data log file for each course, and
- transform the aggregated event data log files into *xAPI event data* format.

Our edX data scrubbing tool is built on top of the HarvardX Tools. We modified several parts of the original scripts to make the tool compatible with the current format of raw edX data, and to speed up the data organizing and transformation time.

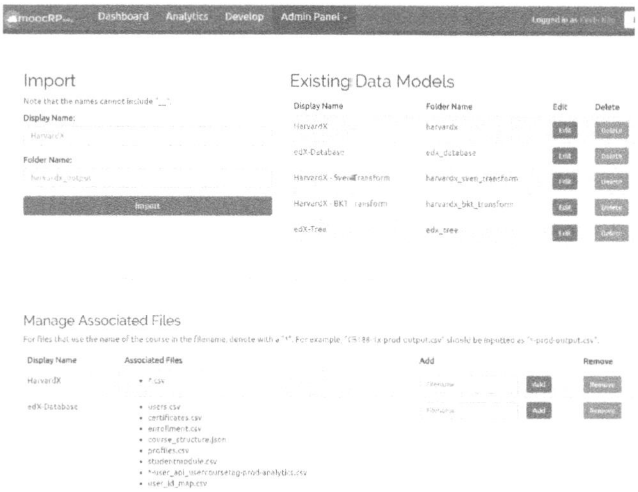

Figure 7. The data models management page, where data models can be added or deleted in a few clicks. Associated files of each data model is also managed here.

TOOL SUSTAINABILITY AND FUTURE WORK

Centralized repositories, such as the LearnLab's DataShop, are not fully supported by an institution and rely on government funding to maintain. The moocRP model instead leverages institutional self-interest to maintain its services. Institutions have an interest in facilitating research from its faculty and staff as well as leveraging value from its data in order to provide a more effective and efficient educational experience to its students. No particular platform buy-in or inter-institutional network is required; rather each institution may utilize the tool and benefit from the analytics modules available for it.

Much work remains to be done to improve moocRP. Some important features to be implemented with community support and continued in-house engineering include:

- Automated analytic module security screening
- Alternative authentication protocols and modularization
- Integration of data pre-processing scripts
- Support for scripts of alternative languages, e.g. Matlab, Perl, Python, that could be used for machine learning analytics
- Additional statistics on data model and analytic usage information
- Various server and implementation optimizations

We will also continue collaborations with interested universities and learning systems through webinars and conferences to gain feedback on the tool.

CONCLUSIONS

In this paper we introduced an open-source analytics platform that adopts the three tenants of open learning analytics; transparency, modularity, and privacy. The platform provides value to; MOOC researchers by allowing for replication of results by providing a simple framework to share and develop analytic modules, to instructors by providing an easy to use interface for applying community generated analytics to their course, and to administrators by providing a workflow for managing secured data repository access controls. The moocRP platform is not a panacea to the problem of open learning analytics or reproducible research, but it is a earnest step towards bringing the power of learner data to bear on both the educational and research objectives of an organization.

ACKNOWLEDGEMENTS

The second author was partially supported by a Google Faculty Research Award (#2014_R1_446).

REFERENCES

[1] Siemens, G., Gašević, D., Haythornthwaite, C., Dawson, S., Buckingham Shum, S., Ferguson,R., et al. (2011) Open Learning Analytics: An Integrated and Modularized Platform (Concept Paper): SOLAR.

[2] Koedinger, K. R., Baker, R., Cunningham, K., Skogsholm, A., Leber, B., & Stamper, J. (2010) A data repository for the EDM community: The PSLC DataShop. *Handbook of educational data mining, 43.*

[3] Veeramachaneni, K., Dernoncourt, F., Taylor, C., Pardos, Z.A. & O'Reilly, U.M. (20213) MOOCdb: Developing data standards for MOOC data science. In *AIED 2013 Workshops Proceedings* (pp. 17-24)

[4] Pardos, Z. A., Heffernan, N. T. (2010) Modeling Individualization in a Bayesian Networks Implementation of Knowledge Tracing. In *Proceedings of the 18th International Conference on User Modeling, Adaptation and Personalization (UMAP)*. Springer. (pp. 255-266)

[5] Daries, J. P., Reich, J., Waldo, J., Young, E. M., Whittinghill, J., Ho, A. D., ... & Chuang, I. (2014) Privacy, anonymity, and big data in the social sciences. *Communications of the ACM, 57*(9), 56-63.

[6] Martin, B., Mitrovic, T., Mathan, S., & Koedinger, K.R. (2011). Evaluating and improving adaptive educational systems with learning curves. *User Model User-Adap Inter* (2011) 21:249–283.

[7] Feng, M., Heffernan, N.T. (2007) Towards Live Informing and Automatic Analyzing of Student Learning: Reporting in ASSISTment System. *Journal of Interactive Learning Research* 18 (2): 207-230.

[8] Gertner, A.S., and VanLehn, K. (2000) Andes: A Coached Problem-Solving Environment for Physics. In *Proceedings of the 5th International Conference on Intelligent Tutoring Systems* (pp. 133-142)

[9] Anderson, J. R., Corbett, A. T., Koedinger, K. R., and Pelletier, R. (1995) Cognitive tutors: Lessons learned. *The Journal of the Learning Sciences* 4 (2): 167-207.

[10] Lovett, M., Meyer, O., & Thille, C. (2008) The Open Learning Initiative: Measuring the effectiveness of the OLI statistics course in accelerating student learning. *Journal of Interactive Media in Education*, no. 14. Special Issue http://jime.open.ac.uk/2008/14

[11] Corbett, A. T., & Anderson, J. R. (2001). Locus of feedback control in computer-based tutoring: Impact on learning rate, achievement and attitudes. In *Proceedings of SIGCHI 2011* (pp. 245-252). ACM.

[12] Bloom, B. S. (1968). Learning for mastery.

[13] Ferguson, R., & Shum, S. B. (2012). Social learning analytics: five approaches. In *Proceedings of the 2nd International Conference on Learning Analytics and Knowledge* (pp. 23-33). ACM.

[14] Breslow, L., Pritchard, D. E., DeBoer, J., Stump, G. S., Ho, A. D., & Seaton, D. T. (2013) Studying learning in the worldwide classroom: Research into edX's first MOOC. *Research & Practice in Assessment, 8*, 13-25.

[15] Daries, J. P., Reich, J., Waldo, J., Young, E. M., Whittinghill, J., Ho, A. D., ... & Chuang, I. (2014) Privacy, anonymity, and big data in the social sciences. *Communications of the ACM*, 57(9), 56-63.

[16] Verbert, K., Govaerts, S., Duval, E., Santos, J. L., Van Assche, F., Parra, G., & Klerkx, J. (2013) Learning dashboards: an overview and future research opportunities. *Personal and Ubiquitous Computing*, 1-16.

[17] The Asilomar Convention for Learning Research in Higher Education (http://asilomar-highered.info/asilomar-convention-20140612.pdf)

[18] edX Research Guide. Data Delivered in Data Packages. http://edx.readthedocs.org/projects/devdata/en/latest/internal_data_formats/package.html, 2014.

[19] Jim Waldo. HarvardX Tools. https://github.com/jimwaldo/HarvardX-Tools

[20] ADL Initiative, Experience API, 2013, https://github.com/adlnet/- xAPI-Spec/blob/master/xAPI.md

[21] Stanford Vice Provost Office for Online Learning. How to Access the VPOL Online Learning Data. http://datastage.stanford.edu

[22] Andreas Paepcke. json_to_relation. https://github.com/paepcke/json_to_relation

[23] MOOCdb. http://moocdb.csail.mit.edu/wiki/index.php?title=MOOCdb

[24] Stephens-Martinez, K., Hearst, M. A., & Fox, A. (2014) Monitoring MOOCs: which information sources do instructors value? In *Proceedings of the first ACM conference on Learning@ Scale* (pp. 79-88)

[25] Xu, Z., Goldwasser, D., Bederson, B. B., & Lin, J. (2014) Visual analytics of MOOCs at Maryland. In *Proceedings of the first ACM conference on Learning@ Scale* (pp. 195-196)

Learning is Not a Spectator Sport: Doing is Better than Watching for Learning from a MOOC

Kenneth R. Koedinger
Carnegie Mellon University
5000 Forbes Avenue
koedinger@cmu.edu

Jihee Kim
Carnegie Mellon University
5000 Forbes Avenue
smile.jihee@gmail.com

Julianna Zhuxin Jia
Carnegie Mellon University
5000 Forbes Avenue
zhuxinj@andrew.cmu.edu

Elizabeth A. McLaughlin
Carnegie Mellon University
5000 Forbes Avenue
mimim@cs.cmu.edu

Norman L. Bier
Carnegie Mellon University
5000 Forbes Avenue
nbier@cmu.edu

ABSTRACT
The printing press long ago and the computer today have made widespread access to information possible. Learning theorists have suggested, however, that mere information is a poor way to learn. Instead, more effective learning comes through doing. While the most popularized element of today's MOOCs are the video lectures, many MOOCs also include interactive activities that can afford learning by doing. This paper explores the learning benefits of the use of informational assets (e.g., videos and text) in MOOCs, versus the learning by doing opportunities that interactive activities provide. We find that students doing more activities learn more than students watching more videos or reading more pages. We estimate the learning benefit from extra doing (1 SD increase) to be more than six times that of extra watching or reading. Our data, from a psychology MOOC, is correlational in character, however we employ causal inference mechanisms to lend support for the claim that the associations we find are causal.

Keywords: Learning by doing; MOOCs; learning prediction; course effectiveness; Open Education; OER

ACM Classification Keywords K.3.1

INTRODUCTION
The use of online learning resources to provide and support instruction is on the rise and spectacularly so [5]. Further, there is a growing recognition and interest in the opportunity to apply and contribute to the learning sciences by conducting education research through online learning environments [29, 16]. While there are notable success stories of online courses that were shown to be more effective than traditional instruction [e.g., 20], the more typical situation is that, at best, online courses achieve the same outcomes at lower cost [e.g., 6, 9]. Perhaps more importantly, we do not know enough about what features of online courses are most important for student learning.

The prototypical feature of a Massive Open Online Course (MOOC) is lecture videos, but many MOOCs also include activities such as questions for students to answer or problems for them to solve, in some cases with immediate online feedback. What is more important for student learning? Is it the information students get from watching lecture videos, the practice and feedback they get from online questions or problems, or some combination. The idea of scaling the best lecturers for open access is a compelling feature of MOOCs. However, in contrast to the passive form of learning characterized by watching video lectures or reading text, a diversity of learning theorists have recommended more active learning by doing [e.g., 3, 11, 28]. Many argue for learning by doing as it focuses on authentic activities that are more representative of knowledge use in the real world. More fundamentally, learning by doing is important because most of human expertise involves tacit knowledge of the cues and conditions for deciding when, where, and what knowledge to bring to bear in complex situations [36]. In this view, there appears to be no verbal shortcut to acquiring expertise It is gained by observing examples (or "models"), attempting to engage in expert activities with feedback and as-needed instruction ("scaffolding"), and having that support be adaptive to advancing proficiency ("fading") [cf., 10].

Intelligent tutoring systems provide such support through adaptive feedback and hints during learning by doing [1, 2, 34]. When well designed, they yield significant learning gains [e.g., 24, 27, 35]. "Well-designed" means designed using theory of learning and instruction [cf., 14, 26], data-driven methods including cognitive task analysis

L@S 2015, March 14–18, 2015, Vancouver, BC, Canada.
ACM 978-1-4503-3411-2/15/03.
http://dx.doi.org/10.1145/2724660.2724681

[8, 17], and classroom design research iterations [4, 19]. Interactive activities in Carnegie Mellon University's *Open Learning Initiative* courses attempt to mimic some of the behavior of intelligent tutors and, importantly, follow these good design practices [21, 31].

In the past few years, much attention has been paid to the demonstrated potential of Massive Open Online Courses (MOOC) to scale access to educational resources [25]. While the exact definition and role of MOOCs continues to be debated, much of the popular dialogue surrounds the three major MOOC platforms – Coursera, Udacity and EdX – who describe MOOCs as online courses with open, unlimited enrollment [23]. Though specific activities vary from course to course, video-based lectures and student discussion forums typically form the core of the MOOC instructional experience. We call this the "lecture model". The Open Learning Initiative, which has offered online learning environments since 2002, takes a different approach focusing on rich and interactive learn-by-doing activities, aligned with student-centered learning outcomes, and designed around science-based learner models. We call this the "learn-by-doing model." Both models offer rich datasets, though with different focuses and capturing different kinds of learner interactions.

An opportunity emerged recently to compare the instructional features of these two different models in terms of how variations in student use of them impacts the learning outcomes they achieve. In 2013, Georgia Institute of Technology and Carnegie Mellon University (CMU) collaborated to incorporate elements of CMU's Open Learning Initiative (OLI) "Introduction to Psychology" learning environment into Tech's *Introduction to Psychology as a Science* MOOC. Taught via the Coursera platform, OLI materials were available as part of the larger course, in addition to lectures, quizzes and other Coursera-based activities. This paper explores the impact of the use of the OLI elements on learning, in comparison to use of MOOC elements (alone or in association with the OLI materials). As part of this exploration, we examine which OLI features are most associated with learning and if we can infer causal relationships between these features. In addition, we analyze the potential for predicting the course dropout using student performance in OLI activities and survey-based demographic information.

The key research questions we pursue are:

1. What factors determine whether or not students stay in the course or dropout?
2. Do students who use OLI features learn more than those using the MOOC only?
3. What variations in course feature use (watching videos, reading text, or doing activities) are most associated with learning? And can we infer causal relationships?

A key goal is to provide evidence relevant to alternative hypotheses about what makes a course effective. The "lecture model" suggests that students' primary source for learning is through listening to lectures. The "learn-by-doing model" suggests that students' primary source for learning comes from answering questions and solving problems with feedback. Of course, it may be that both sources are critical.

COURSE FEATURES AND DESIGN

In considering the features available in the course, we divide components into two broad categories: passive/declarative information and active/interactive activities. Students learn from passive/declarative information by reading, watching or studying; these features include video lectures, lecture slides and other expository materials (text). Active/interactive features by definition require students to be more active, and include quizzes, exams, discussion forum participation and interactive activities that provide targeted feedback and hints. Although engagement with the full range of learning materials assigned was encouraged, the final grade in the course was awarded based upon a combination of quiz scores, final exam score and two written assignments. In addition, the course contained two additional features intended to support research rather than learning: a pre/post test and student background survey. Neither of these elements was factored into students' grades.

Introduction to Psychology as a Science was designed as a 12-week introductory survey course, as is often taught during the first year of college. For each week of class, the course targeted a major topic area (e.g. Memory, Sense and Perception, Abnormal Behavior, Brain Structures and the Nervous System); these topics were broken into 3-4 sub-topics, each supported by a pre-recorded video lecture (10-15 minutes, with downloadable slides) and included assigned modules and learning outcomes in the OLI learning environment. A high-stakes quiz assessed students against these outcomes at the end of each week.

The **Coursera MOOC platform** provided general course structure (registration, syllabus, etc), video lectures and slides, discussion forums, writing assignments, quizzes (with questions drawn from OLI item banks, see Figure 1b for an example), and a final exam (with questions created by the instructor, see Figure 1c for an example). The background survey was also administered via this platform, which focused on demographic information (gender, age, education, occupation) as well as some questions to assess learner intent and opinion.

The **OLI Learning Environment** was embedded in the Coursera platform using Learning Tools Interoperability (LTI) for a seamless learner experience. The corresponding OLI modules included a variety of expository content (text, examples, images, and video clips) and a large number of interactive activities. Broadly, these activities serve two purposes. "Learn By Doing" activities, intended to support student outcome achievement, provide feedback targeted to diagnose misconceptions and robust hints to support students. In Figure 1a, we show a screenshot of a Learn by Doing activity from the unit on Personality covered in week 9 of the course. "Did I Get This" activities provide a self-comprehension check for students. They are introduced at points when students are expected to have achieved mastery and do not provide hints, though they do offer feedback [31].

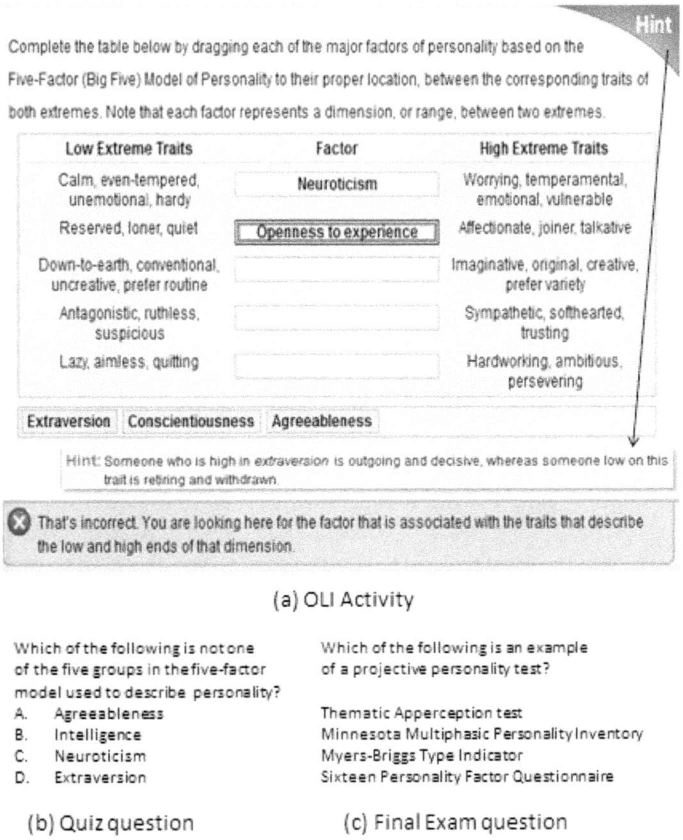

Figure 1. (a) Screen shot of a Learn By Doing OLI activity from the unit on Personality© OLI. (b) Corresponding quiz question © OLI. (c) Related final exam question © Dr. Anderson Smith, GA Institute of Technology.

METHODS

It is important to point out that using data from natural student use of MOOCs adds uncertainty in making inferences about causal relationships as compared to using data from experimental designs. This uncertainty is further increased by the large attrition or dropout that is typical in MOOCs. The sample of students involved in any particular analysis is determined by student participation and effects that might be attributed to other factors (e.g., course features) might instead be so-called "selection effects", that is, effects of sampling differences based on the choices or selections that students make. Nevertheless, there is a real opportunity to use the large and naturally-occurring data that comes from MOOCs to provide initial, if not confirming, evidence of factors of potential importance for course participation and learning outcomes.

Table 1 shows different subsets of students as indicated by different forms of participation in the course. We refer to it in describing how samples were selected to address our research questions.

Our first research question is: What factors determine whether or not students stay in the course or dropout? 27720 students registered in the Coursera MOOC Psychology course while 1154 students completed it (see Table 1). We are interested in what indicators or features may predict dropouts throughout the course, and we use quiz and final exam participation as estimates of student dropout. For example, if a student has a score for quiz 4 but none of the remaining quizzes or the final, we consider that student to have dropped out after quiz 4. We are interested in factors that predict future dropouts. In addition to whether students used the OLI material or not, we also included quiz participation and quiz score in a logistic regression model to predict final exam participation.

Our second research question is: Do students who use OLI learn more than students who only use the MOOC materials? MOOC+OLI students (N=9075) are those who registered to use the OLI materials. MOOC-only students (N=18,645) did not (see Table 1). To address the question, we did a quasi-experimental comparison of learning outcomes between the MOOC+OLI students who took the final (N=939) with the MOOC-only students who took the final (N=215).

Our third research question is: What variations in course feature use (watching videos, reading text, or doing activities) are most associated with learning? And can we infer causal relationships? In the results section, we describe an exploratory data analysis to identify relationships between usage of these features (garnered from the log data [15]) and our two measures of learning, quizzes scores and final exam score. To frame that analysis, we present some global data on feature usage. Of all MOOC registrants, 14,254 (51.4% of total) started to watch at least one lecture video. Of the 9075 students (32.7% of total) registered for OLI material study, 84.5% (7683 students) accessed at least one page of OLI readings and visited or revisited an average of 69 pages with a maximum of 1942 pages (variable *pageview*). On average, 33 unique pages were viewed with a maximum of 192 unique pages. Of the 9075 OLI registered students, 62.3% (5658 students) started at least one interactive

	Students	Percent total (percent subgroup)	Average Score or Feature Usage/Max
All students	27720	100%	
Pre-test	12218	44.89%	6.9/20
Quizzes	2373[1]	8.7%	7.1 /10
Final	1154	4.2%	25.6/ 40
MOOC only	18645	67.3% (100%)	
Pre-test	4872	17.6% (39.9%)	5.8/20
Quizzes	496	1.8% (4.1%)	6.3/10
Final	215	1% (1%)	22.8/40
OLI registered	9075	32.7% (100%)	
Pre-test	7346	26.5% (80.9%)	8.6/20
Quizzes	1876	6.8% (20.7%)	7.5/10
Final	939	3.4%	26.3/40
Playing video	902	(96.1%)	164.4/4460
Reading pages	939	(100%)	296.8/1942
Doing activities	939	(100%)	387.2/695
Non-activity pages	939	(100%)	182/1759

Table 1. Student participation in assessments and in course features; average score or usage.

[1]6912 students took quiz 1 and 1136 students took quiz 11. 2374 is the average across all 11 quizzes.

activity with an average of 127 and a maximum of 695 activities started (variable *activities_started*). Table 1 shows these same activity use statistics for the subset of OLI registered students who took the final exam (939 students).

Because activities sit on pages and students must go to those pages to do the activities, we created a new measure to represent pages accessed beyond those needed to get to a page. A scatterplot between pageview and activities_started indicated a lower bound on pages seen for a given number of activities and the bound is reasonably estimated at the maximum of 695 activities, where no one did this many activities in fewer than 206 pageviews. We used this ratio of about 3.4 activities per page to subtract out the pages due to activity access and computed a new variable, *non_activities_pageview*, that is arguably a more pure measure of the variation in the reading students did.

After the exploratory data analysis, the results present a search for potential causal relationships, including estimates of the strength of these relationships, by using a causal inference system called Tetrad [32]. Tetrad is a program that creates, estimates, tests, predicts with, and searches for causal and statistical models. Tetrad has a distinct suite of model discovery search algorithms that include, for example, an ability to search when there may be unobserved confounders of measured variables, to search for models of latent structure, to search for linear feedback models, and to calculate predictions of the effects of interventions or experiments based on a model[1]. We used Tetrad to infer the causal relationships between pretest score, course feature use variables (watching videos, reading pages, doing activities), quiz scores, and final exam score. To aid causal model search, we specified some extra time-based constraints, particularly that leader measures could not use earlier ones (i.e., the final scores cannot cause quiz scores, quiz scores cannot cause feature use, and feature use cannot cause pre-test score). We used Tetrad's PCD algorithm for causal model search and we normalized the data (using a correlation matrix input to PCD) so that resulting model coefficients could be better compared and interpreted.

RESULTS AND DISCUSSION

Predicting Course DropOut and Completion

From the total number of registered students (27,720), only 4% take the final exam. Of the 9075 students who registered for the OLI materials, only 10% took the final exam. Such high attrition rates in MOOC courses are not uncommon [12] as many students register for reasons other than completing the course (e.g., determine their interest in the material, check their knowledge on the topic, etc.). But, we were interested in examining when students dropout (i.e., is there a crucial point in the course for students to not continue to participate) and what factors might contribute to dropping out.

[1] http://www.phil.cmu.edu/tetrad/

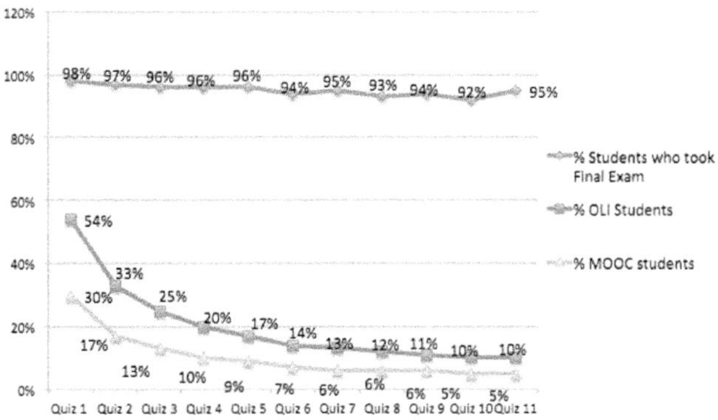

Figure 2. The participation rate in quizzes among three groups of students, registered in MOOC (N = 27720), also registered in OLI (N = 9075), and also taking the final exam (N = 939).

Figure 2 shows different participation rates among three student groups: 1) the 27720 students who registered for the course, 2) the 9075 students who registered to use the OLI materials, and 3) the 939 of those MOOC+OLI students who took the final. Quiz participation decreases over time both for all MOOC students and for the MOOC+OLI subset. The rate of quiz participation is consistently higher for MOOC+OLI students than for MOOC students in general, about twice as high. Seriousness to take the extra step to register in OLI appears *not* to be enough to explain greater MOOC+OLI participation rates. If we further restrict the sample to those who completed the first quiz (another indicator of early seriousness), we still find the MOOC+OLI students are more likely to take quiz 11 (18.5%) than the MOOC-only students (14%). The biggest drop in participation comes between quiz 1 and 2 with 43% of students dropping overall (39% of MOOC+OLI and 50% of MOOC only). Perhaps not surprisingly, the quiz participation of the MOOC+OLI students who attended the final exam (N = 939) is quite high with 98% taking quiz 1 and 95% taking quiz 11.

We also explored whether quizzes' participation and/or quizzes' scores can predict final exam participation. We used a logistic regression model with final exam participation as the outcome variable. The predictor variables were Pretest participation and Pretest score and 22 others for participation in each of the 11 quizzes and for scores on each of the 11 quizzes. Table 2 shows the coefficients, standard errors and P values for all predictors that are highly significant, at the $p<0.01$ level. Participations in quizzes later in the course (i.e., quizzes 7 and 11) are, perhaps not surprisingly, good predictors of final exam participation. Additionally, there is an indication that how well students are doing in the course may also be predictive. A student's score on quiz 1, above and beyond having merely taken it (and taken other quizzes), is associated with higher final exam participation. Given this is the first quiz, this result may suggest that students that are either underprepared for the course or are not engaging sufficiently with the first unit materials to learn from them are unlikely to continue through to the end of the course and take the final exam.

Factors	Estimate	Std. Error	Pr(>|z|)
(Intercept)	-6.34020	0.19564	< 2e-16 ***
Quiz 1 Score	0.24434	0.07698	0.0015 **
Took Quiz 7 or Not	2.95023	0.71933	4.11e-05 ***
Took Quiz 11 or Not	4.95794	0.69094	7.20e-13 ***

Table 2. Significant factors in a logistic regression model predicting final exam *participation*.

Signif. codes: 0 '***' 0.001 '**' 0.01 AIC: 1469

Comparing Learning Outcomes of MOOC-only and MOOC+OLI Students

The first measure of comparison was students' final exam scores. MOOC-only students (N=215) had an average final exam score of 56.9% and the MOOC+OLI students (N=939) averaged 65.7%. This difference is highly significant based on a t-test ($p < .001$), however, applying a t-test directly is not appropriate because the group score distributions are not normally distributed. They are skewed toward higher scores and include a number of low outliers. We employ a simple transformation (a cubic) of the measure ($final\_score^3$) to produce normal distributions. Applying a t-test to the transformed data once again yields a highly significant difference ($p < 0.001$).

As mentioned above, the difference in these self-selected groups may be a consequence of features of the students rather than of the OLI instruction. Students who registered to use the OLI materials may simply be better students. One way to test for (but not completely eliminate) the possibility of such a selection effect is to build a statistical model using all the information we have about student characteristics. We can then test whether a difference based on OLI use still remains after accounting for these other characteristics. In particular, we created a linear regression with final exam score as the outcome variable and, in addition to instructional group (MOOC+OLI vs. MOOC-only), we included six other student characteristic variables: pretest score, Quiz 1 score, occupation, age, education and gender. Because not all students answered the survey, our sample is now reduced to 551 students, 251 in MOOC+OLI and 301 in MOOC-only. Table 3 shows only the significant coefficients in the model and we see that Quiz 1 score and education make significant independent contributions to the final exam score and, importantly, the increase due to

OLI use remains. None of the other variables (pretest score, occupation, age, or gender) make a significant independent contribution to the final exam score.

	Estimate	Std Error	P-value
(Intercept)	16.90	3.32	5.21e-07***
OLI use	1.43	0.55	0.009 **
Quiz 1 score	1.06	0.11	<2e-16 ***
Education = PhD	3.96	1.84	0.032 *

Table 3. Significant factors in a linear regression predicting final exam *score*.

Signif. codes: 0 '***' 0.001 '**' 0.01 '*' 0.05

The model parameters indicate that students with a PhD (N=41) get 3.96 more questions (out of 40) correct on average than students in other educational groups, that every extra point on the pre-test yields 1.06 more questions correct, and that use of OLI (at least registering) produces 1.43 more questions correct. Just because students register to use OLI, does not guarantee that they do. And, similarly, just because students are in the MOOC does not mean they take advantage of the features it provides, such as watching the lecture videos. The next section investigates the log data to explore the impact of estimated student use of such features.

Variations in Course Feature Use Predict Differences in Learning Outcomes

Exploratory Data Analysis: Doing, not Watching, Better Predicts Learning. As a method of exploratory data analysis, we simply performed a median split on each of our metrics of instructional feature use -- videos played, pages accessed (beyond activities), and activities started. A student is a "watcher" if they played more than a median number of videos, a "reader" if they accessed more than a median number of pages, and a "doer" if they started more than a median number of activities. Figure 3a shows that the most frequent combinations are the extremes, either being on the low half for all three, a non-watcher-non-reader-non-doer shown in the leftmost bar (N=201) or being on the high half for all three a watcher-reader-doer shown in the leftmost bar (N=184). The next most frequent combinations are reader-doers (N=120), who are using the OLI features, and watchers (N=105), who are using the distinctive MOOC feature, video lectures.

Which type of student appears to learn the most? Figure 3b shows the results for the total quiz score and indicates that the doers do well on the quizzes (score of about 94 points) even without being on the high half of reading or watching (the red bars are equally high). (Note, however, that the doers tend to read and watch more than the non-doers in the matched reading and watching groups.) Those in the lower half of doing (the non-doers) do not perform as well on the quizzes, but those who are on *either* the high half of reading *or* watching do better (80 points) than those low on both (62 points). In other words, doing the activities may be sufficient to do well on the quizzes, but if you do not do the activities, you will be better off at least reading or watching.

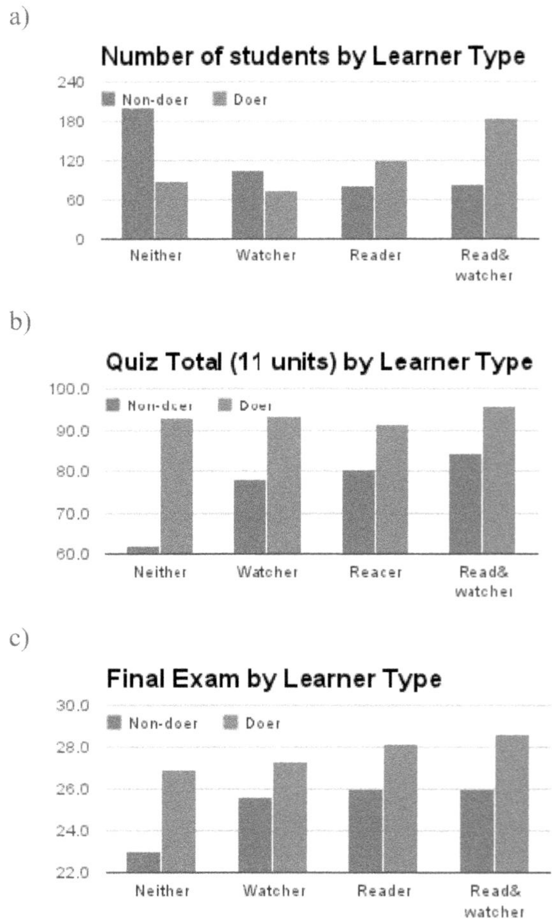

Figure 3. (a) Most students are either on the low half of watching, reading, and doing (the first blue Neither column for Non-doers) or high on all three (the last red Read&watcher column for Doers), but many (>70) are present in the other 6 combinations. (b) Doers consistently do better in the total quiz score and next best is either watching or reading. (c) Final exams appear to show greater sensitivity to reading and watching further boosting the benefits of doing, but doing is still the clear dominant factor.

Figure 3c indicates that, as for quiz score, a higher final exam score is more typical of those on the higher half of doing (about 28 points) and next best is either reading or watching (about 26 points) with low on all being the worst (23 points). In contrast with the quizzes, there is at least a hint in the final exam score showing that simply doing (26.7) is further enhanced by watching (27.4), reading (28.2), and both (28.7).

	Quiz		Final	
	Poor	Excellent	Poor	Excellent
High watcher only	46%	5%	38%	15%
High doer only	13%	42%	13%	16%
High both	2%	52%	0%	31%

Table 4. Percent of students of different extreme types (highest quartile) that do poorly or excellently on the quizzes and final.

Table 4 summarizes an analysis of the extremes that starts by splitting each of the watching, doing, quiz, and final variables into four equal groups of students and focuses on the lowest and highest quarters of these groups. The first row in Table 4 illustrates how watching lots of the videos but doing few activities leaves one quite likely to do poorly on quizzes (46% of such students) or on the final (38%) and quite unlikely to do an excellent job on quizzes (5%) and final (15%). The second row shows how simply doing a lot even without much watching of video lectures avoids poor performance on quizzes and the final (only 13% for both) and enhances excellent performance on quizzes (42%). However, a lot of doing alone does not facilitate excellent performance on the final (16%). As seen in the last column of the third row, reaching excellent levels of transfer to performance on the final is one place where it appears that extensive video watching is beneficial, but only for those who are also extensively engaged in the learning by doing activities (31% as opposed to 15% and 16% for those who are only high watchers or high doers alone).

Why might high video watching along with high doing aid excellent performance on the final, whereas lots of doing without much video watching appears sufficient for excellent performance on the quizzes? One possible reason is that the final was created by the MOOC professor and may have had items on it that are not covered in the OLI material, but only in the lecture videos. Learning by doing activities may generally better support learning, but if certain items on the final involved concepts or skills that were not required in those activities but that were presented in the videos, then students that watched lots of video lectures are more likely to get those items correct. Alternatively, we find that replacing "high watcher" with "high reader" in Table 4 produces similar results, that high doing is enough to increase chances of excellent quiz performance but it takes combining high *reading* along with high doing to increase chances of excellent quiz performance. In other words, it may not be the video lecture per se, but the declarative content present in video *or* reading, that appears important, on top of lots of learning by doing, for excellent performance on the final exam.

Is Course Feature Use Causally Related with Student Outcomes? As introduced in the Methods, we used Tetrad, a tool for causal inference, to evaluate whether associations between key variables, pre-test, course features (doing, reading, and watching), quiz total, and final are potentially causal. Figure 4 shows the causal model that a Tetrad search identified. The model is a good one in that a chi square (df=7) test shows its predictions are not statistically different from the data (p = 0.39)[2].

The model indicates direct causal impacts from all course features, doing activities, reading materials, and watching videos, to a higher total quiz score. The most influential impact comes from doing activities, with a normalized coefficient of 0.44 (a 1 standard deviation increase in doing activities produces 0.44 sd increase in quiz score). The strength of this relationship is more than six times the impact of watching video or reading pages (both with coefficients of about .065) and more than three times the combined impact of watching and reading.

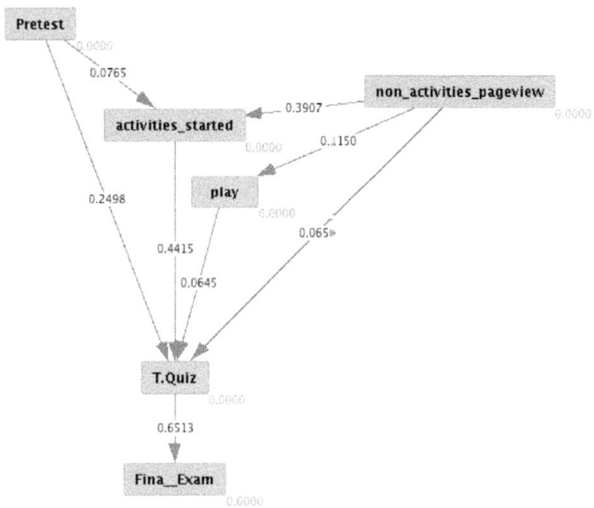

Figure 4. Tetrad inference of causal relationships between pretest score, course features (doing activities, watching videos, reading pages), total quizzes score, and final exam.

Looking at other features of the model, we see that a higher pretest score directly causes a higher quiz score (coefficient = 0.25). Thus, effects of course feature use are adjusted for and above and beyond this influence. Higher pretest also causes greater activity use, though weakly (0.08). Within the three course features, more reading causes both more doing and more watching, with

[2] In Tetrad, the null hypothesis of the chi square test is that the population covariance matrix is equal to the estimated covariance matrix determined as a function of the free model parameters. The test essentially asks whether the predictions for associations between variables that are not linked in the causal graph are different from the actual associations -- a model is good when the prediction is not significantly different from the data.

a larger coefficient for doing (0.39 > 0.12). The higher influence of reading on doing may reflect the proximity of these features within OLI pages, whereas the videos are located in the MOOC proper. Higher quiz scores cause higher final scores and this relationship is quite strong (0.65). The final exam was developed by the MOOC instructor whereas the unit quizzes more directly correspond with the content of the associated OLI modules. The strength of the connection suggests that student-learning improvements as measured by the quizzes (and highly influenced by doing more activities) do well transfer to the final exam.

RELATED WORK, LIMITATIONS AND FUTURE WORK

Our results on the limited value of video watching for learning are particularly interesting given other results suggesting that video watching behavior is predictive of dropout [30]. Those who are motivated to watch lecture videos may well be interested in the course material and may stick with it, however, that is no guarantee that those experiences produce any substantial robust or lasting learning. Consistent with our results, much work on intelligent tutoring systems is premised on the power of learning by doing. A pre-MOOC analysis of course elements found that "electronic homework as administered by CyberTutor is the only course element that contributes significantly to improvement on the final exam" [22]. A recent analysis of two MOOC data sets was less conclusive "the wide distribution of demographics and initial skill in MOOCs challenges us to isolate the habits of learning and resource use that correlate with learning for different students" [7]. One potential important difference between some learning by doing activities in those MOOCs (e.g., use of a circuit simulator) and the ones provided by OLI is the availability of fast feedback and hints in the context of doing. Such interactive (not merely active) experiences may be particularly effective for learning.

An immediate opportunity for future work is to evaluate whether our results generalize to data from a second offering of the same MOOC that was run in Spring 2014 using the same materials and teaching team. In addition, during Spring of 2013, these OLI materials were used in a variety of two-year institutions as part of the OLI Community College evaluation project [13]. An analysis of this data offers an opportunity to consider the generalizability of these results beyond the MOOC setting.

Our analysis to date has not taken advantage of all the available data. In future work, we would like to also explore how student involvement in peer-graded writing assignments and in discussion forums is associated with learning outcomes and dropout. We can also improve on our estimates of the amount of watching, reading, and doing students engage in by not only seeing how often a video, page, or activity is started, but also estimate the amount of time they spend on each (though variation in availability of resource/activity use start and end times makes doing so harder than it may seem).

If more time were spent doing activities than reading, our results may simply be a consequence of this extra time. Preliminary analysis of the log data shows that students, on average, do more activities than read pages (387 vs. 297, respectively), but spend less overall time doing activities than reading (21.6 hrs vs. 25.0 hrs, respectively). In other words, it appears students actually spend substantially less time per activity (3.4 min) than reading a page (5.0 min). Given the improvement we see in our learning outcomes and the exploratory analysis results, this time analysis further supports the notion that doing interactive activities has a greater impact on learning than passive reading. It will be interesting to get the results of a similar analysis to compare lecture video watching time.

Although our analysis considers elements of watching, reading and doing across the entirety of the course, a more fine-grained analysis is likely desirable and it could take advantage of the fact that learning materials in OLI have been carefully mapped to specific learning objectives and skills [cf., 15].

Going beyond this specific psychology MOOC, we look to doing and seeing an expansion of this kind of analysis to other MOOCs, online or blended courses that include both passive declarative elements and interactive problem-solving elements.

CONCLUSION

While many MOOCs do include questions and some online and offline homework assignments, some have argued that a key limitation of many online courses is that they lack sufficiently rich, well-supported activities with adaptive scaffolding for learning by doing [cf., 33, 18]. Our results support the view that video lectures may add limited value for student learning and that providing more interactive activities will better enhance student learning outcomes.

ACKNOWLEDGEMENTS

We thank Dr. Anderson Smith and other members of the Georgia Institute of Technology and Coursera teams that were critical to developing and delivering the Psychology MOOC. We used the 'Psychology MOOC GT' dataset, accessed via DataShop [15] (pslcdatashop.org) at https://pslcdatashop.web.cmu.edu/DatasetInfo?datasetId=863. Support for developing and delivering this course was provided by the Bill and Melinda Gates Foundation. Support for data storage and analytics was provided by LearnLab (NSF grant SBE-0836012).

REFERENCES

1. Aleven, V., Beal, C. R., & Graesser, A. C. (2013). Introduction to the special issue on advanced learning technologies. *Journal of Educational Psychology*, 105(4), 929–931.

2. Anderson, J. R., Corbett, A. T., Koedinger, K. R., & Pelletier, R. (1995) . Cognitive tutors:Lessons learned. *The Journal of the Learning Sciences*, 4, 167-207.

3. Anzai, Y., & Simon, H. A. (1979). The theory of learning by doing. *Psychological Review*, 86, 124–140.

4. Barab, S.A. & Squire, K.D. (2004). Design-based research: Putting a stake in the ground. *Journal of the Learning Science,* 13 (1) 1-14.

5. Bichsel, J. (2013). The State of E-Learning in Higher Education: An Eye toward Growth and Increased Access (Research Report), Louisville, CO: EDUCAUSE Center for Analysis and Research. Available online: http://www.educause.edu/ecar.

6. Bowen, W. G., Chingos, M. M., Lack, K. A., & Nygren, T. I. (2013). Interactive learning online at public universities: Evidence from a six-campus randomized trial. *Journal of Policy Analysis and Management*, 33(1), 94–111.

7. Champaign, J., Fredericks, C., Colvin, K., Seaton, D., Liu, A. & Pritchard, D. Correlating skill and improvement in 2 MOOCs with a student's time on task. In *Proc. Learning@Scale 2014*, Retrieved from: http://dx.doi.org/10.1145/2556325.2566250

8. Clark, R.E., Feldon, D., van Merriënboer, J., Yates, K., & Early, S. (2007). Cognitive task analysis. In J.M. Spector, M.D. Merrill, J.J.G. van Merriënboer, & M.P. Driscoll (Eds.), *Handbook of research on educational communications and technology* (3rd ed., pp. 577–593). Mahwah, NJ: Lawrence Erlbaum Associates.

9. Collins, E.D. (2013) "SJSU Plus augmented online learning environment: Pilot project report." The Research and Planning Group for California Community Colleges. Available online:http://www.sjsu.edu/chemistry/People/Faculty/Collins_Research_Page/AOLE%20Report%20Final%20Version_Jan%201_2014.pdf

10. Collins, A., Brown, J. S., & Newman, S. E. (1989). Cognitive apprenticeship: Teaching the crafts of reading, writing, and mathematics. In L. B. Resnick. *Knowing, Learning, and Instruction: Essays in Honor of Robert Glaser* (pp. 453-494). Hillsdale, NJ: Erlbaum.

11. Dewey, J. (1916), (2007 edition). Democracy and Education, Teddington: Echo Library.

12. Hill, P. (2013). Emerging Student Patterns in MOOCs: A (Revised) Graphical View. *e-literate*. Available online: http://mfeldstein.com/emerging-student-patterns-in-moocs-a-revised-graphical-view/

13. Kaufman, J.; Ryan, R.; Thille, C. and Bier, N. (2013) Open Learning Initiative Courses in Community Colleges: Evidence on Use and Effectiveness. Mellon University, Pittsburgh, PA. Available online: http://www.hewlett.org/sites/default/files/CCOLI_Report_Final_1.pdf

14. Koedinger, K.R., & Aleven V. (2007). Exploring the assistance dilemma in experiments with Cognitive Tutors. *Educational Psychology Review*, 19(3), 239-264.

15. Koedinger, K.R., Baker, R.S.J.d., Cunningham, K., Skogsholm, A., Leber, B., Stamper, J. (2010). A Data Repository for the EDM community: The PSLC DataShop. In Romero, C., Ventura, S., Pechenizkiy, M., Baker, R.S.J.d. (Eds.) *Handbook of Educational Data Mining*. Boca Raton, FL: CRC Press.

16. Koedinger, K.R., Booth, J. L., & Klahr, D. (2013). Instructional Complexity and the Science to Constrain It. *Science,* 342(6161), 935-937.

17. Koedinger, K. R., Corbett, A. C., & Perfetti, C. (2012). The Knowledge-Learning-Instruction (KLI) framework: Bridging the science-practice chasm to enhance robust student learning. *Cognitive Science, 36 (5)*, 757-798.

18. Koedinger, K. R., McLaughlin, E. A., & Stamper, J. C. (2014). Ubiquity symposium: MOOCs and technology to advance learning and learning research: Data-driven learner modeling to understand and improve online learning. *Ubiquity*, Volume 2014, Number May (2014), Pages 1-13. ACM New York, NY, USA. DOI:10.1145/2591682

19. Koedinger, K. R., & Sueker, E. L. F. (2014). Monitored design of an effective learning environment for algebraic problem solving. Technical report CMU-HCII-14-102.

20. Lovett, M., Meyer, O., Thille, C. (2008). The Open Learning Initiative: Measuring the effectiveness of the OLI learning course in accelerating student learning. *Journal of Interactive Media in Education.* http://jime.open.ac.uk/2008/14/.

21. Meyer, O., & Lovett, M. C. (2002). Implementing a computerized tutor in a statistical reasoning Course: Getting the big picture. In B. Phillips (Ed.) *Proc. of the Sixth International Conference on Teaching Statistics.*

22. Morote, E. & Pritchard, D. E. (2002). What Course Elements Correlate with Improvement on Tests in Introductory Newtonian Mechanics? National

Association for Research in Science Teaching – NARST- 2002 Conference.

23. Ng, A. and Widom J. (2014). Origins of the Modern MOOC. http://www.cs.stanford.edu/people/ang/papers/mooc14-OriginsOfModernMOOC.pdf

24. Pane, J.F., Griffin, B., McCaffrey, D.F. & Karam, R. (2014). Effectiveness of Cognitive Tutor Algebra I at Scale. *Educational Evaluation and Policy Analysis*, 36 (2), 127 - 144.

25. Pappano, L. (2012, November 2). *The year of the MOOC*. The New York Times.

26. Pashler, H., Bain, P., Bottge, B., Graesser, A., Koedinger, K., McDaniel, M., & Metcalfe, J. (2007). *Organizing Instruction and Study to Improve Student Learning (NCER 2007-2004)*. Washington, DC: National Center for Education Research, Institute of Education Sciences, U.S. Department of Education.

27. Ritter S., Anderson, J. R., Koedinger, K. R., & Corbett, A. (2007). Cognitive tutor: Applied research in mathematics education. *Psychonomic Bulletin & Review*, 14 (2):249-255.

28. Schank, R. C., Berman, T. R. & Macperson, K. A. (1999). Learning by doing. In C. M. Reigeluth (Ed.), *Instructional Design Theories and Models: A New Paradigm of Instructional Theory (Vol. II)* (pp.161-181). Mahwah, NJ: Lawrence Erlbaum Associates.

29. Singer, S.R. & Bonvillian, W.B. (2013). Two Revolutions in Learning. *Science 22*, Vol. 339 no. 6126, p.1359.

30. Sinha, T., Jermann, P., Li, N., Dillenbourg, P. (2014). Your click decides your fate: Inferring Information Processing and Attrition Behavior from MOOC Video Clickstream Interactions. *Proc. of the 2014 Empirical Methods in Natural Language Processing Workshop on Modeling Large Scale Social Interaction in Massively Open Online Courses*

31. Strader, R. & Thille, C. (2012). The Open Learning Initiative: Enacting Instruction Online. In Oblinger, D.G. (Ed.) *Game Changers: Education and Information Technologies (201-213). Educause.*

32. Tetrad IV. http://www.phil.cmu.edu/tetrad

33. Thille, C. (2014). Ubiquity symposium: MOOCs and technology to advance learning and learning research: opening statement. *Ubiquity*, Volume 2014, Number April (2014), Pages 1-7. ACM New York, NY, USA. DOI: 10.1145/2601337

34. VanLehn, K. (2006). The behavior of tutoring systems. *International Journal of Artificial Intelligence in Education*, 16(3), 227-265.

35. VanLehn, K. (2011). The relative effectiveness of human tutoring, intelligent tutoring systems, and other tutoring systems. *Educational Psychologist*, 46(4), 197-221.

36. Zhu X., Lee Y., Simon H.A., & Zhu, D. (1996). Cue recognition and cue elaboration in learning from examples. In *Proc. of the National Academy of Sciences 93*, (pp. 1346±1351).

Exploring the Effect of Confusion in Discussion Forums of Massive Open Online Courses

Diyi Yang, Miaomiao Wen, Iris Howley, Robert Kraut, Carolyn Rosé
Carnegie Mellon University, Pittsburgh, PA 15213
{diyiy, mwen, ihowley}@cs.cmu.edu, robert.kraut@cmu.edu, cprose@cs.cmu.edu

ABSTRACT
Thousands of students enroll in Massive Open Online Courses (MOOCs) to seek opportunities for learning and self-improvement. However, the learning process often involves struggles with confusion, which may have an adverse effect on the course participation experience, leading to dropout along the way. In this paper, we quantify that effect. We describe a classification model using discussion forum behavior and clickstream data to automatically identify posts that express confusion. We then apply survival analysis to quantify the impact of confusion on student dropout. The results demonstrate that the more confusion students express or are exposed to, the lower the probability of their retention. Receiving support and resolution of confusion helps mitigate this effect. We explore the differential effects of confusion expressed in different contexts and related to different aspects of courses. We conclude with implications for design of interventions towards improving the retention of students in MOOCs.

Author Keywords
Massive Open Online Courses (MOOC); Confusion; Survival Analysis.

ACM Classification Keywords
H.5.m. Information Interfaces and Presentation (e.g. HCI): Miscellaneous

INTRODUCTION
With the recent boom in development of educational resources in industry and academia, Massive Open Online Courses (MOOCs) have rapidly moved into a place of prominence in the media. MOOCs enable thousands upon thousands of students to register for courses to learn at their convenience and with no cost. Despite all the potential, MOOCs have so far suffered from extremely high rates of attrition. The reasons behind the dropout are various, but evidence suggests that a potential culprit is learners' confusion and frustration evidenced in their learning process either explicitly or implicitly [6]. Previous explorations of student affect in educational contexts have demonstrated a strong connection between affect, engagement, and learning. However, little systematic research has been conducted to specify how confusion affects student commitment to their continued participation in MOOCs.

Confusion has a complex influence on learning and engagement. Confusion experienced during learning processes is not always associated with negative outcomes. In certain circumstances, a prompt response to confusion (e.g., support from an instructor or help from other sources), or simply the experience of overcoming confusion through a student's own efforts, may lead to a beneficial effect [8]. On the other hand, students who experience confusion may struggle to stay involved in a course and ultimately drop out, especially if students are already vulnerable to dropout for other reasons. Thus, the focus of our work is to better understand the student participation experience as they struggle, express confusion, and ultimately stop participating in a MOOC course.

Behavior traces during periods of confusion may provide clues that offer the opportunity to observe the process of student struggles with confusion [11, 2]. For example, students may become confused while watching lecture videos or working on assignments. They might express their confusion via the discussion forum with detailed descriptions of the problem (e.g. "I'm stuck on this question.." and "I'm very lost on this concept.."), or through traceable interactions with course affordances, for example, re-watching a video or slowing the video speed. Without receiving help from other students or teaching staff, students might remain confused, and persistent confusion might promote negative attitudes toward the course and ultimately dropout. On the other hand, monitoring the behavior trace for such evidence offers the opportunity to offer just-in-time support, and supporting the participation of these struggling students might increase the overall course success.

Our work focuses on exploring different levels of confusion and their corresponding impact on student retention, which affects the health of the MOOC learning community. Based on two MOOC datasets, we first describe a classifier that predicts the degree of confusion associated with student posts in the MOOC discussion forum. The model takes into account student video watching patterns and the linguistic choices displayed in their posts. We then apply this model to measure the quantity of confusion over all posts. With reasonable accuracy we are able to distinguish different types of confusion,

L@S 2015, March 14–18, 2015, Vancouver, BC, Canada.

http://dx.doi.org/10.1145/2724660.2724677

such as confusion that appears in different contexts or confusion in response to different aspects of courses. This allows us to examine the different effects of this array of confusion experience types on students' continued participation.

The contribution of our work is two-fold. Theoretically, by exploring the impact of confusion on student survival, we have identified several important connections between student confusion and their dropout of MOOC courses. Practically, our findings provide guidance for development of potential interventions that might promote retention by providing just-in-time help and support for confused students.

RELATED WORK

Analysis of Attrition in MOOCs

The recent boom of MOOC platforms such as Coursera and edX raise hopes related to the potential of distance learning and lifelong learning to reach the masses, while at the same time sparking a debate about the extremely high attrition. The level of concern related to MOOC dropout rates is reflected in the attention the research community has dedicated to it [29]. For example, Rose et al. [17] investigate the influence of social positioning factors on student commitment to MOOC courses, and Yang et al. [30] demonstrate that students who share similar behavior patterns influence other students' commitment to the courses through their interaction with them. These analyses focus on social connection and social positioning, but do not deeply explore student affect. Work from Ramesh [16] incorporates content analysis to investigate the correlation between sentiment and subjectivity of user posts and student engagement/disengagement. In finer-grained forum content analysis work [25], the authors explore sentiment mining from forum posts to monitor students' trending opinions towards the course, and find a correlation between measured sentiment and student attrition. Additionally, Wen et al. [24] have used computational linguistic models to measure learner motivation and cognitive engagement from forum posts and their association with student survival rates. Here we see an expected pattern of motivation and cognitive engagement consistently associated with commitment, but weak or inconsistent effects associated with simple measures of sentiment. Prior work provides a multi-faceted understanding of student engagement through examination of discussion forum posts. However, little effort appears to have dealt specifically with understanding students' experience of confusion while participating in MOOC courses.

Confusion and Learning

Student affect, of which confusion is one example, has been investigated in many scenarios related to student learning [2, 27]. It has been pointed out that accurate understanding of student affect has the potential not only to contribute towards improved affect detection, but also to contribute insights towards design of interventions that might increase engagement. Students experience confusion when they are confronted with an anomaly, contradiction, or an impasse; and are uncertain about how to proceed. On the positive side, confusion, as one of the most frequently studied forms of student affect [13], has been found to correlate with learning [12], particularly with learning at deeper levels of comprehension. Confusion causes students to stop, reflect, and begin active problem solving to resolve their confusion. Struggling with confusion as a cognitive activity may enable learners to acquire a deeper understanding of complex topics [12, 8].

The positive effect of confusion occurs when students can effectively regulate their confusion or if the learning environment provides sufficient scaffolding to help them do so [8, 12]. On the other hand, prolonged confusion leads to poorer student achievement [11]. [8] also emphasizes the importance of rapidly resolving confusion when it arises. That is, when a learner becomes confused, a quick instructional strategy is to provide explanations and other scaffolds to alleviate the confusion. Furthermore, confusion associated with failure to resolve an impasse [7] might transition into frustration, boredom, and become a crucial point at which the learner disengages from the learning process [10].

When it comes to the MOOC context, the distant nature and the size of MOOCs introduce limitations on opportunities for students to interact with others as effectively as in traditional classroom learning or intelligent tutor situations [21]. Lacking immediate feedback, interactive communication, or timely support increases the likelihood of members leaving such communities [22, 23], especially when members get confused in the learning process. As we look towards the more successful MOOCs of the future, we require new interventions to provide confused students with feedback, interaction and even instructor interventions [16]. Such interventions will depend on an ability to monitor behavior traces to identify the experience of confusion as well as an understanding of how confusion plays out in the context.

Modeling Confusion and its Relationship to Dropout

As a step towards being able to regulate student confusion and ultimately to increase their engagement, first we must be able to identify confusion, as we track and monitor learner experiences [12]. Building on that, we must model the connection between the experience of confusion and dropout.

Considerable prior research has been directed towards automatic identification of confusion in the context of educational software such as intelligent tutoring systems [2]. Researchers have been investigating student affect changes, including confusion, over extended periods of time by developing models using approaches such as classification or knowledge engineering [14]. Some of the most successful affect detectors are built through physiological sensors, identifying vocal patterns [4] or through log files[2], and conversation cues [9]. For instance, Lee et al. [11] explored the relationship between novice programmer confusion and achievement based on students' compilation logs from their programming courses, and concluded that prolonged confusion is associated with poorer student achievement. Similarly, Conati [5], developed a detector based on a combination of questionnaire and log data to predict self-reported student affect. Their model was better at identifying focused and curious students, but less successful at identifying students who were confused. However, approaches relying upon sensors or self-reported affect are limited in application to datasets for which such things are present, and also have limitations in terms of large-scale deployment. We address these limitations in our work in the

MOOCs by relying only on information readily available in that context.

Our analysis is conducted in the following two steps. First, we train and validate a confusion detection classifier to measure the degree of student confusion revealed in their forum post and click behavior. Then we leverage survival analysis to explore how student confusion predicts continued participation by itself and in connection with receiving support or a resolution to confusion. We also use a similar modeling approach to explore the differential effect of confusion experienced in connection with different course aspects.

DATA PREPARATION

In our investigation, we partnered with faculty at a well-known West Coast state university, which provided the data from two Coursera MOOCs. Our dataset for this paper consists of two Coursera courses: one mathematics course, "Algebra" and one economics course "Microeconomics". Algebra had 2,126 active users (active users refers to those who post at least once in a course forum) and 7,994 forum posts; Microeconomics had 2,155 active users and 4,440 forum posts. A flag that indicates whether the issue was resolved or not was also provided for each thread. The duration of each of the two courses was 12 weeks. Besides forum records, each student's interaction (student clicks) with the course materials is also recorded in a clickstream. Algebra has 8,686,230 student clicks, and Microeconomics has 2,709,053 clicks. This clickstream data provides us with the opportunity to investigate the relationship between click patterns and student confusion. Around 3.4% students in Algebra course and 8.3% students in the Microeconomics have posted at least once in the forum.

CONFUSION PREDICTION

As we have argued, confusion is an important factor in the experiences of students in MOOCs. In order to offer the opportunity to identify students who are experiencing confusion, we built machine learning models to automatically identify the level of confusion expressed in students' posts in the course discussion forums. Such models use statistical procedures to map a set of input features to a set of output categories. In our work, we extract the input features both from students' click behaviors and their posting behaviors, including clicking patterns in courses, presence of domain-specific content words, and high-level linguistic features. The output is a numerical value indicating the degree of confusion expressed in each post. We began our work by creating a human annotated corpus for developing our automated measure of student confusion. Second, we represented each post as a set of features as input for our machine learning models. Finally, we constructed a statistical model based on the hand-coded data and evaluated its performance.

Creating the Human-Coded Dataset: MTurk

We used Amazon's Mechanical Turk (MTurk) to construct a reliable, hand-coded dataset to automatically measure student confusion. Amazon Mechanical Turk[1] is a crowdsourcing Internet marketplace, which allows for requesters to post tasks known as HITs (Human Intelligence Tasks) and workers (Turkers) to browse among existing tasks and complete them for a monetary payment set by the requester. Buhrmester et al. [3] demonstrated that MTurk data quality matched or surpassed psychometric standards of traditional studies, for simple tasks. In addition, Snow et al. [20] showed that the combined ratings of five to seven Turkers yielded judgments of textual content comparable to judgments made by experts, such as expressions of emotion, event timing, similarity of words, disambiguation of word meaning, and language-based entailment/implication.

To increase the annotation quality, we required Turkers to have a United States location and a 98% approval rate for their previous work on MTurk. We randomly sampled 522 posts from the Algebra course forum, and 584 posts form the Microeconomics course forum. Non-English posts were filtered out, and personal identifiers were verified to have been replaced by anonymous unique identifiers. Personal details of student experiences were obscured in order to preserve the privacy of the students in the course. For each post, Turkers judged the level of confusion contained in the message on a 1-4 Likert scale ranging from "No Confusion", "Slightly Confused", "Moderately Confused" to "Seriously Confused". We provided them with explicit definitions and examples to use in helping their judgments. Each post was labeled by five different workers. To encourage workers to take the rating task seriously, we asked Turkers to highlight the portion of the post's text that supported their judgments. Turkers received $0.06 for rating each post.

We aggregated the 5 workers' responses for each post by averaging their ratings. Thus, each post has a 1-4 scale numerical value indicating the level of confusion contained in the message. Following are two examples from our final hand-coded datasets, with one example illustrating serious confusion and another indicating slight confusion.

- Student Confusion = 4.0 (Seriously Confused)

  I am completely lost on quiz 3. (I've never been awesome at math of any kind) Quiz 1 &2 were easy breezy, but 3 is throwing me. I feel like the video barely touched on what this is asking for. Or maybe I am just *that* bad at this...? Anyone want to help me understand better?

- Student Confusion = 2.0 (Slightly Confused)

  Hi, I am having problems running coursera on Chrome from my laptop. I do not have this problem using Explorer or Chrome from another PC. Have anyone else has the same issues?

To evaluate the reliability of the annotations we calculated the intra-class correlation coefficient for the confusion annotation. Intra-class correlation is appropriate to assess the consistency of quantitative measurements when all objects are not rated by the same judges. The intra-class correlation coefficient is 0.745 for Algebra, and 0.801 for Microeconomics, which indicates good agreement. To assess the validity of their ratings, we also had the workers code 50 posts, which had been previously coded by three experts. The correlation between MTurkers' average ratings and the experts' average

[1] `https://www.mturk.com/mturk/welcome`

ratings were 0.86 and 0.80 on the two courses, which is indicates moderate agreement. We divided the set of annotated data into two balanced groups based on the confusion scores: "confused" posts and "unconfused" posts, acting as positive and negative instances respectively.

Classifier Construction: Feature Space Design

Students expressed their confusion explicitly or implicitly via different approaches. For example, post writers could use different language strategies when expressing different levels of confusion in their messages. Students could also demonstrate their learning difficulties via their video watching behavior implicitly, outside of discussion forums. In the following, we describe how we capture these different cues to build a classifier, which can identify the degree of confusion that students express in their messages. This collection of features (e.g. linguistic choices, usage of question marks, behavior as reflected in logfile data, etc.) are given as input into a classifier algorithm which determines how to weight the features to predict confusion. The process requires a test set of human-coded data to determine the accuracy of the feature weighting. Once accuracy is achieved, the algorithm can be applied to un-coded data, allowing us to automatically predict the confusion levels in a nearly infinite number of students based solely on the feature variables and their coefficients. Taking advantage of previous literature, we designed our three types of features as described below.

Click Patterns

Clickstream data in MOOCs describes students' complete interaction with each course component, and can be regarded as a shallow but ever present indication of student experience. This trace log data reveals students' learning patterns, however, researchers are just beginning to investigated how click patterns in MOOCs correlate with student engagement in a meaningful way. [19] focuses on investigating students' information processing behaviors while interacting with video lectures. Effective analysis of such click patterns helps to better identify students' confusion when combined with their language choices in discussion forum posts, and also may eventually provide the means for us to analyze confusion in students enrolled in MOOCs even without their participating in discussion boards. For example, imagine a student becomes confused about a concept when watching class videos. Even though he/she did not make an explicit post about the issue, his/her click behaviors that may have involved re-watching and referring to course lectures may suggest potential confusion.

Based on clickstream data, we distinguish instances where students are taking quizzes (quiz), watching lectures (lecture), participating in forums (forum), and viewing other course materials (course). The complete record of click behaviors within a 3 hour window before the student has made a post are collected to analyze patterns that might be associated with confusion. N-grams of behaviors, with a maximum length of 4, are then extracted from these collections of behaviors. A ceiling of 4 was selected in order to avoid sparsity. The top twenty click patterns are then extracted as predictors of confusion. For example, we observed a student having a specific click pattern such as "quiz-quiz-forum" before making a post *"I try to submit the quiz w1: [...] but it says wrong. Could someone tell me what is wrong here?? Thank you"*. In this case, accessing the forum after taking the quiz reflects that the student encountered problems during the quiz and turned to the forum to seek help from peers. Similarly, another pattern "quiz-lecture-quiz-lecture" might indicate that this student referred to the lectures for clarification and help after working on a quiz.

Linguistic Features

The Linguistic Inquiry and Word Count (LIWC), designed by Pennebaker et al. [15] calculates the degree to which people use different categories of words across a wide array of texts, including emails, speeches, poems, or transcribed daily speech. LIWC dictionaries were selected based on their relevance to confusion affect. For example, "I, my" reflects that the student is describing something related to herself, whereas negative terms such as "depress, struggle" express a negative affect related to learning. Negation words or phrases might act as a proxy for potential confusion, such as not, shouldn't, or did not. Similarly, insight words such as consider or think reflect students' active orientation towards learning. To summarize, the LIWC features we incorporated into our machine learning models may be categorized into the following: (1) Pronouns : "I, we, you, she/he", impersonal pronouns; (2) Sentiment : affective processes (e.g. "happy, cried, abandon"), positive emotion, negative emotion ("anxiety, anger, sadness"); (3) Spoken Language: negation (e.g., no, not, never), disfluencies (e.g., rr, hm, umm), insight words (e.g., "think, know, consider"), assent ("agree, ok, yes"), adverbs (e.g., "very, much"), certainty (e.g., "always, never"), discrepancy (e.g., "should, would, could").

Question Features

Confusion is often conveyed by asking questions [26]. Thus, we counted the number of question marks in the sentences as a question marker feature. In addition, since not all questions are asked directly and end with a question mark, we took advantage of a heuristic rule to detect question sentences (i.e., whether the sentences start with a modal verb or a question word [23]). For example, sentences beginning with "is, was, had, does, can, may, which, why", etc., might provide cues for potential confusion. Additionally, we calculated whether sentences begin with a confusion related fixed expression such as " I am confused", "I was stuck", "I am struggling with" etc.

Classification Performance Discussion

Quantitative Discussion

We began by examining the classifiers' performance on identifying the degree of confusion expressed in each discussion forum post. We trained a Logistic Regression model for these text classification experiments and evaluated performance with a 10-fold cross validation. Accuracy and Cohen's Kappa are used to evaluate model performance. The labeled data for both Algebra and Microeconomics courses were divided into two balanced sets. Thus the baseline performance of random guessing is around 50%. We compared several different models: a unigram feature representation as a baseline feature set (**Unig**), classifiers using click patterns **Click**,

Courses	Algebra Course			Microeconomics Course		
Classifier	Accuracy	Kappa	#Features	Accuracy	Kappa	#Features
Unig	0.791	0.581	2967	0.698	0.375	4921
Click	0.587	0.176	20	0.567	0.049	20
Ling	0.647	0.293	15	0.594	0.056	15
Question	0.683	0.370	4	0.652	0.333	4
CLQ	0.723	0.448	39	0.678	0.309	39
CLQ + Unig	0.796	0.582	3006	0.706	0.388	4960
Reduced(CLQ + Unig)	0.803	0.606	632	0.712	0.403	650

Table 1. Performance of Confusion Classifiers on Two Courses

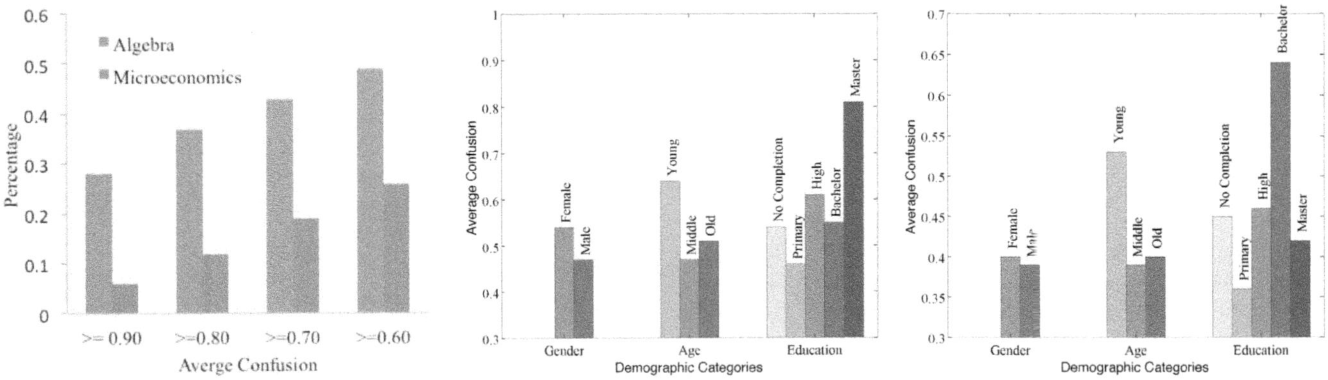

(a) Course Difference (b) Algebra Course (c) Microeconomics Course

Figure 1. Qualitative Confusion Comparison over Courses and Demographics

Courses	Algebra	Microeconomics
Most Important Features (Feature Weight)	question marker count(1.16) 1st pers singular (1.31) question word count(0.52) click pattern (0.38) impersonal pronouns (-0.15) certainty (-0.17) negation (-0.19) adverbs (-0.20)	question marker count(1.30) start with modal words (1.09) 1st pers singular(0.73) question word count(0.17) adverbs (-0.17) affect (-0.18) click pattern(-0.19) negation (-0.20) insight (-0.28)

Table 2. Top Ranked Features for Confusion Detection

linguistic features **Ling**, and question features **Question** individually, a classifier **CLQ** combining Click, Ling, and Question feature sets, and a classifier **CLQ+Unig** taking all the combination of previous feature sets. We also conducted feature selection to reduce the high dimensionality. The reduced model is denoted as **Reduced(CLQ+Unig)**. We present the results in Table 1. **CLQ+Unig** achieves better performance compared to models with individual types of features. In contrast, the performance of the reduced CLQ+Unig model is superior to that of the full CLQ+Unig feature set. Given the Reduced(CLQ+Uing) model achieves adequate levels of accuracy of 80.3% on the Algebra data set and 71.2% on the Microeconomics data, we then applied the model to the task of predicting the confusion degree of all remaining posts in the two courses. Table 2 shows some important features identified by the **CLQ+Unig** model on the two different datasets. This is consistent with our initial analysis that confusion is closely related to viewing quizzes and exams.

Findings and Observations

Course Differences: Considering that Algebra and Microeconomics can be considered technical and less technical courses respectively, we compared the average confusion students expressed in the two forums in Figure 1(a). We found that students expressed more confusion in Algebra and less confusion in Microeconomics. For example, 28% posts in the Algebra course have an average confusion score larger than 0.90, while that score is 6% in Microeconomics. Besides, 54.6% posts in the Alegebra course have expressed confusion (having a confusion score larger than 0.5) and that of Microeconomics is 35.1. A possible explanation might be that technical courses focus more on problem solving, where confusion is natural to discuss as students work through the problems. Nontechnical courses require less problem solving, and thus confusion might be more indirectly expressed via discussion rather than through direct questions.

Demographic Differences: We also examined how confusion varies across different demographic groups, in terms of *Gender*, *Age* and *Highest Education Level*. The average confusion degree comparisons over different demographics are presented in Figure 1(b) and Figure 1(c). We found that females tend to express more confusion than males; young people have the highest expressed confusion; and middle-aged people are the least likely to express confusion. In addition, students who achieved higher education degrees shared a relatively low level of confusion compared to students whose highest education were primary school or no completion.

Courses	Algebra				Microeconomics			
	Mean	Std. Dev	Min	Max	Mean	Std. Dev	Min	Max
TotalPost	8.41	17.18	1	232	6.01	9.56	1	172
Starter	0.26	0.57	0	5	0.16	0.46	0	5
ExprConfusion	0.29	0.34	0	1	0.23	0.28	0	1
UserExpoConfusion	0.10	0.20	0	0.69	0.05	0.14	0	0.69
OtherExpoConfusion	0.21	0.23	0	0.69	0.15	0.17	0	0.69
Resolved	0.36	0.46	0	1	0.25	0.42	0	1
Reply	0.40	0.47	0	1	0.26	0.42	0	1

Table 3. Descriptive Statistics for the Variables in the Survival Analysis

ASSESSING THE INFLUENCE OF CONFUSION

Our hypothesis in this work is that in the MOOC context, different kinds of student confusion may lead to different effects on students' survival in courses. For this purpose, we first investigate how expressing confusion and being exposed to others' confusion influences students' continued participation and how such effects might at least partly be mitigated. Then we explore what students are confused about and examine the influences of confusion expressed within different course contexts. We use survival analysis to explore these quantitatively, controlling for other forum behaviors. For example, the number of posts students contributes within a time period is a strong indicator of a priori level of commitment and thus makes an effective control variable. The constructed models are used to quantify the impact of confusion.

Survival Analysis Design

Survival analysis is generally defined as a set of methods for analyzing data where the outcome variable is the time until the occurrence of an event of interest. In our case, we investigate how measures of student confusion at a time point is associated with propensity of the student to drop out of the course after that time point. More specifically, we want to understand whether our automatic measure of confusion predicts the length of student participation in the course. Survival analysis is known to provide less biased estimates than simpler standard regression techniques that do not take into account the potentially truncated nature of time-to-event data. The Hazard Ratio (HZ) measures the effect of an explanatory variable on the probability of participant drop out. We used the statistical software package Stata [1] to conduct our experiments. Specifically, we used parametric regression survival analysis and assumed a Weibull distribution of survival times. We included all the active students who contributed at least one post to the course forums in the two courses. The time interval is defined as student participation weeks. We considered the timestamp of the first post by each student as the starting point for that student's active participation in the course discussion forums, and the date of the last post as the end of participation unless it is the last course week.

Dependent Variables

- **Dropout**: we consider a student dropping out from participation in the course community if that student has no activities in the course forum (even if they may engage in other forms of engagement with the materials). This dependent variable is a binary indicator, with 1 on a student's last week of active participation unless it is the last course week, and 0 otherwise.

Control Variables

- **TotalPost**: This is the number of posts a student contributes to the forums in one week. It could be regarded as a basic effort measurement of student engagement [24].
- **Starter**: Students who start a discussion thread tend to have a higher probability of being confused compared to those who participate in discussions initiated by others. This variable is defined as the number of threads a student has initiated in a week.

Independent Variables

- **Expressed Confusion** (ExprConfusion):
  This measures the average confusion per post a student has expressed in a week. It was calculated by averaging confusion scores of an individual's posts in that week.
- **User Exposed Confusion** (UserExpoConfusion):
  This measures the average confusion per post a student was exposed to by averaging confusion scores of posts in the threads that student initiated during the time period.
- **Others Exposed Confusion** (OthersExpoConfusion):
  This measures the average confusion a student was exposed to by averaging the measured confusion of posts in all the threads he/she participated in those he/she initiated.
- **Confusion Resolved** (Resolved):
  This variable indicates how many threads are initiated by a student and are later resolved. Students sometimes express confusion through initiating threads with questions. Others providing satisfactory help to such threads might relieve the confusion of those students. Whether a thread was resolved or not is provided in the datasets.
- **Reply** (Reply):
  This variable indicates how many threads a student initiated that have received a response from others. Student communication in the discussion forums is a vital component in MOOCs where personalized interaction is limited.

Table 3 reports the descriptive statistics for the variables entered into the survival regression models.

Commitment Analysis

In addition to validating how students' expressed confusion and confusion exposure affect their participation in the courses, we also examine how their continued participation is affected by the interaction of being confused, experiencing confusion resolution, and receiving instructor support.

Confusion on Commitment

Results of the two survival models from the two courses are shown in Table 4. We investigated the influences of student

	Algebra Model 1		Algebra Model 2		Microeco Model 1		Microeco Model 2	
Variables	HZ	(Std. Err)S.E	HZ	S.E	HZ	S.E	HZ	S.E
TotalPost	0.60***	0.02	0.47***	0.02	0.71***	0.03	0.60***	0.03
Starter	1.29***	0.02	1.38***	0.05	1.19***	0.02	1.45***	0.11
ExprConfusion			1.17***	0.03			1.18***	0.05
UserExpoConfusion			1.06	0.04			1.05	0.04
OthersExpoConfusion			1.85***	0.06			1.51***	0.06

Table 4. Results of Confusion on Students' Survival (*: $p < 0.05$, **: $p < 0.01$, *** $p < 0.001$)

	Algebra						Microeco					
	Model 0		Model 1		Model 2		Model 0		Model 1		Model 2	
Variables	HZ	S.E	HZ	S.E	HZ	S.E	HZ	S.E	HZ	S.E	HZ	S.E
TotalPost	0.58***	0.02	0.59***	0.02	0.60***	0.02	0.66***	0.03	0.67***	0.03	0.68***	0.03
Starter	1.11***	0.02	1.22***	0.03	1.30***	0.04	1.08***	0.03	1.18**	0.04	1.21***	0.04
ExprConfusion	1.64***	0.04	1.69***	0.05	1.59***	0.04	1.54***	0.04	1.54***	0.04	1.54***	0.04
Resolved			0.83***	0.03					0.87**	0.04		
ExprConfusion ×Resolved			0.87*	0.04					0.93**	0.03		
Reply					0.79***	0.03					0.83***	0.04
ExprConfusion ×Reply					0.91***	0.02					0.93**	0.02

Table 5. Results of Survival Analysis for Interaction Effects(*: $p < 0.05$, **: $p < 0.01$, *** $p < 0.001$)

expressed confusion and confusion exposure when controlling for other important distinguishing characteristics of students such as the total number of posts they contributed at the time point. Model 1 reports the effects of the control variables of TotalPost and Starter (i.e., number of threads started by the student per week) on student dropout. The hazard ratio (HZ) for TotalPost is 0.60, indicating that students who contribute a standard deviation more posts than average are 40% more likely to survive compared to students who have lower post counts. HZ 1.29 for Starter indicates that survival rates are $29\%((100\% \times 1.29) - 100\%)$ more likely to dropout for those who have started one standard deviation more thread starters than average. This finding is consistent in Microeconomics. Model 2 shows when controlling for control variables, student expressed confusion and confusion exposure both influence the survival rate negatively. Confusion exposure on threads started by other students has the strongest influence (HZ=1.85) on dropout compared to students expressed confusion (HZ=1.17). The reason behind it might be, expressing confusion reflects students' difficulty in the study process but also indicates their desire to learn and overcome an impasse. Exposure to others' confusion might just communicate to the student that the course materials are low quality, especially when seeing that the lecture/quiz is confusing to other students. For example, a student in the Algebra course is confused about a quiz and the following discussion respond to it by complaining about the same problem: "A: *I dont understand how to write square root for my answer. i saw it put it's been rejected.* B: *I don't understand how to write it either.... Help..* C: *-16-7sqrt(14). Is this correct? Because it's not working.* D: *I am still not getting it to go. Through hand i know that I'm correct*". In the Microeconomics course, cases such as poor presentation in course materials are common, for instance, "A: *Hello! Just trying to watch the lecture now but it always stops in the middle for some reason. Does anyone have the same problem as mine?* B:*my biggest issue is also that the video freezes when I am trying to replay a section to take notes* C: *I think the quality of videos is very bad. This may lead to lost the interest in the course*".

Resolving Threads and Receiving Replies

The research literature shows that confusion might negatively impact learning, and resolvable confusion could enrich the learning experience and might encourage deeper engagement [21]. This motivates us to explore the influence of the interaction between a variable indicating being confused and a variable indicating problems getting resolved. Similarly we explore the interaction between a variable indicating being confused and a variable indicating getting others' replies. We explore both of these interaction effects on student commitment to courses, which results in two variables: ExprConfusion × Resolved and ExprConfusion × Reply. The first variable measures the interaction effect of expressed confusion and confusion resolution and the latter measures the interaction effect of expressed confusion and receiving replies.

The results are presented in Table 5. Taking the Algebra course as an example, the interaction between the problem being resolved and being confused has a Hazard Ratio (HZ) of 1.22, one third of that of simply being confused(1.64) [2]. It indicates that students whose ExprConfusion X Resolved are one standard deviation higher than average are 22% more likely to dropout. Students whose ExprConfusion X Reply are one standard deviation higher have a Hazard Ratio of 1.14, which means that they are one quarter as likely to drop out as the full set of students who express confusion at a level of 1 standard deviation higher than average (1.64). Specifically, students who are measured at 1 standard deviation higher expressed confusion are 14% more likely to dropout. Thus we conclude that, even though being confused

[2] $1.22 = 1.69 * 0.83 * 0.87$

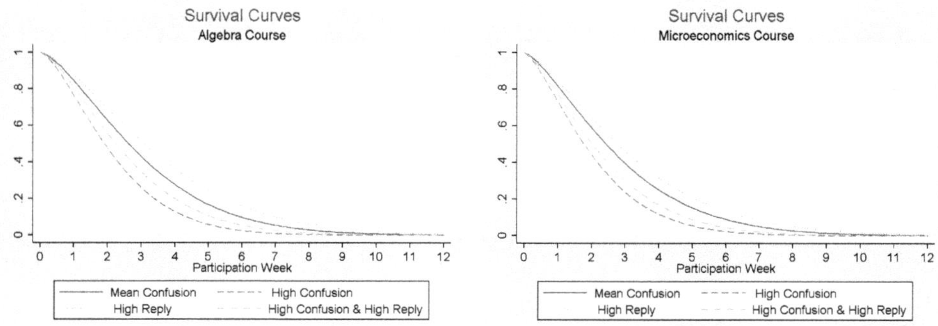

(a) Algebra Course (b) Microeconomics Course

Figure 2. Survival Curves for Students Exposed to Different Levels of Confusion Being Replied

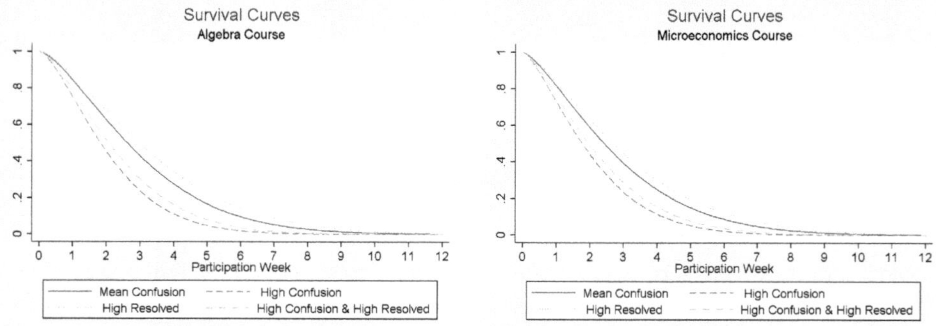

(a) Algebra Course (b) Microeconomics Course

Figure 3. Survival Curves for Students Exposed to Different Levels of Confusion Being Resolved

in courses has a negative influence on one's commitment, providing replies to such confusion and resolving the underlying issues at least partly mitigates that negative effect. Especially in a MOOC context, where instructors provide very limited guidance (Only 13% threads have instructor intervention in the Algebra course and 18% in Microeconomics), how to encourage students to offer help to others and even help unresolved threads get answered is a direction for potential positive impact. Figure 3 and Figure 2 illustrate these results graphically. *High* means that a variable is 1 standard deviation higher than average, and *Low* describes the case of 1 standard deviation lower than average.

Confusion Content Identification

The above correlational confusion analysis demonstrates the statistical association between confusion and student dropout. To take the next step and automatically recommend help, learning partners, and even experts in that specific field to confused students [28], we not only need to know who is confused, but also what students are confused about. For this purpose, first we designed a simple and effective method for identifying what students are talking about by utilizing their recent click behavior. That is, the content of current post is determined by the type of behavior indicated by the previous click before making that post. The intuition is that a student is more likely to express confusion about recently browsed course material or a recent course experience. The targeted types of contents in the posts and clicks can be divided into three categories: (1) *Course*: content about course tools, course settings, course resources, etc; (2) *Lecture*: content about lectures/videos or discussion on problems/content in lectures; (3) *Quiz*: content about quiz questions, such as quiz answers, submission, and deadlines. Post content that does not belong to any of the above types is categorized into *Other*. To validate the effectiveness of recent click type in determining post content, we randomly sampled 300 posts from each course, asked experts to judge what students are talking about, and checked the correlation between human labeling and our method. Results demonstrated that the automated method that refers to recent click behavior can correctly identify 60% and 64% on Algebra and Microeconomics courses respectively. Phi-Coefficient between human labeling and automatically identification is 0.405 with Kappa 0.300 on Algebra; on Microeconomics course, Phi-Coefficient is 0.632, with Kappa 0.308. We conclude that utilizing the previous click behavior before a post was made captures what students are talking about well enough to offer some visibility into the differential effects of confusion related to different course aspect, so we proceed with the analysis.

Once the context of each post has been identified, we then measure the confusion towards Course, Quiz, Lecture and Other by computing the average confusion scores in a user's Course/Quiz/Lecture/Other posts; denoted as *Course Confusion*, *Quiz Confusion*, *Lecture Confusion*, *Other Confusion* separately. We show the average confusion related to the four categories in Figure 4. We conducted the survival analysis again to check how confusion within different course contexts influences dropout, as results shown in Table 6. It can be concluded that, even though confusion distributions are similar across the two courses (quiz is associated with highest confu-

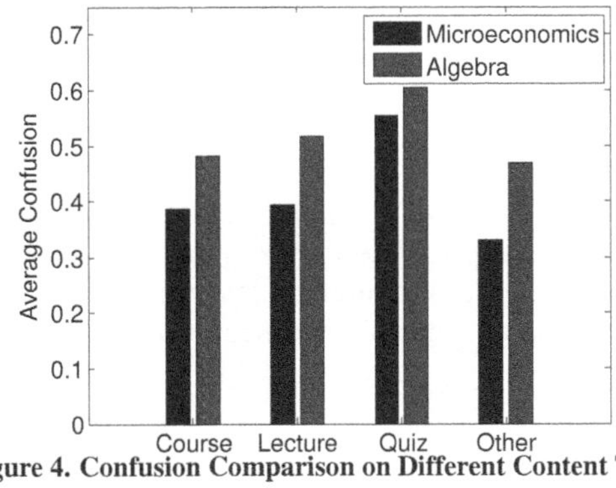

Figure 4. Confusion Comparison on Different Content Types

	Algebra		Microeco	
Variables	HZ	S.E	HZ	S.E
TotalPost	0.51***	0.02	0.63***	0.03
Starter	1.06*	0.02	1.08**	0.03
Course Confusion	1.39***	0.03	1.40***	0.04
Quiz Confusion	1.51***	0.03	1.00	0.03
Lecture Confusion	1.15***	0.02	1.26***	0.03
Other Confusion	1.01	0.03	1.03	0.03

Table 6. Confusion towards Different Course Aspects on Survival

sion), confusion towards different content types do not have similar influence on dropout. Instead, quiz confusion has the biggest impact on dropout in the Algebra course while confusion towards the course more generally leads to the highest dropout in the Microeconomics course. One explanation is that this pattern is a side effect of the fact that mathematical courses emphasize problem solving whereas less technical courses require much more discussion and opinion exchange. Thus we conclude the influence of different types of confusion on dropout is determined by the specifics of course settings, and thus we cannot make strong claims generally about specific types of confusion being more or less damaging than others across courses.

DISCUSSION AND CONCLUSION

Increasing student engagement and facilitating learning is of great importance to future MOOC deployment. In this work, we investigated the effect of student confusion on survival in MOOC courses. We first built a confusion detection classifier to measure the confusion contained in students' forum posts in the course's discussion forums and as indicated by click behavior. Then we examined the effect of different kinds of confusion on students' continued participation in the MOOC courses. Our results demonstrate that: (1) the more students express their confusion and are exposed to confusion in the MOOC forums, the less likely students are to remain active in the learning community; (2) helping resolving or providing responses to student confusion reduces their dropout in the courses; (3) the extent to which different types of confusion affect dropout is determined by specific courses. In our data, quiz confusion leads to the highest dropout in a technical course while confusion towards the course in general contributes more to dropout in a less technical course.

More specifically, compared to traditional classroom learning and many intelligent tutoring systems, students in MOOC courses are less likely to receive immediate feedback when confused. MOOCs have a large number of students in each course and do not often enable face-to-face interaction with instructors or other well-performing students. Such interaction could play an important role in maintaining student engagement because of its directive, facilitative and motivational functions [18]. However, once students get confused, they must choose to either remain confused or attempt to continue course learning, or make their confusion explicit and wait for resolution. Remaining in a confused state without support from instructors and others might easily transition into dropout, while expressing confusion in the forum may not receive a timely response, which might eventually cause disengagement. The effect of being confused and then being given support (e.g. resolving their problems or providing students interaction) has a demonstrated effect to partly mitigate the effect of confusion on dropout. Therefore, in the context of MOOCs, how to encourage students offer help to confused students and even help confusion get resolved, is beneficial for students, instructors and creators of MOOC courses.

Implications and Limitations

Our findings provide guidance for future MOOC deployment. This study sheds light on how to identify student confusion during the learning process. Tracking and monitoring student confusion helps instructors give appropriate feedback to students. Our classifier is able to give a reasonably accurate estimation of students' confusion expressed in the discussion forums. The LIWC features, question features, and click pattern features may be able to be applied to confusion detection in other contexts since they are not tailored to any specific domain. Secondly, our results show that getting students' confusion resolved and providing help reduces their dropout. More interventions that incorporate resolving problems and providing support for students could be developed and deployed, especially tailored to the distant nature and the sheer size of MOOCs.

This study is also subject to the limitation that, all measures of student expression, including expressed confusion, exposed confusion, as well as interaction effect of confusion with reply or resolution, are all judged by Turkers who are not participants and possibly have no experience in MOOC course forums. A natural follow-up is to conduct surveys to collect self-reported confusion when students make posts to see whether such data offer a confirming view.

ACKNOWLEDGEMENT

This research was funded in part from a grant from Google.

REFERENCES

1. 2011, S. C. Stata statistical software release. *7.0: Programming. Stata Corporation* (2011), 418–443.
2. Baker, R. S., Gowda, S. M., Wixon, M., Kalka, J., Wagner, A. Z., Salvi, A., Aleven, V., Kusbit, G. W., Ocumpaugh, J., and Rossi, L. Towards sensor-free affect detection in cognitive tutor algebra. *International Educational Data Mining Society* (2012).
3. Buhrmester, M., Kwang, T., and Gosling, S. D. Amazon's mechanical turk a new source of inexpensive, yet high-quality, data? *Perspectives on Psychological Science 6*, 1 (2011), 3–5.

4. Calvo, R. A., and D'Mello, S. Affect detection: An interdisciplinary review of models, methods, and their applications. *Affective Computing, IEEE Transactions on 1*, 1 (2010), 18–37.

5. Conati, C., and Maclaren, H. Empirically building and evaluating a probabilistic model of user affect. *User Modeling and User-Adapted Interaction 19*, 3 (2009), 267–303.

6. Conole, G. Moocs as disruptive technologies: strategies for enhancing the learner experience and quality of moocs. *Revista de Educación a Distancia 39* (2013), 1–17.

7. DMello, S., and Graesser, A. Dynamics of affective states during complex learning. *Learning and Instruction 22*, 2 (2012), 145–157.

8. DMello, S., Lehman, B., Pekrun, R., and Graesser, A. Confusion can be beneficial for learning. *Learning and Instruction 29* (2014), 153–170.

9. DMello, S. K., Craig, S. D., Witherspoon, A., Mcdaniel, B., and Graesser, A. Automatic detection of learners affect from conversational cues. *User modeling and user-adapted interaction 18*, 1-2 (2008), 45–80.

10. Larson, R. W., and Richards, M. H. Boredom in the middle school years: Blaming schools versus blaming students. *American Journal of Education* (1991), 418–443.

11. Lee, D. M. C., Rodrigo, M. M. T., d Baker, R. S., Sugay, J. O., and Coronel, A. Exploring the relationship between novice programmer confusion and achievement. In *Affective Computing and Intelligent Interaction*. Springer, 2011, 175–184.

12. Lehman, B., DMello, S., and Graesser, A. Interventions to regulate confusion during learning. In *Intelligent Tutoring Systems*, Springer (2012), 576–578.

13. Lehman, B., Matthews, M., DMello, S., and Person, N. What are you feeling? investigating student affective states during expert human tutoring sessions. In *Intelligent Tutoring Systems*, Springer (2008), 50–59.

14. Pekrun, R., Goetz, T., Titz, W., and Perry, R. P. Academic emotions in students' self-regulated learning and achievement: A program of qualitative and quantitative research. *Educational psychologist 37*, 2 (2002), 91–105.

15. Pennebaker, J. W., Francis, M. E., and Booth, R. J. Linguistic inquiry and word count: Liwc 2001. *Mahway: Lawrence Erlbaum Associates 71* (2001), 2001.

16. Ramesh, A., Goldwasser, D., Huang, B., Daumé III, H., and Getoor, L. Modeling learner engagement in moocs using probabilistic soft logic. In *NIPS Workshop on Data Driven Education* (2013).

17. Rosé, C. P., Carlson, R., Yang, D., Wen, M., Resnick, L., Goldman, P., and Sherer, J. Social factors that contribute to attrition in moocs. In *Proceedings of the first ACM conference on Learning@ scale conference*, ACM (2014), 197–198.

18. Shute, V. J. Focus on formative feedback. *Review of educational research 78*, 1 (2008), 153–189.

19. Sinha, T., Jermann, P., Li, N., and Dillenbourg, P. Your click decides your fate: Leveraging clickstream patterns in MOOC videos to infer students' information processing and attrition behavior. *CoRR abs/1407.7131* (2014).

20. Snow, R., O'Connor, B., Jurafsky, D., and Ng, A. Y. Cheap and fast—but is it good?: evaluating non-expert annotations for natural language tasks. In *EMNLP*, Association for Computational Linguistics (2008), 254–263.

21. VanLehn, K., Siler, S., Murray, C., Yamauchi, T., and Baggett, W. B. Why do only some events cause learning during human tutoring? *Cognition and Instruction 21*, 3 (2003), 209–249.

22. Vlahovic, T. A., Wang, Y.-C., Kraut, R. E., and Levine, J. M. Support matching and satisfaction in an online breast cancer support community. In *Proceedings of the 32nd annual ACM conference on Human factors in computing systems*, ACM (2014), 1625–1634.

23. Wang, Y.-C., Kraut, R., and Levine, J. M. To stay or leave?: The relationship of emotional and informational support to commitment in online health support groups. In *Proceedings of the ACM 2012 Conference on Computer Supported Cooperative Work*, CSCW '12, ACM (New York, NY, USA, 2012), 833–842.

24. Wen, M., Yang, D., and Rosé, C. P. Linguistic reflections of student engagement in massive open online courses. In *Proceedings of the International Conference on Weblogs and Social Media* (2014).

25. Wen, M., Yang, D., and Rosé, C. P. Sentiment analysis in mooc discussion forums: What does it tell us? *Proceedings of Educational Data Mining* (2014).

26. Wilson, N. Learning from confusion: Questions and change in reading logs. *English Journal* (1989), 62–69.

27. Woolf, B., Burleson, W., Arroyo, I., Dragon, T., Cooper, D., and Picard, R. Affect-aware tutors: recognising and responding to student affect. *International Journal of Learning Technology 4*, 3 (2009), 129–164.

28. Yang, D., Adamson, D., and Rose, C. Question recommendation with constraints for massive open online courses. In *Recsys*, ACM (2014).

29. Yang, D., Sinha, T., Adamson, D., and Rosé, C. P. Turn on, tune in, drop out: Anticipating student dropouts in massive open online courses. In *Proceedings of the 2013 NIPS Data-Driven Education Workshop* (2013).

30. Yang, D., Wen, M., and Rose, C. Peer influence on attrition in massive open online courses. *Proceedings of Educational Data Mining* (2014).

Uncovering Trajectories of Informal Learning in Large Online Communities Of Creators

Seungwon Yang, Carlotta Domeniconi, Matt Revelle, Mack Sweeney, Ben U. Gelman, Chris Beckley, and Aditya Johri
George Mason University
4400 University Drive, Fairfax, VA 22030, U.S.A.
syang20@gmu.edu, {carlotta, revelle}@cs.gmu.edu,
{msweene2, bgelman, cbeckley, ajohri3}@gmu.edu

ABSTRACT
We analyzed informal learning in Scratch Online – an online community with over 4.3 million users and 6.7 million instances of user-generated content. Users develop *projects,* which are graphical interfaces consisting of interacting programming *blocks*. We investigated two fundamental questions of *how we can model informal learning,* and *which patterns of informal learning emerge*. We proceeded in two phases. First, we modeled learning as a trajectory of cumulative programming block usage by long-term users who created at least 50 projects. Second, we applied K-means++ clustering to uncover patterns of learning and corresponding subpopulations. We found four groups of users manifesting four different patterns of learning, ranging from the smallest to the largest improvement. At one end of the spectrum, users learned more and in a faster manner. At the opposite end, users did not show much learning progress, even after creating dozens of projects. The modeling and clustering of trajectory patterns that enabled us to quantitatively analyze informal learning may be applicable to other similar communities. The results can also support administrators of online communities in implementing customized interventions for specific subpopulations.

Author Keywords
Learning analytics; informal learning; modeling; clustering; programming; Scratch; online community.

ACM Classification Keywords
H.3.3. Information Search and Retrieval: Clustering; K.3.1. Computers and Education: Computer Uses in Education.

L@S 2015, March 14 - 18, 2015, Vancouver, BC, USA
Copyright 2015 ACM 978-1-4503-3411-2/15/03…$15.00
http://dx.doi.org/10.1145/2724660.2724674

INTRODUCTION
Thousands of massive open online courses (MOOCs) [17], Q&A forums [28], tutorial sites [31], and online communities of creators (OCOCs) [29] attract people interested in learning. MOOCs provide a formal learning environment with specific learning goals, rubrics to follow, and assessments on learner performance toward goals. Other online communities such as OCOCs offer platforms with tools and services to create content both individually and in collaboration with others. Although these settings do not provide formally structured instruction, they do provide participants the opportunity to learn important content and skills informally [5, 9, 14, 19].

Within formal contexts, such as MOOCs, assessment of learning outcomes is relatively straightforward as student progress can be measured against educational aims of the course. Consequently, MOOCs incorporate automatic and formal assessments to measure learner progress in order to provide feedback [4, 30]. In contrast, online communities that support informal learning often lack appropriate means to assess progress of their members.

In this paper, we aimed to analyze informal learning occurring in Scratch online [23, 24] by addressing the questions of *how we can model informal learning,* and *which patterns of informal learning may emerge*. Specifically, we focused on measuring and analyzing the three aspects of learning:

- Amount of learning
- Speed of learning
- Potential prior knowledge

Scratch users are mainly kids and teenagers who create and share their 'projects,' which are games, animations, arts, and other media content. Projects are constructed by importing multimedia files and editing/controlling them using a visual programming language called Scratch. The Scratch language consists of various programming 'blocks,' which are the software version of Lego™ bricks. Once created, a project can be shared with other users. Remixing – creating a project based on another's project – is also highly encouraged in the community. Although there may be exceptions (e.g., sophisticated arts project may not require a large vocabulary), we believe that a wider spectrum of vocabulary block use identified from a user's original projects (non-remix) may be an indicator of learning. We developed a two-phase approach to answer our questions:

- Phase I: Model informal learning of a user as a trajectory of cumulative vocabulary block use, as s/he creates more projects over time. Visualize trajectories for all projects, as well as only the original projects.
- Phase II: Find and compare patterns of trajectories using a clustering approach to uncover subpopulations that share similar learning patterns [11, 18]. Examine samples from each cluster for detail analysis.

This study contributes to the learning community by exploring an approach to quantitatively measure informal learning from a large online community – which is difficult due to the nature of online communities (e.g., non-goal directed, less structured). It may also trigger administrators of online communities to implement targeted services for specific subpopulations.

After introducing related studies, we plunge into modeling and clustering the trajectories of programming block use. Then, we present the clustering results and examples in each cluster, followed by the discussions regarding the meaning of our results and limitations. We provide implications of this study, and conclude with an overall summary and future work.

RELATED STUDIES

Scratch Online

A core goal of Scratch is to make the creation and sharing of interactive content easy for users [20]. Within the Scratch programming environment as shown in Figure 1, users program with blocks, which map to programming constructs and allow users to manipulate data including media content (e.g., sounds, videos, images). Users can then share these interactive creations on the Scratch website [23]. The website is an online community where users may run and build on others' ideas and projects. Members can import the source code of any project into their own workspace and remix it.

In addition to the Scratch project's goal of creating and sharing programs, a fundamental element behind its creation has been to provide an alternate model for how the Web can be used for learning. The Scratch team envisioned learning outcomes related to programming and math skills as well as skills in design, creativity, communication, and so on. Learning is inherently a collaborative process that occurs across communities of practice. The Scratch community was created with the goal to foster learning among users through interaction and sharing of ideas and projects [15, 16].

Resnick et al. wrote about the Scratch in 'Programming for all' and their goal has always been to develop an approach to programming that would appeal to people who had not considered themselves programmers [20]. In May 2007, a website was launched to allow for more sharing of projects on the Web. Maloney et al. studied the use of Scratch at a Computer Clubhouse where urban youth between the age of 8-18 used Scratch [13]. The findings from this research indicated that users learned key programming concepts even in the absence of instructional interventions or experienced mentors. The ease of use for the Scratch platform and its interactivity made it attractive for users.

Informal Learning and Assessment

One of the alternate mechanisms that is accepted as central to revising the current model of education is emphasizing and improving learning that occurs in informal settings [2, 6]. Even when in formal learning environments, people gain from participation in informal learning activities [2, 8]. Consequently, informal settings and activities represent an important opportunity for engineering students to develop technical capabilities, social skills, strengthen their engineering identities, and cultivate habits necessary for life-long learning [3]. The lack of research on informal learning within engineering education was highlighted in the Educating the Engineers of 2020 report, which raised

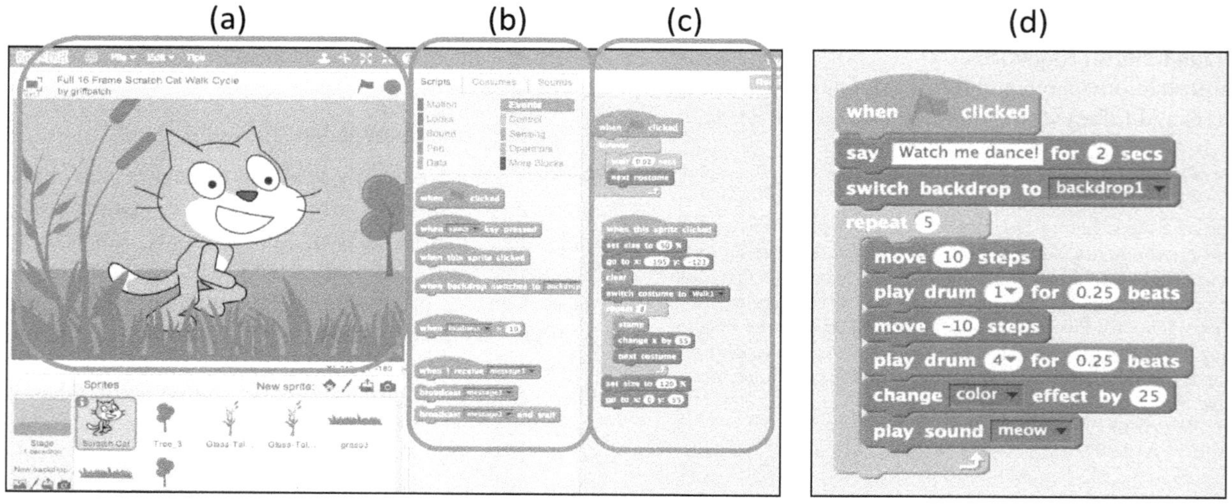

Figure 1. Scratch interface: (a) a project window, (b) blocks, (c) scripts, and (d) a script constructed with blocks.

the question, 'How can formal education be better integrated with informal and lifelong learning by engineering graduates?' [6].

The topic of assessment for online learning (e.g., MOOCs) has already found significant traction within the Learning at Scale community. For instance, Kulkarni et al. investigated ways to scale up peer assessment [12]. Peer assessment is a useful tool in the learning process, but it suffers from quality issues. The authors use machine learning techniques to scale this process whereby the quality is maintained and the burden of grading is not high. Brooks et al. propose a cluster-based interface that allows teachers to read, grade, and provide feedback on large groups of answers at once [4]. Wilkowski et al. looked at grading in MOOCs where the solutions are complex and qualitative items require subjective judgment [30]. They incorporated meta-evaluation, which evaluates the self-evaluation of students, and found that the assessments were accurate. These studies are interesting in that they investigated assessment issues occurring in large online courses. However, the primary setting for these studies was not on informal learning, but on MOOCs that provide formal learning.

Studies do exist for assessing informal learning. For example, Naturalistic Assessments [14] focuses on STEM learning taking place outside institutions. Naturalistic Assessment is focused on people's awareness of who knows how to do what. Carliner [5] proposes self-assessments, process portfolios, and certifications for measuring informal learning occurring in a professional environment. However, these approaches may not scale to large communities, are obtrusive to online community members, or require longitudinal studies to capture the cumulative nature of learning [19].

TRAJECTORIES OF VOCABULARY PROGRESS

Modeling Vocabulary Progress

The Scratch Dataset

The Lifelong Kindergarten Group at the MIT Media Lab created the Scratch dataset from the Scratch Online Community [24, 25]. It contains five years of data between 2007 and 2012, including 1 million users and their 1.9 million projects, grouped in five categories (Table 1). Demographics of users have not been published due to privacy concerns considering that the majority of Scratch users are kids and teens. Data files in each category accompanied their documentation, which describe variable fields, summary statistics, and omitted observations.

In this study, we selected 3,852 long-term users each with at least 50 original projects. In total, there were 618,721 projects of which 145,916 were original and 472,805 were remixed. Each project consists of sprites (characters in a project), imported media files, and programming blocks. Users can stack up blocks and specify variables (e.g., '10 steps', '0.25 beats') embedded in blocks to control sprites and media (Figure 1 (c) and (d)). In total, 170 different types of blocks are available.

Category	Description	Count*
Core	Data files describing the major objects and relationships captured by the Scratch website	18 (1)
Text & Code	User submitted texts useful for text and natural language processing analysis	8 (3)
Project Analytics	Detail data of blocks, drums, media, midi instruments, save history, and sprites of projects	6
Other Scratch Website	Scratch Media wiki dump, forum posts, and Text-based Games forum posts	3(3)
Code	Code used to generate the datasets from the MySQL database used by Scratch	1

Table 1. The Scratch dataset. *The numbers inside parentheses denote the number of data files in preparation (not available).

Assigning Block Weights

Some blocks are commonly used while others appear only rarely in the projects. The question then arises: should the different block types be equally considered when modeling users' progress? We assumed that users create simple projects at the beginning using a set of common blocks. As users create more projects and become familiar with the Scratch editor, they may explore blocks that they have not used before, gradually expanding their vocabulary set. Based on this assumption, we considered the presence of rarely used blocks in a project as a sign of a more advanced progress in learning about blocks, as compared to the presence of common blocks.

To account for this difference of the blocks, we assigned a weight to each block using *Inverse Document Frequency* (IDF) [27], which was computed from the entire set of original projects of all users in our selected data set:

$$w_{b_j} = \log_{10}\left(\frac{1+P}{1+P_{b_j}}\right) \tag{1}$$

where P is the total number of original projects, and P_{b_j} is the number of original projects containing a vocabulary block b_j $(1 \leq j \leq 170)$. We added '1' to both numerator and denominator in (1) as a smoothing term to avoid negative weights and division by zero. Thus, our IDF weight vector **W** has 170 elements, one for each corresponding vocabulary block:

$$\mathbf{W} = [w_{b_1} \quad \cdots \quad w_{b_j} \quad \cdots \quad w_{b_{170}}] \tag{2}$$

The highest weight value is 5.17, and is assigned to the blocks used most rarely, e.g., *changebrightnessshift*; very common blocks, such as *eventhatmorph_startclicked,* receive a weight value that is close to zero (Figure 2). The total sum of weights is 402.94.

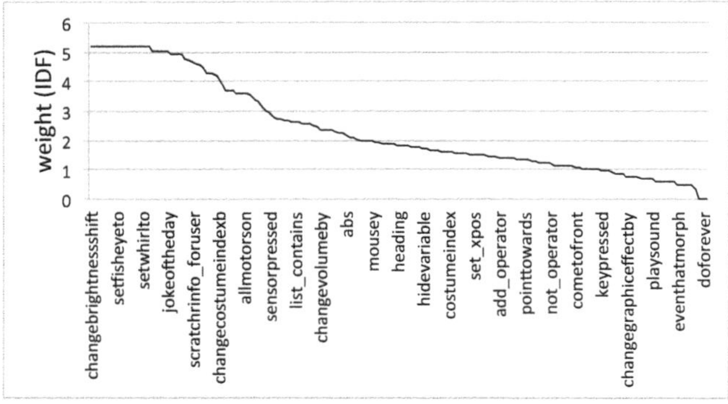

Figure 2. Vocabulary weights computed from IDF.

Modeling Learning Trajectories

We modeled the informal learning of a user as a trajectory of cumulative vocabulary block use. Procedures shown below are based on the analysis of the user's first 50 projects – including original and remix. Since our main focus was to examine the use of blocks as a user creates projects one by one, we used the project sequence, instead of actual time stamps, as the unit of trajectories.

For each user u, we proceed as follows (the user ID ranges from 1 to 3852).

1. Align all projects of a user u including original and remix in sequence from the earliest to the latest.
2. Construct a 50 x 170 matrix $\mathbf{P}_u$ using the first 50 projects and frequencies of their 170 blocks:

$$\mathbf{P}_u = \begin{bmatrix} f_{1,1} & \cdots & f_{1,j} & \cdots & f_{1,170} \\ \vdots & \ddots & \vdots & \ddots & \vdots \\ f_{i,1} & \cdots & f_{i,j} & \cdots & f_{i,170} \\ \vdots & \ddots & \vdots & \ddots & \vdots \\ f_{50,1} & \cdots & f_{50,j} & \cdots & f_{50,170} \end{bmatrix} \quad (3)$$

where $f_{i,j}$ is the frequency of block b_j $(1 \leq j \leq 170)$ in project i $(1 \leq i \leq 50)$.

3. Create a matrix $\mathbf{P}_c$ by cumulatively summing rows in $\mathbf{P}_u$ (e.g., the ith row of $\mathbf{P}_c$ is the element-wise sum of the first i rows in $\mathbf{P}_u$).
4. Create a binary matrix $\mathbf{P}_b$ from $\mathbf{P}_c$ ('1' if frequency of an element > 0, '0' otherwise).
5. Compute a trajectory by applying weights on the elements of $\mathbf{P}_b$ and summing values in each row: $\mathbf{V}_u = (\mathbf{P}_b\mathbf{W}^T)^T$. The final result is a 50-dimensional vector:

$$\mathbf{V}_u = [v_{u,1} \quad v_{u,2} \; \cdots \; v_{u,i} \; \cdots \; v_{u,50}] \quad (4)$$

where $v_{u,i}$ is a cumulative sum of weighted vocabulary blocks for a user u, computed using the first i projects. It is a weighted binary count considering whether a block was ever used (frequency is ignored). We compute $\mathbf{V}_u$ for all 3,852 users to construct a matrix $\mathbf{T}_{all}$ that has 3,852 x 50 dimensions:

$$\mathbf{T}_{all} = \begin{bmatrix} \mathbf{V}_1 \\ \vdots \\ \mathbf{V}_u \\ \vdots \\ \mathbf{V}_{3,852} \end{bmatrix} \quad (5)$$

6. Create a vector $\mathbf{O}_u$, corresponding to a trajectory that uses only original projects, simply by adding another step after step 2 above: Replace the rows of remix projects in matrix $\mathbf{P}_u$ with vectors of zeros:

$$\mathbf{O}_u = [o_{u,1} \quad o_{u,2} \; \cdots \; o_{u,i} \; \cdots \; o_{u,50}] \quad (6)$$

where $o_{u,i}$ is the analogous to $v_{u,i}$ except that it is based only on the original projects. We compute $\mathbf{O}_u$ for all 3,852 users to construct a matrix $\mathbf{T}_{ori}$ that has 3,852 x 50 dimensions:

$$\mathbf{T}_{ori} = \begin{bmatrix} \mathbf{O}_1 \\ \vdots \\ \mathbf{O}_u \\ \vdots \\ \mathbf{O}_{3,852} \end{bmatrix} \quad (7)$$

The trajectory of vocabulary progress – *Original & remix* or *Original only* – of a user u can be plotted using the corresponding rows in $\mathbf{T}_{all}$ and $\mathbf{T}_{ori}$ (Figures 8-11).

Identifying Trajectory Patterns

After inspecting many trajectory graphs, which represent informal learning of blocks over the first 50 projects, we recognized their shapes vary significantly. In order to determine a small number of canonical trajectory patterns, we applied a clustering algorithm on $\mathbf{T}_{ori}$ since we were initially interested in the trajectory patterns from original projects. Using the trajectories in each cluster, we also collected corresponding trajectories from $\mathbf{T}_{all}$.

The trajectory graphs increase monotonically, and the maximum value they reach in the first 50 projects is 402.94 (most trajectories reached a value under 150). Since we were not concerned with outliers, we decided to use the K-means++ algorithm [1] as opposed to the more robust variant, K-medoids [26], which works well in the presence of outliers. Regular K-means is sensitive to initial cluster centroid seeds, which are randomly selected. K-means++ does a bit more intelligent selection by choosing the first centroid seed randomly, the second seed to be the farthest from the first, the third seed to be the farthest from the first and second, and so on. Therefore, the only source of randomness is the first choice of the first seed.

K-means-based algorithms require the number of clusters (k) as an input. To find an appropriate k, we plotted the total Within-Group Sum of Squared Error (SSE) [21] for increasing k values, as shown in Figure 3. A red rectangle box encloses the meaningful portion of the graph. Increasing the value of k from 3 to 4 reduces considerably the value of the total Within-Group SSE. However, further increasing k affects the SSE values only minimally. Thus we chose $k = 4$.

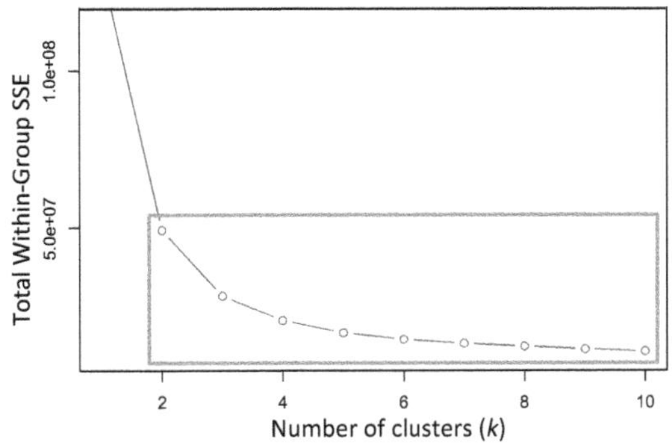

Figure 3. The total Within-Group SSE values by different number of clusters (k). $k = 4$ was selected.

We ran K-means++ 50 times on our matrix $\mathbf{T}_{ori}$, and then selected the model that had the least total Within-Group SSE. Figure 4 illustrates the SSE values achieved at each run of K-means++. Although the first seed centroid of K-means++ is randomly selected at each run, we observed that only a handful of different SSE values were reached. All the multiple runs, which gave the same smallest SSE value at convergence, corresponded to the same partition.

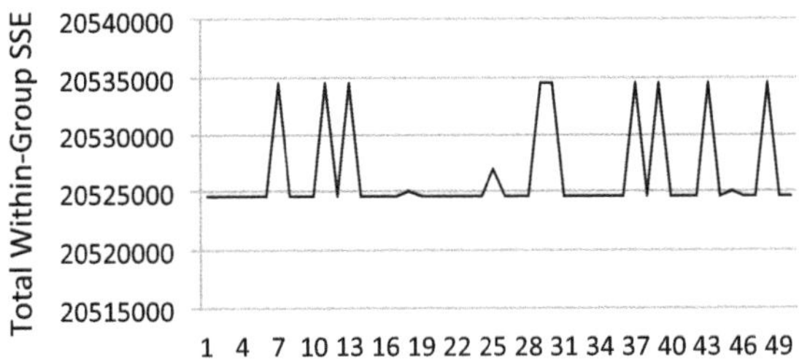

Figure 4. Total Within-Group SSE values for the 50 runs of K-means++.

Table 2 gives the sizes (number of users) of the resulting clusters.

Cluster A	Cluster B	Cluster C	Cluster D
1,304	1,250	941	357

Table 2. Size of clusters.

RESULTS

Figure 5 illustrates average trajectory patterns of users from clusters A-D. For each cluster, we first plotted an *Original only* graph (solid line) using the centroid vector of that cluster since a centroid in K-means++ clustering represents an average of all the members in that cluster. We then plotted the corresponding *Original & remix* graph (dotted line). We recognized interesting differences between graphs in each cluster and across clusters. Since the first 10 projects and the second 10 projects in the graph showed prominent characteristics, we attached regression lines and their slopes for those learning segments.

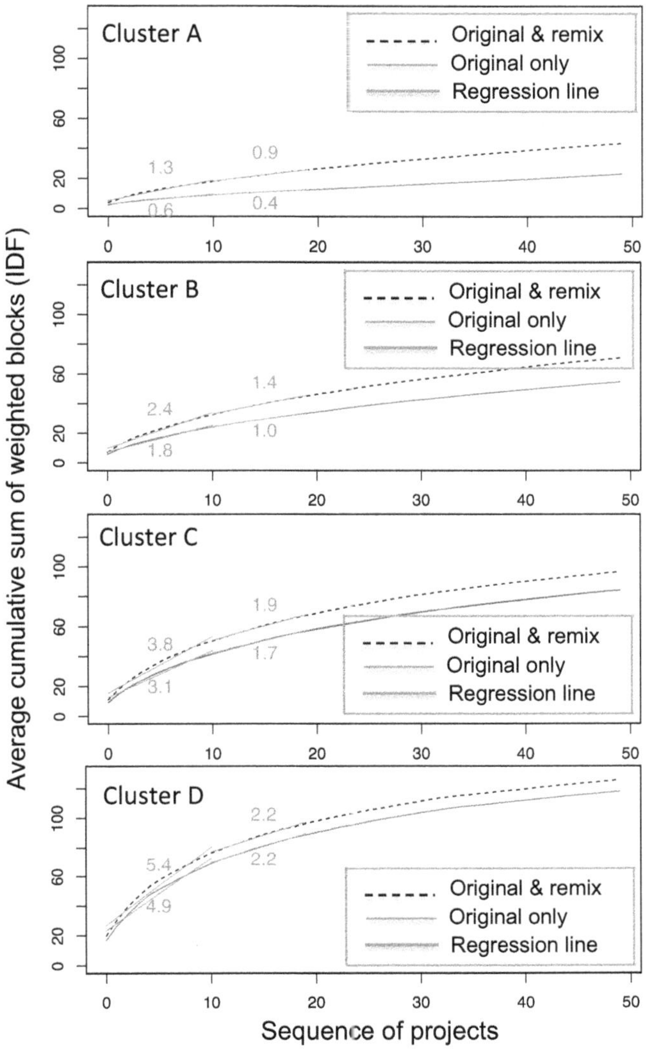

Figure 5. Average trajectory graphs for clusters A-D. Regression lines and slopes are shown for the first 10 and the following 10 projects (p-value << 2.2e-16).

Differences in Amount and Speed of Learning

Based on the value of the graphs at the 49th project, which is the index of the last project, we can measure the average 'amount' of learning of blocks in each cluster (Figure 5). The amount of learning in clusters A-D was proportionally related to the 'speed' of learning occurring in the corresponding clusters, as evidenced by the increasing slopes (from A to D) for the first 10 projects and the following 10. However, the amount and speed of learning were inversely related to the size of clusters in Table 2, which reflects the general trend in groups of learners.

The gap between the upper (*Original & remix*) and lower (*Original only*) graphs at a specific project index represents the corresponding cumulative vocabulary difference up to that point. This gap is smaller in D than in A. Also, the differences in slope between the two curves, measured within the first 10 projects and the following 10 projects, are smaller in D than in A. One reason for this might be that users in cluster D used diverse vocabulary even in their early original projects. This interpretation is supported by the fact that the cumulative sum in the *Original only* graph (cluster D graph in Figure 5) reached 70 at the project index of 10, when the second-most-progressed group of users (cluster C graph in Figure 5) reached the same value at the project sequence of 35. Therefore, it might have been hard to find remix projects with previously unused vocabulary. Another possible explanation for the discrepancy might be that users in cluster D typically remixed projects similar to their original projects, leading to only a small difference between the graphs.

Differences in Initial Vocabulary

Another observation from Figure 5 is that the 'starting value' of the trajectory (*Original only*) at project sequence 0 is higher in cluster D (mean=17.0) than in A (mean=2.5).

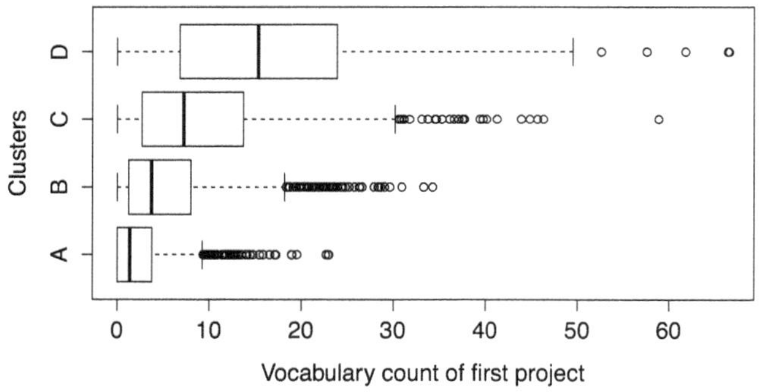

Figure 6. Boxplots summarizing the starting value for the first original projects in each cluster (count is 0 if a trajectory starts with a remix project).

The boxplots in Figure 6 illustrate this further. The median starting values of the trajectories from A to D are 1.4, 3.7, 7.3, and 15.4, showing an exponential increase. Even the outliers of A have lower values than those of D. This may be due to the differences in users' background knowledge. For example, users with prior programming experience already know how to use various vocabulary blocks. Thus, these users can apply a variety of blocks when creating complex Scratch projects. Other factors such as age and gender of users may contribute to this phenomenon as well. We further discuss on this in Discussion and Limitations section.

Characteristics of Block Use by Different Clusters

We computed the percentage of blocks used in the original projects for each cluster to understand the block usage trend among clusters (Figure 7). A total of 145,916 projects (A: 47,097; B: 48,270; C: 36,421; and D: 14,128) were analyzed and the percentages of block use were visualized along with the block names, which were organized in decreasing order of their IDF weights from left (higher weight, rare blocks) to right (lower weight, common blocks). 25 blocks with the highest weights were removed from the computation because they were not used at all.

As we may expect from the definition of IDF weighting, blocks with lower weights were more popular in general than those with higher weights. An interesting tendency was that the D graph (black solid line) was higher than the A graph (red dotted line) until they reached the 'doif' block, where the two lines crossed. After the 'doif' block, the A graph became higher than the D graph, indicating that the users of cluster D used rare blocks more often compared to the users of A. The B and C graphs were located in between the A and D graphs.

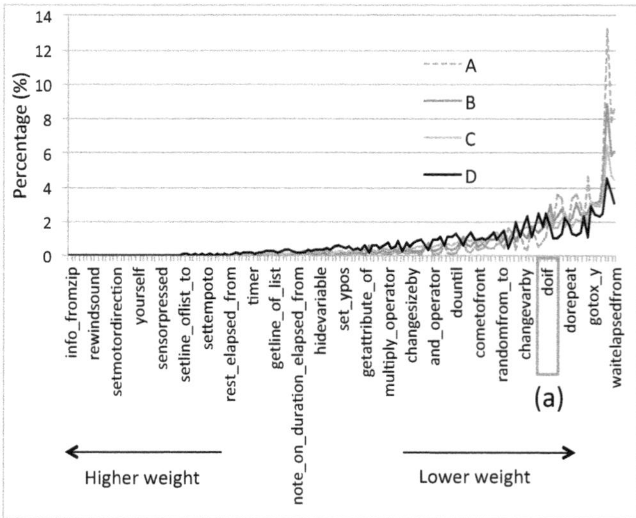

Figure 7. Block use (%) for different clusters. The A graph and the D graph cross at (a) 'doif' block.

Text Analysis of Project Descriptions and Comments

To get a glimpse of how the users in different clusters describe their projects and what kind of comments are posted for those projects, we extracted the 100 most frequent words from the project descriptions and comments. We then compared these 100 words across clusters to uncover unique words (Table 3).

Cluster	Unique Words	Count
A	poor, story, kirby, movie, sad, cookie, anime, car, baby, wolf, shadow, drawing	12
B	king, head, views, meow, dragon, nice	6
C	nyan, spam, watch, astro, darkraiworld, hill, battle, pizza, stick	9
D	color, bros, radas, player, tagger, darkb, mouse, liam, long, version, online, turbo, adventure, survived, scripts, ninja, projects, great, mhm, magic, level, geometry, button, bob, view, erk	26

Table 3. Unique words extracted from the project descriptions and comments in each cluster.

Table 3 shows that the cluster D has the largest number of unique words (26) by a considerable margin. In addition, the unique words from cluster D may have come from games (e.g., player, mouse, adventure, survived, ninja, level, button) and programming (e.g., version, scripts, geometry). Users in cluster B and C create a large number of projects that are related to cats (See the unique words 'meow' in cluster B and 'nyan' in cluster C in Table 3). In fact, 'cat' was a popular topic in Scratch considering that searching with 'cat' returned over 7 million results. The popularity of 'dragon' in cluster B was probably due to over 2.26 million projects about a famous animation "Dragon Ball." 'battle' in cluster C was usually associated with games (e.g., RPG battle, Tank battle, battle training game). The word 'poor' in cluster A was often used in titles along with the name of animation characters (e.g., 'poor foxy', 'poor Pinkie Pie', 'poor snow man'). 'poor' was also used to comment on the quality of projects (e.g., 'poor translation'). The frequent use of word 'poor' may indicate that the users in cluster A are novices who frequently acknowledge the low quality of their projects in relation to those in other clusters.

	Emotion	Project Type	Other
Across A-D	crazy, awesome, love, best, funny, yay, happy, good, evil, cool, rock(s), bad, stupid, fun, weird	art, cat, pokemon, click, contest, music, sonic, super, mario, press, game(s), remix, space, sprites	wuz, random, pie, cant, tag(s), blue, song, waffles, add, stuff, scratch, green, epic, red, real, life, star, big, time, day, eat, man

Table 4. Common words extracted from clusters A-D (a total of 56 words).

Table 4 shows common words across all clusters. They might be divided into three groups: emotion, project type, and other. Combined together, these word groups illustrate a simplified snapshot of the Scratch community, where people create arts, games, animations, and express their emotions towards those content.

Example Trajectory Graphs

Cluster analysis provides us a macroscopic examination of the patterns in the trajectory graphs. For microscopic details of graph variations, we present two examples which are randomly selected from each cluster.

Figure 8 depicts typical patterns of trajectories from the least progress group in cluster A. In Figure 8 (a), the *Original only* graph stayed under 25 cumulative sum of vocabulary even though the user remixed many projects over time. The user in Figure 8 (b) remixed only one project later in the sequence. His/her cumulative sum of vocabulary increased gradually during the first 10 projects, then stabilized for another 30 or so. There was a small vocabulary jump around the 43rd project, but overall progress is slow.

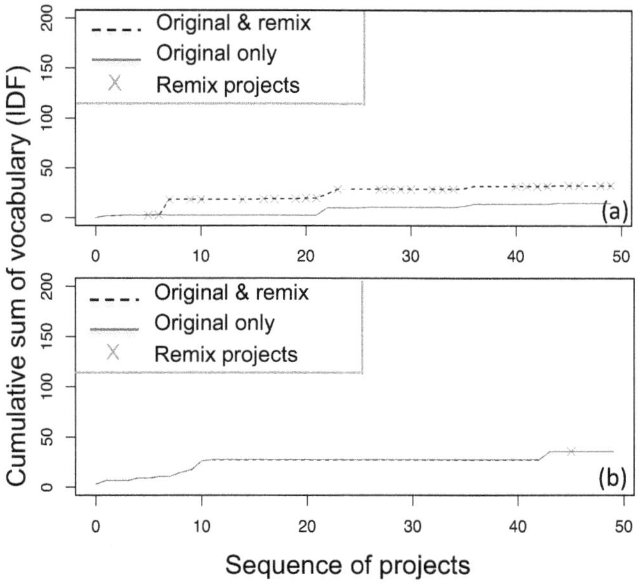

Figure 8. Examples from cluster A (the least progress group). Graphs in (a) and (b) stay under the cumulative sum value of 50.

Figures 9 and 10 illustrate example trajectories from cluster B and C respectively. In the first 10 projects, the two figures show noticeable differences: corresponding portions in Figure 9 (a) and (b) are rather flat; but those in Figures 10 (a) and (b) are increasing. The *Original & remix* graph (dotted line) in Figure 9 (a) has a slight jump at the 21st project due to new vocabulary in a remix project. However, the last two remix projects at 36th and 37th do not contribute to the vocabulary progress very much. Figure 9 (b) shows a sharp jump at the 8th project caused by the vocabulary increase in the original project, but then the progress slows down even after multiple remixes.

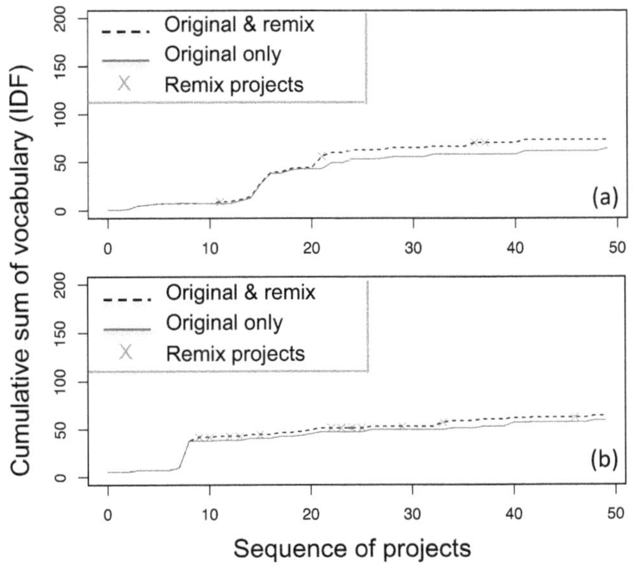

Figure 9. Examples from cluster B. (a) and (b) reach slightly over 50 cumulative sum of vocabulary in the end.

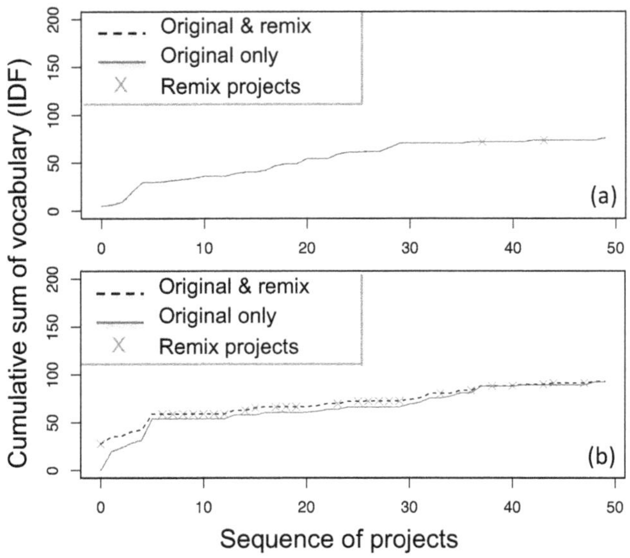

Figure 10. Examples from cluster C. (a) and (b) reach near 70-80 cumulative sum of vocabulary in the end.

The final cumulative values at project index 49 in Figures 9 (a) and (b) reach between 60 and 70. Figures 10 (a) and (b) have similar patterns, but Figure 10 (b) has many more remix projects which do not contribute much to the vocabulary increase. The final cumulative values in Figure 10 (a) and (b) reach between 80 and 90.

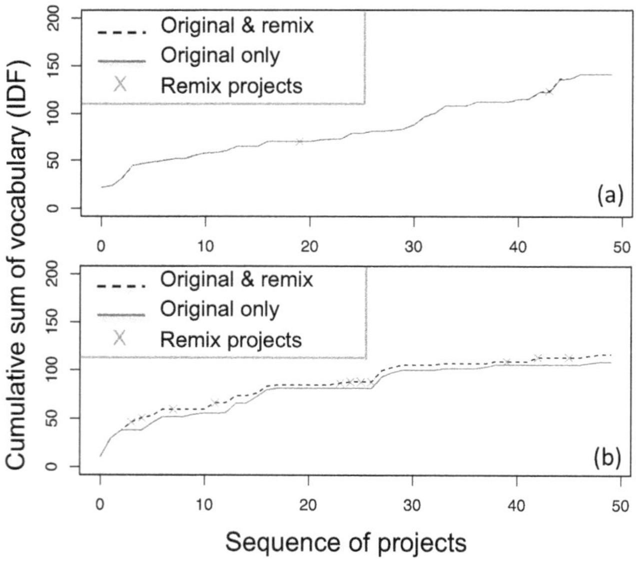

Figure 11. Examples from cluster D (the most progress group). (a) and (b) reach 110-140 cumulative sum of vocabulary in the end.

Figure 11 shows example trajectories from the most progressed group in cluster D. These trajectory graphs start increasing from the beginning and reach over the cumulative value of 50 before the 5th projects. This is a steep increase compared to the corresponding portions in Figures 5, 6, and 7. The graphs in Figure 11 (a) keep increasing until they reach close to 140. Graphs in Figure 11 (b) show a slight jump at the 27th project due to vocabulary increase in the original project. Another observation to note is that four remix projects occur consecutively right before this jump. They do not directly contribute to the vocabulary increase; however, it's possible that those remix projects indirectly helped learning new blocks and contributed to the vocabulary increase in the *Original only* graph.

DISCUSSION AND LIMITATIONS

We found that our approach – modeling and clustering of learning trajectories – was effective in answering our research questions. We could quantitatively measure and analyze the three aspects listed below, both at macroscopic (Figure 5) and microscopic levels (Figures 8-11):

1. The amount of learning using the cumulative sum at the end of a trajectory
2. The speed of learning using the slopes of regression lines of a trajectory
3. Potential prior programming knowledge using the first value of a trajectory

The clustering analysis unveiled four patterns of trajectories and corresponding subpopulations in our dataset – from the least progress (cluster A) to the most progress (cluster D). We observed that the quantities listed above in 1, 2, and 3 were positively correlated with each other. Users in cluster A (least progress) had the smallest amount of vocabulary learning, their learning speed was the slowest, and their starting vocabulary sum was only 2.5 on average (Figure 5 and 6). Referring to vocabulary weights in Figure 2, the vocabulary sum of 2.5 means the projects of users in A contained only one type of vocabulary (e.g., list_contains (IDF=2.5)), or two (e.g., set_xpos (1.5) and keypressed (1)). The trajectory of learning in cluster A shows slow increase in the first 10 (slope = 0.6) and the following 10 projects (slope = 0.4), and then stabilizes after the 20th project for the Original only graph. The larger gap between the two trajectory graphs may indicate that the users in A incorporated only a small number of new vocabulary blocks from the remix projects into their original projects.

Users in D showed characteristics of 'expert' learners – fastest learning, largest amount of vocabulary use, and a highest starting vocabulary sum of 17 (Figure 5-6). A vocabulary sum of 17, for example, means that their first projects contained several types of blocks: 'changecostumeindexb (3.8)', 'allmotorson (3.2)', 'sensorpressed (2.8)', 'mousey (2)', 'hidevariable (1.8)', 'add_operator (1.4)', 'not_operator (1.2)', and 'changegraphiceffectby (0.8).' If a vocabulary of smaller weights were used, many more different types of blocks might have been included in a project. The trajectory of their vocabulary growth shows a steep increase in the first 10 projects, where the slope of 4.9 indicates fast learning. At the 10th project, the trajectory reaches 70, and then it keeps increasing even after the 20th project.

Figure 7 and Table 3 also support that the users in D showed characteristics of expert learners. In Figure 7, users in D tend to use blocks with higher weight for their projects compared to the users in A. It might be interpreted in three ways: (1) users in D use blocks with higher weight in general compared to those in A, (2) the proportion of advanced users using blocks with higher weight was larger in D than in A, or (3) a combination of these two cases. From the unique words of users in D in Table 3, we can also postulate that these users create unique and sophisticated games which require advanced programming skills.

Limitations

Although we identified patterns of learning trajectories, we may not know the reasons behind the different levels of learning outcomes for users with certainty. For example, there can be several reasons for the use of only a small number of vocabulary blocks by the users in cluster A: the characteristics of their projects may not require a large list of vocabulary. This might be the case in art projects, since visualizing pictures only requires a single keystroke to advance to the next picture. Another possibility is that of very inexperienced or very young users who do not understand the usage of more sophisticated blocks (e.g., blocks with high IDF values in Figure 2). We also do not know the reasons for differences in starting values of the first original projects (Figure 6). We were limited by the lack of demographics and user profile data. In addition, the nature of the Scratch platform is flexible and not goal-directed; therefore, users are free to develop the projects they wish over time without concern for vocabulary acquisition.

In our dataset, we included only the long-term users who created at least 50 original projects, and analyzed their first 50 projects. This selection criterion may have limited our scope of analysis to focus on a phenomenon occurring only in a small sub-community of Scratch online. Thus, lowering the user selection/analysis criteria (e.g., original projects < 50, analyzing all projects of a user) may have led to more meaningful and generalizable results.

IMPLICATIONS

Uncovering patterns in trajectories of learning implies that there exist subpopulations in the community, each of which shares similar learning characteristics (i.e., amount, speed, and, potentially, prior programming knowledge). It may allow administrators and designers of online communities to apply interventions and implement services to better support underperforming subpopulations. More importantly, our approach is based on automated modeling and clustering, thus it is scalable and applicable to much larger online communities than Scratch. Since it was successful in quantifying learning in an informal setting, applying this approach to formal settings (e.g., MOOCs) may lead to more robust results and enable deeper analyses. In addition, the patterns of learning trajectories might be connected with the learner engagement patterns [11] to acquire richer information about the users and subpopulations.

CONCLUSION AND FUTURE WORK

In this study, we presented an approach to model informal learning, which takes place in the Scratch online community. We modeled a trajectory of learning by analyzing the cumulative vocabulary block use over the first 50 projects. The K-means++ algorithm was applied to a total of 3,852 users and their learning trajectories to uncover four canonical patterns and corresponding subpopulations. Average trajectory graphs from each cluster indicated the existence of 'elite' users, who learn more vocabulary terms more quickly, and potentially have more prior programming knowledge; whereas the least progress users learn only a small number of vocabulary terms at a slower pace than other groups, and they have almost no prior programming knowledge. The text analysis of the project descriptions and comments, as well as the analysis of block usage by users from each cluster, further evidenced the different characteristics of user groups in the Scratch community. A few examples from each cluster were also analyzed to account for the chance that average graphs might oversimplify patterns of learning trajectories.

Our approach is meaningful in that the modeling and clustering of trajectory patterns enabled us to quantitatively analyze informal learning both at a single-user level (microscopic) as well as at a cluster level (macroscopic). It may also be applicable to much larger communities regardless of whether they are structured (e.g., MOOCs) or less structured (e.g., Q&A). A potential implication of our work is the opportunity for targeted intervention and support for a specific subpopulation, which may lead to an improved experience for the community members.

We aim to extend our study in two ways. First, we will apply our approach to other types of online communities for learning (e.g., Q&A forums) and compare the results with the one presented in this paper. Second, we plan to design a recommender system based on a detailed analysis of blocks and project themes in each cluster, in addition to our approach in this paper. This system will promote learning of users by suggesting programming blocks and projects so that the learning trajectory of users can be aligned with the trajectory pattern of more advanced users within his/her own cluster, as well as from the most advanced cluster.

ACKNOWLEDGMENTS

We appreciate the Lifelong Kindergarten group at MIT for publicly sharing the Scratch datasets. This work is partly based upon research supported by U.S. National Science Foundation (NSF) Award#DUE-1444277 & EEC-1408674. Any opinions, recommendations, findings, or conclusions expressed in this material are those of the author(s) and do not necessarily reflect the views of NSF.

REFERENCES

1. Arthur, D. and Vassilvitskii, S. 2007. K-means++: the advantages of careful seeding. In *Proc. SODA '07.* 1027-1035.
2. Bell, P., Lewenstein, B., Shouse, A. W. and Feder, M. A. (Eds.). 2009. Learning Science in Informal Environments: People, Places, and Pursuits. Washington, D.C.: The National Academies Press. ISBN 978-0-309-11955-9.
3. Bransford, J. D. 2007. Preparing People for Rapidly Changing Environments. Journal of Engineering Education, 2007, 96(1), 1–3.
4. Brooks, M., Basu, S., Jacobs, C., and Vanderwende, L. 2014. Divide and correct: using clusters to grade short answers at scale. In *Proc. L@S 2014.* 89-98.
5. Carliner, S. 2012. How to evaluate informal learning. Newsletters published by the Association for Talent Development. Article retrieved from http://bit.ly/1tBwXUk.
6. Committee on the Engineer of 2020. (2005). Educating the engineers of 2020: adapting engineering education to the new century. Washington, D.C.: The National Academies Press. ISBN 0-309-09649-9.
7. Darling-Hammond, L. 2010. The Flat World and Education: How America's Commitment to Equity Will Determine Our Future. New York, NY: Teachers College Press. ISBN 978-0-8077-4963-0.
8. Dutta, D. 2010. Lifelong Learning Imperative in Engineering Workshop. Summary of workshop conducted in June 17-18, 2009. Arlington, VA U.S.A.
9. Eraut, M. 2004. Informal learning in the workplace. Studies in Continuing Education, 26(2), 247-273.
10. Khalid, S. and Naftel, A. 2005. Classifying spatiotemporal object trajectories using unsupervised learning of basis function coefficients. In *Proc. VSSN 2005.* 45-52.
11. Kizilcec, R. F., Piech, C. and Schneider, E. 2013. Deconstructing disengagement: analyzing learner subpopulations in massive open online courses. In *Proc. LAK 2013*, Suthers, D., Verbert, K., Duval, E., and Ochoa, X. (Eds.). 170-179.
12. Kulkarni, C., Wei, K. P., Le, H., Chia, D., Papadopoulos, K., Cheng, J., Koller, D., and Klemmer, S. R. 2013. Peer and self-assessment in massive online classes. ACM Transactions of Computer-Human Interaction. 20 (6), Article 33, 31 pages.
13. Maloney, J., Peppler, K., Kafai, Y.B., Resnick, M., Rusk, N. 2008. Programming by Choice: Urban Youth Learning Programming with Scratch. In *Proc. SIGCSE 2008*, 367-371. New York, NY: ACM Press.
14. Michalchik, V. and Gallagher, L. 2010. Naturalizing Assessment. Curator: The Museum Journal, 53: 209–219.
15. Monroy-Hernández, A. 2007. ScratchR: sharing user-generated programmable media. In *Proc. IDC 2007.* 167-168.
16. Monroy-Hernández, A. 2009. Designing a website for creative learning. In *Proc. WebSci 2009*: Society On-Line.
17. MOOCs Directory. Retrieved from http://www.moocs.co/.
18. Morris, B. and Trivedi, M. 2009. Learning trajectory patterns by clustering: Experimental studies and comparative evaluation. In *Proc. CVPR 2009.* Miami, FL, USA, 312-319.
19. Rennie, L. J. 2007. Chapter 7: Learning Science Outside of School. In Handbook of Research on Science Education, S. K. Abell and N. G. Lederman. (Eds.). 125-167. Mawah, NJ: Lawrence Erlbaum Associates.
20. Resnick, M., Maloney, J., Monroy-Hernández, A., Rusk, N., Eastmond, E., Brennan, K., Millner, A., Rosenbaum, E., Silver, J., Silverman, B., and Kafai, Y. 2009. Scratch: Programming for All. Commun. ACM 52, 11 (November 2009), 60-67.
21. R Script for K-means Clustering Analysis. Retrieved from http://www.mattpeeples.net/kmeans.html.
22. Salton, G., & Buckley, C. 1988. Term-weighting approaches in automatic text retrieval. Information Processing and Management, 24(5), 513–523.
23. Scratch™ Online. Retrieved from http://scratch.mit.edu.
24. Scratch™ Online Statistics. Retrieved from http://scratch.mit.edu/statistics/.
25. Scratch Research Data Sharing Agreement. Retrieved from http://llk.media.mit.edu/scratch-data/.
26. Singh, S. and Chauhan, N. C. 2011. K-means v/s K-medoids: A Comparative Study. National Conference on Recent Trends in Engineering & Technology.
27. Sparck-Jones, K. 1972. A statistical interpretation of term specificity and its application in retrieval. Journal of Documentation. 28(1), 11-21.
28. StackExchange. Retrieved from http://stackexchange.com/.
29. Sylvan, E. A. 2010. Predicting social influence and project influence in Online Communities of Creators. In *Proc. ICLS 2010*, Kimberly Gomez, Leilah Lyons, and Joshua Radinsky (Eds.), International Society of the Learning Sciences, 455-457.
30. Wilkowski, J., Russell, D. M., and Deutsch, A. 2014. Self-evaluation in advanced power searching and mapping with Google MOOCs. In *Proc. L@S 2014.* 109-116.
31. W3Schools. Retrieved from http://www.w3schools.com/

Probabilistic Use Cases: Discovering Behavioral Patterns for Predicting Certification

Cody A. Coleman
Massachusetts Institute of Technology
Cambridge, MA 02139
colemanc@mit.edu

Daniel T. Seaton
Massachusetts Institute of Technology
Cambridge, MA 02139
dseaton@mit.edu

Isaac Chuang
Massachusetts Institute of Technology
Cambridge, MA 02139
ichuang@mit.edu

ABSTRACT
Advances in open-online education have led to a dramatic increase in the size, diversity, and traceability of learner populations, offering tremendous opportunities to study detailed learning behavior of users around the world. This paper adapts the topic modeling approach of Latent Dirichlet Allocation (LDA) to uncover behavioral structure from student logs in a MITx Massive Open Online Course, 8.02x: Electricity and Magnetism. LDA is typically found in the field of natural language processing, where it identifies the latent topic structure within a collection of documents. However, this framework can be adapted for analysis of user-behavioral patterns by considering user interactions with courseware as a "bag of interactions" equivalent to the "bag of words" model found in topic modeling. By employing this representation, LDA forms probabilistic use cases that clusters students based on their behavior. Through the probability distributions associated with each use case, this approach provides an interpretable representation of user access patterns, while reducing the dimensionality of the data and improving accuracy. Using only the first week of logs, we can predict whether or not a student will earn a certificate with 0.81 ± 0.01 cross-validation accuracy. Thus, the method presented in this paper is a powerful tool in understanding user behavior and predicting outcomes.

Author Keywords
Latent Dirichlet Allocation; Student Behavior; Use Case Modeling; Massive Open Online Courses

ACM Classification Keywords
I.5.2 Design Methodology: Feature evaluation and selection

INTRODUCTION
Massive Open Online Courses (MOOCs) create a tremendous opportunity to study learning from the perspective of large and diverse populations of students. In the first year alone, HarvardX[1] and MITx[2] courses enrolled roughly 600,000 unique users from around the world [10]. Such large numbers, combined with diverse backgrounds and enrollment motivations, implies variation in how users choose to interact with material. Clickstream data – stored records of user interactions with course content – provide the opportunity to understand such variation. Previous studies have aggregated clickstream data to inform broad metrics such as the unique number of resources accessed within a course [5], while others offered more detailed activity such as pause and play clicks within a single lecture video [12]. These data provide a great deal of insight into student behavior, but enumerating all possible student-interaction patterns is nearly impossible. Furthermore, interpreting such patterns remains a daunting task for researchers and course teams alike.

In this paper, we make the problem of modeling student behavior more tractable by adapting the approach of Latent Dirichlet Allocation (LDA) [4]. LDA is an unsupervised probabilistic model, which has had great success illuminating shared topics in large collections of texts [2, 3, 4]. Along with natural language processing, LDA has been adapted in areas such as genetics [15] and web page recommendation [22]. In the latter, LDA discovered latent topics associated with the semantics of user webpage access patterns, while delivering better performance compared to conventional clustering techniques [22]. Inspired by these adaptations, we use LDA to distill user interactions in an educational context by considering user interactions with resources making up a course.

Our adaptation of LDA results in a finite set of use cases representing the probability distributions of a participant interacting with each resource in the courseware. Behavioral patterns can be deduced from the most probable resources within each use case. Within any digital course containing unique resource identifiers, these probabilities offer a natural interpretation of behavioral patterns in a course. An additional feature of LDA is the mixed-membership model, where student behavior is represented as different proportions of a shared set of use cases, rather than hard cluster assignments. This enabled us to compare students by their relative proportions, define behavioral patterns, and reduce the dimensionality of the data for further analysis and prediction. Detecting such patterns is important to handle the openness of MOOCs, which has been tied to a variety of behavioral patterns, as evidenced

[1] Harvard University's institution for creating MOOCs
[2] MIT's institution for creating MOOCs

L@S 2015, March 14–18, 2015, Vancouver, BC, Canada

http://dx.doi.org/10.1145/2724660.2724662

by large initial enrollments, low percentages of completions, and widely varying resource use [14, 10, 18].

In this paper, we adapt LDA to edX clickstream data in order to address the following questions:

- Can LDA serve as an unsupervised approach for discovering the behavioral trends of MOOC participants?

- Can the mixed-membership model from LDA predict certification?

Our application involves one MITx MOOC, an introductory physics course called 8.02x: Electricity and Magnetism from the spring of 2013.

The paper continues as follows. The Related Work section summarizes work related to modeling learner behavior as context for our work. The Course Studied and Dataset section overviews the data examined in this paper. The Methods section describes the theory behind LDA and how it is adapted to and evaluated in an educational context. The Results section provides the outcome from applying LDA to 8.02x. The Discussion section outlines strengths and weaknesses of this approach. The Conclusion section summarizes the key contributions of this paper.

RELATED WORK

Understanding student behavior has been a consistent theme in MOOC research. Most studies aim to group students by their behavior, and then better understand how discovered behavior leads to educational advancement. A central challenge to any study includes significant aggregation of raw data sets, often requiring advanced methods that scale to large data sets.

Many researchers have employed machine learning and pattern recognition techniques to distill raw clickstream data into more interpretable models of student behavior. Kizilcec et al. [13] applied clustering techniques to gain insight into student disengagement and course completion. They represented students by their weekly activity, capturing whether or not students were "on track," "behind," "auditing," or "out" each week. Using these features, they performed k-means clustering and constructed four learner subpopulations: "completing", "auditing", "disengaging", and "sampling". These student subpopulations were then compared in terms of their demographics, surveyed experience, forum activity, and video streaming index to analyze retention. Rameh et al. [16] used the graphical model of Probabilistic Soft Logic (PSL) to distinguish forms of engagement in MOOCs. In contrast to Kizilcec et al., Rameh et al. viewed engagement/disengagement as latent variables and focused on social behaviors such as posting and subscribing in addition to more traditional behaviors such as following course material and completing assessments. Their study illustrated the informative role peer-to-peer interactions can play in user modeling. With a similar methodology Yang et al. [23] used social behavior for a survival analysis of students in MOOCs, finding that social engagement within the course was correlated with retention.

In this paper, we provide another perspective. Rather than rigidly defined feature sets, we use LDA to uncover behavioral patterns directly from the data in a unsupervised manner. This preserves much of the statistical information from the original dataset, while still forming an interpretable representation. Unlike the studies above, we don't sacrifice much granularity for interpretability.

COURSE STUDIED AND DATASET

8.02x: Electricity and Magnetism is an MITx MOOC offered by edX in the spring of 2013, based on an introductory physics course at MIT. Between January, 17 and September 8, enrollment reached 43,758 people (MIT has since removed this course), from around the world with a wide range of educational backgrounds [17]. Courseware interactions from these enrollees led to 37,394,406 events being recorded in the edX tracking logs [19]. Courseware in this context refers to the individual learning components and software features available to 8.02x participants.

The resources in 8.02x included a variety of videos, problems, textual content, and simulation activities. The major assessments consisted of weekly problem sets (18%), interactive simulations with concept questions (2%), and examinations – three midterms (15% each) and a final (30%). To promote engagement and self-assessment, weekly lectures were typically broken into roughly 5-10 video segments, each interspersed with graded multiple choice questions. These resources are organized hierarchically. Chapters, sequences, and verticals are container objects that form organizational units in the course. Within these containers are the course resources [7]. In order to better understand the course structure of 8.02x, a screenshot is provided in Figure 1. Unique resources are navigated in two ways: the left navigation bar provides a link to sequences of content that are organized into chapters (represented by weeks of material), while the top navigation provides access to individual resources and verticals. More information about 8.02x can be found in the MITx Course report [19].

METHODS

This section explains how LDA is adapted to model user behavior in MOOCs and the processes used to predict certification. Beginning with an overview of the theoretical background of LDA, we cover its original use for topic modeling in natural language processing [4] and draw a parallel between topic modeling and user modeling, which forms the basis for probabilistic use cases. Then, we explain how a students interactions are represented and quantified. This representation is evaluated according to their ability to predict certification and serves as a baseline for LDA. The section concludes with an explanation of the two-part evaluation process for LDA.

LDA for Traditional Topic Modeling

Traditionally, LDA has been used to understand the latent topic structure of textual documents. Topics are thought of as probability distributions over a fixed and shared vocabulary. LDA is an unsupervised technique, meaning initially there are no keywords or tags that can be used for categorization

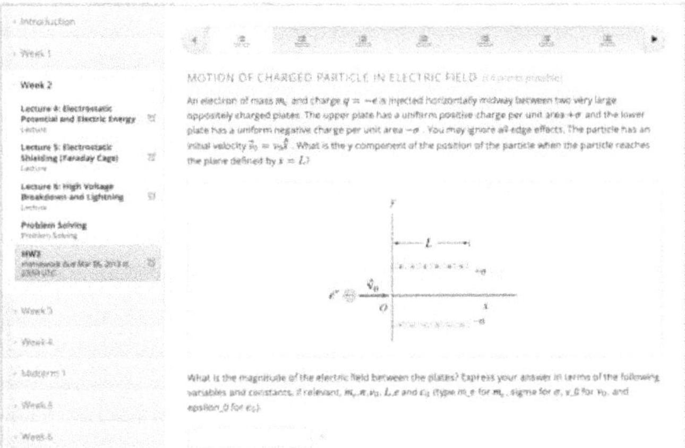

Figure 1: Screenshot of student display for 8.02x courseware. The left navigation bar provides access to weekly chapters, while the main display, to its right, offers videos, problems, and html pages packaged in lecture, problem set, tutorial, and exam sequences.

by topic. Hence, the topics, their distributions, and the topic assignments of each word are hidden variables that need to be estimated. These hidden variables are combined with the observable variables – document word counts for each word of the fixed vocabulary – to form a generative process that defines a joint distribution over the hidden and observable variables. This distribution is used to form a posterior distribution for the hidden variables that is optimized through an approximation to the Expectation-Maximization (EM) Algorithm [3, 4].

More formally, LDA assumes there are K topics in the collection of T documents that have a fixed vocabulary (V). These topics are indexed by $\hat{z} = 1, ..., K$ and represent a probability distribution over V called $\beta_{\hat{z}}$, where each word ($\hat{w}$) has a probability $\beta_{(\hat{w}|\hat{z})}$. Each document ($d^t$) in the collection can be represented as a bag of n_t words, i.e. $d^t = ({w_1}^t, ..., {w_{n_t}}^t)$. Although all of the documents share the same set of topics, each document has its own topic proportions (θ^t). θ^t is a categorical distribution sampled from a Dirichlet distribution with parameters α, where $\theta^t_{\hat{z}}$ is the probability of topic $\hat{z}$ in document d^t. This categorical distribution in turn is the basis for a multinomial distribution used to assign each word in d^t to a topic, i.e. $z^t_1, ..., z^t_{n_t}$. Using this formulation gives rise to an expansion of the joint distribution, $\prod_{t=1}^{T} P(d^t, z^t_1, ..., z^t_{n_t}, \phi^t, \beta; \alpha)$, as shown in Equation 1.

$$\prod_{z=1}^{K} P(\beta_z) \prod_{t=1}^{T} P(\theta^t|\alpha)\{\prod_{i=1}^{n_t} \theta^t_z \beta_{w_i|z}\} \quad (1)$$

Unfortunately, the posterior distribution for hidden variables defined by LDA is normally intractable because of the marginal distribution for the documents [4]. To approximate a solution, we use the python package gensim [8], which implements an online variational Bayes algorithm as proposed by Hoffman et al. [11].

LDA for Probabilistic Use Cases

To model behavior, we represent students as a bag of interactions with the courseware. Each of the static resources in the backbone of the course, as defined in the Course Studied and Dataset section, has a unique module identifier. These module identifiers ($\hat{m}$) form a fixed course vocabulary or structure ($\hat{m} \in C$) for LDA. In 8.02x, there were 1,725 unique module identifiers. With this information, a student in a course with T registrants can be modeled as $s^t = (m^t_1, ..., m^t_{n_t})$, where m^t_i represents an interaction with a course module. By substituting the students in a course for the collection of documents, topics describe behavioral patterns rather than words. For clarity, we refer to these interaction-based topics as *probabilistic use cases*. As such, use cases are similarly indexed by $\hat{u} = 1, ..., K$ and define a probability distribution over C called $\beta_{\hat{u}}$, where each module has an interaction probability of $\beta_{\hat{m}|\hat{u}}$. Students, like documents, share the same set of use cases, but in different proportions defined by ϕ^t. Equation 2 shows the expansion of the the joint distribution, $\prod_{t=1}^{T} P(d^t, u^t_1, ..., u^t_{n_t}, \phi^t, \beta; \alpha)$, that is parallel to the topic modeling application. This model builds on the existing infrastructure for topic modeling and allows us to investigate the hidden behavioral structure within a course.

$$\prod_{u=1}^{K} P(\beta_u) \prod_{t=1}^{T} P(\phi^t|\alpha)\{\prod_{i=1}^{n_t} \phi^t_u \beta_{m_i|u}\} \quad (2)$$

Quantifying Interactions

In applying LDA to model the behavior of MOOC participants, each student is represented as a bag of interactions with the courseware, where we only consider browser issued events. To quantify these interactions, we used time spent in seconds on each course module. Time was calculated by taking the difference between browser event timestamps. Breaks over 30 minutes long were discarded. This use of time spent is unique to the context of modeling user behavior. The traditional topic modeling application are limited to binary indicators or word counts.

While using time spent to quantify user interactions, the bag of interactions model was tested based on its ability to accurately predict whether or not a student would earn a certificate. For each week in 8.02x's 18 week runtime, we separately generated each of the interaction representations using the logs from the beginning of the course to the end of the given week. The performance of each representation was quantified by 5-fold cross validation of a Support Vector Machine (SVM) classifier for certification, where Different Error Costs (DEC) compensated for the class imbalance [20]. This provided a baseline to compare the predictive performance of a student's use case proportions (ϕ^t).

Evaluating Probabilistic Use Cases

Using the best interaction representation from the above process, LDA was evaluated on how well it modeled the data in addition to its predictive performance. Traditionally, model selection, i.e. selecting the optimal number of use cases, is based upon log perplexity [4] per interaction. This method is equivalent to the negative log likelihood of a corpus (approximated by the Evidence Lower Bound) divided by the number of interactions within that corpus, as in Equation 3. This is commonly used in natural language processing to evaluate language models. We use log perplexity per interaction here to reduce perplexity to a reasonable numerical scale.

$$log\{perplexity(corupus)\} = \frac{-log\{P(corpus|\alpha, \beta)\}}{\sum_{corpus} n_t}. \quad (3)$$

Using the models that fit well without an excessive number of use cases, we evaluated how well LDA predicted certification. LDA was trained on a weekly basis, where only the logs from the beginning of the course to the end of the given week were used. Students were then represented by their use case proportions (ϕ^t) in the 5-fold cross validation of a SVM classifier for certification, where DEC compensated for the class imbalance [20]. This approach demonstrated the predictive power of a student's use case proportions (ϕ^t) and quantified the effect that varying the number of use cases has on performance.

RESULTS

The results from applying LDA to 8.02x are broken into 4 subsections. The Interaction Representation subsection evaluates the time spent bag of interactions representation. Employing this representation, the Identifying the Number of Use Cases Through Log Perplexity subsection explores how well LDA fits the data for a varying number of use cases. The Probabilistic Use Cases subsection visualizes and explains the resulting use cases through their probability distribution over the course structure. In the final subsection, Predicting Certification, students' use case proportions are used in order to predict certification.

Predicting Certification with a Bag of Interactions Model

A student's activity within the edX platform can be quantified in a number of ways. In this section, we evaluate the ability of the bag of interactions model to predict certification of students. User interactions are quantified by time spent in seconds on each course module. We use 5-fold cross-validation over the 8.02x's 18 week duration as our primary heuristic. Table 1 shows the average scores broken down into true positive rates (TPR) for identifying certificate earners and true negative rates (TNR) for identifying non-certificate earners. Comparing both metrics illuminates any asymmetries in performance due to class imbalance [1].

Based on Table 1, using time spent for the bag of interactions model achieved high performance on non-certificate earners very early in the course, while performance on certificate earners lagged behind. This asymmetry is likely due to the overwhelming number of non-certificate earners. Only 4.2% of registrants earned a certificate in 8.02x [19], making the classes of non-certificate earners and certificate earners extremely imbalanced. Thus, the early performance of the bag of interactions model must be taken with skepticism because

Time Spent						
Week	1	2	3	4	5	6
TPR	0.38	0.39	0.39	0.45	0.48	0.54
TNR	0.92	0.95	0.97	0.98	0.98	0.98
Week	7	8	9	10	11	12
TPR	0.76	0.81	0.91	0.91	0.93	0.94
TNR	0.97	0.97	0.97	0.97	0.97	0.97
Week	13	14	15	16	17	18
TPR	0.95	0.95	0.96	0.96	0.96	0.97
TNR	0.97	0.97	0.98	0.98	0.97	0.98

Table 1: True positive rates (TPR) and true negative rates (TNR) for identifying certificate earners with different interaction representations.

a trivial majority classifier could achieve 95% overall accuracy by labeling the entire feature space as non-certificate earners. Balanced prediction between class is much more difficult.

Identifying the Number of Use Cases Through Log Perplexity

Using the time spent on modules as the underlying representation, 5-fold cross-validation of log-perplexity per interaction is displayed in Figure 2. The optimal number of use cases appeared to be around 50, however, it is unclear from cross-validation alone how much of effect such a large number of use cases has on our ability to interpret the model. Determining the right balance between predictive performance and interpretability is currently an open issue in probabilistic topic modeling [2]. Although there has been some work that tries to quantify interpretability [6], our vocabulary of course modules is only understood by a small set of individuals, making it difficult for us to apply those strategies here. Hence, in the next section we chose to visually explore how use cases vary and separate as the number of use cases increases.

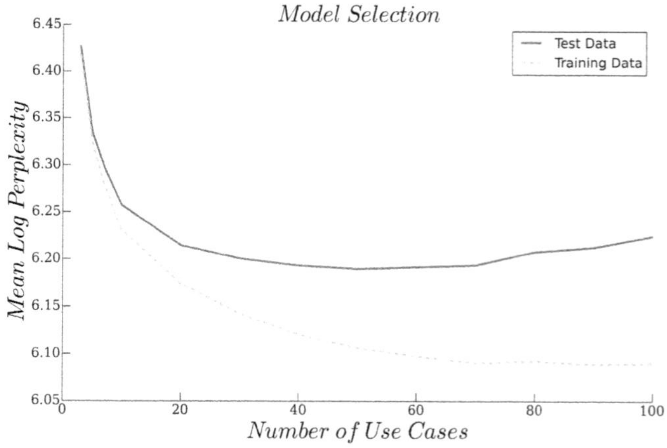

Figure 2: 5-fold log perplexity for a varying number of use cases.

Probabilistic Use Cases

This section illustrates the descriptive power of probabilistic use cases by plotting their probability distributions according to the course structure. With the 3-use case model as a baseline, we describe the resulting behavioral patterns. Subsequently, we investigate how these use cases evolved over the course's duration and subdivide as the number of use cases is increased.

Figure 3 shows the probability distributions of the 3-use case model after all 18 weeks of 8.02x. Each probability distribution is color-coded according to the course structure visual aid at the lower most x-axis. Color indicates the type of resource, and the length of each vertical bar is the weight towards the final grade. In order to ensure consistency, all figures in this section use the same visual aid in conveying course structure within each probability distribution.

Each of the presented use cases in Figure 3 illuminates a distinct behavioral pattern in 8.02x. The use case in Figure 3a concentrated the majority of its probability on videos from the first week of the courses. This skewed distribution resulted from the large population of registrants that only watched the videos at the beginning of the course before stopping activity.

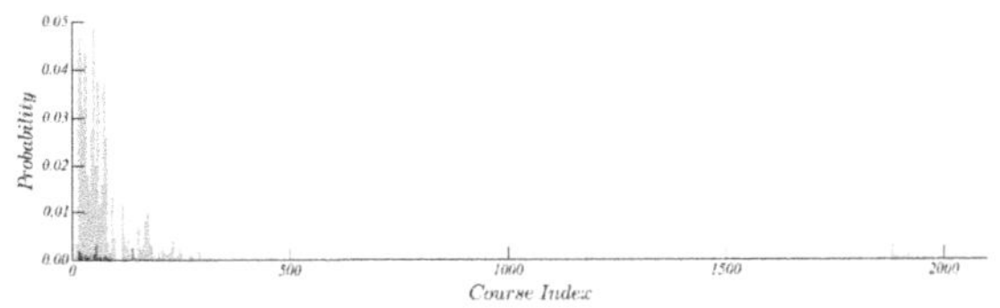

(a) Shopping use case

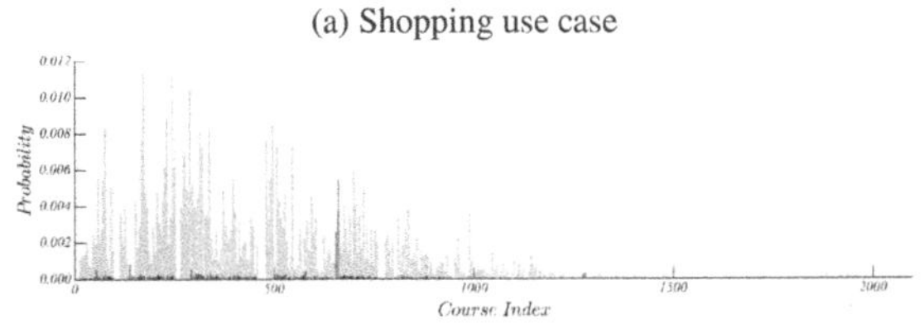

(b) Disengaging use case

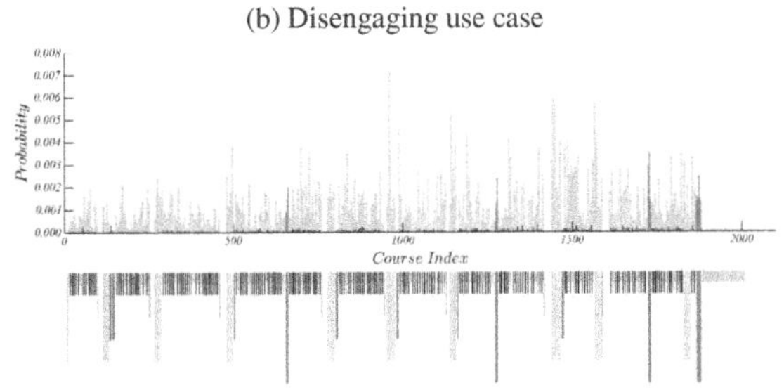

(c) Completing use case

Figure 3: Probability distributions from a 3-Use Case Model of 8.02x over all released content during the 18 week running. A course structure visual aid is below the lowermost probability distribution. Each bar is a set of resources, where color and length represents the type of resource and its weight toward final grade, respectively. Orange - lecture videos, black - lecture questions, gray - homework, green - simulations, red - exams, and blue - problem solving videos.

Based on our observations, we hypothesize that these users were simply "shopping", although many other possibilities exist. Figure 3b captures users who actively participated in the course yet disengaged midway through. Finally, the distribution in Figure 3c remains roughly uniform throughout the course, signifying significant engagement with the majority of the course material. Together these 3 use cases represent intuitive groups (shopping, disengaging, and completing) for students based on their interactions with the courseware.

These three use cases were evident from the very beginning of the course. The shopping use case remained virtually unchanged after the first two weeks of the course, while the disengaging and completing use cases slowly spread their distributions out, as new material was released. Figures for each use-case per week will be made available online. Students in the completing cohort engaged with material as soon as it was released, following the instructor's intentions. The disengaging use case had a similar, although delayed, progression to the completing use cases, where students increasingly lagged behind as new material was released. Overall the behavioral patterns captured in Figure 3 remained well-defined throughout the course, defining consistent archetypes for students.

Increasing the number of use cases breaks these archetypes into additional behavioral patterns based on the types of materials accessed and the percentage of the course utilized. Figure 4 depicts the 10-use case model trained on all 18 weeks of 8.02x. Users that failed to make it to the end of the course are represented by use cases in Figures 4a, 4b, 4c, 4d, and 4e. The shopping use case (see Figure 3a) reemerges most clearly in Figure 4a. Figure 4b potentially illuminates a shopping variant, where users are only attempting the first problem set. Figures 4c, 4d, and 4e resemble the disengaging use case from Figure 3b, highlighting potential inflection points in the course. The remaining 6 use cases embody the completing use case, as they spread their probability distributions across the course. Going from Figure 4f to Figure 4j there is a clear shift in probability from videos to assessments. Such separation indicates the degree to which students depended on videos, ranging from users that primarily audited the class to potential experts that attempted the problem sets and exams with little instruction. Therefore, we get higher granularity into the behavioral trends with the course by varying the number of use cases.

Predicting Certification Through Probabilistic Use Cases

By substituting in students' use case proportions, we effectively reduce the dimensionality of the data from thousands of resources to a small number of use cases. This allows for more accurate predictions of user outcomes. Through 5-fold cross validation, we test this hypothesis on a weekly basis in 8.02x, using certification as our outcome of choice. Table 2 presents the overall accuracy rates (ACC), true positive rates (TPR), and true negative rates (TNR) for 3, 5, 10, and 50-use case models. Despite the initial drop in TNR in comparison to the base representation of time spent in Table 1, the use case formulations yield much higher TPR, providing balanced prediction performance between certificate and non-certificate earners. Moreover, as the number of use cases in-

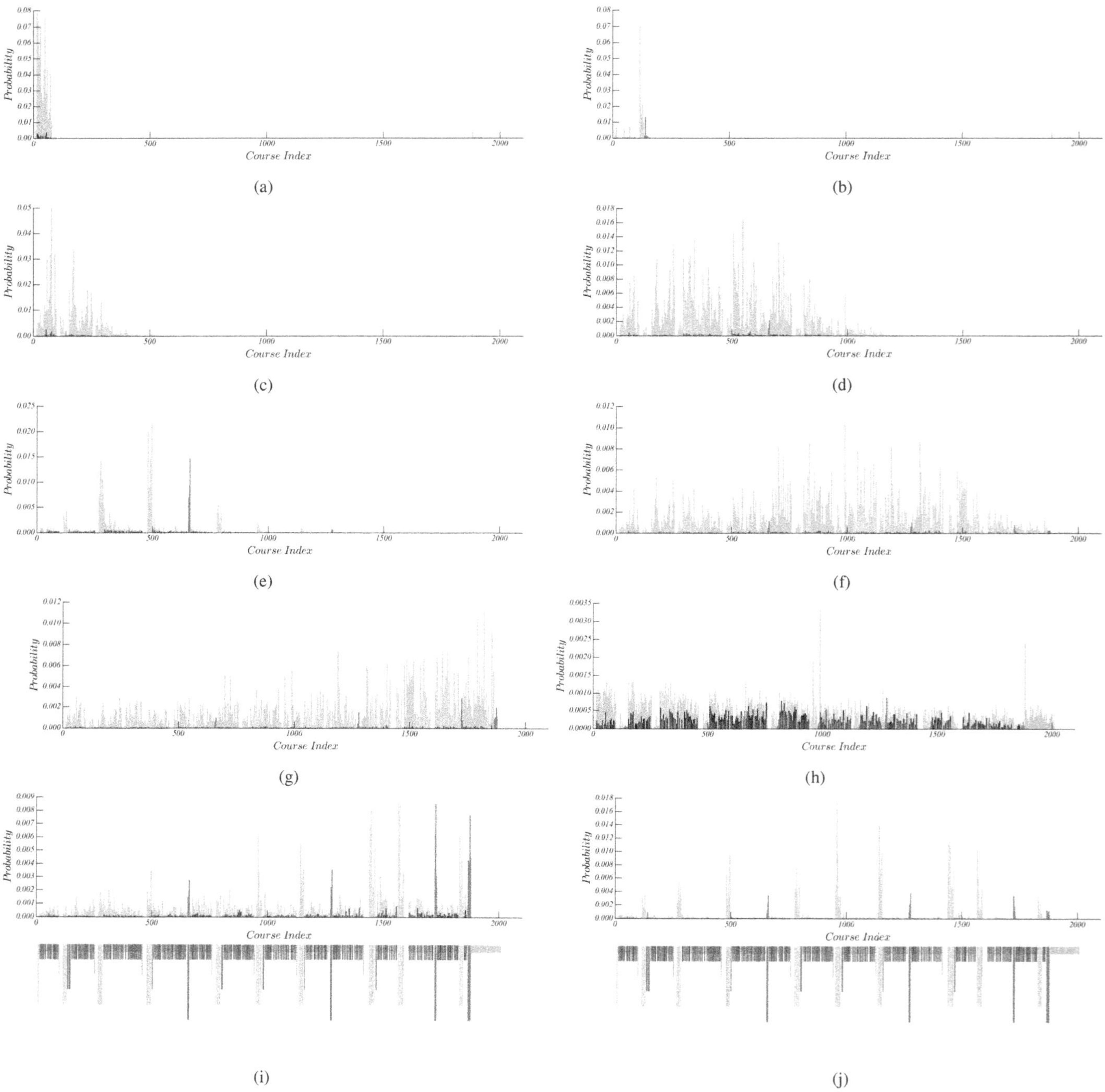

Figure 4: Probability distributions for each use case in a 10-Use Case Model trained on all 18 weeks of logs from 8.02x. In contrast to the 3-Use Case Model, the 10-Use Case model provides higher granularity into disengaged and engaged behavior trends. Figure 4i and Figure 4j contain the course structure visual aid. Each bar is a set of resources, where color and length represents the type of resource and its weight toward final grade, respectively. Orange - lecture videos, black - lecture questions, gray - homework, green - simulations, red - exams, and blue - problem solving videos.

	3-use case model			5-use case model			10-use case model			50-use case model		
Week	ACC	TNR	TPR	ACC	TNR	TPR	ACC	TNR	TPR	ACC	TNR	TPR
1	0.71±0.01	0.70	0.79	0.77±0.01	0.77	0.76	0.81±0.01	0.81	0.75	0.81±0.01	0.81	0.74
2	0.79±0.01	0.78	0.93	0.83±0.01	0.82	0.90	0.83±0.02	0.82	0.89	0.85±0.02	0.85	0.90
3	0.87±0.02	0.86	0.96	0.84±0.02	0.83	0.96	0.88±0.02	0.87	0.96	0.90±0.02	0.90	0.94
4	0.90±0.01	0.89	0.97	0.91±0.02	0.90	0.97	0.91±0.02	0.90	0.97	0.93±0.02	0.93	0.95
5	0.87±0.02	0.86	0.98	0.91±0.02	0.91	0.98	0.91±0.02	0.91	0.96	0.93±0.02	0.93	0.96
6	0.90±0.02	0.90	0.99	0.91±0.02	0.90	0.99	0.92±0.02	0.91	0.98	0.94±0.02	0.94	0.98
7	0.92±0.02	0.91	0.99	0.91±0.02	0.90	0.99	0.92±0.02	0.92	0.98	0.95±0.02	0.95	0.97
8	0.92±0.02	0.91	0.99	0.94±0.02	0.94	0.99	0.94±0.01	0.93	0.99	0.96±0.02	0.96	0.97
9	0.94±0.01	0.93	0.99	0.95±0.01	0.95	0.98	0.94±0.01	0.94	0.99	0.96±0.01	0.96	0.97
10	0.93±0.02	0.93	0.99	0.94±0.02	0.93	1.00	0.96±0.01	0.96	0.98	0.97±0.01	0.97	0.97
11	0.93±0.02	0.93	1.00	0.95±0.01	0.95	1.00	0.96±0.01	0.96	0.99	0.97±0.01	0.97	0.98
12	0.93±0.02	0.93	1.00	0.93±0.02	0.93	0.99	0.96±0.01	0.96	0.99	0.98±0.01	0.98	0.97
13	0.92±0.02	0.91	0.99	0.95±0.01	0.95	0.99	0.97±0.01	0.97	0.99	0.98±0.01	0.98	0.98
14	0.96±0.01	0.95	0.97	0.97±0.01	0.97	0.99	0.97±0.01	0.97	0.99	0.98±0.01	0.98	0.98
15	0.92±0.02	0.92	0.99	0.95±0.01	0.95	0.99	0.96±0.01	0.96	0.99	0.99±0.01	0.99	0.98
16	0.96±0.01	0.96	1.00	0.95±0.01	0.94	1.00	0.97±0.01	0.97	0.99	0.99±0.01	0.99	0.98
17	0.96±0.01	0.95	1.00	0.97±0.01	0.97	0.98	0.97±0.01	0.97	0.99	0.98±0.01	0.98	0.98
18	0.96±0.01	0.96	1.00	0.96±0.01	0.96	1.00	0.97±0.01	0.97	0.99	0.99±0.00	0.99	0.98

Table 2: Overall accuracy rates (ACC), true positive rates (TPR), and true negative rates (TNR) for 3, 5, 10, and 50-use case models at predicting certification.

creases, both the TNR and TPR increase. At the peak of 50 use cases, a SVM classifier with DEC achieves 0.81±0.01 accuracy at predicting certification with just one week of data. Even with only 3 use cases the, prediction accuracy is still at 0.71±0.01 with only one week of data.

DISCUSSION

Applying LDA to 8.02x generates probabilistic use-cases that transform massive amounts of statistical information into a set of behavioral trends that are more easily characterized and communicated. Investigating the probability distributions associated with each use case can help researchers distinguish archetypes such as auditors, completers, and even experts. The true descriptive power of LDA, nevertheless, comes from its mixed-membership model. Because students have their own proportions for each use case, important differences between users are preserved, which is critical in prediction.

Despite the preserved statistical information, the implementation of LDA in this paper involves two assumptions regarding the student data. First, LDA assumes that the order of the interactions does not matter when determining the use cases. The joint distribution in Equation 2 indicates this assumption, as permutations of interactions do not affect the overall likelihood of the model. However, the order of student interactions can encode valuable information about behavioral patterns. For example, consider playing a video in a lecture sequence and answering a follow up question. Answering the question before watching the video alludes to a very different behavior than the reverse. Rather than following the natural order of the course, a student might be trying to optimize their behavior to get through the material as quickly as possible. To relax this constraint, the work of Wallach [21] or Griffiths et al. [9] could be adapted for use case modeling.

The second assumption is that the ordering of the students does not matter. Because enrollment took place throughout the running of 8.02x, this is not entirely true. The release and due dates for course content were spread across roughly 16 weeks, meaning students ultimately had different user experiences depending on the date they enrolled. Such course features could potentially have a dramatic effect on behavior, which traditional LDA does not currently capture.

Nevertheless, the application of LDA in this paper serves as a solid proof of concept. To truly validate the effectiveness of this approach, the methods need to be applied to a broad range of courses. As next steps, we are excited to explore how factors, such as population size, course structure, or material, effect the resulting use cases.

CONCLUSIONS

Our results show that LDA can be adapted to the context of user modeling in MOOCs. The descriptive power of this approach reveals a number of latent use-cases learned from data in the MITx on edX MOOC, 8.02x: Electricity and Magnetism. These use cases have shown distinct patterns of behavior, while preserving important statistical information for additional analysis. Perhaps most important, using only the first week of logs, probabilistic use cases can predict whether or not a student will earn a certificate with 0.81±0.01 accuracy.

Beyond research, it is our hope that this may impact course content teams and platform developers. The probabilistic representation of use cases provides intuition about which course components are utilized and potentially more complex modes of student behavior. The mixed-membership representation of students offered by LDA also has the potential to facilitate similarity queries between students on the basis of their behavior. From a platform perspective, these queries could in turn serve as the basis for intervention studies of specific cohorts. LDA adapted for user modeling provides key insights into behavior via a data-driven approach that could potentially form a foundation for adaptive design in large-scale applications.

ACKNOWLEDGMENTS

We thank the MITx and the HarvardX Research Committee for guidance on this work and computational resources.

REFERENCES

1. Batuwita, R., and Palade, V. Class imbalance learning methods for support vector machines. *Imbalanced Learning: Foundations, Algorithms, and Applications* (2013), 83.
2. Blei, D. M. Probabilistic topic models. *Communications of the ACM 55*, 4 (2012), 77–84.
3. Blei, D. M., and Lafferty, J. D. Topic models. *Text mining: classification, clustering, and applications 10* (2009), 71.
4. Blei, D. M., Ng, A. Y., and Jordan, M. I. Latent Dirichlet Allocation. *Journal of Machine Learning Research 3* (1 2003), 993–1022.
5. Breslow, L., Pritchard, D. E., DeBoer, J., Stump, G. S., Ho, A. D., and Seaton, D. Studying learning in the worldwide classroom: Research into edX's first MOOC. *Research & Practice in Assessment 8* (2013), 13–25.
6. Chang, J., Gerrish, S., Wang, C., Boyd-graber, J. L., and Blei, D. M. Reading tea leaves: How humans interpret topic models. In *Advances in Neural Information Processing Systems* (2009), 288–296.
7. Course XML Tutorial – edX Data Documentation documentation. `http://edx.readthedocs.org/en/latest/course_data_formats/course_xml.html`.
8. gensim: Topic modelling for humans. `http://radimrehurek.com/gensim/`.
9. Griffiths, T. L., Steyvers, M., Blei, D. M., and Tenenbaum, J. B. Integrating topics and syntax. In *Advances in Neural Information Processing Systems* (12 2004), 537–544.
10. Ho, A. D., Reich, B. J. F., Nesterko, S. O., Seaton, D. T., Mullaney, T. P., Waldo, J. H., and Chuang, I. HarvardX and MITx: The first year of open online courses, fall 2012-summer 2013. *Social Science Research Network* (1 2014). `http://ssrn.com/abstract=2381263`.
11. Hoffman, M., Bach, F. R., and Blei, D. M. Online learning for Latent Dirichlet Allocation. In *Advances in Neural Information Processing Systems* (12 2010), 856–864.
12. Kim, J., Guo, P. J., Seaton, D. T., Mitros, P., Gajos, K. Z., and Miller, R. C. Understanding in-video dropouts and interaction peaks inonline lecture videos. In *Proceedings of the first ACM conference on Learning@Scale conference*, ACM (3 2014), 31–40.
13. Kizilcec, R. F., Piech, C., and Schneider, E. Deconstructing disengagement: analyzing learner subpopulations in massive open online courses. In *Proceedings of the third international conference on learning analytics and knowledge*, ACM (2013), 170–179.
14. Koller, D., Ng, A., Do, C., and Chen, Z. Retention and intention in massive open online courses: In depth. *Educause Review 48*, 3 (2013).
15. Pritchard, J. K., Stephens, M., and Donnelly, P. Inference of population structure using multilocus genotype data. *Genetics 155*, 2 (2000), 945–959.
16. Ramesh, A., Goldwasser, D., Huang, B., Daumé III, H., and Getoor, L. Modeling learner engagement in MOOCs using probabilistic soft logic. In *NIPS Workshop on Data Driven Education* (2013).
17. Rayyan, S., Seaton, D. T., Belcher, J., Pritchard, D. E., and Chuang, I. Participation and performance in 8.02x electricity and magnetism: The first physics MOOC from MITx. *arXiv preprint arXiv:1310.3173* (2013).
18. Seaton, D., Nesterko, S., Mullaney, T., Reich, J., and Ho, A. Characterizing video use in the catalogue of MITx MOOCs. *European MOOC Stakeholders Summit, Lausanne* (2014), 140–146.
19. Seaton, D. T., Reich, J., Nesterko, S. O., Mullaney, T., Waldo, J., Ho, A. D., and Chuang, I. 8.02x electricity and magnetism – spring 2013 MITx course report (MITx working paper# 10). *Social Science Rsearch Network* (1 2014). `http://ssrn.com/abstract=2382328`.
20. Veropoulos, K., Campbell, C., Cristianini, N., et al. Controlling the sensitivity of support vector machines. In *Proceedings of the international joint conference on artificial intelligence*, vol. 1999 (1999), 55–60.
21. Wallach, H. M. Topic modeling: beyond bag-of-words. In *Proceedings of the 23rd international conference on Machine learning*, ACM (2006), 977–984.
22. Xu, G., Zhang, Y., and Yi, X. Modelling user behaviour for web recommendation using LDA model. In *Web Intelligence and Intelligent Agent Technology, 2008. WI-IAT'08. IEEE/WIC/ACM International Conference on*, vol. 3, IEEE (2008), 529–532.
23. Yang, D., Sinha, T., Adamson, D., and Rosé, C. P. Turn on, tune in, drop out: Anticipating student dropouts in massive open online courses. In *Proceedings of the 2013 NIPS Data-Driven Education Workshop* (2013).

Bayesian Ordinal Peer Grading

Karthik Raman
Department of Computer Science
Cornell University, Ithaca NY 14853
karthik@cs.cornell.edu

Thorsten Joachims
Department of Computer Science
Cornell University, Ithaca NY 14853
tj@cs.cornell.edu

ABSTRACT
Massive Online Open Courses have become an accessible and affordable choice for education. This has led to new technical challenges for instructors such as student evaluation at scale. Recent work has found *ordinal peer grading*, where individual grader orderings are aggregated into an overall ordering of assignments, to be a viable alternate to traditional instructor/staff evaluation [23]. Existing techniques, which extend rank-aggregation methods, produce a single ordering as output. While these rankings have been found to be an accurate reflection of assignment quality on average, they do not communicate any of the uncertainty inherent in the assessment process. In particular, they do not to provide instructors with an estimate of the uncertainty of each assignment's position in the ranking. In this work, we tackle this problem by applying Bayesian techniques to the ordinal peer grading problem, using MCMC-based sampling techniques in conjunction with the Mallows model. Experiments are performed on real-world peer grading datasets, which demonstrate that the proposed method provides accurate uncertainty information via the estimated posterior distributions.

Author Keywords
Peer Grading, Ordinal Feedback, Rank Aggregation

ACM Classification Keywords
H.4 Information Systems Applications: Miscellaneous

General Terms
Algorithms, Experimentation, Theory

INTRODUCTION
MOOCs (Massive Online Open Courses) offer the promise of affordable higher education, across a breadth of disciplines, for anyone with access to the Internet. The introduction of MOOCs has forced instructors to adapt conventional classroom logistics in order to scale to classrooms of 10,000+ students. One such key logistic is the *evaluation of students* in MOOCs. Given the orders of magnitude difference in scale, conventional assessment techniques such as instructor/staff-based grading are simply infeasible for MOOCs. While scalable automatic-grading schemes — such as multiple-choice questions — exist, they are not suitable in all settings [4, 25, 12, 13]. For instance, research-oriented classes require more open-ended testing such as essays and reports, which are very challenging to evaluate automatically. A lack of reliable assessment techniques for these types of assignments may limit the kinds of courses offered as MOOCs.

Peer grading, where students — not instructors or staff — provide feedback on the work of other students in the class, has been proposed as a solution. Peer grading naturally overcomes the problem of scale [11, 16], since the number of "graders" matches the number of students. Despite this inherent scalability of peer grading, a key obstacle for peer grading to work is the fact that the students are not trained graders and are just learning the material themselves. To ensure good-quality grades it is therefore imperative that grading guidelines are easy to communicate and apply, making the feedback process a easy and unambiguous as possible. Towards this goal, recent work has proposed eliciting ordinal feedback from graders [23] (e.g. "project A is better than project B") rather than cardinal grades (e.g. "project A should get 87 out of 100"), since ordinal feedback has been shown to be more reliable than cardinal feedback [15, 3, 24, 6], and avoids having to communicate absolute grading scales.

This leads to the **ordinal peer grading problem**, where given the grader feedback (partial orderings over a subset of the assignments), the goal is to infer the overall ordering of all assignments. Rank-aggregation techniques have been extended to this task [23] and shown to not only be comparable to (if not better than) cardinal-grading based techniques but also traditional evaluation practices such as course-staff (TAs) based grading. It is important to note than unlike other rank aggregation problems, peer grading requires accuracy throughout the ranking and not just at the top.

While existing ordinal peer grading techniques were shown to estimate rankings that are accurate on average, they merely output a single ranking without communicating the uncertainty inherent in the assessment process. In particular, they do not provide instructors with an estimate of the uncertainty of each assignment's position in the ranking. To overcome this limitation, this paper presents a method for inferring the posterior distribution of where each assignment falls in the overall ranking. This information can, for example, be visualized as shown in Figure 1. Most importantly, the height of the blue bars shows the probability with which each assignment falls at a specific rank. This information allows instructors to ascertain the algorithm's confidence in the grade (*i.e.,* percentile/position in ranking) of each assignment and discern the uncertainty of the underlying peer grades for each assignment. For instance, in the above example, while there

ACM 978-1-4503-3411-2/15/03 ...$15.00.
http://dx.doi.org/10.1145/2724660.2724678

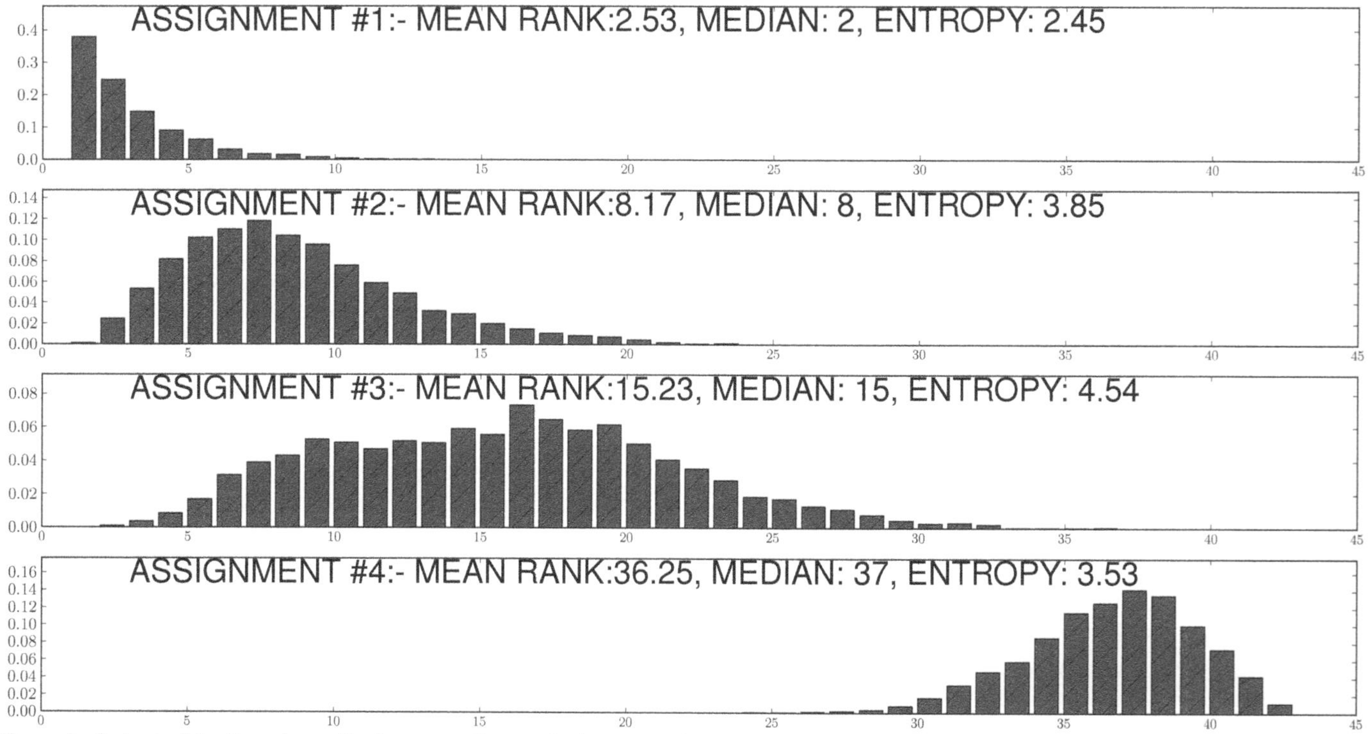

Figure 1. Output of the Bayesian ordinal peer grading method proposed in this paper. Having the peer grading algorithm produce more detailed information of each individual assignment's performance can be very useful for instructors when it comes to determining final grades. The above figure is one such example, where for each assignment the *posterior marginal distribution* (over position in the overall ranking) is shown (rank on x-axis, marginal probability on y-axis) along with statistics such as *posterior mean, median and entropy* of the marginal distribution.

is a high probability that assignment 1 is the best of the four assignments, it is less certain that assignment 2 is better than assignment 3. This is because of the high uncertainty in the position of assignment 3 (as evidenced by its' high entropy of 4.54). If presented with such information, instructors could intervene and improve certainty by soliciting additional reviews for specific assignments, or at least by accounting for the uncertainty when deriving their grades from the ranking.

In this work, we address the problem of uncertainty modeling by employing Bayesian techniques for the ordinal peer grading problem. In particular we propose a Metropolis-Hastings [8] based Markov Chain Monte-Carlo (MCMC) method, for sampling from the posterior of a Mallows model [20]. The resulting samples allow us to empirically estimate the posterior rank distribution of each assignment, allowing us to report confidences and uncertainty information.

We empirically study the efficacy of the proposed method on peer grading datasets, collected from a university-level class. In addition to studying the quality of the learned posterior orderings, we also analyze the resulting confidences and uncertainty information, both qualitatively and quantitatively.

BAYESIAN METHODS FOR ORDINAL PEER GRADING

In this section, we first describe the ordinal peer grading problem from a machine learning perspective. We then briefly review existing techniques for the ordinal peer grading problem. Our proposed Bayesian version of these techniques is then presented, followed by an empirical evaluation of these techniques in the Experiments section.

Ordinal Peer Grading (OPG) Problem

In the *ordinal peer grading* problem, we are given a set of $|D|$ *assignments* $D = \{d_1, ..., d_{|D|}\}$ (*e.g.*, project reports, essays) which we need to grade. The grading is performed by a set of $|G|$ graders $G = \{g_1, ..., g_{|G|}\}$ (*e.g.*, student peer grader, reviewers). Each grader receives a subset of assignments $D_g \subset D$ to assess. The subsets D_g can be determined randomly, by a sequential mechanism or a deterministic policy. As feedback, each grader provides an ordering $\sigma^{(g)}$ (possibly with ties) of their assignments D_g.

The *primary goal* of OPG is *ordinal grade estimation* [23] *i.e.*, to produce an overall ordering [1] of the assignments $\hat{\sigma}$ using the individual grader orderings $\sigma^{(g)}$. While we would like this inferred ordering $\hat{\sigma}$ to accurately match some (latent) true ordering σ^*, we are faced with a couple of challenges. First, the individual grader orderings are only partial orderings *i.e.*, the orderings only cover a small subset of the assignments ($|D_g| \ll |D|$). The second challenge is the fact that not all graders do an equally good job of grading, be it due to effort, skill or understanding of the material.

[1]Producing an overall ordering of the assignments can be used to infer, for each assignment, a percentile rank as the grade (a common performance metric reported by standardized tests).

$G, g(\in G)$	Set of all graders, Specific grader
$D, d(\in D)$	Set of all assignments, Specific assignment
$D_g(\subset D)$	Set of items graded by grader g
$\sigma^{(g)}$	Ranking feedback (with possible ties) from g
$\eta_g(\in \Re^+)$	Predicted reliability of grader g
$r_d^{(\sigma)}$	Rank of assignment d in ordering σ (rank 1 is best)
$d_2 \succ_\sigma d_1$	d_2 is preferred/ranked higher than d_1 (in σ)
$\pi(A)$	Set of all rankings over $A \subseteq D$
$\sigma_1 \sim \sigma_2$	$\exists$ way of resolving ties in σ_2 to obtain σ_1
$\hat{\sigma}$	Estimated ordering of assignments
σ^*	(Latent) True ordering of assignments

Table 1. Notation overview and reference.

This leads to the secondary goal of *grader reliability estimation*, where we would like to estimate the accuracy/quality $\eta_g \in \Re^+$ of the feedback of each grader g. This should allow us to improve the ordinal grade estimation quality by identifying unreliable graders and thus reduce the impact of their feedback on the estimated ordering $\hat{\sigma}$. Furthermore, the ability to identify unreliable graders enables the instructor to incentivize good and thorough grading by making peer grading itself part of the overall grade.

Relation to existing rank aggregation literature

The ordinal grade estimation problem in OPG can be viewed as a specific kind of rank aggregation problem. Rank aggregation [17] covers a class of problems where the goal is the combination of ordinal (ranking) information from multiple different sources. **Voting Systems** (or **Social Choice** [1]) are one of the most common applications of rank aggregation techniques. The goal of these systems is to merge the preferences of a set of individuals. Condorcet voting methods such as *Borda count* amongst others [10, 19] are commonly used to tackle these problems. **Search Result Aggregation** (also known as **Rank Fusion** or **Metasearch** [2]) is perhaps the most well-known rank-aggregation problem. Given rankings from different sources (typically different algorithms), the goal is to merge them and produce a single output ranking. Extensions of classical techniques such as the Mallows model [20] and Bradley-Terry model [5] have become popular for these problems [18, 7] and have been used to improve ranking performance in different settings [22, 26, 21].

While our work also extends the classical Mallows model, there are some fundamental differences to the these other rank aggregation problems, which make existing methods ill-suited for the OPG problem. First and foremost is the fact that while the success of search result aggregation and voting systems depend on correctly identifying the top item(s), in ordinal grade estimation it is imperative to accurately estimate the **full ranking**. In other words, we cannot afford to do any worse of a job identifying the 50th percentile assignments than we do identifying the top assignments.

A second key difference (and the main focus of this work) is the fact that unlike other rank aggregation problems, **a single ordering** of assignments **may not suffice** for the purpose of determining grades. Before determining the final grades of assignments, instructors would like to have access to other information such as the uncertainty in the rank of an assignment. In other words, they would like to know more about the distribution of $r_d^{(\hat{\sigma})}$ (for instance a visualization such as Figure 1).

Existing Approaches to OPG

Different approaches [23] to the OPG problem include extensions of classical models such as the Mallows and Bradley-Terry model. We focus on the Mallows-based methods, as they form the basis for the techniques proposed in this work. In particular, the proposed Mallows-based peer grading model defines a distribution over rankings in terms of the **Kendall-Tau** distance [14] from the true ranking σ^* of assignments.

DEFINITION 1. *The Kendall-τ Distance δ_K between rankings σ_1 and σ_2 is the number of incorrectly ordered pairs between the two rankings and is given by*

$$\delta_K(\sigma_1, \sigma_2) = \sum_{d_1 \succ_{\sigma_1} d_2} \mathbb{I}[[d_2 \succ_{\sigma_2} d_1]]. \quad (1)$$

Given the grader orderings $\sigma^{(g)}$, we can define the data likelihood (if the overall ranking was σ) as

$$P(\{\sigma^{(g)}; \forall g\}|\sigma) = \left\{ \prod_{g \in G} \frac{\sum_{\sigma' \sim \sigma^{(g)}} e^{-\delta_K(\sigma, \sigma')}}{Z_M(|D_g|)} \right\}, \quad (2)$$

where the normalization constant Z_M is easy to compute as it only depends on the ranking length.

$$Z_M(k) = \prod_{i=1}^{k} \left(1 + e^{-1} + \cdots + e^{-(i-1)}\right) = \prod_{i=1}^{k} \frac{1 - e^{-i}}{1 - e^{-1}} \quad (3)$$

Note that in Equation 2, **ties in the grader rankings** are modeled as *indifference* (*i.e.,* agnostic to either ranking), which leads to the summation in the numerator is over all total orderings σ' consistent with the weak ordering $\sigma^{(g)}$. While computing the Maximum-Likelihood Estimator (MLE) of Equation 2 is NP-hard [10], several simple and tractable approximations that are shown to work well in practice are presented in [23].

While this model does not produce grader reliability estimates, an extension to the model is proposed in [23] and computed using a MAP estimator (rather than MLE estimator):

$$P(\{\sigma^{(g)}; \forall g\}|\sigma, \{\eta_g\}) = \left\{ \prod_{g \in G} \frac{\sum_{\sigma' \sim \sigma^{(g)}} e^{-\eta_g \delta_K(\sigma, \sigma')}}{Z_M(\eta_g, |D_g|)} \right\}.$$

However, both models (with and w/o reliability estimates) suffer from the same issue, in that they both produce **point estimates** *i.e.,* a single ranking as output. In the next section, we will propose and study a Bayesian version of these models that estimates the posterior distribution of the predicted ranking and reliabilities.

Mallows MCMC using Metropolis-Hastings

To help provide more detailed information to instructors, we would like to have access to the posterior distribution of the orderings. In other words, instead of the data likelihood probability we have in Equation 2 (ignoring the grader reliabilities

Algorithm 1 Sampling from Mallows Posterior using Metropolis-Hastings

1: **Input:** Grader orderings $\sigma^{(g)}$, Grader reliabilities η_g and MLE ordering $\hat{\sigma}$.
2: Pre-compute $x_{ij} \leftarrow \sum_{g \in G} \eta_g \mathbb{I}[d_i \succ_{\sigma^{(g)}} d_j] - \sum_{g \in G} \eta_g \mathbb{I}[d_j \succ_{\sigma^{(g)}} d_i[$
3: $\sigma_0 \leftarrow \hat{\sigma}$ ▷ Initialize Markov Chain using MLE estimate
4: **for** $t = 1 \dots T$ **do**
5: Sample σ' from (**MALLOWS**) jumping distribution: $J_{MAL}(\sigma'|\sigma_{t-1})$
6: Compute ratio $r_t = \frac{P(\sigma'|\{\sigma^{(g)}; \forall g\})}{P(\sigma_{t-1}|\{\sigma^{(g)}; \forall g\})}$ using Equation 5
7: With probability $\min(r_t, 1)$, $\sigma_t \leftarrow \sigma'$ else $\sigma_t \leftarrow \sigma_{t-1}$
8: Add σ_t to samples (if burn-in and thinning conditions met)

for now), we would like to know the posterior distribution of the inferred rankings σ *i.e.,* $P(\sigma|\{\sigma^{(g)}; \forall g\})$. We can safely assume a uniform prior on all orderings (for academic fairness), which gives us

$$P(\sigma|\{\sigma^{(g)}; \forall g\}) = \frac{P(\{\sigma^{(g)}; \forall g\}|\sigma)P(\sigma)}{\sum_{\sigma' \in \pi(D)} P(\{\sigma^{(g)}; \forall g\}|\sigma')P(\sigma')}$$
$$= \frac{P(\{\sigma^{(g)}; \forall g\}|\sigma)}{\sum_{\sigma' \in \pi(D)} P(\{\sigma^{(g)}; \forall g\}|\sigma')}. \quad (4)$$

With the posterior distribution in hand, we can derive the desired marginal rank distributions of each assignment, or we can predict a single ranking that minimizes posterior expected loss.

However, exact computations with this posterior are infeasible given the combinatorial number of possible orderings of all assignments. To help us ascertain information from the posterior, we will employ MCMC based sampling. Markov Chain Monte Carlo (or MCMC in short) are a set of techniques for sampling from a distribution by constructing a Markov Chain which converges to the desired distribution asymptotically. **Metropolis-Hastings** is a specific MCMC algorithm which is particularly common when the underlying distribution is difficult to sample from (as is the case here) especially for multi-variate distributions.

Thus to help us estimate properties of the posterior we will design a Markov Chain whose stationary distribution is the distribution of interest: $P(\sigma|\{\sigma^{(g)}; \forall g\})$. Along with the theoretical guarantees accompanying these methods, an added advantage is the fact that we can control the desired estimation accuracy (by selecting the number of samples).

This results in a simple and efficient algorithm, shown in Algorithm 1. To begin with we pre-compute statistics of the net cumulative weighted total each assignment d_i is ranked above another assignment d_j. We then initialize the Markov Chain using the MLE estimate of the ordering: $\hat{\sigma}$. At each timestep, to propose a new sample σ' given the previous sample σ_{t-1}, we sample from a jumping distribution (Line 5). In particular, we use a **Mallows**-based jumping distribution:

Data Statistic	Poster	Report
Number of Assignments	42	44
Number of Peer Reviewers	148	153
Total Peer Reviews	996	586

Table 2. Statistics for the two datasets "Poster" and "Report"

.

$\rightarrow \quad J_{MAL}(\sigma'|\sigma) \propto e^{-\delta_K(\sigma', \sigma)}$.
This is a simple distribution to sample from and can be done efficiently in $|D|log|D|$ time. Furthermore as this is a symmetric jumping distribution (*i.e.,* $J_{MAL}(\sigma'|\sigma) = J_{MAL}(\sigma|\sigma')$), the acceptance ratio computation is simplified.

When it comes to computing the (acceptance) ratio r_t (Line 6), we can rely on the pre-computed statistics to do so efficiently. In particular, we can simplify the expression for the ratio to:

$$\frac{P(\sigma_a|\{\sigma^{(g)}; \forall g\})}{P(\sigma_b|\{\sigma^{(g)}; \forall g\})} = \prod_{g \in G} e^{\delta_K(\sigma^{(g)}, \sigma_b) - \delta_K(\sigma^{(g)}, \sigma_a)}$$
$$= \prod_{i,j} e^{x_{ij}(\mathbb{I}[d_i \succ_{\sigma_a} d_j] - \mathbb{I}[d_i \succ_{\sigma_b} d_j])} \quad (5)$$

This expression is again simple to compute and can be done in time proportional to the number of flipped pairs between σ_a and σ_b, which in the worst case is $O(|D|^2)$. Overall, the algorithm has a **worst-case time complexity** of $O(T|D|^2)$.

The resulting samples produced by the algorithm can be used to *estimate* the posterior distributions including the marginal posterior of the rank of each assignment *i.e.,* $P(r_d|\{\sigma^{(g)}; \forall g\}$, as well as statistics such as the entropy of the marginal, the posterior mean and median etc.

In order to improve the quality of the resulting estimates, we ensure proper mixing by targeting a moderate acceptance rate and by thinning samples (in our experiments we thin every 10 iterations). Furthermore we draw samples once the chain has started converging *i.e.,* we use a burn-in of around 10,000 iterations.

We also derive a Metropolis-Hastings based extension of the Mallows model with grader reliabilities. In addition to sampling the orderings, we also sample the reliabilities using a Gaussian jumping distribution (also symmetric). However the acceptance ratio computation is now more involved and hence less efficient than that for Algorithm 1, but nonetheless can be computed fairly efficiently. We omit the precise equation and computations for the purpose of brevity.

Software and an online service that implements these methods is available at `http://www.peergrading.org/`.

EXPERIMENTS

In this section, we empirically evaluate the performance of the Bayesian Mallows-based peer grading method. In particular, we study a) the quality of its predicted rankings in comparison with existing peer-grading methods as measured with regards to conventional instructor grades; and b) the accuracy of the confidence intervals and uncertainty information.

Experimental Setting

We used the peer-grading datasets introduced in [23]. These datasets were collected in a real-classroom setting from a large university class. The class which consisted of about 170 students and 9 Teaching Assistants (TAs), used peer grading to evaluate the course projects (done in groups of 3-4 students) The advantage of this class size is the availability of conventional instructor based grades for assignments, in addition to the peer grades (performed individually by each student). Having these instructor grades allows us to provide a more robust evaluation of the educational impact of these techniques, beyond what previous work has done.

We used both the **Poster** and **Final Report** datasets in this work. The two datasets correspond to different parts of the course. Students were incentivized to do a good job grading, by incorporating their peer grading performance into their overall grade for the course. The peer grading was done on a 10-point (cardinal) Likert scale so as to compare cardinal and ordinal peer grading methods. The ordinal peer grading methods merely used the ordering implies by the cardinal grades.

Table 2 provides some of the key statistics of the two datasets. On average each poster and final report received roughly 24 and 13 peer reviews respectively. For both datasets there was a single instructor grade for each assignment. As described in [23], the instructor grades for the reports were determined completely independent of the peer grades. For the posters the instructor grades utilized the TA grades, which were partly influenced by student grades.

The Bayesian Mallows MCMC method was run with identical (fixed) parameters for both datasets. In total, 5000 sample orderings were drawn from the Markov Chain using Algorithm 1. These samples were used to estimate the posterior distributions and for obtaining the statistics in the following subsections.

Are the inferred orderings accurate?

A key benefit of the Bayesian approach is that the posterior distribution of the orderings provides uncertainty information. But we can also use the posterior distribution to predict a single ordering of the assignments. How does the accuracy of the orderings predicted by the Bayesian model compare to the accuracy of the orderings estimated via maximum likelihood estimation (MLE)? To address this question, we compare the following techniques:

- **MLE:** Maximum-Likelihood Estimator of the Mallows model [23]. This is a single point estimate, and it is also used to initialize the Markov Chain.
- **Mode-MAL:** (One of the) Modes of the posterior of the Mallows distribution. Ties are broken randomly.
- **Mode-MAL+G:** (One of the) Modes of the posterior of the Mallows distribution with grader reliability estimates. Ties are broken randomly.

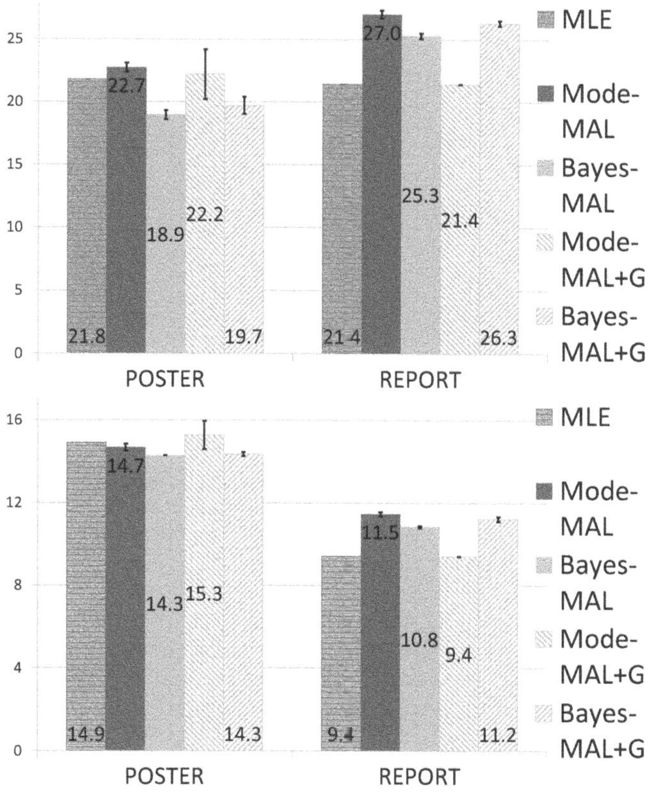

Figure 2. (*Top*) Normalized Kendall-Tau performance of all methods against the instructor grades for both datasets: Poster (Left) and Report (Right). Figure on the *Bottom* is similar but reports a *weighted* version of the Kendall-Tau error. Note: Performance of a *random baseline* would be 50% for both metrics. For both figures, the lower value is better.

- **Bayes-MAL:** This is the Bayes estimate minimizing posterior expected δ_K over the posterior learned by Alg 1. Formally, the predicted ordering is

$$\hat{\sigma} = \texttt{argmin}_\sigma \sum_{\sigma'} \delta_K(\sigma', \sigma) P(\sigma'|D),$$

where $P(\sigma'|D)$ represents the estimated posterior distribution (as output by the Bayesian MCMC method).

- **Bayes-MAL+G:** This is the Bayes estimate minimizing posterior expected τ_{KT} over the posterior of the Mallows model with grader reliability estimates.

While computing the Bayes-MAL and Bayes-MAL+G predictions is an NP-hard problem, as it requires computing the Kemeny-optimal aggregate [10], we can approximate the optimal solution of the minimization problem efficiently. In particular, we used the simple and efficient Borda-Count technique, which is known to be a 5-approximation [9]. In our case, this also carries a nice semantic meaning as it amounts to simply ordering the assignments by their posterior mean ranks.

The results are shown in Figure 2. As the measure of prediction accuracy, we use the Kendall-Tau error with regards to the instructor rankings. We also compute a *weighted* version of the Kendall-Tau error, where misordering items with

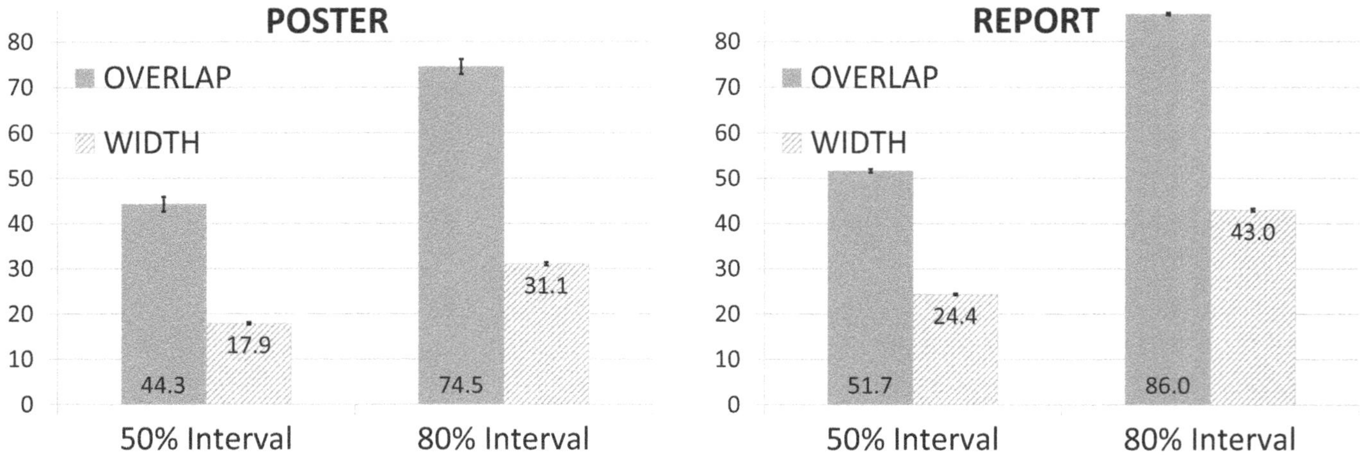

Figure 3. Average Overlap (solid green bars) of the 50% and 80% Bayesian credible intervals with the instructor rank distribution, for the intervals produced by the Bayesian Mallows MCMC method for the POSTER (*Left*) and REPORT (*Right*) datasets. Along with the overlap is the average size (width) of the interval (as a percentage) of the overall ranking length (the red striped bars).

a larger (instructor) score difference leads to a worse performance measure. Note that both of these measures are normalized to lie between 0 (indicating perfect agreement with instructors) and 100 (indicating a complete reversal of the instructor ranking). On both datasets, the performance of the proposed Bayesian methods are not substantially different from that of the MLE. There appears to be no clear trend that one method is superior to the others, and the differences are probably due to fact that the instructor grades used as a gold standard are themselves subject to uncertainty. One issue to note is that the "Mode" techniques tend to have larger variance, as performance can vary with the mode that was selected (as the distribution tends to be multi-modal).

Lastly, we also note that the performance does not vary much with adding grader reliability estimation. This observation agrees with a similar finding made in [23] (for both ordinal and cardinal grading techniques). The most likely reason for observing this behavior is the explicit incentive in terms of grade credit that the students were given for doing a thorough job with the peer reviews, such that the number of truly substandard reviews in the data may be low.

How good are the estimated confidence intervals?

While the previous experiment indicated that the overall quality of the orderings tends to be quite good (with regards to instructor grades), it does not tell us how accurately the Bayesian approach models the uncertainty of the predicted ranks. To address this question, we now evaluate how good the Bayesian confidence intervals (*i.e.,* credible intervals) of the inferred posterior marginal distributions (over position in the overall ranking) for individual assignments are. To evaluate these uncertainty estimates, we again utilize the instructor grades [2]. In particular we evaluate the quality of the 50% and 80% credible intervals.

[2] Since these also have ties, we treat ties as indifference and hence have a uniform probability distribution over all possible *valid* rank positions.

For each assignment, we first compute the (posterior) marginal distribution over the ranking positions as shown in Figure 1 from the introduction. We then compute the overlap of the credible intervals of these marginals with the instructor ranking distribution *i.e.,* an assignment whose credible interval contains (all) the instructor-provided ranks has a 100% overlap, whereas an interval with no overlap scores a 0%. We report this overlap averaged over all assignments. In addition to this, we also report the size of these intervals (as a percentage of the overall ranking length).

The results are shown in Figure 3. We find that the intervals produced by the Bayesian MCMC based Mallows technique have are well calibrated. In particular, for both the posters and the reports, the 50% and 80% interval cover roughly that percentage of the instructor grades as desired (as indicated by the overlap values). The observed overlap is far greater than the size of the interval, which indicates predictive performance that is far better than random. These results show that the estimated intervals are meaningful and convey accurate uncertainty information. The results when incorporating grader reliability information are similar and hence left out to avoid redundancy.

How peaked are the posterior distributions?

The results in Figure 3 show that the confidence interval for the reports have larger width than those for the posters *i.e.,* there is more uncertainty in the marginals of the reports than the posters. This suggests that the posterior distributions are more peaked around the mode for the posters as compared to the reports. To verify this, we computed the *expected* values of the Kendall-Tau error (and the *weighted* Kendall-Tau error) under the posterior distribution:

$$\sum_{\sigma} \delta_K(\sigma^*, \sigma) P(\sigma|D)$$

Note that σ^* refers to the instructor ranking and $P(\sigma|D)$ is the learned posterior. We refer to these values as *EXP-MAL*

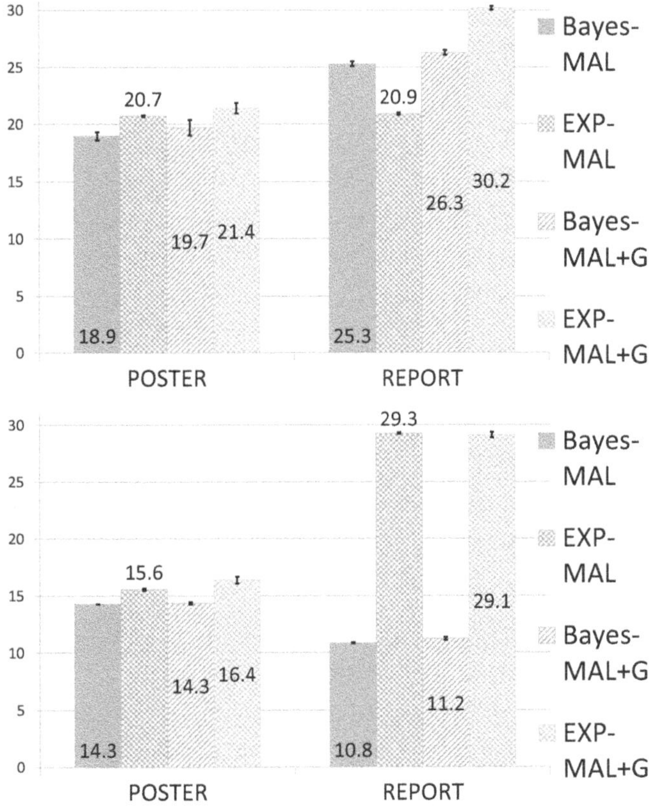

Figure 4. Kendall-Tau (*Top*) and Weighted Kendall-Tau (*Bottom*) performance of the Bayesian point estimate rankings versus the expected performance of the posterior ranking distribution. For both figures, the lower value is better.

(without grader reliabilities) and *EXP-MAL+G* (with grader reliability estimation). The results are shown in Figure 4.

We find that the difference in performance between the Bayes estimate (Bayes) and the expected value (EXP) of the full posterior is typically larger for the reports than for the posters. For the posters, it appears that the posterior is so narrow that almost any sample from the posterior is close to the Bayes estimate. For the reports, the posterior is less peaked. One explanation is the larger number of reviews available for the posters.

Finally, we would like to investigate which assignments the Bayesian peer grading method is most uncertain about, and how this uncertainty relates to the scores given by the instructors. To provide some insight, we compute the posterior marginal entropies of all assignments, and then average the entropies for all assignments with the same cardinal instructor grade. The result is visualized in Fig. 5. The assignments that receive the highest and the lowest instructor scores tend to be the assignments with the lowest posterior marginal entropy. The assignment in the middle tend to have higher entropies, indicating that the method is less certain about their position in the ranking. Based on these findings, our conjecture is that it is "easy" to for both students and instructors to identify very good and very bad assignments. The assignments in the middle are more difficult to grade, since they require careful

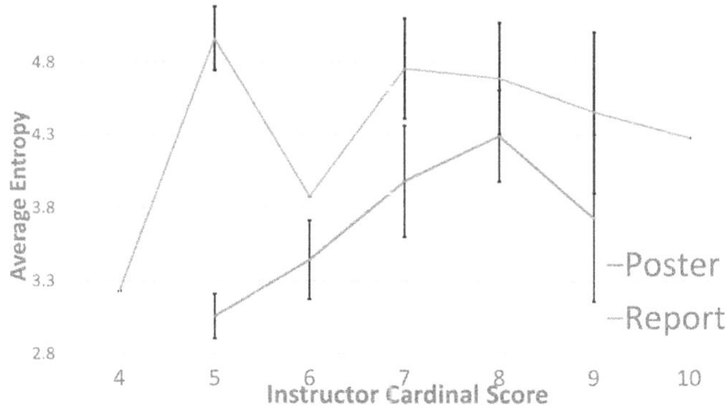

Figure 5. Distribution of the *average entropies* of the marginals when aggregated by the cardinal instructor grades. Points with no error bars indicate just a single assignment with that score.

tradeoff between different types of errors. It may also be the case that some of the assignments in the middle are difficult to compare, since they are so different in topic that a meaningful comparison is difficult.

CONCLUSIONS AND FUTURE WORK

In this work we proposed the use of Bayesian techniques for the problem of ordinal peer grading so as to provide instructors richer information that communicates uncertainty in addition to the predicted ordinal grades. Our proposed method utilizes a Metropolis-Hastings based MCMC sampler for the peer grading Mallows model. We empirically validated the proposed techniques and show the inferred posteriors to agree with instructor grades and to convey an accurate amount of uncertainty.

In addition to further empirical studies into the quality of the learned posteriors, we are exploring how to develop Bayesian inference methods also for other ordinal peer grading models. An open question regards the quality of the credible intervals of the estimated grader reliabilities. Furthermore, there are many interesting questions regarding how to elicit the feedback from the students. For example, it may be cognitively less demanding on the students to break their ordinal assessment task into pairwise comparisons [15], especially if the number of items to assess is large.

ACKNOWLEDGMENTS

This research was funded in part by NSF Awards IIS-1217686 and IIS-1247637, the JTCII Cornell-Technion Research Fund and a Google PhD Fellowship.

REFERENCES

1. Arrow, K. J. *Social Choice and Individual Values*, 2nd ed. Yale University Press, Sept. 1970.
2. Aslam, J. A., and Montague M. Models for metasearch. In *SIGIR* (2001), 276–284.
3. Barnett, W. The modern theory of consumer behavior: Ordinal or cardinal? *The Quarterly Journal of Austrian Economics 6*, 1 (2003), 41–65.
4. Birenbaum, M., and Tatsuoka, K. K. Open-ended versus multiple-choice response formatsit does make a

difference for diagnostic purposes. *Applied Psychological Measurement 11*, 4 (1987), 385–395.

5. Bradley, R. A., and Terry, M. E. Rank analysis of incomplete block designs: I. the method of paired comparisons. *Biometrika 39*, 3/4 (1952), pp. 324–345.
6. Carterette, B., Bennett, P. N., Chickering, D. M., and Dumais, S. T. Here or there: Preference judgments for relevance. In *ECIR* (2008), 16–27.
7. Chen, X., Bennett, P. N., Collins-Thompson, K., and Horvitz, E. Pairwise ranking aggregation in a crowdsourced setting. In *WSDM* (2013), 193–202.
8. Chib, S., and Greenberg, E. Understanding the Metropolis-Hastings Algorithm. *The American Statistician 49*, 4 (1995), 327–335.
9. Coppersmith, D., Fleischer, L. K., and Rurda, A. Ordering by weighted number of wins gives a good ranking for weighted tournaments. *ACM Trans. Algorithms 6*, 3 (July 2010), 55:1–55:13.
10. Dwork, C., Kumar, R., Naor, M., and Sivakumar, D. Rank aggregation methods for the web. In *WWW* (2001), 613–622.
11. Freeman, S., and Parks, J. W. How accurate is peer grading? *CBE-Life Sciences Education 9*, 4 (2010), 482–488.
12. Haber, J. `http://degreeoffreedom.org/between-two-worlds-moocs-and-assessment`.
13. Haber, J. `http://degreeoffreedom.org/mooc-assignments-screwing/`, Oct. 2013.
14. Kendall, M. *Rank correlation methods*. Griffin, London, 1948.
15. Krosnick, J. A. Survey research. *Annual Review of Psychology 50*, 1 (1999), 537–567. PMID: 15012463.
16. Kulkarni, C., Wei, K., Le, H., Chia, D., Papadopoulos, K., Cheng, J., Koller, D., and Klemmer, S. Peer and self assessment in massive online classes. *ACM Trans. CHI 20*, 6 (Dec. 2013), 33:1–33:31.
17. Liu, T.-Y. Learning to rank for information retrieval. *Found. Trends Inf. Retr. 3*, 3 (Mar. 2009), 225–331.
18. Lu, T., and Boutilier, C. Learning mallows models with pairwise preferences. In *ICML* (June 2011), 145–152.
19. Lu, T., and Boutilier, C. E. The unavailable candidate model: A decision-theoretic view of social choice. In *EC* (2010), 263–274.
20. Mallows, C. L. Non-null ranking models. *Biometrika 44*, 1/2 (1957), pp. 114–130.
21. Niu, S., Lan, Y., Guo, J., and Cheng, X. Stochastic rank aggregation. *CoRR abs/1309.6852* (2013).
22. Qin, T., Geng, X., and Liu, T.-Y. A new probabilistic model for rank aggregation. In *NIPS* (2010), 1948–1956.
23. Raman, K., and Joachims, T. Methods for ordinal peer grading. In *KDD*, KDD '14, ACM (New York, NY, USA, 2014), 1037–1046.
24. Stewart, N., Brown, G. D. A., and Chater, N. Absolute identification by relative judgment. *Psychological Review 112* (2005), 881–911.
25. Veloski, J. J., Rabinowitz, H. K., Robeson, M. R., and Young, P. R. Patients don't present with five choices: an alternative to multiple-choice tests in assessing physicians' competence. *ACADEMIC MEDICINE-PHILADELPHIA- 74*, 5 (1999), 539–546.
26. Volkovs, M. N., and Zemel, R. S. A flexible generative model for preference aggregation. In *WWW* (2012), 479–488.

An Automated Grading/Feedback System for 3-View Engineering Drawings using RANSAC

Youngwook Paul Kwon
UC Berkeley
Berkeley, CA 94720
young@berkeley.edu

Sara McMains
UC Berkeley
Berkeley, CA 94720
mcmains@berkeley.edu

ABSTRACT
We propose a novel automated grading system that can compare two multiview engineering drawings consisting of three views that may have allowable translations, scales, and offsets, and can recognize frequent error types as well as individual drawing errors. We show that translation, scale, and offset-invariant comparison can be conducted by estimating the affine transformation for each individual view within drawings. Our system directly aims to evaluate students' skills creating multiview engineering drawings. Since it is important for our students to be familiar with widely used software such as AutoCAD, our system does not require a separate interface or environment, but directly grades the saved DWG/DXF files from AutoCAD. We show the efficacy of the proposed algorithm by comparing its results with human grading. Beyond the advantages of convenience and accuracy, based on our data set of students' answers, we can analyze the common errors of the class as a whole using our system.

Author Keywords
Autograder, multiview engineering drawing, affine transformation estimation, RANSAC.

ACM Classification Keywords
I.4 Computing Methodologies: IMAGE PROCESSING AND COMPUTER VISION

INTRODUCTION
Multiview drawing is an international standard "graphical language" to represent 3D objects with 2D drawings. By following the rules of the graphical language, people can communicate the shape of three-dimensional objects without ambiguity. A multiview drawing consists of orthogonal projections to mutually perpendicular planes, typically the *front*, *top*, and *right* views. In the U.S., these are arranged on the page using so-called third angle projection, as if orthogonal projections onto the sides of a transparent glass box containing the object had been unfolded onto the page [1]. The three typical projections of a simple 3D object under third angle projection are shown in Figure 2. Sometimes additional projections are drawn for interpretation convenience. At the University of California at Berkeley, multiview drawing is taught in the lower division course "Basic Engineering Design Graphics," Engineering 28 (E28).

L@S 2015, March 14–18, 2015, Vancouver, BC, Canada.

ACM 978-1-4503-3411-2/15/03...$15.00.
http://dx.doi.org/10.1145/2724660.2724682

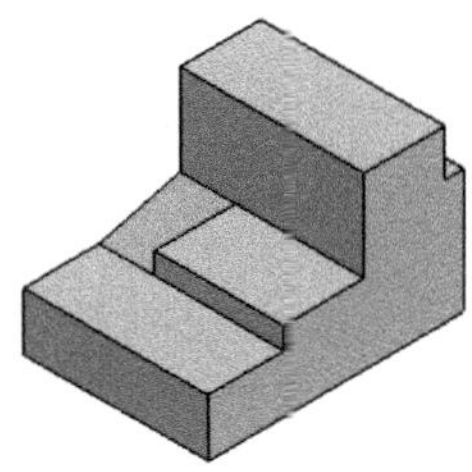

Figure 1. 3D geometry represented in multiview drawings in Figure 2-4.

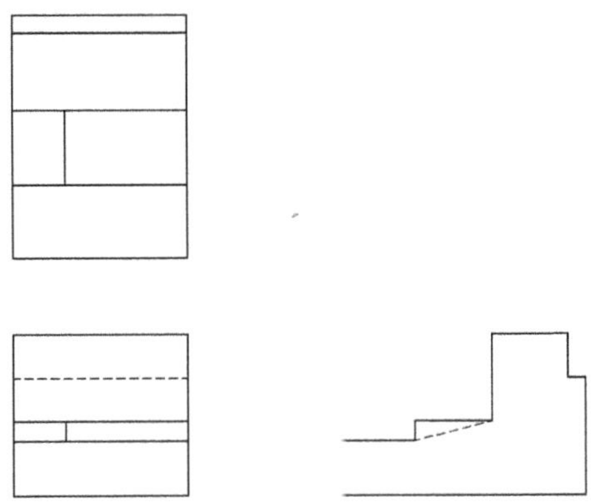

Figure 2. An example of a formal multiview drawing. Note that in multiview engineering drawings the views are not labeled; the placement and alignment communicates the relative viewpoints.

Due to the fundamental importance of engineering drawing for design and communication, E28 is a large class serving students majoring in fields including mechanical engineering, electrical engineering, computer science, industrial engineering, civil engineering, nuclear engineering, and architecture. Manually grading students' multiview drawing submissions and manually giving feedback to them is very time consuming, and the feedback is not always precise or timely. In the era of Massive Open Online Courses (MOOCs), we ex-

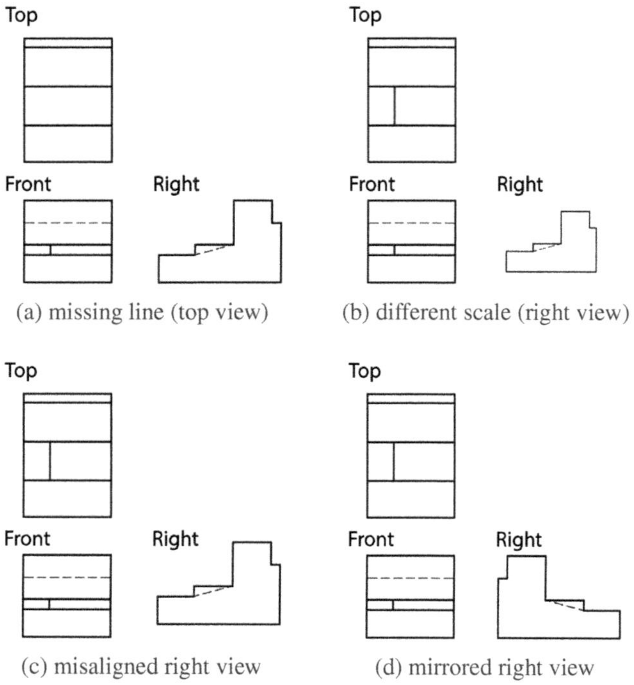

(a) missing line (top view)
(b) different scale (right view)
(c) misaligned right view
(d) mirrored right view

Figure 3. Four typical cases of mistakes. Note that the labels on the views are not present in the actual multiview drawing.

pect high future demands for this type of engineering drawing course on an even larger scale, for which an automated grading/feedback tool would be critical. Particularly in a MOOC, but also with the large variety of backgrounds of students taking our on-campus course, different levels of students are engaged in the same curriculum. For effective education, we envision a system that should be able to distinguish them and provide specialized additional focused instruction and practice problems for different groups of students. To understand where students make mistakes frequently, an automated grading tool is essential not only for grading but also for analyzing big data.

Our autograder addresses several frequent error types that inexperienced engineers and designers make [11], summarized below.

Missing and Incorrect Lines
A common problem with hand-created or 2D Computer-Aided Design (CAD) software-created drawing is that one or more lines may be missing. Figure 3a shows this error type. This error is especially difficult to recognize when someone else made the drawing [1]; even when a grader has a solution to compare with, the grader may miss such a subtle mistake.

Mismatched View Scales
Each view of a drawing must have the same scale. Figure 3b shows an example when the scale of the right view is different, which makes for misaligned features between views. This is not permitted in multiview drawings. Note that as long as a drawing has the same scale throughout the views, the scale itself can be arbitrary for undimensioned drawings. So an automated grading tool should be *scale-invariant*, yet recognize mismatched scales between views in the same drawing.

Misaligned Views
Misaligned views, as shown in Figure 3c, also make it difficult for a human to match up features between adjacent views; they are not permitted in multiview drawings. The orthogonal views must be aligned both horizontally and vertically. Note that once the views are aligned appropriately, the offset distances between pairs of adjacent views do not need to match. So an automated grading tool should be *offset-invariant*. Moreover, because the entire drawing can be translated anywhere relative to the origin, the grading tool should be *translation-invariant*, up to alignment and relative location of views.

Views in Incorrect Relative Locations
Each view in a drawing must be located appropriately with respect to each other view. One possible mistake is caused by confusion of views (e.g., mistakenly placing a left view in the right view location). Sometimes students mistakenly rotate an entire view, typically by 90°. Another mistake is mirroring a view, as shown in Figure 3d.

These subtle mistakes are very easy for students to make, and are also easy for graders to miss. Especially with the traditional grading method where each student's printed drawing is graded by comparing it with a printed solution, a human grader can not guarantee a perfect comparison.

We show an example of a solution drawing and a student's drawing in Figure 4. Since they have different scale, translation, and offsets, the naïve comparison shown in Figure 4(c) does not work. Therefore we propose that an automated grading tool should be translation, scale, and offset-invariant when grading individual views, yet take these factors into account between views.

In this paper, we propose a simple and flexible automated grading/feedback system, which is translation, scale, and offset-invariant in the sense described above. The proposed algorithm determines the transformation information for each view (top, front, and right) in a drawing (Section "Algorithm"). We implement the automated grading/feedback system using MATLAB and address how the student errors detailed above can be graded using the transformation information (Section "Grading Checks").

RELATED WORK
To our knowledge, no existing work addresses machine grading of multiview engineering drawings. AutoCAD provides a plug-in called Drawing Compare [20], but it just visualizes the temporal changes of edits to a single drawing, and therefore it is not suitable to compare two drawings that include scale, translation, and offset differences.

There has been research on multiview engineering drawing interpretation in the context of using the drawings as input to reconstruct 3D models [15, 18, 18, 6, 19, 10]. However, none

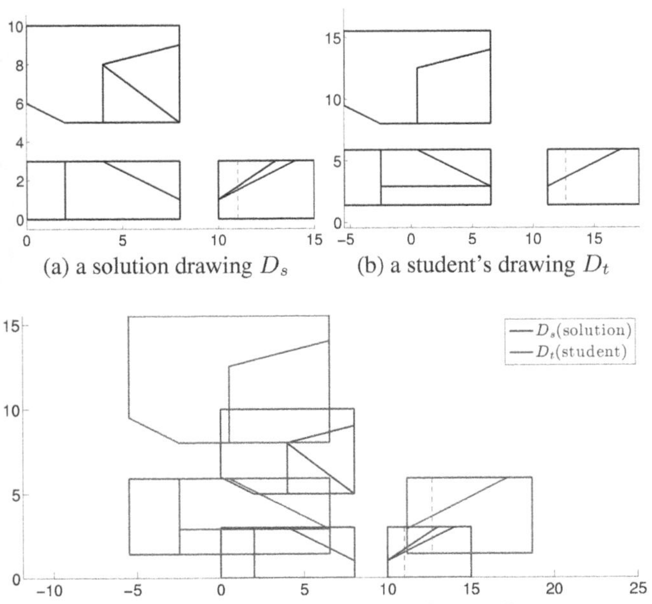

(a) a solution drawing D_s (b) a student's drawing D_t

(c) naïve comparison between D_s and D_t

Figure 4. An example of (a) a solution drawing and (b) a student's drawings and (c) their naïve comparison. Because they have different scales, translations, and offsets, a naïve comparison does not work.

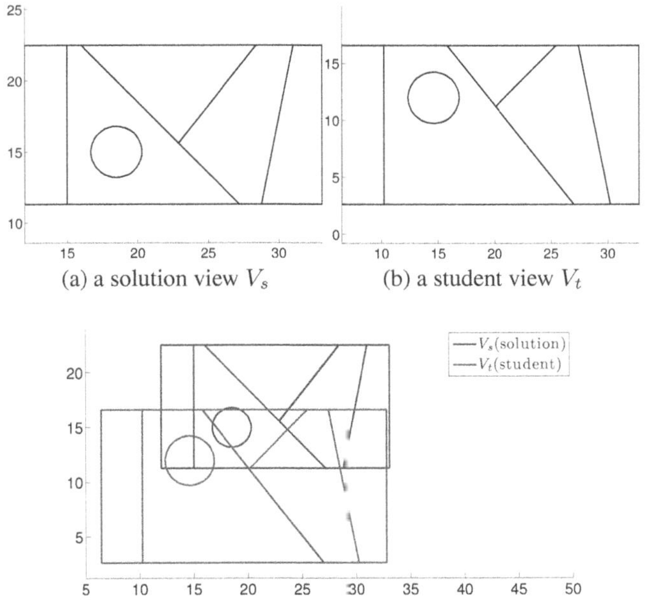

(a) a solution view V_s (b) a student view V_t

(c) naïve comparison

Figure 5. An example pair of views for transformation estimation.

of these techniques are useful to compare and grade multiview drawings given that the reconstruction algorithms may fail when they face the incompleteness of students' drawings. Moreover the computation would be very intensive (both reconstruction and 3D object comparison).

On the educational side, Suh and McCasland developed education software to help train students in the interpretation of multiview drawings [16]. In their software, complete multiview drawings are given as input, and students are asked to draw the corresponding 3D models. This is very useful to enhance and evaluate students' multiview-drawings interpretation skills, the inverse of our purpose of evaluating students' multiview creation skills when 3D models are given as input. Since it is important for students to be familiar with popular CAD software such as AutoCAD, we chose to compare and grade native format AutoCAD files, which is easily extended to batch processing.

We use the random sample consensus (RANSAC) method [5] to estimate an affine transformation between the individual views of the two given drawings. RANSAC is an iterative method used to estimate parameters of a mathematical model from a set of data. RANSAC is very popular due to its effectiveness when the data has a high percentage of noise. The fact that much research in the computer vision field relies on RANSAC, for example, estimating the fundamental matrix [2], recognizing primitive shapes from point-clouds [14], or estimating an affine transformation between two line sets [4, 9], shows RANSAC's efficacy in multiple contexts. There have also been many variations introduced such as MLESACK [17] and Preemptive RANSAC [12], as well as research comparing the performance of the variations [3, 13].

In our current application, we have found that the original RANSAC concept is efficacious enough. We next discuss the basic RANSAC algorithm and how we apply it to estimate parameters of the transformation between single view drawings.

ALGORITHM

Single View Transformation Estimation

Initially we ignore the offset-invariant problem by assuming a drawing consists of only one view (e.g., front, top, or right). Let V_s be a single view from the source drawing (solution), and V_t be a single view from the target drawing (student's). Then the task here is to estimate the optimal transformation T^* between V_s and V_t in order to address the translation and scale-invariant problems. Once we know this transformation, we can transform V_s into the coordinate system of V_t. Let V_s' be the transformed version of V_s. We denote this as

$$T^* : V_s \rightarrow V_s'$$

or equivalently,

$$V_s' = T^*(V_s).$$

We can then compare V_s' and V_t fairly. (In the next section, we will discuss how to apply this single view transformation in the context of full multiview drawings to address the flexible offsets permitted between views.)

As a transformation model between the two views, we assume an affine transformation. Its parameters are translation in x and y (t_x, t_y), scale in x and y (s_x, s_y), rotation θ, and skew k.

We take the pair of drawings in Figure 5 as an illustrative example for this section. V_t (Figure 5(b)) was obtained from V_s (Figure 5(a)) by applying a uniform scale, mirroring, and

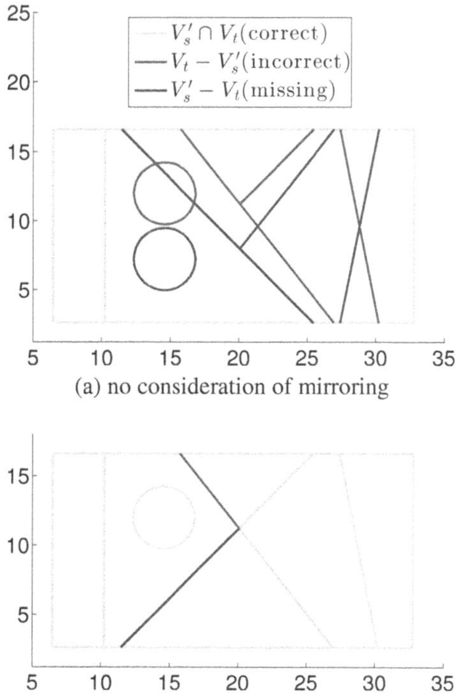

(a) no consideration of mirroring

(b) appropriate consideration of mirroring

Figure 6. (a) Even if we align the two views in terms of scale and translation, it is not easy to compare them at a glance; here half the elements still appear to be slightly off. (b) In fact, most elements match perfectly if the correct affine transformation is applied. The real problem is mirroring and two lines that only partially differ.

translation to V_s, and then editing two lines. It is not easy for a human to recognize what changes are there. The naïve comparison (Figure 5(c)) does not work at all. Even if scale and translation is properly considered, a grader may simply think most lines are slightly wrong as shown in Figure 6(a). However, better feedback can be provided by recognizing that the overall representation is in fact correct, except for mirroring and partially differing lines, as shown in Figure 6(b). Therefore, for a fair comparison that correctly identifies what conceptual errors led to the student's mistake, we need to estimate the affine transformation and use it to align the two drawings first, before comparing individual line elements.

The affine transformation estimation procedure is based on RANSAC, which consists of the following generically described four steps:

1. At each iteration, randomly select a subset $\mathcal{S}$ of the data set $\mathcal{D}$. Hypothesize that this subset (called *hypothetical inliers*) satisfies the ground truth model we seek.
2. Solve (or fit) the hypothetical model parameters Θ based on the hypothetical inliers $\mathcal{S}$. Note that $\mathcal{S}$ is the only input for choosing Θ, so if $\mathcal{S}$ includes incorrect of "noisy" elements, naturally the estimated model parameters Θ will not be high quality.
3. Evaluate the estimated model parameters Θ using all data $\mathcal{D}$. The subset $\mathcal{C} \subseteq \mathcal{D}$ whose members are consistent with the estimated model parameters Θ is called a *consensus set.*
4. Iterate steps 1-3. The optimal choice of model parameters Θ^* is that with the largest consensus set. Terminate when the probability of finding a better consensus set is lower than a certain threshold.

Our data set $\mathcal{D}$ is obtained by extracting certain points related to the elements in the drawings. The element types that we currently consider are *line*, *circle*, and *arc*. The point set consists of the two endpoints of line elements and the center points of circle and arc elements. Let P_s and P_t be the point sets extracted from all elements (lines, circles and arcs) from V_s and V_t, respectively. P_s and P_t together comprise the data set $\mathcal{D}$.

2D Affine transformations have six degrees of freedom (DOFs): two each for translation and scale, and one each for rotation and skew: therefore three noncolinear point pairs (correspondences between the two views) will give a unique solution. We randomly pick three ordered points from both P_s and P_t, and pair them in order. The three randomly selected point pairs are the hypothetical inliers $\mathcal{S}$, and we solve for the (hypothetical) affine transformation matrix T based on the three pairs of points. The full 3×3 affine transformation matrix can be solved for by using the homogeneous coordinate representation of the three pairs of points. (See for example [8] for more details.)

To evaluate T, we now transform the entire point set P_s by T. Let P_s' be the transformed version of P_s. If T is the optimal transformation, then most or even all points of P_s will be coincident with those of P_t. We define the consensus set $\mathcal{C}$ as $\mathcal{C} = P_s' \cap P_t$. Our evaluation metric is the cardinality of the consensus set (that is, the number of coincident points). We iterate this process; the optimal affine transformation T^* is the T with the largest $|\mathcal{C}|$. We can denote this as

$$\begin{aligned} P_s' &= T(P_s) \\ T^* &= \arg\max_T |\mathcal{C}| \\ &= \arg\max_T |P_s' \cap P_t)| \\ &= \arg\max_T |T(P_s) \cap P_t)| \end{aligned}$$

where arg max stands for the argument of the maximum, the argument element(s) of the given argument space for which the given function attains its maximum value.

We terminate the iteration when $|C| > R * \min(|P_s|, |P_t|)$, where R is the minimum match rate, or all the cases are checked. We have found $R = 80\%$ to work well in practice. Once we have found a transformation that matches more than 80% of the points in the solution subview with points in the target drawing, we have found the region of interest that we are searching for, and there is no need to search further.

Consider the example of Figure 5; the optimal affine transformation is

$$T^* = \begin{bmatrix} 1.2494 & 0 & -8.5118 \\ 0 & -1.2494 & 30.7256 \\ 0 & 0 & 1 \end{bmatrix},$$

or equivalently, $t_x = -8.5118, t_y = 30.7256, s_x = 1.2494, s_y = -1.2494, \theta = 0$, and $k = 0$. Figure 6(b) shows the comparison between the transformed version of V_s, $V_s' = T^*(V_s)$, and V_t. In other words, we know that V_s should be scaled by 1.2494 and -1.2494 along the x and y axes respectively, and translated by (-8.5118, +30.7256) in order to compare it to V_t. The opposite signs for the x and y scales indicates mirroring. There is no skew or rotation.

Application to Multiview Drawings

In this section, we discuss how to apply the transformation estimation process to multiview drawing grading. Again, let the source drawing D_s be the solution drawing and the target drawing D_t be a student's drawing.

First a grader must manually subdivide the solution drawing (but not the student's drawing) into the front, right, and top views. Call them V_{front}, V_{right}, and V_{top}, respectively:

$$D_s = V_{front} \cup V_{right} \cup V_{top}.$$

In the general case, a view can be any subset of the solution drawing. One can specify arbitrary views V_i depending on the complexity of the solution drawing:

$$D_s \supseteq \bigcup_i V_i.$$

We individually estimate optimal transformations $T^*_{V_i}$ between each view V_i ($\subseteq D_s$) and the entire student drawing D_t. By calculating separate transformations for each view, we can address offset flexibility.

Consider the example input shown in Figure 4. For the front view, we have $t_x = -5.4785, t_y = 1.4114, s_x = 1.5, s_y = 1.5, \theta = 0$, and $k = 0$. For the top view, we have $t_x = -5.4785, t_y = 8.0145, s_x = 1.5, s_y = 1.5, \theta = 0$, and $k = 0$. For the right view, we have $t_x = 11.1657, t_y = 1.4114, s_x = 1.5, s_y = 1.5, \theta = 0$, and $k = 0$.

We next discuss how these components, and their relationships, can be used to grade the student drawing.

GRADING CHECKS

Once the optimal transformations $T^*_{V_i}$ (and their components) are calculated, one can set up a flexible set of rubrics. The checks described here correspond to the common student errors presented in the introduction.

Element Comparison

By applying each transformation $T^*_{V_i}$ to the corresponding view V_i from the solution D_s, we can compare individual elements of the two full multiview drawings. Suppose we have $T^*_{V_{front}}$, $T^*_{V_{top}}$ and $T^*_{V_{right}}$ from D_s. The transformed version D_s' is:

$$D_s' = \bigcup_{V_i} T^*_{V_i}(V_i)$$
$$= T^*_{V_{front}}(V_{front}) \cup T^*_{V_{top}}(V_{top}) \cup T^*_{V_{right}}(V_{right}).$$

Figure 7 shows the transformed version of the solution, D_s', super imposed on the student's drawing D_t. The transformed version has the same location, offset and scales as the student's. In Figure 7(c), red highlights the missed elements (elements that exist in the solution, but not in the student's drawing: $D_s' - D_t$), and blue highlights the incorrect elements (elements that exist in the student's drawing, but not in the solution, $D_t - D_s'$). If both set differences are the empty sets, the two drawings are the same up to scale, translation, rotation, and skew.

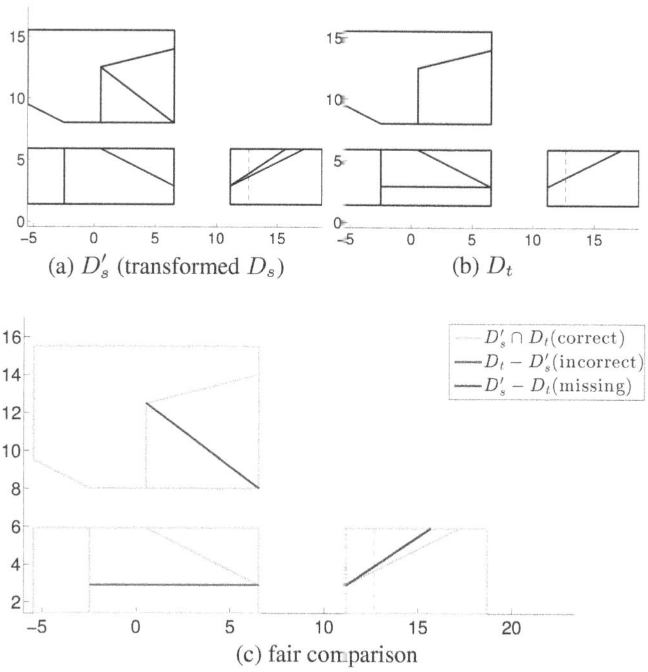

Figure 7. We estimate the transformation for each view individually using RANSAC. By applying the transformations to the views in D_s, we get the transformed version D_s'. Then the elements of D_s' and D_t can be compared one by one.

Front-Right View Alignment

The front view and right view should be aligned horizontally. This can be checked by confirming that the t_y components of $T^*_{V_{front}}$ and $T^*_{V_{right}}$ are the same. We also need to check if the right view is in fact to the right side of the front view in the student's drawing (in other words, t_x of $T^*_{V_{right}}$ should be greater than t_x of $T^*_{V_{front}}$.)

Front-Top View Alignment

The front view and top view should be aligned vertically. This can be checked by confirming that the t_x components of $T^*_{V_{front}}$ and $T^*_{V_{top}}$ are the same. We also need to check if the top view is on the upper side of the front view in the student's drawing (in other words, t_y of $T^*_{V_{top}}$ should be greater than t_y of $T^*_{V_{front}}$.)

Uniform Scale

In multiview drawings, the aspect ratio must be preserved, and all views must have the same scale, even though the scale factor itself can be arbitrarily. This can be checked by confirming that all six scale components (s_x and s_y of $T^*_{V_{front}}$, $T^*_{V_{top}}$, and $T^*_{V_{right}}$) are the same.

Mirroring
By confirming that the signs of all six scale components are positive, we can recognize mirroring, which should not be present.

Rotation / Skew
The rotation and skew components of the transformations of all views should be zero, as long as the homework assignment is to reproduce the typical front, top, and right views.

COMPUTATION FILTERING
Suppose we estimate a transformation between point sets P_s and P_t. Let n_s and n_t be the cardinality of P_s and P_t, respectively. In the hypothesis generation step in RANSAC, there are $6\binom{n_s}{3}\binom{n_t}{3}$ possible cases, and for each case we need $n_s n_t$ comparisons to calculate the consensus set. This requires a huge number of iterations in the worst case. But we can filter out some hypotheses to reduce computation, as follows.

Choice Filtering
We store two simple attributes with each point: the element type ($\in \{line, circle, arc\}$) that gave rise to the point, and the number of intersecting elements at the point (in the case of the center points of circle and arcs, the number is zero). In the hypothesis generation step, we skip a hypothesis if these attributes of any of the pairs are inconsistent.

Transformation Filtering
Because the hypothesis transformations are acquired from the randomly chosen set of three pairs of points, most of them imply severe distortions, which are not typical of student errors. We can skip the evaluation step for this kind of unrealistic transformation. To filter out these cases, when we solve for T, we decompose T into its six components (DOFs). The unrealistic cases include when the absolute value of translations are too big, scales are too big, too small, or too imbalanced, etc. We skip those where:

- translation: $|t_x|, |t_y| > 300$;
- scale: $|s_x|, |s_y| < 1/3$ or $|s_x|, |s_y| > 3$;
- skew: $|k| > 0.1$; and
- rotation: no constraint.

Here the thresholds for t_x, t_y, s_x and s_y are practically determined based on the default visible canvas size when AutoCAD is opened. Students do not make mistakes such that the skew is nonzero, so theoretically k should be always zero, but due to numerical errors, the k value may be a very small number, e.g. 10^{-8}. Note that this is solely to reduce the search space, and one can shrink/expand the permissible ranges if analysis of a larger dataset indicates smaller/larger valid variations in students' drawings.

IMPLEMENTATION ISSUES
In practice, there are additional steps that needed to be implemented to fully automate the grading/feedback system. We briefly mention some of them below.

Converting DWG → DXF
Students draw using AutoCAD, which by default saves files in DWG format. Because AutoCAD is commercial software and DWG is its binary file format, to our knowledge, there is no open source code for accessing DWG files directly. So we need to convert DWG files to DXF file format, which is a file format developed by AutoDesk for enabling data interoperability between AutoCAD and other programs. For an automated batch process of this conversion on all students' submissions, we also implemented an AUTOLISP script, which runs in AutoCAD.

Loading DXF in MATLAB
We extract drawing elements from each DXF file using MATLAB. Currently the loading operation is based on the open source code in the MATLAB CENTRAL File Exchange website [22, 21].

Merging Elements
Some elements may be drawn (partially) duplicated, overlapping, or decomposed into sub-segments. Especially in the case of lines/arcs, one may have several connected or overlapping partial lines/arcs instead of one long line/arc. For this reason, we merge objects into one if they can be represented as a simpler one. This also makes the point set smaller, which reduces computation time.

Pre-defining Layer Names
Currently we do not autograde dimensioning and header parts of multiview drawings, only visible and hidden lines. Since visible and hidden lines should be drawn with different line styles and thickness, we teach students to put them in separate layers and define these properties to apply to the entire layer. For autograding, we provide a template with the layer names, and only load elements drawn on the visible and hidden layers. Even though giving predetermined layer names is a constraint for the autograding system, declaring layers and grouping objects of the same type into a single layer is an important skill for student to learn regardless.

RESULTS
We show another grading example in Figure 8. The solution drawing D_s (Figure 8a) and the student drawing D_t (Figure 8b) can not be compared using a naïve algorithm due to translation, scale, and offsets (Figure 8c). Using the estimated transformation for each view, we take our transformed version of the solution, D'_s, and compare D_s and D_t (Figure 8d).

Grading result visualization
Beyond the advantages of more accurate, timely feedback to students, another advantage of an autograding tool will be its ability to analyze and summarize the grading results. As an example, we can visualize which elements of a drawing were most frequently drawn incorrectly by students, which can be useful information for instructors. We ran our algorithm in batch mode on the submissions in Fall 2013 for two problems assigned in homeworks #2 and #3 in E28. These assignment batches consisted of 115 and 113 students' submissions

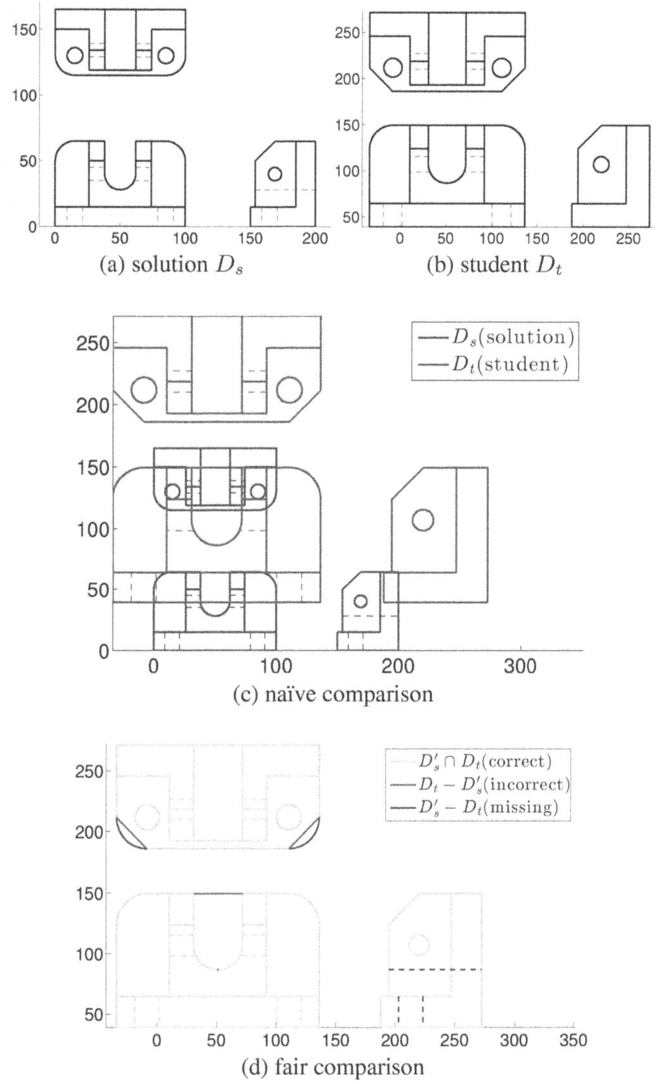

Figure 8. Comparing the solution to a student's drawing. To be compared to D_t, all views in D_s are scaled 1.7 times larger. The top, front, and right views are translated (-33.8, +186.2), (-33.8, +39), and (+187.7, +39), respectively. All views have zero rotation and skew. By aligning them, the algorithm finds incorrect and missing lines, which are represented in blue and dark red.

respectively. For each element in the solution drawing, we count in how many student submissions it is "missing." Similarly, for each "incorrect" element in the student drawing, we count how many student submissions have it. Figure 9 shows the solution with the elements color coded: the most difficult elements — that are most frequently missing/incorrect — are represented in dark red/blue, and those less frequently missing/incorrect are represented in light red/blue. In the problem from assignment #2 we can see that the top view causes more mistakes than the other views, and that students miss the diagonal and hidden lines in the front and right view most frequently (Figure 9a). Figure 9b shows that the diagonal features are frequently misdrawn. In the problem from assignment #3, many times students get confused in the upper part of the front view, and hidden lines are frequently missed.

Comparison with human grading

To verify the efficacy of the proposed algorithm, we compare the autograding results with human grading. A human grader with a full semester of experience grading for the course graded the 115 submissions of the homework #2 problem introduced above, using gradescope [7] with pdf files of the submission.

Manual vs. autograding

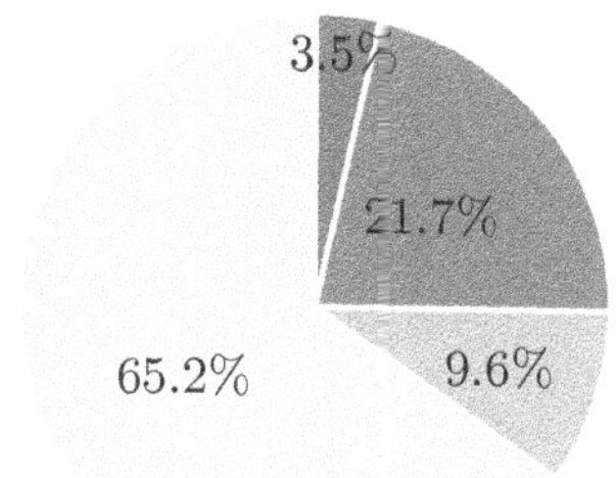

- Category A: Same feedback
  Both give the same feedback.
- Category B: Similar feedback.
  The same errors are identified, but described differently.
- Category C: Better autograding feedback.
  Manual grading fails to catch some mistakes.
- Category D: Incorrect autograding feedback.
  Autograding fails to estimate proper transformation.

We divide the comparison results into four categories. In the case of category A and B, autograding and human grading find the same errors, which account for 74.8% of the total 115 submissions. In the case of category B, although the same drawing elements are identified as errors, the human grader described them differently in her grading feedback to the student. Figure 10 shows two examples of category B. While the human grader interprets the mistake as "lines not aligned," the autograder reports it as the number of missing lines and incorrect lines. The human's interpretation can be more flexible,

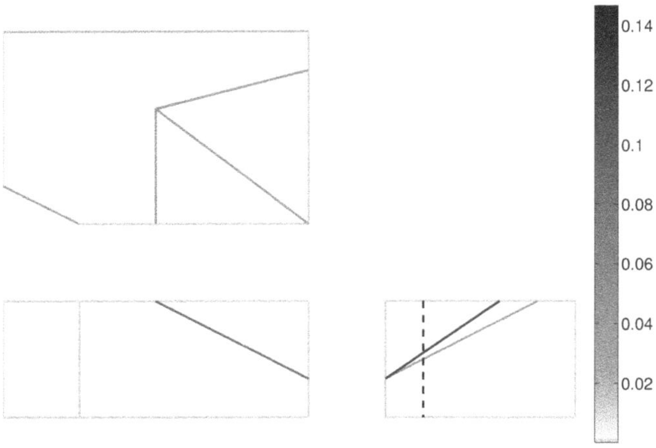

(a) visualization of missing errors on a problem from assignment #2

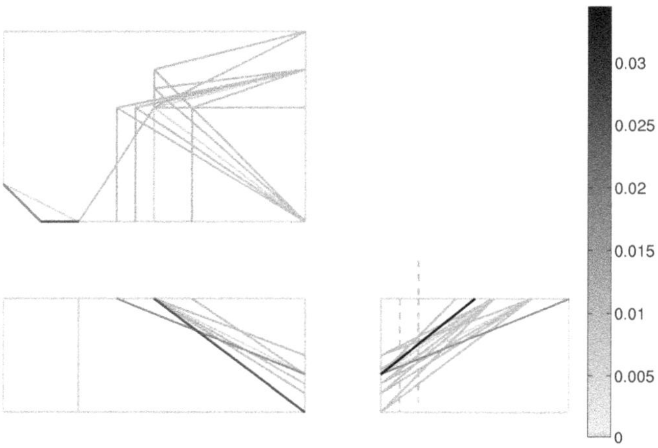

(b) visualization of incorrect errors on a problem from assignment #2. Correct lines (solution) are shown in green.

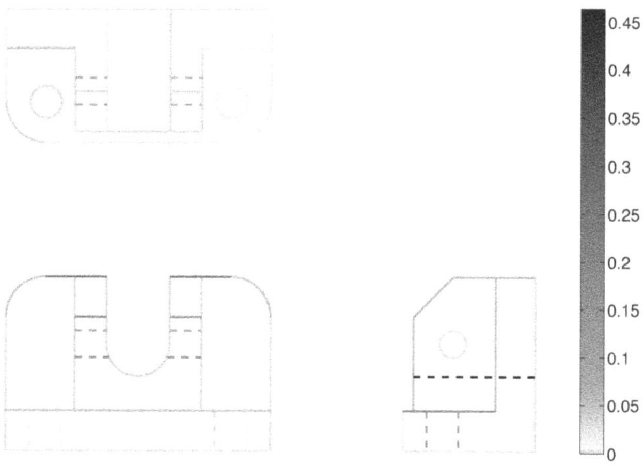

(c) visualization of missing errors on a problem from assignment #3

Figure 9. Color coded difficulty. The elements that are most frequently "missing" are shown in dark red, and those less frequently missing are shown in light red (a and c). The elements that are most frequently "incorrect" are shown in dark blue, and those less frequently incorrect shown in light blue (b). The numbers in the color bar indicate the fraction of student submissions that made the mistake for each element.

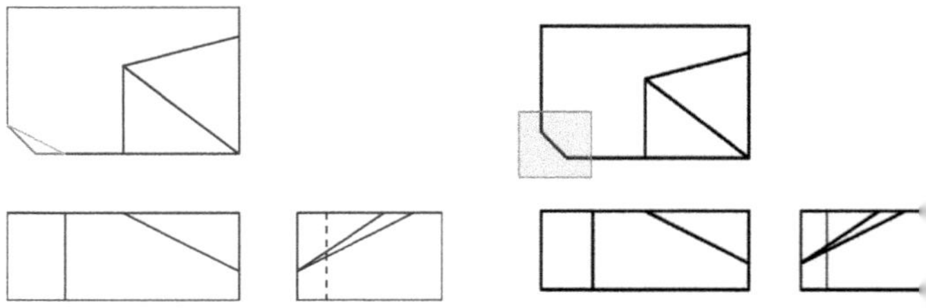

(a) While autograding (left) reports "1 missing line, 2 incorrect lines a human grader (right) reports "1 incorrect position."

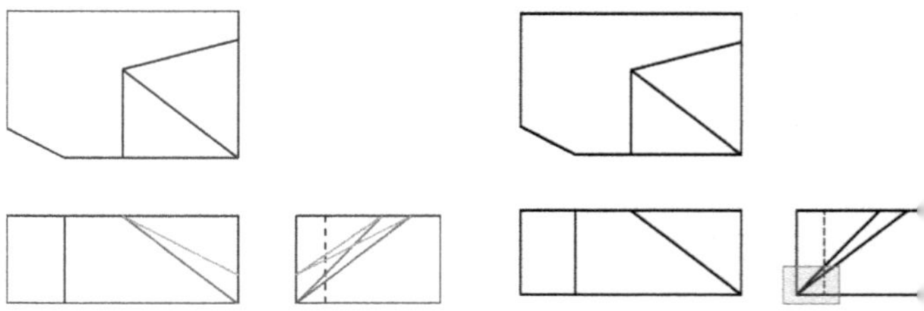

(b) While autograding (left) reports "3 missing line, 3 incorrect lines a human grader (right) reports "1 line not aligned."

Figure 10. Two examples of category B. Even though different rubrics are applied, errors are identified.

nuanced, and higher level. We leave more advanced emulation of such human grading rubrics as future work.

The most dramatic result is category C. For 21.7% of the submissions, the new autograding system catches students' mistakes that the human grader misses. We show two examples in Figure 11. This happens especially when a drawing includes subtle mistakes such as a slightly incorrect location, and/or when a drawing includes incorrect locations that are nonetheless consistent in neighboring views. In these cases, human graders may not notice them on the printed drawing.

For 3.5% of the submissions, the autograding system failed to estimate the appropriate transformation, and gave incorrect feedback. We show an example in Figure 12. The student drawing (Figure 12b) has an incorrect front view. Note that our RANSAC evaluation metric is the number of coincident points. When a student drawing has several wrong elements, the RANSAC algorithm may regard a strange transformation as the best transformation for the reason that it yields the maximum number of coincident points. We expect that this problem can be solved by extending the RANSAC evaluation metric to consider lines as well as points in future work. Note that even though the proposed algorithm fails to give correct feedback for 3.5% of the submissions, this happens only when the student drawing has multiple errors. In these cases, a whole view was reported as incorrect by the autograder, where in fact some partial credit should have been given. The proposed algorithm never failed to recognize perfect drawings as such.

CONCLUSION

Motivated by the importance of an automated grading system for multiview drawings, we propose a novel system that can compare two multiview drawings, a reference solution and a student's submission. These drawings may have inconsistent translations, scales, mirroring, skew, and/or rotation, all of

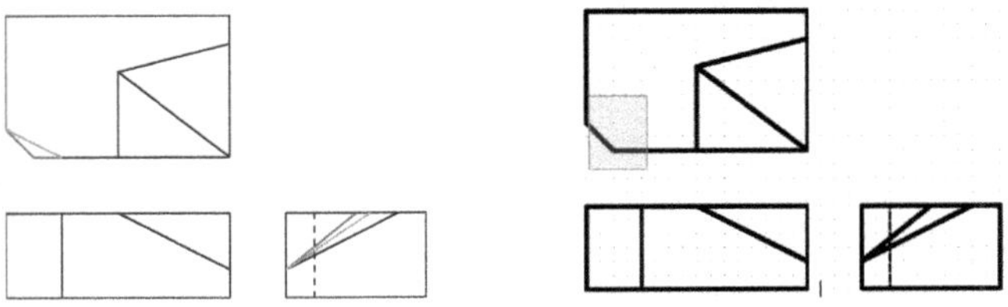

(a) A human grader (right) succeeded in recognizing the incorrect elements in the top view, but failed to catch the element in a slightly incorrect position in the right view.

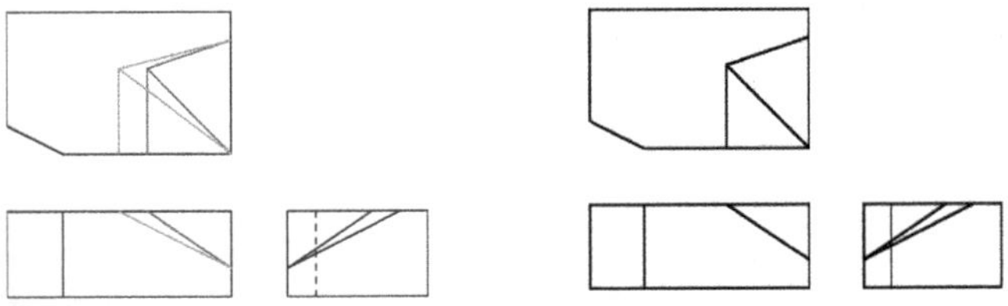

(b) A human grader (right) failed to notice elements in incorrect positions and gave a perfect score. Such errors are difficult for humans to catch because the positions are consistent with the neighboring view.

Figure 11. Two examples of category C. While a human grader failed to notice these mistakes, our autograding system found them.

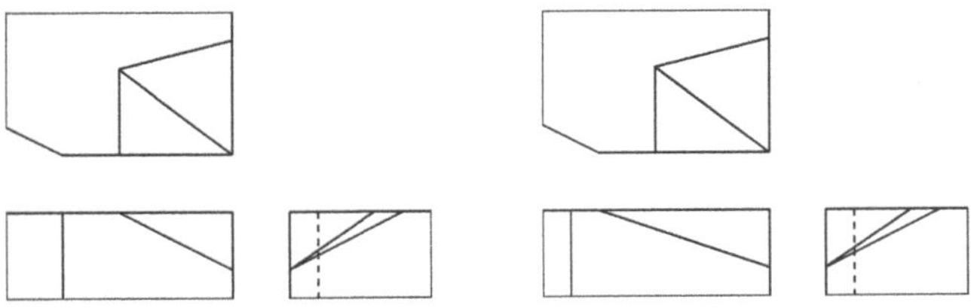

(a) solution drawing

(b) student drawing

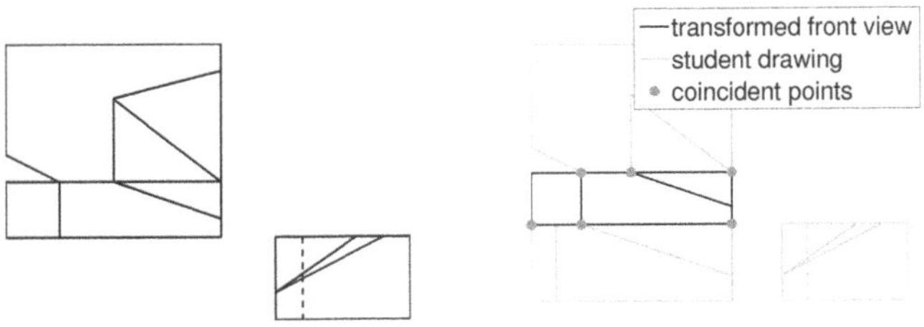

(c) transformed solution. The transformation estimate for the front view is wrong.

(d) The wrong transformation is chosen because it matches six points among the total eight points of the front view.

Figure 12. An example of category D. Our algorithm failed to estimate an appropriate transformation for the front view of the solution drawing. Note that the student drawing (b) has multiple mistakes in the front view.

which must be distinguished from allowable differences in scale, offset, and translation to reliably identify and classify errors in the students' drawings.

Our system provides fair comparison and grading checks for students' drawings, which can be used as input for a flexible scoring system. For example, in many cases, a grader may not want to reduce scores for duplicate errors of the same type. A grader may want to place different scores (emphasis) on different elements. One possibility would be to use our element-wise difficulty analysis to assign an appropriate score to each element.

The proposed system can be useful for large classes, eliminating time consuming manual grading and incomplete feedback, and for MOOCs on engineering drawing, which currently do not exist.

ACKNOWLEDGMENTS

We thank Zhongyin Hu for performing the manual grading for comparison. We also thank Armando Fox for offering an inspiring course on online education and autograding. We also thank many E28 students who tested submission instructions for autograding and whose assignments provided us with test data, and Anastasia Shuller for beta testing the autograder. This work was funded in part by UC Berkeley's vice provost for teaching and learning.

REFERENCES

1. Bertoline, G., Wiebe, E., Hartman, N., and Ross, W. *Technical Graphics Communication*. McGraw-Hill Science/Engineering/Math, 2002.
2. Brown, M., and Lowe, D. G. Unsupervised 3D object recognition and reconstruction in unordered datasets. In *Fifth International Conference on 3-D Digital Imaging and Modeling* (2005), 56–63.
3. Choi, S., Kim, T., and Yu, W. Performance evaluation of RANSAC family. *Journal of Computer Vision* (1997).
4. Coiras, E., Santamar, J., and Miravet, C. Segment-based registration technique for visual-infrared images. *Optical Engineering 39*, 1 (2000), 282–289.
5. Fischler, M. A., and Bolles, R. C. Random sample consensus: a paradigm for model fitting with applications to image analysis and automated cartography. *Communications of the ACM 24*, 6 (June 1981), 381–395.
6. Geng, W., Wang, J., and Zhang, Y. Embedding visual cognition in 3D reconstruction from multi-view engineering drawings. *Computer-Aided Design* (2002).
7. gradescope.com. `https://gradescope.com`, Last accessed on Jan 16, 2015.
8. Hartley, R., and Zisserman, A. Multiple View Geometry in Computer Vision, 2003.
9. Kwon, Y. P. Line segment-based aerial image registration. Master's thesis, EECS Department, University of California, Berkeley, May 2014.

10. Lee, H., and Han, S. Reconstruction of 3D interacting solids of revolution from 2D orthographic views. *Computer-Aided Design 37*, 13 (Nov. 2005), 1388–1398.
11. Lieu, D., and Sorby, S. *Visualization, Modeling, and Graphics for Engineering Design*, 3rd ed. Delmar Learning, 2009. Chapter 10.
12. Nistér, D. Preemptive RANSAC for live structure and motion estimation. *Machine Vision and Applications* (2005).
13. Raguram, R., Frahm, J.-M., and Pollefeys, M. A comparative analysis of RANSAC techniques leading to adaptive real-time random sample consensus. In *ECCV 2008*. 2008, 500–513.
14. Schnabel, R., Wahl, R., and Klein, R. Efficient RANSAC for point-cloud shape detection. *Computer Graphics Forum* (2007).
15. Shin, B. S., and Shin, Y. G. Fast 3D solid model reconstruction from orthographic views. *Computer-Aided Design 30*, 1 (Jan. 1998), 63–76.
16. Suh, Y. S., and McCasland, J. Interactive Construction of Solids from Orthographic Multiviews for an Educational Software Tool. *Computer-Aided Design and Applications 6*, 2 (Jan. 2009), 219–229.
17. Torr, P. H. S., and Zisserman, A. MLESAC: A new robust estimator with application to estimating image geometry. *Computer Vision and Image Understanding 78*, 1 (Apr. 2000), 138–156.
18. Wang, W., and Grinstein, G. G. A survey of 3D solid reconstruction from 2D projection line drawings. *Computer Graphics Forum 12*, 2 (May 1993), 137–158.
19. Wang, Z., and Latif, M. Reconstruction of a 3D solid model from orthographic projections. In *2003 International Conference on Geometric Modeling and Graphics, 2003. Proceedings* (2003), 75–82.
20. AutoCAD Drawing Compare Plug-in. `https://apps.exchange.autodesk.com/VLTC/en/Detail/Index?id=appstore.exchange.autodesk.com%3Adrawingcompare%3Aen`, Last accessed on Oct 20, 2014.
21. MATLAB CENTRAL, File Exchange. `http://www.mathworks.com/matlabcentral/fileexchange`, Last accessed on Oct 20, 2014.
22. Read DXF File Data. `http://www.mathworks.com/matlabcentral/fileexchange/24572-read-dxf-file-data`, Last accessed on Oct 20, 2014.

Mathematical Language Processing: Automatic Grading and Feedback for Open Response Mathematical Questions

Andrew S. Lan, Divyanshu Vats, Andrew E. Waters, Richard G. Baraniuk
Rice University
Houston, TX 77005
{mr.lan, dvats, waters, richb}@sparfa.com

ABSTRACT

While computer and communication technologies have provided effective means to scale up many aspects of education, the submission and grading of assessments such as homework assignments and tests remains a weak link. In this paper, we study the problem of automatically grading the kinds of *open response mathematical questions* that figure prominently in STEM (science, technology, engineering, and mathematics) courses. Our data-driven framework for *mathematical language processing* (MLP) leverages solution data from a large number of learners to evaluate the correctness of their solutions, assign partial-credit scores, and provide feedback to each learner on the likely locations of any errors. MLP takes inspiration from the success of natural language processing for text data and comprises three main steps. First, we convert each solution to an open response mathematical question into a series of numerical *features*. Second, we *cluster* the features from several solutions to uncover the structures of correct, partially correct, and incorrect solutions. We develop two different clustering approaches, one that leverages generic clustering algorithms and one based on Bayesian nonparametrics. Third, we *automatically grade* the remaining (potentially large number of) solutions based on their assigned cluster and one instructor-provided grade per cluster. As a bonus, we can track the cluster assignment of each step of a multistep solution and determine when it departs from a cluster of correct solutions, which enables us to indicate the *likely locations of errors* to learners. We test and validate MLP on real-world MOOC data to demonstrate how it can substantially reduce the human effort required in large-scale educational platforms.

Author Keywords

Automatic grading, Machine learning, Clustering, Bayesian nonparametrics, Assessment, Feedback, Mathematical language processing

L@S'15, March 14–March 15, 2015, Vancouver, Canada.
Copyright © 2015 ACM 978-1-4503-3411-2/15/03...$15.00.
http://dx.doi.org/10.1145/2724660.2724664

INTRODUCTION

Large-scale educational platforms have the capability to revolutionize education by providing inexpensive, high-quality learning opportunities for millions of learners worldwide. Examples of such platforms include massive open online courses (MOOCs) [6, 7, 9, 10, 16, 42], intelligent tutoring systems [43], computer-based homework and testing systems [1, 31, 38, 40], and personalized learning systems [24]. While computer and communication technologies have provided effective means to scale up the number of learners viewing lectures (via streaming video), reading the textbook (via the web), interacting with simulations (via a graphical user interface), and engaging in discussions (via online forums), the submission and grading of assessments such as homework assignments and tests remains a weak link.

There is a pressing need to find new ways and means to automate two critical tasks that are typically handled by the instructor or course assistants in a small-scale course: (*i*) grading of assessments, including allotting partial credit for partially correct solutions, and (*ii*) providing individualized feedback to learners on the locations and types of their errors.

Substantial progress has been made on automated grading and feedback systems in several restricted domains, including essay evaluation using natural language processing (NLP) [1, 33], computer program evaluation [12, 15, 29, 32, 34], and mathematical proof verification [8, 19, 21].

In this paper, we study the problem of automatically grading the kinds of *open response mathematical questions* that figure prominently in STEM (science, technology, engineering, and mathematics) education. To the best of our knowledge, there exist no tools to automatically evaluate and allot partial-credit scores to the solutions of such questions. As a result, large-scale education platforms have resorted either to oversimplified multiple choice input and binary grading schemes (correct/incorrect), which are known to convey less information about the learners' knowledge than open response questions [17], or peer-grading schemes [25, 26], which shift the burden of grading from the course instructor to the learners.[1]

[1]While peer grading appears to have some pedagogical value for learners [30], each learner typically needs to grade several solutions from other learners for each question they solve, in order to obtain an accurate grade estimate.

$$
\begin{aligned}
&((x^3+\sin x)/e^x)' \\
&= ((x^3+\sin x)e^{-x})' \\
&= (x^3+\sin x)'e^{-x} + (x^3+\sin x)(e^{-x})' \\
&= (3x^2+\cos x)e^{-x} + (x^3+\sin x)(-e^{-x}) \\
&= (3x^2+\cos x - x^3 - \sin x)e^{-x} \\
&= \frac{3x^2+\cos x - x^3 - \sin x}{e^x}
\end{aligned}
$$

(a) A correct solution that receives 3/3 credits

$$
\begin{aligned}
&((x^3+\sin x)/e^x)' \\
&= \frac{(3x^2+\cos x)e^x - (x^3+\sin x)e^x}{e^{2x}} \\
&= \frac{2x^2 - x^3 + \cos x - \sin x}{e^x}
\end{aligned}
$$

(b) An incorrect solution that receives 2/3 credits due to an error in the last expression

$$
\begin{aligned}
&((x^3+\sin x)/e^x)' \\
&= ((x^3+\sin x)e^{-x})' \\
&= -e^x(x^3+\sin x) + e^{-x}(3x^2+\cos x) \\
&= -e^x x^3 - e^x \sin x + 3e^{-x}x^2 + e^{-x}\cos x
\end{aligned}
$$

(c) An incorrect solution that receives 1/3 credits due to an error in the second expression

$$
\begin{aligned}
&((x^3+\sin x)/e^x)' \\
&= x
\end{aligned}
$$

(d) An incorrect solution that receives 0/3 credits

Figure 1: Example solutions to the question "Find the derivative of $(x^3 + \sin x)/e^x$" that were assigned scores of 3, 2, 1 and 0 out of 3, respectively, by our MLP-B algorithm.

$$
\begin{aligned}
&(x^2+x+\sin^2 x+\cos^2 x)(2x-3) \\
&= (x^2+x+1)(2x-3) \\
&= 2x^3 - 3x^2 + 2x^2 - 3x + 2x - 3 \\
&= 2x^3 - x^2 - x - 3
\end{aligned}
$$

(a) A correct solution that makes the simplification $\sin^2 x + \cos^2 x = 1$ in the first expression

$$
\begin{aligned}
&(x^2+x+\sin^2 x+\cos^2 x)(2x-3) \\
&= 2x^3 + 2x^2 + 2x\sin^2 x + 2x\cos^2 x \\
&\quad - 3x^2 - 3x - 3\sin^2 x - 3\cos^2 x \\
&= 2x^3 - x^2 - 3x + 2x(\sin^2 x + \cos^2 x) \\
&\quad - 3(\sin^2 x + \cos^2 x) \\
&= 2x^3 - x^2 - 3x + 2x(1) - 3(1) \\
&= 2x^3 - x^2 - x - 3
\end{aligned}
$$

(b) A correct solution that makes the the simplification $\sin^2 x + \cos^2 x = 1$ in the third expression

Figure 2: Examples of two different yet correct paths to solve the question "Simplify the expression $(x^2 + x + \sin^2 x + \cos^2 x)(2x - 3)$."

Main Contributions

In this paper, we develop a data-driven framework for *mathematical language processing* (MLP) that leverages solution data from a large number of learners to evaluate the correctness of solutions to open response mathematical questions, assign partial-credit scores, and provide feedback to each learner on the likely locations of any errors. The scope of our framework is broad and covers questions whose solution involves one or more mathematical expressions. This includes not just formal proofs but also the kinds of mathematical calculations that figure prominently in science and engineering courses. Examples of solutions to two algebra questions of various levels of correctness are given in Figures 1 and 2. In this regard, our work differs significantly from that of [8], which focuses exclusively on evaluating logical proofs.

Our MLP framework, which is inspired by the success of NLP methods for the analysis of textual solutions (e.g., essays and short answer), comprises three main steps.

First, we convert each solution to an open response mathematical question into a series of *numerical features*. In deriving these features, we make use of symbolic mathematics to transform mathematical expressions into a canonical form.

Second, we *cluster* the features from several solutions to uncover the structures of correct, partially correct, and incorrect solutions. We develop two different clustering approaches. MLP-S uses the numerical features to define a *similarity score* between pairs of solutions and then applies a generic clustering algorithm, such as spectral clustering (SC) [22] or affinity propagation (AP) [11]. We show that MLP-S is also useful for visualizing mathematical solutions. This can help instructors identify groups of learners that make similar errors so that instructors can deliver personalized remediation. MLP-B defines a *nonparametric Bayesian model* for the solutions and applies a Gibbs sampling algorithm to cluster the solutions.

Third, once a human assigns a grade to at least one solution in each cluster, we automatically *grade* the remaining (potentially large number of) solutions based on their assigned cluster. As a bonus, in MLP-B, we can track the cluster assignment of each step in a multistep solution and determine when it departs from a cluster of correct solutions, which enables us to indicate the likely locations of errors to learners.

In developing MLP, we tackle three main challenges of analyzing open response mathematical solutions. First, solutions might contain different notations that refer to the same mathematical quantity. For instance, in Figure 1, the learners use both e^{-x} and $\frac{1}{e^x}$ to refer to the same quantity. Second, some questions admit more than one path to the correct/incorrect solution. For instance, in Figure 2 we see two different yet correct solutions to the same question. It is typically infeasible for an instructor to enumerate all of these possibilities to automate the grading and feedback process. Third, numerically verifying the correctness of the solutions does not always apply to mathematical questions, especially when simplifications are required. For example, a question that asks to simplify the expression $\sin^2 x + \cos^2 x + x$ can have both $1+x$ and $\sin^2 x + \cos^2 x + x$ as numerically correct answers, since both these expressions output the same value for all values of x. However, the correct answer is $1+x$, since the question expects the learners to recognize that $\sin^2 x + \cos^2 x = 1$. Thus, methods developed to check the correctness of computer programs and formulae by specifying a range of different inputs and checking for the correct outputs, e.g., [32], cannot always be applied to accurately grade open response mathematical questions.

Related Work

Prior work has led to a number of methods for grading and providing feedback to the solutions of certain kinds of open response questions. A linear regression-based approach has been developed to grade essays using features extracted from a training corpus using Natural Language Processing (NLP) [1, 33]. Unfortunately, such a simple regression-based model does not perform well when applied to the features extracted from mathematical solutions. Several methods have been developed for automated analysis of computer programs [15, 32]. However, these methods do not apply to the solutions to open response mathematical questions, since they lack the structure and compilability of computer programs. Several methods have also been developed to check the correctness of the logic in mathematical proofs [8, 19, 21]. However, these methods apply only to mathematical proofs involving logical operations and not the kinds of open-ended mathematical calculations that are often involved in science and engineering courses.

The idea of clustering solutions to open response questions into groups of similar solutions has been used in a number of previous endeavors: [2, 5] uses clustering to grade short, textual answers to simple questions; [23] uses clustering to visualize a large collection of computer programs; and [28] uses clustering to grade and provide feedback on computer programs. Although the high-level concept underlying these works is resonant with the MLP framework, the feature building techniques used in MLP are very different, since the structure of mathematical solutions differs significantly from short textual answers and computer programs.

This paper is organized as follows. In the next section, we develop our approach to convert open response mathematical solutions to numerical features that can be processed by machine learning algorithms. We then develop MLP-S and MLP-B and use real-world MOOC data to showcase their ability to accurately grade a large number of solutions based on the instructor's grades for only a small number of solutions, thus substantially reducing the human effort required in large-scale educational platforms. We close with a discussion and perspectives on future research directions.

MLP FEATURE EXTRACTION

The first step in our MLP framework is to transform a collection of solutions to an open response mathematical question into a set of numerical features. In later sections, we show how the numerical features can be used to cluster and grade solutions as well as generate informative learner feedback.

A solution to an open response mathematical question will in general contain a mixture of explanatory text and core mathematical expressions. Since the correctness of a solution depends primarily on the mathematical expressions, we will ignore the text when deriving features. However, we recognize that the text is potentially very useful for automatically generating explanations for various mathematical expressions. We leave this avenue for future work.

A workhorse of NLP is the *bag-of-words* model; it has found tremendous success in text semantic analysis. This model treats a text document as a collection of words and uses the frequencies of the words as numerical features to perform tasks like topic classification and document clustering [4, 5].

A solution to an open response mathematical question consists of a series of *mathematical expressions* that are chained together by text, punctuation, or mathematical delimiters including $=$, $\leq$, $>$, $\propto$, $\approx$, etc. For example, the solution in Figure 1(b) contains the expressions $((x^3 + \sin x)/e^x)'$, $((3x^2 + \cos x)e^x - (x^3 + \sin x)e^x))/e^{2x}$, and $(2x^2 - x^3 + \cos x - \sin x)/e^x$ that are all separated by the delimiter "=".

MLP identifies the unique mathematical expressions contained in the learners' solutions and uses them as features, effectively extending the bag-of-words model to use mathematical expressions as features rather than words. To coin a phrase, MLP uses a novel *bag-of-expressions* model.

Once the mathematical expressions have been extracted from a solution, we parse them using SymPy, the open source Python library for symbolic mathematics [36].[2] SymPy has powerful capability for simplifying expressions. For example, $x^2 + x^2$ can be simplified to $2x^2$, and $e^x x^2/e^{2x}$ can be simplifed to $e^{-x}x^2$. In this way we can identify the equivalent terms in expressions that refer to the same mathematical quantity, resulting in more accurate features. In practice for some questions, however, it might be necessary to tone down the level of SymPy's simplification. For instance, the key to solving the question in Figure 2 is to simplify the expression using the Pythagorean identity $\sin^2 x + \cos^2 x = 1$. If SymPy is called on to perform such a simplification automatically, then it will not be possible to verify whether a learner has correctly navigated the simplification in their solution. For such problems, it is advisable to perform only arithmetic simplifications.

After extracting the expressions from the solutions, we transform the expressions into numerical features. We assume that N learners submit solutions to a particular mathematical question. Extracting the expressions from each solution using SymPy yields a total of V unique expressions across the N solutions.

We encode the solutions in a integer-valued *solution feature matrix* $\mathbf{Y} \in \mathbb{N}^{V \times N}$ whose rows correspond to different expressions and whose columns correspond to different solutions; that is, the $(i, j)^{\text{th}}$ entry of $\mathbf{Y}$ is given by

$$Y_{i,j} = \text{times expression } i \text{ appears in solution } j.$$

Each column of $\mathbf{Y}$ corresponds to a numerical representation of a mathematical solution. Note that we do not consider the ordering of the expressions in this model; such an extension is an interesting avenue for future work. In this paper, we indicate in $\mathbf{Y}$ only the presence and not the frequency of an expression, i.e., $\mathbf{Y} \in \{0, 1\}^{V \times N}$ and

$$Y_{i,j} = \begin{cases} 1 & \text{if expression } i \text{ appears in solution } j \\ 0 & \text{otherwise.} \end{cases} \qquad (1)$$

The extension to encoding frequencies is straightforward.

To illustrate how the matrix $\mathbf{Y}$ is constructed, consider the solutions in Figure 2(a) and (b). Across both solutions, there are 7 unique expressions. Thus, $\mathbf{Y}$ is a 7×2 matrix, with each row corresponding to a unique expression. Letting the first four rows of $\mathbf{Y}$ correspond to the four expressions in Figure 2(a) and the remaining three rows to expressions 2–4 in Figure 2(b), we have

$$\mathbf{Y} = \begin{bmatrix} 1 & 1 & 1 & 1 & 0 & 0 & 0 \\ 1 & 0 & 0 & 1 & 1 & 1 & 1 \end{bmatrix}^T.$$

[2]In particular, we use the `parse_expr` function.

We end this section with the crucial observation that, for a wide range of mathematical questions, many expressions will be shared across learners' solutions. This is true, for instance, in Figure 2. This suggests that there are a limited number of types of solutions to a question (both correct and incorrect) and that solutions of the same type tend tend to be similar to each other. This leads us to the conclusion that the N solutions to a particular question can be effectively clustered into $K \ll N$ clusters. In the next two sections, we will develop MLP-S and MLP-B, two algorithms to cluster solutions according to their numerical features.

MLP-S: SIMILARITY-BASED CLUSTERING

In this section, we outline MLP-S, which clusters and then grades solutions using a solution similarity-based approach.

The MLP-S Model

We start by using the solution features in $\mathbf{Y}$ to define a notion of similarity between pairs of solutions. Define the $N \times N$ *similarity matrix* $\mathbf{S}$ containing the pairwise similarities between all solutions, with its $(i,j)^{\text{th}}$ entry the similarity between solutions i and j

$$S_{i,j} = \frac{\mathbf{y}_i^T \mathbf{y}_j}{\min\{\mathbf{y}_i^T \mathbf{y}_i, \mathbf{y}_j^T \mathbf{y}_j\}}. \quad (2)$$

The column vector $\mathbf{y}_i$ denotes the ith column of $\mathbf{Y}$ and corresponds to learner i's solution. Informally, $S_{i,j}$ is the number of common expressions between solution i and solution j divided by the minimum of the number of expressions in solutions i and j. A large/small value of $S_{i,j}$ corresponds to the two solutions being similar/dissimilar. For example, the similarity between the solutions in Figure 1(a) and Figure 1(b) is $1/3$ and the similarity between the solutions in Figure 2(a) and Figure 2(b) is $1/2$. $\mathbf{S}$ is symmetric, and $0 \leq S_{i,j} \leq 1$. Equation (2) is just one of any possible solution similarity metrics. We defer the development of other metrics to future work.

Clustering Solutions in MLP-S

Having defined the similarity $S_{i,j}$ between two solutions i and j, we now cluster the N solutions into $K \ll N$ clusters such that the solutions within each cluster have high similarity score between them and solutions in different clusters have low similarity score between them.

Given the similarity matrix $\mathbf{S}$, we can use any of the multitude of standard clustering algorithms to cluster solutions. Two examples of clustering algorithms are *spectral clustering* (SC) [22] and *affinity propagation* (AP) [11]. The SC algorithm requires specifying the number of clusters K as an input parameter, while the AP algorithm does not.

Figure 3 illustrates how AP is able to identify clusters of similar solutions from solutions to four different mathematical questions. The figures on the top correspond to solutions to the questions in Figures 1 and 2, respectively. The bottom two figures correspond to solutions to two signal processing questions. Each node in the figure corresponds to a solution, and nodes with the same color correspond to solutions that belong to the same cluster. For each figure, we show a sample solution from some of these clusters, with the boxed solutions corresponding to correct solutions. We can make three interesting observations from Figure 3:

- In the top left figure, we cluster a solution with the final answer $3x^2 + \cos x - (x^3 + \sin x))/e^x$ with a solution with the final answer $3^{x^2} + \cos x - (x^3 + \sin x))/e^x$. Although the later solution is incorrect, it contained a typographical error where $3 * x \wedge 2$ was typed as $3 \wedge x \wedge 2$. MLP-S is able to identify this typographical error, since the expression before the final solution is contained in several other correct solutions.

- In the top right figure, the correct solution requires identifying the trigonometric identify $\sin^2 x + \cos^2 x = 1$. The clustering algorithm is able to identify a subset of the learners who were not able to identify this relationship and hence could not simplify their final expression.

- MLP-S is able to identify solutions that are strongly connected to each other. Such a visualization can be extremely useful for course instructors. For example, an instructor can easily identify a group of learners who lack mastery of a certain skill that results in a common error and adjust their course plan accordingly to help these learners.

Auto-Grading via MLP-S

Having clustered all solutions into a small number K of clusters, we assign the same grade to all solutions in the same cluster. If a course instructor assigns a grade to one solution from each cluster, then MLP-S can automatically grade the remaining $N - K$ solutions. We construct the index set $\mathcal{I}_S$ of solutions that the course instructor needs to grade as

$$\mathcal{I}_S = \left\{ \arg\max_{i \in \mathcal{C}_k} \sum_{j=1}^{N} S_{i,j},\ k = 1, 2, \ldots, K \right\},$$

where $\mathcal{C}_k$ represents the index set of the solutions in cluster k. In words, in each cluster, we select the solution having the highest similarity to the other solutions (ties are broken randomly) to include in $\mathcal{I}_S$. We demonstrate the performance of auto-grading via MLP-S in the experimental results section below.

MLP-B: BAYESIAN NONPARAMETRIC CLUSTERING

In this section, we outline MLP-B, which clusters and then grades solutions using a Bayesian nonparameterics-based approach. The MLP-B model and algorithm can be interpreted as an extension of the model in [44], where a similar approach is proposed to cluster short text documents.

The MLP-B Model

Following the key observation that the N solutions can be effectively clustered into $K \ll N$ clusters, let $\mathbf{z}$ be the $N \times 1$ cluster assignment vector, with $z_j \in \{1, \ldots, K\}$ denoting the cluster assignment of the jth solution with $j \in \{1, \ldots, N\}$. Using this latent variable, we model the probability of the

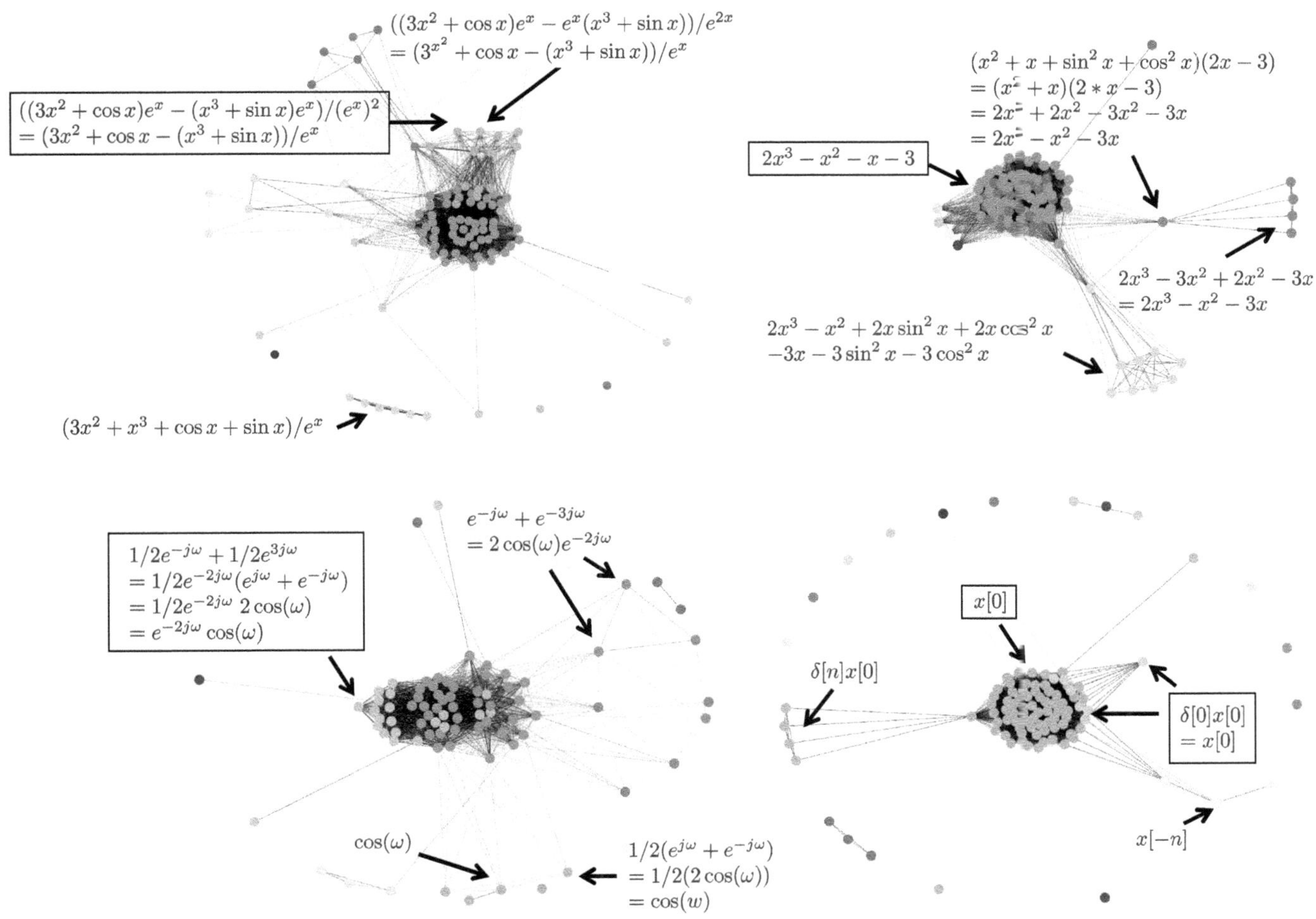

Figure 3: Illustration of the clusters obtained by MLP-S by applying affinity propagation (AP) on the similarity matrix $\mathbf{S}$ corresponding to learners' solutions to four different mathematical questions (see Table 1 for more details about the datasets and the Appendix for the question statements). Each node corresponds to a solution. Nodes with the same color correspond to solutions that are estimated to be in the same cluster. The thickness of the edge between two solutions is proportional to their similarity score. Boxed solutions are correct; all others are in varying degrees of correctness.

solution of all learners' solutions to the question as

$$p(\mathbf{Y}) = \prod_{j=1}^{N}\left(\sum_{k=1}^{K} p(\mathbf{y}_j|z_j=k)p(z_j=k)\right),$$

where $\mathbf{y}_j$, the jth column of the data matrix $\mathbf{Y}$, corresponds to learner j's solution to the question. Here we have implicitly assumed that the learners' solutions are independent of each other. By analogy to topic models [4, 35], we assume that learner j's solution to the question, $\mathbf{y}_j$, is generated according to a *multinomial* distribution given the cluster assignments $\mathbf{z}$ as

$$\begin{aligned} p(\mathbf{y}_j|z_j=k) &= \mathit{Mult}(\mathbf{y}_j|\phi_k) \\ &= \frac{(\sum_i Y_{i,j})!}{Y_{1,j}!Y_{2,j}!\ldots Y_{V,j}!}\Phi_{1,k}^{Y_{1,j}}\Phi_{2,k}^{Y_{2,j}}\ldots\Phi_{V,k}^{Y_{V,j}}, \end{aligned} \tag{3}$$

where $\mathbf{\Phi} \in [0,1]^{V\times K}$ is a parameter matrix with $\Phi_{v,k}$ denoting its $(v,k)^{\text{th}}$ entry. $\phi_k \in [0,1]^{V\times 1}$ denotes the kth column of $\mathbf{\Phi}$ and charcterizes the multinomial distribution over all the V features for cluster k.

In practice, one often has no information regarding the number of clusters K. Therefore, we consider K as an unknown parameter and infer it from the solution data. In order to do so, we impose a Chinese restaurant process (CRP) prior on the cluster assignments $\mathbf{z}$, parameterized by a parameter α. The CRP characterizes the random partition of data into clusters, in analogy to the seating process of customers in a Chinese restaurant. It is widely used in Bayesian mixture modeling literature [3, 14]. Under the CRP prior, the cluster (table) assignment of the jth solution (customer), conditioned on the

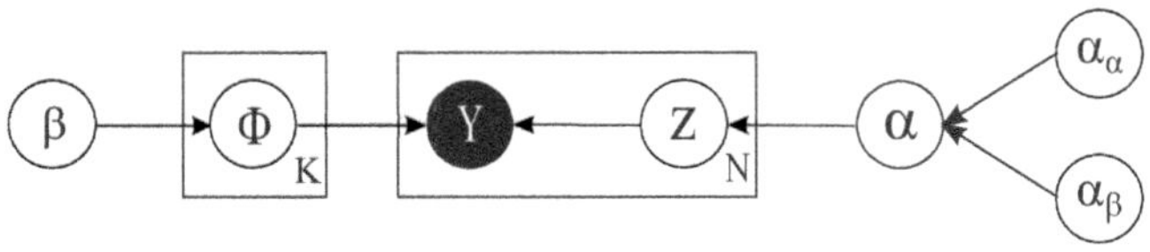

Figure 4: Graphical model of the generation process of solutions to mathematical questions. α_α, α_β and β are hyperparameters, $\mathbf{z}$ and $\mathbf{\Phi}$ are latent variables to be inferred, and $\mathbf{Y}$ is the observed data defined in (1).

cluster assignments of all the other solutions, follows the distribution

$$p(z_j = k|\mathbf{z}_{\neg j}, \alpha) = \begin{cases} \frac{n_{k,\neg j}}{N-1+\alpha} & \text{if cluster } k \text{ is occupied,} \\ \frac{\alpha}{N-1+\alpha} & \text{if cluster } k \text{ is empty,} \end{cases} \tag{4}$$

where $n_{k,\neg j}$ represents the number of solutions that belong to cluster k excluding the current solution j, with $\sum_{k=1}^{K} n_{k,\neg j} = N-1$. The vector $\mathbf{z}_{\neg j}$ represents the cluster assignments of the other solutions. The flexibility of allowing any solution to start a new cluster of its own enables us to automatically infer K from data. It is known [37] that the expected number of clusters under the CRP prior satisfies $K \sim O(\alpha \log N) \ll N$, so our method scales well as the number of learners N grows large. We also impose a Gamma prior $\alpha \sim \mathit{Gam}(\alpha_\alpha, \alpha_\beta)$ on α to help us infer its value.

Since the solution feature data $\mathbf{Y}$ is assumed to follow a multinomial distribution parameterized by $\mathbf{\Phi}$, we impose a symmetric Dirichlet prior over $\mathbf{\Phi}$ as $\boldsymbol{\phi}_k \sim \mathit{Dir}(\boldsymbol{\phi}_k|\beta)$ because of its conjugacy with the multinomial distribution [13].

The graphical model representation of our model is visualized in Figure 4. Our goal next is to estimate the cluster assignments $\mathbf{z}$ for the solution of each learner, the parameters $\boldsymbol{\phi}_k$ of each cluster, and the number of clusters K, from the binary-valued solution feature data matrix $\mathbf{Y}$.

Clustering Solutions in MLP-B

We use a Gibbs sampling algorithm for posterior inference under the MLP-B model, which automatically groups solutions into clusters. We start by applying a generic clustering algorithm (e.g., K-means, with $K = N/10$) to initialize $\mathbf{z}$, and then initialize $\mathbf{\Phi}$ accordingly. Then, in each iteration of MLP-B, we perform the following steps:

1. **Sample z**: For each solution j, we remove it from its current cluster and sample its cluster assignment z_j from the posterior $p(z_j = k|\mathbf{z}_{\neg j}, \alpha, \mathbf{Y})$. Using Bayes rule, we have

$$p(z_j = k|\mathbf{z}_{\neg j}, \mathbf{\Phi}, \alpha, \mathbf{Y}) = p(z_j = k|\mathbf{z}_{\neg j}, \boldsymbol{\phi}_k, \alpha, \mathbf{y}_j)$$
$$\propto p(z_j = k|\mathbf{z}_{\neg j}, \alpha) p(\mathbf{y}_j|z_j = k, \boldsymbol{\phi}_k).$$

The prior probability $p(z_j = k|\mathbf{z}_{\neg j}, \alpha)$ is given by (4). For non-empty clusters, the observed data likelihood $p(\mathbf{y}_j|z_j = k, \boldsymbol{\phi}_k)$ is given by (3). However, this does not apply to new clusters that are previously empty. For a new cluster, we marginalize out $\boldsymbol{\phi}_k$, resulting in

$$\begin{aligned} p(\mathbf{y}_j|z_j = k, \beta) &= \int_{\boldsymbol{\phi}_k} p(\mathbf{y}_j|z_j = k, \boldsymbol{\phi}_k) p(\boldsymbol{\phi}_k|\beta) \\ &= \int_{\boldsymbol{\phi}_k} \mathit{Mult}(\mathbf{y}_j|z_j = k, \boldsymbol{\phi}_k) \mathit{Dir}(\boldsymbol{\phi}_k|\beta) \\ &= \frac{\Gamma(V\beta)}{\Gamma(\sum_{i=1}^{V} Y_{i,j} + V\beta)} \prod_{i=1}^{V} \frac{\Gamma(Y_{i,j} + \beta)}{\Gamma(\beta)}, \end{aligned}$$

where $\Gamma(\cdot)$ is the Gamma function.

If a cluster becomes empty after we remove a solution from its current cluster, then we remove it from our sampling process and erase its corresponding multinomial parameter vector $\boldsymbol{\phi}_k$. If a new cluster is sampled for z_j, then we sample its multinomial parameter vector $\boldsymbol{\phi}_k$ immediately according to Step 2 below. Otherwise, we do not change $\boldsymbol{\phi}_k$ until we have finished sampling $\mathbf{z}$ for all solutions.

2. **Sample $\mathbf{\Phi}$**: For each cluster k, sample $\boldsymbol{\phi}_k$ from its posterior $\mathit{Dir}(\boldsymbol{\phi}_k|n_{1,k} + \beta, \ldots, n_{V,k} + \beta)$, where $n_{i,k}$ is the number of times feature i occurs in the solutions that belong to cluster k.

3. **Sample α**: Sample α using the approach described in [41].

4. **Update β**: Update β using the fixed-point procedure described in [20].

The output of the Gibbs sampler is a series of samples that correspond to the approximate posterior distribution of the various parameters of interest. To make meaningful inference for these parameters (such as the posterior mean of a parameter), it is important to appropriately post-process these samples. For our estimate of the true number of clusters, $\widehat{K}$, we simply take the mode of the posterior distribution on the number of clusters K. We use only iterations with $K = \widehat{K}$ to estimate the posterior statistics [39].

In mixture models, the issue of "label-switching" can cause a model to be unidentifiable, because the cluster labels can be arbitrarily permuted without affecting the data likelihood. In order to overcome this issue, we use an approach reported in [39]. First, we compute the likelihood of the observed data in each iteration as $p(\mathbf{Y}|\mathbf{\Phi}^\ell, \mathbf{z}^\ell)$, where $\mathbf{\Phi}^\ell$ and $\mathbf{z}^\ell$ represent the samples of these variables at the ℓth iteration. After the algorithm terminates, we search for the iteration $\ell_{\max}$ with the largest data likelihood and then permute the labels $\mathbf{z}^\ell$ in the other iterations to best match $\mathbf{\Phi}^\ell$ with $\mathbf{\Phi}^{\ell_{\max}}$. We use $\widehat{\mathbf{\Phi}}$ (with columns $\hat{\boldsymbol{\phi}}_k$) to denote the estimate of $\mathbf{\Phi}$, which is simply the posterior mean of $\mathbf{\Phi}$. Each solution j is assigned to the cluster indexed by the mode of the samples from the posterior of z_j, denoted by $\hat{z}_j$.

Auto-Grading via MLP-B

We now detail how to use MLP-B to automatically grade a large number N of learners' solutions to a mathematical question, using a small number $\widehat{K}$ of instructor graded solutions. First, as in MLP-S, we select the set $\mathcal{I}_B$ of "typical solutions" for the instructor to grade. We construct $\mathcal{I}_B$ by selecting one solution from each of the $\widehat{K}$ clusters that is most representative of the solutions in that cluster:

$$\mathcal{I}_B = \{\arg\max_j p(\mathbf{y}_j|\hat{\phi}_k), k = 1, 2, \ldots, \widehat{K}\}.$$

In words, for each cluster, we select the solution with the largest likelihood of being in that cluster.

The instructor grades the $\widehat{K}$ solutions in $\mathcal{I}_B$ to form the set of instructor grades $\{g_k\}$ for $k \in \mathcal{I}_B$. Using these grades, we assign grades to the other solutions $j \notin \mathcal{I}_B$ according to

$$\hat{g}_j = \frac{\sum_{k=1}^{\widehat{K}} p(\mathbf{y}_j|\hat{\phi}_k) g_k}{\sum_{k=1}^{\widehat{K}} p(\mathbf{y}_j|\hat{\phi}_k)}. \quad (5)$$

That is, we grade each solution not in $\mathcal{I}_B$ as the average of the instructor grades weighted by the likelihood that the solution belongs to cluster. We demonstrate the performance of auto-grading via MLP-B in the experimental results section below.

Feedback Generation via MLP-B

In addition to grading solutions, MLP-B can automatically provide useful feedback to learners on where they made errors in their solutions.

For a particular solution j denoted by its column feature value vector $\mathbf{y}_j$ with V_j total expressions, let $\mathbf{y}_j^{(v)}$ denote the feature value vector that corresponds to the first v expressions of this solution, with $v = \{1, 2, \ldots, V_j\}$. Under this notation, we evaluate the probability that the first v expressions of solution j belong to each of the $\widehat{K}$ clusters: $p(\mathbf{y}_j^{(v)}|\hat{\phi}_k), k = \{1, 2, \ldots, \widehat{K}\}$, for all v. Using these probabilities, we can also compute the expected credit of solution j after the first v expressions via

$$\hat{g}_j^{(v)} = \frac{\sum_{k=1}^{\widehat{K}} p(\mathbf{y}_j^{(v)}|\hat{\phi}_k) g_k}{\sum_{k=1}^{\widehat{K}} p(\mathbf{y}_j^{(v)}|\hat{\phi}_k)}, \quad (6)$$

where $\{g_k\}$ is the set of instructor grades as defined above.

Using these quantities, it is possible to identify that the learner has likely made an error at the vth expression if it is most likely to belong to a cluster with credit g_k less than the full credit or, alternatively, if the expected credit $\hat{g}_j^{(v)}$ is less than the full credit.

The ability to automatically locate *where* an error has been made in a particular incorrect solution provides many benefits. For instance, MLP-B can inform instructors of the most common locations of learner errors to help guide their instruction. It can also enable an automated tutoring system to generate feedback to a learner as they make an error in the early steps of a solution, before it propagates to later steps. We demonstrate the efficacy of MLP-B to automatically locate learner errors using real-world educational data in the experiments section below.

EXPERIMENTS

In this section, we demonstrate how MLP-S and MLP-B can be used to accurately estimate the grades of roughly 100 open response solutions to mathematical questions by only asking the course instructor to grade approximately 10 solutions. We also demonstrate how MLP-B can be used to automatically provide feedback to learners on the locations of errors in their solutions.

Table 1: Datasets consisting of the solutions of 116 learners to 4 mathematical questions on algebra and signal processing. See the Appendix for the question statements.

	No.of solutions N	No.of features (unique expressions) V
Question 1	108	78
Question 2	113	53
Question 3	90	100
Question 4	110	45

Auto-Grading via MLP-S and MLP-B

Datasets

Our dataset that consists of 116 learners solving 4 open response mathematical questions in an edX course. The set of questions includes 2 high-school level mathematical questions and 2 college-level signal processing questions (details about the questions can be found in Table 1, and the question statements are given in the Appendix). For each question, we pre-process the solutions to filter out the blank solutions and extract features. Using the features, we represent the solutions by the matrix $\mathbf{Y}$ in (1). Every solution was graded by the course instructor with one of the scores in the set $\{0, 1, 2, 3\}$, with a full credit of 3.

Baseline: Random sub-sampling

We compare the auto-grading performance of MLP-S and MLP-B against a baseline method that does not group the solutions into clusters. In this method, we randomly sub-sample all solutions to form a small set of solutions for the instructor to grade. Then, each ungraded solution is simply assigned the grade of the solution in the set of instructor-graded solutions that is most similar to it as defined by $\mathbf{S}$ in (2). Since this small set is picked randomly, we run the baseline method 10 times and report the best performance.[3]

Experimental setup

For each question, we apply four different methods for auto-grading:

- Random sub-sampling (RS) with the number of clusters $K \in \{5, 6, \ldots, 40\}$.
- MLP-S with spectral clustering (SC) with $K \in \{5, 6, \ldots, 40\}$.
- MLP-S with affinity propagation (AP) clustering. This algorithm does not require K as an input.
- MLP-B with hyperparameters set to the non-informative values $\alpha_\alpha = \alpha_\beta = 1$ and running the Gibbs sampling algorithm for 10,000 iterations with 2,000 burn-in iterations.

[3]Other baseline methods, such as the linear regression-based method used in the edX essay grading system [33], are not listed, because they did not perform as well as random sub-sampling in our experiments.

MLP-S with AP and MLP-B both automatically estimate the number of clusters K. Once the clusters are selected, we assign one solution from each cluster to be graded by the instructor using the methods described in earlier sections.

Performance metric

We use mean absolute error (MAE), which measures the "average absolute error per auto-graded solution"

$$\text{MAE} = \frac{\sum_{j=1}^{N-K} |\hat{g}_j - g_j|}{N-K},$$

as our performance metric. Here, $N - K$ equals the number of solutions that are auto-graded, and $\hat{g}_j$ and g_j represent the estimated grade (for MLP-B, the estimated grades are rounded to integers) and the actual instructor grades for the auto-graded solutions, respectively.

Results and discussion

In Figure 5, we plot the MAE versus the number of clusters K for Questions 1–4. MLP-S with SC consistently outperforms the random sampling baseline algorithm for almost all values of K. This performance gain is likely due to the fact that the baseline method does not cluster the solutions and thus does not select a good subset of solutions for the instructor to grade. MLP-B is more accurate than MLP-S with both SC and AP and can automatically estimate the value of K, although at the price of significantly higher computational complexity (e.g., clustering and auto-grading one question takes 2 minutes for MLP-B compared to only 5 seconds for MLP-S with AP on a standard laptop computer with a 2.8GHz CPU and 8GB memory).

Both MLP-S and MLP-B grade the learners' solutions accurately (e.g., an MAE of 0.04 out of the full grade 3 using only $K = 13$ instructor grades to auto-grade all $N = 113$ solutions to Question 2). Moreover, as we see in Figure 5, the MAE for MLP-S decreases as K increases, and eventually reaches 0 when K is large enough that only solutions that are exactly the same as each other belong to the same cluster. In practice, one can tune the value of K to achieve a balance between maximizing grading accuracy and minimizing human effort. Such a tuning process is not necessary for MLP-B, since it automatically estimates the value of K and achieves such a balance.

Feedback Generation via MLP-B

Experimental setup

Since Questions 3–4 require some familiarity with signal processing, we demonstrate the efficacy of MLP-B in providing feedback on mathematical solutions on Questions 1–2. Among the solutions to each question, there are a few types of common errors that more than one learner makes. We take one incorrect solution out of each type and run MLP-B on the other solutions to estimate the parameter $\hat{\phi}_k$ for each cluster. Using this information and the instructor grades $\{g_k\}$, after each expression v in a solution, we compute the probability that it belongs to a cluster $p(\mathbf{y}_j^{(v)}|\hat{\phi}_k)$ that does not have full credit ($g_k < 3$), together with the expected credit using (6). Once the expected grade is calculated to be less than full credit, we consider that an error has occurred.

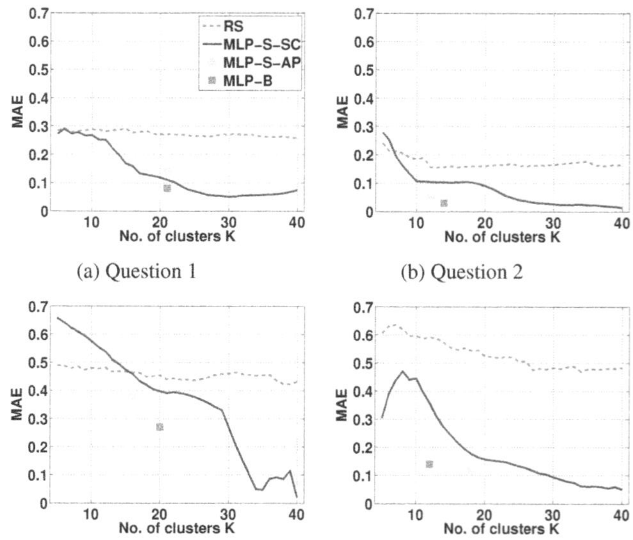

(a) Question 1 (b) Question 2 (c) Question 3 (d) Question 4

Figure 5: Mean absolute error (MAE) versus the number of instructor graded solutions (clusters) K, for Questions 1–4, respectively. For example, on Question 1, MLP-S and MLP-B estimate the true grade of each solution with an average error of around 0.1 out of a full credit of 3. "RS" represents the random sub-sampling baseline. Both MLP-S methods and MLP-B outperforms the baseline method.

Results and discussion

Two sample feedback generation process are shown in Figure 6. In Figure 6(a), we can provide feedback to the learner on their error as early as Line 2, before it carries over to later lines. Thus, MLP-B can potentially become a powerful tool to generate timely feedback to learners as they are solving mathematical questions, by analyzing the solutions it gathers from other learners.

CONCLUSIONS

We have developed a framework for mathematical language processing (MLP) that consists of three main steps: (*i*) converting each solution to an open response mathematical question into a series of numerical features; (*ii*) clustering the features from several solutions to uncover the structures of correct, partially correct, and incorrect solutions; and (*iii*) automatically grading the remaining (potentially large number of) solutions based on their assigned cluster and one instructor-provided grade per cluster. As our experiments have indicated, our framework can substantially reduce the human effort required for grading in large-scale courses. As a bonus, MLP-S enables instructors to visualize the clusters of solutions to help them identify common errors and thus groups of learners having the same misconceptions. As a further bonus, MLP-B can track the cluster assignment of each step of a multistep solution and determine when it departs from a cluster of correct solutions, which enables us to indicate the locations of errors to learners in real time. Improved learning outcomes should result from these innovations.

$$((x^3+\sin x)/e^x)'$$
$$= (e^x(x^3+\sin x)' - (x^3+\sin x)(e^x)')/e^{2x}$$
prob.incorrect = 0.11, exp.grade = 3
$$= (e^x(2x^2+\cos x) - (x^3+\sin x)e^x)/e^{2x}$$
prob.incorrect = 0.66, exp.grade = 2
$$= (2x^2+\cos x - x^3 - \sin x)/e^x$$
prob.incorrect = 0.93, exp.grade = 2
$$= (x^2(2-x)+\cos x - \sin x)/e^x$$
prob.incorrect = 0.99, exp.grade = 2

(a) A sample feedback generation process where the learner makes an error in the expression in Line 2 while attempting to solve Question 1.

$$(x^2+x+\sin^2 x+\cos^2 x)(2x-3)$$
$$= (x^2+x+1)(2x-3)$$
prob.incorrect = 0.09, exp.grade = 3
$$= 4x^3+2x^2+2x-3x^2-3x-3$$
prob.incorrect = 0.82, exp.grade = 2
$$= 4x^3-x^2-x-3$$
prob.incorrect = 0.99, exp.grade = 2

(b) A sample feedback generation process where the learner makes an error in the expression in Line 3 while attempting to solve Question 2.

Figure 6: Demonstration of real-time feedback generation by MLP-B while learners enter their solutions. After each expression, we compute both the probability that the learner's solution belongs to a cluster that does not have full credit and the learner's expected grade. An alert is generated when the expected credit is less than full credit.

There are several avenues for continued research. We are currently planning more extensive experiments on the edX platform involving tens of thousands of learners. We are also planning to extend the feature extraction step to take into account both the ordering of expressions and ancillary text in a solution. Clustering algorithms that allow a solution to belong to more than one cluster could make MLP more robust to outlier solutions and further reduce the number of solutions that the instructors need to grade. Finally, it would be interesting to explore how the features of solutions could be used to build predictive models, as in the Rasch model [27] or item response theory [18].

APPENDIX: QUESTION STATEMENTS

Question 1: Multiply
$$(x^2+x+\sin^2 x+\cos^2 x)(2x-3)$$
and simplify your answer as much as possible.

Question 2: Find the derivative of $\dfrac{x^3+\sin(x)}{e^x}$ and simplify your answer as much as possible.

Question 3: A discrete-time linear time-invariant system has the impulse response shown in the figure (omitted). Calculate $H(e^{j\omega})$, the discrete-time Fourier transform of $h[n]$. Simplify your answer as much as possible until it has no summations.

Question 4: Evaluate the following summation
$$\sum_{k=-\infty}^{\infty} \delta[n-k\ x[k-n].$$

Acknowledgments

Thanks to Heather Seeba for administering the data collection process and Christoph Studer for discussions and insights. Visit our website **www.sparfa.com**, where you can learn more about our project and purchase t-shirts and other merchandise.

REFERENCES

1. Attali, Y. Construct validity of e-rater in scoring TOEFL essays. Tech. rep., Educational Testing Service RR-07-21, May 2007.
2. Basu, S., Jacobs, C., and Vanderwende, L. Powergrading: A clustering approach to amplify human effort for short answer grading. *Trans. Association for Computational Linguistics 1* (Oct. 2013), 391–402.
3. Blei, D., Griffiths, T., and Jordan, M. The nested chinese restaurant process and Bayesian nonparametric inference of topic hierarchies. *J. ACM 57*, 2 (Jan. 2010), 7:1–7:30.
4. Blei, D. M., Ng, A. Y., and Jordan, M. I. Latent Drichlet allocation. *J. Machine Learning Research 3* (Jan. 2003), 993–1022.
5. Brooks, M., Basu, S., Jacobs, C., and Vanderwende, L. Divide and correct: Using clusters to grade short answers at scale. In *Proc. 1st ACM Conf. on Learning at Scale* (Mar. 2014), 89–98.
6. Champaign, J., Colvin, K., Liu, A., Fredericks, C., Seaton, D., and Pritchard, D Correlating skill and improvement in 2 MOOCs with a student's time on tasks. In *Proc. 1st ACM Conf. on Learning at Scale* (Mar. 2014), 11–20.
7. Coursera. https://www.coursera.org/, 2014.
8. Cramer, M., Fisseni, B., Koepke, P., Kühlwein, D., Schröder, B., and Veldman, J. The Naproche project – Controlled natural language proof checking of mathematical texts, June 2010.
9. Dijksman, J. A., and Khan, S. Khan Academy: The world's free virtual school. In *APS Meeting Abstracts* (Mar. 2011).
10. edX. https://www.edx.org/, 2014.
11. Frey, B. J., and Dueck, D. Clustering by passing messages between data points. *Science 315*, 5814 (2007), 972–976.
12. Galenson, J., Reames, P., Bodik, R., Hartmann, B., and Sen, K. CodeHint: Dynamic and interactive synthesis of code snippets. In *Proc. 36th Intl. Conf. on Software Engineering* (June 2014), 653–663.
13. Gelman, A., Carlin, J., Stern, H., Dunson, D., Vehtari, A., and Rubin, D. *Bayesian Data Analysis*. CRC Press, 2013.

14. Griffiths, T., and Tenenbaum, J. Hierarchical topic models and the nested chinese restaurant process. *Advances in Neural Information Processing Systems 16* (Dec. 2004), 17–24.

15. Gulwani, S., Radiček, I., and Zuleger, F. Feedback generation for performance problems in introductory programming assignments. In *Proc.22nd ACM SIGSOFT Intl. Symposium on the Foundations of Software Engineering* (Nov. 2014, to appear).

16. Guo, P., and Reinecke, K. Demographic differences in how students navigate through MOOCs. In *Proc. 1st ACM Conf. on Learning at Scale* (Mar. 2014), 21–30.

17. Kang, S., McDermott, K., and Roediger III, H. Test format and corrective feedback modify the effect of testing on long-term retention. *European J. Cognitive Psychology 19*, 4-5 (July 2007), 528–558.

18. Lord, F. *Applications of Item Response Theory to Practical Testing Problems*. Erlbaum Associates, 1980.

19. Megill, N. *Metamath: A computer language for pure mathematics*. Citeseer, 1997.

20. Minka, T. Estimating a Drichlet distribution. Tech. rep., MIT, Nov. 2000.

21. Naumowicz, A., and Korniłowicz, A. A brief overview of MIZAR. In *Theorem Proving in Higher Order Logics*, vol. 5674 of *Lecture Notes in Computer Science*. Aug. 2009, 67–72.

22. Ng, A., Jordan, M., and Weiss, Y. On spectral clustering: Analysis and an algorithm. *Advances in Neural Information Processing Systems 2* (Dec. 2002), 849–856.

23. Nguyen, A., Piech, C., Huang, J., and Guibas, L. Codewebs: Scalable homework search for massive open online programming courses. In *Proc. 23rd Intl. World Wide Web Conference* (Seoul, Korea, Apr. 2014), 491–502.

24. OpenStaxTutor. https://openstaxtutor.org/, 2013.

25. Piech, C., Huang, J., Chen, Z., Do, C., Ng, A., and Koller, D. Tuned models of peer assessment in MOOCs. In *Proc. 6th Intl. Conf. on Educational Data Mining* (July 2013), 153–160.

26. Raman, K., and Joachims, T. Methods for ordinal peer grading. In *Proc. 20th ACM SIGKDD Intl. Conf. on Knowledge Discovery and Data Mining* (Aug. 2014), 1037–1046.

27. Rasch, G. *Probabilistic Models for Some Intelligence and Attainment Tests*. MESA Press, 1993.

28. Rivers, K., and Koedinger, K. A canonicalizing model for building programming tutors. In *Proc. 11th Intl. Conf. on Intelligent Tutoring Systems* (June 2012), 591–593.

29. Rivers, K., and Koedinger, K. Automating hint generation with solution space path construction. In *Proc. 12th Intl. Conf. on Intelligent Tutoring Systems* (June 2014), 329–339.

30. Sadler, P., and Good, E. The impact of self-and peer-grading on student learning. *Educational Assessment 11*, 1 (June 2006), 1–31.

31. Sapling Learning. http://www.saplinglearning.com/, 2014.

32. Singh, R., Gulwani, S., and Solar-Lezama, A. Automated feedback generation for introductory programming assignments. In *Proc. 34th ACM SIGPLAN Conf. on Programming Language Design and Implementation*, vol. 48 (June 2013), 15–26.

33. Southavilay, V., Yacef, K., Reimann, P., and Calvo, R. Analysis of collaborative writing processes using revision maps and probabilistic topic models. In *Proc. 3rd Intl. Conf. on Learning Analytics and Knowledge* (Apr. 2013), 38–47.

34. Srikant, S., and Aggarwal, V. A system to grade computer programming skills using machine learning. In *Proc. 20th ACM SIGKDD Intl. Conf. on Knowledge Discovery and Data Mining* (Aug. 2014), 1887–1896.

35. Steyvers, M., and Griffiths, T. Probabilistic topic models. *Handbook of Latent Semantic Analysis 427*, 7 (2007), 424–440.

36. SymPy Development Team. Sympy: Python library for symbolic mathematics, 2014. http://www.sympy.org.

37. Teh, Y. Drichlet process. In *Encyclopedia of Machine Learning*. Springer, 2010, 280–287.

38. Vats, D., Studer, C., Lan, A. S., Carin, L., and Baraniuk, R. G. Test size reduction for concept estimation. In *Proc. 6th Intl. Conf. on Educational Data Mining* (July 2013), 292–295.

39. Waters, A., Fronczyk, K., Guindani, M., Baraniuk, R., and Vannucci, M. A Bayesian nonparametric approach for the analysis of multiple categorical item responses. *J. Statistical Planning and Inference* (2014, In press).

40. WebAssign. https://webassign.com/, 2014.

41. West, M. Hyperparameter estimation in Drichlet process mixture models. Tech. rep., Duke University, 1992.

42. Wilkowski, J., Deutsch, A., and Russell, D. Student skill and goal achievement in the mapping with Google MOOC. In *Proc. 1st ACM Conf. on Learning at Scale* (Mar. 2014), 3–10.

43. Woolf, B. P. *Building Intelligent Interactive Tutors: Student-centered Strategies for Revolutionizing E-learning*. Morgan Kaufman Publishers, 2008.

44. Yin, J., and Wang, J. A Drichlet multinomial mixture model-based approach for short text clustering. In *Proc. 20th ACM SIGKDD Intl. Conf. on Knowledge Discovery and Data Mining* (Aug. 2014), 233–242.

BayesRank: A Bayesian Approach to Ranked Peer Grading

Andrew E. Waters[1], **David Tinapple**[2], **and Richard G. Baraniuk**[1]
[1] Rice University, Houston, TX
[2] Arizona State University, Tempe, AZ
[1] Houston, TX 77005, [2] Tempe, AZ 85281
{andrew.e.waters@rice.edu, dtinapple@asu.edu, richb@rice.edu}

ABSTRACT

Advances in online and computer supported education afford exciting opportunities to revolutionize the classroom, while also presenting a number of new challenges not faced in traditional educational settings. Foremost among these challenges is the problem of accurately and efficiently evaluating learner work as the class size grows, which is directly related to the larger goal of providing quality, timely, and actionable formative feedback. Recently there has been a surge in interest in using peer grading methods coupled with machine learning to accurately and fairly evaluate learner work while alleviating the instructor bottleneck and grading overload. Prior work in peer grading almost exclusively focuses on numerically scored grades – either real-valued or ordinal. In this work, we consider the implications of *peer ranking* in which learners rank a small subset of peer work from strongest to weakest, and propose new types of computational analyses that can be applied to this ranking data. We adopt a Bayesian approach to the ranked peer grading problem and develop a novel model and method for utilizing ranked peer-grading data. We additionally develop a novel procedure for adaptively identifying which work should be ranked by particular peers in order to dynamically resolve ambiguity in the data and rapidly resolve a clearer picture of learner performance. We showcase our results on both synthetic and several real-world educational datasets.

Author Keywords

Automatic grading; peer grading; Bayesian methods; rank aggregation; adaptive recommender systems

INTRODUCTION

In the shifting landscape of higher education we are seeing advances in online and hybrid forms of teaching and learning. From the flipped classroom to the MOOC, these new formats present opportunities to provide not only high quality online courses to larger and larger numbers of students, but also more engaging classroom experiences for 21st century learners.

L@S'15, March 14–15, 2015, Vancouver, BC, Canada.

http://dx.doi.org/10.1145/2724660.2724672

A common challenge in these experimental formats is how to meaningfully evaluate student work. The traditional method of having the instructor evaluate and grade or score each work is increasingly untenable. In the case of the large classroom or the online MOOC, having an instructor or team grade by hand creates an enormous workload bottleneck, leading to delayed and/or inadequate feedback. Even when the grading workload can be distributed among teams of assistants, the central experience for the student is the same – a single centralized expert makes an often rapid and subjective judgement on the work, returning a grade and, at best, some qualitative feedback.

Two common approaches to overcoming the traditional grading bottleneck are machine automation and peer grading. In machine automation, software is used, most typically to determine right and wrong answers on a test. Often these methods focus on easy-to-grade question formats such as multiple choice or true/false. Increasingly, these techniques rely on natural language processing [20] to assess or estimate the quality of essays or answers. In peer grading, by contrast, the assessment is "crowdsourced" to the group itself, usually by providing a rubric or scoring guide to students and asking them to evaluate one or more peer works, giving one or more ratings to the work. In addition to being useful in efficiently evaluating student work, it has been in several educational contexts the act of *giving* peer feedback is at least as beneficial to the giver to the receiver of the feedback [12].

While many peer review systems allow for direct written feedback from peers, they often utilize a rating system as the primary mode of evaluation. Even with a clearly communicated rubric or guide provided to raters, the ratings can vary greatly from reviewer to reviewer creating significant noise in the overall rating data. One way to combat the problem of rater reliability is to calibrate the raters themselves using a carefully created demonstration assignment. Raters responses to this example content are then used to evaluate the quality of the raters themselves. While this form of calibrated peer review (CPR) has been shown to be effective [10], it does require the creation of sample assignments and detailed multi-question rubrics for each new type of assignment. In a larger sense, CPR assumes that a students conformity to the right answers provided by the instructors determines their value as reviewers. Many kinds of creative work, however, can be viewed and reviewed from multiple valid viewpoints, which may serve as the primary value of using peer review in the classroom.

An alternative to traditional peer grading in which graders rate items on a numerical [14] or ordinal scales [8] is to use *ranked* peer grading [18]. In this approach, graders rank the quality of a small number of items in order from best to worst. While reviewers are often less comfortable providing a ranked assessments of items [9, 5], ranked approaches have been shown to often yield significantly more reliable data with much higher discriminative power than rating data [2]. Given a set of potentially partially observed ranked data from a set of graders on a set of items, the goal of the ranked peer grading problem is to assess the quality of each item relative to all others.

Prior Work

There has been considerable prior work in the field of rank aggregation, an excellent summary of which is available in [16]. These methods include the Mallows method (MAL [13]) which places a probabilistic distribution over a set of observed rankings given a ground truth ranking. It can be shown that using the Kendall's-τ distance metric that computation can be carried out quickly for the MAL method, allowing one to find a maximum likelihood estimate of the global rankings from a set of partially observed rankings. An augmentation of the MAL method is the score-based Mallows method (MALS, [16]) which estimates pairwise distances between item to improve the overall robustness of the inference. Another important method is the Plackett-Luce (PL) model introduced in [15], which is in turn a generalization of the Bradley-Terry method [3]. This model has the advantage of being convex and can be solved quickly using optimization techniques.

There are three important limitations in the prior rank aggregation and ranked peer grading literature. First, these methods rely on maximum likelihood estimation and output a singular point estimate of the true ranking of all items. While this is useful, it is generally difficult to assess the *reliability* of the estimate provided. This reliability information can be extremely useful to course instructors when assigning grades or to learners who wish to understand the quality of their work relative the rest of the class. Second, these methods do not explicitly model the reliability of the graders themselves, but rather focus exclusively on finding a ranking of the items that makes sense given the ranked data. Not all graders in a course are equally reliable, and by modeling grader reliability explicitly one can improve the overall inference quality while additionally relaying this reliability information to course instructors. Third, these methods typically assume a random assignment of items to graders which, especially in the case of ranked peer grading, fails to take capitalize on the ability of graders to distinguish between closely related items. This, in turn, leads to suboptimal inference of item quality.

Contributions

In this paper we develop the *BayesRank* model and method for overcoming the limitations of prior work in rank aggregation and ranked peer grading. Concretely, we make the following three contributions:

- We develop a novel Bayesian model for partially observed ranked data. This Bayesian model has the advantage of explicitly modeling reliability of each grader in addition to the intrinsic quality of each item.
- We develop a novel Markov-Chain Monte Carlo (MCMC) method for fitting the BayesRank model to partially observed ranking data. This MCMC method has the advantage of providing not only inference for all model parameters of interest but also reliability estimates for those parameters.
- We develop a novel procedure for adaptively selecting a set of items to present to a grader in order to reduce our uncertainty about item quality. We will demonstrate that this method can provide great improvements over the standard practice of assigning items to graders randomly.

THE BAYESRANK MODEL FOR RANKED PEER GRADING

We now detail the BayesRank generative model for partially observed ranked data. We assume throughout this work that we are given ranked peer grading data consisting of I items being ranked by G graders. We further assume that each grader only ranks a small subset $K \ll I$ items. Let $\Omega^g \in \{1, \ldots, I\}^K$ denote the indices of the items ranked by grader g. We are ultimately interested in determining the *quality* of each item as well as the *reliability* of each grader in a given dataset.

We model each item $i \in \{1, \ldots, I\}$ item as possessing an underlying latent quality score $s_i \in \mathbb{R}$, where items that have higher scores are said to have higher quality. We model grader g as observing a noisy version of the true score $s_i, \forall i \in \Omega^g$. Let $\mathbf{z}^g$ denote a random vector of observed item qualities observed by grader g, with z_i^g denoting the observation for item i. We model $z_i^g \sim \mathcal{N}(s_i, \sigma_g^2)$, where $\mathcal{N}(s_i, \sigma_g^2)$ denotes the standard normal distribution with mean s_i and grader-specific noise variance σ_g^2 that determines how accurately grader g observes the true score s_i. Graders with lower σ_g^2 are said to be more reliable than graders with higher σ_g^2. Grader g then returns a ranked set of indices according to the observations z_i^g. Let $\mathcal{T}_{(j)}[\mathbf{z}]$ denote the index of the jth largest index of $\mathbf{z}$. Then, grader g returns the rankings $\mathbf{r}^g = [r_1^g, r_2^g, \ldots, r_K^g] = [\mathcal{T}_{(1)}[\mathbf{z}^g], \mathcal{T}_{(2)}[\mathbf{z}^g], \ldots, \mathcal{T}_{(K)}[\mathbf{z}^g]]$. As we take a Bayesian approach to our model, all that remains is to specify appropriate prior distributions for all parameters of interest. For this we choose standard prior distributions typically used in Bayesian literature. We formally write our model as:

$$\begin{aligned} s_i &\sim \mathcal{N}(0, \sigma_I^2), \\ \Omega^g &\propto 1, \\ \sigma_g^2 &\sim \mathcal{IG}(\alpha, \beta), \\ z_i^g &\sim \mathcal{N}(s_i, \sigma_g^2), \\ \mathbf{r}^g &= \left[\mathcal{T}_{(1)}[\mathbf{z}^g], \mathcal{T}_{(2)}[\mathbf{z}^g], \ldots, \mathcal{T}_{(K)}[\mathbf{z}^g]\right] \end{aligned} \quad (1)$$

where $\mathcal{IG}(\alpha, \beta)$ denotes the inverse-gamma distribution with shape parameter α and scale parameter β, and where σ_I^2, α, and β are tunable hyperparameters. We dub our generative

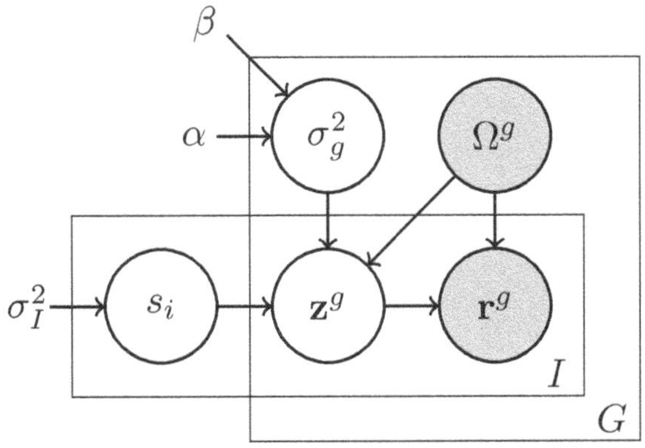

Figure 1: Graphical model for the generative BayesRank model

model BayesRank and display this model graphically in Figure 1.

We note that the BayesRank model is not strictly identifiable. As a concrete example, a set of scores $\{s_i\}$ and $\{s_i + \delta\}$ will achieve the same data likelihood. Similarly we can inversely scale the grader variance and latent score variance by any constant $a > 0$ while maintaining the same data likelihood. Consistent with prior art in Bayesian literature, we rely on our choice of prior and hyperparameters to circumvent these issues [8].

INFERENCE METHOD

Given a set of observations $\{r_k^g\}$ for $k = 1, \ldots, K$ and $g = 1, \ldots, G$, we wish to infer the latent parameters of the BayesRank model (1). There are many methods available for doing this, including expectation-maximization and variational Bayesian approaches. In this work we will use a MCMC technique [6] which is simple to implement, efficient, and provides rich posterior information for all of the model parameters of interest. This posterior information provides a wealth of statistical information unavailable under many other methods and enable us to assert not only an estimate for each model parameter but also the degree of confidence that we can assert for these parameter estimates. This posterior information can be used by course instructors to evaluate the strength of a given item or the reliability of a particular grader relative to other items and graders in the course.

Our MCMC approach is based on the Gibbs sampler [7] and estimates the posterior distributions of s_i and σ_g^2 for $i = 1 \ldots I$ and $g = 1 \ldots G$. We can considerably simplify our inference by using data augmentation [1] and additionally sampling the noisy latent observations z_i^g. Our method proceeds by sequentially sampling each random variable of interest conditioned on all other latent variables in the model. It can be shown that for our method these distributions are given by:

$$z_{r_k}^g|\cdot \sim \mathcal{N}^+(s_{r_k}, \sigma_u^2; z_{r_k-1}^g, z_{r_k+1}^g), (k,g) \in \Omega^g,$$

$$s_i|\cdot \sim \mathcal{N}(\widehat{\mu}, \widehat{\sigma}^2), i \in \{1, \ldots, I\}$$

$$\sigma_g^2|\cdot \sim \mathcal{IG}(\widehat{\alpha}, \widehat{\beta}), g \in \{1, \ldots, G\}$$

where $\widehat{\sigma}^2 = 1/\sigma_I^2 + \sum_{g:i\in\Omega^g} \in (1/\sigma_g^2)$, $\widehat{\mu} = \sum_{g:i\in\Omega^g} \frac{z_i^g}{\sigma_g^2}$, $\widehat{\alpha} = \alpha + K$, and $\widehat{\beta} = \beta + \sum_{i:i\in\Omega^g} \frac{1}{z_i^g}$. The notation $\mathcal{N}^+(\mu, \sigma^2; a, b)$ denotes a normal distribution with mean μ and variance σ^2 truncated below at a and truncated above at b. This distribution results from the ordering constraint imposed by the observations $\mathbf{r}^g$. We adopt the convention that $z_0 = -\infty$ and $z_{K+1} = \infty$, consistent with our initial modeling assumption $s_i \in \mathbb{R}$.

POST PROCESSING

After sufficient burn-in, the MCMC produces samples drawn approximately from the true posterior distribution of each parameter of interest conditioned on the data in $\{r_k^g\}$. We can obtain simple estimates of the latent score quality $\widehat{s}_i$ and grader reliability $\widehat{\sigma}_g$ via simple posterior averaging. Additionally, we can produce a global ranking of the items at each iteration of the MCMC which can be used to evaluate the rank stability of each item relative to all other items in the dataset.

ADAPTIVELY SELECTING ITEMS TO RANK

In formulating the BayesRank model in (1) we assumed explicitly that graders were assigned items uniformly and independently, consistent with the implementation of most peer grading systems. However, we can hope to do better than a purely random assignment strategy in practice. First, some learners in a class may choose not complete their ranked grading assignment. In this scenario, there may be a variable number of rankings for each item, which can lead to the scoring of certain items being more reliable than others. Second, a ranking of a randomly selected set of items may provide very little information to a rank aggregation algorithm. As a concrete example, the quality difference between the best and worst item in a dataset may be quite stark. Repeatedly asking graders to compare these two items yields little useful information since there will be little to no diversity in the rankings provided by multiple graders.

A more powerful approach than random assignment is to assign the items to graders adaptively. Such an adaptive assignment has the potential to capitalize on the ability of a grader to resolve ambiguous items. Furthermore, this approach is entirely feasible in many a practical grading scenarios. A specific example of such a scenario is when graders have some time frame (e.g., one week) to log into a computer-based system to receive and rank a set of items. In this scenario, we can use knowledge obtained from the last $g-1$ graders to adaptively select items for grader g to rank.

Our selection strategy is based on selecting the items for grader g that maximize the entropy [4] of the ranking that grader g will provide. Given a set of K items we can have $K!$ potential rankings. Let $\mathcal{I}$ denote the current set of items and let $\mathbf{s}_\mathcal{I}$ denote the random variable of the latent quality scores over the items contained in $\mathcal{I}$. Now let $\mathbf{r}_\mathcal{I}^j$, $j \in \{1, \ldots, K!\}$ denote one of the possible ranking permutations over the set

$\mathcal{I}$. The entropy of the ranking is then given by

$$H(\mathbf{r}_\mathcal{I}|\mathbf{s}_\mathcal{I}) = \sum_{j=1}^{K!} p(\mathbf{r}_\mathcal{I}^j) \log \left(p(\mathbf{r}_\mathcal{I}^j) \right). \quad (2)$$

We then find the entropy-maximizing set $\widetilde{\mathcal{I}}$ by solving the following optimization problem

$$\widetilde{\mathcal{I}} = \arg \max_{\mathcal{I}, |\mathcal{I}|=K} \mathcal{H}(\mathbf{r}_\mathcal{I}|\mathbf{s}_\mathcal{I}). \quad (3)$$

This optimization problem, however, is intractable in most practical scenarios for two reasons. First, in the case of I items, we would be required to search over all $\binom{I}{K}$ sets. Second, evaluating the rank-entopy in (2) itself requires computation on a $K+1$-dimensional normal cumulative distribution function for which there is no closed form solution. Using full posterior information on $\mathbf{s}_\mathcal{I}$ renders this computation even more complicated.

We propose two simple approximations that enable us to find a tractable approximation to the optimization problem (3) given our MCMC inference method. First, we will use the posterior mean $\widehat{\mathbf{s}}$ rather than full posterior information when calculating the entropy. Thus, $H(\mathbf{r}_\mathcal{I}|\mathbf{s}_\mathcal{I}) \approx H(\mathbf{r}_\mathcal{I}|\widehat{\mathbf{s}}_\mathcal{I})$. Second, we note that it is simple to construct the entropy maximizing set $\mathcal{I}$ for each element item i by searching for the $K-1$ nearest neighbors of item i whose quality scores s_j are closest to s_i. Once this is computed for each item, we choose the item (and neighbors) the minimize the overall square distance. We display the steps of this procedure in Algorithm 1.

Algorithm 1: Finding the approximate rank-entropy maximizing set

Data: Item quality means $\widehat{s}_i, i = \{1, \ldots, I\}$, Set cardinality K
Result: Approximate rank-entropy maximizing set $\mathcal{I}$
Compute pairwise distance matrix $\mathbf{D}$, s.t. $D_{ij} = (\widehat{s}_i - \widehat{s}_j)^2$
for $i \leftarrow 1$ **to** I **do**
  $\mathcal{I}_i' = [i, \mathcal{T}_{(2)}[D_i], \ldots, \mathcal{T}_{(K)}[D_i]]$;
  $d_i = \sum_{k=1}^{K} D_{i,\mathcal{T}_{(k)}[D_i]}$
end
$\widehat{i} = \arg\min d_i$;
$\mathcal{I} = \mathcal{I}_{\widehat{i}}$

For practical purposes, we would initialize our beliefs about the item scores to 0 for all items, which would initially cause our adaptively selection strategy to behave similarly to a randomized selection strategy. As ranked comparisons begin to be made, however, and the MCMC inference method begins to infer the quality scores for the individual items, the adaptive procedure of Algorithm 1 will begin to start assigning items to graders that it believes are close together and use the grader rankings to better resolve those items.

EXPERIMENTS

Here we characterize the BayesRank model and method using both synthetic and real-world data experiments.

Synthetic Data

We first examine the performance of BayesRank on synthetic data generated according to the model described in (1) under a variety of problem configurations. We will compare our results to the known ground truth item ordering using Kendall's-τ metric, which examines the general agreement between two ordered sets of items of size I. For any two orderings σ and $\widetilde{\sigma}$, Kendall's-τ is defined by:

$$D_\tau(\sigma, \widetilde{\sigma}) = \frac{1}{\frac{1}{2}I(I-1)} \sum_{i,j} \text{sgn}(\sigma_i - \sigma_j) * \text{sgn}(\widetilde{\sigma}_i - \widetilde{\sigma}_j),$$

where $\text{sgn}(\cdot)$ denotes the signum function. In words, Kendall's-τ looks at each pair in one ranking and compares the same items in the second ranking to check for consistency. We note that $-1 \leq D_\tau \leq 1$, with the case $D_\tau = 1$ corresponding to perfect agreement between σ and $\widetilde{\sigma}$, the case $D_\tau = -1$ corresponding to perfect disagreement between σ and $\widetilde{\sigma}$, and the case $D_\tau = 0$ corresponding to no correlation between σ and $\widetilde{\sigma}$.

In each synthetic experiment we will compare BayesRank using both adaptive and non-adaptive item assignment. Random assignment is done to ensure that all items receive the same number of rankings. For the adaptive scenario we employ an additional constraint that only the items with the fewest number of rankings be considered for assignment in order to keep the total number of rankings per item equal, consistent with both the randomized approach and what would be done in a real classroom scenario.

We first look at performance as the problem size increases. We assume here that $G = I = N$ and sweep $N \in \{10, 30, 50, 100\}$. We set $K = 5$, $\sigma_I = 10$, and $\alpha = \beta = 5$ in all experiments. We repeat each configuration over 50 randomized trials and plot the average performance with error bars in Figure 2(a). We see that both methods degrade gracefully as the class size grows, but note that the adaptive item assessment considerably mitigates this effect, achieving superior performance over all class sizes.

We next examine the performance of BayesRank as the number of peer rankings, K, varies. We assume a single problem size of $G = I = 50$ with $\sigma_I = 10$ and $\alpha = \beta = 5$ and sweep $K \in \{2, 3, 5, 10\}$. We again repeat each configuration over 50 randomized trials and display our results in 2(b). As expected, performance improves as the number of peer rankings grows. Importantly, we note that performance begins to level off at around $K = 5$, meaning that we can achieve good performance with a very reasonable number of rankings that is not burdensome to learners. As before, the adaptive item selection strategy outperforms the random selection strategy.

We further examine performance as we vary the grader reliability. We again assume a problem size of $G = I = 50$ with $K = 5$ ratings per grader and with $\sigma_I = 10$. We set $\alpha = \beta$ and sweep $\alpha \in \{1, 5, 10\}$. Note that all cases correspond to

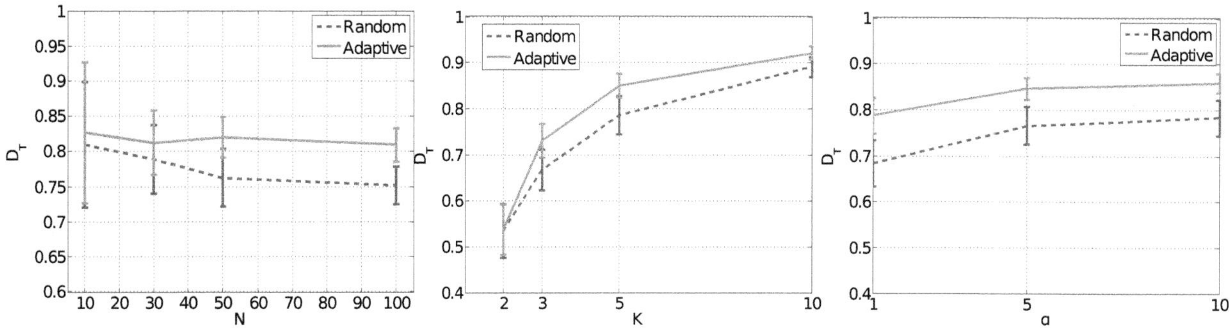

(a) D_τ vs. N (b) D_τ vs. K (c) D_τ vs. α

Figure 2: BayesRank synthetic experiments using both random and adaptive item assignment. a) D_τ as a function of the class size N, b) D_τ as a function of the number of items K ranked by each grader, c) D_τ as a function of the grader reliability parameter α.

Table 1: D_τ for various rank aggregation techniques for all four class projects. Size is measured as $G \times I$. BayesRank wins across all datasets.

Dataset	Size	BayesRank	Rank Avg	MAL	MALS	PL
Proj. 1	47×56	**0.2971**	0.2468	0.2390	0.2948	0.2779
Proj. 2	57×60	**0.4463**	0.4328	0.4034	0.4362	0.4413
Proj. 3	48×60	**0.4373**	0.3243	0.3096	0.4011	0.4153
Proj. 4	46×53	**0.4441**	0.4122	0.3570	0.4412	0.4354

an expected grader variance of 1 but that we have less prior variance as α increases. Higher values of α correspond to the case of less variability in the graders. We repeat each configuration over 100 trials and display our results in 2(c). As expected, performance improves as grader reliability improves. The adaptive selection strategy again outperforms the random selection strategy.

Real-World Educational Data

We now present the results of the analysis of a classroom of 60 learners in a computer programming class taught at Arizona State University. A part of this class consisted in learners completing four projects that were subsequently evaluated via ranked peer grading by other learners in the course. During the peer grading phase, each learner who completed their project was then asked to rank 5 other projects. Not all learners in the course completed every project, nor did all learners who completed their project complete their assigned peer grading task. Thus, for these datasets $G \neq I$ and not every item received the same number of rankings. The ranked peer grader data was collected using the CritViz peer review system [19].

In addition to the ranking scores provided by peer graders, the course instructor and assistants also assigned numerical quality scores to each project on a (non-integer) scale of 0—3. This additional numerical scores provide us a ground truth that can be used for comparison — by sorting the numerical grades in order we can compare the ranking estimated by BayesRank to the ground truth under the Kendall's-τ metric.

We compare BayesRank against four other rank aggregation models: Rank Averaging (in which the final score is simply the average of the ranks given to each item), MAL, MALS, and PL. Our results are displayed in Table 1, where we see that the BayesRank method achieves superior performance for all projects under consideration. To put these results in perspective, recall that the Kendall's-τ metric counts the number of ranking agreements between two sets of I items (a total of $I(I-1)$ comparisons). For many of our datasets, the global improvement is relatively small. As an example, the improvement in BayesRank over MALS for Project 1 is only 7 rankings. For Project 3, however, the improvement of BayesRank over MALS is much larger with 76 additional rankings matching the ground truth.

As discussed previously, our method enables us to make useful inference not only about the final quality of each project but also how reliably we can make such assertions. We compute this reliability information for each project by computing the ranking of each item at each iteration of the MCMC. We examine the statistics of these rankings in Figure 3. Here we have sorted the items in order by their average ranking (denoted by the black dot). We additionally show a 50% Bayesian credible interval as a blue bar showing which rankings are most likely for each item. We note that there is quite a bit of certainty for objects with very high and very low ranking, while there is considerable variation for item in the middle rankings.

Finally we show histograms for posterior mean grader reliability parameters σ_g^2 for all graders and each project in Figure 4. Here we find that most graders are highly reliable, with a small number being less reliable. As discussed previously, an advantage of the BayesRank approach is that the rankings

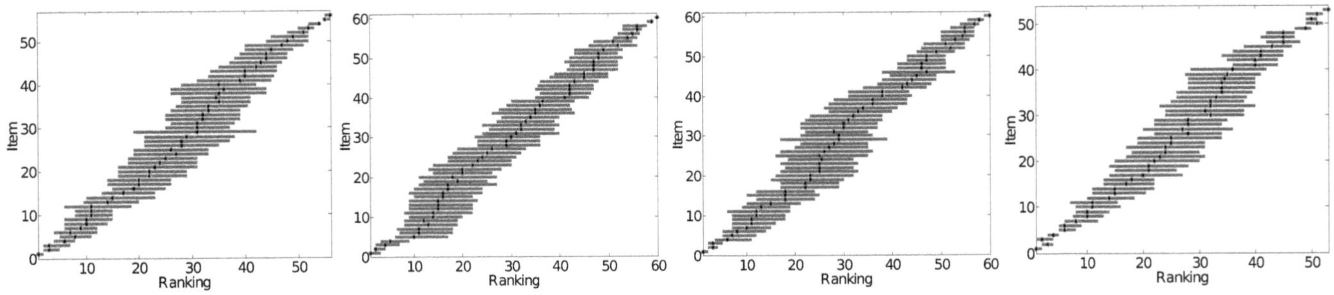

(a) Project 1 (b) Project 2 (c) Project 3 (d) Project 4

Figure 3: Item ranking credible intervals all four projects. Items are sorted in order of decreasing rank, with rank 1 corresponding to the highest quality project. The credible is small for high-tier and bottom-tier items, with larger variance for mid-tier items.

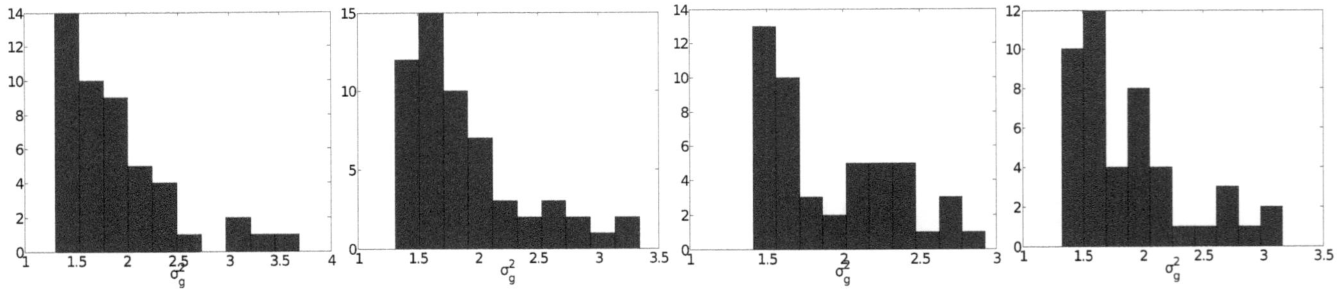

(a) Project 1 (b) Project 2 (c) Project 3 (d) Project 4

Figure 4: Histogram of average grader reliability σ_g^2 for each grader across all projects. Most graders are highly reliable, but a small number of graders are less reliable. The BayesRank model naturally uses this information to better assess the quality of all items.

from the less-reliable graders are naturally de-weighted when determining the latent item quality parameters.

CONCLUSIONS

Peer grading is a valuable tool for alleviating instructor workload in large courses while maintaining a fair standard of grading. We have developed the BayesRank model and method for ranked peer grading data which jointly infers the quality of student as well as the reliability of each peer grader. Additionally, we have developed a simple method for adaptively recommending items to graders that improves the overall reliability of the ranked peer grading method.

Our findings point toward several exciting directions for future work. First is determining the optimal number of items to be graded in a single ranking session. The optimal number is a practical question and must balance not only the needs of the model but also the cognitive limits of human graders. Ranking too many items might easily lead to sloppy ranking and, thus, bad data.

Next, we will pilot a study of an adaptive peer review assignment strategy in which during the review period, reviewers are assigned to look at specific clusters of work rather than randomized selections. Our work here points towards the possibility of greatly increasing the effectiveness of reviews by using reviewers to tease out the subtle differences between closely ranked works. In addition, we seek to understand how students would respond to such a system.

Similarly, the instructors can be asked to perform a small number of timely and carefully selected reviews that might serve as a real-time calibration, improving overall estimation not only by direct exposure to instructor review but by anchoring the entire network of review activity. Additionally, the model for item quality considered in this work is single dimensional with every item is modeled by a single quality parameter. Extensions to the multi-dimensional case [11, 17], where graders are asked to evaluate over multiple criteria, is a yet unexplored area. Finally, there may be useful ways to blend ranking and rating, fusing both ranked (comparing works) and numerically rated (isolated works) grading data, allowing for a balance between these two distinct cognitive activities.

Acknowledgments

The authors would like to thank Pavan Turaga and Mr. Lan for many helpful discussions regarding this work. This research was supported in part by NSF grant # 1431856.

REFERENCES

1. Albert, J. H., and Chib, S. Bayesian analysis of binary and polychotomous response data. *Journal of the American Statistical Association 88*, 422 (1993), 669–679.
2. Bass, B. M., and Avolio, B. J. Potential biases in leadership measures: How prototypes, leniency, and general satisfaction relate to ratings and rankings of transformational and transactional leadership constructs. *Educational and Psychological Measurement 49*, 3 (1989), 509–527.
3. Bradley, R. A., and Terry, M. E. Rank analysis of incomplete block designs: I: The method of paired comparisons. *Biometrika* (1952), 324–345.
4. Cover, T. M., and Thomas, J. A. *Elements of information theory*. John Wiley & Sons, 2012.
5. Elig, T. W., and Frieze, I. H. Measuring causal attibutions for success and failure. *Journal of Personality and Social Psychology 37*, 4 (1979), 621.
6. Gelman, A., Carlin, J., Stern, H., Dunson, D., Vehtari, A., and Rubin, D. *Bayesian Data Analysis*. CRC press, 2013.
7. Hoff, P. D. *A First Course in Bayesian Statistical Methods*. Springer, 2009.
8. Johnson, V. E., and Albert, J. H. *Ordinal Data Modeling*. Springer, 1999.
9. Krosnick, J. A. Survey research. *Annual review of psychology 50*, 1 (1999), 537–567.
10. Kulkarni, C., Wei, K. P., Le, H., Chia, D., Papadopoulos, K., Cheng, J., Koller, D., and Klemmer, S. R. Peer and self assessment in massive online classes. *ACM Transactions on Computer-Human Interaction (TOCHI) 20*, 6 (2013), 33.
11. Lan, A. S., Waters, A. E., Studer, C., and Baraniuk, R. G. Sparse factor analysis for learning and content analytics. *J. Machine Learning Research 15* (June 2014), 1959–2008.
12. Lundstrom, K., and Baker, W. To give is better than to receive: The benefits of peer review to the reviewer's own writing. *Journal of Second Language Writing 18*, 1 (2009), 30–43.
13. Mallows, C. L. Non-null ranking models. i. *Biometrika* (1957), 114–130.
14. Piech, C., Huang, J., Chen, Z., Do, C., Ng, A., and Koller, D. Tuned models of peer assessment in MOOCs. *arXiv preprint arXiv:1307.2579* (2013).
15. Plackett, R. L. The analysis of permutations. *Applied Statistics* (1975), 193–202.
16. Raman, K., and Joachims, T. Methods for ordinal peer grading. *arXiv preprint arXiv:1404.3656* (2014).
17. Reckase, M. D. *Multidimensional Item Response Theory*. Springer, 2009.
18. Shah, N. B., Bradley, J. K., Parekh, A., Wainwright, M., and Ramchandran, K. A case for ordinal peer-evaluation in MOOCs. In *NIPS Workshop on Data Driven Education* (2013).
19. Tinapple, D. *The CritViz Peer Review System*, 2014 (accessed October 21, 2014). `http://critviz.com/`.
20. Xiong, W., Litman, D., and Schunn, C. Improving research on and instructional quality of peer feedback through natural language processing. *Journal of Writing Research 4*, 2 (2012), 155–176.

Staggered Versus All-At-Once Content Release in Massive Open Online Courses: Evaluating a Natural Experiment

Tommy Mullaney
Harvard University
tmullaney@post.harvard.edu

Justin Reich
Harvard University
bjr795@mail.harvard.edu

ABSTRACT
We report on an experiment testing the effects of releasing all of the content in a Massive Open Online Course (MOOC) at launch versus in a staggered release. In 2013, HarvardX offered two "runs" of the *HeroesX* course: In the first, content was released weekly over four months; in the second, all content was released at once. We develop three operationalizations of "ontrackness" to measure how students participated in sync with the recommended syllabus. Ontrackness in both versions was low, though in the second, mean ontrackness was approximately one-half of levels in the first HeroesX. We find few differences in persistence, participation, and completion between the two runs. Controlling for a students' number of active weeks, we estimate modest positive effects of ontrackness on certification. The revealed preferences of students for flexibility and the minimal benefits of ontrackness suggest that releasing content all at once may be a viable strategy for MOOC designers.

Author Keywords
MOOCs; natural experiment; ontrackness; synchronicity

ACM Classification Keywords
K.3.1 Distance Learning.

BACKGROUND AND CONTEXT
One of the distinctive features of open online courses is their asynchronicity. Most credit-bearing courses, whether residential or online, have a registration date, a start date, a drop-date, an end date, and a series of due dates for assignments and exams along the way. These structures create a synchronous cohort of students who proceed through a course at roughly the same pace; "falling behind" in this synchronous regime is considered a warning sign for students. As a result, many learning analytics systems are designed to rapidly identify off-pace students, so they can be remediated [1]. By contrast, many non-credit-bearing online learning environments are totally asynchronous. Students can engage with Khan Academy or MIT's OpenCourseWare at any pace, and these platforms make no efforts to support a synchronous community of learners.

Many of the MOOCs offered on platforms like edX and Coursera walk a middle ground between the tight synchronicity of credit-bearing residential courses and the total asynchronicity of OpenCourseWare. MOOCs have what might be described as "partially asynchronous" structures. They include mechanisms to encourage synchronicity, but without the strict pacing typical of credit-bearing courses. MOOCs have start dates, but students can often also register late without penalty. Some courses have intermediate due dates, but many MOOCs have only a final due date at the end of the course. Some courses sequentially release content every week, which prevents people from racing ahead but allows laggards to catch up. Other courses release all materials at once, a model akin to hosting open courseware with an auto-grading mechanism and a final due date. Some courses use norming mechanisms—such as recommended syllabi and reminder emails—rather than enforcement mechanisms to keep students moving as a cohort. Indeed, Cormier in his original video definition of a MOOC describes such a course as "an event," but one in which students are admonished to "find your own path" [2].

Partially asynchronous MOOCs attempt to balance two competing and worthy goals. On the one hand, instructors try to create a sense of community by encouraging students to progress as a cohort. When students move at the same pace, discussion forums can offer a sense of ongoing dialogue, and course teams can produce "office hours" videos and other media to address common issues raised in a given week. Many programs in computer-supported collaborative learning, where online tools help students learn with and from their peers [11], depend upon nearly synchronous peer interactions. From this perspective, the signature advantage of online learning environments is the ability to leverage peer networks at scale [10].

On the other hand, these time-based structures are not necessary in many MOOCs—especially when computers can automatically assess student work at any time—so some instructors attempt to accommodate learners'

L@S 2015, March 14–18, 2015, Vancouver, BC, Canada.

ACM 978-1-4503-3411-2/15/03…$15.00
http://dx.doi.org/10.1145/2724660.2724663

schedules by offering flexibility in completing the course. From this perspective, the signature advantage of using computers in education is to personalize student learning. In this vision, technologists hope that permitting students to choose their own path and pace will enable them to optimize their individual progress and learning. Early research on course-taking patterns in MOOCs indicates that students often do proceed through courses in non-linear ways, particularly by moving forward to assessments and then backwards to relevant lecture material [4]. Whether exercising this flexibility produces better student learning outcomes remains an open question.

The effects of MOOC course design on community-building or individual flexibility are little understood, in part because of the nature of access to MOOC data. While most MOOCs serve many thousands of students, few researchers have data from more than a dozen courses. Thus, while researchers can conduct rich investigations of individual variation within courses, comparisons between courses are limited by the paucity of public data [6]. For example, Nesterko and colleagues examined the relationship between the use of strict due dates in MOOCs and course completion rates, and they found a modest positive correlation [8]. But the ten courses they examined differed not only by their use of due dates, but also by their enrollment size, subject matter, university affiliation, and many other dimensions. Researchers need data from hundreds of courses to begin drawing reasonable inferences about cross-course differences from naturalistic observation.

While cross-course MOOC research awaits greater university collaboration, one way that researchers can study the impact of course design is by exploiting the methodological opportunities afforded by repeat runs of the same course. In this study, we address several questions about the tradeoffs between community-centered and individual-centered design by taking advantage of a natural experiment conducted in 2013 with the HeroesX course offered by HarvardX on the edX platform. In the first version of the course, the content was released in weekly or semi-weekly bundles over five months between March and August of 2013. In the second version of the course, the content was identical, but it was all released on the course start date in September 2013. From this natural experiment, we can evaluate the impact of one mechanism for enforcing partial asynchronicity—the timed release of content—on student behavior and performance.

Student *ontrackness*, which we define as the degree to which students cohere with the recommended syllabus in a course, is one important dimension of student behavior. A perfectly on-track student will move through the course at exactly the recommended pace, whereas a student with low ontrackness will move at a highly idiosyncratic pace. In Figure 1, we illustrate the wide variation in ontrackness in HeroesX by showing sample pathways of six students who

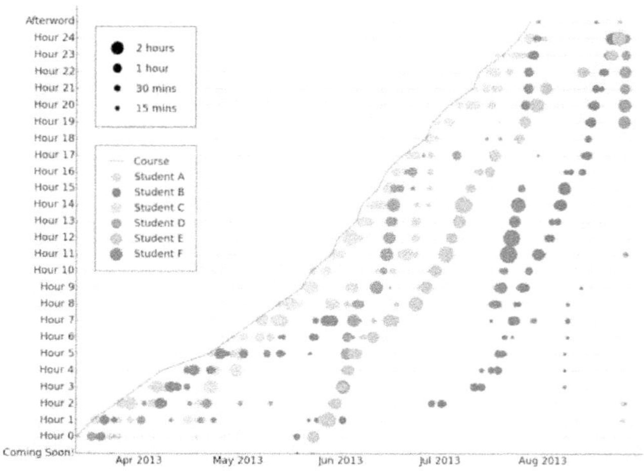

Figure 1: Sample student pathways from HeroesX v1

completed the course and earned a certificate with very different paces. We plot calendar time on the x-axis, and the 27 chapters—high-level organizational units of the course called "Hours"—on the y-axis. Each circle represents a session of time spent in a chapter, and larger circles indicate longer sessions. None of these six students display perfect ontrackness; a student perfectly on-track would have the bulk of their time each week following the grey line that represents the release of content. Student C comes closest: though C has a late start in mid-April, by early May, the student consistently spends time on the most currently released units. By contrast, students A and F both start on-track, but then fall behind. Student A catches up to being on-track towards the end of the course, whereas Student F takes a six week break and then makes a major push to finish. Students B and E both start quite late, remain well behind the release of content, but ultimately finish the course. That six students with very different course-taking patterns all completed the course provides a proof of concept that students with low ontrackness can complete a course, and that when given flexibility in course pacing, at least some students will take advantage. However, there remain open questions as to whether such flexibility is desirable and whether students are more likely to persist, participate, learn, or earn a certificate if the structures of a course encourage or compel students to stay on-track.

To investigate the effect of different content-release paradigms (sequential versus all-at-once) on students' ontrackness, we investigated data from the two versions of HeroesX with two research questions. First, does releasing all content at the beginning of a course lead to more individual variation in student progress and less ontrackness? Second, are these changes consequential? Can we identify benefits to staying on-track in a course even when instructors allow for individual variation in path and pace? In addressing these questions, we propose novel ways to visualize and operationalize ontrackness and asynchronicity in MOOCs.

THE HEROESX NATURAL EXPERIMENT

Since 1978, Professor Gregory Nagy has taught a General Education course at Harvard University on conceptions of the hero in ancient Greek literature. In 2013, Prof. Nagy adapted the most recent version of that course into a MOOC. HeroesX: The Ancient Greek Hero first launched in March of 2013 as the third HarvardX course offered through the edX platform [9]. The goal of the course is to address the question, "What does it mean to be human?" by examining one model of humanity, the ancient Greek hero. The course is designed to invite both novices and committed Hellenic scholars into a community of inquiry exploring the world described by ancient Greek texts.

HeroesX is divided into 24 chapters called "Hours" (corresponding to lecture hours in the residential class), plus two introductory chapters and one concluding chapter. Each Hour includes a package of materials, such as video lectures from Nagy, dramatic readings of ancient texts from students, and discussions among Nagy and course staff. These videos are complemented by readings in two online books. *The Ancient Greek Hero in 24 Hours* guides student learning through the material, and the *Sourcebook of Original Greek Texts Translated into English* includes all 55 primary sources from the course. Each Hour also includes two sets of assessment questions: Content Questions test a student's recall of important features of the texts, and Annotation Exercises evaluate a student's ability to interpret ancient texts. These two sets of multiple-choice assessments have four questions each, amounting to a total of eight questions per Hour. Students must earn a grade of at least 50 percent on these questions to earn a certificate for the course.

Registration for the first version of HeroesX opened on December 19, 2012, and the course opened 83 days later on March 12, 2013. When the course launched, not all of the content was finished, so it was released at a rate of roughly two chapters per week, though delays occasionally meant a week would go by without new content. Regular messages to participants announced the arrival of new content, creating a sense of shared syllabus. All content was available by July 24, 2013, and students were given until August 26, 2013 to complete assignments in consideration of a certificate. While the sequential release of content created a ceiling on how quickly students could progress, no due dates or other structures prevented students from falling behind or enrolling late. A student who registered on the final day of the course could still earn a certificate. When the course finished, 43,563 students had registered, and 1,399 students had earned certificates, yielding a completion rate of 3.2 percent for all registered students.

Even before the completion of the first version (v1) of the course, the HeroesX course team announced plans for a second run (v2). On August 7, 2013, registration opened for HeroesX v2, which launched on September 8, 2013.

	v1	v2 (online)	v2 (college)
Structure			
Start date	March 12, 2013	Sept. 8, 2013	Sept. 8, 2013
End date	8-26-2013	12-8-2013	12-8-2013
Total weeks	20	13	13
Total chapters	27	27	27
Total videos	295	294	294
Total hours of video	34.532	34.585	34.585
Content release	Sequential	All-at-once	All-at-once
Demographics			
Registrants	43,563	22,975	236
Active students	24,905	11,473	236
Median age	30	30	20
Median Education	Bachelors degree	Bachelors degree	High school

Table 1: Structure and demographics of HeroesX

In terms of content and sequence, HeroesX v2 was almost identical to v1. Because of the short turnaround between the two runs of the course, there was no time to make substantive changes to the content. Structurally, however, HeroesX v2 differed from v1 in several important ways: for instance, v2 had a shorter registration window and a smaller enrollment. The most important difference, however, was that content was released all-at-once, rather than sequentially.

In ideal experimental conditions, students would have been randomly assigned to HeroesX v1 or v2, and the timing of content release would be the only difference between the two course runs; unfortunately, this was not the case. Table 1 compares v1 and v2 in terms of timing, demographics, content, and other features of the course. HeroesX v2 had a much shorter registration window than v1 and had far fewer students; only 22,975 online students registered for v2 before the course ended. The composition of student bodies, however, was quite similar. Both populations had a median age of 30, a median level of education of a Bachelor's degree, and slightly more men than women. It is possible that students in v1 and v2 may differ in unobservable ways in terms of motivation, aptitude, or other dimensions, and this could have impacted their overall performance and biased our findings. Causal inferences about the effect of changing the content release pattern depend upon the assumption, which appears reasonable but cannot be proven, that edX students in v1 and v2 are similar.

The second course run also included several smaller populations of interest. The courseware for HeroesX v2 was used simultaneously by three groups of learners: students registered for the residential version of the course in Harvard College (n=236); students registered for a credit-bearing online version of the course in Harvard's Division of Continuing Education (n=37); and edX students online (n=22,975). The two credit-bearing groups proceeded along a defined syllabus, which also guided the edX students. Regular emails and messages from the course staff announced the Hours that were featured in the credit-bearing courses each week, creating a set of norms around course pace but providing no strict controls for edX students' pacing. Residential students were also assigned to post to the discussion forums associated with particular Hours, creating another norming-mechanism to define a course pace. Within the group of online edX students, another special population was repeat enrollees. There were 4,319 students from HeroesX v1 that registered for v2, including 429 who earned a certificate in v1.

Given the many similarities between HeroesX v1 and v2, and especially given the pedagogical consistency between the two versions, the second run of HeroesX provides an exciting opportunity to evaluate two different versions of the same MOOC. That said, HeroesX v2 contained a bundle of changes—content release timing, several special populations, and a smaller total student body—so we must be cautious in attributing differences from v1 to v2 to any particular, specific change. Nonetheless, one of the most substantial changes to the course was the shift in content-release timing, and in the next section we examine differences in pacing and ontrackness that are likely to be attributable to this shift.

BEHAVIOR AND ONTRACKNESS IN HEROESX

The pathways of students in HeroesX v2 were much more diverse, and much less on-track, than the pathways of students in HeroesX v1. We demonstrate this finding in three parts. First, we clarify what it means to be on-track in a given week of the course. Second, we offer descriptive visualizations illustrating that far fewer active students in v2 were on-track compared with v1. Finally, we define several operationalizations of student-level ontrackness to quantify these differences and link to student outcomes.

In any week of either version of HeroesX, some chapters are defined as on-track. In HeroesX v1, we define chapters as *strictly on-track* if they were released that week; likewise, in v2, we define chapters as strictly on-track if they were assigned that week in the course's recommended schedule, thus corresponding to the pace of the residential students. For both versions of the course, we define chapters as *loosely on-track* if they were released or assigned that week, the previous week, or the next week. In effect, there is a one-week buffer on either side of the schedule (note this buffer only extends backwards in v1 because future content wouldn't be released yet). Table 2 illustrates these definitions for the closing weeks of v1. These two definitions of ontrackness allow us to conduct at least one form of sensitivity analysis on our findings.

Week	Released	On-track	Loosely On-track
17	Hour 20	…	…
18	Hour 21 Hour 22	Hour 21 Hour 22	Hour 20 Hour 21 Hour 22
19	Hour 23	Hour 23	Hour 21 Hour 22 Hour 23
20	Hour 24 Afterword	Hour 24 Afterword	Hour 24 Afterword
21	(None)	Hour 24 Afterword	Hour 24 Afterword

Table 2: Strict and loose ontrackness in the idealized schedule from HeroesX v1

In the first version of HeroesX, three trends characterized student pathways through the course: staying on-track, progressing off track, and "shopping." In Figure 2, we show where students spent the plurality of their time in each week of the course. On the x-axis we show the week relative to course launch, and on the y-axis we plot the 27 chapters for the course. For each week, we estimate the time spent on each chapter by each student by examining the event logs from the edX platform. For each student, the time spent on a chapter is the sum of the time differences between events in that chapter, excluding differences greater than 30 minutes, an inactivity threshold standard in the web analytics literature [5, 7]. From these estimates, we identify the chapter of the course that students spent the plurality of their time in for each week. In Figure 2, each student contributes to one circle per week—to the circle corresponding to the chapter where he or she spent the plurality of his or her time. Thus, a large circle on Week 1, Hour 0 indicates that a large fraction of students spent the plurality of their time in Week 1 in Hour 0.

Three important groups can be seen in Figure 2. Chapters that are strictly and loosely on-track are shaded in dark and light gray, respectively, and a distinct cluster of students proceeds on-track with the release of content. In every week of the course, there is a separate cluster of students spending the plurality of their time in Hours 0 and 1, the introductory material to the course. Some of these are students getting a late start (such as students B and E from Figure 1), but many of these students are "shoppers" [3] who examine introductory materials but never return. As

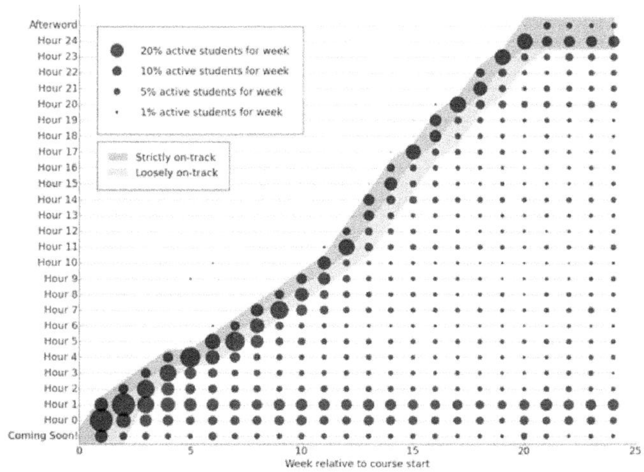

Figure 2: Where students spent the plurality of their time each week, HeroesX v1

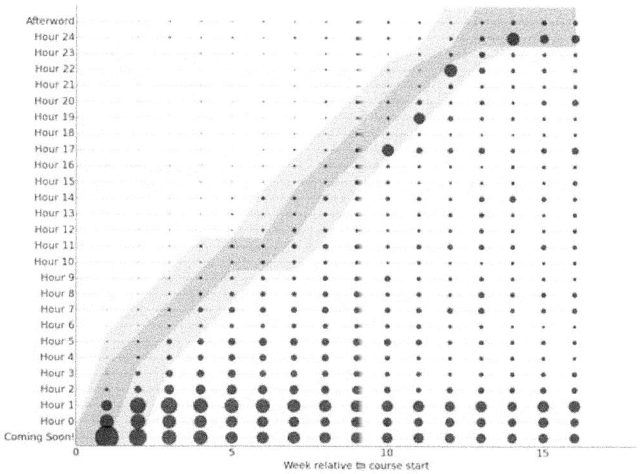

Figure 3: Where students spent the plurality of their time each week, HeroesX v2 (online)

the course advances, student activity becomes more diffuse and spread out across the various Hours. By Week 8, most students were spending the plurality of their time "off-track." So even though several mechanisms, like sequential content release and regular emails, attempt to keep students on-track, asynchronous pacing was the norm rather than the exception by the middle of the course.

Figure 3 shows the same distribution of time for all HeroesX v2 students who were not enrolled in either of the two credit-bearing options. The visual difference with v1 is stark. First, the dense cluster of activity defined by the sequential release of content in v1 diminishes substantially. The cluster of activity around the schedule defined by the syllabus of the course becomes very faint, and from the early weeks of the course, student activity is already widely distributed across all chapters of the course. As with v1, though, a cluster of "shoppers" (and late entrants) in Hours 0 and 1 is visible in every week. The activity of students in the online version of HeroesX v2 contrasts sharply with the behavior of residential HeroesX v2 students, shown in Figure 4. Here, notice that residential students maintain almost perfect synchronicity with the course syllabus until exam preparations begin in Weeks 14 and 15.

A potential limitation of these visualizations is that each student is assigned to a single chapter (and circle) each week. Even if a student spends his or her time relatively evenly across many chapters in a given week, he or she only counts towards one of the circles. As a result, we complement our scatter plots with two additional visualizations that address this limitation. In Figure 5, we show the unweighted average time spent by students across the course each week in three categories. Time spent in Hour 1 and earlier is defined as "Shopping"; time spent loosely on-track is defined as such; and time spent in all other chapters is defined as "Elsewhere." Each week, we calculate the fraction of time spent by each active student across these three categories, and then we plot the average percentage time spent in each category for each week.

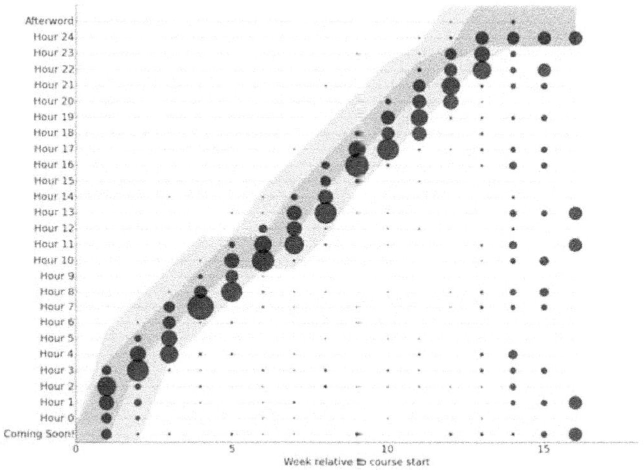

Figure 4: Where students spent the plurality of their time each week, HeroesX v2 (college)

(Note that in the first few weeks, time spent shopping overlaps with time spent loosely on-track, so this time is counted twice.)

As with the trio of scatter plots, Figure 5 shows the striking difference in time allocation between the students in HeroesX v1, the edX students in HeroesX v2, and the credit-bearing students in HeroesX v2. Time spent loosely on-track in HeroesX v1 is noticeably higher than that in HeroesX v2. By contrast, nearly all of student time is spent loosely on-track for most of the credit-bearing, residential version of HeroesX v2. Again, in both v1 and v2, there is a substantial fraction of student time spent "shopping" each week, and the fraction of student time spent neither shopping nor on-track increases rapidly in the first 8 weeks of both courses, and then steadily after that point.

To characterize how our analyses might change with strict and loose definitions of ontrackness, in Figure 6 we plot the fraction of active students who spent the plurality of their time in strictly and loosely on-track chapters. Between 30 and 40 percent of students are at least loosely on-track in

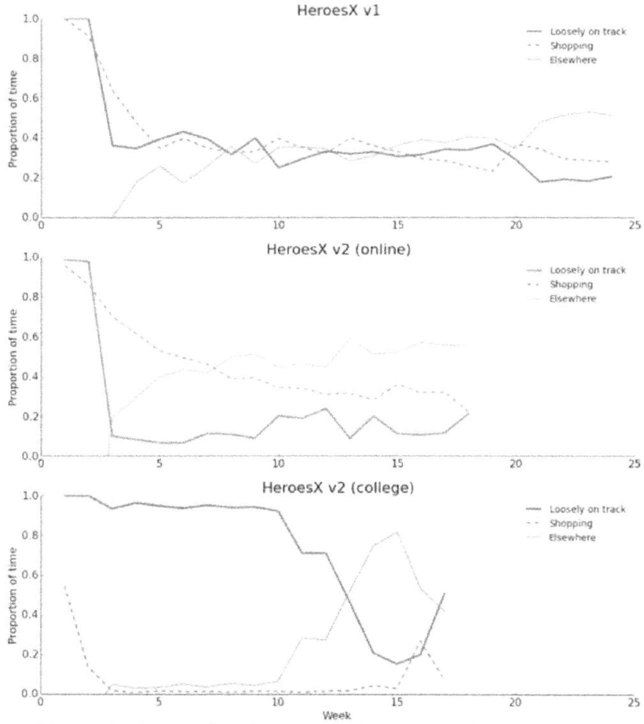

Figure 5: Unweighted average allocation of time by active students, by week

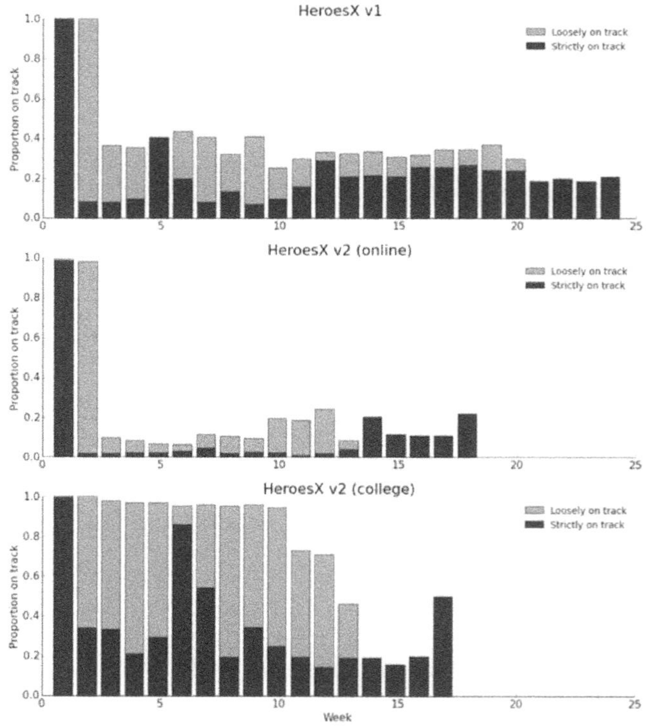

Figure 6: Proportion of active students spending the plurality of their time on-track, by week

most weeks in v1, and the proportion of those who are strictly on-track varies. In v2, by contrast, 20 percent or fewer of edX students are loosely on-track during the course, and very few are strictly on-track until the end, while college students in the HeroesX v2 were by far the most synchronized.

So far we have examined ontrackness through the perspective of a course week, but we can also evaluate the overall ontrackness for each student. Summarizing a student's ontrackness is challenging because students often start at different times, are on-track one week and off-track the next, skip certain weeks of the course, and finish the course in different weeks. Consequently, we propose three possible operationalizations, shown in Table 3.

In the first two definitions of student ontrackness, we consider weeks spent on-track. First, we define ontrackness as the proportion of weeks, after a student starts, with the plurality of time spent in on-track chapters. Since this measure includes all weeks a student is active in the course, it "penalizes" students who skip weeks or finish early. Thus, in our second operationalization we examine the proportion of active weeks (weeks with at least one log event) where the plurality of time is spent on-track, excluding the first two weeks of the course. We exclude these weeks because of the large numbers of "shoppers" at course launch who briefly view the first two chapters and then leave.

We can also examine student ontrackness by calculating the proportion of total time, rather than weeks, spent on-track. In our third operationalization in Table 3, we show the fraction of total time spent in chapters defined as on-track, excluding the first two weeks. This metric could be biased

Operationalization	v1		v2 (online)		v2 (college)	
	Strictly	Loosely	Strictly	Loosely	Strictly	Loosely
(1) Proportion of *weeks after first activity* with plurality of time on-track	0.0190	0.0404 (n=24,782)	0.0052	0.0231 (n=11,457)	0.2331	0.6133 (n=236)
(2) Proportion of *active weeks* with plurality of time on-track (excluding first two weeks)	0.0594	0.1386 (n=17,773)	0.0249	0.0758 (n=6,959)	0.3174	0.8312 (n=235)
(3) Proportion of *total time* spent on-track (excluding first two weeks)	0.0552	0.1396 (n=17,773)	0.0227	0.0739 (n=6,959)	0.3233	0.8437 (n=235)

Table 3: Mean student ontrackness, by three operationalizations

by students who spend an inordinate amount of time in a single on-track chapter, but the similarity between operationalizations (2) and (3) suggests this is not the case.

By each of these operationalizations, we find that students in HeroesX v1 exhibit greater ontrackness than those in v2. These differences are statistically significant ($p < 0.001$) and substantial: across all operationalizations, students in HeroesX v1 spent about twice as much time on-track as students in v2. Both students in v1 and the edX students in v2 were far less on-track then the residential students in v2. The majority of college student time in all operationalizations was at least loosely on-track.

WAS THE DECREASE IN ONTRACKNESS CONSEQUENTIAL?

In the previous section, we showed that student course-taking behaviors in HeroesX v2 showed substantially more variation than in HeroesX v1, and that fewer students in v2 spent time on-track than in v1. The next key question for researchers, practitioners, and students is whether or not these changes are consequential. Was HeroesX v2 improved or weakened by releasing all content at the beginning? Who might have benefited and who might have been harmed?

When looking across the two courses as a whole, we see very few differences in performance, persistence, and participation across the two versions of the course. In Table 4 we display several aggregate measures of these categories: certification rate, median grade, mean days of activity in the courseware (defined as discrete 24 hour UTC-demarcated periods with at least one event log), mean hours on site, mean videos watched, the percentage of students active on the forums, and the mean posts and comments per forum-using student. Generally, these measures are very similar between the two runs of the course. The certification rate, hours on site, and video watching behavior are slightly higher in v2. The proportion of students using the forums at least once, and the number of posts per active forum user are slightly higher in v1. In comparing the two edX versions of HeroesX from this high-level view, it appears that the bundle of changes made

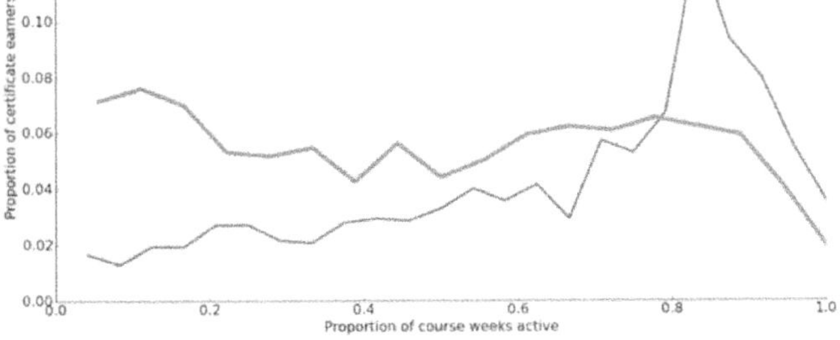

Figure 7: Normalized distributions of weeks active for certificate earners (n=1,399 for v1, n=658 for v2 online)

	v1	v2 (online)	v2 (college)
Active students	24,905	11,473	236
Performance			
Certificate earners	1,399	658	57
Certification rate	0.055	0.057	0.242
Median grade (excluding grade=0)	0.090	0.100	0.260
Persistence			
Median days active	3	3	51
Median hours on site	0.673	0.777	22.525
Mean videos watched	7.934	6.718	10.127
Participation			
Students active on forums	3,190 (12.8%)	869 (7.6%)	226 (95.8%)
Mean posts	3.130	2.509	4.146
Mean comments	8.127	8.272	1.456

Table 4: Aggregate statistics of performance, persistence and participation for active students in HeroesX v1 & v2.

between the versions of HeroesX (the shorter registration window, the smaller course size, the inclusion of credit-seeking Harvard college students, the return of participants from v1, the release of all content at once, and the additional experience of the course team) had minimal impact on persistence, performance, and participation. It is possible that some elements within that bundle of changes might be counteracting each other, and that certain positive changes might be rendered unobservable by negative ones. Figure 7, for instance, shows that the two versions of HeroesX had very different distributions of weeks active for certificate earners, suggesting that the parity in overall certification rates may mask underlying mechanisms that impacted student performance. On the whole, however, the high level statistics about the course suggest minimal differences in student outcomes.

One critical caveat to this observation is that we have very little insight into student learning from each version of the course. For instance, there were no diagnostic tests to establish baseline student knowledge, and it is unclear whether strong performance on the highly structured multiple-choice assessments reflects student learning and not the application of test-taking strategies. In short, although performance, persistence, and participation may be proxies for learning, the degree to which they lend themselves to making valid inferences about student learning is unknown [9].

	Model A	Model B	Model C	Model D	Model E	Model F	Model G
Intercept	-5.537*** (0.079)	-5.406*** (0.079)	-5.429*** (0.079)	-5.311*** (0.084)	-5.321*** (0.084)	-5.239*** (0.082)	-5.247*** (0.082)
Version	0.851*** (0.115)	0.767*** (0.115)	0.774*** (0.115)	0.845*** (0.129)	0.91*** (0.128)	0.816*** (0.126)	0.851*** (0.115)
Proportion of Weeks Active	9.677*** (0.175)	8.189*** (0.227)	8.345*** (0.197)	8.631*** (0.189)	8.495*** (0.18)	9.092*** (0.199)	9.677*** (0.175)
Ontrackness Proportion		Loose	Strict	Loose	Strict	Loose	Strict
Weeks on Track		2.773*** (0.299)	4.957*** (0.411)				
Active Weeks on Track				0.869*** (0.134)	2.104*** (0.168)		
Total Time On Track						0.102 (0.146)	1.379*** (0.204)
Version* Weeks Active	-1.812*** (0.274)	-1.179*** (0.323)	-1.134*** (0.296)	-1.606*** (0.292)	-1.423*** (0.286)	-2.051*** (0.299)	-1.596*** (0.289)
Version* Ontrackness		2.317** (0.72)	4.373*** (1.191)	0.56* (0.227)	0.218 (0.332)	1.07*** (0.241)	0.666 (0.389)
n		36738	36738	24732	24732	24732	24732
Pseudo R2		0.5592	0.5641	0.5398	0.5334	0.5292	0.5319
Log Likelihood		-3485	-3446	-3228	-3274	-3303	-3284

Note: Cell contents are logits and (standard errors). * $p < .05$ ** $p < .01$ *** $p < .001$

Table 5: Taxonomy of logistic regression models predicting completion rates by six operationalizations of ontrackness, controlling for the proportion of weeks active and course version.

One way to examine the effect of the all-at-once content release on course outcomes in HeroesX v2 is to specifically examine how ontrackness relates to student course performance, and then to examine whether there appear to be any benefits or costs associated with staying on or falling off track. If there are substantial benefits to staying on-track, then the marked decrease in ontrackness in HeroesX v2 might be seen as problematic.

To begin to address this question, we estimated a series of logistic regression models examining the relationship between weeks on-track and certificate attainment, shown in Table 5. In Model A, we present a baseline model including the proportion of weeks active, course version (coded as "0" for the Spring v1 and as "1" for the Fall v2), and an interaction term. We find that there is a significant, positive relationship between weeks on-track and certification, and a complex interaction between version and weeks active. For all students, there is a positive relationship between weeks active and certificate attainment. The negative term on the interaction between version and weeks active indicates that for students with few weeks active, students in v2 are more likely to earn a certificate, but for students with many weeks active, students in v1 are more likely to earn a certificate. This finding is consistent with the distributions of certificate attainment by weeks active shown in Figure 7. Computing adjusted risk ratios from these logit parameter estimates, we estimate that students active in 75 percent of weeks are 17 times more likely to earn a certificate than students active in 25 percent of weeks.

In the subsequent six models, Model B through Model G, we include an additional term for each of our three approach to measuring ontrackness (each proportions that can range from 0 to 1), with both strict and loose definitions. We also include an additional interaction term between version and weeks on-track. The results are very similar across all six models. In all models, the proportion of weeks active is a stronger predictor of certification than the proportion of weeks on-track. The proportion of weeks on-track is positively associated with certificate attainment

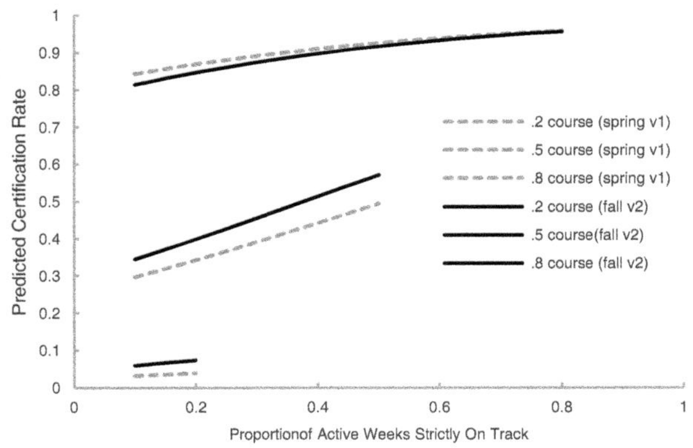

Figure 8: Predicted certification rates by proportion of active weeks strictly on track for six prototypical students.

in all models. The first operationalization of ontrackness, the proportion of weeks on track, has the largest positive parameter estimates and the third operationalization, the proportion of active time on track has the smallest parameter estimates. Parameter estimates are smaller for the loosely on-track definitions relative to the strictly on-track ones. In all models, the interaction term with version and weeks active is negative, and the interaction term with version and weeks on track is positive (though not always significant) indicating that the effect of ontrackness is stronger for students in v2 than in v1.

To illustrate these interactions, we display plots of six prototypical groups of students in Figure 8, drawn from Model E, where ontrackness is defined as the proportion of active weeks a student spends the plurality of his or her time strictly on-track. We chose this model since the parameter estimates were in the middle of the range of effect sizes. Students in v1 are displayed in solid black, and students in v2 are displayed in dashed grey. For each version of the course, we plot the effect of ontrackness (the x-axis) on the probability of earning a certificate (the y-axis), for students who are active 20 percent of course weeks, 50 percent of course weeks and 80 percent of course weeks. Notice the substantial gaps between the line pairs, indicating the strong effect of weeks active on predicted certificate rates. The effect of ontrackness (the slope of these lines) is modest at low and high levels of weeks active, and more substantial for students with half of weeks active. Students with 20 and 50 percent weeks active have higher predicted certificate probabilities in v2, while students with 80 percent weeks active have higher predicted certificate probabilities in v1. Although the nuances of version and ontrackness are of interest, the most striking finding is the positive effect of weeks active on predicted certification probabilities in both versions of HeroesX.

CONCLUSION: GUIDELINES FOR COURSE DEVELOPERS AND DIRECTIONS FOR FUTURE RESEARCH

The most striking difference between HeroesX v1 and v2 is seen in the variable student pathways through the course material over time. In the first version of HeroesX, which released course content in a staggered fashion over several months, a cohort of students stayed on-track with the syllabus throughout the course, but many students pursued their own individually paced pathways through the material. After the first few weeks of the course, the majority of students spent the plurality of their time in chapters other than the most current, assigned chapters. In HeroesX v2, where all content was released at once, this asynchronicity was even more extreme, and nearly all online edX students pursued their own individual paces throughout the course. By several measures of ontrackness, students in the second version of HeroesX were on-track half as much as students in the original. The pacing of edX students in HeroesX v2 stands in stark contrast to the Harvard students enrolled in credit-bearing courses using the same courseware, who moved through the material in lockstep.

While these differences in pacing are striking, their effects on student attainment are substantively modest (though statistically significant). In all of our models of certificate attainment, the strongest predictor of certification is weeks active. Students with many weeks active were slightly more likely to earn a certificate in v1, and students with few weeks active were slightly more likely to earn a certificate in v2. This may simply reflect that the full release of the content in v2 allowed students to finish with fewer weeks of effort—whereas students in v1 were forced to return after many weeks to see the full content. Staying on-track in both v1 and v2 had a small positive effect on certificate attainment. From the narrow perspective of certificate attainment (which again, we must be careful not to treat as a perfect proxy for learning), staying on-track appears preferable to being off-track. These effects, however, were modest, and they may not apply equally to different types of learners. Moreover, the better performance of those who stayed on-track must be weighed against the revealed preferences of students whose actions indicate that they prefer a more flexible schedule.

From these findings, we offer three observations for course developers and faculty in creating open online courses. First, we suggest that instructional designers should assume that students will take advantage of any flexibility offered to proceed at their own pace. Even in courses with a recommended syllabus and norming mechanisms to encourage students to follow that syllabus, course developers should assume that most students will not stay on-track. Collaborative activities and discussions should assume a dimension of asynchronicity that can extend over the whole length of the course run.

A second important, if somewhat incidental, finding from our investigations is that in every week of the course, a substantial portion of visitors engage with the very first contents of the course. For many students, it is the only part of the course they see. Faculty and course teams should consider carefully, therefore, how they use this privileged piece of educational real estate, both to entice students to stay in the course but also to make a meaningful impact on students who might only engage with that small portion of content. One possible approach might be to have the first chapter of a course summarize the important ideas from the whole course, rather than simply introducing the first topic to be discussed.

Finally, for those course developers considering whether to release content in stages versus all-at-once, we found very few differences in student performance, persistence, or participation resulting from changing the pattern of content release. Increasing flexibility does lead to having fewer students stay on-track, and there does appear to be some evidence of modest benefits to keeping students on-track in terms of certificate attainment. Thus, there appears to be at least a modest tradeoff between offering students greater flexibility and encouraging students to stay on-track, where they are slightly more likely to complete the course. If we can make any statement with confidence, it is that students will take advantage of whatever flexibility in pacing is offered. There appear to be advantages to returning to the courseware over multiple weeks, suggesting that even if students don't stay on-track, engaging frequently from week to week is correlated with certificate attainment.

It is important, however, to return to the caveat that we did not comprehensively examine all possible student outcomes and cannot be sure that there are not systematic unobservable differences in students in each run of the course. We cannot definitively say that staying on-track enriches student learning, only that staying on-track has a modest positive correlation with earning a certificate in HeroesX. We also cannot comment on changes to the overall quality of the learning experience resulting from greater flexibility. For instance, one reason for keeping students together as a more synchronous cohort is to enrich the quality of online discussions. While we saw no evidence of major changes in the proportion of students participating in discussions or in the quantity of participation from each student, we did not measure the quality of student discussions. This would be a fruitful avenue for further research.

Moreover, while the particular conditions of the HeroesX natural experiment, especially the stability in the content of both offerings, made it an interesting site for examination, no study of a single course can generalize to the full range of MOOC offerings. Courses in different subjects and with different structures—different assessments, stricter due dates—might be differentially impacted by structures that increase student flexibility in completing the course.

There are many MOOC faculty and course developers who have completed one run of a course and are pondering a repeat run. For faculty in those circumstances considering releasing all of their content at the beginning of the second run, our research offers some guidance. For those who wish to maximize student flexibility, releasing all content at once appears to allow students more flexibility in their pathways through a course. For those who wish to keep students as a more synchronous cohort, our findings suggest that releasing all content at once will further diminish the size of the student cohort that proceeds through a course on-track, and that there may be modest benefits to keeping students on-track.

REFERENCES

[1] Bienkowski, M., Feng, M. and Means, B. Enhancing Teaching and Learning through Educational Data Mining and Learning Analytics: An Issue Brief. United States Department of Education, Washington, DC, 2012.

[2] Cormier, D. What is a MOOC? YouTube (2009).

[3] DeBoer, J., Ho, A. D., Stump, G. S. and Breslow, L. Changing "Course": Reconceptualizing Educational Variables for Massive Open Online Courses. Educational Researcher, 43, 2 (03 2014), 74-84. DOI=10.3102/0013189X14523038.

[4] Guo, P. J. and Reinecke, K. Demographic Differences in How Students Navigate Through MOOCs. In Anonymous Proceedings of the First ACM Conference on Learning @ Scale Conference. (Atlanta, Georgia, USA). ACM, New York, NY, USA, 2014, 21-30.

[5] Interactive Advertising Bureau. IAB Audience Reach Measurement Guidelines. 2014 (2009).

[6] Jordan, K. Initial trends in enrolment and completion of massive open online courses. The International Review of Research in Open and Distance Learning, 15, 1 (2014).

[7] Mullaney, T. Making Sense of MOOCs: A Reconceptualization of HarvardX Courses and Their Students. 2014.

[8] Nesterko, S. O., Seaton, D., Reich, J., McIntyre, J., Han, Q., Chuang, I. and Ho, A. Due dates in MOOCs: does stricter mean better? In Anonymous Proceedings of the first ACM conference on Learning@ scale conference. ACM, 2014, 193-194.

[9] Reich, J., Emanuel, J., Nesterko, S. O., Seaton, D. T., Mullaney, T., Waldo, J., Chuang, I. and Ho, A. D. Heroesx: The Ancient Greek Hero: Spring 2013 Course Report. (2014).

[10] Siemens, G. Activating Latent Knowledge Capacity. Elearnspace, (2014), August 5, 2014.

[11] Stahl, G., Koschmann, T. and Suthers, D. Computer-supported collaborative learning: An historical perspective. Cambridge handbook of the learning sciences, 2006 (2006).

Autonomously Generating Hints by Inferring Problem Solving Policies

Chris Piech
Stanford University
piech@cs.stanford.edu

Mehran Sahami
Stanford University
sahami@cs.stanford.edu

Jonathan Huang
Stanford University, Google
jonathanhuang@google.com

Leonidas Guibas
Stanford University
guibas@cs.stanford.edu

ABSTRACT
Exploring the whole sequence of steps a student takes to produce work, and the patterns that emerge from thousands of such sequences is fertile ground for a richer understanding of learning. In this paper we autonomously generate hints for the Code.org 'Hour of Code,' (which is to the best of our knowledge the largest online course to date) using historical student data. We first develop a family of algorithms that can predict the way an expert teacher would encourage a student to make forward progress. Such predictions can form the basis for effective hint generation systems. The algorithms are more accurate than current state-of-the-art methods at recreating expert suggestions, are easy to implement and scale well. We then show that the same framework which motivated the hint generating algorithms suggests a sequence-based statistic that can be measured for each learner. We discover that this statistic is highly predictive of a student's future success.

Author Keywords
Problem solving policy; Hint generation; Educational data mining.

ACM Classification Keywords
K.3.1 Computer Uses in Education

INTRODUCTION
In massive online courses that have thousands and sometimes millions of students it is often unfeasible to provide feedback on assignments of any complexity [10]. As a result simple multiple choice questions, not open ended assessments, are the staple of online learning. The inability to provide feedback even applies to richly-structured assignments (such as math proofs or computer programs) where students create responses in a highly expressive, formalized grammar. Beautiful assessments can inspire students and add artistry to a course. This gulf between what is currently possible and what we think would improve open access learning suggests a research challenge: imagine and evaluate ways to give feedback to richly-structured assessments at scale. We believe that data of how previous students navigated their way to a final answer can be leveraged to autonomously understand the landscape of such assessments and enable hints for future students.

L@S 2015, March 14–18, 2015, Vancouver, BC, Canada.
ACM 978-1-4503-3411-2/15/03.
http://dx.doi.org/10.1145/2724660.2724668

A motivating case study is the set of assessments in the Code.org Hour of Code course. Code.org is a non-profit organization that led a coordinated effort to have every K-12 student in the United States complete an hour worth of computer science. As part of the initiative Code.org hosted an Hour of Code curriculum: a series of twenty introductory programming "challenges" with instructional videos. In the year and a half since they launched, over 27 million learners have tried their curriculum and it has been taught in over 90 thousand classrooms making it, to the best of our knowledge, the largest MOOC to date. In the challenges students generate programs by putting together blocks of code. The open ended nature of coding, and the many avenues that students can take to get to the solution both make the challenges appealing learning activities, and prevent Code.org from being able to provide expert feedback to stuck students.

The Hour of Code challenges take several steps for a student to solve. At each point in time, the student's current work constitutes a partial solution $\psi \in S$ where S is the set of all possible responses. As the student works on the assessment they will transition through a series $T = \{\psi_0, \psi_1, ..., \psi_n\}$ of partial solutions from step 0, when they have done no work, to step n when they have either reached the solution or given up. We propose that generating feedback autonomously for an assessment of this nature can be seen as the composition of two tasks:

1. Deciding for any learner what partial solution an educational expert would suggest they transition to next.
2. Choosing how to communicate that information to the student such that they improve on a learning objective.

We suggest that both of the decoupled tasks can be solved and tested independently. The objective of this paper is to solve the former problem by learning what we call a Problem Solving Policy (PSP): a decision for any partial solution as to what next partial solution a student should take (see definition 1 and the example in figure 1). Using historical data we generate PSPs for challenges in the Hour of Code and evaluate to what extent they capture expert opinion.

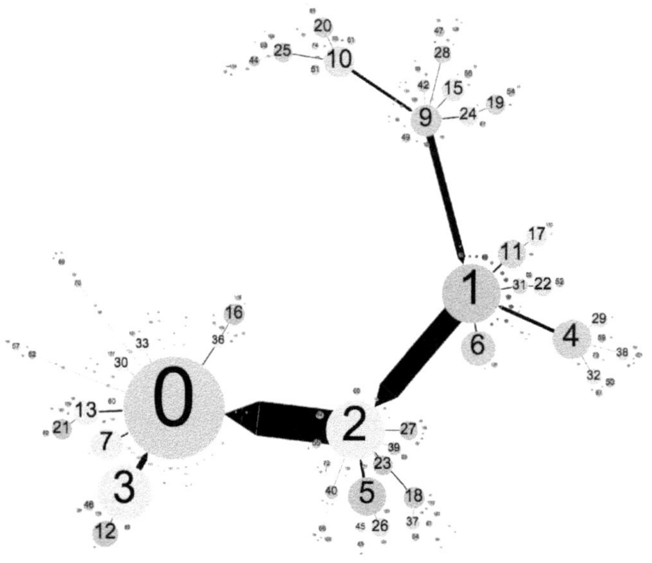

Figure 1: A visualization of a problem solving policy generated for an early Hour of Code challenge (P_A). Each node is a unique partial solution, node 0 is the correct answer. The edges show what next partial solution we think an expert would suggest students move towards.

DEFINITION 1. *Problem Solving Policy (PSP).*

Let S be the set of partial solutions. A problem solving policy $\pi : S \to S$ specifies a partial-solution $s' = \pi(s)$ for all $s \in S$.

Note that the definition for a PSP makes the Markov assumption as no partial solution other than a student's current state is considered in the policy mapping.

A PSP provides a foundation for generating formative feedback. For a given partial solution, there are many types of issues a student could have: they may have missed a step, made a mistake, have compounded mistakes, or possibly they are on the right path and simply need to keep going. An ideal PSP captures these diverse needs. It selects the single part of the partial solution the student should work on first and denotes how they should do so. Importantly, the PSP can also be evaluated independently from the actual feedback given to students (e.g. via a hint generation) given a ground truth dataset composed of expert evaluations on how they would push a student forward.

Our hypothesis is that for large classes like Code.org there are patterns which materialize in how the many previous students have navigated from an empty project to the final answer which can be leveraged to learn how students should move forward from any $\psi \in S$. For example, if ten thousand students had at some point all submitted the exact same partial solution with the same set of mistakes, it seems reasonable that the best way forward is illuminated by the way that crowd then went on to fix their programs. Surprisingly, we found that many of the most obvious statistics that could be calculated from historical data or static analysis were not particularly useful.

The main contributions of this work are: (1) a family of algorithms which can accurately predict how experts believe learners should make forward progress from a partial solution (a PSP), based on historical data (2) a related per-student statistic generated from how a student solves a challenge that correlates strongly with future performance and (3) a unified comparison of previously published algorithms. These results speak to a deeper theme: *how* students solve assignments is an under utilized, important lens into what students know and what feedback future students will need.

Related Work

Giving automated hints for richly-structured assessments at scale is a task with a long history of research that includes fields as diverse as intelligent tutors, theorem provers, crowd sourcing and peer grading.

This work expands upon research towards data-driven PSPs by the Intelligent Tutor (IT) community. In particular a similar problem was posed in Rivers' and Koedinger's paper Automating Hint Generation with Solution Space Path Construction [15]. Rivers et al presented an algorithm which introduces the heuristic that popular partial solutions tend to correspond to good next steps. The Hint Factory by Barnes et al uses a historically trained Markov Decision Problem (MDP) formulation [3]. While both papers present algorithms, the PSPs they generate were not directly measured for quality and the algorithms have previously not been compared to one another. There has been research from the field of static analysis which present alternative ways to generate PSPs. Singh et al suggest ways to find shortest path edits to a solution for programming problems, work which builds off a community of static analysis and theorem prover research [18] [4]. One contribution of this paper is to recreate the IT algorithms and a static analysis algorithm so that we can evaluate them all on the same dataset.

There are a range of ways to generate feedback for richly-structured assessments at scale that do not involve first learning a PSP. One particularly interesting approach is to crowd source feedback for students [21], an idea which can be extended to the programming domain [20]. While it would take a substantial amount of work to give feedback to all answers in rich assessments Nguyen et al suggests ways to identify functionally equivalent programs which can share annotations [9] [14]. An appealing idea is to have students reflect on what mistakes they made after solving a problem, but this idea does not apply to our setting where students are as young as five years old. At what point is a student ready to consciously reflect on the challenges that they faced? Peer grading is one of the most common solutions for giving feedback to complex assignments at scale in massive open online courses [8]; however, it can only be used to give feedback on a final submissions, not hints to a stuck student. Moreover asking students to peer grade programs would have a dramatic impact on the experience of the Hour of Code if used for each challenge.

Cognitive tutors are a compelling approach towards hint generation [13] [2]. They are well rooted in educational theory and have been shown to be pedagogically successful. However, the effort required to author a cognitive model, a neces-

Figure 2: Schematic of the maze and example solution for P_A (left) and P_B (right). The arrow is the agent and the heart is the goal.

Statistic	P_A	P_B
Students Studied	509,405	263,569
Submissions	1,138,506	1,263,360
Unique Submissions	10,293	79,553
Pass Rate	97.8%	81.0%

Table 1: Summary of the dataset analyzed.

sary component, increases with the number of unique answers a student can produce. For richly-structured assignments such as the one in Code.org this approach does not scale well. Similarly there is a literature of scientists trying to understand, via observation, how student's solve programming challenges. The frameworks developed have engendered better teaching techniques but not at-scale autonomous hints [5] [1].

The problem of generating a PSP can be seen as an instance of more general problems. There is a clear parallel between generating a PSP and autonomous decision making [12]. Finding a PSP could be expressed as a route planning task [19] and historical data could be viewed as item responses where students vote on ways to make forward progress [22].

One of the aims of this work is to enable further comparative research. To this end we will share relevant code and annonomized, aggregate data: `http://stanford.edu/~cpiech/codedotorg.html`

DATA

In the Hour of Code website, students write programs to solve maze world puzzles. Each time a learner runs their program, a symbolic representation of their current work is recorded. When the learner submits a final answer, or stops working on a challenge, the learners partial solutions are composed into a raw series. There is a simple mechanism to test if two symbolic representations are identical.

The dataset for this paper is the series of partial solutions from all logged in students from December 2013 to March 2014. In that time Code.org gathered over 137 million partial solutions. Retention was quite high relative to other contemporary open access courses, see figure 3(a). Volunteered information from 19.5% of the logged in users gives us a window into the demographic makeup of the learners: 59% are male and 41% are female. The average age is μ = 13.2, σ = 4.3 years old with the age range spanning from 5 to 98 years old.

In this analysis we focus on two problems P_A and P_B which are representative of different levels of complexity. See figure 2 for a schematic of the problems, and the solution code. The solution to P_A , which was the fourth challenge in the twenty challenge curriculum, requires students to string together a series of moves and turns. The solution to P_B , which was the eighteenth challenge, requires an if/else condition inside a for loop: the most advanced concept in the hour of code.

Surprisingly, while the challenges only required a few lines of code, the number of unique partial solutions submitted by the logged in users was in the tens of thousands (See table 1). We define unique submissions to be ones with unique abstract syntax trees. For P_B , even if we only look at programs with ten lines of fewer, there are around 10 million hypothetical unique partial solutions. It is partially for this reason that it is so difficult to crowd source hints. However, the occurrence of partial solutions is not evenly distributed and notable impact could be had by annotating the most popular partial solutions. Figure 3(b) shows the percent of submissions that would be covered by generating hints for the most popular partial submissions. In order to cover 90% of submissions for P_B one would need to annotate 7,127 unique programs. Code.org crowd sources hints but to this date has only solicited tens of annotations per challenge.

In the raw series of data, a student could make incremental changes between runs or make large changes between runs. To normalize out this difference we interpolated each student's series so that transitions between partial solutions constituted exactly one program edit (as allowed by the website interface). To interpolate we first made a "legal move graph" of all the ways that users can move between partial solutions using single edits. The legal move graphs for P_A and P_B have average out-degrees of 8.5 and 4.3 respectively. Then for every sequence of states (a, b) in the raw series that is not in the legal move graph, we replaced the sequence with the most likely path that a student would have taken along the legal move graph to get from a to b. Transition probabilities were calculated through the observed transitions along the legal move graph with a baysian prior. We made a Markovian assumption that the probability of each transition was independent of previous transitions taken. Interpolation results in a new series $T = \{\psi_0, \psi_1, ..., \psi_n\}$. We define a student to have been "successful" if ψ_n was the challenge solution.

To evaluate policies, we gathered expert gold standard data for both challenges. A group of seven computer science educators each labelled hundreds of student programs (225 for P_A and 268 for P_B) with the partial solution they suggest a student who ran that program should transition to next. Inter rater reliability showed a notable degree of agreement. The Fleiss Kappa score [6] was 0.58. All conflicting codings were discussed and multiple correct ways forward were allowed when there was disagreement.

METHODS

The main objective of our research is to find the best algorithm for generating a PSP. We tested three classes of solutions: Desirable Path algorithms, previously proposed algo-

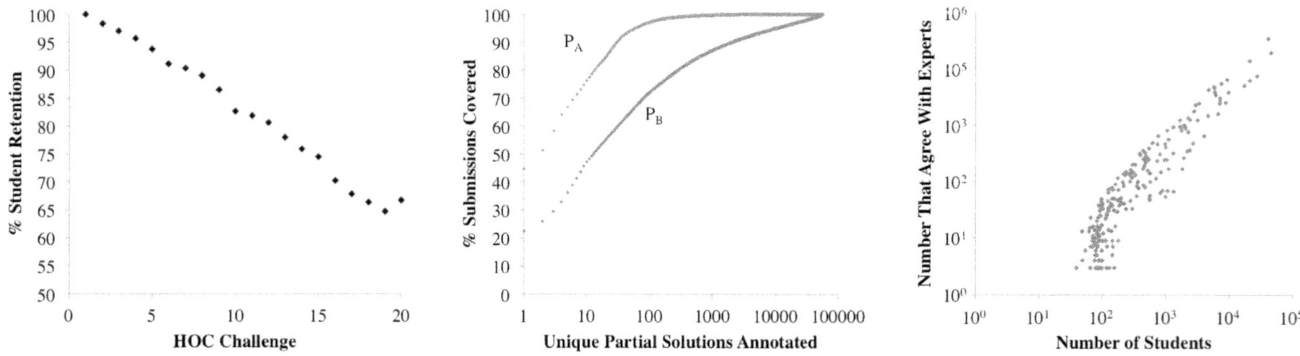

(a) (b) (c)

Figure 3: (a) Percent of students who finished the first problem in the hour of code that solve the remaining ones. (b) The percent of submissions that are covered by annotating the most popular partial solutions. (c) How does node popularity relate to number of students who agree with experts?

rithms and vanilla baseline algorithms. The general intuition is that though individuals navigate partial solutions in misleading ways, wisdom emerges from the cohort of students.

Desirable Path Algorithms

Historical data of students shows many interesting patterns. But turning that data into a prediction of how experts would suggest a learner make forward progress is a complicated task. Students are learning. Many students are working through systematic misunderstandings and this process is reflected in their navigation through partial solutions.

Moreover, partial solutions that are further off the most common path-to-solution, are visited by students that are less likely to act like experts. See figure 3(c). This is an especially salient confound as these are precisely the partial solutions where feedback to a student would be most necessary. One way to think about this problem is that uncommon partial solutions usually reflect mistakes on the part of a student. Knowing that a student has made a mistake, one can suppose that they are less likely than the average student to make future transitions which agree with expert suggestions. For example: in P_A a common incorrect partial solutions is a program that makes the agent move twice (and thus crash into the wall) before turning left. The population of students who have submitted a program that crashes into a wall already have misconceptions as to the dynamics of the challenge. Though the expert recommended way to make forward progress is to remove one of the move statements, by far the most common next transition that those students make is to change their turn left to a turn right, which takes them even further from the solution.

If we base our policy off of the transitions of students, we will often be trusting a group of learners that we know have already made a mistake. This biased sample limits our ability to understand the path-to-solution that *would* have been the most popular *if* partial solutions were all visited by ideal students. This raises a question: how can we know anything about a given partial solution that isn't collected solely from the students that submit said partial solution?

One answer to that question is that we know the relative popularity of a partial solution based on how often it was submitted. Unlike transition counts, which sample from a biased population, the number of times a partial solution is seen in our dataset, "partial solution counts," reflect a property of that partial solution for the average student in the dataset. A relatively high popularity suggests that the average student in the sample found the partial solution to be a useful way-point on a path-to-solution. A relatively low popularity suggests that the average student did not. By creating algorithms based off of this statistic we can avoid the confound that arises from the uneven distribution of ability across partial solutions.

Even if we make the assumption that partial solution counts reflect a global desirability of that partial solution how can we turn that intuition into a PSP? The solution is not as easy as: for any partial solution, chose the legal move such that the next partial solution has a high count. That strategy, more often than not, would encourage the student to delete any progress they have made. The most popular partial solution is the empty program and partial solutions which are further from the empty program tend to be less popular. Instead, to generate a PSP we must seek a balance between visiting desirable partial solution and making forward progress. We believe that teachers strike this balance by considering the entire path that they would expect a student to go down. Algorithmically this can be interpreted as searching for an optimally desirable path-to-solution. Once a path-to-solution is decided upon, the PSP function is simply the first step in that path.

We propose a desirable path theory which assumes that (a) desirability of a partial solution to the average student is a function of historical counts and (b) experts suggest that learners make progress along the most desirable path-to-solution. We present two algorithms that derive from this theory.

Poisson Path

The first algorithm that we propose based on the desirable path theory is the Poisson Path.

We define the Poisson Path from a partial solution s to be the path from s to a perfect solution with the smallest expected time to be generated by the average successful student. We assume that the amount of time required for an average student to generate a partial solution is a Poisson process whose rate parameter can be estimated via the partial solution count from the student's population. This assumption is founded in the belief that the prototypical student prefers partial solutions that are easy to generate.

Given these assumptions the Poisson Path $\gamma(s)$ is:

$$\gamma(s) = \arg\min_{p \in Z(s)} \sum_{x \in p} \frac{1}{\lambda_x}$$

Where $Z(s)$ are all the paths-to-solution from s and λ_x is the number of times partial solution x is seen in successful student data. To generate a PSP we set $\pi(s)$ to be the first partial solution in the path $\gamma(s)$.

> DEFINITION 2. *Poisson Path.*
>
> *Let G be a graph traversed by agents. Assume for a node $x \in G$, the time required for an agent to visit that node varies as an $exponential(\lambda_x)$ where λ_x is a Poisson rate parameter.*
>
> *The expected time until an agent visits a given node x is $\frac{1}{\lambda_x}$ and the expected time until an agent generates each node in a path p is $\sum_{x \in p} \frac{1}{\lambda_x}$*
>
> *The Poisson Path is the path from a node s to a terminal with the smallest expected time required to be generated by an agent. Of all the paths $Z(s)$ from s to the terminal, the path with the smallest expected time is*
>
> $$\gamma(s) = \arg\min_{p \in Z(s)} \sum_{x \in p} \frac{1}{\lambda_x}$$

Computing the Poisson Path can be solved using a simple reduction to Dijkstra's shortest path algorithm. We construct a graph where for all legal transitions $a \to b$ we add an edge with cost $\frac{1}{\lambda_b}$. A Dijkstra search for the shortest path to any solution over this graph will return the Poisson Path. Dijkstra's algorithm is easy to implement and runs in $O(n \log n)$ time for a graph with n partial solutions. To prevent repeat submissions from having an undue influence on our partial solution counts we remove all cycles from student series before we count occurrences.

Independent Probable Path

A second algorithm that we propose based on the desirable path theory, is the Independent Probable Path.

This algorithm tries to find the path-to-solution from a given partial solution that would have been the most probable for an average successful student who we would hypothetically start at that partial solution. For the average student we do not know partial solution transition probabilities. We instead know that the probability of the average student submitting a partial solution is proportional to the partial solution count. Using these submission probabilities we can calculate the markov-zero most likely path-to-solution for a randomly sampled student in the class. The Independent Probable Path $\gamma(s)$, is calculated as:

$$\begin{aligned}\gamma(s) &= \arg\max_{p \in Z(s)} \prod_{x \in p} p(\psi_t = x) \\ &= \arg\max_{p \in Z(s)} \sum_{x \in p} \log(\frac{\lambda_x}{k}) \\ &= \arg\min_{p \in Z(s)} \sum_{x \in p} -\log(\frac{\lambda_x}{k})\end{aligned}$$

Where $Z(s)$ are all paths in the legal move graph from s to the solution, λ_x is the count of successful students who submitted x and k is the total number of submissions. This algorithm can also be reduced to an instance of Dijkstra's shortest path.

Baseline Algorithms

Several algorithms for generating PSPs have been proposed in recent publications. Here we provide a brief overview of the algorithms and any modifications that were made to better fit the algorithms to the Code.org context. We also explore a series of simpler, direct measures.

Markov Decision Problem

As proposed by Barnes and Stamper we can generate a PSP by formulating student transitions as a Markov Decision Problem (MDP) and learning an optimal policy. An MDP is defined by specifying states, actions, rewards over states and transition probabilities. In the Barnes et al formulation the states are the set of partial solutions, actions are the legal changes to a program allowed in the interface and the reward of a partial solution is set to be 100 if it is a correct answer, 0 otherwise. Of note, the transition probability between partial solutions a and b is defined as $p(\psi_{t+1} = b | \psi_t = a)$.

In a standard MDP the transition probability is the chance of ending up in a state given one's previous state *and* an action the policy decided to perform. Applied to this setting we would need to know the probability of a student going from one partial solution to another if we were to suggest a particular next state. In the historical data available to Barnes et al and in the Code.org context that conditional probability is unknown; we can't observe how our suggestions would effect student transitions. Instead, as in Barnes et al, we assume that a student's transition probability is independent of the partial solution we chose for them. The MDP has a single hyper-parameter, the discount factor. We use standard value iteration [17] inference on the MDP which results in a PSP.

Rivers Policy

In a paper recently published Rivers et al provided an algorithm for choosing the ideal next step [15]. For a given partial solution, the algorithm computes a score for all potential next partial solutions and selects the argmax. The score is a weighted sum of features. We adapted their score to utilize the legal move graph which results in the following policy function:

$$\pi(x) = \arg\max_{n \in N(x)} \theta_0 \lambda_n + \theta_1(1 - \delta(n, g)) + \theta_2 v(n)$$

Where $N(x)$ are the neighbors of x in the legal move graph, λ_n is the popularity of the partial solution, $\delta(n, g)$ is the minimum Abstract Syntax Tree edit distance between a neighbor n and a correct answer g and $v(n)$ is the unit-test score of the neighbor. Though specific settings for parameters θ are provided in the paper, after trying the values given we considered the weights to be hyper-parameters.

Static Analysis

Given the simple nature of the hour of code problems, especially P_A, we hypothesized that the optimal PSP could be chosen by a static analysis solution. For P_A there was a single optimal sequence of commands that solved the maze. Given any partial solution, we believed that the expert labels could be perfectly predicted by a sequence alignment algorithm which compares the sequences of actions in the partial solution to the answer and selects the first divergence. We did our best to statically recreate human labels for P_A. The algorithm allowed for reductions of equivalent blocks of code and had different insert and delete costs depending on relative position in the sequence. This algorithm was originally developed to generate gold standard data.

Most Likely Next

For each partial solution x, select the partial solution that most successful students transitioned to from x. This is equivalent to choosing the next state that has maximal probability $\pi(x) = \arg\max_n p(\psi_{t+1} = n|\psi_t = x)$.

Most Common Path

Find the the most common entire path to a solution in the dataset and set $\pi(x)$ to be the first partial solution in the path from x to the correct answer.

Expected Success

For each partial solution x, select the legal next partial solution y that maximizes the probability of a student arriving at the final answer given that they transition from x to y.

Min Time

Since all of our data was timestamped, for a given partial solution x we can compute the expected time $J(x)$ between when a student submits x and when they submit the correct solution. We chose $\pi(x) = \arg\min_{n \in N(x)} J(n)$ to be the legal next partial solution that has minimal expected time until the student arrives at the solution.

Ability Model

We modified the inference algorithm for an item response model with unknown correct answers presented by Whitehill et al to learn a problem solving policy [22]. Let t_j be the true next step for partial solution j. Let α_i be the ability of student i and let β_j be the difficulty of choosing right answer for partial solution j. Let l_{ij} be the next step taken by student i from state j. We model the probability of student i being correct on item j to be:

$$p(l_{ij} = t_j|\alpha_i, \beta_j) = \frac{1}{1 + e^{\alpha_i \beta_j}}$$

We chose values for α, β and t that best fit the data using expectation maximization. The policy was set as $\pi(x) = t_x$.

Evaluation

All ten of the algorithms listed–the Desirable Path algorithms, the previously proposed algorithms and the vanilla baseline algorithms–were run and the PSPs that they generated were tested against the gold standard data that we had collected.

For both P_A and P_B we use the gold standard data collected to generate an expert map $t : T \to S$ where $T \subset S$ is the set of partial solutions annotated by experts. For each partial solution $k \in T$, $t(k)$ is the set of partial solutions that experts say a student should ideally transition to from k.

To evaluate a PSP π we calculate the percent of overlap between the policy and the expert map, weighted by number of students who submitted partial solutions. Let λ_k be the number of students that submitted partial solution k. We computed accuracy as:

$$acc_\pi = \frac{\sum_{k \in T} \lambda_k \delta(k)}{\sum_{k \in T} \lambda_k}$$

$$\delta(k) = \begin{cases} 1, & \text{if } \pi(k) \in t(k) \\ 0, & \text{otherwise} \end{cases}$$

Four of the baseline policies that we tested (MDP, Static Analysis, Rivers Policy and Ability Model) had hyper-parameters. To maximally benefit the baseline methods we optimize hyper-parameters with respect to accuracy on P_A. This means that for those algorithms, it is possible that their performance numbers will be artificially higher on P_A due to over-fitting.

RESULTS

The best algorithm for both P_A and P_B was the Poisson Path policy which had accuracy of 95.9% and 84.6% respectively despite making the desirable path assumptions and only using submission counts. Indeed, the second best performing algorithm also made such assumptions and had almost identical accuracies. See table 2 for the full results. The structure of the policies learned by the Desirable Path Algorithms tended to push students towards a backbone pathway of partial solutions. This pattern is visible in figure 1 which depicts the Poisson Path PSP for P_A. You can see the backbone through partial solutions [10, 9, 1, 2, 0] that the algorithm favored.

The other algorithms had notably lower scores. Interestingly, algorithms that were based on transition dynamics, eg MDP and Most Common Next were less effective even though we had enough historical data to accurately approximate transition probabilities. This result seemed related to the observation that outside the mainstream paths-to-solution students systematically made transitions which disagreed with expert suggestions. We observed that for most partial solutions, the majority of students did not take an action which agreed with the expert label. In fact for P_A, for over 51% of the expert labelled partial solutions, the most popular next partial solution was not one that experts said students should transition to, and for 34% of labelled partial solutions, the incorrect most popular next step was over three times as popular as any expert recommended next step.

	P_A Accuracy	P_B Accuracy
Algorithm		
Random	8.2%	4.3%
Shortest Path	49.5%	33.6%
Min Time	67.2%	42.2%
Rivers Policy†	72.9%	78.2%
Expected Success	77.9%	56.2%
MDP†	80.5%	47.6%
Most Common Next	81.1%	49.0%
Static Analysis†	86.3%	-
Most Popular Path	88.3%	52.8%
Ability Model	88.4%	63.3%
Independent Probable Path ‡	**95.5%**	**83.3%**
Poisson Path ‡	**95.9%**	**84.6%**
Variation		
Unconditioned on Success	72.2%	68.3%
No Interpolation	86.8%	70.5%
Allow Cycles	94.3%	82.0%
Poisson Interpolation	94.6 %	83.2%

Table 2: Percent submissions with the ground truth edge correctly predicted. † Algorithms applied to learning PSP's in other papers. ‡ Desirable Path Algorithms.

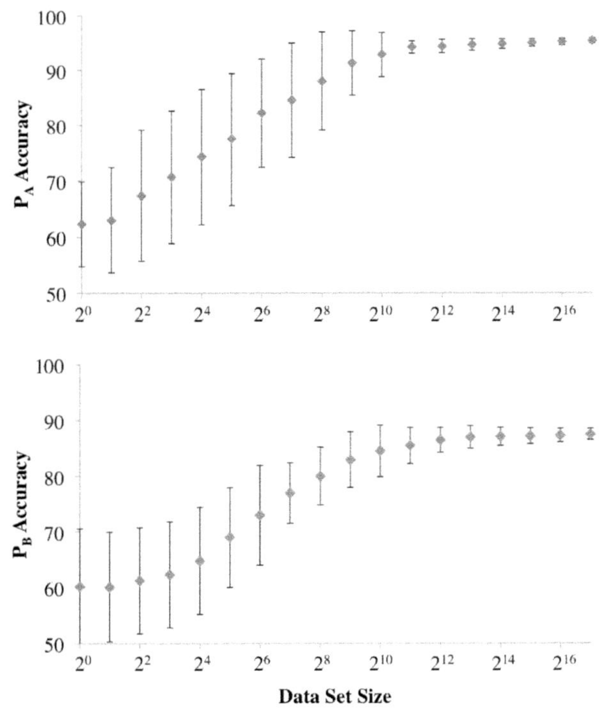

Figure 4: Learning curve for P_A (above) and P_B (bellow). Students are subsampled randomly from dataset. Error bars are standard error.

While the Rivers Policy performed well on the P_B in many instances in P_A it would suggest a student undo something constructive from their partial solution. The optimal static analysis algorithm was worse than the best trajectory based algorithm and it would have been very difficult to design such a system for P_B. There is a lot of nuance that goes into deciding what a student should do. The experts seem to be working in a formulaic way, but it is very difficult to codify their decision making.

There are several variations of the Poisson Path that we tested to understand what preprocessing was most important. The two steps that were necessary were: (1) interpolate each student series over the graph of single legal moves and (2) condition node counts on success (see table 2). Removing cycles from student partial solution series is less important. We applied the same pre-processing for all algorithms tested.

We ran an experiment to understand the effect of dataset size on accuracy. On both P_A and P_B we subsampled students from our dataset and reran the entire policy learning process (including the interpolation). The policy generated by the subsampled students was evaluated for accuracy on the same gold standard expert data. We started with a training dataset size of two students and continually doubled the number of students. For each size we repeated the experiment 100 times to estimate accuracy mean and standard deviation. See figure 2. Even if we were given historical data from substantially fewer students the Poisson Path PSP would have had comparable accuracy. With a dataset of only two thousand students accuracy is similar to the results from running the algorithm on hundreds of thousands of students. While two thousand students may be sufficient, as more data is collected the algorithm monotonically improves in accuracy and accuracy variance. Since the Poison Path algorithm can be cast as an instance of Dijkstra's shortest path the running time will be reasonable even for courses that are orders of magnitude larger than the Hour of Code.

Summative Assessment

The same insights that allow us to predict how experts would suggest students make forward progress can be used to understand how well each student progressed through the assignment. The desirable path theory that inspired both the Poisson Path and the Independent Probable Path algorithms suggests a statistic that can be measured per student. Assuming that path counts of a partial solution are a function of desirability, we can then calculate the desirability of the path of partial solutions a student took through as they worked through a challenge.

Based on the Poisson interpretation of desirability used in the Poisson Path, we define the "path score" of a student's series T to be the time we expect an average successful student would take to complete the series. Assuming that each state is generated via a Poisson process, expected time until we see the series of states that constitute a path is the sum of the inverse of the rate of each partial solution:

$$pathScore(T) = \sum_{x \in T} \frac{1}{\lambda_x}$$

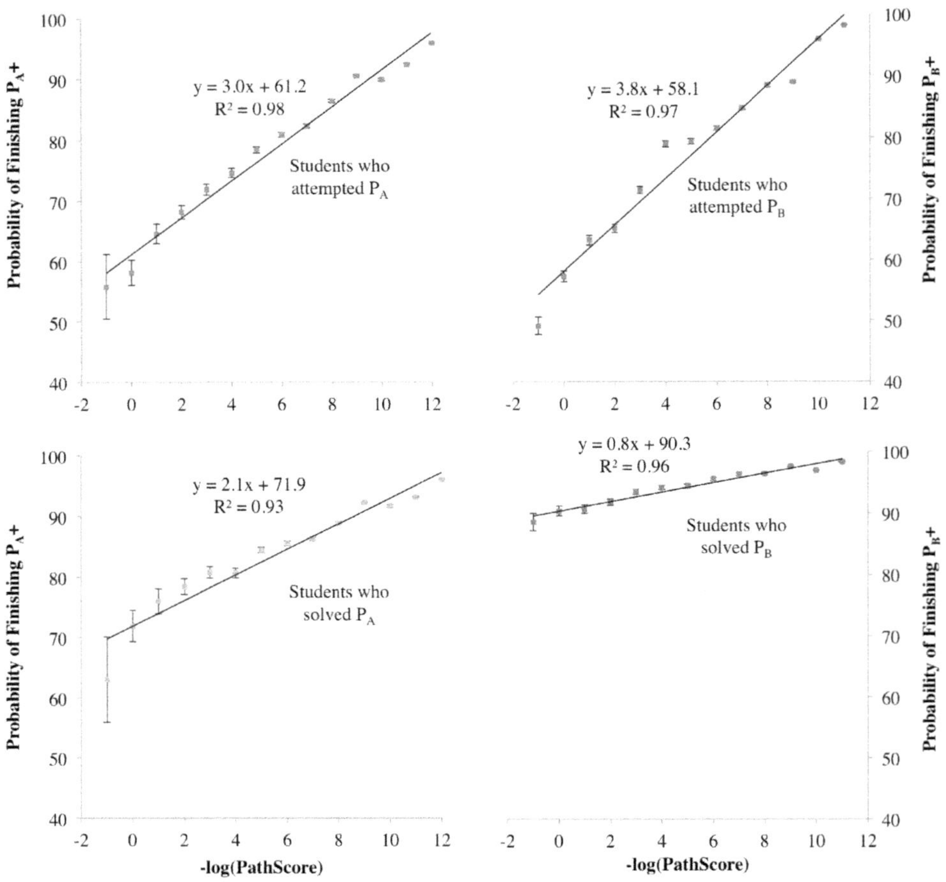

Figure 5: Student path scores vs probability of completion of subsequent problems. Error bars are standard error.

We calculated the path score for each student and explored how the scores were related to the probability that the student would complete the next challenge. For example P_A is the fourth challenge in the Hour of Code. We computed a path score for each student that completed P_A and observed which of those students went on to solve the fifth challenge (P_A +).

From simple visualization it was clear that the negative log of the path score had a strong linear relationship with probability of completing the next challenge for students in both P_A and P_B. For the population of students who attempted P_A, their probability of completing the next challenge P_A+ increased by 3% with each per unit increase in $-\log(pathScore)$. Linear regression between $\log(pathScore)$ and the probability of completing the next challenge had an R^2 of 0.98. Learners with the worst paths had a 58% chance of completing the next problem and learners with the best paths had a 95% chance: an effect size of 37pp. P_B similarly had an straight line pattern ($R^2 = 0.97$) and an effect size of 43pp. See figure 5.

This trend is especially interesting when we only look at the scores of students who arrived at a solution to the challenge from which we calculate the path scores. These are the students who, if it were a traditional classroom, would have received a perfect grade. For P_A the successful students with the worst and the best path scores had a 25.1pp difference in the probability of completing the subsequent problem. Again there was a linear relationship between the negative log of the path score and probability of success ($R^2 = 0.93$). P_B also had a linear relationship ($R^2 = 0.96$), with an effect size that was 9.7pp between the best and the worst path scores. It seems plausible that many students who may have disengaged from the curriculum because of a factor related to low path score may not have stayed in the course until the 18th challenge. In both problems the Path Score shows predictive signal towards retention beyond what we could know from simply observing whether a students solved the challenge.

Generating Hints

In the introduction of this paper we proposed that the challenge of autonomously providing hints could be decoupled into (1) Deciding how a learner should make forward progress and (2) Choosing how to communicate that information to the student such that they improve on a learning objective. Given that we can solve the first task sufficiently well, we are pursuing research on the second: how to turn our PSP into hints. This latter task combines education and UI decisions.

Having a PSP for a given challenge substantially simplifies the task of generating hints. It tells the hint generation algorithm which part of a student's current partial solution they should work on, and how they should modify their work. Often, students have multiple issues. A policy allows an automated system to know what is the first issue the student should work on. Moreover, knowing the exact edit we believe an expert would like a student to make means that generating a hint is reduced to deciding how directly we should tell the student what to do. Based off of a simple template we turned $\pi(x)$ into English text hints. We are currently running an A/B study with thousands of students where they either receive hints generated autonomously from the policy, hints hand-crafted by humans, or placebo hints.

DISCUSSION

One of the more surprising results of this research is that even with hundreds of thousands of students, it turns out that many reasonable statistics on learner trajectories are not particularly useful for predicting what experts say is the correct way forward. Most interestingly, the transitions that learners take after encountering a problem do not tend to correspond with what experts think learners should do. The wisdom of the crowd of learners, as seen from this angle, is not especially wise. This result raises the question: What is so good about the Poisson Path? Why does it, and the Independent Probable Path work when other methods do not? In designing both of the Desirable Path Algorithms, we followed our intuition that a useful algorithm would be able to predict what an *average* successful student would do if we were to place her in a partial solution. We first assumed that partial solution submission counts are uniquely important as they are a statistic which reflects how desirable a partial solution is to the *average* student (or rather the inverse is a measure of how relatively undesirable). Many baseline algorithms instead relied on transition counts, but that number captures what the biased population of students who had arrived at a given partial solution, *not* the average student, would do. Previous research suggests that transition-based algorithms are limited by lack of data. We now believe that their shortcomings are instead a result of reliance on subpopulations with systematic predispositions. When designing the Desirable Path Algorithms we also assumed that when deciding on a next step it is best to search for an entire path to solution. Many baseline algorithms only consider neighboring partial solutions and do not see the bigger picture. We propose that the success of the Desirable Path Algorithms is evidence that both assumptions are important, operable properties of historical student trajectories.

Code.org is a compelling case study as tens of millions of students are expected to use the website next year. However, it is only one course and as such is not a proof of our ability to provide feedback for general richly-structured assignments. Even for the Hour of Code where the problems are simple and there are huge numbers of students, the solution space is almost too disperse for statistical methods. Though there may be millions of students, outside the most common partial solutions there is a sharp drop-off in both the density of students per partial solution, and the proportion of students who took reasonable next steps. For more complicated programming tasks, or written language tasks, there would be too few students that would submit the same partial solutions [7]; feedback based on historical patterns over raw partial solutions has its limits. One way in which we could further extend the boundary of assignments for which we could provide at scale feedback using the Desirable Path Algorithms would be to develop a better representation for partial solutions and/or a more intelligent way to find patterns in submissions. In general the AI challenges in education are hard and the field can make faster progress if we decouple the evaluation of machine learning tasks so that we can make progress without continuously paying the heavy cost of user studies.

A limitation of our approach is that it is not clear that students need hints and it is not clear that pushing a student towards the answer is the right objective [16]. A lot of learning happens when we struggle and go off on tangents. In the Code.org context, hints that push students towards the solution are useful because the goal of the Hour of Code is primarily motivation. The course intends to provide learners with an exposure to programming. Being able to give a stuck student a hint is useful for fostering retention and interest in the subject. One way to approach the uncertainty of knowing whether a hint would be useful for a student is through a reinforcement-agent hint-giving system. Such a system would be integrated into the website and would dynamically decide whether to give a hint (and if so, which hint). There are well studied ways to balance the need to explore the impacts of giving different hints to learners at different times, and to exploit what is known to work.

Beyond the capacity to generate hints, the process of finding signals in historical data has interesting side-products. The most important corollary we presented is that the same intuition that guides generating PSPs can help us understand individual learners and predict retention. Piech et al found prototypical clusters of ways in which students solve problems that were predictive of exam scores [11]. This paper goes beyond that result by calculating a continuous valued path score which can make more fine grained predictions. Our ability to predict both retention and teacher suggestions are results that lend credibility to one another. The Path Score metric has obvious utility as a diagnostic measure that could help identify learners that may need more attention. Of course, knowing that a student has a bad path score does not imply *why* the student has a low probability of completing a subsequent challenge. It is only a correlation. It is not clean why Path Scores and probability of retention are exponentially related. One interpretation is that there is a monotonic ability scale and that each unit decrease in ability has compounding, and therefore exponential, impact on how well a student navigates through partial solutions.

There are more undiscovered patterns in how students navigate richly-structured assessments. Student trajectories remain a great mystery.

Conclusion

In this paper we explored ways to solve the machine learning question: how can we predict the way a teacher would encourage a student to make forward progress? The ability to make such prediction is useful for generating feedback at scale. We show that in the Code.org case study two algorithms with the same theoretical backing are accurate at recreating expert opinion. These algorithms can be applied to logs of learners working on problems for which there are no expert labels, and will produce an intelligent strategy for what learners ought to do. We then claim that the same theory can be used to calculate a statistic on how well a student navigated the assignment and show that this statistic predicts future retention. The way in which students solve problems is fertile ground for research in learning at scale. Instead of looking solely at a student's final answer, education of the future will take note of the journey the learner took to get there.

ACKNOWLEDGMENTS

We thank Code.org. Especially Ellen Speritus and Nan Li. We would also like to thank Steve Cooper, John Mitchell, Peter Norvig and Andy Nguyen for helpful advice. Chris is supported by NSF-GRFP grant number DGE-114747.

REFERENCES

1. Ahmadzadeh, M., Elliman, D., and Higgins, C. An analysis of patterns of debugging among novice computer science students. In *ACM SIGCSE Bulletin*, vol. 37, ACM (2005), 84–88.
2. Aleven, V. A., and Koedinger, K. R. An effective metacognitive strategy: Learning by doing and explaining with a computer-based cognitive tutor. *Cognitive science 26*, 2 (2002), 147–179.
3. Barnes, T., and Stamper, J. Toward automatic hint generation for logic proof tutoring using historical student data. In *Intelligent Tutoring Systems*, Springer (2008), 373–382.
4. Cheang, B., Kurnia, A., Lim, A., and Oon, W.-C. On automated grading of programming assignments in an academic institution. *Computers & Education 41*, 2 (2003), 121–131.
5. Fitzgerald, S., Lewandowski, G., McCauley, R., Murphy, L., Simon, B., Thomas, L., and Zander, C. Debugging: finding, fixing and flailing, a multi-institutional study of novice debuggers. *Computer Science Education 18*, 2 (2008), 93–116.
6. Fleiss, J. L., Levin, B., and Paik, M. C. The measurement of interrater agreement. *Statistical methods for rates and proportions 2* (1981), 212–236.
7. Huang, J., Piech, C., Nguyen, A., and Guibas, L. Syntactic and functional variability of a million code submissions in a machine learning mooc. In *AIED 2013 Workshops Proceedings Volume*, Citeseer (2013), 25.
8. Kulkarni, C., Wei, K. P., Le, H., Chia, D., Papadopoulos, K., Cheng, J., Koller, D., and Klemmer, S. R. Peer and self assessment in massive online classes. *ACM Transactions on Computer-Human Interaction (TOCHI) 20*, 6 (2013), 33.
9. Nguyen, A., Piech, C., Huang, J., and Guibas, L. Codewebs: scalable homework search for massive open online programming courses. In *Proceedings of the 23rd international conference on World wide web*, International World Wide Web Conferences Steering Committee (2014), 491–502.
10. Pappano, L. The year of the mooc. *The New York Times 2*, 12 (2012), 2012.
11. Piech, C., Sahami, M., Koller, D., Cooper, S., and Blikstein, P. Modeling how students learn to program. In *Proceedings of the 43rd ACM technical symposium on Computer Science Education*, ACM (2012), 153–160.
12. Puterman, M. L. *Markov decision processes: discrete stochastic dynamic programming*, vol. 414. John Wiley & Sons, 2009.
13. Ritter, S., Anderson, J. R., Koedinger, K. R., and Corbett, A. Cognitive tutor: Applied research in mathematics education. *Psychonomic bulletin & review 14*, 2 (2007), 249–255.
14. Rivers, K., and Koedinger, K. R. A canonicalizing model for building programming tutors. In *Intelligent Tutoring Systems*, Springer (2012), 591–593.
15. Rivers, K., and Koedinger, K. R. Automating hint generation with solution space path construction. In *Intelligent Tutoring Systems*, Springer (2014), 329–339.
16. Roll, I., Baker, R. S., Aleven, V., and Koedinger, K. R. On the benefits of seeking (and avoiding) help in online problem-solving environments. *Journal of the Learning Sciences*, just-accepted (2014).
17. Shapley, L. S. Stochastic games. *Proceedings of the National Academy of Sciences of the United States of America 39*, 10 (1953), 1095.
18. Singh, R., Gulwani, S., and Solar-Lezama, A. Automated feedback generation for introductory programming assignments. In *ACM SIGPLAN Notices*, vol. 48, ACM (2013), 15–26.
19. Szczerba, R. J., Galkowski, P., Glicktein, I., and Ternullo, N. Robust algorithm for real-time route planning. *Aerospace and Electronic Systems, IEEE Transactions on 36*, 3 (2000), 869–878.
20. Watson, C., Li, F. W., and Godwin, J. L. Bluefix: Using crowd-sourced feedback to support programming students in error diagnosis and repair. In *Advances in Web-Based Learning-ICWL 2012*. Springer, 2012, 228–239.
21. Weld, D. S., Adar, E., Chilton, L., Hoffmann, R., Horvitz, E., Koch, M., Landay, J., Lin, C. H., and Mausam, M. Personalized online educationa crowdsourcing challenge. In *Workshops at the Twenty-Sixth AAAI Conference on Artificial Intelligence* (2012).
22. Whitehill, J., Wu, T.-f., Bergsma, J., Movellan, J. R., and Ruvolo, P. L. Whose vote should count more: Optimal integration of labels from labelers of unknown expertise. In *Advances in neural information processing systems* (2009), 2035–2043.

Problems Before Solutions: Automated Problem Clarification at Scale

Soumya Basu
UC Berkeley
soumyab@berkeley.edu

Albert Wu
UC Berkeley
albert12132@berkeley.edu

Brian Hou
UC Berkeley
brian.hou@berkeley.edu

John DeNero
UC Berkeley
denero@berkeley.edu

ABSTRACT
Automatic assessment reduces the need for individual feedback in massive courses, but often focuses only on scoring solutions, rather than assessing whether students correctly understand problems. We present an enriched approach to automatic assessment that explicitly assists students in understanding the detailed specification of technical problems that they are asked to solve, in addition to evaluating their solutions. Students are given a suite of solution test cases, but they must first unlock each test case by validating its behavior before they are allowed to apply it to their proposed solution. When provided with this automated feedback early in the problem-solving process, students ask fewer clarificatory questions and express less confusion about assessments. As a result, instructors spend less time explaining problems to students. In a 1300-person university course, we observed that the vast majority of students chose to validate their understanding of test cases before attempting to solve problems. These students reported that the validation process improved their understanding.

Author Keywords
automated assessment; behavioral analytics; online learning

INTRODUCTION
Instructors of massive courses must be frugal and efficient with their attention to individuals in all aspects of course delivery. For assignments, automatic assessment of solutions can dramatically reduce or even eliminate the individual attention required for assigning scores, allowing instructors to focus on content delivery and interaction design. This paper describes the scaling benefits of another form of automated assessment for technical assignments: automatic verification of problem understanding. By validating each student's understanding of each problem statement automatically, our system substantially reduces the instructor intervention required for clarification and explanation of assignments.

L@S 2015, March 14–18, 2015, Vancouver, BC, Canada.

ACM 978-1-4503-3411-2/15/03 ... $15.00
http://dx.doi.org/10.1145/2724660.2724679

This paper describes a particular implementation of our approach to validating problem understanding. Our system, called OK[1], performs automatic assessment for programming-based assignments. Each assignment in our course is distributed with a suite of test cases that are designed to verify a student's proposed solution; OK applies these test cases and summarizes the results. However, students are not able to view these results unless they first validate their understanding of each test case. As a result, they cannot check their solution until after they demonstrate that they are at least attempting to solve the right problem.

Through an interactive process, the student is presented with a series of short-answer questions that ask about the potential behaviors of their program. Each question corresponds to a "locked" test case. By responding with the correct intended behavior, they "unlock" the test case and can then apply it to their proposed solution.

This unlocking process is designed to encourage students to understand details of the problem specification fully before attempting to develop a solution. Automating this process gives students instant feedback about their interpretation of each problem's description, feedback that is intended to reduce the amount of time that students spend developing solutions for misinterpreted variants of a problem. We found that students overwhelmingly chose to validate their problem understanding using our system before attempting to solve each problem. In addition, 78% of students responded positively to the system in an end-of-semester survey, despite the fact that unlocking test cases is an extra step in the process of completing their projects.

Creating an unlocking process for an assignment requires only a small amount of additional effort beyond the creation of test cases for automatic assessment, but provides substantial time savings. When students more often arrive at correct interpretations of problems independently and have increased confidence in their interpretation, they ask fewer clarificatory questions. For example, forum questions about one problem

[1] OK is hosted on `https://okpy.org`. Open-source development is hosted on `https://github.com/Cal-CS-61A-Staff/ok`.

in our course decreased by 79% in the semester after we deployed OK. Adding the unlocking process to all major assignments helped us scale our introductory computer science course[2] from 500 to 1300 students per semester in three years.

RELATED WORK

The sheer scale of massive open online courses (MOOCs) has increased demand for tools and techniques that automate aspects of course administration. Automated assessment now extends beyond multiple-choice to include free-response short answers [1]. Assessment at scale has also successfully leveraged the large pool of enrolled students as a source of human judgment [9]. These innovations in assessment allow for broader flexibility in assignment design.

The purpose of assignments is not only to assess progress, but also to support learning, and assessment is integral to the learning process [2]. Assignments are useful to students in validating their understanding [13]. In addition, assignments and their assessments highlight and even influence learning goals of a course [5]. Open-ended assignments that require integration of past concepts with current concepts are particularly effective for learning and retention [8]. This collection of prior research highlights the value of designing assessment systems that support learning directly. When learning to solve technical problems, a student will ideally receive feedback throughout the problem solving process.

Considerable prior research has focused on automated assessment of programming-based assignments, which are typically found in computer science courses, but increasingly appear in other technical fields. Automated assessment of programming assignments was first suggested more than 50 years ago [6]. In a recent survey, Ihantola *et al.* identify a wide range of recent features in automated program assessment systems, including test case construction assistance, submission management, automated scoring, and security features [7]. Noticeably absent from these features is any attempt to specifically provide feedback about problem understanding, rather than student solutions.

To scale a course to a massive size, instructors often rely on peer forums to assist students in understanding assignments. Indeed, online forums have been hailed as an essential component of a massive course [12]. However, the forums in massive courses often raise their own challenges. Mak *et al.* describe how large differences in skill between novices and experienced students can lead to friction and frustration among students, often requiring instructor moderation to maintain a productive discussion [12]. They found that half of students stopped participating in online forums, primarily because of "unacceptable behavior" from other participants. In our experience, peer forums can be particularly hostile to students who ask clarificatory questions that are similar to previous questions. Online forums certainly have a central role to play in massive courses, but the need for problem clarification may be addressed more effectively using an automated system that allows students to reach understanding independently or in small groups.

[2] `https://cs61a.org`

SOLVING TECHNICAL PROBLEMS

Technical problems appear in many disciplines and many varieties, but we focus here on problems that have descriptions written in natural language (e.g., English), but have solutions expressed in a formal language. For such problems, validating solutions is typically straightforward: the formal language is interpreted by a computer, which judges correctness based on a series of criteria. While programming problems are the focus of this paper, our approach could also apply to other assignments that use formal languages, such as constructing a logical proof.

Solving technical problems is an acquired skill that challenges many students. We seek to teach our students an effective multi-stage problem-solving process, and the OK system is designed to encourage and support that process.

Step 1: Problem Understanding

The first step in solving a technical problem is to understand the required properties of the solution from the problem description. Beyond just reading the prose, problem understanding involves identifying corner cases, clarifying details, and considering interactions with existing implementations.

For programming problems that involve implementing a function, the textbook *How to Design Programs* suggests first writing down a data representation, then writing down the purpose of the function, then illustrating its use with examples, then taking inventory of available inputs to the function [3]. All of these activities are examples of problem understanding, and they are useful activities that occur before any attempt at solving the problem.

In our experience, students often attempt to forego this step and focus immediately on writing a solution. With only a solution assessment tool at their disposal, they may attempt to reach a satisfactory solution through a process of trial-and-error. By contrast, including an automated assessment tool that explicitly targets this stage of the process not only encourages problem understanding before solution attempts, but also highlights problem understanding as a skill to be learned as part of a technical course.

Step 2: Planning

This second step involves developing a solution strategy, which may involve stating a natural language description or choosing among possible approaches. At this stage, the problem is understood, but the mechanics of how to solve it are still undetermined.

Assessment can also have a role to play here. The approach to designing a general solution can often be inspired by certain illustrative examples. The OK system asks students to predict the intended behavior of a program for specific cases. In doing so, they must work by hand through the process of computing some desired result. In our experience, selecting examples judiciously can provide automated guidance toward a solution.

We do not attempt to evaluate this effect, as the activity of solution planning is particularly difficult to measure. Indeed, past research has shown that hinting toward solutions does not necessarily improve student performance [10].

Step 3: Implementation

Finally, the plan must be expressed in the formal language required to satisfy the original problem. In programming assignments, this step requires detailed knowledge of a programming language.

If steps 1 and 2 are carried out successfully, automatic assessment of solutions is often sufficient to support students in this final stage. Small issues with language syntax or boundary conditions can be identified by applying a suite of well-designed test cases. The OK system also provides this support, as do many other automated assessment tools.

Solution assessment can also provide feedback about earlier stages, as students may identify issues with their solution plan or problem understanding based on the failure of a solution test case. However, this feedback is only offered after the student has invested significant time developing a proposed solution. Moreover, students who misunderstand a problem may fail to attribute a test case failure to this earlier misunderstanding. Therefore, we hypothesized that providing earlier feedback would be beneficial to students.

EXAMPLE PROBLEMS

The remainder of this paper describes the details and empirical evaluation of the OK system, focusing on its application to a single programming assignment that was used in our course before and after deploying OK.

The assignment involves implementing a simulator and several strategies for a jeopardy dice game called Hog [11]. In this game, players alternate turns in which they select some number of dice and roll them to score points. If at least one of the dice outcomes is 1, then the current player scores only 1 point that turn. Otherwise, the player scores the sum of the dice outcomes.

The first problem in the assignment is to implement a function called `roll_dice` that computes a player's score on a single turn, using the player's choice of how many dice to roll and a random function that simulates each roll. The description of the problem includes a specification of exactly how many times to simulate a dice roll, a detail often overlooked by students.

The second problem we consider in our evaluation, which appears near the end of the project, is to implement a function called `swap_strategy`. This function encodes a strategy for playing the game by specifying how many dice to choose under various score conditions. The strategy can be illustrated effectively using a handful of test cases.

This assignment is implemented in Python. Students are given less than two weeks to complete all problems, which are released together during the second week of the course. The Appendix contains further details of the parts of the assignment used in our evaluations.

```
=====================================================================
Assignment: Project 1: Hog
OK, version v1.3.10
=====================================================================

~~~~~~~~~~~~~~~~~~~~~~~~~~~~~~~~~~~~~~~~~~~~~~~~~~~~~~~~~~~~~~~~~~~~~
Unlocking tests

At each "? ", type what you would expect the output to be.
Type exit() to quit

---------------------------------------------------------------------
Question 1 > Suite 1 > Case 1
(cases remaining: 4)

>>> roll_dice(2, make_test_dice(4, 6, 1))
? 3
-- Not quite. Try again! --

? 10
-- OK! --

---------------------------------------------------------------------
```

Figure 1. An unlocking session where the student wishes to unlock question 1, initially provides an incorrect response, then provides a correct response.

SYSTEM DESIGN

The design of the OK assessment system includes a student interface, an instructor interface, and a mechanism for test-case locking and unlocking.

Interface for Students

The OK system integrates two kinds of assessments in a single interactive text-based interface presented in a terminal window and invoked from the command line.[3] Initially, test cases are locked, and the only available assessment focuses on problem understanding. As a byproduct of the understanding assessment, test cases are unlocked and become available for solution assessment.

Students start an assessment by selecting a problem. They are free to run the assessments at any time, before or after they attempt to implement a solution. When developing the system, we hoped that students would run the understanding assessment before attempting to solve the problem; observational results in the next section show that this order does indeed hold for most students.

Figure 1 contains a screenshot of this initial assessment, which we call an *unlocking session*. The system presents the student with a series of short-answer questions. Most of these questions consist of an expression to be evaluated and are answered by typing the correct value of the expression according to the problem description. In this example, the intended result is 10, the score received in a game of Hog by rolling a 4 and a 6. If the student is able to correctly state the intended result, then the interface advances to the next question. When students respond incorrectly, they are prompted to try again. This phase of the assessment is unaffected by whether or not the student has attempted a solution.

[3]The system could easily be adapted to the web, but one of our course goals is to build students' competence with command-line interfaces.

```
=====================================================================
Assignment: Project 1: Hog
OK, version v1.3.10
=====================================================================

~~~~~~~~~~~~~~~~~~~~~~~~~~~~~~~~~~~~~~~~~~~~~~~~~~~~~~~~~~~~~~~~~~~~~
Running tests

---------------------------------------------------------------------
Question 1 > Suite 1 > Case 1

>>> from hog import *
>>> roll_dice(2, make_test_dice(4, 6, 1))

# Error: expected
#     10
# but got
#

---------------------------------------------------------------------
Question 1
    Passed: 0
    Failed: 1
    Locked: 3
[k.........] 0.0% passed

There are still locked tests! Use the -u option to unlock them

---------------------------------------------------------------------
Test summary
    Passed: 0
    Failed: 1
    Locked: 3
[k.........] 0.0% passed
```

Figure 2. While there are still some tests that are locked, the OK system applies only the unlocked test cases for each question, but also reports the number of test cases that are still locked.

```
=====================================================================
Assignment: Project 1: Hog
OK, version v1.3.10
=====================================================================

~~~~~~~~~~~~~~~~~~~~~~~~~~~~~~~~~~~~~~~~~~~~~~~~~~~~~~~~~~~~~~~~~~~~~
Unlocking tests

At each "? ", type what you would expect the output to be.
Type exit() to quit

---------------------------------------------------------------------
Question 5 > Suite 1 > Case 1
(cases remaining: 12)

Q: The variables score0 and score1 are the scores for both
players. Under what conditions should the game continue?
Choose the number of the correct choice:
    0) While score0 and score1 are both less than goal
    1) While at least one of score0 or score1 is less than goal
    2) While score0 is less than goal
    3) While score1 is less than goal
? 3
-- Not quite. Try again! --

Choose the number of the correct choice:
    0) While score0 and score1 are both less than goal
    1) While at least one of score0 or score1 is less than goal
    2) While score0 is less than goal
    3) While score1 is less than goal
? 0
-- OK! --

---------------------------------------------------------------------
```

Figure 3. For this test case, it is rather difficult to predict the intended behavior without writing a program to do so. Therefore, we include conceptual questions in order to check the student's understanding, rather than requiring a tedious amount of computation by hand.

Each correctly answered question unlocks a corresponding test case. In Figure 1, the test case would evaluate a call to `roll_dice` using the student's implementation and report whether or not the result matched the intended result of 10.

After unlocking one or more test cases for a question, the student can run a solution assessment, as shown in Figure 2. This phase has the typical behavior of an automated program assessment tool. The student's solution is loaded automatically from the current directory. Test cases are executed in order. Each test case failure generates a description of the problem, typically comparing the expected and observed results.

Interactive questions to assess understanding are not limited to evaluating Python expressions. Some problems are sufficiently complex so evaluating an example by hand is arduous or unfeasible. Despite this constraint, the system can validate problem understanding by asking conceptual multiple-choice or short-answer questions. An example of a conceptual question is shown in Figure 3. In this example, rather than supplying the value of an expression, the student selects an answer choice. To dissuade random guessing, the order of answer choices is randomized.

Interface for Instructors

Instructors create test cases for both types of assessment: problem understanding and solution verification. However, the unlock-then-apply structure allows the same test case to be used for both phases of assessment. As a result, the additional effort required from the instructor to support both kinds of assessment is minimal, beyond the effort required just for solution assessment.

The only additional work needed is to construct the conceptual questions that substitute for particularly complex test cases. For the Hog project, we created 58 test cases and 5 conceptual questions. Thus, the only additional instructional effort came from designing the 5 conceptual questions and deciding which test cases were too complicated to predict by hand. In OK, test cases are specified as string pairs indicating expression and value, along with a small amount of set-up and comparison code.

Unlocking Mechanism

The design of the underlying unlocking mechanism was chosen to satisfy several constraints. First, we wanted to make sure that the unlocking phase was not trivial to circumvent by students. Second, we wanted to ensure that the test cases were correct once unlocked. In this way, all tests remain reliable, so students don't have to determine whether or not an issue lies within their implementation or the test itself. Our design makes it very difficult to extract the answers from the codebase while making sure that using the resulting answers only creates valid test cases for their solutions. In addition to the above, we designed our system to run locally on each student's computer, so that students can proceed through the project without a network connection.

Our mechanism relies on hashing in order to meet these constraints. Specifically, the staff knows every question Q (an input to a test case) and the answer to each question, A (the output to a test case). Let H be an irreversible hash function. We chose a hash-based message authentication code (MAC) [4]. The instructor distributes both Q and $H(A)$ to the students, along with the OK system which includes an implementation of H. When the student provides a guess G for a question, OK computes $H(G)$. If $H(G) = H(A)$, then we assume $G = A$ and use G as the test-case output for Q.

Our hash-based unlocking mechanism provides a fully-local way to check student answers for our questions. In addition, the mechanism has proven resilient to any method of unlocking test cases automatically without knowing the correct responses, as far as we have been able to observe.

EVALUATION

We sought to measure the effectiveness of our approach on two dimensions: whether or not the instructor workload actually decreased and whether or not students used the unlocking system and found it valuable. In order to measure whether or not the instructor workload decreased, we monitored the class forum and kept track of the number of questions asked.

We measured our students' experience in two ways. First, we checked to see whether or not students were unlocking in the correct stage of the problem solving process—at the beginning. Then, we looked at the types of questions that were asked on the class message board. Finally, we asked the students how helpful they found the unlocking process in an online survey.

Usage Pattern

Students had the option to attempt a solution before assessing their understanding or vice versa. The OK system allowed us to measure this ordering directly. With permission from students, the system would send both their solution progress and unlocking session information to an instructional server. We received data on whether the student was unlocking a question or not, what question they were unlocking, and which problems they had attempted to solve from the assignment.

Our analysis was complicated by the fact that not all unlocking sessions were reported to the server. Students had the option of unlocking tests for all problems at once; if they did so, we collected no data. Students could also choose not to share their session data with us. In addition, students may have started to implement solutions in a way that we could not record. To determine when a student started a question, we looked for edits to the files submitted to our server by OK. It is possible that students began solutions in another external file, in which case we would have been unable to detect their progress. However, we believe that very few students did so, because of convenience. When students edited the files we tracked, they could easily check their solutions using OK.

For all of these events, we recorded the time when they happened, which allowed us to assess whether or not students unlocked test cases before attempting to solve problems.

In this class, we had 1287 students who received grades for this project and 1272 students who sent usage statistics to our server for at least one problem—the completion rate is lower than these numbers suggest because some students dropped

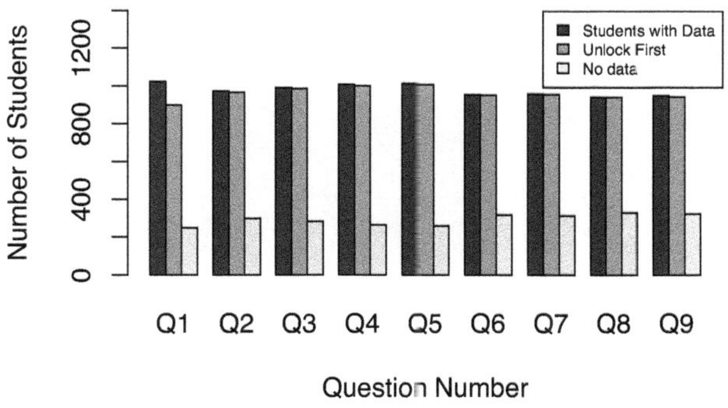

Figure 4. The total number of students who provided unlocking data for each question, as well as the number of students that interacted with the autograder, but did not provide data for that question.

the class during this project. Usage statistics were not collected when students opted out or had a slow network connection; attempts to contact our server were limited to less than a second.

Figure 4 shows the fraction of students for which we have data who unlocked test cases for a problem, verifying their understanding, before attempting to solve the problem. For Question 1, 88% of students unlocked the test cases before they started writing code. That fraction increased to 99.5% by the end of the project, where almost all students unlocked test cases before attempting a solution.

While these numbers are encouraging, we also note the large number of students with no unlocking data, and we believe that some of these students might also not follow our expected behavior. However, even a pessimistic assumption where all unknown students fail to follow our expected behavior shows that 70% to 79% of students meet our expectations, which is still a strong majority.

The usage statistics show students are using the unlocking mechanism at the beginning of the problem solving process, implying that it is serving its true purpose.

Class Forum

In our course, we use the Piazza online forum. A student can make a post with his or her question and receive a response from one of the staff members or a fellow student, usually in under an hour. The average response time in our course is about 11 minutes.

Due to the short response times, different students often make similar posts because they have the same misunderstanding about the project specifications. One common use of Piazza is for students to post their autograder test failures and ask for debugging help. If the initial response does not fully answer their question, then they are able to post a follow-up question.

To evaluate changes in student behavior, we counted and classified posts about two problems from the Hog assignment described earlier. In Fall 2013, students received test cases

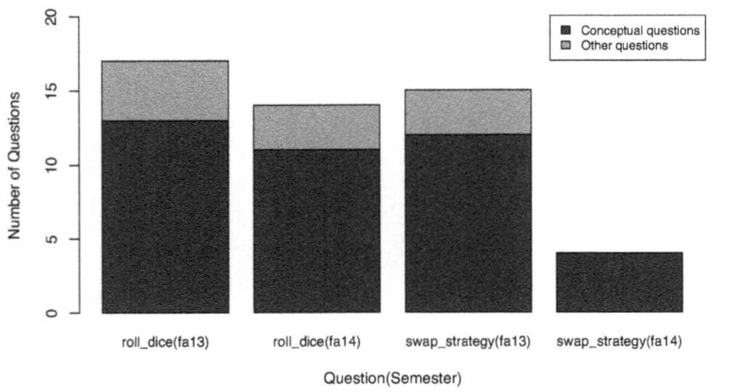

Figure 5. Number of forum questions posted about each problem, by semester. Each bar shows the total number of questions on Piazza, classified as conceptual questions (misunderstanding or clarification of the problem) or other kinds of questions.

embedded in a source code file, but they were not explicitly encouraged to read those tests. In Fall 2014, similar test cases were provided, but students had to unlock them before using them to check correctness. We focused our analysis on two problems that students historically had trouble understanding, `roll_dice` and `swap_strategy`. We classified all forum posts about these two problems as either conceptual questions (misunderstanding or clarification of the problem) or other questions (usually issues with implementation).

To find all of the relevant posts, we looked at all forum posts that were posted after the project was released until when the project was due. Two of this paper's authors independently went through all of the posts related to the project for each problem. A post was only classified for that problem if it specifically asked about that problem, not whether the final issue was actually in that problem. Both authors independently decided whether or not the question was a misunderstanding or clarification of the problem description (or some other type of question) based on the response and any follow-up questions that were asked. After finishing classification, the authors compared their judgments for each question and resolved discrepancies through discussion.

In the posts from Fall 2014, we classified questions that asked for help unlocking the tests as conceptual questions. Since students' Piazza questions about these two problems were usually a result of misunderstanding the prompt, we expected to see fewer questions asked about them.

In Fall 2013, we had 1011 students with a submission for this project. In Fall 2014, we had 1287 students. Despite this 27% increase in students, Figure 5 shows that the number of forum posts about these questions decreased substantially. In particular, Piazza questions about `swap_strategy` dropped significantly after unlocking was introduced. In addition, we have observed that many forum questions are repeated in other settings as well (discussion sections and office hours). These results imply that significant instructor time was saved through other venues.

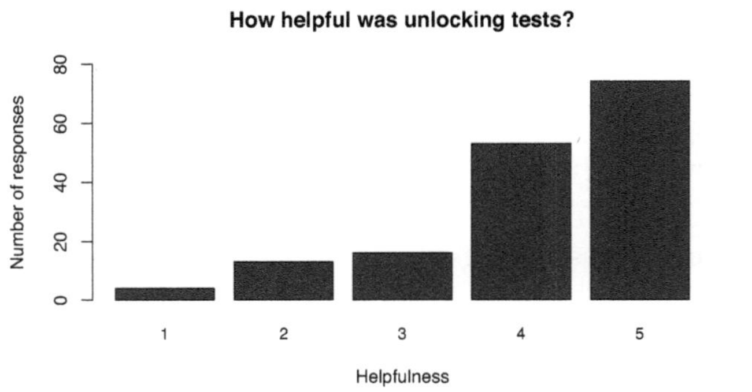

Figure 6. Survey results for the question "How helpful do you find unlocking test cases to be in improving your understanding of the project?" Answers are based on a scale from 1 ("completely unhelpful") to 5 ("very helpful").

The ratio of conceptual questions versus other questions remained fairly constant between semesters. However, in Fall 2014, the overwhelming majority of the conceptual Piazza questions were asked by students that were having trouble unlocking the tests, rather than by students who unlocked the tests and implemented a function that did not match our specifications. This trend imples that students who are able to unlock our tests understand what the problem statement was asking. In addition, since unlocking a test case is not implementation specific, these questions can be asked to other classmates and answered by instructors in small groups as well, without students sharing their code.

Survey Results

In the Spring 2014 offering of the course, we had unlocking partially implemented for all projects. While many simple questions were locked, we had not written any conceptual questions. After the completion of four projects that used the partially implemented unlocking mechanism, we issued a student survey to measure the effectiveness of the unlocking mechanism and to garner suggestions from students. Due to the partial implementation, these students were able to compare how much unlocking helped.

The results shown in Figure 6 indicate the unlocking mechanism reinforced students' conceptual understanding of project questions. Students were asked to answer the question "How helpful do you find unlocking test cases to be in improving your understanding of the project?" from a scale of 1 ("completely unhelpful") to 5 ("very helpful"). Out of 160 responses, 74 (46%) students chose a score of 5 and 53 (33%) students chose a score of 4.

In addition, we were also interested in how students interacted with unlocking when working in groups. Two of our four projects allowed students to work in pairs, the rationale being that project partners can provide each other with different insights on problem solving. In the context of unlocking, partners would ideally complete the unlocking procedure together and address any misunderstandings in the process.

Responses to the question "If you worked with a partner, how did you and your partner unlock tests?" are shown in Fig-

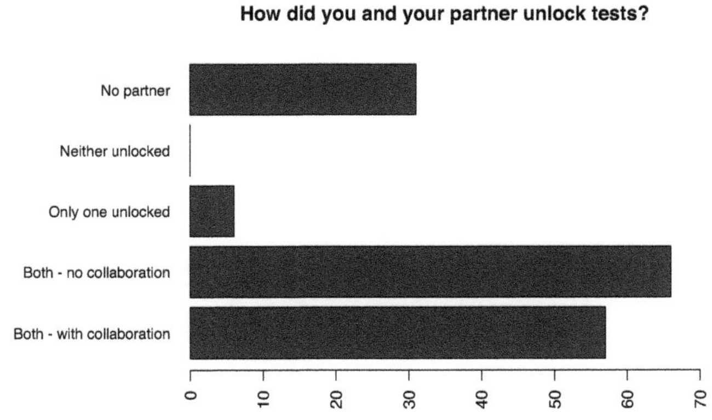

Both my partner and I unlocked tests with each other's help	**57**	36%
Both my partner and I unlocked tests without each other's help	**66**	41%
Only one partner in our group unlocked tests	**6**	4%
Neither of us unlocked tests	**0**	0%
I did not work with a partner	**31**	19%

Figure 7. Survey results for the question "If you worked with a partner, how did you and your partner unlock tests?"

ure 7. Out of 160 responses, only 6 students (4%) reported that "one partner in our group unlocked tests." Few students progressed through the projects without interacting with the unlocking mechanism. In order to simply gain access to the test case, the fastest way to do so would be to only have one partner be responsible for all of the unlocking. Since both partners went through the unlocking process, this suggests that a majority of students made a conscious decision to reinforce their conceptual understanding of the project prompts before advancing to program implementation. Of the project groups where both partners unlocked, 57 students (36%) "unlocked tests with [their partner's] help," while 66 students (41%) "unlocked tests without [their partner's] help."

We also included the option for students to provide free-form responses. The responses generally verified that unlocking "helped [students] work through the thought process" and "[got students] to understand what [they] need to do first." We had one project that did not use unlocking at all; one student suggested "add[ing] this feature" to that project, as unlocking aided in "understand[ing] the question...much better, especially since some of the instructions can be confusing or unclear." In addition to supplementing instructor guidance, the unlocking mechanism can also clarify unexpected ambiguities in assignment instructions.

One student noted that "unlock[ing does not] help with implementation" and instead is better suited for students who are "totally lost." While the comment may have been intended as a complaint, it actually reinforces the distinction between unlocking for assessing conceptual understanding and applying test cases for assessing implementation correctness.

CONCLUSION

As class sizes increase, automated feedback becomes increasingly important to both students and instructors. Our work complements prior efforts to assess solutions by also assessing problem understanding. This additional feedback encourages an effective approach to solving technical problems by providing feedback early in the problem solving process in order to make sure that students do not waste their time trying to solve an incorrect interpretation of the given problem.

Our approach has multiple benefits to both students and instructors. First of all, instructional effort is reduced while feedback is given instantaneously and consistently. Students save time by avoiding incorrect solutions based on misunderstandings, and instructors avoid helping students debug implementations that are based on misinterpretation.

Through our evaluations, we found this additional form of automated assessment to have positive effects. The number of questions instructors were asked decreased, and students stated that unlocking test cases was helpful. Perhaps most encouraging of all, the usage patterns we observed suggested that our students were adopting an effective approach to solving technical problems.

APPENDIX

The Game of Hog

The game of Hog is our first project and the project that we used during our evaluation of the unlocking mechanism. The rules were described to the students as follows:

In Hog, two players alternate turns trying to reach 100 points first. On each turn, the current player chooses some number of dice to roll, up to 10. Her turn score is the sum of the dice outcomes, unless any of the dice come up a 1, in which case the score for her turn is only 1 point (the **Pig out** rule).

To spice up the game, we will play with some special rules:

1. **Free bacon.** If a player chooses to roll zero dice, she scores one more than the largest digit in her opponent's score. For example, if Player 1 has 42 points, Player 0 gains 1 + max(4, 2) = 5 points by rolling zero dice. If Player 1 has 48 points, Player 0 gains 1 + max(4, 8) = 9 points.

2. **Hog wild.** If the sum of both players' total scores is a multiple of seven (e.g., 14, 21, 35), then the current player rolls four-sided dice instead of the usual six-sided dice.

3. **Swine swap.** If at the end of a turn one of the player's total score is exactly double the other's, then the players swap total scores. Example 1: Player 0 has 20 points and Player 1 has 5; it is Player 1's turn. She scores 5 more, bringing her total to 10. The players swap scores: Player 0 now has 10 points and Player 1 has 20. It is now Player 0's turn. Example 2: Player 0 has 90 points and Player 1 has 50; it is Player 0's turn. She scores 10 more, bringing her total to 100. The players swap scores, and Player 1 wins the game 100 to 50.

The project prompt and rules are the same for the two semesters that we are comparing.

Roll Dice Function

The `roll_dice` function is a problem about simulating simultaneous dice rolls. The exact prompt that we gave them is as follows:

Implement the `roll_dice` function in hog.py, which returns the number of points scored by rolling a fixed positive number of dice: either the sum of the dice or 1. To obtain a single outcome of a dice roll, call dice(). You should call this function exactly `num_rolls` times in your implementation. The only rule you need to consider for this problem is *Pig out*.

In Fall 2014, since we had the unlocking mechanism, we added a few questions in order to aid understanding of our testing suite. Specifically, the test scenarios that we checked in Fall 2013 were the following:

```
>>> counted_dice = make_test_dice(4, 1, 2)
>>> roll_dice(2, make_test_dice(4, 6, 1))
10
>>> roll_dice(3, make_test_dice(4, 6, 1))
1
>>> roll_dice(3, make_test_dice(1, 2, 3))
1
>>> roll_dice(3, counted_dice)
1
>>> roll_dice(1, counted_dice)
4
>>> test_dice = make_test_dice(4,2,3,3,4,1)
>>> roll_dice(5, test_dice)
16
>>> roll_dice(2, make_test_dice(1))
1
```

In addition, in Fall 2014, we added some more scenarios in order to help students understand the Fall 2013 tests that were only used for unlocking purposes:

```
>>> test_dice = make_test_dice(4, 1, 2)
>>> test_dice()
4
>>> test_dice() # Second call
1
>>> test_dice() # Third call
2
>>> test_dice() # Fourth call
4
```

Swap Strategy Function

The `swap_strategy` function asks students to implement a strategy that takes advantage of the Swine swap rule. The exact prompt that we gave them is as follows:

A strategy can also take advantage of the Swine swap rule. Implement `swap_strategy`, which

1. Rolls 0 if it would cause a beneficial swap that gains points.
2. Rolls `BASELINE_NUM_ROLLS` if rolling 0 would cause a harmful swap that loses points.
3. If rolling 0 would not cause a swap, then do so if it would give at least `BACON_MARGIN` points and roll `BASELINE_NUM_ROLLS` otherwise.

In Fall 2013, we had the following scenarios:

```
>>> swap_strategy(23, 60)
0
>>> swap_strategy(27, 17)
5
>>> swap_strategy(50, 80)
0
>>> swap_strategy(12, 12)
5
>>> swap_strategy(12, 34)
0
>>> swap_strategy(8, 9)
4
>>> swap_strategy(32, 43)
0
>>> swap_strategy(20, 32)
4
```

In Fall 2014, we had the following scenarios:

```
>>> swap_strategy(23, 60)
0
>>> swap_strategy(27, 17)
5
>>> swap_strategy(50, 80)
0
>>> swap_strategy(12, 12)
5
>>> swap_strategy(15, 34, 5, 4)
0
>>> swap_strategy(8, 9, 5, 4)
4
>>> swap_strategy(32, 40, 5, 4)
0
>>> swap_strategy(20, 32, 5, 4)
4
```

For all of the above tests, students had to unlock them in order to clarify their understanding.

ACKNOWLEDGMENTS

This work was supported by a Google Research Cloud Credits Award.

REFERENCES

1. Brooks, M., Basu, S., Jacobs, C., and Vanderwende, L. Divide and correct: Using clusters to grade short answers at scale. In *Proceedings of the First ACM Conference on Learning @ Scale Conference*, L@S '14, ACM (New York, NY, USA, 2014), 89–98.
2. Earl, L. M. *Assessment As Learning: Using Classroom Assessment to Maximize Student Learning*. Corwin, 2003.
3. Felleisen, M., Findler, R. B., Flatt, M., and Krishnamurthi, S. *How to Design Programs: An Introduction to Programming and Computing*. MIT Press, Cambridge, MA, USA, 2001.
4. H. Krawczyk, M. Bellare, R. C. HMAC: Keyed-Hashing for Message Authentication. RFC 2104.

5. Heywood, J. *Assessment in higher education: Student learning, teaching, programmes and institutions.* 2000.
6. Hollingsworth, J. Automatic graders for programming classes. *Commun. ACM 3*, 10 (Oct. 1960), 528–529.
7. Ihantola, P., Ahoniemi, T., Karavirta, V., and Seppälä, O. Review of recent systems for automatic assessment of programming assignments. In *Proceedings of the 10th Koli Calling International Conference on Computing Education Research*, Koli Calling '10, ACM (New York, NY, USA, 2010), 86–93.
8. Karpicke, J. D., and Roediger, H. L. The critical importance of retrieval for learning. *Science 319*, 5865 (2008), 966–968.
9. Kulkarni, C. E., Socher, R., Bernstein, M. S., and Klemmer, S. R. Scaling short-answer grading by combining peer assessment with algorithmic scoring. In *Proceedings of the First ACM Conference on Learning @ Scale Conference*, L@S '14, ACM (New York, NY, USA, 2014), 99–108.
10. O'Rourke, E., Ballweber, C., and Popović, Z. Hint systems may negatively impact performance in educational games. In *Proceedings of the First ACM Conference on Learning @ Scale Conference*, L@S '14, ACM (New York, NY, USA 2014), 51–60.
11. Parlante, N., Zelenski, J., Dodds, Z., Vonnegut, W., Malan, D. J., Murtagh, T. P., Neller, T. W., Sherriff, M., and Zingaro, D. Nifty assignments. In *Proceedings of the 41st ACM Technical Symposium on Computer Science Education*, SIGCSE '10, ACM (New York, NY, USA, 2010), 478–479.
12. Sui Fai John Mak, Roy Williams, J. M. Blogs and forums as communication and learning tools in a MOOC. In *Proceedings of the Seventh International Conference on Networked Learning 2010* (2010), 275–284.
13. Thorpe, M. Assessment and third generation distance education. *Distance Education 19*, 2 (1998), 265–286.

Machine Learning for Learning at Scale

Peter Norvig
Director of Research, Google Inc.

Abstract
There is great enthusiasm for the idea that massive amounts of data from online interactions of learners with material can lead to a rapid improvement cycle, driven by analysis of the data, experimentation, and intervention to do more of what works and less of what doesn't. This talk discusses techniques for working with massive amounts of data.

Bio
Peter Norvig is a Director of Research at Google Inc. Previously he was head of Google's core search algorithms group, and of NASA Ames's Computational Sciences Division, making him NASA's senior computer scientist. He received the NASA Exceptional Achievement Award in 2001. He has taught at the University of Southern California and the University of California at Berkeley, from which he received a Ph.D. in 1986 and the distinguished alumni award in 2006. He was co-teacher of an Artificial Intelligence class that signed up 160,000 students, helping to kick off the current round of massive open online classes.

His publications include the books Artificial Intelligence: A Modern Approach (the leading textbook in the field), Paradigms of AI Programming: Case Studies in Common Lisp, Verbmobil: A Translation System for Face-to-Face Dialog, and Intelligent Help Systems for UNIX. He is also the author of the Gettysburg Powerpoint Presentation and the world's longest palindromic sentence. He is a fellow of the AAAI, ACM, The California Academy of Science and The American Academy of Arts & Sciences.

L@S 2015, March 14–18, 2015, Vancouver, BC, Canada.
ACM 978-1-4503-3411-2/15/03
http://dx.doi.org/10.1145/2724660.2735205

Towards Capturing Learners Sentiment and Context

Jaye Clarkes-Nias
Bowie State University
14000 Jericho Park Road
Bowie, MD 20715-9465
jclarknias@gmail.com

Oliver Bent
IBM Research | Africa.
Nairobi, Kenya
oliverbent@ke.ibm.com

Juliet Mutahi
IBM Research | Africa.
Nairobi, Kenya
julimuta@ke.ibm.com

Komminist Weldemariam
IBM Research | Africa.
Nairobi, Kenya
k.weldemariam@ke.ibm.com

Andrew Kinai
IBM Research | Africa.
Nairobi, Kenya
andkinai@ke.ibm.com

Saurabh Srivastava
IBM Research | India
New Dehli, India
saurabhsrivastava@in.ibm.com

L@S 2015, March 14–18, 2015, Vancouver, BC, Canada.
ACM 978-1-4503-3411-2/15/03.
http://dx.doi.org/10.1145/2724660.2728662

Abstract
We report on the motivation and qualitative studies that examine the design of a sentiment and context collection tool in a mobile-enabled blended learning technology. The tool concept emerged from field studies with teachers and students from two primary schools in Kenya. In this paper, we discuss the background and motivation of learners sentiment and context. Next, we present the overall design of the proposed module and its prototype implementation in a blended learning environment. Detailed discussions on the algorithms underlying the tool are beyond the scope of this paper.

Author Keywords
Education; blended learning; context; sentiment; user interface; mobile computing.

ACM Classification Keywords
H.5.m [Information interfaces and presentation (e.g., HCI)]: Miscellaneous.

Introduction
Students learning outcomes vary based on multiple factors such as skill levels, motivation, demography, teacher affinity, etc. In significant parts of the world such as Africa, varying socio-economic, cultural,

political, religious and social factors continue to be dominant threats to learning outcomes in most public schools.

Currently, teachers are expected to perform various activities to understand their student sentiment, context and emotion. These include monitoring attendance and behavior; intervening for poorly performing students; conducting parent counseling for multiple student groups at multiple grades and varying skill levels.

Most sentiment data collection solutions (e.g., [3, 7, 1]) explicitly collect learner's sentiment (such as happy, excited, anxious) through feedback or user input; use a gamification approach to collect learners current affective state, interpret learners behavioral indicators and assess learners cognitive context through an adaptive approach [5]; or interactive context dialogue systems to share contextual situations and sentiment, experiences and knowledge [4, 6]. From our experience and as noted in [5], explicit-based data collection (e.g. by presenting questionnaires on the screen) tends to disrupt the learners experience of flow. Moreover, while novel, none of the deployed systems designed to collect sentiment data in a blended learning model.

In this paper, we combine both implicit and explicit means of collecting learner sentiment and context. The rapid adoption of digital learning delivered through web and now on handheld devices (e.g. smart phones, tablets) allows for the collection of sentiment and context data by instrumenting user-interactions with learning resources.

In what follows, first we report on our field studies that resulted in a conceptual view of a sentiment module within a blended learning environment. Next, we present the design and implementation of a sentiment and context data collection module. Finally, we discuss and conclude the paper.

Motivation and Field Study

Our vision for the sentiment module was influenced by (i) extensive interactions we had with a group of students and teachers from primary schools in Kenya, and (ii) the lack of existing adaptive tool-support for collecting such data.

We conduced field studies with teachers and students from two primary schools, Nairobi, Kenya. One public school with poor school infrastructure and one private school with nationally recognized infrastructure. With the teachers, our goal was to study how they identify a student struggling (*at-risk*) with sentiment/context and the perceived impact of this aspect on their students learning outcomes. With students, we experimented how they can express their sentiment with a given context using visual representations.

A key observation we made in the course of our discussions with teachers was all the teachers agreed that the sentiment and context of a student is one of the most important factors that could impede their learning progress. Upon discussion of the factors determining a student is at risk; the teachers indicated that academic performance is not the highest indicator of risk. In their experience, students from their communities may not be academically inclined but may still be successful in life due to effort. The biggest challenge for the teachers however is, how to identify the issue as early as possible, and how and when it has started. Currently, the only time they notice

Table 1: Sample sentiment scores.

Sentiment	Very -ve (-2)	-ve (-1)	Neutral (0)	+ve (1)	Very +ve (2)	# Pupil	Results (rounded)
Confused	0	7	0	0	0	7	**-1**
Excited	0	0	0	0	8	8	**2**
Smart	0	0	0	4	6	10	**2**
Great	0	0	0	1	6	7	**2**
Frustrated	2	6	1	0	0	9	**-1**
Hungry	2	5	3	0	0	10	**-1**

sentimental or contextual problems is either the student performance drops significantly or he or she showed some degree of behavioral changes.

With the students, we studied the interpretation of sentiment to create a broader classification based on semantic orientation on a 5-point scale. To assess how locally relevant the sentiments are we translated the English meaning of each sentiments to their Swahili (the national language of Kenya) counterpart.

Thirty-three (33) pupils from public primary school participated in this workshop. We further divided them into 4 groups, where each group was given a subset of the sentiment list (36 in total) and asked them to give polarity values on scale 1 to 5.

Table 1 shows sample sentiment scoring results from the student workshop. The sentiment score is calculated for each pupil based on a weighted average. In addition to the polarity value given to each sentiment, it also has an associated image and weighted sentiment value that is assigned.

A key observation we made in the course of this workshop with pupils was some sentiments (like scared, alone, shocked and sleepy) often considered negative mood were ranked *neutral* by the majority of the pupils. We even have had one student who considered *alone* as the highest possible positive sentiment. All in all, 83% of the ranks as compared to our expectation. However, different results were found when the pupils were given the same sentiments in Swahili (Table 2), with 98% close to what we initially expected.

Table 2: Comparison between English and Swahili sentiment weights.

Sentiment (English)	Weight	Sentiment (Swahili)	Weight
Alone	0	Peke yangu	0
Confused	-1	Changanikiwa	0
Good	1	Vizuri	1
Happy	1	Furaha	2
Loved	2	Pendo	2
Sad	-1	Huzuni	-1
Scared	0	Uoga	-1
Sleepy	0	Uzingizi	0

The findings provided great insights to our team on how we should approach the development of a dynamic sentiment and context capturing system in a blended learning environment. Most importantly, it convinced us of the need to rigorously track student sentiment and context along with performance and engagement factors to generate a student's holistic profile.

Design and Implementation

As mentioned in the previous section, discussions with teachers resulted in the requirement to identify the contextual factors that can affect the learning performance of students beyond academic constraints.

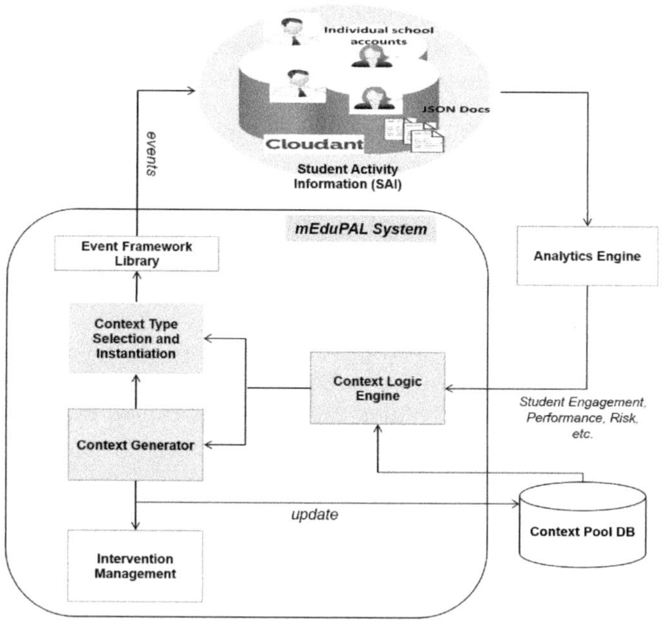

Figure 1: Simplified view of the sentiment module architecture.

Figure 1 shows an overview of the sentiment module architecture designed with this requirement. The *Context Logic Engine* interprets two levels of explicit and implicit sentiment from the output of the *Analytics Engine*, by matching to known contexts contained in the *Context Pool DB*. The *Analytics Engine* contains a number of analytics models to describe the sentiment, engagement, performance of the student. The *Context Type Selection and Instantiation* considers which context (e.g., classroom, outside classroom or interactive context) and renders the appropriate questions on the sentiment dialog interface within the blended learning environment (i.e. mEduPAL system).

The *context generator* module draws deeper inferences on what caused a particular sentiment (e.g. if a student repeatedly indicates that "I feel sick", the module may make use of external data sources such as demographics, available in the student longitudinal record) in order to further explore and reason about the sentiment and content of the student.

The sentiment module is designed to capture three forms of sentiment: *generic*, *content-centric* and *poll-based* sentiments.

The *generic sentiment* is meant to allow students to express their general feeling (e.g., annoyed, bored, confused, excited, happy, sad). Depending on their assessment how they feel, second level context questions will be instantiated through feedback from the *Analytics Engine*. For example *"How are you feeling today?"* is presented as an opportunity for a student to update their status. The response might be *"confused"*, the *Context Logic Engine* would then determine if further questioning based on the current context may better describe this status, e.g. "Tell me more about the source of your feelings?".

The *content-centric* sentiment is captured in relation to engagement which is computed based on user interactions with content on the mobile device. Upon completion of a learning activity (reading, performing a quiz, watching a video, etc.), based on the engagement level and/or performance results of the student (computed by the *Analytics Engine*), the student may be prompted to answer a question regarding their understanding of the topic presented (Figure 2). More specifically, the *Context Logic Engine* receives a dynamic input from the analytics engine, to then interpret. For example, the student's completion index for the content just viewed, along with past values of completion index in similar content items. This information is used to describe any change of the student's current learning context.

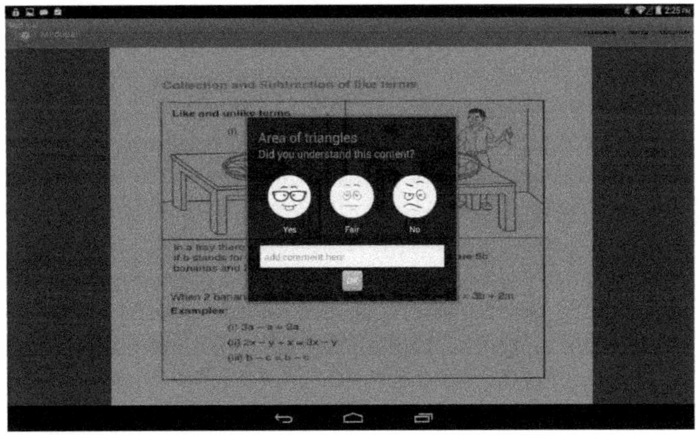

Figure 2: Example: Content-centric sentiment query interface.

Finally, the *poll-based* sentiment is specifically meant for in-classroom mode, to assess classroom engagement and learning outcomes. During classroom instruction the teacher can now instantiate a question and poll the class as each topic is covered, to address the specific feedback they may seek on how the students are following the in class material. This can give the chance for the teacher to revise their instruction in realtime, with a more complete insight into the whole classes understanding, through combination with the inferences already made by the sentiment module.

It should be noted that the collected sentiment and context data are captured through the *Event Framework Library*, which is a customisable and extensible event generation and collection library. It automatically syncs the event data with the *Student Activity Information (SAI)* on cloud.

Discussion and Future Work

We ran a limited pilot in a classroom composed of 18 students attending Grade 5 Mathematics and Science classes. Two lessons in Mathematics (topic "Area of Shapes") and Science (topic "States of Matter") were conducted. We tested the usability of the sentiment module as a component of the overall learning system.

For each lesson, students were given learning resources (contents and assessments/quizzes). The students posted their feeling/sentiment using the context interface when interacting with the learning system (generic sentiment). The engine further interacted with students to understand their context of the reported feeling/sentiment. Similarly, the sentiment engine was able to collect content-centric (Figure 2) and poll-based sentiments while the students interact with the content and the teachers sent poll questions to the classroom, respectively. All the collected data are sent to the cloud storage (i.e. Cloudant, a globally distributed database-as-a-service [2]). Using the collected sentiments, we defined MapReduce functions on Cloudant, extracted views, generated visualizations and rendered on the teacher device along with performance and engagement visualizations.

Currently, we are in the process of launching a pilot at school using our technology. The availability of this data produces new opportunities for learning at scale in education where such data has not been available in blended learning environments. The opportunities are to create historic/longitudinal sentiment data for holistic student profiles (contained in the *Context Pool DB*), to better understand their learning styles/preferences and assist in the generation of interventions for struggling (or at-risk) students. Finally, using the data we will harden our technology platform and improve underlying algorithms based on field data.

References

[1] Altrabsheh, N., Cocea, M., and Fallahkhair, S. Learning sentiment from students' feedback for real-time interventions in classrooms. In *Adaptive and Intelligent Systems - Third International Conference, ICAIS 2014, Bournemouth, UK, September 8-10, 2014. Proceedings*, Springer (2014), 40–49.

[2] Cloudant. `https://cloudant.com/`.

[3] The eSpark platform. `https://esparklearning.com/`.

[4] Jaques, P. A., and Vicari, R. M. A BDI Approach to Infer Student's Emotions in an Intelligent Learning Environment. *Comput. Educ. 49*, 2 (2007), 360–384.

[5] Michael Bedek, Paul Seitlinger, S. K. D. A. Inferring a Learner's Cognitive, Motivational and Emotional State in a Digital Educational Game. *Electronic Journal of e-Learning 10*, 2 (2012), 172–184.

[6] Qu, L., and Johnson, W. L. Detecting the Learner's Motivational States in An Interactive Learning Environment. In *AIED*, IOS Press (2005), 547–554.

[7] Qu, L., Wang, N., and Johnson, W. L. Choosing when to interact with learners. In *IUI*, ACM (2004), 307–309.

[8] Uwezo Kenya. Are Our Children Learning? Annual Learning Assessment Report., 2011. `http://goo.gl/ocxYTP`.

Measuring and Maximizing the Effectiveness of Honor Codes in Online Courses

Henry Corrigan-Gibbs
Stanford University
Stanford, CA, USA
henrycg@stanford.edu

Edward Cutrell
Microsoft Research India
Bangalore, Karnataka, India
cutrell@microsoft.com

Nakull Gupta
Microsoft Research India
Bangalore, Karnataka, India
t-nakgup@microsoft.com

William Thies
Microsoft Research India
Bangalore, Karnataka, India
thies@microsoft.com

Curtis Northcutt
MIT EECS
Cambridge, MA, USA
cgn@mit.edu

L@S 2015, March 14–18, 2015, Vancouver, BC, Canada.
ACM 978-1-4503-3411-2/15/03.
http://dx.doi.org/10.1145/2724660.2728663

Abstract
We measure the effectiveness of a traditional honor code at deterring cheating in an online examination, and we compare it to that of a stern warning. Through experimental evaluation in a 409-student online course, we find that a pre-task warning leads to a significant decrease in the rate of cheating while an honor code has a smaller (non-significant) effect. Unlike much prior work, we measure the rate of cheating directly and we do not rely on potentially inaccurate post-examination surveys. Our findings demonstrate that replacing traditional honor codes with warnings could be a simple and effective way to deter cheating in online courses.

Author Keywords
cheating; honeypot; honor code; online course; MOOC

ACM Classification Keywords
K.3 [Computers and Education]; J.4 [Social and behavioral sciences]: Psychology.

Introduction
Honor codes are surprisingly effective at discouraging cheating [9] and encouraging truth-telling [6] in physical encounters. In online environments, however, prior work has not found that honor codes have a discernible impact on cheating behavior [7, 8]. In spite of the lack of

evidence supporting the use of traditional honor codes on the Web, online education platforms are adopting and deploying conventional honor codes for online use [3, 4].

In this work, we use a randomized controlled trial to rigorously evaluate the effectiveness of a conventional honor code at deterring cheating in an online course. In addition, we evaluate a potential alternative to traditional honor codes: a stern pre-task *warning*. By priming test-takers with a warning that details the potential consequences of cheating, we aim to increase the perceived costs and decrease the expected benefits of cheating. We evaluated the effectiveness of our pre-task honor code and warning in the context of the final examination for an online course in India.

Along the way, we introduce a new a method for directly measuring rates of cheating in online courses that does not rely on potentially inaccurate *post hoc* self-reporting. To measure cheating, we created a Google-indexed "honeypot" website containing key words and phrases from the online exam. Using a tracking cookie, we were able to identify students who visited our honeypot website while taking the exam—in violation of the rules of the exam. We also manually analyzed answers to a free-response question to detect copying from peers and online resources (other than the honeypot).

Prior work on physical-world cheating informs our approach. Mazar et al. theorize that people decide to cheat based on (1) the expected payout (estimated costs and benefits) of cheating and (2) "the manner in which the act of" acting dishonestly makes a person "perceive themselves" [9]. Honor codes target the latter mechanism: by reminding participants of their ethical standards, an honor code makes it more difficult to maintain a positive self concept and still cheat. The warnings we used in this work target the former mechanism: by informing participants of the consequences of cheating, we aimed to increase the perceived costs and decrease the expected benefits of cheating.

Our primary finding is that *a pre-task warning led to a statistically significant decrease* in the rate of cheating in a real online examination in India. Application of the warning decreased the rate of cheating to 15.5% from a baseline of 34.4%. The rate of cheating under an honor code was 25.5%, suggesting a potential benefit; however, consistent with prior work [7, 8], we did not find this benefit to be statistically significant. Our results indicate that a simple warning may be more effective at deterring would-be cheaters than a traditional honor code. With the application of appropriate warnings, administrators of online courses may be able to effectively promote honest test-taking behavior at negligible cost.

Related Work

Prior work has investigated the prevalence of cheating in unsupervised tasks and the question of how to influence cheating behavior by modifying the task. In particular, past studies find pre-task honor codes effective in *physical encounters*. Mazar et al. demonstrated that having students recall the Ten Commandments or sign an honor code before completing a self-graded task reduced the rate of cheating in a classroom setting [9]. Pruckner and Sausgruber demonstrated that placing an appeal to honor on the price tag of a newspaper box decreased the rate of newspaper theft [10].

In contrast, there is scant evidence that honor codes are effective *online*. Mastin et al. did not observe any effect of an honor code in the context of an online psychology experiment [8]. LoSciavo and Shatz were unable to find

Honor Code: Please show that you will respect the rules of the exam by typing the following text into the box below:

I promise not to visit other websites or take help from other people during the exam.

Figure 1: Honor Code.

Warning: **Do not** visit other websites or take help from other people during the exam. If we discover that you did either of these things, we may:

- Cancel your exam.
- Cancel your account on MEC.
- Notify your institution.

Please show that you understand the rules of the exam by typing the following text into the box below:

I understand the consequences of visiting other websites or taking help from other people during the exam.

Figure 2: Warning.

any effect of an honor code on *self-reported* cheating in an online exam [7]. Other work found an honor code ineffective in by-mail interactions [5].

This paper demonstrates that a simple warning can have an effect on rates of cheating, even in situations in which an honor code does not offer commensurate benefits. There is some precedent for the idea that increasing the perceived risks of cheating can decrease the cheating rate. For example, Braumoeller and Gaines find that overt use of plagarism detection software may deter cheating in the classroom [2].

Methods

In the spring of 2014, we conducted a free online course ("The Design and Analysis of Algorithms") targeted at undergraduate engineering students in India. We gave students who completed the online lectures and activities the option of taking a final exam to qualify for a certificate. We offered proctored in-person versions of the exam in five different cities and offered an online version of the exam for students who were not able to travel to a test site.

The exam consisted of fifteen multiple-choice questions[1] and one free-response question. All questions were original, required critical thinking, and would not easily benefit from third-party reference materials.

We required that students taking the exam: (1) not consult other materials (books, notes or other websites) while taking the test, and (2) neither give nor receive aid from other people during the exam. To explore the effect of honor codes and warnings on students' compliance with these rules, we randomly assigned all students taking the online exam to one of three conditions:

- **No additional instructions.** This was identical to exams provided to students in the proctored setting.
- **Honor code.** For this condition, students were asked to read and type out an honor code at the beginning of the exam (Figure 1). This code was designed to appeal to their sense of integrity to follow the rules of the exam.
- **Warning.** For this condition, students were asked to read and type out a warning statement at the beginning of the exam (Figure 2). This statement emphasized the negative consequences of breaking the rules by cheating.

To ensure that students in the latter two conditions actually read the honor code or warning, we asked students to type one sentence of the honor code or warning into a text box. We displayed the relevant text as an embedded image to prevent students from copying-and-pasting the sentence.

We employed two different techniques to estimate the prevalence of cheating:

1. Examination of "free response" questions. The free response question was one of the harder questions on the exam. It required students to design a graph algorithm and describe it informally in a few sentences (our solution was 38 words long). To catch students who copied their answer directly from an Internet website, we identified responses with idiosyncratic language or symbols and entered them into an Internet search engine.

[1] Due to an ambiguity in one question, only 14 multiple-choice questions were graded.

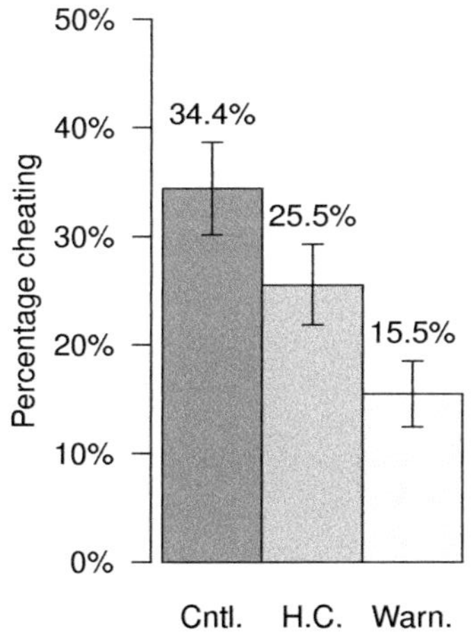

Figure 3: Rates of cheating on the online exam. Error bars indicate the standard error of the proportion.

We labeled students who submitted responses that exactly matched the text on a website as cheaters. To identify students who copied answers from other students, we performed manual comparison of responses. We ranked all response pairs by longest common substring, and also by longest common subsequence, and inspected pairs with high scores. In addition, we sorted all responses alphabetically, and also by total length, and examined adjacent entries. Three of the authors, all blind to treatment condition, jointly examined similar responses for cheating. For each pair that evidenced cheating, we labelled both students as cheaters.

2. **"Honeypot" website.** To help detect students who consulted the Web to seek help on the exam, we placed all of the exam questions on a public-facing website (the "honeypot") that was indexed by Google. If students searched for the exact text of any exam question, our website was the first hit returned. The website did not include the answers to the questions, but it did include a button ("Click to show answer") for each question on the test; when that button was pressed, the website paused and simulated a timeout, without showing the answer. We instrumented the honeypot website to check for a cookie set by our online exam platform. The cookie allowed us to identify the students who tried to download the exam answers from the honeypot page.

Ethical Issues

Prior to the exam we sent an email to all participating students. The email explained that we would be performing a research study during the final exam to test features designed to improve the fairness and reliability of future online examinations. Students had the opportunity to opt out of the study, in which case they received a default version of the exam (following other MOOCs, the default version used the honor code). When we communicated the scores to students, we debriefed them on the purpose of the experiment and on the methods we used to conduct it.

We did not take any disciplinary actions against students who we labeled as cheaters on the exam. Our experimental protocol received approval from our institutions' ethics review boards.

Participants

There were 409 students who took the online exam (and 674 students who took the in-person exam). We exclude from our analysis two students who opted out of the experiment, and three students who did not advance past the exam's instructions page. Thus we analyze data for 404 students.

Results

Overall, we classified 24% of students taking the exam as cheaters. The breakdown of cheaters by experimental condition is shown in Figure 3. Cheating was highest in the baseline condition (34% of students), followed by the honor code condition (25% of students), followed by the warning condition (15% of students). The difference between the baseline condition and the warning condition was significant[2] ($\chi^2(1, 267) = 11.9$, $p < 0.001$). The difference between the honor code and the warning has borderline significance without correction ($\chi^2(1, 279) = 3.74$, uncorrected $p = 0.053$) but is not significant with correction ($p = 0.11$).

Of the 100 students who we classified as cheaters, 84% were connected to plagiarism on the free response

[2] We present p values for the χ^2 tests as adjusted using the Bonferroni-Holm correction.

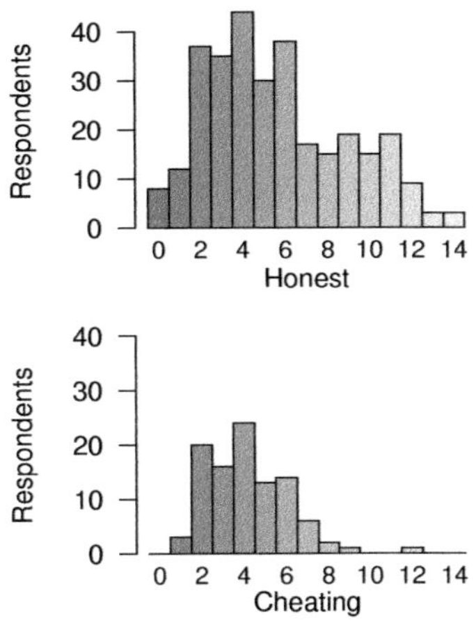

Figure 4: Histogram showing the number of correct exam answers for honest and cheating participants in the online exam.

question, 18% visited the honeypot, and 2% were connected to both plagiarism and the honeypot. Of the 23 unique IP addresses that visited the honeypot site during the exam, there were 5 that we could not associate with any student. These may represent visitors who were not taking the exam, or may correspond to additional devices used by exam participants to access the honeypot but not to access the exam site.

Among the plagiarized responses, most (80%) showed similarity to another student's response, 42% showed similarity to an Internet website, and 21% fell into both categories. The vast majority of repeated answers were submitted by exactly two students, though six responses were submitted by 3-5 students and one answer (copied from Wikipedia) had overlap between 8 students. Often the responses were identical, though sometimes they were reworded slightly, suggesting that students may have intentionally tried to avoid detection by a plagiarism check. For example, one student wrote "find the path though all safe edges using dijikshraw's algorithm" while another wrote "find the path using safe edges only by dijikshraw's algorithm". In addition to similarity in sentence structure, both of these responses had a unique misspelling of "Dijkstra's algorithm".

The set of online resources copied by students included Wikipedia, a tutorial, a course book, and peer-reviewed publications. None of the plagiarized responses were correct and many were nonsensical. For example, two students submitted a response copied from a paper published in the *Wilson Journal of Ornithology*. The response begins, "edges are often associated with a high risk of brood parasitism by Brown-headed Cowbirds". We later discovered that this paper is the top search hit for "risky edges", a phrase that appeared in the question.

Figure 4 illustrates the distribution of exam scores for cheaters and non-cheaters. Despite their efforts to cheat, the average score for cheaters (30% correct, $SD = 14\%$) was lower than the average score for non-cheaters (40% correct, $SD = 23\%$). This difference is statistically significant ($t(402) = 4.18, p < 0.0001$). We conjecture that the weaker students felt more inclined to cheat, but due to the questions (and random variations) on the exam, cheating did not offer large benefits to their scores. These results are in concert with prior work, which found that students who abuse digital learning systems perform poorly on subsequent assessments [1].

Discussion and Future Work

Although our results demonstrate that warnings can deter cheating online, further study is needed to fully understand the implications for online courses. One open question is how the effectiveness of a warning changes over time. If users see the same pre-task warning repeatedly, they may become numb to the warning's threat of negative consequences. In addition, if the consequences are difficult to impose or if it is difficult to detect cheating behavior, users may cheat in spite of the warning. Studying how the effect of online warnings changes over time presents an interesting challenge for future work.

A second issue with adopting warnings as an alternative to honor codes is that they may intimidate or alienate well-intentioned users of an online education platform. If the warning deters cheating at the cost of "scaring off" honest students, it may not be a beneficial solution overall. It would be valuable to study the effect of an honor code versus a warning on drop-out rates in the context of an online course.

Finally, we would like to study if and how the effect of an honor code or warning varies with demographic factors (country, age, education level, etc.). Our study targeted undergraduate engineering students living in India. Replicating the experiment with a more diverse participant population would give insight into how demographics affect our results.

Conclusions

We measure the rates of cheating in a 409-student online course using an online "honeypot" combined with analysis of a free-response text question. We found that displaying a pre-task warning that focused users on potential negative outcomes of dishonesty deterred cheating in the context of an online exam in India. Consistent with prior studies, we did not find a significant benefit of a traditional honor code (though we did see a trend that may suggest smaller benefits). Our results indicate that pre-task warnings may be an effective and easy-to-implement alternative to honor codes in online examinations.

Acknowledgements

We would like to thank Srinath Bala, Andrew Cross, Viraj Kumar, Madhusudan Parthasarathy, Shambwaditya Saha, Sumit Gulwani, and the whole MEC team for help creating and administering the online exam. We would like to thank David Nemer for helpful conversations about the study design and we thank the reviewers for their suggestions for future work. The first author received support from an NSF Graduate Research Fellowship under Grant No. DGE-114747 and from an NDSEG Fellowship. This work was also supported by the Catalyst Center for Sustainable Development at Microsoft Research India.

References

[1] Baker, R. S., Corbett, A. T., Koedinger, K. R., and Wagner, A. Z. Off-task behavior in the cognitive tutor classroom: When students "game the system". In *CHI*, ACM (2004), 383–390.

[2] Braumoeller, B. F., and Gaines, B. J. Actions do speak louder than words: Deterring plagiarism with the use of plagiarism-detection software. *Political Science & Politics 34*, 04 (2001), 835–839.

[3] Coursera Student Support Center: What is the honor code? Retrieved 20 September 2014. http://help.coursera.org/customer/portal/articles/1164381-what-is-the-honor-code-.

[4] edX honor code pledge. Retrieved 20 September 2014. https://www.edx.org/edx-terms-service.

[5] Fellner, G., Sausgruber, R., and Traxler, C. Testing enforcement strategies in the field: Threat, moral appeal and social information. *J. of the European Economic Association 11*, 3 (2013), 634–660.

[6] Jacquemet, N., Joule, R.-V., Luchini, S., and Shogren, J. F. Preference elicitation under oath. *J. Environ. Econ. and Mgmt. 65*, 1 (2013), 110–132.

[7] LoSchiavo, F. M., and Shatz, M. A. The impact of an honor code on cheating in online courses. *MERLOT Journal of Online Learning and Teaching 7*, 2 (2011).

[8] Mastin, D. F., Peszka, J., and Lilly, D. R. Online academic integrity. *Teaching of Psychology 36*, 3 (2009), 174–178.

[9] Mazar, N., Amir, O., and Ariely, D. The dishonesty of honest people: A theory of self-concept maintenance. *J. Marketing Research 45*, 6 (2008), 633–644.

[10] Pruckner, G. J., and Sausgruber, R. Honesty on the streets: A field study on newspaper purchasing. *J. Euro. Econ. Assoc. 11*, 3 (2013), 661–679.

Technology-Enhanced Learning: Evidence-based Improvement

Eileen Scanlon
Open University
Milton Keynes, UK
MK7 6AA
Eileen.Scanlon@open.ac.uk

Tim O'Shea
University of Edinburgh
Edinburgh, UK EH3 6HP
Principal@ed.ac.uk

Patrick McAndrew
Open University
Milton Keynes, UK
MK7 6AA
Patrick.Mcandrew@open.ac.uk

L@S 2015, March 14–18, 2015, Vancouver, BC, Canada.
ACM 978-1-4503-3411-2/15/03.
http://dx.doi.org/10.1145/2724660.2728664

Abstract
The design of learning materials and researching their efficacy involves the application of both theoretical learning principles and ways of working or practices to move towards evidence based improvement. This paper abstracts 4 categories from our on-going work of educational technology research which we have found to be important in considering what constitutes a successful Technology-Enhanced Learning implementation. These considerations influence the likelihood or feasibility of the wider adoption a particular Technology-Enhanced Learning implementation in the longer term. We also discuss how these considerations relate to the scalability of the development.

Author Keywords
Technology-Enhanced Learning; Learning Analytics; Interdisciplinarity

ACM Classification Keywords
K.3.1 distance learning

Introduction
Educational technology has become big business. Forty years of research has delivered a wealth of working prototypes and accounts of their efficacy [7, 8]. In the multidisciplinary area of Technology-Enhanced Learning (TEL) the aim is to find practical solutions based on

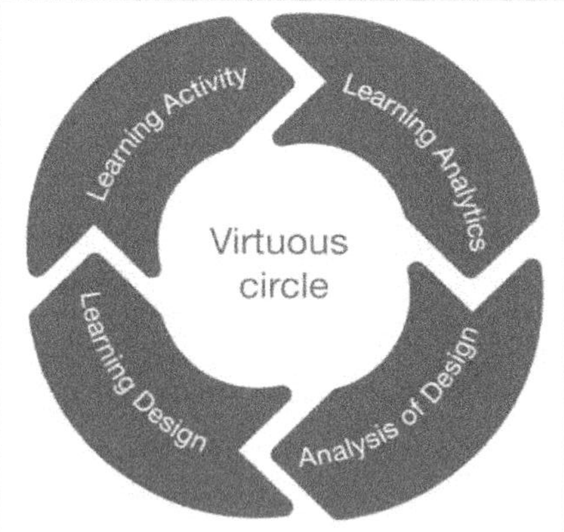

Figure 1. The *virtuous circle* that links learning design with learning analytics (building on ideas discussed in [2]).

technology to educational problems. TEL consists of much more than a set of research-informed products that use technology under a belief in its efficacy or possibilities for enhancement. It is a complex system, which includes communities, technologies and practices that are informed by pedagogy (the theory and practice of teaching, learning and assessment) and an evidence base of research into its efficacy. Today we need to improve the process of moving from innovative prototypes arising from academic research to effective and sustainable products and practices. The *Beyond prototypes* report [8] describes the outcomes of an international research study designed to help us understand this transfer process. In tandem with this study we have brought out a consideration of the role of interdisciplinary working [6] in TEL and how teams working on research and development can be helped with this process. In this paper we will discuss 4 themes that we are exploring in our work in progress.

Interdisciplinarity

There is a growing recognition of the need for a cross discipline approach in solving complex research problems. In particular work in TEL seeks collaboration from the disciplines of learning, cognition, human computer interaction and computer understanding of the nature of learning, and whether or how it is changing. There has been a move towards interdisciplinarity in many areas but there are few studies of interdisciplinarity in TEL. The need for interdisciplinarity in TEL research is recognized in practical terms, e.g. working in teams on projects and the benefits these bring. Rarer are more complex cases such as the development of a Model of Game Motivation (MGM), explaining digital play motivation [3] by applying a multidisciplinary approach. In that case the choice of a mixed methods research design was reinforced by critical review of literature which revealed that a combination of evidence from multiple disciplines (psychology, sociology, technology) would contribute to a more comprehensive understanding of player motivation.

Learning design and learning analytics

Educational technology research has absorbed working methods from HCI such as participatory design, design-based research and socio-cultural approaches building on an evaluation model featuring context, interactions and outcomes [4]. Theories in use in educational technology influence principled decisions about the design of learning materials and the way we frame our research on learning. Work related to the design of materials has close links with the paradigm of design-based research. Learning design has emerged from the instructional design, computing and learning sciences communities [9] to provide both a way to study the range of actions involved in the specification of learning activities, and a means to represent the design of learning. It resonates (Figure 1) with a description of design-based research that captures the spirit of the endeavor of participatory design as iterative cycles of improvement [1]. As a process design-based research expects researchers to *'systemically adjust various aspects of the designed context so that each adjustment served as a type of experimentation that allowed the researchers to test and generate theory in naturalistic contexts'* [1, p4]. This way of working also can be used to aid design of TEL systems on a large scale, such as in The Open University where improvement cycles are supported by collection of data by educational technologists as Data Wranglers [2]. In this role they make sense of a range of data sources,

Beyond Prototypes [8]

Method: Existing critiques of TEL have focused on whether the innovations created in research and development projects have become embedded in educational practice going forward. In the *Beyond prototypes* investigation an expert analysis of TEL projects gives an in-depth examination of the processes of innovation.

Data: Case studies of projects were combined with systematic analysis of data collected from in-depth interviews with key figures from research and industry.

Key factors: Several factors are identified for the success of TEL projects: we highlight here *persistent intent* in working through successive projects and an understanding of the complexity of the infrastructure around TEL and the process of *bricolage*.

More information: http://beyondprototypes.com

including demographic data from students, survey feedback data and activity data and information on the mode of delivery and the structure of courses and completion and pass rates. They produce reports that summarize important points and make recommendations, recognizing the importance of human sense-making to turn data into something which is actionable. In addition if patterns in the data can be identified which are highly predictive of learning outcomes, and especially if those patterns occur at particular points in a module, interventions and redesign of a module can be identified and planned. This model leads to connected research in learning design and in learning analytics, "*...the analysis and representation of data about learners in order to improve learning...*" [2.p683] Learning design makes explicit the process of planning and provides a means of describing underlying pedagogy. Learning analytics provides measures that help judge impact and motivate interventions that target improvements in aspects such as learner retention, satisfaction or attainment.

Persistent intent

The *Beyond prototypes* project (see Side Bar) reports as follows: "*Success in TEL is associated with 'persistent intent' – efforts by a group to develop inspirational ideas and turn them into products and practices over an extended period of time. ... Teams of researchers need persistent intent in order to develop their work over time with a shared educational goal in mind. Many [...] research projects may be aligned in order to work towards the same educational goal. Persistent intent motivates researchers to work closely with the communities that will be involved in implementation, developing a shared vision that is owned not only by the project team, but also by those who will take it forward once the research programme is complete and the development team has left. To carry out this work successfully, researchers need opportunities to develop the skills that will enable them to bridge the gaps between those different groups.*" [8.p6] What this means in practice is that significant innovations are developed and embedded over periods of years rather than months, and changing teaching practices in a sustainable way is not a straightforward roll–out of a product. This contrasts with the perceived rapid change cycle in technology itself.

Bricolage

The *Beyond prototypes* project identifies how *"Successful TEL innovations, both in academia and in business, are developed by a process of bricolage [5] in which educational goals are achieved by bringing together pedagogic approaches, diverse technological elements, frameworks and social practices.*" [8, p7] TEL is a complex system. There is a need to consider communities which build up, technologies which become available and day to day learning and teaching practices that can be informed by theory or practice. "*The work involved in successful TEL innovation can be characterised as bricolage or tinkering. This productive and creative innovation process involves bringing together and adapting technologies and pedagogies, experimentation to generate further insights and a willingness to engage with local communities and practices.*" [8, p6] The connection of bricolage to tinkering is illustrated by the term bricoleur [5]:*"Bricoleurs do not typically start a project and then consider which tools and materials will be required to achieve their goals. Rather, they review their available materials and tools and work out how to use them to achieve their goal or something close to their goal*

Above all, bricolage is rooted in engagement with the concrete properties of a situation and the available materials, rather than with an abstract model of how they will behave...." [8 p31]. Interviews conducted during the project revealed successful TEL innovators as ..." *bricoleurs who achieve educational goals by bringing together diverse technological elements, frameworks and social practices*." [8, p32]. Viewing successful TEL innovation as a form of tinkering is a challenge to a researcher, interested in making planned adjustments to teaching activities that can then be evaluated for effectiveness. However the term captures the reality of a learning process in flux and subject to multiple influences. A key challenge for the researcher is the move from controlled experimentation for small groups in the laboratory setting to the investigation of large-scale naturalistic experiments 'in the wild'.

Work in progress

This work in progress involves refining the key factors influencing the success of TEL projects through case studies of successful TEL projects that examine the relationship between interdisciplinary working and progress and knowledge creation. A further intended outcomes is to develop a good practice guide for researchers new to interdisciplinary working. This approach, in combination with further case study work, is expected to extend the combined use of learning analytics with learning design to enhance designs and improve support for learner progress.

Acknowledgements

We are grateful to the UK ESRC for their support for achievement of impact under the TEL Teaching and Learning Research Programme.

References and Citations

[1] Barab, S. and Squires, K. Design-Based Research: Putting a Stake in the Ground, *The Journal of the Learning Sciences*, 13, 1 (2004), 1–14.

[2] Clow, D. An overview of learning analytics. *Teaching in Higher Education*, 18, 6 (2013), 683–695.

[3] Herodotou, C., Winters, N. and Kambouri, M. An iterative, multidisciplinary approach to studying digital play motivation: The Model of Game Motivation, *Games and Culture,* (2014).

[4] Jones, A., Scanlon, E., Butcher, P., Murphy, P., Greenberg, J., Ross, S. Evaluating CAL: a distance education perspective, *Interacting with Computers*, Special issue on evaluation, 11, 5 (1999) 499-516.

[5] Levi-Strauss, C. *The Savage Mind*, University of Chicago Press, 1962.

[6] O'Shea, T. Keynote on Interdisciplinarity, Horizon 2020 meeting, (2013).

[7] McAndrew, P. and Scanlon, E. Open learning at a distance: lessons for struggling MOOCs. *Science*, 342 (2013) 1450–1451.

[8] Scanlon, E. Sharples, M. Fenton-O'Creevy, M., Fleck, J. Cooban, C., Ferguson, R., Cross, Simon and Waterhouse, P. *Beyond Prototypes: enabling innovation in technology-enhanced learning*, TEL-TLRP, 2014.

[9] Scanlon, E., McAndrew, P. and O'Shea, T. Designing for educational technology to enhance the experience of learners in distance education, *Journal of Interactive Media in Education,* (in press).

A Modern Student Experience in Systems Programming

Vaishaal Shankar
UC Berkeley
vaishaal@berkeley.edu

David Culler
UC Berkeley
culler@berkeley.edu

L@S 2015, Mar 14-18, 2015, Vancouver, BC, Canada
ACM 978-1-4503-3411-2/15/03
http://dx.doi.org/10.1145/2724660.2728665

Abstract
The study of Operating Systems and Systems Programming provides invaluable software engineering experience and crucial conceptual understanding that make it an essential component of an undergraduate computer science curriculum. It is also imperative that classroom course material and infrastructure keep pace with rapidly evolving technology. A "modern" course will provide an accurate software engineering experience and prevent the study of outdated concepts. With the recent increase in size and popularity of computer science courses, all course material must also be appropriately scalable. In order to create such a "modern" systems course, we redesigned UC Berkeley's CS 162, a 300 student Introduction to Operating Systems & Systems Programming course. In this paper we detail our unique curriculum layout, our advanced infrastructure support for students, and future work on extending our infrastructure for other large computer science courses

Author Keywords
systems, teaching, operating systems, infrastructure

Introduction
A course on Operating Systems & Systems programming is arguably one of the most fundamental hands-on courses for an computer science education. Yet the wide breadth and deep complexity of Operating Systems makes designing effective course curriculum and infrastructure a difficult task. The principle challenge on the curriculum side is dividing and

scheduling the material across lecture, discussion sections, individual homework assignments, and group projects to provide a cohesive and effective learning experience. On the infrastructure side, students should be given real world tools for testing, submitting, and evaluating their work.

We present CS 162, an operating systems course redesigned from the ground up to specifically address these issues. The Fall 2014 iteration of CS 162 had 271 undergraduate students supported by 8 TAs and 1 Professor. The sections below detail our primary contributions: innovative layout of curriculum, and a modern course infrastructure based on current industry practices.

Curriculum

Approaches to teaching Operating Systems generally fall along two axes: whether the treatment of material is abstract (revolving around conceptual exercises) or concrete (revolving around large programming projects) and whether the students take on the role of the OS designer, modifying parts of the OS or a user-level programmer using OS APIs [7]. However there merits of a hybrid approach: our course balances the conceptual and practical elements of operating systems and allows the student to work as both an OS designer and OS user. We organized the four components of the course: lectures, sections, individual assignments, and group projects to achieve this balance. We introduced all concepts in lecture, served conceptual exercises and practice problems in section, and finally give concrete practice via programming assignments. This "conceptual pipeline" is shown in Figure 1.

Our lecture schedule follows a "helical" pattern in that the first few lectures gave a holistic introduction of concepts we cover throughout the semester. The high level overview provides the students with a basic understanding of systems. It also provides a review of assumed programming and machine structures knowledge, and tools for the rest of the course. After the initial overview, a basic understanding of future material can be assumed, which can greatly help motivate certain concepts. For example, we can use file I/O and communication to motivate the use of threads and concurrency beyond merely parallel computation. These conceptual bridges allows us to create more cohesive and effective lectures. We used Anderson and Dahlin's new operating systems book [2] as a backbone for much of the lecture material, and as the primary textbook of the class. The book's excellent balance of conceptual overview and low-level implementation details proved a good fit for our course model. The sample "helical" lecture schedule is show in Figure 2.

We carefully constructed a variety of programming assignments that captured important concepts above and below the operating system abstraction level. Individual assignments were small user level programs that used OS abstractions. We had five such assignments: wordcount, shell, http server, memory allocator and an improved http server. We found these smaller assignments crucial in contextualizing the larger design projects. [1].

For our bigger projects, the students took on the role of systems designers and worked through the architecture and implementation of a scheduler, system call interface, and distributed key value store. We borrowed our first two projects from Stanford's excellent Pintos projects, and developed the final project our self [7].

For both individual and group assignments we heavily monitored student progress by mandating use of version control. Our autograder infrastructure tied into the version control system and allowed for periodic progress evaluation and regression tests over the span of a three week project. We believe this provides both a natural introduction to modern development practice and a better way to provide visibility and timely feedback.

[1] In hindsight, we should have done more concurrency and use of abstractions within the kernel at user level

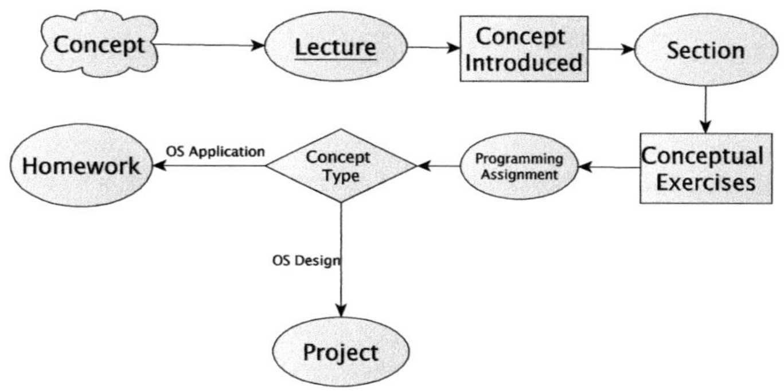

Figure 1: Evolution of a concept through our course model

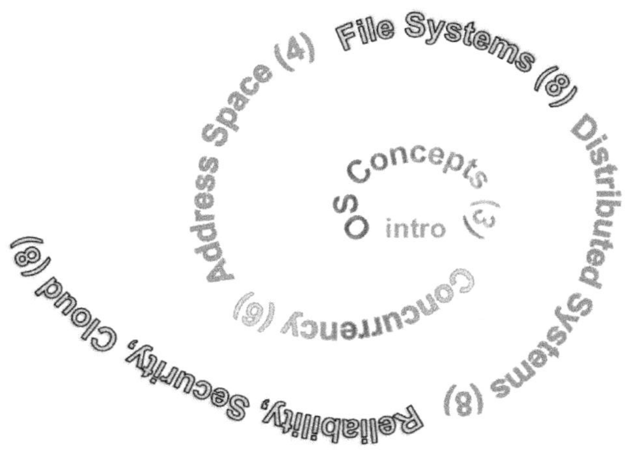

Figure 2: Our lecture schedule has a helical structure, initially introducing a wide breadth of concepts and later diving into them

Infrastructure

Our goal for course infrastructure was to adhere closely to modern industry practices, while still maintaining a positive and educational student experience.

Version control is an essential component of software development for large projects [5, 4]. Thus, we have based our entire assignment submission system on the popular version control system, Git. We generated Git repositories for all students on Github, and distributed assignments by pushing skeleton code to the student repositories. Students were instructed to use their Git repository to manage their own progress, and to push their completed assignment to a "release" branch. Our instructional machines used Git's post-receive hook system to trigger a build on the continuous integration system (CI), Jenkins. Jenkins would run the appropriate tests to evaluate the students' work, and finally email the students a summary of their build. By integrating the assignment submission system seamlessly into the existing version control system, we get students acclimated to working closely with both continuous integration tests and a version control system, both of which are commonplace in industry. An overview of our submission system can be found in Figure 3

In industry it is common to provide a separate machine for development work. Unfortunately this is neither practical nor financially feasible in a classroom environment. Instead we opted to provide students a *virtual machine* preloaded with all necessary dependencies. Virtual machines have been successfully used in other systems courses, for specific assignments centered around the virtual machine [1, 6]. Our approach was different, we distributed the virtual machine in the beginning of the semester using *vagrant* and instructed students to carry out all course related activities within that virtual machine. By imposing a standard student platform, we mitigated problems arising from heterogeneous student machines. The use *vagrant* greatly simplified the virtual machine distribution process.

Future Work

We have only had the chance to build and evaluate our system over the course of one semester. Needless to say there are many avenues for improvement, especially on the infrastructure front. Though functional for a first iteration,

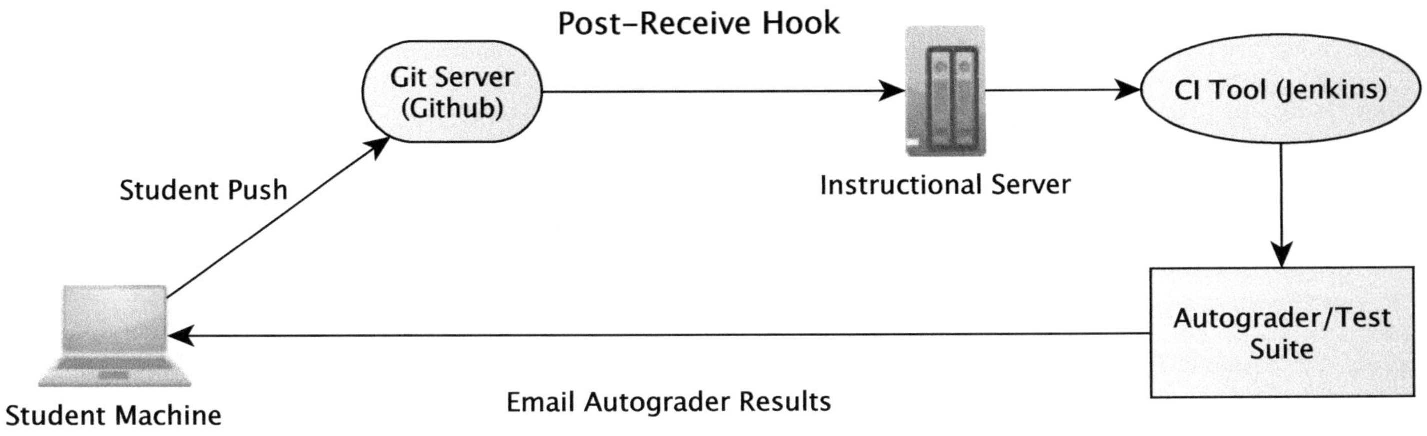

Figure 3: A flow chart for our general purpose submission system

our goal for our "industry-esque" student experience is to create a flexible system that can be ported to other computer science courses. Currently we are working closely with other UC Berkeley computer science courses to package, refine and port our infrastructure for other courses. Though we thought of the course infrastructure as separate from the course curriculum, we found a big challenge for many students to be getting acclimated to the variety of tools we presented. Git for example, can be extremely challenging to pick up [3]. Thus, the usage of tools may need to integrated into the conceptual pipeline presented in Figure 1 in some manner.

References

[1] Adams, J. C., and Laverell, W. D. Configuring a multi-course lab for system-level projects. *ACM SIGCSE Bulletin 37*, 1 (2005), 525–529.

[2] Anderson, T., and Dahlin, M. *Operating Systems: Principles and Practice*. Recursive books, 2012.

[3] Isomöttönen, V., and Cochez, M. Challenges and confusions in learning version control with git. In *Information and Communication Technologies in Education, Research, and Industrial Applications*. Springer, 2014, 178–193.

[4] Kelleher, J. Employing git in the classroom. In *Computer Applications and Information Systems (WCCAIS), 2014 World Congress on*, IEEE (2014), 1–4.

[5] Lawrance, J., Jung, S., and Wiseman, C. Git on the cloud in the classroom. In *Proceeding of the 44th ACM technical symposium on Computer science education*, ACM (2013), 639–644.

[6] Nabhen, R., and Maziero, C. Some experiences in using virtual machines for teaching computer networks. In *Education for the 21st CenturyImpact of ICT and Digital Resources*. Springer, 2006, 93–104.

[7] Pfaff, B., Romano, A., and Back, G. The pintos instructional operating system kernel. In *ACM SIGCSE Bulletin*, vol. 41, ACM (2009), 453–457.

Educational Evaluation in the PKU SPOC Course "Data Structures and Algorithms"

Ming Zhang
School of EECS
Peking University
Beijing, 100871, China
mzhang@net.pku.edu.cn
+86-10-62765825

Jile Zhu
School of EECS
Peking University
Beijing, 100871, China
zhujile0918@163.com

Yanzhen Zou
School of EECS
Peking University
Beijing, 100871, China
zouyz@pku.edu.cn

Hongfei Yan
School of EECS
Peking University
Beijing, 100871, China
yhf@net.pku.edu.cn

Dan Hao
School of EECS
Peking University
No.5 Yiheyuan Road
haodan@pku.edu.cn

Chuxiong Liu
School of SESS
Peking University
No.5 Yiheyuan Road
cxliu@pku.edu.cn

L@S 2015, Mar 14-18, 2015, Vancouver, BC, Canada
ACM 978-1-4503-3411-2/15/03.
http://dx.doi.org/10.1145/2724660.2728666

Abstract
In order to learn the impact of MOOCs, we conducted a SPOC experiment on the course of Data Structures and Algorithms in Peking University. In this paper, we analyze student online activities, test scores, and two surveys using statistical methods (t-test, analysis of variance, correlation analysis and OLS regression) to understand what factors will foster improvements in student learning. We find that the "SPOC + Flipped" is a helpful mode to teach algorithm, time spent on the course and students' confidence had a positive impact on learning effect, and SPOC resource should be made full use of.

Author Keywords
SPOC; Flipped Classroom; Algorithms; Education

ACM Classification Keywords
K.3.0 Computers and Education

Introduction
A SPOC (Small Private Online Course) [1] was proposed by Armando Fox in 2013, which was referred as a version of MOOC and used locally by only on-campus students. And Fox argued that a SPOC can supplement the classroom experience by combining with online resources [2]. SPOCs can take the online approach to smaller, targeted and revenue generating classes [3].

Konstan et al. tried a flipped classroom model and constructed an OLS (Ordinary Least Squares) regression model to predict the completion, knowledge gains and final grades [4].

As the students of a SPOC course usually come from the same school or university, the difference among learners is much smaller. Reducing the influence from the background and purpose of the students, the analysis of the course is more reliable. Our analysis in this paper will show a positive meaning for the application of SPOCs.

In 2014 spring, we conducted an experiment on the course of Data Structures and Algorithms in Peking University (PKU in short) to evaluate the learning effectiveness of SPOCs. In particular, 828 undergraduate students majoring in science or engineering took this course: 397 of them attended the five SPOC classrooms, and the others attended the five traditional classrooms, which means they didn't use the online materials.

We collected the data through students' online behaviors and the surveys. We aimed to find out how to improve students' learning effectiveness.

Research Questions

We will analyze the data of the course and discuss the following issues in details.

1. Compared with the students of traditional classrooms, did the students of SPOC classrooms who used online materials perform better?
2. To what degree does the factors play a role in students' learning effect and why did them work?
3. Among the students of SPOC classrooms, did the students who were asked to finish the online quizzes and assignments make greater progresses than those who just used online quizzes and assignments as optional supplements?

Statistical Analysis Results

The impact of SPOC learning mode on learning effect

In order to measure how much students had learned from the course, we collected the score of their final examination. We divided the final examination into two parts, concept questions and algorithm questions. The former part focus on students' memorizing, while the latter one focus on students' understanding.

We used the t-test to analyze the performance difference between the students of SPOC classrooms and traditional classrooms in the concept questions and algorithm questions.

We find that the performance of the concept questions of two kinds of classrooms may not have any difference ($P = 0.067$), but there might be a difference between the performances of algorithm questions of two classrooms ($P = 2.97E\text{-}08$). Namely, the performance of algorithm questions of students of SPOC blended learning classroom (the mean is 33.99) is significantly better than that of the students of traditional classroom (the mean is 31.35). And the score variance of concept questions and algorithm questions of SPOC classroom is smaller than that of traditional classroom, which means that the students of SPOC classroom have better overall appearance and more stable performance. The average score of concept/algorithm questions of ten classrooms are shown in Figure 1.

The students were partitioned into the ten classes based on their schools, and the students of SPOC classroom perform better in the College Entrance Examination in average. Since the grade of Class B2 far lower than others, we hold another t-test excluding class B2, and the P-value is 0.027, which also shows that SPOC classroom perform better.

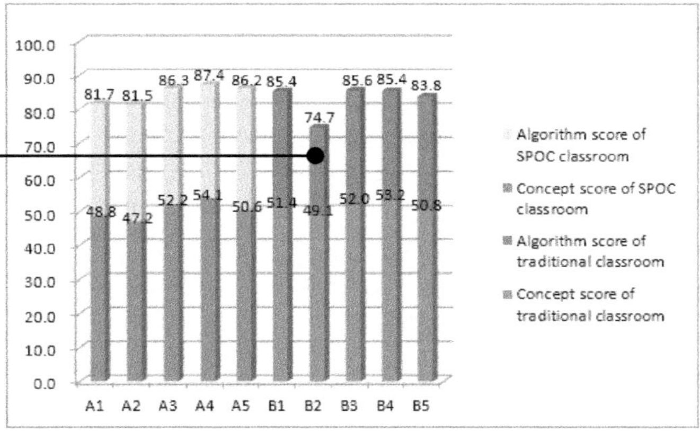

Figure 1. The comparison of the final scores between different classrooms

So, the t-test above to some extent shows that the learning mode of SPOC may help students grasp the knowledge more deeply.

Factors that impact on the students' learning effect

Students' learning effect will be influenced by many aspects. In order to understand better what kind of factors may impact learning effect significantly or what kind of characteristics better students owned, we used an OLS regression model to fit the students' final score, as an evaluation of the final learning effect of students. The regression was based on four kinds of features, students' learning background, students' basic information, students' attitude to the course, and the level of effort of the students.

According to the students' online learning activities, their offline learning situation (fetched by two questionnaires) and the performance in the final exam, we took the intersection of students who attended all the activities above as the sample.

We find that the total time of students spent in the course has a significant positive effect on students' learning effects (Co = 0.845****), which means that the students' efforts were rewarded. In addition, both the confidence of students at the beginning and the end of the course had a significant positive impact on learning effect (Co = 2.595*, 2.029*). Confidence motivates students to learn, and it is also an evaluation of students' own learning situation. Finally, we find whether he or she was a freshman had a significant positive impact on the learning effect of students (Co = 3.733*). Because this course is delivered for freshman, they usually communicated with each other, which would produce the effect of collaborative learning. And it also may be due to that seniors focused more on the professional courses of study.

Finally, note that the adjusted R-square is only 0.174, which means that some factors that influence the learning effect had not been taken into account or observed, such as collaborative learning and review time. The discussion between students may deepen the understanding of knowledge, help students learn from each other and play a supervisory role. The review before the final exam helps to consolidate the knowledge. We plan to collect these information through questionnaires in the next term of the course.

The impact of SPOC resource utilization

In order to further analyze the impact of SPOC teaching mode, we divided the five SPOC classrooms into flipped classrooms and resource utilization classrooms based on the actual teaching situation. The main difference is that the online quizzes and programming labs were rigidly required to complete in flipped classroom, while the quizzes and programming labs are supplement of learning materials in resource utilization classroom. In

	SPOC flipped classroom	SPOC resource utilization classroom
Mean	0.30	-0.24
Variance	1.05	0.88
N	154	192
Degree	344	
P-value	4.12E-07	

Table 1. T-test for the difference in means between SPOC flipped classroom and SPOC resource utilization classroom

general, the latter's utilization of SPOC resources was not sufficient. Because *Introduction to Computing* was taught in different forms among students, we measured students' progresses by their z-scores of the courses.

We used the t-test to analyze the progresses difference between the students from two kinds of classrooms, to see whether resource utilization of SPOC impacted on students' learning effect significantly. The progress was defined as follows. The progress of a student equals to his z-score of our course minus his z-score of *Introduction to Computing*, which is the prerequisite of our course. The result is shown in Table 1.

The result shows that the average progress of z-score in flipped classroom is 0.30, which shows the general increase in student grades, while the average progress of z-score in resource utilization classroom is -0.24, which shows a slight decrease of student grades. And the difference between the two kinds of classrooms is significant, for the P-value is 4.12E-07.

Therefore, the analysis to some extent shows that if students can make full use of SPOC platform resources, including video resources, after-school practices, they will have a significant improvement on learning effect.

Conclusion

This paper presents a SPOC experiment of Data Structures and Algorithms in Peking University, and gets the following findings:

"SPOC + Flipped" is helpful in teaching algorithms. Since the blended "SPOC + Flipped" teaching mode asked students to preview the lecture before the class, it gives students more opportunities to discuss with teachers and classmates, so that they can understand the knowledge better.

Students' time spent on the course was rewarded and the confidence of students is important in learning. Thus, we should encourage students to pay more efforts and put more positive words in their assignment comments.

Making full use of SPOC resources improved the learning effect. The quizzes and assignments were carefully chosen and contains most knowledge points, which would correct students' inaccurate understanding, so that students who practices more will perform better.

Through the analysis, our research shows a positive meaning for the application of SPOCs.

Acknowledgements

This paper is partially supported by the National Natural Science Foundation of China (NSFC Grant Number 61472006), the Doctoral Program of Higher Education of China (the Special Fund for Fast Sharing of Science Paper in Net Era, "FSSD" Grant No. 20130001110113) and the National Basic Research Program (973 Program No. 2014CB340405).

References

[1] Fox, A., Patterson, D. A., Ilson, R., Joseph, S., Walcott-Justice, K., & Williams, R. (2014). Software Engineering Curriculum Technology Transfer: Lessons learned from MOOCs and SPOCs.

[2] Fox, A. (2013). From MOOCs to SPOCs. Communications of the ACM, 56(12), 38-40.

[3] Goral, T. (2013). Make Way for SPOCS: Small, Private Online Courses May Provide What MOOCs Can't. University Business, 16(7).

[4] Konstan, J. A., Walker, J. D., Brooks, D. C., Brown, K., &Ekstrand, M. D. (2014, March). Teaching recommender systems at large scale: evaluation and lessons learned from a hybrid MOOC. In Proceedings of the first ACM conference on Learning@ scale. pp. 61-70.

Learn With Friends: The Effects of Student Face-to-Face Collaborations on Massive Open Online Course Activities

Christopher Brooks
School of Information
University of Michigan
Ann Arbor, MI 48103
brooksch@umich.edu

Tawanna Dillahunt
School of Information
University of Michigan
Ann Arbor, MI 48103
tdillahu@umich.edu

Caren Stalburg
Department of Learning Health Sciences, Medical School
University of Michigan
Ann Arbor, MI 48103
carens@med.umich.edu

Lionel Robert
School of Information
University of Michigan
Ann Arbor, MI 48103
lprobert@umich.edu

L@S 2015, Mar 14-18, 2015, Vancouver, BC, Canada
ACM 978-1-4503-3411-2/15/03.
http://dx.doi.org/10.1145/2724660.2728667

Abstract
This work investigates whether enrolling in a Massive Open Online Course (MOOC) with friends or colleagues can improve a learner's performance and social interaction during the course. Our results suggest that signing up for a MOOC with peers correlates positively with the rate of course completion, level of achievement, and discussion forum usage. Further analysis seems to suggest that a learner's interaction with their friends compliments a MOOC by acting as a form of self-blended learning.

Author Keywords
MOOC; student success; collaboration; social learning; blended learning

ACM Classification Keywords
K.3.1 Computer Uses in Education

Introduction
Unlike traditional courses where learners attend classes together in real-time, form cohorts, and share classroom activities, learners enrolled in MOOCs interact asynchronously across geographical and

temporal boundaries. Given the low rates of completion associated with MOOCs, we investigated whether enrolling with friends or colleagues would be associated with improvements in both course completion and social interaction in a professional development MOOC. We also explored the types of collaborative activities that learners, their friends and/or colleagues engaged in and how these activities might map onto social learning theories.

We surveyed learners in a single offering of a professional development MOOC to determine whether they signed up with friends or colleagues and, if so, what type of collaborative activities they engaged in outside of the MOOC environment. We used these responses, along with quantitative behavior data collected directly from the Coursera MOOC environment, to answer the following research questions:

RQ1: Do learners who sign up with friends/colleagues have higher completion rates than those who do not?

RQ2: Do learners who sign up with friends/colleagues have different discussion forum posting ratings than those who did not?

RQ3: When users engage in a MOOC with friends, what activities do they do outside of the MOOC environment?

Methodology

In this work, we explore the topic of peer collaboration in a professional skills development MOOC, *Instructional Methods in Health Professions Education.* [1]

[1] https://www.coursera.org/course/instructmethodshpe

This MOOC has video lectures and quizzes, and uses a heavily structured discourse forum where learners respond to questions the instructor scaffolds. The majority of learners have a background in the health field and practice both as teachers (the focus of the MOOC) and professionals (e.g. nurses, doctors, dentists, etc.). For the session analyzed, the course came at no cost to learners. Our analysis is based on surveys administered at two points within the semester: one at the beginning of the semester (Entrance Survey) and the other midway through the course (Midterm Survey). The surveys were delivered as optional course quizzes. We also analyzed learners' performance data within the MOOC.

Results

The first survey resulted in a 20% response rate and the second survey resulted in a 6% response rate. In the authors' experiences, this is a reasonable response rate for surveys in MOOC environments. Table 1 shows the breakdown of respondents based on whether they signed up with friends or colleagues (*Friends*) or whether they did not sign up with friends or colleagues (*Alone*).

	Entrance Survey	Midterm Survey
Friends	243 (23.4%)	76 (24.6%)
Alone	797 (76.6%)	233 (75.4%)

Table 1: Survey Response Rate by Condition

RQ1: Completion Rates

We measured the completion rate by end of course credential, which could be either none (learner either did no evaluative exercises or did not pass the course threshold for minimum grade), normal (user achieved a grade above 80% but below 95%) or distinction (user achieved a grade equal to or above 95%). A χ^2 contingency test suggests that the two population responses were different ($p = 0.006$).

	Distinction	Normal	None
Friends	34.2%	5.3%	60.5%
Alone	24.2%	4.5%	71.3%

Table 2: Achievement Level by Condition

Table 2 shows the proportions for each category of achievement. Most notable is that those learners who signed up with friends or colleagues achieved higher rates of distinction and normal completion than those who did not sign up with others.

RQ2: Sociability in Discussion Forums

Our expectation was that learners who signed up with friends would be less likely to use the MOOC-based discussion forums as they would prefer to interact with their friends. Our results show that this is not the case. When comparing the number of postings to the discussion forums, an independent t-test was statistically significant ($p = 0.03$) and the mean number of postings per user was higher for those who signed up with friends (**Table 3**).

	$\bar{x}$	σ
Friends	6.96	8.83
Alone	4.86	5.06

Table 3: Mean and Standard Deviation of Number of Posts per Condition

RQ3: How Learners Collaborated Outside of the MOOC

The survey responses from those who signed up with friends also provided an open-ended question asking how learners interacted outside of the course. A qualitative analysis of the results suggested several themes of interaction including:

- Casual discussions with family members who were in similar job roles and who were co-enrolled in the course;
- Formal study group discussions with colleagues who had signed up for the course, sometimes around specific professional practices such as the planning of teaching assignments;
- Ad-hoc discussions with colleagues who did not sign up for the course, suggesting that the MOOC could impact others in the workplace;
- Formal professional development activities, with learners using this content directly in their teaching practice (e.g. within related higher education courses or mentorship duties);
- Collaborative lecture viewing activities, where learners enrolled in the MOOC would gather in a collocated space to engage with the content.

Conclusions

Through this work we have shown there is an effect on learner academic achievement and online interaction when learners sign up with friends or colleagues. Additional qualitative analysis seems to suggest that learners use their interaction with their friends/colleagues as a type of self-blended learning to complement or perhaps supplement the MOOC. Although social learning theory suggests that individuals can learn by interacting with others [0], more work is needed to fully understand the mechanisms that underlie the peer learning that happens outside of the MOOC environments. Prior research has consistently shown that both the size and actions of one's peer group can alter an individual's level of engagement [4]. For example are the potential benefits associated with signing up with friends or colleagues due mainly to social support, informational peer tutoring, or a combination of both? Perhaps the differences in completion rates are due to social proof – if this class is important enough for a peer to work on, it must be worth the learner's time too.

In addition, other questions emerge about the mechanisms that may or may not facilitate these learning benefits due to peer collaboration. Do these potential benefits materialize through greater engagement with in-course activities or simply provide benefits derived entirely outside of the course structure? Are these benefits dependent on environmental factors? For example, is the ability to take advantage of peer collaboration related to a learner's social structure [0]? Learners with access to more friends who have better educational experiences may benefit more from peer collaborations. Do some environments offer richer opportunities for peer learning than others (e.g. some employers may setup in-house learning programs/incentives to support peer learning)?

We believe future work in this area has implications for design. For example, the learners in this study interacted with their friends/colleagues in many different ways. Some interactions were technology mediated, such as the co-viewing of lectures in a shared space, while others were not, such as the discussion of topics over a meal. Prior research has shown that the context in which communications take place can influence the quality of interpersonal interactions [3]. By better understanding the ways in which learners collaborate outside of the MOOC we may be able to design collaboration technologies which can be made available to learners to help support their own learning experiences.

Our future work involves designing studies to provide more detailed analysis and replicating this with other sections of the same MOOC and with other types of MOOCs. Perhaps professional skills courses, such as the one we studied here, are different from general interest MOOCs or MOOCs that are aimed at college replacement courses. The potential improvements due to peer collaboration may be dependent on the level of the learner's education. Nonetheless, the results of this preliminary work open up several potential avenues of research we hope to explore.

References

[1] Bandura, A. *Social learning theory.* Englewood Cliffs, N.J.: Prentice-Hall, 1977.

[2] Rosé, C. P., Carlson, R., Yang, D., Wen, M., Resnick, L., Goldman, P. & Sherer, J. (2014). Social Factors that Contribute to Attrition in MOOCs, in Proceedings of the First ACM Conference on Learning@ Scale.

[3] Robert, L. P., Dennis, A. R. Paradox of Richness: A Cognitive Model of Media Choice, IEEE Transactions on Professional Communication, vol. 48, no. 1 (March 2005), pp. 10–21.

[4] Alnuaimi, O. A., Robert, L. P., Maruping, L. M. (2010) Team size, dispersion, and social loafing in technology-supported teams: A perspective on the theory of moral disengagement. Journal of Management Information Systems.

Who You Are or What You Do: Comparing the Predictive Power of Demographics vs. Activity Patterns in Massive Open Online Courses (MOOCs)

Christopher Brooks
School of Information
University of Michigan
Ann Arbor, MI 48103
brooksch@umich.edu

Stephanie Teasley
School of Information
University of Michigan
Ann Arbor, MI 48103
steasley@umich.edu

Craig Thompson
Department of Computer Science
University of Saskatchewan
Saskatoon, SK S7N 5C9
craig.thompson@usask.ca

L@S 2015, Mar 14-18, 2015, Vancouver, BC, Canada
ACM 978-1-4503-3411-2/15/03.
http://dx.doi.org/10.1145/2724660.2728668

Abstract
Demographics factors have been used successfully as predictors of student success in traditional higher education systems, but their relationship to achievement in MOOC environments has been largely untested. In this work we explore the predictive power of user demographics compared to learner interaction trace data generated by students in two MOOCs. We show that demographic information offers minimal predictive power compared to activity models, even when compared to models created very early on in the course before substantial interaction data has accrued.

Author Keywords
MOOC; learning analytics; predictive modeling; student success; demographics, interaction data mining; activity

ACM Classification Keywords
K.3.1 Computer Uses in Education

Introduction

Demographics, which we broadly construe here to be information known about learners that does not change while they interact with learning systems, are a valuable tool in building models to predict learner success. For example, [1] used performance demographics, such as previous grade point averages, to predict student success in traditional higher education courses, while [2] used sociocultural demographics, such as gender and military service, with the same goal. A major theme of the research in this area is to inform the development of *early warning systems* [3] which can identify when learners are struggling and intervene, typically through dashboards or providing awareness cues.

MOOCs provide a very different learning environment than traditional place-based educational institutions; the stakes are lower, attrition rates are higher, learners have different motivations and goals, and the information about the prior educational experience of learners is limited. In attempts to better understand MOOC students, vendors and institutions offering MOOC content have begun to actively survey learners in an attempt to generate demographic profiles as well as to identify students' goals and preferences. However survey response rates tend to be quite low, and the usefulness this information is unknown. Therefore, the question we address here is:

To what extent is demographic information valuable for building predictive models of student success in MOOCs?

To explore this question, we compare the value of demographic data versus learner activity data when building predictive models of student success. Because definitions of success are numerous (perhaps more so in MOOCs than in traditional higher education), we contextualize this work around the basic concept of academic success: the student passes a course. In a MOOC, this means that the student has scored high enough on tests or quizzes to earn a certificate of completion.

Activity data in online learning systems is collected through clickstream logging, and we use the temporal interaction modeling techniques described in [4] to process MOOC clickstreams and generate comparative models. These models are absent of learner demographics, and are based only on the regularity by which a learner interacts with resources in the online courseware. Finally, we compare both the demographic and activity approaches to a hybrid model that includes both demographic and activity data.

Methodology

We considered data from a MOOC course which was a broadly accessible introduction on Internet technologies. This MOOC ran three times each over 11 weeks, with tens of thousands of learners enrolled in each offering.

To capture demographic data, we used three sources including (i) the Coursera demographic survey, which asks questions about student gender, age, race, and language capabilities, (ii) data about whether a learner was paying for the course or not (e.g. in the *signature track*) as well as their signup date, and (iii) geolocation information derived from the learners clickstream data, including country, state/province, and city. The total number of demographic attributes (features) used for our models was 97.

Week	1	2	3	4	5	6	7	8	9	10	11	End
Hybrid	0.344	0.502	0.595	0.645	0.687	0.698	0.711	0.711	0.741	0.751	0.743	0.755
Activity	0.328	0.495	0.591	0.639	0.686	0.689	0.705	0.725	0.754	0.775	0.781	0.810
Difference	0.016	0.007	0.004	0.006	0.000	0.010	0.007	-.014	-.014	-.024	-.037	-.054

Table 1: Weekly average κ for hybrid and activity models.

For the activity-based models, three different kinds of content accesses were considered: lecture video views, quiz attempts, and discussion forum accesses. As the data is based on end-user activity, predictive models were generated for each day of the course. The total number of attributes (features) used for data mining ranged between 371 (for the first day of the course) and 1,091 (for the last day of the course). The third comparison, the hybrid models, were created through the merger of the data from the demographic and activity-based models described previously.

The first two sessions of the course were used to train models to predict success, while the third session of each course was used as a validation set. The Weka toolkit version 3.7.12 was used with the J48 classifier. The training of the model was done by restricting the data to only those who had filled out both the demographics (7,791 of 61,820 learners, 12.6%) and those who had interacted in the course (23,818 of 61,280 learners, 38.9%) which was a total of 4,130 learners (6.7%) after balancing. The validation was done on the full unbalanced third session of the course (23,902 learners), to simulate the performance of an actual early warning system.

Results

Shown in Figure 1 are the accuracies (in Fliess' κ) of all three models over time. The dotted straight line in the figure is the accuracy of demographics features alone, which does not change over time. The dashed line is the activity-based modeling approach, while the solid line is the hybrid model.

The demographics model performed poorly, with $\kappa=0.17$. Even at the beginning of the course when the clickstream data is minimal, the activity model has a $\kappa=0.24$ which outperformed demographics models considerably. Interestingly, the addition of demographics to the activity model made minimal difference. Table 1 shows the difference in accuracy between the activity and hybrid models broken down on a weekly averages. It is notable that for the first seven weeks of the course the hybrid model has a slight ($\kappa\leq0.01$) benefit over the activity model, but for the last five weeks of the course it has a slight ($\kappa\leq0.05$) disadvantage over the activity model.

Conclusions

Demographics, including your location and whether you are paying for a certificate, have minimal predictive power when determining the academic achievement of learners enrolled in MOOCs. While there are many exciting questions this work surfaces (e.g. Is this true in other kinds of MOOCs, or just this one? Are some demographics of particular value versus others?), the one most interesting to us for follow up is understanding whether this is true for traditional residential education as well. In traditional early warning systems, student demographics (which include

Figure 1: Fliess' κ versus time in days.

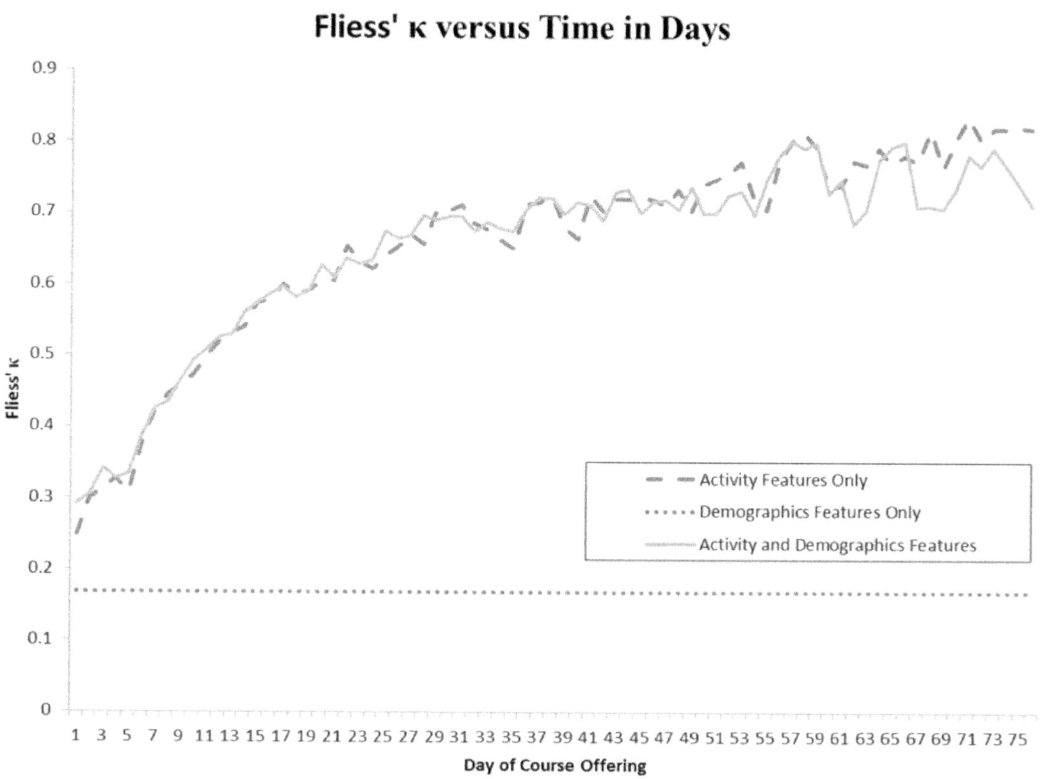

prior achievement, a value often not available in MOOCs) models) are used for predictive modeling. Is this simply because activity models are starved of data in traditional blended formats, or are there key demographic features, such as prior achievement, which may help increase the quality of success models in MOOC environments as well?

References

[1] S. Jayaprakash, E. Moody, E. Lauría, J. Regan and J. Baron, "Early Alert of Academically At-Risk Students: An Open Source Analytics Initiative," *Journal of Learning Analytics,* vol. 1, no. 1, 2014.

[2] M. Sharkey, "Academic analytics landscape at the University of Phoenix," in *1st International Conference on Learning Analytics and Knowledge (LAK11)*, Banff, AB, 2011.

[3] L. Macfadyen and S. Dawson, "Mining LMS data to develop an "early warning system" for educators: A proof of concept," *Computers & Education,* vol. 54, no. 2, pp. 588-599, 2010.

[4] C. Brooks, C. Thompson and S. Teasley, "A Time Series Interaction Analysis Method for Building Predictive Models of Learners using Log Data," in *5th International Conference on Learning Analytics and Knowledge 2015 (LAK15)*, Poughkeepsie, NY, 2015.

Connecting the Dots: Predicting Student Grade Sequences from Bursty MOOC Interactions over Time

Tanmay Sinha
ArticuLab
Carnegie Mellon University
5000 Forbes Avenue
Pittsburgh, PA 15213 USA
tanmays@andrew.cmu.edu

Justine Cassell
ArticuLab
Carnegie Mellon University
5000 Forbes Avenue
Pittsburgh, PA 15213 USA
justine@cs.cmu.edu

L@S 2015, March 14–18, 2015, Vancouver, BC, Canada.
ACM 978-1-4503-3411-2/15/03.
http://dx.doi.org/10.1145/2724660.2728669

Abstract

In this work, we track the interaction of students across multiple Massive Open Online Courses (MOOCs) on edX. Leveraging the "burstiness" factor of three of the most commonly exhibited interaction forms made possible by online learning (i.e, video lecture viewing, coursework access and discussion forum posting), we take on the task of predicting student performance (operationalized as grade) across these courses. Specifically, we utilize the probabilistic framework of Conditional Random Fields (CRF) to formalize the problem of predicting the sequence of grades achieved by a student in different MOOCs, taking into account the contextual dependency of this outcome measure on students' general interaction trend across courses. Based on a comparative analysis of the combination of interaction features, our best CRF model can achieve a precision of 0.581, recall of 0.660 and a weighted F-score of 0.560, outweighing several baseline discriminative classifiers applied at each sequence position. These findings have implications for initiating early instructor intervention, so as to engage students along less active interaction dimensions that could be associated with low grades.

Introduction and Motivation

The potential of MOOCs, despite their impact on education worldwide, is still relatively untapped. There

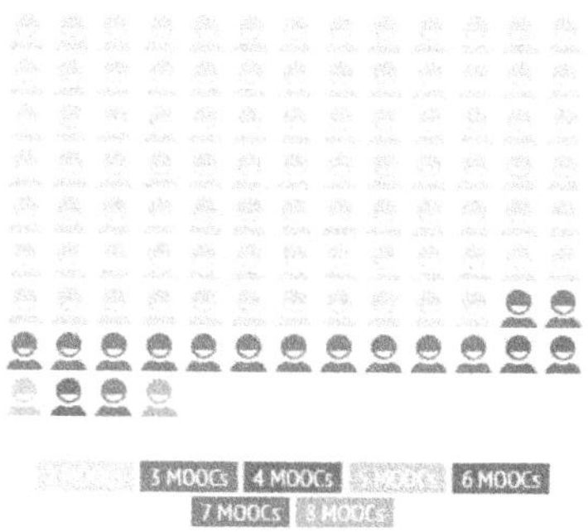

Figure 1: Pictorial Depiction of Data Distribution of Students who took more than 1 course on the edX platform in 2013 ([#MOOCs,#Students]: [2,8906], [3,1259], [4,202], [5,41], [6,7], [7,5], [8,1])

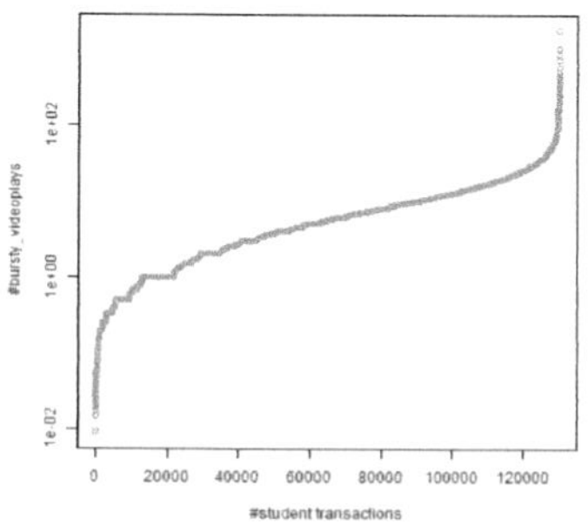

Figure 2: Scatterplot of #student transactions (Linear X axis) vs #burstyvideoplays (Logarithmic Y axis)

has been considerable commentary about gauging achievement in MOOCs and trying to improve retention, while accommodating participation differences and degrees of commitment along the modalities that have been made affordable. One salient assessment measure that indexes performance levels and is conventionally used to incentivize participation is grade. In this paper we consider the problem of "grade sequence prediction" or "grade labeling": to classify a students' grade points scored in multiple MOOC courses into one of the several defined categories. Such a labeling requires contextual information, because the labels are dependent on students' generic online learning strategy across courses.

Prior work predicting student performance from event traces has utilized measures such as motivation for signing up, obtaining help on discussion forums, and course features such as video lecture presentation and course content coverage. However, most of the focus has been on the student's current MOOC. If we were to rely on these analytics alone, it would be hard to capture any inherent student learning styles that might hold across different MOOCs. And we believe that these learning styles, if they match MOOC characteristics, will be a strong contributor to achievement. For example, if a student has been achieving high grades (say, >80%) by following a consistent participation pattern of spending more time watching video lectures and posting to the discussion forums, while never accessing chapters related to the coursework, it is legitimate to hypothesize that effective predictions of his grades in future MOOCs can be made based on those behaviors in prior courses.

Furthermore, there may be dependencies among the interaction features themselves, for instance, higher video lecture viewing might be related to heavy discussion forum clarifications for a MOOC on specialized topics, while it may not hold for a more introductory level MOOC.

Because including such interdependent interaction features is difficult to do while retaining tractability and making independence assumptions can affect performance, we are interested in estimating the posterior over grade labels achieved by a student across different MOOCs, given the observed interaction. This motivates the use of Conditional Random Fields (CRF), originally proposed by [3] for labeling text sequences. As a contrast to generative modeling approaches that capture the joint probability distribution $p(y,x)$, CRF follow a discriminative modeling approach to capture the conditional probability distribution $p(y|x)$ of label sequences $(y_1, y_2...y_n)$, given the input sequences $(x_1, x_2...x_n)$, without requiring calculation of potentially dependent features in $p(x)$ that are not required for classification.

We focus on the "burstiness" dimension of students' behavior in MOOCs, by which we mean unusually high rates of interaction. For example, some students usually post to MOOC forums once a week for course X, yet suddenly exhibit a posting pattern of 10 posts/day for course Y. Or some students usually watch 3-5 video lectures/course, and then suddenly start watching 20-25 video lectures/course. Such a longitudinal variance, along with the potential to represent "short-term" interest spikes dynamically driven by either a)captivating aspects in a particular MOOC, or b)problems in understanding course content, makes "burstiness" an important dimension to consider. Our interest is in making "long-term" predictions on grade points that a student achieves, by leveraging this aspect of the interaction.

Study Context

Our study context comprises of de-identified data from the first year (Academic Year 2013: Fall 2012, Spring 2013, and Summer 2013) of 13 MITx and HarvardX courses offered on the edX platform [4]. This is the first

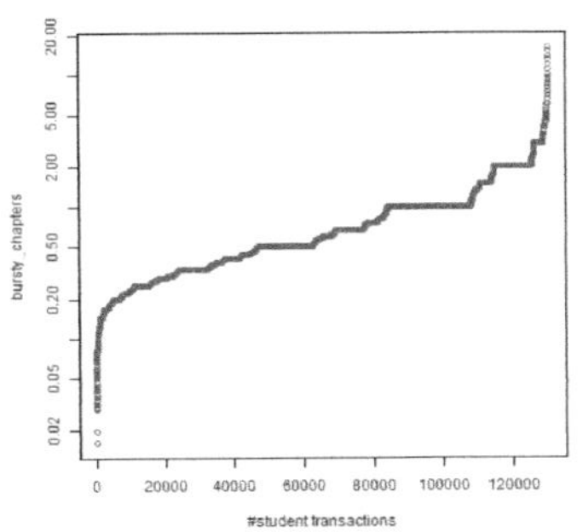

Figure 3: Scatterplot of #student transactions (Linear X axis) vs #burstychapters (Logarithmic Y axis)

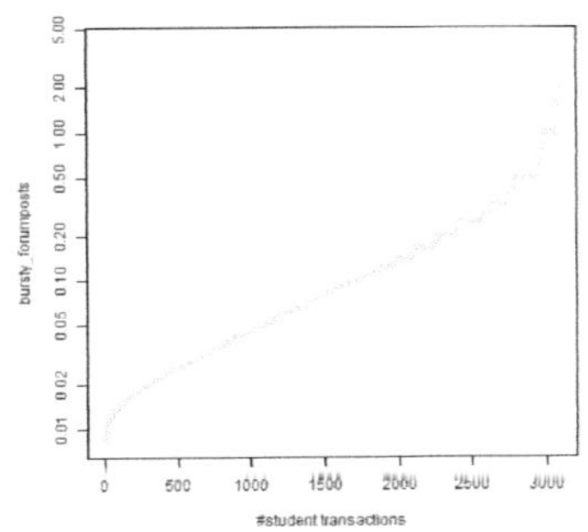

Figure 4: Scatterplot of #student transactions (Linear X axis) vs #burstyforumposts (Logarithmic Y axis)

large scale public MOOC data repository that contains information (aggregated records) about diverse kinds of learning interactions and outcome measures for the same students who took multiple courses on the platform. Our study is confined to ≈ 10000 students who took at least 2 or more courses on the edX platform and had some form of interaction with the particular MOOCs (Figure 1).

Methodology

We first operationalize three kinds of "burstiness" indices from students' interactions for all their MOOC courses taken. For all the 3 indices, a higher value denotes more "burstiness" and vice versa. Firstly, bursty number of play video events/clicks **(Bursty #videoplays)** is defined as the total number of play video events within a course, divided by the number of unique days student interacted with the particular course (Figure 2). In an analysis of video lecture viewing behavior across 4 edX courses, prior work [2] has shown that sudden spikes in video play events can be triggered both by type of students accessing the lecture (first time watchers versus re-watchers) and by the type of video lecture itself (such as tutorials versus lectures). Secondly, bursty number of chapters **(Bursty #chapters)** is defined as the total number of chapters (within the Courseware) with which the student interacted, divided by the number of unique days student interacted with the particular course (Figure 3). For edX MOOCs, Courseware tab is the home of the videos lectures, problem sets and exams. In an analysis of navigational differences across the same 4 edX courses, [1] found evidence for students over 40 accessing the digital course textbook 27% more frequently than those under 40 and thus exhibiting more bursty behavior. Thirdly, bursty number of discussion forum posts **(Bursty #forumposts)** is the total number of posts to the discussion forum, divided by the number of unique days student interacted with the particular course (Figure 4). Prior literature suggests that more burstiness on MOOC discussion forums is associated with greater likelihood of attrition [6], which we in turn expect to affect the grade points scored by a student. Next, we discretize the above burstiness indices into four categories based on equal frequency: Low (L), Medium (M), High (H) and Very High (V). Additionally, we also discretize the grade points scored by students in each course into the same 4 categories by equal frequency. To account for variability in course activity levels and course grading criteria, the discretization for each course is performed separately.

We then use a generic sequence of tokens representation for our input to the CRF framework. Figure 5 depicts this representation. For every student, each token represents a)3 feature values (Bursty #videoplays, Bursty #chapters, Bursty #forumposts) for the particular MOOC taken, and b)grade category (tag) for that course which is going to be trained by CRF. Thus, a sequence of tokens represents feature values and grade labels for all MOOCs taken in a sequential order by the student. Additionally, to specify the associations between output grade sequences (denoted by y) and input feature sequences (denoted by x), we utilize the following 4 feature templates for each of the 3 "burstiness" features: a)**1I**: current feature value, previous feature value, next feature value (input ± 1) and independence assumptions among y, b)**2I**: current feature value, previous 2 feature values, next 2 feature values (input ± 2) and independence assumptions among y, c)**1D**: current feature value, previous feature value, next feature value (input ± 1), combinations of previous output token (grade label) and current output token (dependence assumptions among y), d)**2D**: current feature value, previous 2 feature values, next 2 feature values (input ± 2), combinations of previous output token (grade label) and current output token (dependence assumptions among y). The intuition is to a)differentiate both long

	#Videoplays	#Chapter	#Forumposts	Grade
Course 1	L	M	V	H
Course 2	M	L	H	V
Course 3	M	L	M	M
Course 4	V	M	M	V
⋮				

Figure 5: Example depicting "sequence of tokens" representation of input feature sequence along with the grade points sequence for a student who has taken 4 MOOCs. Burstiness indices & Grade points are discretized into four categories based on equal frequency: Low (L), Medium (M), High (H) and Very High (V).

and short term interaction dependencies, and b)accommodate potentially correlated features of the inputs, while performing the training discriminatively.

Results

We do a 70:30 split of the data into training and test sets. The feature cutoff for training the CRF is 5. The output consists a)marginal probabilities for grade label achieved by a student in each course, and b)conditional probability for the grade sequence, given the interaction feature sequence. Evaluation of the grade sequence tagging is done using precision, recall and weighted F-score measure to account for label imbalance. As **baselines**, we also employ Logistic Regression and Sequential Minimal Optimization (SMO with exponent 1) discriminative classifiers that treat the grade sequence labeling problem as a sequence of classification problems, one for each of the labels in the sequence (5 fold cross validation). The results in Table 1 substantiate that the **1I** CRF feature template configuration out-performs these baseline approaches that are myopic about the impact of current decision on later decisions. CRF improves predictability by allowing for a much richer input feature set.

Conclusion

In summary, we showed that "burstiness" factors can make significant predictions on students' grade sequence across different MOOCs. This can be used to facilitate real-time remediation from instructors, by a)combining finer grained features from video viewing, navigational and forum activities [5], b)augmenting such behavioral traces gathered up till specific course time points, with interactions from prior courses, to predict potential grades and tailor course content for students falling in high and low grade clusters, c)filtering these clusters by motivation to precisely gauge the intervention type (for e.g, pointers to applications and challenging learning materials would be a more preferable strategy for students who intended to specialize on certain topics and are likely to score average grade, than those who made an informed commitment for course completion and will score similarly).

Model	Precision	Recall	F-Score
LogReg (baseline)	0.588	0.659	0.558
SMO (baseline)	0.522	0.647	0.521
CRF 1I	**0.581**	**0.660**	**0.560**
CRF 2I	0.568	0.659	0.560
CRF 1D	0.584	0.655	0.551
CRF 2D	0.570	0.656	0.554

Table 1: Evaluation measures on test set using baselines (Logistic Regression & SMO) and 4 different CRF templates.

References

[1] Guo, P. J., and Reinecke, K. Demographic differences in how students navigate through moocs. In *Proceedings of ACM L@S* (2014).

[2] Kim, J., Guo, P. J., Seaton, D. T., Mitros, P., Gajos, K. Z., and Miller, R. C. Understanding in video dropouts and interaction peaks inonline lecture videos. In *Proceedings of ACM L@S* (2014), 31–40.

[3] Lafferty, J., McCallum, A., and Pereira, F. C. Conditional random fields: Probabilistic models for segmenting and labeling sequence data.

[4] MITx, and HarvardX. Harvardx-mitx person-course academic year 2013 de-identified dataset, version 2.0. In *http://dx.doi.org/10.7910/DVN/26147*, Harvard Dataverse Network [Distributor] V10 [Version] (2014).

[5] Sinha, T., Li, N., Jermann, P., and Dillenbourg, P. Capturing attrition intensifying structural traits from didactic interaction sequences of mooc learners. *Proceedings of EMNLP* (2014).

[6] Yang, D., Sinha, T., Adamson, D., and Rosé, C. P. Turn on, tune in, drop out: Anticipating student dropouts in massive open online courses. In *Proceedings of the NIPS* (2013).

Connecting Stories and Pedagogy Increases Participant Engagement in Discussions

Vineet Pandey
UC San Diego Design Lab
La Jolla, CA 92093-0404
vipandey@ucsd.edu

Michael S. Bernstein
Stanford University HCI Group
Stanford, CA 94305-9035
msb@cs.stanford.edu

Yasmine Kotturi
UC San Diego Design Lab
Atkinson Hall 1601
La Jolla, CA 92093-0436
ykotturi@ucsd.edu

Scott Klemmer
UC San Diego Design Lab
Atkinson Hall 1601
La Jolla, CA 92093-0436
srk@ucsd.edu

Chinmay Kulkarni
Stanford University HCI Group
Stanford, CA 94305-9035
chinmay@cs.stanford.edu

L@S 2015, March 14–18, 2015, Vancouver, BC, Canada.
ACM 978-1-4503-3411-2/15/03.
http://dx.doi.org/10.1145/2724660.2728670

Abstract
Student discussions over video in massive classes allow students to explore course content, share personal experiences and get feedback on their ideas. However, such discussions frequently turn into casual conversations without focusing on the curriculum and the learning objectives. This short paper explores whether students can achieve multiple learning objectives by solving challenges collaboratively during discussions. We introduce 'think-pair-share' technique for video discussions. Our pilot results, drawn from a Coursera class, suggest that participants prefer to exchange information with their peers using personal stories and connecting stories with curriculum increases participant engagement.

Author Keywords
video; discussion; small groups; synchronous collaboration

ACM Classification Keywords
K.3.1 [Computer Uses in Education]: Collaborative Learning

Video discussions: popular, but under-utilized
In online discussion groups, students receive feedback, brainstorm ideas, share personal experiences and develop greater empathy, leading to deeper understanding of course material [1].

Current discussions [1] use a discussion agenda to guide the participants while providing them the ability to structure discussions. With this structure, participants moderate discussions themselves, which sometimes devolve into conversations independent of the course material. For example, students feel pressed to fill moments of awkward silence with casual banter. These casual conversations help students build empathy and developing alternate viewpoints, but lack the opportunity to think deeply about a topic.

Seeding discussions with challenge questions

This paper explores whether more structured discussions can help achieve other learning objectives such as transfer of concepts [3], better collaboration/teamwork and faster cognition, while still preserving the benefits of a global conversation such as empathy and perspective-sharing. To achieve these learning goals, we introduce collaborative 'challenge-solving' to global discussions, where students see a specific challenge to be solved and a rigidly enforced discussion structure. This discussion structure enforces individual accountability and helps participants generate relevant ideas broadly and share them with peers.

We chose challenge questions with three learning goals: conceptual transfer of knowledge, building empathy among participants, and to encourage students to think in diverse ways. To help students transfer conceptual knowledge, challenge questions required participants to apply their understanding of course concepts to a problem. To build empathy and diversity in ideas, questions encouraged sharing (geographically) local ideas, which has been successful in prior work [1]. Furthermore, to help students with differing familiarity with content, the question draws from the relevant course content, but is chosen to be approachable without being pedantic.

Even given a specific challenge, participants might not automatically arrange their discussions productively. Instead, software could organize and moderate these discussions. Using software to organize discussions also helps enforce the discussion structure at scale and maintain consistency in participant experience. For our pilot, we built an embedded hangout application to provide the correct structure and provide participants cues at relevant times. This application displayed different parts of the discussion to participants, but we manually switched the discussion from one part to the next. This high-touch approach also allowed us to understand the requirements for the software.

Our work is the first to introduce software to enable specific active learning discussion structure for MOOC discussion groups.

Discussion structure for active learning

We turn to experiences in physical classrooms for insight on how software should structure discussions. In brick and mortar classrooms, discussions that emphasize active learning share features like collaborative goal, individual responsibility and feedback to improve self-esteem [4].

Collaborative goal requires students to work together towards solving a challenge. Individual responsibility requires every student to contribute to the discussion and to the final solution. An open feedback environment allows students to explain their ideas and improve them to to feel better about their contribution. A word of praise or spirit of comradeship is a positive step towards combating the "alone together" phenomenon [5]. Furthermore, while physical classrooms may experiment with elaborate discussion structures, online discussion structures should also be simple so that participants can use them without

How 'Think-pair-share' works

Think-pair-share enables students to collaboratively construct potential answers to an open-ended question. Consider the question: "Why are there few women leaders in global organizations?". In the first, **think**, phase, students formulate their list of ideas alone. In the **pair** phase, each student discusses their answer with a peer to develop it further with their feedback. In the final, **share**, phase, students share their answers with the whole class.

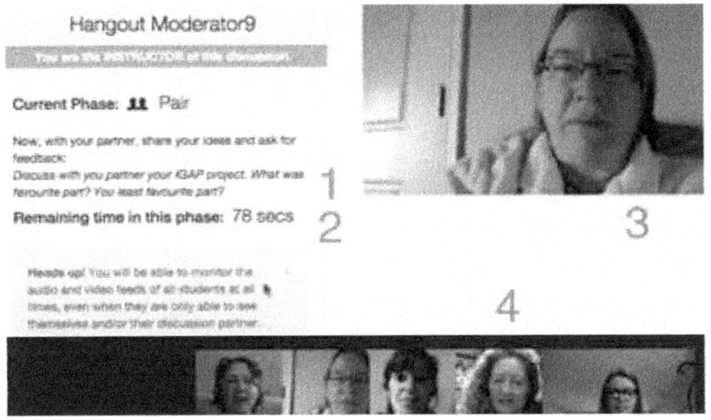

Figure 1: Moderator's view in the 'think-pair-share' discussion structure added to Talkabout [1]. In the pair phase, a participant can only see/hear another participant. The interface includes: 1. Discussion topic 2. Time remaining in the phase 3. Video feed of current speaker 4. Video feeds of all participants (and moderator).

training from in-person instructors. With these requirements, our pilot uses the 'think-pair-share' [2] structure, an active learning classroom technique named for its three sequential phases.

Pilot results: Focus on motivation and stories

We tested our pilot with students in a Philanthropy MOOC on Coursera, "Giving 2.0", which taught students *"..to practice philanthropy more effectively"*. The course uses the online discussion group platform Talkabout [1]. Having observed discussions and interacted with the instructors, we knew the course objectives and the nature of discussions. We used this information to run pilots with different discussion structures. An app in the Talkabout platform provides the think-pair-share structure as shown in Figure 1. Using our app, a moderator (researcher) starts the 'think-pair-share' discussion after the participants have introduced themselves. Each of the three phases (think, pair, share) had time limits enforced to encourage students to focus on the important ideas and to make progress in the discussion. The think time was set as 1 minute, pair time as 2 minutes and share time was 5 minutes which moved to the free-flowing discussion format. The challenge question was *"In your community, how do you make people passionately follow and contribute to causes of their interest. Think about the principles mentioned in the course as well as your unique understanding of your community. "*

We piloted with three discussions, with a total of 11 participants. In our first two discussions, we tried the challenge-solving exercise but realized that participants were not very motivated. Therefore, in the third discussion, we built the discussion structure around participant goals (e.g. sharing their projects and getting feedback). Given the small number of participants and course settings, our results are suggestive rather than rigorous, and have provided us insights into next steps and the challenges with this discussion structure.

In the first two discussions, participants discussed their ideas broadly and asked some questions in the pair and share phases. However, they did not seem motivated and did not complete the challenge exercise to create a final solution list. Some participants preferred getting feedback on their ideas while others wanted to hear their peers' experiences and insights in philanthropy. One participant said, *"I am attending this discussion to get feedback on my idea. I cannot spend time on this challenge exercise."*

Participants preferred sharing stories to solving a specific challenge. Ideas from course lectures were explicitly mentioned infrequently. Students' stories served to illustrate their ideas with events in their professional or personal lives; the personal nature of such narratives made peers supportive and curious. Consequently, we structured the third discussion as a collaborative exercise towards discussing end of the course projects. This seemingly allowed participants to have longer, detailed conversations that shared experiences in context of their projects.

Pilot results: Personal interactions matter

In our think phase, video and audio from other participants were blocked to allow participants to think by themselves. The inherently lonely nature of think phase and our interface made this phase awkward to participants who joined the discussion to "talk" to their peers. The pair phase allowed participants to talk in greater depth with a peer and participants seemed to enjoy such interactions. Participants preferred getting to know their classmates better through the pair phase, leading to stronger pair bonds later in the discussion. This suggests using a prompt that lets students relate to each other; for instance, using the pair phase to discuss their project which allowed them to describe their experiences. In our experience, this yielded higher participant engagement than putting up a hypothetical challenge.

Participants were most comfortable in the share phase possibly because it was easy to follow and seemed familiar from previous discussions. In the share phase, participants also encouraged their paired partners to speak up if they were not actively participating. Finally, different classes may benefit from different lengths of each phase. For instance, classes that require greater empathy among participants (e.g. a human rights class) might benefit from a longer pair phase, and a shortened think phase.

Conclusion and Future Work

This research aims to explicitly structure discussions to maximize learning goals. To be successful, our experience suggests that such structures must also satisfy students' desire to connect with classmates and share stories.

A primary obstacle in comparing different structures is finding metrics that capture the learning benefits. For instance, grades in open-ended work can measure students' performance, the post-discussion diversity amongst participants' work provides a measure for creative fixation. The difference in student work before and after discussions may help measure how well discussions transfer new perspectives. The fraction of students who choose each discussion format provides one measure of adoption, other measures include post-discussion surveys with measures of enjoyment and motivation.

With these metrics, future work will attempt to find structures which satisfy these student desires and leverage them to achieve learning goals.

Acknowledgements

We thank Julia Cambre, who initially developed the 'think-pair-share' app and UC San Diego Design Lab for supporting this research. This research was funded in part through NSF grants #1351131 and #1444865 and the Hasso Plattner Design Thinking Program, and conducted under the Stanford IRB protocol #30319.

References

[1] Kulkarni, C., Cambre, J., Kotturi, Y., Bernstein, M. S., and Klemmer, S. Talkabout: Making distance matter with small groups in massive classes. In *Proc. CSCW* (2015).

[2] Lyman, F. Think-pair-share: An expanding teaching technique. *MAA-CIE Cooperative News* (1987).

[3] Schwartz, D., Bransford, J., and Sears, D. Efficiency and innovation in transfer. *Transfer of learning from a modern multidisciplinary perspective* (2005).

[4] Slavin, R. E. *Student Team Learning: An Overview and Practical Guide*. National Education Assoc., 1988.

[5] Turkle, S. *Alone Together: Why We Expect More from Technology and Less from Each Other*. Basic Books, Inc., (2011).

Source Effects in Online Education

Nakull Gupta[1]
t-nakgup@microsoft.com

Jacki O'Neill[1]
jackioniell@micrososft.com

Andrew Cross[1]
across@micrososft.com

Edward Cutrell[1]
cutrell@microsoft.com

William Thies[1]
thies@micrososft.com

[1]Microsoft Research India
Bangalore, Karnataka, India

Abstract

While most MOOCs rely on world-famous experts to teach the masses, in many circumstances students may learn more from people who share their context such as local teachers or peers. Here, we describe an experiment to explore how the "source" of video content, the teacher, affects online learning, specifically in the context of higher education in Indian colleges. The proposed experiment will compare three content sources – a local lecturer (teacher from an Indian engineering college), a local peer (both male and female students similar to the targeted audience), and an internationally recognized expert (a Stanford lecturer). Students will watch videos by the various source authors, after which we will measure differences in their preference, engagement, and learning. In addition, we discuss our experiences with helping students prepare video lectures and describe the support and processes we used to curate interesting and clear peer-generated content.

L@S 2015, Mar 14-18, 2015, Vancouver, BC, Canada
ACM 978-1-4503-3411-2/15/03.
http://dx.doi.org/10.1145/2724660.2728671

Author Keywords

Online education; peer learning; source effects; MOOCs

ACM Classification Keywords

H.5.m. Information interfaces and presentation (e.g., HCI): Miscellaneous.

Introduction and motivation

One of the motivating philosophies behind the MOOC movement is that the best teachers are singular, internationally recognized subject-matter experts. However, in many educational contexts, learning from a local peer has been shown to be a highly effective method of teaching. Given these two conflicting notions, we describe an experiment to examine how the "source", or lecturer, of video content might impact learning outcomes in online education. Our aim is to understand how students react to content produced by different sources such as local teachers, international

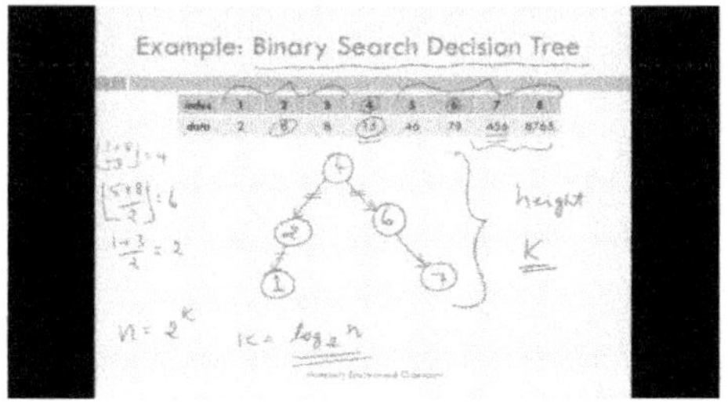

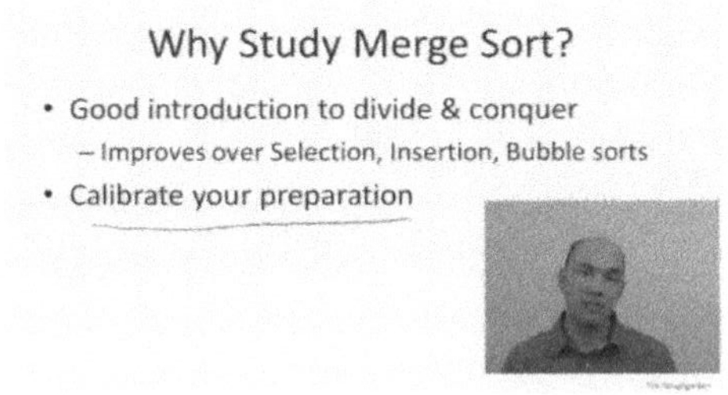

Figure 1: Screenshots of (from top to bottom) a sample MEC video, peer video and a Stanford professor's video.

experts, and peers ("local" and peers referring to individuals from similar cultural and educational backgrounds), and to explore how effective these alternative teaching sources might be for learning.

Engineering students in India naïve to MOOCs frequently tell us that if they were to watch online lectures, they would prefer to learn from international experts (i.e., professors from recognized universities, such as those who would normally teach a course on edX or Coursera). However, after actual exposure to such lectures in MOOCs, Indian students often find those same lecturers difficult to learn from, citing language or accent, pace, examples, and divergence from their college curriculum. This seeming contradiction motivated us to explore how peer learning might bootstrap or even replace "expert" teaching in some scenarios, something that has not yet been evaluated. Another strong motivation to explore peer learning is that there are relatively few international subject-matter experts, which makes content creation difficult for even a single language, much less the native languages of many online learners. Conversely, peers represent a potential low-cost, unharnessed resource for content creation.

Peer learning has been demonstrated as a powerful teaching tool in a variety of domains. Work by Gandhi et al. [1] showed the effectiveness of videos of local farmers demonstrating best practices in farming and animal husbandry relevant for the local context and in the local dialect of that region. They showed that peer learning at scale is not only an effective tool for disseminating information and behavior change, but is also more cost-effective. Similarly, in traditional educational contexts researchers have explored the applications of peer learning in higher education [2], as well as peer and self-assessment in massive online classes [3], showing that in certain contexts, peer learning is an effective tool for learning. While there will always be a place for world-class lecturers in MOOCs, we wonder if peer-generated content in online learning might supplement or even replace expert content in certain cases to be more culturally relevant, understandable, linguistically appropriate, and cheaper to produce at scale.

Before exploring these themes, key questions remain regarding whether students can produce quality content, and how best to support peer production. While MOOC professors have significant teaching experience, and often have professional recording equipment and editing teams, students are usually novice teachers with very limited equipment. Given these disparities, can peers produce educational content which is as good as, or even better than, existing sources of content for certain audiences? Also, how might students actually produce such content?

In the following section we describe our experimental design motivated by these research questions. We plan to conduct the study on a platform called Massively Empowered Classrooms (MEC), an experimental educational platform designed to support MOOC-like functionality and blended learning for Indian colleges. The experiment focuses on content for teaching the Design and Analysis of Algorithms course which is a foundational course in computer science with ample existing online material allowing comparisons across sources.

Topic and Sequencing	Sources Compared
Binary Search *(shown first or second with 50/50 chance)*	MEC vs. Peer
Merge Sort *(shown first or second with 50/50 chance)*	MEC vs. Stanford
Quick Sort *(shown third)*	MEC vs. Peer vs. Stanford

Table 1: Experiment design. For each lecture, students are randomly assigned to one of the sources listed (with equal likelihood). Those assigned to the "peer" condition are further divided between four peers.

Experiment Design

The proposed study seeks to explore the role of "source effects" in online education by comparing three sources – a MEC lecturer (teacher from a local college - People's Education Society Institute of Technology, Bangalore), a peer (both female and male Indian students, who had recently taken the same class) and an internationally recognized expert (Stanford professor). We have prepared the content and study design, though have not begun the experiment.

The videos cover three topics from the three sources and students will be randomly allocated to different videos for a given topic. As noted in Table 1, each lesson topic compares at least two versions. The MEC version is present for all three topics and serves as a control. Lectures from four students (two male and two female) were prepared for Binary Search and Quick Sort. We used the Merge Sort and Quick Sort lectures from Tim Roughgarden's online algorithms class (with consent from Prof. Roughgarden and Stanford). The presentation order of the Binary Search and Merge Sort topics are randomized to control for potential order effects.

The first few seconds of all the peer-generated videos contain an introduction by the student (name, college and topic) along with a video capture of his/her face. The Stanford videos also have a video capture of the professor throughout the video. While some other MEC videos contain video capture, those used in our experiment do not. All three sources of the videos comprise either a combination of slides and handwritten text, or handwritten text only. Though the visual presentation and pedagogy differ across versions, the technical points explained are similar (students exposed to any of the videos of a particular topic would learn the same subtopics).

Each student will see only one version for any given topic, the allocation of a video being done on the basis of his/her unique user ID on MEC (using a hash function) and completely independent from other students and demographics.

We will concentrate on measuring three aspects for each video: engagement, preference, and learning. Our metric for engagement is the number of seconds watched, which we compare across videos for a given topic. Students always have the option to stop watching a video, as many do for videos they find unengaging or otherwise difficult to understand. To measure preference, we ask in-video questions, including a Likert scale to rate the video with additional space for writing qualitative feedback. At the end of the video students can also fill out a more detailed survey. To measure learning outcomes, we will count the number of correct and incorrect responses to two in-video questions which are the same for all versions.

Although we take care to facilitate a fair comparison, we are still left with many confounds such as varying lengths of the videos, different production quality, recency bias, the particular topics chosen for the experiment, and many more.

It should also be noted that throughout the experiment design we have tried to pay attention to the associated ethical concerns. Students will have an option to opt out of the experiment and it will also be made clear that opting out will not have any negative influence on their grades or performance.

Sample Peer Content (produced by a female student from a college in Bangalore): http://mlxstorage.blob.core.windows.net/mec-v3/seBinarySearchf2.mp4

Sample content on MEC by a local professor: http://mlxstorage.blob.core.windows.net/mec-v3/seBinarySearchMEC.mp4

Sample content from Stanford professor: https://class.coursera.org/algo-004/lecture/1

Figure 2: Links to sample content used

We had six students record videos for Binary Search and Quick Sort, fundamental topics in the course that all students would learn. The content and narrative of the lectures was decided entirely by the students. We provided some logistical support (sound proof rooms and touch screen laptops) and helped fix and point out errors in the videos. Students were given options to use slides, webcams and touch screen input tools as well.

Recording error-free videos that were of acceptable quality was an iterative process. The students, just like expert content producers for MOOCs, had to prepare lecture notes before recording a video, have sufficient recording material, and sometimes rerecord multiple takes. We provided some students with laptops and webcams, reviewed initial recordings to check for technical correctness, and gave basic guidance for post-processing to create a video of reasonable quality. While this overhead was managed by the researchers and not students (peers), any MOOC lecturer would undergo similar background and post-processing work. We believe much of this overhead could be handled at scale through a set of guidelines, some faculty or staff supervision, and by other students' inputs (e.g., through notes on errors or a rating system to weed out low-quality videos).

Current Status and Learnings

We deployed an initial pilot to test the feasibility of running this experiment and get feedback to improve our design. While we did not observe any significant differences in engagement or learning for this limited number of students, we did have some qualitative responses to our in-video questions. For instance a student commented on a video by the expert: *"I did not like the video. Reason: The lecturer's talking speed was very fast, I hardly followed 1 or 2 statements in the whole lesson. The lecturer's voice modulation was also not good."* Other students commented on peer videos: *"Her voice was very clear and I can understand her lecture"*; and, *"it precisely explains the concept in very less time and yes I didn't get bored"*. These comments suggest that there may be important differences from sources, based on the audience, which may impact our three key measures.

While iterating our experiment design, we have also discussed modifying the experiment to force users to make more explicit choices (e.g. watch all versions of a lecture for a few seconds and then choose one), reach out to a larger student population outside of Indian engineering colleges, have more direct interventions, and perhaps use more sources for lecture delivery, such as voice actors or celebrities.

References

[1] A Gandhi, R., Veeraraghavan, R., Toyama, K., & Ramprasad, V. Digital green: Participatory video for agricultural extension. *ICTD* 2007

[2] Boud, D., Cohen, R., & Sampson, J. (Eds.). *Peer learning in higher education: Learning from and with each other.* Routledge, 2014

[3] Kulkarni, C., Wei, K. P., Le, H., Chia, D., Papadopoulos, K., Cheng, J., & Klemmer, S. R. Peer and self-assessment in massive online classes. *ACM TOCHI*, 2014.

AutoStyle: Toward Coding Style Feedback At Scale

Joseph Moghadam
UC Berkeley
jmoghadam@berkeley.edu

Rohan Roy Choudhury
UC Berkeley
rrc@berkeley.edu

HeZheng Yin
The Institute for Theoretical Computer Science, Institute for Interdisciplinary Information Sciences, Tsinghua University
yhz11@mails.tsinghua.edu.cn

Armando Fox
UC Berkeley
fox@berkeley.edu

L@S 2015, Mar 14–18, 2015, Vancouver, BC, Canada.
ACM 978-1-4503-3411-2/15/03.
http://dx.doi.org/10.1145/2724660.2728672

Author Keywords
coding style; MOOCs; autograding

ACM Classification Keywords
K.3.2 [Computer and Information Science Education]: Computer science education.

Abstract
While large-scale automatic grading of student programs for correctness is widespread, less effort has focused on automating feedback for good programming *style:* the tasteful use of language features and idioms to produce code that is not only correct, but also concise, elegant, and revealing of design intent. We hypothesize that with a large enough (MOOC-sized) corpus of submissions to a given programming problem, we can observe a range of stylistic mastery from naïve to expert, and many points in between, and that we can exploit this continuum to automatically provide hints to learners for improving their code style based on the key stylistic differences between a given learner's submission and a submission that is stylistically slightly better. We are developing a methodology for analyzing and doing feature engineering on differences between submissions, and for learning from instructor-provided feedback as to which hints are most relevant.

Introduction

Massive Open Online Courses (MOOCs) provide a powerful way to reach thousands of students simultaneously. UC Berkeley's SaaS MOOC "Engineering Software as a Service", based on a campus course for juniors and seniors, teaches fundamentals of software engineering. The MOOC relies heavily on autograding of complete programming assignments. However, good software engineering also requires developing good coding style, and the current autograders only evaluate correctness and completeness. We would like to automatically provide learners with hints for improving their coding style.

By "style" we refer not to mechanical coding conventions (indentation, punctuation, naming of variables, and so on), but to the effective use of programming idioms [14] that make code readable, concise, and elegant by the standards of an experienced practitioner of a given language or framework. For example, consider a simple programming assignment that groups strings in an array so that all strings in a group are anagrams of each other. In a corpus of about 800 submitted solutions from a recent offering of the SaaS MOOC, correct solutions varied in length by an order of magnitude: Figure 1 shows actual submissions from pseudonymous students Alice, Bob, and Charles.

```
def combine_anagrams(words)
  words.group_by { |word| word.chars.sort }.values
end
```

```
def combine_anagrams(words)
  dict = {}
  words.each do |word|
    letters = word.downcase.each_char.sort
    if dict.has_key?(letters) then
      dict[letters] += [word]
    else
      dict[letters] = [word]
    end
  end
  return dict.values
end
```

```
def combine_anagrams(words)
  rtn = Array.new
  words.each do |word|
    p(word)
    wordDowncase = word.downcase
    letters = wordDowncase.split("")
    exist = false
    rtn.each do |rtnAry|
      rl = rtnAry[0].downcase.split("")
      if (rl.length == letters.length) then
        p(rl)
        rl.sort!
        letters.sort!
        match = true
        i = 0
        rl.each do |rli|
          p(((rli + "-") + letters[i]))
          match = false if (rli != letters[i])
          i = (i + 1)
        end
        if (match == true) then
          (rtnAry << word)
          exist = true
        end
      end
    end
    (rtn << [word]) if (not exist)
  end
  return rtn
end
```

Figure 1: A 3-line solution from "Alice," representative of the best possible solution for this assignment; a 12-line solution from "Bob"; and a 30-line solution from "Charles." While longer solutions were more likely to be clumsy and riddled with stylistic problems, stylistic variation was present even among shorter solutions, and excessive terseness is often worse than verbosity, so program length is an insufficient proxy of code style.

Simply showing Charles the solutions from Alice or Bob is not useful, because too many conceptual gaps separate those from his own 30-line solution. Instead, we present a method for automatically using the corpus of submissions to provide Charles with *actionable* style hints—ones that name a specific concept, language construct, or standard-library facility—that, if properly followed, could improve the style of his code incrementally.

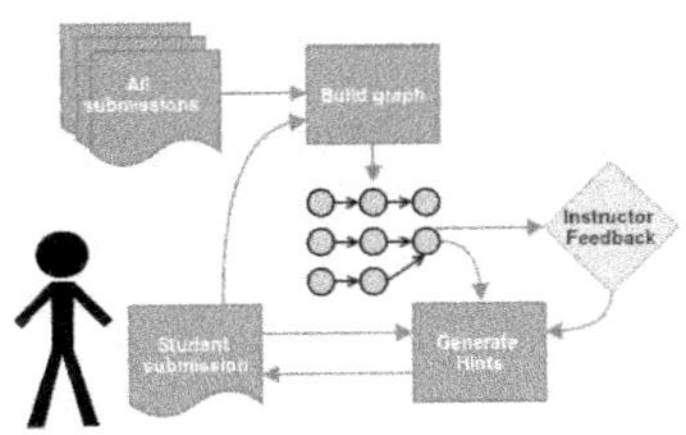

Figure 2: We generate a graph of stylistic improvement across all submissions, which is used to help generate hints for any particular submission. The instructor can provide feedback to train the hint generating system to react to the features of the graph differently.

Problem Formulation

At the level of an individual function or method, we can quantify code style using well-known software engineering metrics such as ABC complexity (assignments, branches, conditions) [3], absence of redundant code blocks [1], and cyclomatic complexity [8], which measures the number of distinct paths through a piece of code. Existing static analysis tools readily compute these metrics, but do not suggest solutions to the problems they report. Indeed, as the example above suggests, in many cases the "solution" lies not in simple substitution of one token or keyword for another, but of substitution of one idiom or data structure for another.

We hypothesize that with a large enough (MOOC-sized) corpus of submissions to a given programming problem, we can observe a range of stylistic mastery from naïve to expert, and many points in between, and that we can offer advice to a learner by extracting hints from other submissions in the corpus that are "just a little better" than that learner's own submission. Specifically, we use automated techniques to find a "chain" from Charles's solution to Alice's. At each link in the chain, we identify a specific language concept or idiom that is introduced and improves the code's style, while bounding how much the overall code structure changes at each point.

Our approach requires a measure of structural similarity between two moderate-length pieces of code and one or more measures of stylistic quality. We currently use Zhang-Shasha tree-edit distance [16] as our similarity metric and a variant of ABC (assignment-branch-condition) complexity as a proxy for stylistic quality, but we are experimenting with other choices.

Our approach assumes that all solutions in the corpus are functionally correct—easily enforceable by our existing autograders—and that at least one submission represents the best possible style achievable for the given assignment, as measured by whatever quality metric is used. We call these *stylistically optimal* solutions and recognize that multiple distinct solutions may achieve the same level of code quality.

We first compute the stylistic quality of every submission and the structural similarity between every pair of submissions. We then construct a directed graph of the submissions such that an arc $A \mapsto B$ is present iff B differs structurally from A by no more than a preset threshold, *and* B's quality score improves on A's by at least a preset threshold. (We say "improves on" because lower is better for some metrics whereas higher is better for others.)

Figure 2 illustrates how we envision using this graph in an instructional setting. From any given learner's submission, we find a path through the graph starting at that submission that eventually reaches a stylistically optimal submission; the intuition is that since each successive link in that chain differs from its predecessor by a bounded amount and improves the style of the submission, the chain represents a possible path of "successive refinement" from the learner's submission to a stylistically optimal one. The goal is to identify which of the various structural differences between adjacent nodes is the "best" hint to give the learner to nudge him or her along that path.

Markers

Manual examination revealed that a common pattern underlying needlessly complex code was the learner's lack of awareness of the language's support for a particular data structure, set of operations, or library functions, leading them to code the functionality by hand. Building on standard Abstract Syntax Tree (AST) analysis libraries, our code looks for *markers* such as the presence of particular calls to the standard library, the presence of local groupings of calls to the standard library, and the presence of certain data structures or operators/library calls that manipulate them. We note which markers are present at each link in the chain (the list of *marker diffs* between adjacent links). We must then decide which marker diffs should be the basis of a hint, which might take the form "Consider using library function x here."

Observe that the usefulness of a particular marker-based hint may be specific to a particular programming assignment. The example given earlier can be solved easily with hash tables, but only awkwardly if learners are unfamiliar with hash tables and use linear arrays. For this particular assignment, then, hints based on markers for hashes and their associated operators are likely to be useful.

We say a marker is more *relevant* if a hint based on that marker, properly instantiated, is more likely in the instructor's opinion to call attention to the most important stylistic deficiency in the current submission. We frame the problem of determining the relevance of marker diffs as a classification problem solved with a perceptron [9], where each marker diff is classified as relevant or not. The features the pereptron considers for each marker have to do with the presence of the marker across the chain of submissions associated with the learner's submissions. The reason we construct an entire chain of length n starting at the learner's submission is that one possible indicator of a marker's relevance is its *persistence:* if a marker is absent from submission i in the chain, indicators for its presence in submissions $i+1$, $i+2$, $\ldots$, n are each a distinct feature. This allows the perceptron to learn, for example, that it should prefer hints of concepts that do not appear in the current submission but appear in later submissions in the chain *and persist* after they appear. We initialize the perceptron to already know this, though it can learn more refined behavior for specific markers through the feedback it receives.

Instructor-Facing GUI

We have implemented the analyses described above as well as an instructor-facing GUI for embedding the analyses in an instructional setting. First, an offline batch computation generates the ASTs, quality scores, and pairwise similarities between submissions in the corpus as described above. Then, as the screenshot in Figure 3 shows, the instructor can visualize the chain associated with a given submission and the marker diffs between adjacent submissions in the chain. The instructor can also use sliders to change hyperparameters of the chains, such as adjusting the thresholds for similarity and style improvement: a tighter threshold for structural differences means that instantiating the hints will require the learner to make only minor changes in the code, while a looser threshold implies larger changes in the code.

The instructor provides feedback about which hints are not helpful in the example chains. The tool learns from this feedback by adjusting the perceptron weights, and adjusts the hints. When the instructor is satisfied with the automated hint generation, the tool is used to generate hints for students. The students can then resubmit their assignments; the revised submissions are incorporated into the corpus, and the process is repeated.

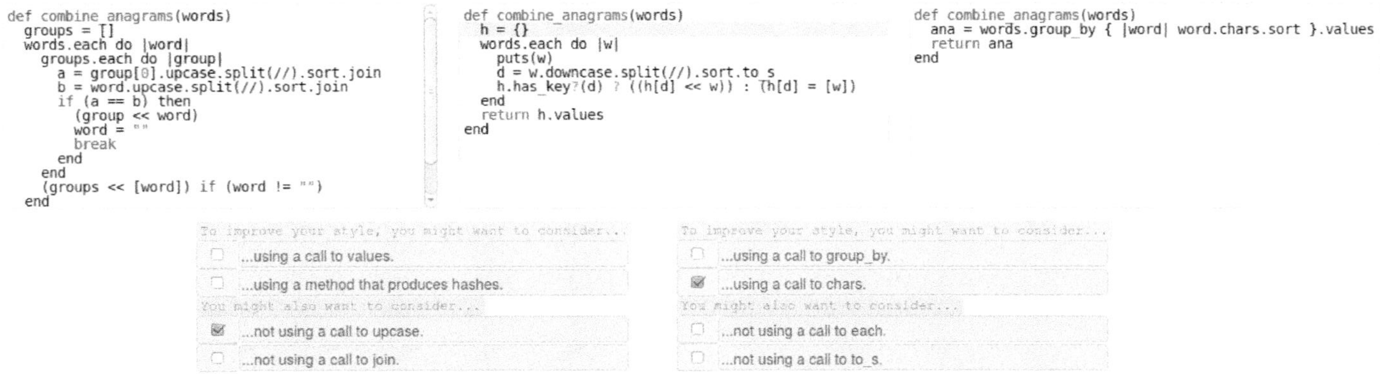

Figure 3: This instructor-facing GUI used to train the perceptron, as described in the text.

Related Work

One of the earliest tools for checking programming style (albeit at a low level of abstraction) is `lint` [6], a static checker that used a set of rules to detect suspicious constructs in C code. The Wikipedia entry *List of tools for static code analysis* lists dozens of `lint`-inspired tools for other languages.

More recently, the intelligent tutoring systems community has focused on generating hints from student solution data by canonicalizing or abstracting aspects of the solution space and using solution-space traversal techniques [11], code synthesis techniques [13], or transformation of the original student submissions [15] to generate the hints. This work generally focuses on helping students turn their incorrect solutions into a correct solution; we focus on proper use of programming idioms, which is both somewhat more subjective and evolves over time. Closer in spirit to our work is Codex [2], which indexes public repositories of Ruby code to extract emergent programming practices, which we can think of as representing "stylistic trends" in a language.

One of the first attempts to visualize variation among submissions to a particular programming assignment from a MOOC cohort was by Huang et al. [5]. Glassman et al. proposed using variation theory to cluster student solutions to an assignment [4], and subsequently produced OverCode [12], a GUI that helps visualize major groupings of variation among student submissions to a code assignment. Codewebs [10] tries to determine "probabilistic semantic equivalence" of two pieces of code by comparing "code phrases," or subgraphs of ASTs. Both of these inherit from much previous work using AST analysis to detect duplicated code or code plagiarism [7].

Status and next steps

We have been developing the tool against one corpus of about 800 submissions to a simple Ruby programming assignment and another corpus of about 200 submissions to a simple Python assignment from an introductory-level course. The front-end parsers and marker extractors are different for Ruby and Python, but the hint generation and classification logic are the same. We expect to alpha-test the tools with TAs and students in Spring 2015.

Acknowledgments

We thank Andrew Huang for providing anonymized submissions from Berkeley's introductory programming course, and our colleagues Ken Goldberg, Björn Hartmann, and John Canny for feedback on the approach and paper.

References

[1] Baxter, I. D. Clone detection using abstract syntax trees. In *Proceedings of ICSM'98*, IEEE (1998).

[2] Fast, E., Steffee, D., Wang, L., Brandt, J., and Bernstein, M. S. Emergent, crowd-scale programming practice in the IDE. In *CHI 2014* (Toronto, Canada, 2014).

[3] Fitzpatrick, J. Applying the ABC metric to C, C++, and Java. In *More C++ Gems*, R. C. Martin, Ed. Cambridge University Press, New York, NY, USA, 2000, 245–264.

[4] Glassman, E. L., Singh, R., and Miller, R. C. Feature engineering for clustering student solutions. In *Learning At Scale (L@S)* (Atlanta, GA, Mar 2014). Work-in-progress submission.

[5] Huang, J., Piech, C., Nguyen, A., and Guibas, L. Syntactic and functional variability of a million code submissions in a machine learning MOOC. In *MOOCshop Workshop, International Conference on Artificial Intelligence in Education (AIED)* (Memphis, TN, 2013).

[6] Johnson, S. Lint, a C program checker. Tech. Rep. 65, Bell Laboratories, Dec 1977.

[7] Lancaster, T., and Culwin, F. A comparison of source code plagiarism detection engines. *Computer Science Education 14*, 2 (2004), 101–112.

[8] McCabe, T. J. A complexity measure. *IEEE Transactions on Software Engineering*, 4 (1976), 308–320.

[9] McCulloch, W. S., and Pitts, W. A logical calculus of the ideas immanent in nervous activity. *The bulletin of mathematical biophysics 5*, 4 (1943), 115–133.

[10] Nguyen, A., Piech, C., Huang, J., and Guibas, L. Codewebs: Scalable code search for moocs. ACM (2014), 491–502.

[11] Rivers, K., and Koedinger, K. Automating hint generation with solution space path construction. In *12th Intl. Conf. on Intelligent Tutoring Systems* (2014).

[12] Scott, J., Singh, R., Guo, P. J., , and Miller, R. C. OverCode: Visualizing variation in student solutions to programming problems at scale. *ACM Transactions on Computer-Human Interaction (TOCHI)* (2014). Special issue: online learning at scale (to appear).

[13] Singh, R., Gulwani, S., and Solar-Lezama, A. Automated semantic grading of programs. Tech. rep., MIT/Microsoft Research, 2012.

[14] WikipediaContributors. Programming idiom.

[15] Xu, S., and Chee, Y. S. Transformation-based diagnosis of student programs for programming tutoring systems. *Software Engineering, IEEE Transactions on 29*, 4 (April 2003), 360–384.

[16] Zhang, K., and Shasha, D. Simple fast algorithms for the editing distance between trees and related problems. *SIAM journal on computing 18*, 6 (1989), 1245–1262.

Assessment of KNOWLA: Knowledge Assembly for Learning and Assessment

Meredith Thompson
Harvard University
13 Appian Way
Cambridge MA 02138
Meredith_thompson@
gse.harvard.edu

Eric Braude
MET College 755 Comm. Ave.
Boston University
Boston MA 02215
ebraude@bu.edu

Christopher D. Canfield
MET College 755 Comm. Ave.
Boston University
Boston MA 02215
cdcanfie@bu.edu

Jay Halfond
MET College 755 Comm. Ave.
Boston University
Boston MA 02215
jhalfond@bu.edu

Aparajita Sengupta
MET College 755 Comm. Ave.
Boston University
Boston MA 02215
asgupta@bu.edu

L@S 2015, Mar 14-18, 2015, Vancouver, BC, Canada
ACM 978-1-4503-3411-2/15/03.
http://dx.doi.org/10.1145/2724660.2728673.

Abstract
The assessment of learning in large online courses such as Massive Online Open Courses, or MOOCs, requires tools that are valid, reliable, and can be automatically administered and scored. We have developed and assessed a tool called Knowledge Assembly for Learning and Assessment, or KNOWLA. The tool measures a student's knowledge in a particular subject by having her assemble a set of scrambled phrases into a logical order. Initial testing indicates that KNOWLA is reliable, and can be used to measure learning gains. KNOWLA also shows promise as a learning tool.

Author Keywords
Assessment; learning aids; scrambled text; automatic scoring; college-level; massive online open source courses

ACM Classification Keywords
Student assessment, adult education, measurement, arts and humanities

Introduction
The advent of online education, and the hope that digital technology can extend the reach of higher education, present a new challenge for finding assessment tools beyond traditional multiple-choice questions that can also be automatically scored.

Although many advances have been made in the areas of intelligent tutoring systems [1] and digital dashboard displays [2], additional assessment and learning strategies are needed. This study describes a dynamic tool called Knowledge Assembly for Learning and Assessment or *KNOWLA*, originated by Braude and implemented by Braude and Canfield. In a KNOWLA assessment, the test-taker demonstrates knowledge of a topic by unscrambling a series of sentences, phrases, or fragments via an online interface. KNOWLA allows instructors to (1) scramble a text or procedure (such as a text passage, science experiment, or computer program), (2) develop rubrics, (3) provide each student with a different scrambled order that can be dragged and dropped, (4) automatically score the results based on the rubrics, and (5) automatically provide comments.

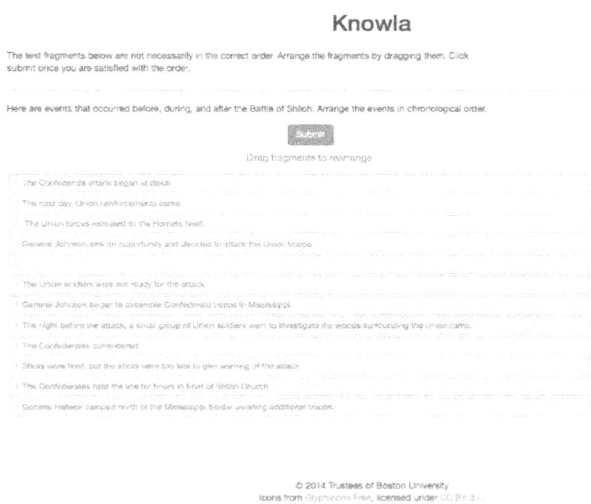

Figure 1: A full screen KNOWLA layout.

Instructors upload a plain text file in which a delimiter indicates how it should be fragmented. Instructors can select one of two possible KNOWLA displays for students. In both configurations, instructions appear at the top of the window, and segments of text that may be phrases or sentences are displayed in boxes that can be dragged and dropped into the desired order. In the full screen version shown in Figure 1, the boxes of text span the entire screen. In the side-by-side configuration shown in Figure 2, the moveable boxes appear on the left side of the screen and the statements appear as unboxed text in the same order on the right side of the screen.

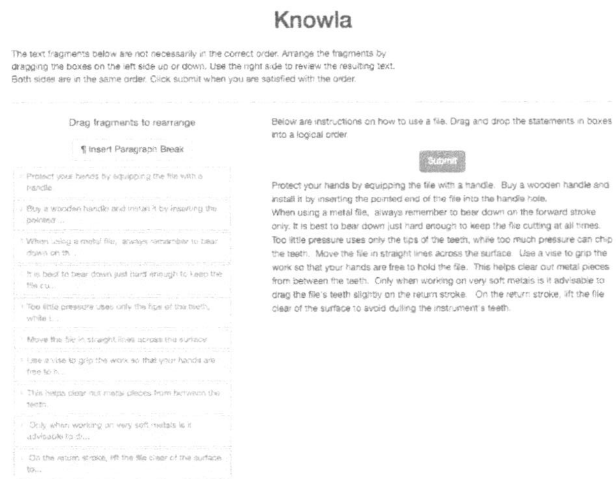

Figure 2: A side-by-side KNOWLA layout.

KNOWLA Grading Scheme

KNOWLA tests are scored according to the level of importance that the instructor associates with the order of fragments, and in such a way that a perfectly ordered answer receives 100%. The default (or standard) scoring gives equal weight to every correctly ordered (though not necessarily consecutive) pair. Suppose, for example, that the correct response of a 5-fragment test is *1-2-3-4-5*. A *1-4-2-3-5* response would receive a score of 80% when default scoring is used since two of the ten correct pair orderings (1-2, 1-3, 1-4, 1-5, 2-3, 2-4, 2-4, 3-4, 3-5, and 4-5) are missing. The tests discussed in this paper were graded with the default rubric. The instructor can impose two kinds of rubrics in addition (other kinds will be considered at a later time). An *order* rubric allows the instructor to give the weight of an order. A *consecutivity* rubric allows the instructor to specially value pairs that occur consecutively in the response. These types of rubrics will be discussed in detail elsewhere.

Study

KNOWLA is designed to be one tool to assess learning, and a KNOWLA question can be used alone either as a formative tool such as a quiz or as one question on a larger summative tool such as a final test or exam [3]. This study examines whether KNOWLA can show evidence of short-term learning using a pre-test/ post-test design. In particular, we want to answer the following questions: How does studying a passage influence performance on a KNOWLA assessment? Does performance improve on KNOWLA assessment if the passage is not studied?

Method

Fifty graduate students in the School of Education at Boston University participated in this sub study during the course "Introduction to Educational Research Methods". After written consent was obtained, students took two KNOWLA tests and answered multiple questions about two topics, an inauguration speech by Theodore Roosevelt, and a historical account of the Battle of Shiloh in the Civil War. The researcher Thompson then gave a short presentation reviewing the passage about the Battle of Shiloh using four PowerPoint slides. Students were then asked to take the same two KNOWLA tests and answer the same multiple-choice questions as in the pre-test. The pre-test post test study design with two forms of assessment (a set of multiple choice questions and a KNOWLA assessment) for each topic allowed us to identify whether learning happened as a result of the teaching event as indicated by an increase in multiple choice question scores for the topic studied. The study design also allowed us to identify whether a KNOWLA assessment could capture learning gains. Learning gains are indicated by an increase in the correct ordering of the statements in the KNOWLA test for the passage that was studied.

Results

The results from the online survey and KNOWLA tests were downloaded and queried together in Excel. Data were imported into SPSS 22.0 for windows for the analysis. The mean KNOWLA scores on the post-test of the Battle of Shiloh (M=75.85, SD=11.74, n=43) were higher than the mean pre KNOWLA tests (M=65.54, SD = 15.86, n=43, p<0.001). For the passage that was not studied, participants did equally well on the pre (M=48.22, SD=15.47) and the post (M=48.50, SD=18.23, p=0.902) for the Theodore Roosevelt (TR) passage that was not studied. The effect size was calculated using Cohen's d for paired t-tests [1]. The results was a Cohen's d of .55, (95% CI=0.115 to 0.988, v=0.0497), which is considered to be a large effect [4]. The results of the t-test are summarized in Figure 1. Error bars in the figure show standard error.

A series of multiple choice questions were also asked about the Shiloh and TR topics for a point of comparison. Participants did slightly better on the post-test multiple choice questions about Shiloh (M=1.63, SD=1.02) than on the pre-test (M=1.30, SD=1.01), but the difference was not statistically significant (p=0.12). Participants did worse on the post questions about Theodore Roosevelt (M=2.72, SD=1.07) than they did on the pre questions about the Theodore Roosevelt topic (M=2.89, SD=0.85). That difference was statistically significant (p=0.038). The slight gain for the Shiloh questions suggests that learning occurred as a result of the short lesson. The statistically significant decrease for the Theodore Roosevelt questions cannot be explained with the information gathered through the current study and will have to be explored through additional research.

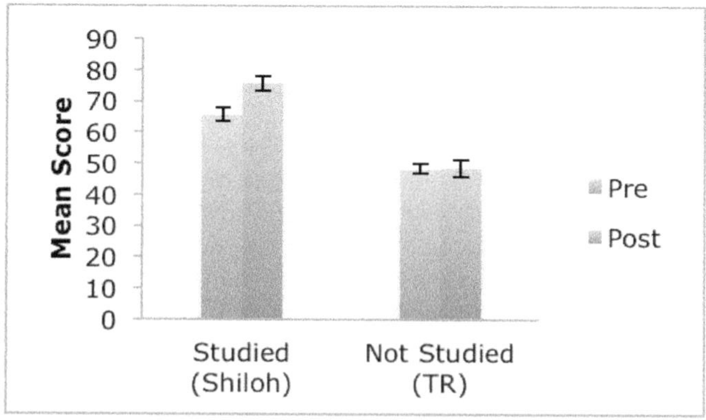

Figure 1: Paired t-test results from the studied (Shiloh) and non-studied (TR) passages

Overall, the participants made significant gains on the KNOWLA test of the passage that was studied, and they scored almost exactly the same on the pre- and post-KNOWLA test for the passage that was not studied.

Discussion

A principal goal for the study was to examine whether KNOWLA can be used as a reliable tool to measure learning. Students completed KNOWLA assessments on two passages, learned about one passage, and then completed two additional sets of multiple choice and KNOWLA questions. Since participants scored higher on the post-test for the studied passage than the pre-test and maintained the same average scores for the non-studied passage, we can conclude that KNOWLA may be useful as a reliable and valid measure of learning about a specific topic.

This study does not provide a clear picture of what specific attributes a KNOWLA assessment does test; however, scrambled text has been used as a measure of academic literacy [6], reading comprehension [7, 8], and writing skill [8] in other studies. We are currently investigating the link between KNOWLA scores and those skills.

Some of the participants noted that they learned more about the topic from doing the test than had they simply read the paragraph quickly. In fact, scrambled text has been used for self-assessment in medical education [9]. Students who engaged more deeply in scrambled reading material are more likely to learn from it than from even well-organized text [10]. The KNOWLA format may become a useful learning tool, as well as a means of assessment.

Conclusion

These preliminary findings support KNOWLA as a reliable tool that can be used to measure learning. Future research could explore other constructs that may provide a better match for the type of critical thinking captured by a KNOWLA test. Since KNOWLA tests require students to engage deeply with the material, KNOWLA also has potential as an engaging tool for learning and reviewing content.

Acknowledgements

We thank the Digital Learning Institute (DLI) at Boston University for project funding and Chrysanthos Dellarocas and Romy Ruukel for their support. We thank Bruce Fraser, Laura Jimenez, Matthew Parfitt, Natalie McKnight, Gillian Pierce, John McGrath, Davida Pines, Tejvir Sekhon, the Behavioral Lab at the School of Management, and the study participants.

References

[1] Bajzek, D., Brooks, J., Jerome, W., Lovett, M., Rinderle, J., Rule, G. & Thille, C. (2008). *Assessment and Instruction: Two Sides of the Same Coin.* In G. Richards (Ed.), Proceedings of World Conference on E-Learning in Corporate, Government, Healthcare, and Higher Education 2008 (pp. 560-565). Chesapeake, VA: AACE.

[2] Psotka, J., Massey, L.D., and Mutter, S. A. eds. *Intelligent tutoring systems: Lessons learned.* Psychology Press, 1988.

[3] Gronlund, N.E. *How to make achievement tests and assessments. Needham Heights, MA, USA, 1993.*

[4] Wilson, D.B. *Practice Meta-analysis Effect Size Calculator*. 2014. [cited 2014 Dec 17]; Available from: http://www.campbellcollaboration.org/escalc/html/EffectSizeCalculator-SMD25.php.

[5] Cohen, J. A power primer. *Psychological Bulletin*, 1992. **112** (1): p. 155-159.

[6] van der Silk, F. , Weideman, A., The refinement of a test of academic literacy. *Per Linguam*, 2005. **21**(2). p 23-35.

[7] Gernabacher, M.A., Varner, K.R., Faust, M.E., Investigating differences in general comprehension skill. *Journal of Experimental Psychology: Learning, Memory, and Cognition*, 1990. 16(3): p. 430.

[8] Kibby, M.W., Intersentential processes in reading comprehension. *Journal of Literacy Research, 12(4)* (1980) p 299-312.

[9] Coirier, P., Favart, M., Chanquoy, L., Ordering and structuring ideas in text: From conceptual organization to linguistic formulation. *European Journal of Psychology of Education,* 2002. 17(2): p. 157-175.

[10] Cairncross, R., Harden, R.. Preparation of scrambled text for use in self-assessment exercises. *Medical Education,* 1983. 17(4): p. 277-279.

[11] Kintsch, W. Text comprehension, memory, and learning. *American Psychologist.* 1994. 49(4) p 294.

An E-Report Scoring Method based on Student Peer Evaluation using Groupware

Yuanyuan Wang
Kyoto Sangyo University
Motoyama, Kamigamo
Kita-ku, Kyoto
603-8555 Japan
yuanw@cc.kyoto-su.ac.jp

Setsuko Miyamoto
University of Hyogo
1-1-12 Shinzaike-honcho
Himeji, Hyogo
670-0092 Japan
miyamoto@shse.u-hyogo.ac.jp

Yukiko Kawai
Kyoto Sangyo University
Motoyama, Kamigamo
Kita-ku, Kyoto
603-8555 Japan
kawai@cc.kyoto-su.ac.jp

Kazutoshi Sumiya
University of Hyogo
1-1-12 Shinzaike-honcho
Himeji, Hyogo
670-0092 Japan
sumiya@shse.u-hyogo.ac.jp

L@S 2015, March 14–18, 2015, Vancouver, BC, Canada.
ACM 978-1-4503-3411-2/15/03.
http://dx.doi.org/10.1145/2724660.2728674

Abstract
Nowadays, many universities utilize groupware support for students to post and share their e-reports, and the students can browse and vote other students' reports in e-learning. Teachers then need to evaluate all students' reports, but this will require a great deal of time and effort for a fair evaluation of the reports. Therefore, we propose an e-report scoring method based on student peer evaluation by considering the relationship between voting and posting time of the e-reports, to promote the quality of the votes and prevent unfair votes. Then, the method can provide scores of reports based on a voting graph by analyzing students who vote the reports. In this paper, we perform a student peer evaluation using groupware based on voting with a "Like" button in a course practice, and compare the results with teachers' evaluation.

Author Keywords
e-reports; groupware; student peer evaluation; voting

ACM Classification Keywords
K.3.2 [Computers and Education]: Computer and Information.

Introduction
Web-based report systems, such as Bulletin Board Systems (BBSs) and groupware, are now one of the most

frequently used tools in e-learning currently. Students then post and share their reports at anytime and from anywhere in a given period, i.e., after a lecture and before the next lecture, and the students can browse and vote other students' reports through these online systems. However, teachers need to evaluate all students' reports, but this will require a great deal of time and effort for a fair and multi-faceted evaluation of the reports.

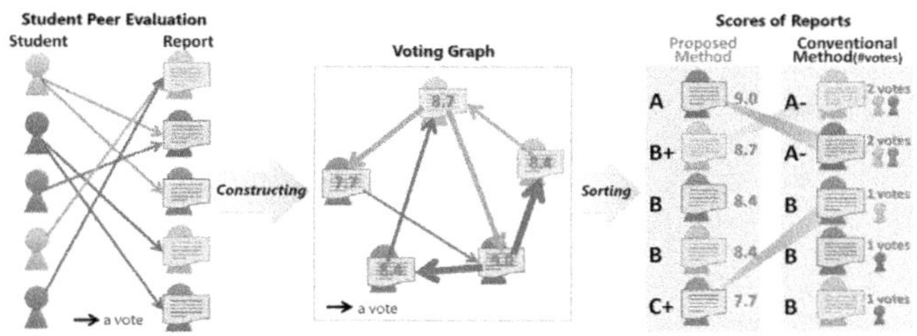

Figure 1: Conceptual diagram of our report scoring method.

As depicted in Figure 1, we propose a report scoring method to enable students instead of teachers to evaluate their reports by voting with each other. It provides scores of reports by analyzing the relationship between voting and posting time of the reports based on a voting graph of the reports, to promote the quality of the votes and prevent unfair votes. For this, the voting graph is constructed by the votes between a student and his or her voted reports. In this paper, we perform a student peer evaluation using groupware based on voting with a "Like" button in a course practice. Students can vote on the others' reports by pressing a "Like" button, when they think the report is good [3]. It can reduce the students' burden of evaluating others' reports without specific points. During a course using the groupware system, the following steps are followed: 1) posting reports after lectures in a certain period, 2) voting reports written by other students and voting with a "Like" button; and 3) receiving votes for their own reports.

The next section describes our proposed report scoring method based on student peer evaluation. In Section 3, we summarize the results of the proposed method in a course practice. Finally, in Section 4, we conclude this paper with suggestions for future work.

Report Scoring Method using Groupware

Voting Graph Construction

A voting graph is first constructed. The nodes of the directed graph consist of students' reports, and the links can be considered as votes from students for the others' reports. In our previous work, we built a system that evaluates users who browse the Web pages based on their links between a user and his or her browsing pages [5]. In this work, in order to evaluate the reports based on student peer evaluation; we focused on the students who vote on the others' reports. If one student u_i is voting another student u_j's report, then, a link from u_i's report to u_j's report (arrows in left and center parts of Figure 1), and the element of its corresponding adjacency matrix $(u_j,\ u_i)$ is set to 1 (left matrix of Figure 2).

Adjacency Matrix

	u_1	u_2	u_3	u_4	u_5
u_1	0	0	0	1	1
u_2	1	0	1	0	0
u_3	1	0	0	0	0
u_4	0	1	0	0	0
u_5	0	1	0	0	0

Constructing

Transition Probability Matrix

	u_1	u_2	u_3	u_4	u_5
u_1	0	0	0	w_4*1	w_5*1
u_2	w_1*0.5	0	w_3*1	0	0
u_3	w_1*0.5	0	0	0	0
u_4	0	w_2*0.5	0	0	0
u_5	0	w_2*0.5	0	0	0

Figure 2: Adjacency matrix and transition probability matrix.

We next describe the construction of transition probability matrix from the adjacency matrix. For example, it can be transformed to a transition probability matrix as shown in the right matrix of Figure 2. In general, before the students post their reports, they often refer to previous others' reports, then, we should reduce the scores of the last posting reports. Then, w_i is the weight assigned to each student's report by considering its posting time.

Student Peer Evaluation for their Reports
We next calculate the scores of students' reports by the following formula based on the concept of PageRank [2] and ObjectRank [1].

$$S(r) = (1-d) + d \times (S(v_1)/T(v_1) + \cdots + S(v_i)/T(v_i)) \quad (1)$$

- r: a student's report, i.e., the report of u_1, u_2, u_3, u_4, or u_5
- $v_1, \cdots, v_i$: the set of the votes of r, i.e., the votes of u_1's report by u_4 and u_5
- $T(v_i)$: the number of votes from a student, i.e., $T(v_1)$=2
- w_i: the weight of posting time of a report, i.e., w_1 is the weight of u_1's report. There are two methods:
    1. w_i=$1/n_i$, n_i is the posting number of u_i's report in the posted order
    2. w_i=$(m$-n_i+$1)/n_i$, m is the total number of students in a course
- d: a damping factor adjusts the derived value downward. Various studies have tested different damping factors, but it is generally assumed that the damping factor is approximately set as 0.85

Initially, the weight of each vote is 1, if a student votes multiple report, the weight distributes through each vote evenly, e.g., if u_1 votes reports of u_2 and u_3, the weight of each vote becomes 0.5. Finally, we normalize the score of each report between 0–10.0.

Results of Student Peer Evaluation

In this section, we present our findings from the results of our proposed report scoring method based on student peer evaluation in a course practice. This is a course of Applied Informatics, which consists of 10 lectures on different topics, and 23 students who participated in this course. Using the "Like" button as a vote through an online groupware, A) we calculated the score of each report based on the sum of the number of "Like" from students; B) we calculated the score of each report based on our proposed method by Equation 1 without the weight w_i considering the quality of votes only; C) we calculated the score of each report based on our proposed method by Equation 1 with the weight $w_i(=1/n_i)$; and D) we calculated the score of each report based on our proposed method by Equation 1 with the weight $w_i(=(m$-n_i+$1)/n_i)$ considering both the quality of votes and the posting time.

For each report scoring method, we then calculated the Spearman's rank correlation coefficient [4] between the score rankings by the teacher considering the posting time and the above methods of Lecture #3 in the same criteria. The correlation value ranges from -1 to 1, where -1 indicates that two rankings are completely reversed, whereas 1 indicates that the rankings are exactly the same. The correlation results are listed in Table 1, and the results can be explained as follows:

Table 1: Correlation results

Report Scoring Method	Correlation Value
A)	0.417
B)	0.465
C)	**0.488**
D)	**0.475**

- The correlation values of all methods (i.e., A), B), C), and D)) were not very close to 1.
- The correlation values of proposed methods (i.e., C) and D)) and the teacher's evaluation, become higher than those of baseline A) and our previous method B).

Although our proposed methods did not reach a very high correlation value, this experiment indicated that our proposed report scoring methods have the potential to support teachers easily and efficiently evaluate students' reports based on student peer evaluation using groupware in Japan. Since our proposed methods by considering both the quality of the votes and the posting time of the reports (strategy aspect by utilizing the cultural psychology of Japanese), achieved a good performance compared with the conventional report scoring methods by counting the total number of votes or considering the quality of votes only.

Future work will deeply analyze the correlation between our proposed methods based on student peer evaluation and teachers' evaluation with large datasets. In the teachers' evaluation, we need to adopt different methods by considering the posting time of reports or not. In order to verify the reliability of our proposed methods, we should do an interview of the students who participated in the student peer evaluation of their reports.

Conclusions

In this paper, we proposed a report scoring method based on student peer evaluation using groupware. In a course practice, students performed a peer evaluation for their reports by voting for valuable reports using a "Like" button. Therefore, it is not only a total number of votes for evaluating the reports, but also considering both the relationship between voting and posting time of the reports. It can lead to a new method rooted in indigenous culture of review by the student peer evaluation.

In the future, we need to measure inter-rater reliability of our proposed report scoring method based on student peer evaluation by combining teachers' evaluation and the student peer evaluation.

Acknowledgements

This work was supported by the Strategic Information and Communications R&D Promotion Programme (SCOPE) of the Ministry of Internal Affairs and Communications of Japan, and JSPS KAKENHI Grant Number 26280042.

References

[1] Balmin, A., Hristidis, V., and Papakonstantinou, Y. Objectrank: Authority-based keyword search in databases. In *Proc. VLDB 2004* (2004), 564–575.

[2] Brin, S., and Page, L. The anatomy of a large-scale hypertextual web search engine. *Computer Networks 30*, 1–7 (1998), 107–117.

[3] Iturrioz, J., Azpeitia, I., and Díaz, O. Generalizing the like button: empowering websites with monitoring capabilities. In *Proc. SAC 2014*, ACM (2014), 743–750.

[4] Myers, J. L., and Well, A. D. *Research Design and Statistical Analysis*. Lawrence Erlbaum Associates, 2003.

[5] Shiraishi, Y., Zhang, J., Kawai, Y., and Akiyama, T. Simultaneous realization of page-centric communication and search. In *Proc. CIKM 2012* (2012), 2719–2721.

Adding Third-Party Authentication to Open edX: A Case Study

John Cox
Google, Inc.
1600 Amphitheatre Parkway
Mountain View, CA 94043 USA
johncox@google.com

Pavel Simakov
Google, Inc.
1600 Amphitheatre Parkway
Mountain View, CA 94043 USA
psimakov@google.com

Abstract
In this document, we describe the third-party authentication system we added to Open edX. With this system, Open edX administrators can allow their users to sign in with a large array of external authentication providers. We outline the features and advantages of the system, describe how it can be extended and customized, and highlight reusable design principles that can be applied to other authentication implementations in online education.

Author Keywords
API design; authentication; authorization; education; identity; privacy; security; testing.

L@S 2015, Mar 14-18, 2015, Vancouver, BC, Canada
ACM 978-1-4503-3411-2/15/03.
http://dx.doi.org/10.1145/2724660.2728675

ACM Classification Keywords
D.2.13 [Reusable Software]: Reusable libraries; K.6.5 [Security and Protection]: Authentication.

Introduction
User authentication is the process whereby a user of a computer system proves their identity to that computer system so they can then be granted the ability to make certain protected actions within that system. It is a difficult problem because maximizing the security an authentication system delivers in practical terms requires balancing two factors: first, the strength of the

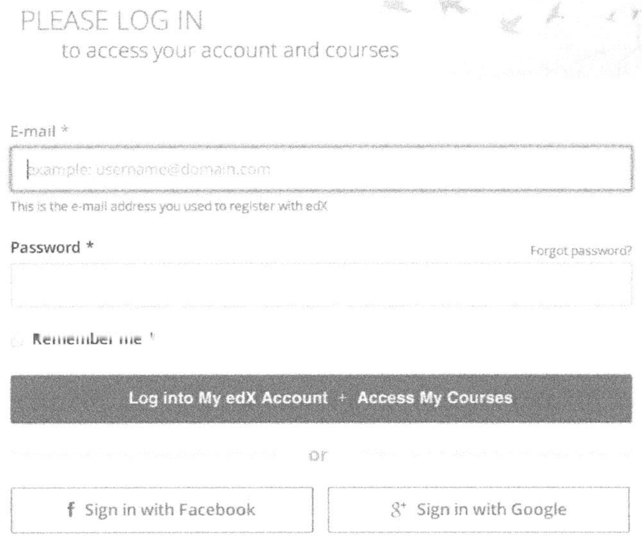

Figure 1. edx.org sign-in page with third-party authentication.

security provided by the system itself, often through strict adherence to ever-evolving cryptological standards; and second, user convenience.

These factors are often in tension: user convenience is maximized by not having an authentication step at all, and security is maximized often by creating systems that are very difficult for users to satisfy. If a system is too hard for users to use, they will opt either not to use the system at all, or they will take steps that increase their convenience but decrease the effective security of the system, such as constructing weak passwords, re-using passwords between systems, and so on.

Finding the balance between these factors, in addition to implementing authentication correctly in the first place, is very difficult. Many authors of computer systems lack the expertise or the time necessary to do this, so they may deliver authentication implementations in their products that are not secure.

Authentication in the online education space is further complicated by the need to integrate with legacy authentication systems at educational institutions. Moving off these systems is impractical, so new online education tools must be able to interoperate with them.

Below we outline an approach we took to creating a secure, configurable, extensible authentication solution for use in the online education space. We cover the features of our implementation, and explain the design principles that can be applied to implementations beyond our own.

Background

Open edX [1] is an open-source, freely-available platform for authoring and delivering educational content at scale. Until 2014, it provided only first-party authentication. "First-party authentication" means the system that requires user authentication is the same as the system that provides user authentication. First-party authentication systems are both common and simple:

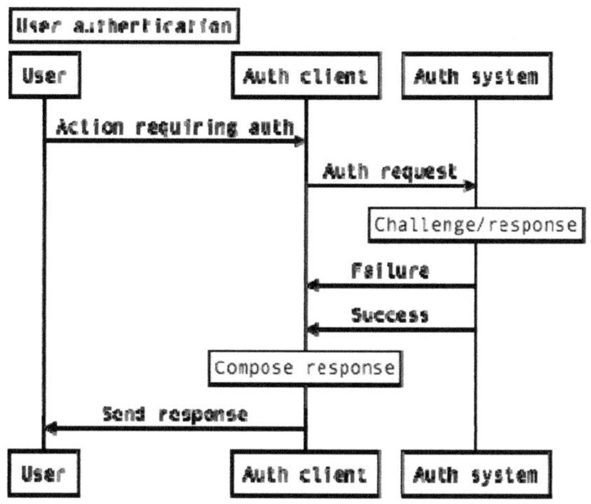

Figure 2. In a first-party authentication system, when a user takes an action that requires authentication, they are first taken to the authentication system component. In this component they are challenged to provide their identity, and they provide a response to that challenge. If they fail the challenge, the system composes a response notifying them of failure. If they succeed, the system composes a success response, which is often the resource they requested with their initial action.

Users of a first-party authentication system will have a user account with that system. That account will store an identifier for that user, their credentials (such as a nonreversible hash of their password), and other user data.

This is distinct from third-party authentication, where the system that requires user authentication (hereafter the "authentication consumer") are different from the system that users authenticate with (hereafter the "authentication provider"). The steps the user goes through under third-party authentication are the same as in Figure 2 above, except they undergo challenge/response with the authentication provider. Consequently, the authentication consumer does not need to store or validate user credentials.

This has two advantages. First, it is more convenient for the user because they do not have an additional set of credentials to manage. Second, the authentication implementation of the provider system is often more secure than authentication systems written by the authors of the consumer system, since authentication is the provider system authors' core competency.

Implementation details

At the core of our implementation [2] is python-social-auth [3], an open-source library that supports third-party authentication, written in the Python programming language. We picked python-social-auth because it supports three open authentication protocols (OpenID, OAuth 1, and OAuth 2 [4]) and over 60 authentication providers [5], is also written in Python, and provides good abstractions for the two biggest extension points we identified when gathering requirements.

First, by using an abstraction called the authentication pipeline, which comes from python-social-auth, future implementers can hook into the authentication flow at any point and insert custom code. This is done by exposing the behavior of the authentication code as a re-entrant stack of function calls via a Python API, each representing a conceptual step in the authentication process. This set of steps can be extended and re-ordered, and the pipeline as a whole can be paused and resumed on an ad-hoc basis by custom authentication code in the containing system.

Second, python-social-auth provides abstractions for additional authentication protocols or providers, also via Python APIs. These are vital because many organizations in the educational space have vast pre-existing computing infrastructure, including custom single-sign on (SSO) systems for user authentication. These systems may speak a host of different protocols, of which Central Authentication Service (CAS) [6] and Shibboleth [7] are the most common. Switching away from their legacy authentication systems is both impractical and undesirable for these organizations.

We wrapped python-social-auth in a thin layer that manages configuration details for a given deployment. This is where, for example, any deployment of Open edX selects the set of providers it will use from the full set of available providers. We then refactored the Open edX codebase to optionally use python-social-auth for authentication actions alongside the existing first-party authentication implementation. We adapted the Open edX user interface to account for a small number of new user actions, like managing associations between an existing Open edX account and any number existing provider accounts. Once these associations are established, users can sign in to their Open edX account with any of the associated provider accounts. Users may revoke an association at any time.

Finally, we provided an extensive set of tests [8]. A major feature of our tests is a comprehensive suite that is executed once per known authentication provider. This makes it easier to test new providers against the system as a whole with a minimal investment of new code: provider developers extend one class with a few dozen lines of provider-specific detail, and the full suite is executed against that provider. This limits the knowledge of the underlying Open edX system that a provider author needs to have in order to write a new provider, and at the same minimizes the risk that they will miss important edge cases during development.

Conclusions

The approach outlined above proved successful. This third-party authentication system has been live on edx.org, the largest deployment of Open edX, since September of 2014. Members of the Open edX community have used the abstractions detailed above to author and deploy customized versions of Open edX with additional authentication providers and customized user authentication flows.

While the system has been extended beyond its initial implementation to account for new requirements, real-world use found no gaps in the overall design. We therefore consider this design approach successful and recommend it to other developers in the online education space who require integrations with third-party authentication providers.

Acknowledgements

We are very grateful to our partners at edX who worked with us on the development of this feature. As well, we'd like to extend our thanks to the university and industry staff we interviewed while gathering requirements. Finally, we would like to thank Matías Aguirre and the other authors of python-social-auth. The library is excellent, and most of the ideas in this paper are very strongly influenced by the design choices and abstractions it established.

References

[1] Open edX. http://code.edx.org.

[2] Open edX third_party_auth module. https://github.com/edx/edx-platform/tree/master/common/djangoapps/third_party_auth.

[3] Python Social Auth. https://github.com/omab/python-social-auth.

[4] Python Social Auth documentation. http://psa.matiasaguirre.net/docs/backends/implementation.html.

[5] Python Social Auth documentation. http://psa.matiasaguirre.net/docs/backends/index.html#social-backends.

[6] CAS Protocol 3.0 Specification. https://github.com/Jasig/cas/blob/master/cas-server-documentation/protocol/CAS-Protocol-Specification.md.

[7] Shibboleth. https://shibboleth.net/.

[8] Open edX third_party_auth module tests. https://github.com/edx/edx-platform/tree/master/common/djangoapps/third_party_auth/tests.

Game Theory Based Peer Grading Mechanisms For MOOCs

William Wu
Acton Boxborough Regional High School
36 Charter Rd
Acton, MA 01720, USA
willy.vvu@gmail.com

Constantinos Daskalakis
Massachusetts Institute of Technology
77 Massachusetts Avenue
Cambridge, MA 02139
costis@csail.mit.edu

Nicolaas Kaashoek
Lexington High School
251 Waltham Street
Lexington, MA 02421, USA
nick.kaashoek@gmail.com

Christos Tzamos
Massachusetts Institute of Technology
77 Massachusetts Avenue
Cambridge, MA 02139
ctzamos@gmail.com

Matthew Weinberg
Massachusetts Institute of Technology
77 Massachusetts Avenue
Cambridge, MA 02139
smweinberg@csail.mit.edu

L@S 2015, Mar 14-18, 2015, Vancouver, BC, Canada
ACM 978-1-4503-3411-2/15/03.
http://dx.doi.org/10.1145/2724660.2728676

Abstract

An efficient peer grading mechanism is proposed for grading the multitude of assignments in online courses. This novel approach is based on game theory and mechanism design. A set of assumptions and a mathematical model is ratified to simulate the dominant strategy behavior of students in a given mechanism. A benchmark function accounting for grade accuracy and workload is established to quantitatively compare effectiveness and scalability of various mechanisms. After multiple iterations of mechanisms under increasingly realistic assumptions, three are proposed: Calibration, Improved Calibration, and Deduction. The Calibration mechanism performs as predicted by game theory when tested in an online crowd-sourced experiment, but fails when students are assumed to communicate. The Improved Calibration mechanism addresses this assumption, but at the cost of more effort spent grading. The Deduction mechanism performs relatively well in the benchmark, outperforming the Calibration, Improved Calibration, traditional automated, and traditional peer grading systems. The mathematical model and benchmark opens the way for future derivative works to be performed and compared.

Author Keywords
Massive Open Online Courses; MOOC; game theory; mechanism design; peer grading; learning at scale;

ACM Classification Keywords
K.3.m. [Computers and Education]: Miscellaneous. See: `http://www.acm.org/about/class/1998/` for help using the ACM Classification system.

Introduction
Over the past few years, there has been a tremendous increase in the popularity of MOOCs (Massive Open Online Courses) and their importance to education as a whole. Popular MOOC systems such as Coursera or EdX are well funded, which explains their rapid growth: 60 million dollars were invested in EdX when it started in May of 2012 [8]. The main importance of MOOCs is their ability to educate massive numbers of students worldwide [3]: by the end of 2012, 1.7 million students had attended a course through Coursera [6]. This leads to high student-professor ratios, reaching 150,000:1 in some courses.

High student-professor ratios lead to problems for professors, who are simply unable to grade hundreds of thousands of submissions. Currently, two types of solutions are used to remedy the problem: automated grading and peer grading [7]. Automated grading relies on machines, which can only check certain types of answers (i.e. multiple choice), severely limiting the depth of the questions asked [1]. Even though automated grading for written essays is an active area of research with much recent progress, the quality and accuracy of such systems is under heavy debate [4]. Students who know the machine's grading criteria can fool the system [9], yielding inconsistent grades. On the other hand, peer grading can grade any type of question. However, such systems can easily be "hacked" by the students [3]. Additionally, lack of feedback from peer grading is an area of complaint in systems such as Coursera [10]. These limitations render the students unable to effectively evaluate mastery of course material.

We propose several peer grading mechanisms based on game theory and our student model - a set of assumptions we believe students abide by. We also create a benchmark to compare between our and existing mechanisms. Although a theoretical model cannot predict exactly what will happen in practice, game theory and mechanism design have a history of generally determining mechanisms that work in practice from ones that do not [5]. Mechanisms that do not follow game theoretic constraints may work in the short-term, but they will be exploited if possible in the long term [2].

Model and Assumptions
Our student model consists of assumptions we believed students abide by, as follows:

1. Let H be a function of a student's grade, returning a student's happiness, such that a grade of zero yields zero happiness ($H(0) = 0$).
   Happiness is an arbitrary numerical unit.
2. Students want to maximize their happiness.
3. Grading an assignment costs 1 (one) happiness.
4. Happiness is not affected by external factors, such as the grades of peers.
5. Students can communicate with their peers.
6. Students are not perfect graders.

7. There is no such thing as partial-grading. Students either grade or do not grade.
8. Students can report their level of uncertainty (U) when they grade.
9. More effort spent in grading lowers uncertainty.
10. The chance of a student-assigned grade G being N off from the actual grade is proportional to U.

With a student model in place, it is now possible to simulate student behavior with game theory.

Benchmark

In order to eventually determine the effectiveness of various mechanisms, as well as to compare mechanisms, we created a numerical benchmark (objective function) where a lower score is better. The score is computed by adding the highest possible error in student grading to the most work done by any person. Mathematically:

$$\max_{i\geq1}\{|H(g_i) - H(o_i)|\} + \max_{i\geq1}\{w_i\}$$

where w_i is the work done (assignments graded) by the ith person, g_i is the grade given by student grader on the ith assignment, and o_i is the accurate "objective" grade that would have been given by the professor on the ith assignment. H is the happiness function defined in the *Models and Assumptions* section.

Mechanisms

Calibration Mechanism

The Calibration mechanism, described visually in Figure 1,achieves a low benchmark score of 4, consisting of a 2 in max work done and 2 in max error in grade.

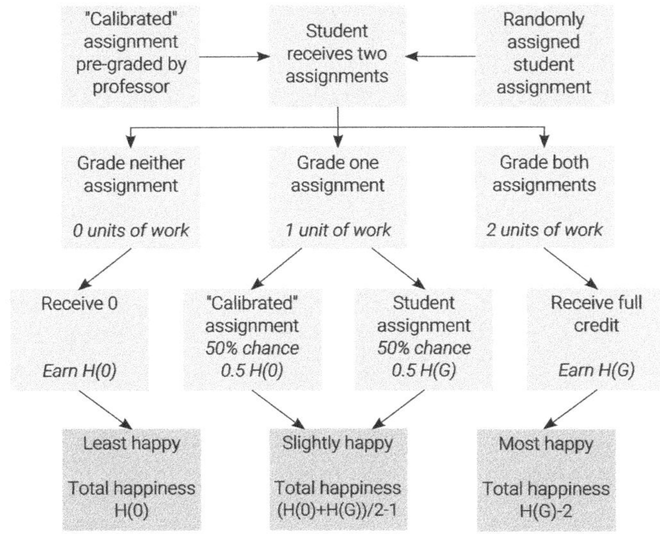

Figure 1: A flowchart of the Calibration Mechanism from the student perspective.

We tested and verified the Calibration mechanism through an anonymous crowd-sourced experiment. We wrote a program that presented participants with two sets of randomly generated orange and blue colored objects. Each set represented an assignment, and "grading" an assignment involved counting the number of orange objects in each set. After observing the set for a randomly chosen amount of time, participants were asked to input the number of orange objects they thought they saw in each set. Initially unknown to the participant, one set is "calibrated" and will be used to reward the participant based on the accuracy of the grading. This reward, awarded for accurately grading the Calibrated set, is synonymous to the punishment administered by the professor upon improperly grading the Calibrated set.

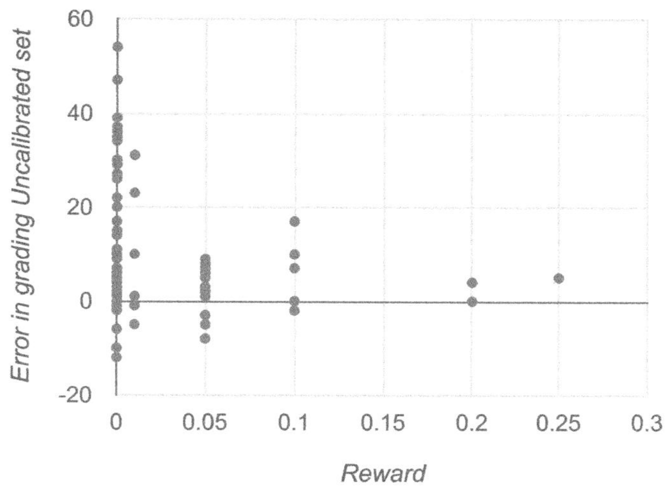

Figure 2: Uncalibrated Error vs Reward

The results of this experiment can be seen in Figure 2, where grading error is plotted against relative magnitude of reward. This shows that a higher reward correlates to lower error. As the reward is administered based on the grader's performance on the Calibrated set, the correlation implies that the graders who perform well on the Calibrated set also perform well on the non-calibrated set. This verifies that the Calibration mechanism indeed works.

Improved Calibration Mechanism
Originally designed with the assumption that students cannot communicate, the Calibration mechanism quickly breaks when student conspire to reveal the calibrated assignment to circumvent grading. The Improved Calibration mechanism mitigates this issue by introducing multiple calibrated papers at the expense of more work, raising the objective score. However, since the work created by this mechanism does not scale well with class size, the Deduction mechanism was developed.

Deduction Mechanism
The Deduction mechanism (Figure 3) achieves a very low benchmark score of 2, with 2 in max work done and a 0 in max error in grade. Incapable graders will raise the benchmark score, as they issue refutations that add work to the professor.

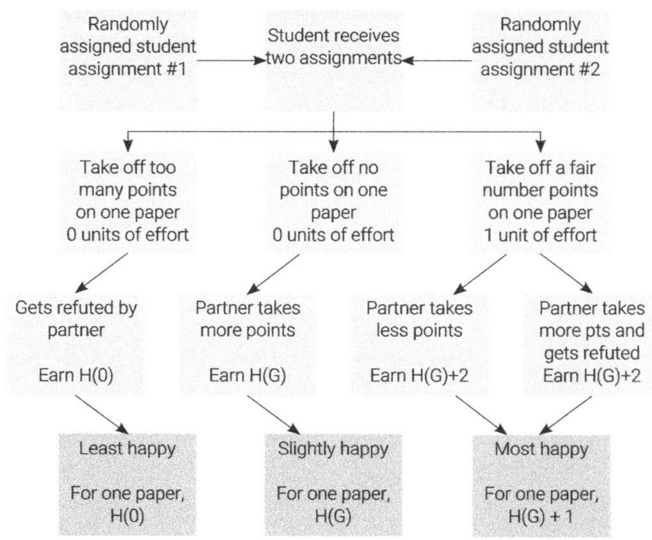

Figure 3: A flowchart of the Deduction Mechanism from the student perspective.

Results

The comparison of existing solutions and those proposed in this work can be seen in Figure 4. Each mechanism will be explained below.

Traditional Professor Grading involves one professor grading all assignments. In an online class of 1000 students, this method is extremely inefficient.

In Traditional Peer Grading, each student grades another's assignment without any supervision. However, as in this mechanism, the objective score is high due to the potential error caused by lack of motivation to grade properly.

Although without requiring effort from either professor or student, Traditional Automated Grading of open-ended responses are still under heavy research. Current solutions are quite preliminary, though can arrive at a grade within approximately 25 percent [4].

The Calibration Mechanism requires one calibrated paper from the professor and two papers graded by each student. The objective score is raised to 4 instead of 2 because students are incentivized by increasing their grade, thus sacrificing accuracy.

The Improved Calibration Mechanism requires each student to grade a subset of the other student's assignments, and the teacher to grade another subset. This mechanism addresses the flaw in the Calibration Mechanism that occurs when students can communicate, at the expense of more work. Thus, leading to poor scalability.

The Deduction Mechanism rewards graders for grading more harshly than their peers, and relies on a voting system to reject grades that are below the expected grade to be reviewed by the professor. In the dominant strategy behavior of the system, no grades should be rejected, leading to no work for the professor. Again, incentive given to the students comes at the cost of accuracy, raising the objective score by two points.

Overall, our Calibration and Deduction mechanisms vastly outperform existing solutions with the exception of Improved Calibration.

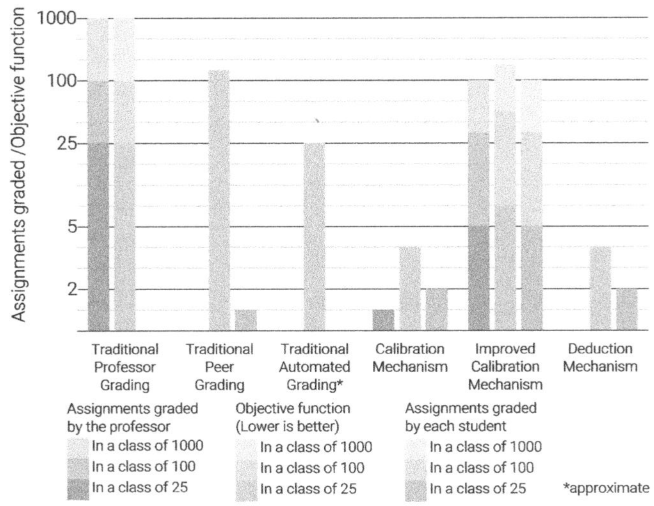

Figure 4: A comparison of mechanisms in terms of effectiveness and scalability.

Conclusion

In this paper, a student model was first created - a set of assumptions that approximate the realistic behavior of students. Based on this model, various grading mechanisms were developed: Calibration, Improved Calibration, and Deduction. These mechanisms incentivize students to grade accurately and efficiently as proven by game theory. The Calibration mechanism was tested with a crowd-sourced experiment, showing that it could work in practice. The student model can easily be reused and improved upon by future researchers who wish to develop more efficient solutions to more realistic scenarios. Mechanism efficiency can be measured in terms of benchmark defined in this paper. The benchmark is a numerical score encompassing both the accuracy of grades and the effort spent by any one person. The inclusion of effort spent by any one person in the benchmark enables the grading system scalability to be taken into account. To the best of our knowledge, these are the first game-theory-based peer-grading mechanisms.

Future Work

The further improvement and development of mechanisms may involve adding more realistic assumptions to the student model, which in turn may require more complex mechanisms. For example, a more complex mechanism may be required to generate accurate grades from incompetent graders. Of course, more testing and validation of mechanisms with crowd-sourced experiments is necessary. Eventually, new mechanisms based off the student model or existing mechanisms could be implemented in commercial MOOCs such as EdX or Coursera.

Acknowledgments

We would like to thank MIT and the MIT PRIMES program for providing the research opportunity, as well as our parents for their support. Of course, none of this is possible without the original idea proposed by our advisor, Constantinos Daskalakis.

References

[1] Bates, T. What's right and what's wrong about coursera-style moocs. *Online Learning and Distance Eductation Resources* (2012).

[2] Budryk, Z. Dangerous curves. *Inside Higher Ed* (2013).

[3] Daniel, S. J. Making sense of moocs: Musings in a maze of myth, paradox and possibility. *Journal of Interactive Media in Education* (2012).

[4] Herrington, A., and Moran, C. Writing to a machine is not writing at all. *National Writing Project* (2012).

[5] Nisan, N., Roughgarden, T., Tardos, E., and Vazirani, V. V., Eds. *Algorithmic Game Theory*. Cambridge University Press, 2007.

[6] Odom, L. A swot analysis of the potential impact of moocs. *EdITLib* (2013).

[7] Randall, E. Edx now has software to grade your essays. *Boston Magazine* (2013).

[8] S, R. Can moocs and existing e-learning paradigms help reduce college costs? *International Journal of Technology in Teaching and Learning* (2012), 21–32.

[9] Theophrastus. The problems with moocs 1: Robo essay-grading. *BLT - Bible*Literature*Translation* (2013).

[10] Watters, A. The problems with peer grading in coursera. *Inside Higher Ed* (2012).

Peers in MOOCs: Lessons Based on the Education Production Function, Collective Action, and an Experiment

Betsy A. Williams
Stanford University
Center for Education Policy Analysis
520 Galvez Mall, 5th Floor,
Stanford, CA, 94301
betsyw@stanford.edu

L@S 2015, March 14–18, 2015, Vancouver, BC, Canada.
ACM 978-1-4503-3411-2/15/03.
http://dx.doi.org/10.1145/2724660.2728677

Abstract
Economic theory about peers can help learning scientists and designers scale their work from the scale of small classrooms to limitless learning experiences. I propose: 1. We may increase productivity in online learning by changing technologies around peers; many structures around peers can scale with class size. 2. It is not always in students' best interests to be good peers, and collective action failures may worsen with class size. I conducted an experiment in a NovoEd MOOC for teachers that was motivated by these propositions; it leads to future questions about unintended and emergent effects.

Author Keywords
Peers; Teams; Learning; Education Production Function; Economics; Collective Action; Incentives; MOOCs

ACM Classification Keywords
K.3.1 [Computer Uses in Education]: Collaborative Learning

Introducing Two Propositions
Advances in online learning have been forecast to solve problems in higher education by bringing down costs [3, 24] while providing unprecedented access to elite coursework. Since peer interactions can be important to many students' motivation, persistence, and learning

[25, 22], I investigate how online classes can make the best use of peer relationships to further these goals; using frameworks from economics highlights how individual incentives affect peer interactions. I propose:

1. We may increase productivity in online learning by changing technologies around peers; many structures around peers can scale with class size.
2. It is not always in students' best interests to be good peers, and collective action failures may worsen with class size.

These propositions motivate a randomized experiment in a MOOC for teacher professional development; I describe the hypothesis, data, and results of this experiment, then discuss implications for future work in online learning.

Technology Around Peers

Economists' "production function" describes how people combine inputs to make things. The model foregrounds two issues. First, producers already optimize given known ways of organizing production, and so higher productivity requires new technologies (e.g., reorganizing curriculum, class, or system, or substituting intelligent tutors for instructors) [4]. Second, students are inputs into their own and peers' educations [28], and technologies could use them more efficiently.

How can we improve technology around peers to improve learning? Already, designers and researchers have focused on building community in the course forum [20, 5, 23, 19]. A study of learner motivations on a question and answer site reveals that altruism, social interaction, and community norms encourage contribution; the conclusion inspires further design to improve collaboration there [27]. Few MOOC platforms support teams, and so evidence there is extremely limited. However, some have considered how to implement effective team-formation algorithms [2] and facilitate small groups with clear goals [11, 26].

Proposition 1 and Its Implications

While designing online learning to improve interaction with peers is not new, the economic production function suggests useful ways to think about this:

1. We may increase productivity in online learning by changing technologies around peers; many structures around peers can scale with class size.

The most practical implications for online learning follow:

1. Students have skills beyond academic background; successful technologies might tap into these.
2. Peer contact may substitute for some inputs (e.g., one-on-one encouragement from the instructor)and complement other inputs (e.g., complex analytical assignments may work better with peer discussion). Productive peer technologies will consider the affordances of peers and of available resources.
3. The number of students is the number of peers, so technologies that place people in fixed-size groups may work similarly even as the course scales.
4. Not all technologies scale constantly in students. For instance, network effects [13, 1] in a course forum may be large and positive when additional students join a small class, but perhaps negative in a large class, where congestion sets in [18].

Peer Effects as a Shared Good

Classes often force strangers with different ability and effort levels to contribute jointly to a project; they can and will give different amounts. This situation is especially susceptible to a collective action problem [9, 15], in which individuals benefit if everyone cooperates, but each has stronger incentives not to cooperate, either by taking more or by giving less than is socially optimal.

Peers share many goods while learning together. These resources are informal, like contributing to an engaging campus life or creating distractions during lectures,and formal, like working on shared projects or joining study groups. All students could benefit from the shared good of a richer learning environment, but helping produce that environment costs individuals and may not pay off as directly as private study strategies.

Motivating Example: MOOC Forums
Having an active MOOC forum is a shared good, but posting constructively has few direct personal benefits. Indeed, posting is a rare activity in MOOC forums [14] and students have few reasons to invest time doing so rather than to read relevant posts or study on one's own.

Fame or attention might induce posts, but not necessarily useful ones.[1] Superposters on Coursera forums often post valuable comments [12], but superposters in the MOOCs for this study post misleading comments or even spam.

Proposition 2 and Its Implications
Online learning teams will face collective action problems.

2. It is not always in students' interests to be good peers, and collective action failures may worsen with class size.

This proposition suggests specific takeaways for design:

1. Cooperation is not guaranteed, especially if a contribution has more costs than direct benefits.
2. Voluntary students may not offer consistent, sustained effort; mechanisms relying on a particular student's contribution are unlikely to succeed.
3. But offering direct *quid pro quo* can extinguish cooperation stemming from norms of cooperation.
4. Known strategies to fix collective action problems include strong group identity, accountability to a small group, accolades, public reputation, having a leader give first, social norms, and opportunities to punish teammates; which strategies work depends on the context of the environment and its users.
5. Students may not have experience, information, or authority to coordinate productive collective outcomes even when they recognize them.
6. Cooperation is likely harder to elicit as online education scales up: cooperation drops as anonymity increases, shirking is less visible, and contributions are shared across too many recipients.

[1] Game theory about attention can explain Twitter use [8].

Experiment

Data and Context
To explore and apply these two propositions, I ran an experiment in online courses with teams. Three related connectivist MOOCs [22] on the NovoEd platform in spring 2014 targeted practicing teachers and were available for free. There were 387 participants were on 78 teams (size 2 to 8) that qualified for the experiment.[2]

Personal data tell whether they teach (and content area taught, etc.), have colleagues in the course, have taken prior courses on this content, took the presurvey, and have Internet access and familiarity with online courses. On the pre- and post-surveys they do a relevant task and rate their knowledge of the course topic and their preparation to implement changes in their classroom.

[2] Teams disqualified if they were smaller than 2; if only 1 or no members wrote out a goal on the pre-survey; and if a team member, simultaneously enrolled in another class, had already been assigned to a treatment or control team through that course.

Foremost among outcomes is completion: did a participant submit all individual assignments and the final team assignment? Other outcomes are peer ratings on assignments, growth in task score, and amount of activity.

Intervention
To induce participants to engage in greater teamwork, the intervention made teammates' goals known and salient. The treatment and control groups were asked to consider their own goals and how to achieve them, and they received lists of several classmates' goals. Only treatment teams knew they had received their own teammates' goals and were prompted to consider how to help each other achieve these goals. Follow-up messages from teaching assistants were sent according to a protocol; treatment teams again got an emphasis on helping teammates.

The treatment was intended to facilitate initial introductions (cf. [21]), provide information to lower the cost of teamwork, increase belonging (which increases levels of costly cooperation in experiments), and make salient the idea of exchanging resources with teammates.

Experiment Design and Model
Whole teams are block-randomized into treatment or control; this eliminates bias from self-selection into teams and improves statistical precision [7]. Teams were blocked on being in a partnering school district, majority US or international participants[3], majority real-life colleagues, and a team of 5 or more, and doing an optional team task.

For binary outcomes, results are robust to linear (shown) and logistic specifications. For individual i on team g in randomization block k, I estimate this model:

$$Y_{igk} = \alpha + \beta Treatment + \gamma X_i + \eta W_g + \delta Z_k + \theta_k + \varepsilon$$

[3]The course mentions U.S. policy, but practices work anywhere.

θ_k is a dummy variable (fixed effect) to adjust for different mean performance across blocks. Z is the vector of team-level characteristics which determine assignment to blocks, while X contains individual-level pretreatment variables. Standard errors cluster at block and team levels.

Results and Discussion
The treatment had no significant effect on completing assignments, nor peer grades, nor learning gain. Yet two aspects of behavior changed significantly with treatment (see Table 1): those in treatment teams spent five *fewer* days on teams and were more likely to become auditors: 4.3% in the control audited, versus 11.6% in treatment.

Outcomes	Coefficient on Treatment	P-Value	Adjusted R^2
Completed Assignments	0.0039	0.948	0.20
Days on Team	-4.85**	0.017	0.16
Switched to Auditing	0.074***	0.009	0.05

Table 1: Treatment effect on completion of required assignments, on number of days participant belonged to original team, and switching to auditing. Note: Each regression has 367 observations. Team- and individual-level covariates are included. Standard errors are clustered by team. * $p < 0.10$, ** $p < 0.05$, *** $p < 0.01$

The significant side effects are counterintuitive effects of providing information and encouragement to teams. The probability of successfully completing the class did not change, but the number of auditors rose with treatment: the simplest interpretation is that some people who would have lingered in class without completing assignments instead audited, if they got the treatment.

The treatment might cause some to dislike their teams (if teammates' goals showed lack of fit), feel guilty (knowing they would not finish, they did not want to disappoint team members later), or feel intimidated (feeling unable to help with goals others had listed or embarrassed by their own goals in relation). Also, perhaps providing this goal information took away some of the topics that teammates otherwise would have used to introduce themselves.

These results take us beyond the simple question of who will finish: what emotional valence and expectations do teams inspire? Interpersonal strategies may provide a way to induce effort in an otherwise impersonal MOOC.

Conclusion and Implications

We should design technologies that complement peers' strengths and perhaps substitute peer time for instructor time. Peer participation is prone to collective action problems: thus classes must have incentives or norms to promote cooperation, or be robust to students leaving.

The experiment reminds us of unintended effects of interventions. Further, emergent behavior (cf. [10]) or general equilibrium effects (cf. [17]) may arise as online learning scales? Who are the next wave of course joiners: those not taking courses now but who will as education quality at scale rises? How will formal schooling change with ubiquitous blended and open online courses? What effects will this have on labor markets and workplace practices? What will today's participants do next, and how will the next waves of online learners differ from earlier waves? In the study and design of online education, the tools of economics can provide a useful analytical lens.

Acknowledgments

I thank the Understanding Language team; the Stanford Lytics Lab; NovoEd & Stanford's Vice Provost of Online Learning for data; the Gerhard Casper Stanford Graduate Fellowship in Sciences & Engineering, the Institute for Education Sciences Predoctoral Training Program (IES Award R305B090016), & Kenji Hakuta for support.

References

[1] Afuah, A. Are network effects really all about size? The role of structure and conduct. *Strategic Management Journal 34* (2013), 257–273.

[2] Agrawal, R., Golshan, B., and Terzi, E. Forming beneficial teams of students in massive online classes. In *L@S*, ACM Press (New York, New York, USA, 2014), 155–156.

[3] Bowen, W. G. The Cost Disease in Higher Education: Is Technology the Answer? Tech. Rep. October, The Tanner Lectures, Stanford University, 2012.

[4] Bowles, S. Towards an educational production function. In *Education, income, and human capital*, W. L. Hanson, Ed., vol. I. National Bureau of Economic Research, 1970, 9–70.

[5] Brooks, C., Teasley, S. D., Lonn, S., and Koo, E. Educational Discourse at Scale: Design Considerations to Support Discussions in Massive Open Online Course (MOOC) Environments. *Innovation at Scale Workshop at CHI* (2014).

[6] Cambre, J., Kulkarni, C., Bernstein, M. S., and Klemmer, S. R. Talkabout : Small-group Discussions in Massive Global Classes. In *L@S 2014* (2014).

[7] Duflo, E., Glennerster, R., and Kremer, M. Using randomization in development economics: A toolkit. *Handbook of Development Economics 4*, 07 (2008), 3895–3962.

[8] Goel, A., and Ronaghi, F. A Game-Theoretic Model of Attention in Social Networks. In *Algorithms and Models for the Web Graph: WAW 2012*, Springer Berlin Heidelberg (2012), 78–92.

[9] Goetze, D. Comparing Prisoner's Dilemma, Commons Dilemma, and Public Goods Provision Designs in Laboratory Experiments. *Journal of Conflict Resolution 38*, 1 (Mar. 1994), 56–86.

[10] Goldstein, J. Emergence as a Construct: History and Issues. *Emergence 1*, 1 (1999), 49–72.

[11] Hmelo-Silver, C. E., Rosé, C. P., and Levy, J. Fostering a Learning Community in MOOCs. In *LAK Workshops* (2014).

[12] Huang, J., Dasgupta, A., Ghosh, A., Manning, J., and Sanders, M. Superposter behavior in MOOC forums. In *L@S '14*, ACM Press (New York, New York, USA, 2014), 117–126.

[13] Katz, M. L., and Shapiro, C. Network Externalities, Competition, and Compatibility. *American Economic Review 75*, 3 (1985), 424–440.

[14] Kizilcec, R. F., Piech, C., and Schneider, E. Deconstructing Disengagement: Analyzing Learner Subpopulations in Massive Open Online Courses. In *Proceedings of the Third International Conference on Learning Analytics and Knowledge*, ACM (New York, NY, USA, 2013), 170–179.

[15] Ledyard, J. Public Goods: A Survey of Experimental Research. In *The Handbook of Experimental Economics*, A. E. Roth and J. H. Kagel, Eds., vol. 85. Princeton University Press, Princeton, NJ, 1995, 111–194.

[16] Lim, S., Coetzee, D., Hartmann, B., Fox, A., and Hearst, M. A. Initial experiences with small group discussions in MOOCs. In *L@S '14*, ACM Press (New York, New York, USA, 2014), 151–152.

[17] Mas-Colell, A., Whinston, M. D., and Green, J. R. *Microeconomic Theory*. Oxford University Press, New York, 1995.

[18] Miller, K., Zyto, S., Karger, D., and Mazur, E. Improving online class forums by seeding discussions and managing section size. In *L@S*, ACM Press (New York, New York, USA, 2014), 173–174.

[19] Rosé, C. P., Carlson, R., Yang, D., Wen, M., Resnick, L., Goldman, P., and Sherer, J. Social factors that contribute to attrition in MOOCs. In *L@S*, ACM Press (New York, New York, USA, 2014), 197–198.

[20] Rosson, M. B. Building Community within Large Groups of Online Learners. *Innovation at Scale Workshop at CHI* (2014).

[21] Salmon, G. *E-moderating: the key to online teaching and learning*, 3rd ed. Routledge, New York, 2011.

[22] Siemens, G., and Tittenberger, P. Handbook of Emerging Technologies for Learning. Tech. rep., University of Manitoba, Manitoba, 2009.

[23] Speck, J., Gualtieri, E., Naik, G., Nguyen, T., Cheung, K., Alexander, L., and Fenske, D. ForumDash : Analyzing Online Discussion Forums. In *L@S* (2014), 139–140.

[24] Thille, C., and Smith, J. Learning Unbound : Disrupting the Baumol / Bowen Effect in Higher Education. In *Forum Futures 2010* (2009), 31–38.

[25] Tinto, V. Student Success and the Building of Involving Educational Communities. 2003.

[26] Trumbore, A. Rules of Engagement: Strategies to Increase Online Engagement at Scale. *Change: The Magazine of Higher Learning 46*, 4 (2014), 38–45.

[27] Walker, E., Girotto, V., Zhang, C., Fernandez, A., Chen, G., and Hsieh, G. Understanding Peer Help in an Online Learning Community. In *Innovation at Scale Workshop at CHI* (2014).

[28] Winston, G. C. Subsidies , Hierarchy and Peers : The Awkward Economics of Higher Education. *Journal of Economic Perspectives 13*, 1 (1999), 13–36.

TELLab: An Experiential Learning Tool for Psychology

Na Li
School of Engineering and Applied Sciences,
Harvard University
nali01@fas.harvard.edu

Ken Nakayama
Department of Psychology,
Harvard University
ken@wjh.harvard.edu

Krzysztof Z. Gajos
School of Engineering and Applied Sciences,
Harvard University
kgajos@eecs.harvard.edu

Ryan Enos
Department of Government,
Harvard University
renos@gov.harvard.edu

L@S 2015, Mar 14-18, 2015, Vancouver, BC, Canada
ACM 978-1-4503-3411-2/15/03.
http://dx.doi.org/10.1145/2724660.2728678

Abstract
In this paper, we discuss current practices and challenges of teaching psychology experiments. We review experiential learning and analogical learning pedagogies, which have informed the design of TELLab, an online platform for supporting effective experiential learning of psychology concepts.

Author Keywords
Experiential learning, analogical learning, online experimentation

Introduction
Teaching psychology concepts is currently mostly done through direct instruction. In natural sciences, in contrast, more experiential methods of instructions are common: teachers often give demonstrations in lectures and offer hands-on laboratory sessions. There are also online learning tools that provide interactive demonstrations and building blocks for students to practice, such as Molecular Workbench [1] for chemistry experiments and Go-LAB [2] for physics experiments. Such hands-on experiences are less of a practice in psychology and other social sciences, particularly when human subjects are involved. Recruiting subjects and scheduling experiments are costly. It requires substantial time, effort and expenses.

	Steps	Activities
1	Concrete experience	Taking experiments.
2	Observation and reflection	Review results. Answering questions about the experiment.
3	Forming abstract concepts	Comparing the experiment with other experiments that belong to the same paradigm.
4	Testing in new situations	Designing new experiment.

Table 1. The four steps of ELM and corresponding activities.

Another challenge of teaching psychology experiments is to transfer the deep structures of those experiments to students. Most psychology experiments have a lot of surface information, such as vivid contexts and images, which distract novice learners from seeing the underlying mechanism that make an experiment works properly.

Let's take the Stroop Test as an example. The original Stroop test [3] presents color words that are printed in either the color that the word indicates (e.g., RED) or another color (e.g., GREEN), and subjects are either asked to name the color of the word, or to read the word. For example, if the word 'red' is printed in green color, then the subject should choose green if asked to name the color of the word and choose red if asked to read the word. The results of the Stroop test showed that people are significantly faster reading a word than naming the color it is printed in. The deep knowledge about this test is that word processing and color processing can interfere with each other, and word processing is dominant to color processing when interference occurs. If we can see this mechanism, then we can use it to test if word processing interferes with image processing, or if auditory processing interferes with image processing, or if word processing interferes with emotional processing. And we can test which processing mechanisms are dominant with respect to others. The Stroop effect is one of the best-known experimental paradigms in psychology. There are many other paradigms like Stroop test—each representing a broad underlying concept—and it is crucial for students to learn these paradigms in order to select the right one to develop new novel interesting experiments.

In this work-in-progress, we discuss the design of TELLab [4], a new platform for supporting effective experiential learning of psychology concepts. We review two pedagogies that have informed the design of TELLab. We then summarize existing resources for experiential learning of psychology concepts. Led by the theoretical discussion, we describe a conceptual design of TELLab and its key features.

Experiential Learning and Analogical Reasoning

The Experiential Learning Model (ELM) [5] provides four steps for constructing effective experiential learning activities. In Table 1, we show these four steps and possible activities to implement them. Let's put the discussion of ELM in the context of learning a psychology paradigm. First, a student needs to generate a concrete experience of the paradigm, for example, taking an experiment that belongs to the paradigm. Second, the student needs to review the experience and reflect on it. To facilitate reflection of experience, there are some practical questions to ask [6], the questions that encourage students to think about what happened, why did that happen, and how does that relate to everyday life.

The third step is to form abstract concepts. As we have discussed above, it is hard for novice learners to grasp the deep knowledge from single experiment. Therefore, we propose to apply another learning pedagogy, Analogical Learning, to facilitate learning the deep knowledge. A central activity of analogical learning is to scaffold the process of analogical mapping—a process of finding common structures between two different examples. It has been shown that people can learn a common underlying principle and apply it to new prob-

Figure 1. Each paradigm page shows a list of experiments (A) for students to learn. Students can copy (B) an experiment design to their workspaces and adapt it to create their own experiment. Students can tag (C) an experiment design to help improve the experiment recommendation system.

lems by comparing two examples, even if the common principle is only partially understood in either example [7].

Resources for Experiential Learning

Online experiment platforms, such as LabInTheWild [8], TestMyBrain [9], and The Norton Psychology Labs [10], provide hands-on opportunities for students to experience psychology concepts. They also provide participants with meaningful feedback on their results. Participants can see how their results conform to or differ from the general public. This approach proved effective for attracting broad participation: LabInTheWild, for example, has more than 2 million visitors and nearly 750,000 visitors have taken experiments on the website [11]. These platforms provide experiential learning opportunities, where students are motivated to learn by taking the experiments and see their results. They get to sense the cause and effect in a phenomenon by themselves. One problem of these platforms is that each experimental paradigm is represented by a single experimental design. It would be hard for students to abstract the deep structure from taking a single experiment.

Besides demonstrative experiment websites, there are also authoring tools that can be used as learning tools. For example, *Qualtrics [12], Open Sesame [13]* and *Paradigm [14],* provide graphic user interfaces for novice users to design and conduct psychology experiments. Qualtrics, a survey authoring tool, is widely used among students. However, it limits the kinds of experiments that could be pursued. Open Sesame and Paradigm are both dedicated desktop tools for designing psychology and neuroscience experiments, however the experiments can only run on individual desktops. It is hard to disseminate experiments and it is hard to attract participation at a scale comparable to the online experiment websites. If there is an online platform that enables easy fast psychology experiment design and holds user-generated experiments in a central space with easy access, it will help students to more easily practice designing experiments and collecting data.

TELLab: An Experiment-Learning Tool

We are building TELLab, an online platform for students to experience and build online psychology experiments. TELLab has a curated collection of expert-generated psychology experiments, with several diverse designs for each major experimental paradigm. For example, Figure 1 shows the Implicit Association Test (IAT) paradigm page, where the Race IAT and Gender IAT are two experiments that both use the IAT paradigm. Building on the analogical learning pedagogy, TELLab encourages students to try multiple diverse instances of the same experimental paradigm. This, in turn, should divert their attention away from the surface features of each experiment and help them identify the general psychological concept underlying the instances. To provide students with hands-on experiences of designing experiments, TELLab allows students to easily copy an experiment using a copy function (shown in Figure 1B) and alter it to create their own experiment. We expect that students who come to the website as participants will eventually become creators of new experiments, and the novel interesting experiments will in turn attract more participants.

Based on the previous discussion, we also propose some design features to support experiential and analogical learning. To support reflection, the system can prompt students to answer questions that help them reflect on their experience. Moreover, the system should prompt students to compare the experiment that they have just finished with one that they had done before. For example, when a student finishes an experiment, the system can show a snippet of another experiment under the same paradigm that the student completed earlier. And then the system can ask the student to identify the similarities and differences of the two experiments. The student can continue the analogical reasoning activity until no more experiments can be found under the same paradigm. As our system grows bigger with more user-generated experiments, students can benefit with more examples to compare.

Research has found that analogical reasoning is particularly successful when the two examples differ in surface features (i.e., salient objects and aspects of the context), but share the same underlying principle [7]. A problem with a growing collection of student-created experiments is that there may be more similar experiments under a paradigm. A mechanism is therefore needed to help students select sets of experiments that are substantially different in surface features. To make automatic selection of appropriately diverse sets of experiments possible, the system can encourage users to tag the features of any experiment using the tagging function (shown in Figure 1C). Alternatively, it can ask students to provide similarity feedback on some pairs of experiments and use the information to automatically generate sets of diverse exemplars [15].

There are many challenges in teaching and learning psychology experiments; we hope to use the TELLab design as a starting point to explore more ways to facilitate learning.

Acknowledgement
This work is supported by the Harvard Initiative on Learning and Teaching under a HILT grant and Google under a Faculty Research Award.

References

[1] Retrieved on Feburary 4th, 2015. http://mw.concord.org/modeler/
[2] Retrieved on Feburary 4th, 2015. http://www.golabz.eu/
[3] Stroop, J. R. Studies of interference in serial verbal reactions. *Journal of Experimental Psychology*, 18, 6 (1935), 643-662.
[4] Retrieved on Feburary 4th, 2015. http://tellab.org
[5] Kolb, D. A. *Experiential learning: experience as the source of learning and development*. Prentice Hall, Englewood Cliffs, NJ, 1984.
[6] Jacobson, M. and Ruddy, M. *Open to outcome*. Wood 'N' Barnes, Oklahoma City, OK, 2004.
[7] Gentner, D., Loewenstein, J. and Thompson, L. Learning and transfer: A general role for analogical encoding. *Journal of Educational Psychology*, 95, 2 (2003), 393-408.
[8] Retrieved on Feburary 4th, 2015. http://labinthewild.org/
[9] Retrieved on Feburary 4th, 2015. https://http://www.testmybrain.org
[10] Retrieved on Feburary 4th, 2015. http://www.wwnorton.com/college/psych/zaps/
[11] Reinecke, K. and Gajos, K. Z. LabintheWild: Conducting large-scale online experiments with uncompensated samples. In *Proceedings of the CSCW '15* (Vancouver, BC, Canada, 2015). ACM.
[12] Retrieved on Feburary 4th, 2015. http://www.qualtrics.com

[13] Retrieved on Feburary 4th, 2015. http://osdoc.cogsci.nl/

[14] Retrieved on Feburary 4th, 2015. http://www.paradigmexperiments.com/

[15] Siangliulue, K., Arnold, K. C., Gajos, K. Z. and Dow, S. P. Toward Collaborative Ideation at Scale: Leveraging Ideas from Others to Generate More Creative and Diverse Ideas. In *Proceedings of the CSCW '15* (Vancouver, Canada, 2015). ACM.

Identifying Content-Related Threads in MOOC Discussion Forums

Yi Cui
Faculty of Education
Simon Fraser University
250-13450 102nd Avenue
Surrey, B.C. V3T 0A3
CANADA
yca231@sfu.ca@sfu.ca

Alyssa Friend Wise
Faculty of Education
Simon Fraser University
250-13450 102nd Avenue
Surrey, B.C. V3T 0A3
CANADA
alyssa_wise@sfu.ca

Abstract
This study investigated the extent to which students asked and instructors answered content-related questions in MOOC discussion forums; subsequently a classification model was built to identify such questions based on extracted linguistic features. Results showed content-related threads were a minority and under-addressed by instructors. However, linguistic modeling was promising in identifying them with high reliability.

L@S 2015, Mar 14-18, 2015, Vancouver, BC, Canada
ACM 978-1-4503-3411-2/15/03.
http://dx.doi.org/10.1145/2724660.2728679

Author Keywords
Massive open online courses; social interaction; natural language processing; machine learning

ACM Classification Keywords
H.3.1 Content analysis and indexing: Indexing methods; H.3.3 Information search and retrieval: Selection process; I.2.7 Natural language processing: Text analysis; I.6.4 Model validation and analysis; I.6.5 Model development: Modeling methodologies.

Introduction
Massive Open Online Courses (MOOCs) are online learning environments that provide a set of curated learning materials and experiences [3]. The lack of barriers to enter or abandon MOOCs has led to both enrollment figures and attrition rates far greater than those seen in traditional educational settings [2]. As a result, much of the early MOOC research has been targeted at identifying the factors predicting student retention. However, all MOOC learners do not necessarily have an intention to complete the full class experience [3]. MOOC registrants enroll with varied motivations and goals that can both align with and diverge from the standards set by the instructor and conventionally expected participation patterns [4]. Thus it is important to investigate how learning occurs for those who *do* participate, and the value of a MOOC to them, whether they complete the course or not.

Course Discussion Forums
General Discussion Discuss general aspects of the course.
Q&A Ask and answer questions about course material.
Assignments Discuss details of the course assignments.
Technical Issues Post any issues with, or questions about, technical aspects of the course website.
OLI Textbook Questions Post any issues with, or questions about, technical aspects of the OLI Textbook.
Student Bios Introduce yourself and learn about other students.

Figure 1. Course discussion forum structure

Looking at Learning in MOOCs

MOOCs are often characterized as cMOOCs or xMOOCs based on whether they follow a connectivist or more traditional pedagogy. In xMOOCs (the focus of this work) learners take part in courses through varied elements. Different to the many pre-prepared and largely static elements (e.g. videos, readings and quizzes), discussion forums are an interaction platform that can be used responsively to meet emergent needs. Discussion forums are not monolithic however; as with any tool, they can be used in different ways to meet a variety of purposes [5]. One common use of forums in xMOOCs is for Q&A about the course content; such use addresses learners' cognitive needs (e.g. resolving misconceptions or clarifying difficult concepts; [1]. Other uses (e.g. making social connections or resolving logistical / technical questions) can be important for course management and community building, but mainly address non-cognitive needs. Because of their profoundly different natures, many MOOCs design separate forums for these different kinds of uses (content, social, logistical etc.). However users often post in unexpected ways that overlook these boundaries. This is one factor contributing to the problem of information overload in online discussion [6] and a lack of sufficient indicators to help users choose which posts to read [7]. This in turn can lead to important learning questions going unanswered.

Research Purpose

The goal of this study was to investigate the extent to which students asked and instructors answered content-related questions in the discussion forums of a MOOC. Different features of discussion forum threads were then explored as potential markers to help instructors more easily find content-related threads.

Research Context

The study was conducted on discussion forum data extracted from an introductory psychology course with 27,739 users offered through Coursera. Course materials included video lectures and readings from the Open Learning Initiative [oli.cmu.edu] online textbook. Assessment consisted of weekly timed multiple-choice quizzes and a final exam. The course was 12 weeks long and all materials were in English.

Six discussion forums were provided as an optional interactive element (see Figure 1). Students were encouraged to post questions about the course content to the Q&A forum and vote-up the questions they wanted answered by the instructors. A total of 2,112 users posted in the forums.

Research Questions

1. What proportion of student questions were substantially content-related?
2. What proportion of students' content-related questions were responded to by the instructors?
3. What proportion of instructor responses overall were to content-related questions?
4. Do starting posts of content-related threads have distinguishing linguistic features?
5. Can linguistic and/or automatically tracked features be used to reliably identify content-related threads?

Methods

Data was received in SQL format. Initial inspection revealed that learners used both the General Discussion (GD) and Q&A (QA) forums to ask content-related questions while the other forums were used exclusively for social and logistical concerns. Thus data analysis

Content	Non-Content
but	course
more	i
by	my
in_the	this_course
why	final
as	BOL_i
what	quiz
is	the_course
that	exam
or	thanks
then	i_am
in	videos
when	grade
of_the	certificate
of	BOL_hi
and_the	BOL_hello
question	hello
between	everyone
age	will
correct	final_exam
than	i_just
were	hi
by_the	i_can
an	find
answer	coursera
does	courses
mental	i_have
research	grades
to_the	material
their	quizzes

Table 1. Top 30 linguistic features for content-related and non-content-related threads (BOL = Beginning of line).

was limited to these two forums. Queries extracted the following data by thread: title and content of starting post; content of all reply posts; number of times the thread was viewed; net number of votes received (upvotes minus downvotes); and whether an instructor replied to thread. After cleaning, the data set contained 439 threads with 1797 posts.

Each discussion thread was coded by two researchers as relating substantively to course content or not. Content-related questions included asking for clarification about course materials, expanding on course concepts, and discussing shared resources. Non-content-related purposes were unrestricted but generally involved asking logistical questions about assessments and credentialing, socializing and initiating study groups, or sharing links. Inter-rater reliability was very good (92%; κ=0.81). All disagreements were discussed and reconciled with borderline cases included as content-related.

Lightside Researcher's Workbench v2.2.1 was used to perform feature extraction on the contents of each thread starting post using the basic bag-of-words feature set and a rare threshold of 5. Unigram and bigrams alone were most useful for characterizing and modeling posts; parts-of-speech tagging was explored but discarded for a lack of additional explanatory power. A total of 1573 features were extracted and used to train a binary Support Vector Machines classification model [thread starting post content-related or not]. The number of views, votes, and replies a thread received were tested as additional features to the base model. All models were evaluated using ten-fold cross-validation.

Results and Discussion

Student Questions

Only a small proportion (28%) of the learners' questions in GD and QA were content-related. This indicates that although there were other forums designed for non-content concerns (see Figure 1) students still used these designated forums in unexpected ways. As a result, content-related and noncontent-related posts were mixed in two forums, with noncontent posts dominating both.

Instructor Replies

The instructors replied to 62 (14%) of all threads. Of these, 22 responses (35%) were directed at content-related threads while 40 responses (65%) addressed non-content based concerns. With these 22 replies, the instructors addressed 18% of all content-related threads. This result reveals two problems: 1. during the learning experience, when students asked for academic support, most of the time they didn't get it from the instructors; 2. when the instructors attended to the forums, most of their time was not spent addressing learning questions. This suggests that either the instructors were having difficulty finding the content threads where they could influence learning most directly, or that this was not their primary concern in forum interaction.

Features Distinguishing Content-Related Posts

The linguistic features extracted from the starting posts in content-related and non-content-related threads showed stark differences (Table 1). While the top features of content-related starting posts were dominated by questions words (e.g. "why"), comparison words (e.g. "than") and connection bigrams (e.g. "of_the"), the top features of non-content-related

	Base model	+# VI	+# VO	+# RE
A*	0.86	0.84	0.85	0.85
K*	0.64	0.6	0.62	0.62
R*	0.71	0.68	0.69	0.69
P*	0.76	0.74	0.75	0.76

Table 2. Evaluation metrics for four models classifying threads as content-related or non-content-related

A*=Accuracy
K*=Kappa
R*=Recall
P*=Precision
VI=Views
VO=Votes
RE=Replies

ones were dominated by first person expressions (e.g. "i_have"), greetings (e.g. "hello") and words referring to course and its evaluation at a global level (e.g. "quizzes," "grades").

Modeling Content-Related Posts

The base classification model (using only linguistic features) provided promising accuracy, recall and precision in identifying content-related threads; the model was not improved by the addition of the automatically tracked thread features (Table 2).

Conclusions and Future Work

In the vast sea of MOOC forums, it can be challenging for users interested in asking and answering questions about the course content to find the threads in which such interactions are occurring. The results of this preliminary work showed that while automatically-tracked thread features were unhelpful in this regard, linguistic modeling was promising as a method to find content-related threads more effectively. Simple as our model was, it identified almost three quarters of all content-related starting posts in the studied forums, with a false positive rate below twenty-five percent. Application in a live course situation could either provide indications that allow instructors and students to make more efficient and informed decisions about which threads to read and respond to, or act as a just-in-time intervention at the moment of posting to create more organized and orderly discussion forums. In both cases the academic support needed by the learners could be addressed more sufficiently by the instructor and the instructor would face a much smaller reading load when trying to provide this support.

While this study provided initial validation of the model, it remains for future work to test its application to data fully external to the training set and to explore its extensibility across courses and domains of learning. We are optimistic in this regard, since the vast majority of top linguistic features identified are not domain-specific words. Future work could also leverage the content of all the posts in a thread (as opposed to just the starting post) to improve classification accuracy and build models to identify other particular kinds of discussion threads. In summary, this work presents a promising first step in supporting learning interactions in MOOC discussion forums by modelling posts' linguistic features to help instructors and students find where learning interactions are most likely to occur and thus can be most directly influenced.

Acknowledgements

We thank the Open Learning Initiative for their assistance in accessing and working with the data.

References

[1] Breslow, L., et al., Studying learning in the worldwide classroom: Research into edX's first MOOC. *Research & Practice in Assessment*, 8(1) (2013), 13-25.

[2] Conole, G., MOOCs as disruptive technologies: Strategies for enhancing the learner experience and quality of MOOCs. *RED. Revista de Educación a Distancia, Septiembre-Diciembre*, 39 (2013), 1-17.

[3] Deboer, J., et al., Changing "course": Reconceptualizing educational variables for Massive Open Online Courses. *Educational Researcher*, 43(2) (2014), 74-84.

[4] Koller, D., et al., Retention and intention in Massive Open Online Courses. *EduCause Review Online*, (2013).

[5] Lockyer, L.et al., Informing pedagogical action: Aligning learning analytics with learning design. *American Behavioral Scientist*, (2013), 1439-1459.

[6] Peters, V.L. and Hewitt, J., An investigation of student practices in asynchronous computer conferencing courses. *Computers & Education*, 54(4) (2010), 951-961.

[7] Wise, A.F., et al., A survey of factors contributing to learners' "listening" behaviors in asynchronous discussions. *Journal of Educational Computing Research* 47(4) (2012), 461-480.

Understanding Learners' General Perception Towards Learning with MOOC Classmates: An Exploratory Study

Soon Hau Chua
NUS-HCI Lab
School of Computing
National University of Singapore
13 Computing Drive
Singapore 117417
chuasoonhau@nus.edu.sg

Toni-Jan Keith Monserrat
NUS-HCI Lab
School of Computing
National University of Singapore
13 Computing Drive
Singapore 117417
tjmonsi@gmail.com

Juho Kim
MIT CSAIL
Cambridge, MA 02139 USA
juhokim@mit.edu

Shengdong Zhao
NUS-HCI Lab
School of Computing
National University of Singapore
13 Computing Drive
Singapore 117417
zhaosd@comp.nus.edu.sg

L@S 2015, March 14–18, 2015, Vancouver, BC, Canada.
ACM 978-1-4503-3411-2/15/03.
http://dx.doi.org/10.1145/2724660.2728680

Abstract
In this work-in-progress, we present our preliminary findings from an exploratory study on understanding learners' general behavior and perception towards learning with classmates in MOOCs. One-on-one semi-structured interview designed with grounded theory method was conducted with seven MOOC learners. Initial analysis of the interview data revealed several interesting insights on learners' behavior in working with other learners in MOOCs. We intend to expand the findings in future work to derive design implications for incorporating collaborative features into MOOCs.

Author Keywords
Massive Open Online Courses; MOOCs; Online Learning; Collaborative Learning; Learning Behavior

ACM Classification Keywords
H.5 [Information Interfaces and Presentation] (e.g., HCI); K3.1 [Computer Uses in Education]: Collaborative Learning; J.4 [Social and Behavioral Sciences]

Introduction

Extended Massive Open Online Course (xMOOCs), or just MOOCs as we know now, is an online learning environment based primarily on the instructivist approach, featuring video lectures, quizzes, assignments, and exams as primary learning activities, with discussion forums to support collaborative learning and social interaction. Since its introduction in 2011, MOOCs has attracted millions of learners worldwide, and has been touted as the next disruptive innovation in the education sector [10].

One of the primary issues with MOOCs at the moment is the low learner engagement and retention, resulting in a very high dropout rate across different courses [11]. Incorporating effective collaborative learning into the learning environment has been shown to improve student engagement in previous contexts such as CSCL and physical classroom [1,7]. Motivated by the prospect, there has been a lot of work studying the use of existing collaborative learning features such as forums [3,6] and synchronous group discussions [2,4,8] in MOOCs. While these works have demonstrated respective benefits in MOOCs that were originally found in physical classroom and CSCL settings, most of them found mixed results in improving learners' engagement, retention, grades, and sense of community, suggesting that a major rethinking and redesigning of collaborative features in MOOCs might be necessary.

To provide some preliminary insights and initial direction on redesigning collaborative features in MOOCs, in this work-in-progress we conducted an exploratory investigation on MOOC learners' general perception and behavior towards learning with MOOC classmates from a qualitative standpoint. Based on our knowledge this is the first study to investigate this problem in the MOOC context. In the following sections, we present our study methodology followed by the preliminary findings.

Methods

Participants

Seven participants (mean age = 30, $\boldsymbol{\sigma}$ = 5) with tertiary education and completed at least 1 MOOC were recruited through snowball sampling method. We only recruited participants with a tertiary degree since they are likely to have participated in collaborative activities both outside and inside the classroom. At the same time, we also recruited participants who have completed a MOOC since they are more likely to have engaged in collaborative activities (forums, social network, chats) in MOOCs.

#	Age	Nationality	Gender	Occupation
P1	38	Canada	Male	Faculty
P2	25	China	Male	Research Staff
P3	25	Netherlands	Male	Designer
P4	27	South Korea	Male	Grad Student
P5	30	South Korea	Male	Grad Student
P6	35	US	Female	Faculty
P7	28	Phillipines	Male	UX Researcher

Table 1. Demographic Information of Participants.

Recruited participants were asked to provide demographic data (e.g., gender, occupation, country of origin) and experience on MOOCs (e.g., completed and uncompleted course and etc.) using Google Form before the interview (see Table 1). The primary objective of the pre-study survey was to understand the participants' background and experience in MOOCs before the study.

Study Design and Protocol
To obtain a deep understanding of learners' perception towards learning with classmates in MOOCs, a semi-structured one-on-one interview methodology was adopted in our study. Since the study was exploratory in nature, we employed the grounded theory method in the interview throughout the investigation [9]. Each interview was conducted after the participants have completed the demographic survey and been briefed on the objectives of the study. Since participants could carry different ideas about collaborative learning, we explained our definition of collaborative learning derived from [5] as "a learning process where two or more people work together to create meaning, explore a topic, or improve skills" in the beginning of the interview.

During the interview, we first asked participants to describe their experiences in learning with classmates in schools and universities. Participants were told to share some of the real life practices, frustrations, and concerns. After describing their real life experiences, we proceeded to interview their experiences in MOOCs. Focuses of the interview were allocated on understanding their perceptions, attitudes, behaviors, and user experiences on collaborative features in MOOCs.

Data Collection and Analysis
On average, each one-on-one interview lasted between 90 minutes to 2 hours. The conversations were recorded through audio and written notes were made during the interview. Data from the interviews were transcribed and coded to establish concepts and categories recurring in the interview.

Preliminary Findings
In this section, we present our findings from the first stage of data collection and analysis from the 7 interviews we conducted.

Most participants we interviewed were not optimistic towards the usefulness of collaborative learning on the learning objectives in MOOCs. Participants felt that the learning in MOOCs focuses on critical thinking skills and is not targeted towards communication & teamwork skills. Besides, three participants thought that face-to-face discussion takes a lot of time, and felt they have no time to engage in social learning activities in general. However, using forums was perceived to save more time. While participants felt that peer learning could be useful, they are reluctant to spend time in coordinating peer activities as well as restricted by the schedule set by these activities.

Participants opined that having the right amount of peer pressure from collaborative learning activities and social interactions could motivate themselves to complete the course. Two participants suggested that the ability to compare their progress with their peers adds positive pressure to continue learning. Apart from peer pressure, classmates' knowledge level in MOOCs was brought up in many occasions during the interviews. Participants told us that the knowledge and skill level of their classmates is important and has to be at some level with the learners in order to grow as a group in face-to-face discussions.

Conclusion

In conclusion, our initial analysis has revealed several interesting preliminary insights on learners' behavior and perception towards learning with other classmates in MOOCs. In the future we intend to conduct subsequent rounds of analysis as well as a more systematic investigation to derive guidelines for redesigning collaborative features that take MOOC learners' expectations and assumptions into account.

References

[1] Boud, D., Cohen, R., and Sampson, J. *Peer learning in higher education: Learning from and with each other.* Routledge, 2014.

[2] Coetzee, D., Fox, A., Hearst, M.A., and Hartmann, B. Chatrooms in MOOCs: all talk and no action. *In Proc. of ACM L@S '14*, (2014), 127–136.

[3] Coetzee, D., Fox, A., Hearst, M.A., and Hartmann, B. Should your MOOC forum use a reputation system? *In Proc. of ACM CSCW '14*, ACM Press (2014), 1176–1187.

[4] Coetzee, D., Lim, S., Fox, A., Hartmann, B., and Hearst, M. Structuring Interactions for Large-Scale Synchronous Peer Learning. *In Proc. of ACM CSCW '15*, ACM CSCW 2015 (2015).

[5] Harasim, L.M. *Learning networks: A field guide to teaching and learning online.* MIT press, 1995.

[6] Huang, J., Dasgupta, A., Ghosh, A., Manning, J., and Sanders, M. Superposter behavior in MOOC forums. *In Proc. of ACM L@S '14*, ACM Press (2014), 117–126.

[7] Ke, F. and Xie, K. Toward deep learning for adult students in online courses. *The Internet and Higher Education 12*, 3 (2009), 136–145.

[8] Kulkarni, C., Cambre, J., Kotturi, Y., Bernstein, M.S., and Klemmer, S. Talkabout: Making Distance Matter with Small Groups in Massive Classes. *In Proc. of ACM CSCW '15*, (2015).

[9] Strauss, A. and Corbin, J.M. *Basics of qualitative research: Grounded theory procedures and techniques.* Sage Publications, Inc, 1990.

[10] Yuan, L., Powell, S., and CETIS, J. MOOCs and open education: Implications for higher education. *Cetis White Paper*, (2013).

[11] Zheng, S., Rosson, M.B., Shih, P., and Carroll, J. Understanding Student Motivation, Behaviors, and Perceptions in MOOCs. *In Proc. of ACM CSCW '15*, (2015).

M-CAFE: Managing MOOC Student Feedback with Collaborative Filtering

Mo Zhou
IEOR Department
UC Berkeley
mzhou@berkeley.edu

Alison Cliff
IEOR Department
UC Berkeley
alisoncliff@berkeley.edu

Allen Huang
IEOR Department
UC Berkeley
hunallen@berkeley.edu

Sanjay Krishnan
EECS Department
UC Berkeley
sanjaykrishnan@berkeley.edu

Brandie Nonnecke
CITRIS Data&Democracy Initiative
UC Berkeley
nonnecke@berkeley.edu

Kanji Uchino
Fujitsu Laboratories of America
Kanji@us.fujitsu.com

Sam Joseph
Hawaii Pacific University
sjpseph@hpu.edu

Armando Fox
EECS Department
UC Berkeley
fox@cs.berkeley.edu

Ken Goldberg
IEOR & EECS Department
UC Berkeley
goldberg@berkeley.edu

L@S 2015, March 14-18, 2015, Vancouver, BC, Canada.
ACM 978-1-4503-3411-2/15/03.
http://dx.doi.org/10.1145/2724660.2728681

Abstract
Ongoing student feedback on course content and assignments can be valuable for MOOC instructors in the absence of face-to-face-interaction. To collect ongoing feedback and scalably identify valuable suggestions, we built the MOOC Collaborative Assessment and Feedback Engine (M-CAFE). This mobile platform allows MOOC students to numerically assess the course, their own performance, and provide textual suggestions about how the course could be improved on a weekly basis. M-CAFE allows students to visualize how they compare with their peers and read and evaluate what others have suggested, providing peer-to-peer collaborative filtering. We evaluate M-CAFE based on data from two EdX MOOCs.

Author Keywords
Course assessment; Collaborative filtering; Instructor support; MOOCs

ACM Classification Keywords
K.3.1 Computers Users in Education: Distance learning. H.5.3 Information Interfaces and Presentation (e.g. HCI): Group and Organization Interfaces

Introduction
Student engagement with course material is important for effective teaching [1]. However, assessing engagement is particularly challenging in the context of MOOCs because of the lack of face-to-face interaction.

The online structure of MOOCs encourages development of novel course evaluation methods and timely feedback systems.

Apart from quantitative data from course evaluations, instructors often find qualitative (textual) data to be a valuable supplement [4]. Stephens-Martinez et al. suggest that qualitative data such as discussion forums, class surveys, and discussions with students are considered the most useful [2]. However, the vast quantity of qualitative data produced by these sources impedes professors from obtaining valuable information efficiently. New tools must be developed that allow MOOC instructors to efficiently collect and analyze data.

In this work-in-progress report, we present a new platform, the MOOC Collaborative Assessment and Feedback Engine (http://opinion.berkeley.edu/m-cafe-2), which encourages students to check in weekly to numerically assess the course, provide qualitative (textual) suggestions on course improvements, and rate each other's suggestions.

As a pilot study, we evaluate M-CAFE with 2 EdX MOOCs by testing the following hypotheses:

1. The ranking of textual input using peer-to-peer collaborative filtering will be significantly closer to expert human performance than NLP methods.

2. The temporal trends of quantitative input will be significantly correlated with events and changes in the course (i.e. material difficulty, homework assignments, quizzes, etc.).

M-CAFE User Interface

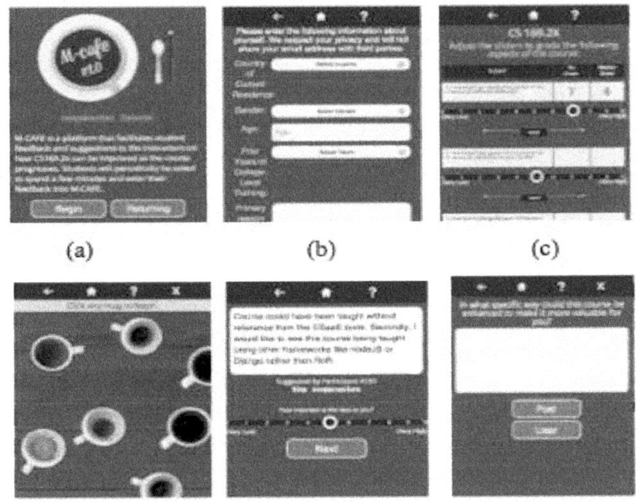

(a) (b) (c) (d) (e) (f)

Figure1: Screenshots of M-CAFE

Upon entering M-CAFE (Figure 1 (a)), new students are required to register by email and are given the option to provide their age, gender, home country, years of college-level education, and the primary reason why they are taking the course (Figure 1 (b)). Returning students can login with their email address. Students are then directed to a page (Figure 1 (c)) where they rate the following 5 quantitative assessment topics (QAT) about the course on a scale of 1-10 (1 represents "Very Low" and 10 represents "Very High"):

(1) How would you grade this course so far in terms of technical difficulty? (Course Difficulty)
(2) How would you grade this course so far in terms of usefulness to your career? (Course Usefulness)
(3) How would you grade your enthusiasm so far for this course? (Self-Enthusiasm)

(4) How would you grade your performance so far in this course? (Self-Performance)
(5) How would you grade the effectiveness of course assignments to help you develop your skills? (HW Effectiveness)

Next, students are directed to a virtual "cafe" interface (figure 1 (d)) where mugs representing other students are arranged on a coffee table [18]. In the cafe, qualitative (textual) suggestions from students are solicited around a Discussion Question: "In what specific ways could this course be enhanced to make it more valuable for you?"

Students click on mugs to view the textual suggestions of their peers and then evaluate how valuable the suggestions are on a scale of 1 -10 (Figure 1 (e)). After rating two suggestions, a new mug appears in the middle of the table, prompting the student to enter his or her own suggestion (Figure 1 (f)).

Case Study

We utilized M-CAFE during the June-July 2014, 6-week EdX MOOC course CS 169.2x and the October-December 2014, 8-week EdX MOOC course CS 169.1x: Engineering Software as a Service. Each week students were invited via email to visit or revisit M-CAFE to enter feedback about the course.

Qualitative Textual Feedback

Data

Students provided a total of 83 suggestions for CS 169.1x and 132 suggestions for CS 169.2x to answer the question "In what specific way could this course be enhanced to make it more valuable for you?" We also observed a total of 1,691 and 3,564 peer-to-peer ratings for the two courses respectively.

We ranked the suggestions using the lower bound of the binomial proportion confidence interval (also called the Wilson Score). This score incorporates both the mean and the variance of the ratings received. We took the mean grade **g** and then calculated the 95% confidence interval of **g** using standard error: **g +/- 1.96*SE(g)**. We ranked the comments by the lower bound **g - 1.96*SE(g)** since it is more robust when suggestions are contentious and receive a different number of ratings.

Collaborative Filtering

Various online platforms with crowd-sourcing ability have adopted collaborative filtering as an alternative approach to Natural Language Processing (NLP) [3]. While NLP of qualitative data hints at the important words or phrases, it fails to identify the underlying meaning of the sentences. Given the complicated nature of natural language, collaborative filtering has gained popularity for content-based items, such as customer recommendations and solution rankings on online QA platforms. Unlike most cases where the items are rated dichotomously, in M-CAFE, we adopted a 10-point scale to better capture rating differences between items in a setting with hundreds of participants.

We hypothesize that peer-to-peer collaborative filtering is capable of identifying valuable suggestions in M-CAFE. Our work will assess the performance of collaborative filtering based on three questions:

1. Are novel comments receiving higher ratings?

2. Is the top-rated set of comments representative of the entire dataset in terms of topics covered?
3. Are comments with higher quality (e.g. conciseness, clarity and completeness) receiving higher ratings?

If the answer is yes to all of the above questions, looking at the top-rated comments would provide us most of the information contained in the entire set, thus addressing the scale issue of qualitative data by reducing the dataset to a representative subset.

Demographic Influence

We will also evaluate the demographic influence on the students' behavior in M-CAFE. How does gender, age, country, or years of training affect the number of peer-to-peer ratings provided? Which types of students are more likely to provide insightful suggestions and what aspects of the course are students from similar backgrounds mostly concerned with?

Quantitative Feedback

There are numerous studies on the danger of purely quantitative course evaluations [3]. Stark and Freishtat [4] argue that quantitative rating data from course evaluations are subject to significant self-selection bias. Though our data nonetheless suffer from self-selection bias, the temporal nature of M-CAFE allows for relative analysis of quantitative data (i.e. increases and decreases) that may be less susceptible to biases.

We will explore the relative relationship of the QATs between weeks throughout each course and attempt to link the quantitative observations to the qualitative feedback in the corresponding weeks to ensure the validity of quantitative trends. In addition, we will study the inter-relationship between the QATs and the correspondence of the QATs to the schedule of the course, aiming to identify other aspects of the course that could explain and validate the trends presented by the quantitative data.

Acknowledgment

This work is supported in part by the Blum Center for Developing Economies and the Development Impact Lab (USAID Cooperative Agreement AID-OAA-A-12-00011) as part of the USAID Higher Education Solutions Network, UC Berkeley's Algorithms, Machines, and People (AMP) Lab, a grant from Fujitsu, and the UC CITRIS Data and Democracy Initiative. Thanks to all students who participated and colleagues who provided feedback on earlier drafts.

References

[1] Angelo, T.A. Cross, P.K. Classroom assessment techniques: A handbook for faculty. National Center for Research to Improve Teaching and Learning 1993. Ann Arbor, MI, 1993.

[2] Kristin, S.M., Hearst, M.A., and Fox, A. Monitoring MOOCs: which information sources do instructors value? *Proceedings of the First ACM conference on Learning @ Scale Conference.* (2014), 79-88.

[3] Marsh, H.W., and Roche, L.A. Making students' evaluations of teaching effectiveness effective: The critical issues of validity, bias, and utility. *American Psychologist, 52(11).* (1997), 1187-1197.

[4] Stark, P.B. and Richard F. An Evaluation of Course Evaluations. *UC Berkeley Technical Report; Center for Teaching and Learning.* (2014)

Item Ordering Effects with Qualitative Explanations using Online Adaptive Tutoring Data

Steven Tang
UC Berkeley
Tolman Hall
Berkeley, CA 94720
steventang@berkeley.edu

Hannah Gogel
UC Berkeley
Tolman Hall
Berkeley, CA 94720
hgogel@berkeley.edu

Elizabeth McBride
UC Berkeley
Tolman Hall
Berkeley, CA 94720
bethmcbride@berkeley.edu

Zachary A. Pardos
UC Berkeley
Tolman Hall 4641
Berkeley, CA 94720
pardos@berkeley.edu

Abstract
Online computer adaptive learning is increasingly being used in classrooms as a way to provide guided learning for students. Such tutors have the potential to provide tailored feedback based on specific student needs and misunderstandings. Bayesian knowledge tracing (BKT) is used to model student knowledge when knowledge is assumed to be changing throughout a single assessment period; in contrast, traditional Item Response Theory (IRT) models assume student knowledge to be constant within an assessment period. The basic BKT model assumes that the chance a student transitions from "not knowing" to "knowing" after each item is the same, and problems are considered learning opportunities. It could be the case, however, that learning is actually context sensitive, where students' learning might be improved when the items and their associated tutoring content are delivered to the student in a particular order. In this paper, we use BKT models to find such context sensitive transition probabilities from real data delivered by an online tutoring system, ASSISTments. After empirically deriving orderings that lead to better learning, we qualitatively analyze the items and their tutoring content to uncover any mechanisms that might explain why such orderings are modeled to have higher learning potential.

L@S 2015, March 14–18, 2015, Vancouver, BC, Canada.
ACM 978-1-4503-3411-2/15/03.
http://dx.doi.org/10.1145/2724660.2728682

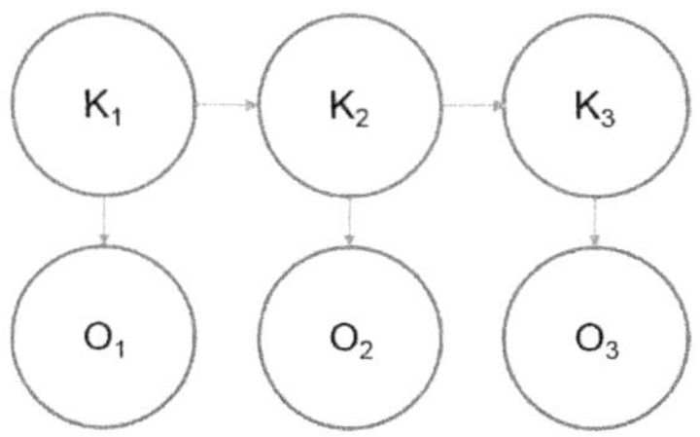

Figure 1: Basic BKT Model. O_1, O_2, and O_3 are binary indicators of correctness at opportunities 1, 2, and 3. K_1, K_2, and K_3 represent the latent knowledge of the KC (assumed to be 0 or 1) at opportunities 1, 2, and 3.

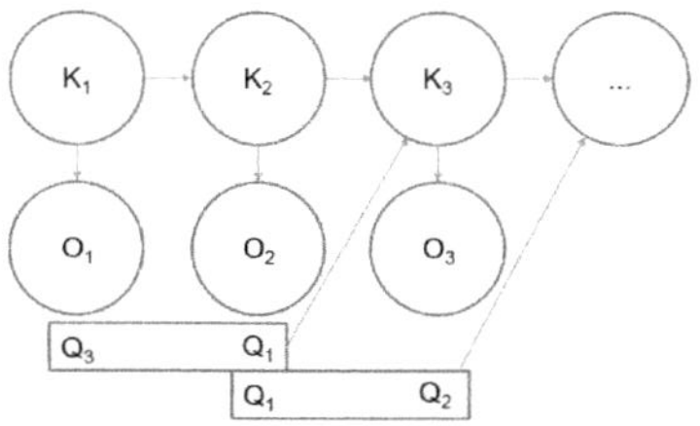

Figure 2: Item Order BKT Model. This student sees items from templates in the order of (3, 1, 2). Q_3 and Q_1 represent items from the 3rd and 1st template respectively, and are boxed together to show that this particular order affects the probability of knowledge at K_3. Then, Q_1 and Q_2 are boxed together to show that K_4 would be affected by seeing items in the order (1, 2).

Author Keywords
Item Ordering; Bayesian Knowledge Tracing; Item Difficulty

ACM Classification Keywords
K.3.1 [Computers and Education]: Computer Uses in Education.

Introduction
Online computer adaptive learning is increasingly being used in K-12 as a supplement to classroom instruction. Online systems, such as various MOOCs and the ASSISTments [4] platform, provide scaffolding and hints to students upon request or when the student answers a question incorrectly. This opportunity for learning after each question provides immediate formative feedback to the students, similar to how a human tutor might provide feedback during a lesson. In this paper, we focus on employing the Bayesian knowledge tracing (BKT) model of student learning typically used when students are expected to learn between assessment opportunities, but with the hypothesis that learning in between assessment opportunities could be *context sensitive*. In particular, we are interested in the qualitative mechanisms that might make one ordering of administered items better than another ordering. As such, after finding large differences in learning parameters of certain item orderings, we inspect the particular tutoring items and their associated learning content to find potential explanations.

ASSISTments Data
The data set analyzed in this paper comes from the publicly available ASSISTments 2012-2013 data set which has been used for numerous other research projects [5, 6]. In this paper, we focus on the Skill Builder sequences (SBs) used in ASSISTments, where a sequence contains a set of problems assumed to address one concept which we refer to as a knowledge component (KC). SBs are made up of problems generated from a randomly selected set of problem templates.

Bayesian Knowledge Tracing
Bayesian knowledge tracing [3] assumes a binary representation of student knowledge. There are noise parameters in the model that affect the relationship between knowledge and performance. For example, the model assumes that even when a student knows a KC, they might answer a question incorrectly (modeled as a *slip* parameter), and that when a student does not know a KC, they might guess and answer a question correctly (modeled as a *guess* parameter). Figure 1 depicts a BKT model representation as a hidden Markov model (HMM). In between each K_i and K_{i+1}, there is an arrow representing a probability of *transition*, or learning.

Item Ordering Effects
It is our hypothesis that there may exist pedagogically more advantageous orderings of problems than the default random orders. The BKT model can be extended to model a transition probability per particular item ordering. For example, the BKT model can estimate a transition probability after a student has specifically seen templates in the order (3, 1) and (1, 3). If one order has a higher transition probability than its reverse order, this could be seen as evidence that one ordering promotes more effective learning than another. Figure 2 depicts how this new model, drawn from work by Pardos and Heffernan [6], might be formulated as an HMM. Each item template is given their own set of guess of slip parameters.

Assignment: Problem #PSAJCFZ

Problem ID: *PRAJCFZ*

Find the sum:

$10\frac{7}{12} + 2\frac{7}{36}$

Assignment: Problem #PSAJCFA

Problem ID: *PRAJCFA*

Find the sum:

$2\frac{1}{2} + 1\frac{1}{2}$

Figure 3: Example of Effective Item Ordering. The learn rate of this ordering (top problem then the bottom problem) was .38 higher than the learn rate of its reverse.

Empirical Results

Only student data within 24 hours of the student's first response in a SB was included. SBs with more than 2000 student responses, at least 16 unique students, and between 2 and 6 (inclusive) template types were used for this analysis resulting in 112 SBs.

Two BKT models were run on each SB using the edX-hmm codebase. The first baseline model used standard BKT, where every item was assumed to have the same transition probability and the second model assumed a different transition probability based on the order of the previous two items administered.

Qualitative analysis

We looked at the 48 problem pair orderings where the difference between one order and its reverse was between 0.3 and 0.7 (avoiding the uninteresting and degenerate cases). We examined each of the templates with the associated template hints and qualitatively coded for certain phenomena that included: the number of hints available, if there was context for the problem (e.g. a story problem), whether the answer to the problem was given in any of the hints, whether there were visualizations or images present in the problem or its hints, whether or not one template in the pair was more difficult than the other, and which item in the pair was more difficult (first or second). Due to the large range of grade levels and mathematical topics covered in the templates we analyzed, any qualitative coding by topic left us with 5 or fewer items per group. This was not enough data to make any conclusions based on the item order and the subject matter. Cohen's kappa between the two unique raters was found to be above .80 on all coded values, ensuring inter-rater agreement.

The sample size for this analyses was quite small, so significance testing on many of these criteria were inconclusive. However, 33 out of the 48 template orderings were found by both raters to have significant differences in difficulty between the two templates in the pair. Of these 33 more effective orderings, the first template was more difficult in 17 orderings and the second template was more difficult in 16 orderings. Theoretically, assigning a guess and slip for each problem template, as was done with this BKT item ordering extension, should control for problem difficulty. That is, if a problem is particularly easy, it should receive a high guess value from the fitting procedure. Thus, in order for the model to assume learning has occurred when a hard question is followed by an easy one, the expected performance on the easy question must outperform the expected independent outcome for the problem.

An example of an effective item ordering is shown in Figure 3. Although the exact numbers within a template can change, the templates can have certain consistencies. In this example, the second ordered template shown always has equal denominators across its addends making it a lower difficulty item than the first ordered template.

One potential hypothesis that can help explain these findings is that of "desirable difficulties". In a series of studies, Bjork and colleagues determined that some challenges to performance during learning activities may actually contribute to greater learning [1, 2]. By introducing "desirable difficulties" that help learners engage in more active processing of information, learning tasks that may be perceived as challenging or inefficient may prove more beneficial than those completed with high fluency. In the case of item orderings where the first problem is more difficult than the second, the first (more difficult) problem may introduce a desirable difficulty, leading the student to learn more than they would with an easier problem. This learning then carries over into the second problem in the pair, thus leading to a higher overall rate of learning than found in the reverse order. When the first problem is easier than the second, this might be an instance where the material is better learned through a gentler or simpler introduction, as perhaps the second problem might be too difficult to be "desirable".

Testing whether an item is of a "desirable" difficulty would likely require a careful experimental design, rather than a post-hoc analysis of item properties when items are administered at random. Thus, numerous future research opportunities abound to further investigate how to best order items; in particular, it could be pertinent to explicitly engineer items with particular difficulty differences and test which orderings lead to the quickest learning of a KC.

Limitations and future work

The work presented in this paper attempted to explain why effective item orderings might exist in a tutoring design like that of the ASSISTments platform. We successfully found interesting effective item orderings, where items in one order tended to produce much higher learning than items presented in a reverse order, which is in line with previous findings of potentially meaningful orderings done by Pardos and Heffernan [6] in 2010.

Finding qualitative properties of those effective item orderings, however, proved to be difficult. In particular, scaffolding techniques significantly varied between different subjects and SBs. Due to this variation, determining general causal mechanisms of learning through different item pairs was mostly inconclusive.

Given that we noted that different templates within a SB tended to vary in difficulty, we hypothesized that "desirable difficulties" might help explain why some orderings might be better than others. Future research with a careful experimental design would be the best way to test this hypothesis, where the difficulty of the item is hypothesized a priori.

References

[1] Anderson, M., Neely, J., Bjork, E., and Bjork, R. *Memory, Chapter 6: Interference and inhibition in memory retrieval.* Academic Press, 1996.

[2] Christina, R. W., and Bjork, R. A. *In D. Druckman and R. A. Bjork (Eds.), In the mind's eye: Enhancing human performance: Optimizing long-term retention and transfer.* Washington, DC: National Academy Press, 1991.

[3] Corbett, A. T., and Anderson, J. R. Knowledge Tracing: Modeling the Acquisition of Procedural Knowledge. *The Journal of User Modeling and User-Adapted Interaction 4* (1995), 253–278.

[4] Feng, M., Heffernan, N., and Koedinger, K. R. Addressing the assessment challenge in an Intelligent Tutoring System that tutors as it assesses. *The Journal of User Modeling and User-Adapted Interaction 19*, 243–266.

[5] Ocumpaugh, J., Baker, R., S., G., Heffernan, N., and Heffernan, C. Population validity for Educational Data Mining models: A case study in affect detection. *British Journal of Educational Technology 45*, 3 (2014), 487–501.

[6] Pardos, Z. A., and Heffernan, N. T. Determining the significance of item order in randomized problem sets. In *Proc. of the 2nd International Conference on Educational Data Mining* (2009).

Learnersourcing of Complex Assessments

Piotr Mitros
edX
141 Portland St
Cambridge, MA 02139
pmitros@edx.org

 L@S 2015, March 14–18, 2015, Vancouver, BC, Canada.
ACM 978-1-4503-3411-2/15/03.
http://dx.doi.org/10.1145/2724660.2728683

Abstract
We present results from a pilot study where students successfully created complex assessments for a MOOC in introductory electronics – an area with a very large expert-novice gap. Previous work in learnersourcing found that learners can productively contribute through simple tasks. However, many course resources require a high level of expertise to create, and prior work fell short on tasks with a large expert-novice gap, such as textbook creation or concept tagging. Since these constitute a substantial portion of course creation costs, addressing this issue is prerequisite to substantially shifting MOOC economics through learnersourcing. This represents one of the first successes in learnersourcing with a large expert-novice gap. In the pilot, we reached out to 206 students (out of thousands who met eligibility criteria) who contributed 14 complex high-quality design problems. This results suggests a full cohort could contribute hundreds of problems. We achieved this through a four-pronged approach. (1) pre-selecting top learners (2) community feedback process (3) student mini-course in pedagogy (4) instructor review and involvement.

ACM Classification Keywords
K.3.1 [Computer Uses in Education]: Collaborative Learning.

Introduction

There are 4,706 degree-granting institutions in the United States. A specialized introductory course such as circuits and electronics is taken by 10k-100k students every year [8]. This gives 3-4 orders of magnitude inefficiency on tasks such as creation of lectures and assessments, and 4-5 orders of magnitude on per-student tasks such as grading. Open educational resources (OER) and at-scale learning organizations (such as MOOC providers) attempt to improve the quality of education by leveraging those inefficiencies to provide higher-quality resources at lower cost. The OER approach has met limited adoption due to lack of coherence – finding and adapting relevant and quality OERs is often more time-intensive than creating new resources [4].

In contrast, institutional Massive Open On-line Courses (xMOOCs) use a centralized approach where a single course team creates a complete, coherent course. xMOOCs are typically taught by top instructors, and many employ research-based pedagogies such as active learning, constructive learning, and mastery-learning [5]. They are further enhanced with data-driven techniques. Initial evidence suggests that well-designed xMOOCs can lead to high levels of student learning and satisfaction in both on-line and blended settings [3][5][1]. In contrast to OERs, xMOOCs are traditionally not open, and do not substantially leverage the creative input of external contributors. xMOOCs have been limited by to the high cost of creating evidence-based resources, combined with a lack of well-developed economic models.

Mitros [6] introduced a hybrid model of course creation where a central staff provides a common course skeleton, and a community of learners, educators, and researchers builds and improves on that skeleton. This approach has been shown successful across a range of areas such as student remediation, translation, subtitling, and peer grading of simple assessments, but as predicted in expert-novice literature [7], had lackluster results for tasks such as concept tagging or text creation. Cormier [2] piloted how this model may work in courses with a large community of instructors, such as an introductory physics course. More esoteric courses, as found at a university level, often do not have such communities.

In this pilot, we explore ways to source content with a large expert-novice gap. To do this, we first pre-screen students for ones who showed a high level of mastery in the MOOC. Second, we train those students in best practices for creating high-quality assessments. Third, we have a process by which those resources are improved based on both community and instructor feedback.

In order to maximize the expert-novice gap, we choose contribution of assessments to 6.002x, the MITx course in circuits and electronics. 6.002x has a small number of complex assessments involving design and analysis. To give an idea of complexity of those problems, most weekly graded assignments consist of three problems and one laboratory. Students self-report spending an average of 11 hours per week on the course (including ungraded work).

The creation of assessments is a complex process:

- Students are taught basic concepts, such as linearity and nodal analysis. A large part of the goal of the course is to begin to develop design intuition for how circuits work and physical intuition for realistic component values. Course creators must be familiar with a range of circuits in order to be able to find ones which illustrate concepts taught in the course,

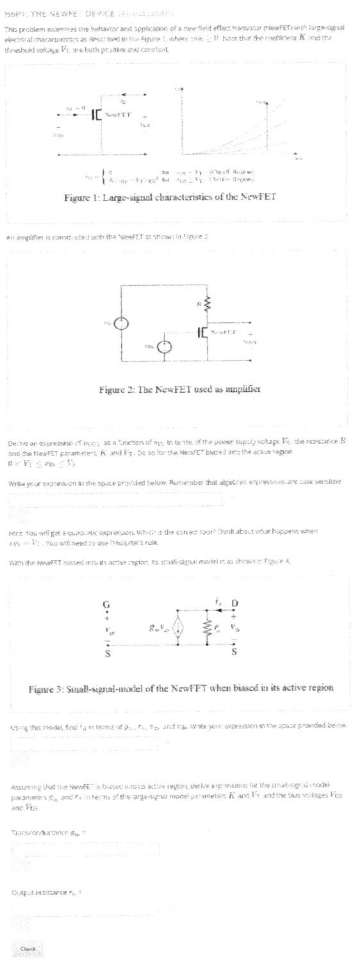

Figure 1: A representative mid-semester problem from the edX offering of 6.002x. Students are asked to analyze an amplifier based on a device they have not seen in the course.

and to be able to create simplified, realistic, variants of those circuits. Finding or creating interesting circuits is the bulk of the assessment creation time.

- Students can continue to work on problems until they reach a correct answer, and receive immediate feedback if they do not. Problems must lend themselves to automated grading, mastery learning, and infinite attempts (e.g. numeric and equations, rather than multiple choice or freeform pictures).
- Quality problem creation requires extensive pedagogical content knowledge.
- Problems should be fun and interesting.

An example problem from 6.002x is shown in Fig. 1. The complexity of this process is such that the assessment creation for the first run of 6.002x required 1.5 semesters of full-time effort from MIT instructors. Creating new exam problems is the major limiting factor on how often the course can be re-offered.

Process and Results

We e-mailed two groups of students:

- 106 students from the fall 2014 run of 6.002x (contacted one week after course completion) who achieved >97.5% on the final exam.
- 100 students from the original spring 2012 run of 6.002x who had achieved an 'A' grade in the course, and had volunteered to participate in such projects in the end-of-course survey (out of 2833 eligible).

Students were invited to participate in a short course about how to create good autograded assessments in introductory electronics, including content about pedagogy, capabilities of the platform, as well as subject-specific advice, such as finding good analog circuits to use as the basis of problems. Students were given a 10 day window within which to submit first drafts. Registered students were sent a reminder three days before this deadline. Assessments had three possible formats:

- Simple practice problems
- Mid-term exam problems (complex multiconcept)
- Final exam problems (complex multiconcept)

Students could submit problems either through the edX peer assessment tool, or the discussion forums. Students almost exclusively favored the discussion forum. Course staff and peers were active on forums, reviewing problems and providing feedback. Problems, on average, received 3-4 comments. This process was critical – few of the submitted problems were directly usable in the first iteration. Students and instructors formed a community in which they reviewed problems, learned from each other, and through the process, many of the problems improved dramatically. Several students indicated a very high level of value from participation in those forums, and found it helped for learning about both electronics and pedagogy.

At the time of the deadline, 57 students had registered for the course, and submitted a total of 17 problems, of which 2 were excellent as evaluated by the course staff[1], 12 were usable or excellent with relatively small tweaks or changes, and 3 were incomplete or unusable. Contributions and community continued beyond the deadline. The level of participation is typical of previous experiments in sourcing from MOOC students[6], but at a much higher task complexity. If we maintained similar

[1]Neither independent nor blind evaluation. The author of this paper is a co-creator of the course.

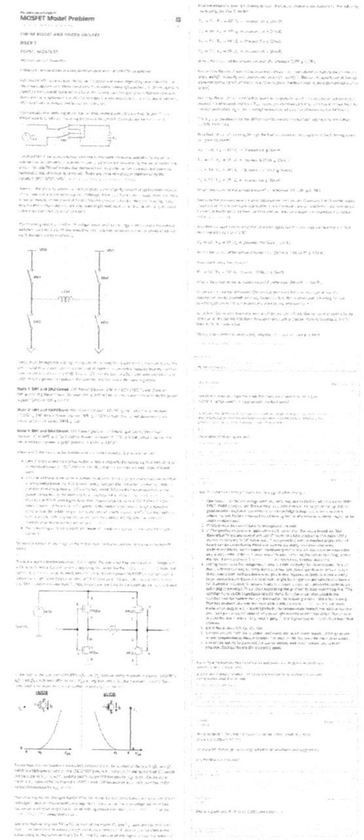

Figure 2: A representative problem contributed by a student, followed by the discussion around that problem. The problem walks through the design of an H-bridge driver. The author rewrote the first draft as a result of feedback.

levels of participation as we scaled out to more participants, we'd expect 28±6% to enroll in the course, and to receive problems corresponding to 30±12% of the registrants (25±11% usable problems). For all eligible students, the number of contributed problems would be many times greater than required for the overall course.

The problems ranged from simple single-concept practice problems to complex multiconcept problems based on real-world circuits, such as edge detector, a motor driver, an envelope detector, and a range of amplifiers, but most tended towards the more complex end. An example problem is shown in Fig. 2. In most cases, the very high quality was the result of the community process. Most of the initial submissions had good ideas, but suffered from any of a range of issues such as ambiguity, inappropriate level of difficulty, technical errors, and pedagogical short-comings. The community process allowed contributors to discover and resolve those issues.

Conclusion

We successfully demonstrated the ability to source complex assessments from MOOC learners. Since this was a pilot study, we used a small sample of 206 eligible learners. The results suggest that using the full cohort of eligible contributors would have allowed us to substantially accelerate the creation of complex assessments – the most resource-intensive portion of the course, assuming we were able to maintain similar contribution levels. A rough guess (with no data) is that the time spent per assessment is roughly an order of magnitude lower than fully manual creation, but also not zero, due to the need for review and editing. Based on the pilot results, learnersourcing appears to be a viable strategy for improving MOOC costs of creation, including those with a large expert-novice gap.

Acknowledgments

We thank all of the 6.002x students for their active engagement in both the course, and in community efforts to improve the course.

References

[1] Cima, M. A mastery-based learning and assessment model applied to 3.091r (introduction to solid-state chemistry). *MIT Interim Report* (2014).

[2] Cormier, D., Mitros, P., and Pritchard, D. Teaching physics at scale. *Physics Education Research Conference* (2014).

[3] Ghadiri, K., Qayoumi, M. H., Junn, E., Hsu, P., and Sujitparapitaya, S. The transformative potential of blended learning using MIT edX's 6.002x online MOOC content combined with student team-based learning in class. *environment 8* (2013), 14.

[4] Harley, D., Head, A., Nasatir, D., Paletz, S., Henke, J., Miller, I., Sheng, X., and Guo, J. Understanding the use of digital collections in undergraduate humanities and social science education: Status report, preliminary analyses, and next steps. *CSHE Digital Resource Study, Center for Studies in Higher Education, University of California at Berkeley* (2004).

[5] Mitros, P., Affidi, K., Sussman, G., Terman, C., White, J., Fischer, L., and Agarwal, A. Teaching electronic circuits online: Lessons from MITx's 6.002x on edX. In *ISCAS*, IEEE (2013), 2763–2766.

[6] Mitros, P., and Sun, F. Creating educational resources at scale. *IEEE Conf. on Adv. Learning Technologies* (2014).

[7] National Research Council. *How People Learn*. National Academy Press, 2000, 31–50.

[8] Snyder, T., and Dillow, S. *Digest of Education Statistics 2012*. NCES 2012-001. NCES, IES, U.S. DOE, Washington, DC, 2012.

Supporting Face-to-Face Like Communication Modalities for Asynchronous Assignment Feedback in Math Education

Bernie Randles
Cornell University, Academic Technologies
Ithaca, NY 14850
bmb256@cornell.edu

Dongwook Yoon
Cornell University, Information Science
Ithaca, NY 14850
dy252@cornell.edu

Amy Cheatle
Cornell University, Academic Technologies
Ithaca, NY 14850
ac2288@cornell.edu

Malte Jung
Cornell University, Information Science
Ithaca, NY 14850
mfj28@cornell.edu

François Guimbretière
Cornell University, Information Science
Ithaca, NY 14850
francois@cs.cornell.edu

L@S 2015, March 14–18, 2015, Vancouver, BC, Canada.
ACM 978-1-4503-3411-2/15/03.
http://dx.doi.org/10.1145/2724660.2728684

Abstract
The digitization of educational course content has proved to be problematic for math instructors due to the lack of quality feedback tools that can accommodate the commenter to efficiently express math formulae and convey descriptions about complex ideas contextualized in situ. This paper proposes that RichReview, a document annotation system which creates inking, voice and deictic gestures on top of the student's submitted work, is a possible formative math feedback solution, because it enables face-to-face like commentary within the contexts of the document at hand. A preliminary qualitative evaluation study conducted while having students receive RichReview feedback showed promise to our approach to enhance the quality of feedback, with the implication that incorporating multi-modal feedback into workflows can be an effective method to address elements of feedback submissions lacking in coursework that has moved online.

Author Keywords
Math education; Formative feedback; Multi-modal user interfaces; Asynchronous communication

ACM Classification Keywords
H.5.2 Information Interfaces and Presentation (e.g. HCI): User Interfaces. - Graphical user interfaces.

Introduction
The importance of *formative* feedback in teaching and learning has been well-established in the field of education [6]. The term *formative* with respect to this field can be nebulous, but we employ Black and Wiliam's definition of assessments being formative when they are used to communicate to students with subsequent teaching practices modified to adapt to the student's input [2]. As educational practices develop in fully-digital online spaces, face-to-face like (having qualities of face-to-face interaction in an asynchronous digital environment) interaction is particularly important in mathematics because the iterative, communicative and gestural nature of the learning of science has been well-documented [4, 7, 8]. The process of formative feedback encourages a relationship or partnership to exist between the educator and the student, and hence reinforces constructive learning practices [11].

One major challenge of formative math feedback tools is the input methods which instantiate the dialogue. Hand-written mathematical formulae or graphical representations require ample real estate for document-based feedback. As a result, many comments are written on margins, white spaces, or separate pages that are remote from the target text. However, educational researchers stress that for feedback to be effective, it should be contextual, meaning it is placed in proximity to the appropriate area in the document under review [5].

An alternative solution to the writing math by hand is keyboard input. However, text-based annotation software lacks scientific symbols to render math properly. A few solutions capable of symbol input, such as Word Equation editor or LaTex, offer the functionality of symbolic representation, but speed of output, level of difficulty, and a possible steep learning curve are factors in using these writing tools.

Another area of concern surrounds the idea that feedback should be *communicative* in nature. It is imperative for the formative feedback tools to support teacher-student dialogues to reinforce learning practices [12]. For example, a student who receives feedback from an instructor may want to respond within the document to ask questions.

RichReview, a tablet-based multimodal annotation system for text [13], addresses these issues in several ways (Figure 1). The tool allows for handwritten feedback, with space-creating (text-tearing) and deictic pointing (Spotlighting) components to ensure contextual feedback, as well as collaborative features that enable a dialog between student and teacher. It is unknown whether the face-to-face like experience will engender a positive learning experience, but preliminary results show this is a possibility.

In this paper, we provide a new perspective on the application area of RichReview, which was originally designed for reviewing written documents, by connecting pedagogical requirements of a formative math feedback tool with the features of the RichReview system. To do this, we conducted a preliminary study to examine the potential useful features of the system, and provide implications in educational contexts.

Furthermore, we suggest future plans for design and implementations of additional features that can make the system better accommodate math feedback and support use cases at scale.

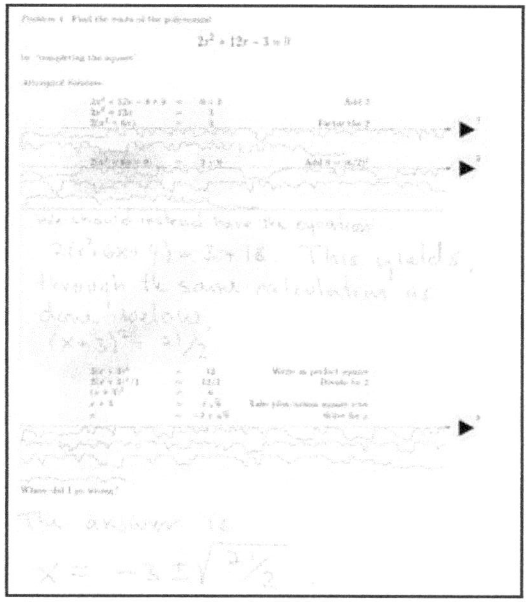

Figure 1. Screenshot from RichReview, the tablet feedback generating interface. The TA has provided written feedback via text-tearing, as well as gestural and voice feedback (notice waveforms of actual audio). The gestures will animate in accordance with the audio file.

Previous Works

There has been much work in technology-based tools for enhancing math education. These tools are specifically designed for the necessity of a digital environment which acknowledges the importance of pen and paper functionality.

Classroom presenter is a classroom communication system for gathering/sharing/presenting students' responses via pen and tablet which was successfully deployed to many classes including math courses [1].

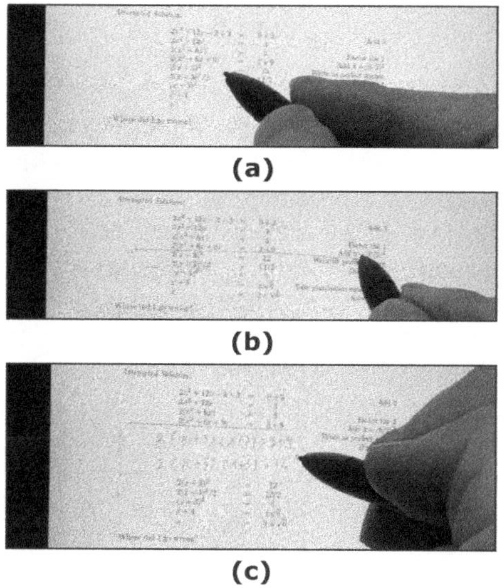

Figure 2. Text-tearing creates space for annotations within the document space. The user has created an annotation space, and has added written feedback with the pen. Steps in text-tearing: (a) screenshot of pdf document demonstrating text-tearing: the user decides at what point to create more space; (b) the user draws a line with the pen to initiate the tearing procedure; (c) the user has annotated in the created space with the stylus.

Hands-on-math is a tabletop system to help problem-solving and conceptualization with user interactions over math equations augmented by the Computer Algebra System [15]. The goal of Hands-on-math is to provide a paper-like environment, including a built-in math solving tool within the document itself.

Both of these tools recognize the various issues ingrained into the process of learning math, especially the notion that the handwritten, step-wise methods of solving problems and minimizing transfer between environments is a crucial part of the design.

RichReview is a collaboration tool at heart, focusing on ways of enabling a back and forth communication built into the document itself; which inherently lends itself to the iterative process of learning math. Dialogues reinforce learning practices, and successful feedback enables this capacity [8].

Rethinking RichReview as a Math Feedback Tool

We explain how RichReview, developed by our research team [13], contains features which address the specific requirements that successful feedback contains. We leverage the core features of the RichReview system as following:

Features of RichReview for Math Feedback

- *TextTearing* feature [14], which provides extra white space in the document (Figure 2), and allows for more 'real estate' for writing mathematical expressions or graphs at relevant points of the documents.
- Voice comments are fast and effective for delivering complex notions or procedures of math problem solving. The spoken comments can also better convey the commenter's intentions, since voice can deliver expressive and rich nuances.
- Spotlight feature supports recording of deictic gesture in sync with voice. Pointing at a particular place in a document is helpful for drawing one's attention to a specific part of the problem, graph, or diagram, enriching contexts of speech with better localization of the verbal description over documents.

Results of Preliminary Study

Our preliminary evaluation study explored the efficacy of RichReview as a feedback tool.

We conducted a qualitative evaluation study which explored experiences 9 university students had receiving feedback on writing samples they provided, in pdf format and emailed to the reviewer. Students were divided into groups and received feedback using three tools: RichReview, traditional pen and paper, and a commercially available grading tool with annotation capabilities, Turnitin. The 'RichReviewed' paper used comments in the margin, and text tearing. The pen and paper assignment provided hand-written comments in the margin, and at the end of the paper. The Turnitin assignment provided text annotation layered over the document, there is no handwritten functionality. After the study, students were surveyed on their experiences with the tool, including how they preferred to receive feedback, how they generally received feedback in their coursework, and ideally how they would like to receive feedback, as well as comments about the specific tool they used. None of the three students receiving feedback with Turnitin thought it was a preferable way to receive feedback, and the other 6 respectively thought that RichReview and pen and paper were acceptable ways to receive feedback.

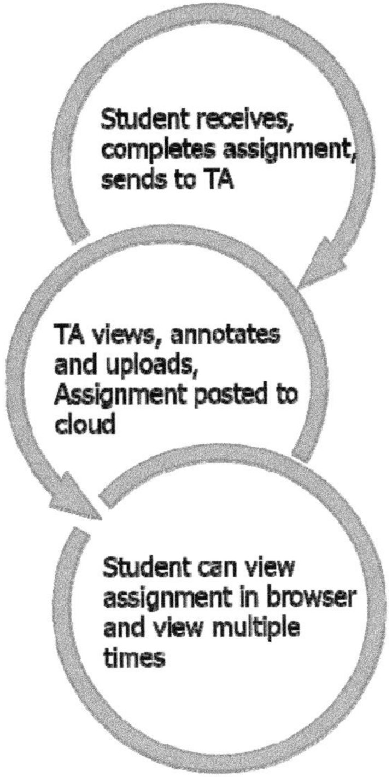

Figure 3. Online course digital workflow for math assignments feedback

Concerning preferences relating to modes of receiving feedback, one student said, "written comments are helpful", another said," I like hearing feedback verbally", and yet another preferred "written or verbal feedback from the professor." We conclude that when given the opportunity, students prefer a variety of modes of receiving feedback, with 6 of the 9 students preferring to receive both written and verbal feedback. In regards to RichReview as a feedback tool, the 3 students using RichReview yielded valuable input, including verification that the tool: 1) is an effective way of providing feedback, 2) purveyed a level of care that was perceived as thoughtful, and 3) made participants feel valued as people upon receiving their feedback [2]. This is in line with findings from a previous study, that participants collaborating with RichReview asynchronously felt remote presence as if the person was there, helping them [13].

This preliminary study involved a written assignment, and now we propose RichReview to be used for a mathematics course.

Online Math Feedback Workflow

By using RichReview as an enabling technology, we outline a method for providing face-to-face like comments on students' assignment submissions (Figure 3). The student writes up the assignment and scans the paper as a pdf. Note that the student could also use LaTex or even MS Word, or a combination of type and handwritten elements. The homework is then sent to the grader, who uses the RichReview tool to provide feedback. The commented paper is then submitted to a cloud storage area, and a link to the paper is sent to the student, who can then view (in a web browser) the annotated homework, listen to the voice comments, and view the gestural components that relate to the comments in the paper.

Making it Scalable: Future Work

Our approach to tackle the issue of effective feedback for mathematics courses in a scalable fashion is to develop a system of reusable feedback elements that the instructor or TA can utilize. It is common for students to make similar errors in their work per assignment, and so a bank of visual elements and voice instructions can be created to be embedded into the document. In this way, the process of providing feedback can leverage existing solution templates, yet still provide a personalized level of care in the giving of feedback.

Secondly, for future work, we theorize that RichReview could be deployed in a MOOC environment. MOOCs often employ peer assessments to combat the lack of TAs to assess homework. We propose a feedback system with peers using an instructor-created grading template which is designed to retain the human-interactive elements at scale. For example, we envision a multi-modal rubric designed to teach the student how to provide feedback to others, and in doing so, participating in the iterative learning process. RichReview is designed for a back and forth collaboration between reviewer and recipient of feedback, and this would be an integral part of the browser-based design. Research has shown that, when implemented properly, peer and self-assessment can be an effective part of a student's learning experience [9,10]. More research is needed to ascertain the best pedagogical practices to utilize self and peer assessments within MOOC courses.

Conclusion

In conclusion, we hypothesize that the features of the RichReview tool will provide an encouraging way of receiving feedback, as well as new learning opportunities generated by the multi-modal functionality of RichReview. The ability for the student to review verbal comments repeatedly is a useful feature in learning math. In addition, the extra data tracked in digitizing homework sets will enhance future teaching of the course. We aim to show that the improved workflow and increased feedback will foster a better online learning environment than currently exists today, particularly in the field of mathematics.

Acknowledgements

This study was made possible by a generous gift from Microsoft Research. Yoon gratefully acknowledges support from the Kwanjeong Educational Foundation.

References

[1] Anderson, R., et al. "Classroom presenter: Enhancing interactive education with digital ink." *Computer* 40.9 (2007): 56-61.

[2] Black, P & Wiliam, D; Inside the Black Box: Raising Standards through Classroom Assessment. *The Phi Delta Kappa International* 80, 2 (1998), 139-148.

[3] Cheatle, A. and Randles, B. "A Further Examination of RichReview: Comparing Tools Instructors Use to Provide Feedback." manuscript (2014).

[4] Crowder, E. Gestures at Work in Sense-Making Science Talk. *Journal of the Learning Sciences,* 5(3) (1996). 173-208.

[5] Edmison, B., and Edwards, S., et al. Using a Rubric-based assessment system to improve feedback and student performance in course-management systems. *ASEE Southeast Section Conference,* (2010).

[6] Hattie, J, and Timperley, H. "The power of feedback." *Review of educational research* 77.1 (2007), 81-112.

[7] Halliday, M.A.K. "Towards a language-based theory of learning." *Linguistics and education* 5.2 (1993): 93-116.

[8] Kress, G., ed. Multimodal teaching and learning: The rhetorics of the science classroom. Bloomsbury Publishing, 2001.

[9] Kulkarni, C.,et al. "Peer and self assessment in massive online classes." *Design Thinking Research*. Springer International Publishing, 2015. 131-168.

[10] Nicol, D. From monologue to dialogue: improving written feedback processes in mass higher education. *Center for Academic Practice and Learning Enhancement (CAPLE)* (2010).

[11] Price, M., et al. "Feedback: all that effort, but what is the effect?."*Assessment & Evaluation in Higher Education* 35.3 (2010): 277-289.

[12] Sadler, P., and Good, E. "The impact of self-and peer-grading on student learning." *Educational assessment* 11.1 (2006): 1-31.

[13] Yoon, D, Chen, N., Guimbretiere, F., and Sellen, A. "RichReview: blending ink, speech, and gesture to support collaborative document review." *Proceedings of the 27th annual ACM symposium on User interface software and technology*. ACM, (2014).

[14] Yoon, D., Chen, N. and Guimbretière, F. "TextTearing: Opening white space for digital ink annotation." *Proceedings of the 26th annual ACM symposium on User interface software and technology*. ACM, (2013).

[15] Zeleznik, R., et al. "Hands-on math: a page-based multi-touch and pen desktop for technical work and problem solving." *Proceedings of the 23nd annual ACM symposium on User interface software and technology*. ACM, (2010).

Practical Measures of Learning Behaviors

Andrew E. Krumm
SRI International
333 Ravenswood Ave. BN388
Menlo Park, CA 94025
andrew.krumm@sri.com

Cynthia D'Angelo
SRI International
333 Ravenswood Ave. BN313
Menlo Park, CA 94025
cynthia.dangelo@sri.com

Timothy E. Podkul
SRI International
333 Ravenswood Ave. BN366
Menlo Park, CA 94025
timothy.podkul@sri.com

Mingyu Feng
SRI International
333 Ravenswood Ave. BN378
Menlo Park, CA 94025
mingyu.feng@sri.com

Hiroyuki Yamada
Carnegie Foundation for the Advancement of Teaching
51 Vista Lane
Stanford, CA 94305
yamada@carnegiefoundation.org

Rachel Beattie
Carnegie Foundation
51 Vista Lane
Stanford, CA 94305
beattie@carnegiefoundation.org

Heather Hough
Carnegie Foundation
51 Vista Lane
Stanford, CA 94305
hough@carnegiefoundation.org

Chris Thorn
Carnegie Foundation for the Advancement of Teaching
51 Vista Lane
Stanford, CA 94305
thorn@carnegiefoundation.org

L@S 2015, March 14–18, 2015, Vancouver, BC, Canada.
ACM 978-1-4503-3411-2/15/03
http://dx.doi.org/10.1145/2724660.2728685

Abstract
This paper argues that improving learning reliably and at scale requires a specific orientation toward measurement, understood broadly. Drawing on examples from a partnership between SRI International and The Carnegie Foundation for the Advancement of Teaching, this paper describes measures of student behaviors that are being used by researchers and instructors to improve learning environments at more than 50 community colleges and four-year universities for thousands of students.

Author Keywords
Practical measurement; learning behaviors; developmental mathematics

ACM Classification Keywords
K.3.1 Computers and Education: Computer Uses in Education–Computer-assisted instruction

Introduction
This paper describes how SRI and Carnegie developed *practical measures* of learning behaviors used to support improvement efforts within Carnegie's Community College Pathways (CCP) Networked Improvement Community (NIC) [4]. The CCP NIC is a coordinated effort to improve developmental math learning opportunities for thousands of students in

colleges throughout the United States. Statway, one of two CCP Pathways, is an accelerated, two-term course that combines both developmental mathematics and statistical reasoning content. Below, we address how using data to support improvement efforts, such as those undertaken in the CCP NIC, is often different from using data for the purposes of accountability (which is often typified by the use of outcome measures), theory-development (which can be focused on the reliability of self-report items), or developing early warning systems (which are often focused on identifying students and not directing subsequent actions).

Along with multiple drivers of student success, CCP courses seek to enhance students' productive persistence, which is defined as the *tenacity* to persist, and the *learning strategies* to do so productively [3]. To improve upon and accelerate in-class interventions directed at improving productive persistence, formative measures were needed that could be acted on in a relatively short time frame and help instructors work with students around specific mindsets and learning strategies.

In this project, we sought to go beyond identifying students at risk—typical of many early warning systems—and help instructors take specific next steps with students [1]. With this goal in mind, we developed measures of key elements associated with productive persistence, namely, the use of good strategies. Using data from the online learning platform supporting Statway courses, we identified and validated key learning strategies evoked by students that were interpretable and pointed to specific actions that instructors could take.

Data and Methods

In this paper, we report on data collected from 2013-2014 Statway courses that were hosted by Carnegie Mellon's Online Learning Initiative (OLI) platform. We used historical data to develop proof-of-concept measures, and we are currently exploring how well the measures continue to perform with updated data. Over 1,600 Statway students in fall 2013 generated more than 12 million rows of data as they read course materials, engaged in practice activities, and completed assessments called "Checkpoints." In order to leverage the data coming from the OLI platform, it was important to first understand how instructors intended to use the platform in their instruction. Understanding instructors' intentions helped in identifying whether or not students' behaviors in the system were on or off track and if some data collected by the system should be attended to more than others [1].

We initially distilled multiple features from students' Checkpoint scores, reading and practice activities before and after Checkpoints, combinations of activities within sessions, and days between logins. Sessions are defined as the time between students logging in and out of the system. Within a session, students can engage in multiple learning behaviors. Drawing on theory and face-validity checks, we translated behaviors into features, and once validated, these features served as data-driven examples of students productively persisting.

To identify the practicality of measures for instructors, we codified features as actions students would take within the system (e.g., number of times students re-read course material after failing a Checkpoint) and identified whether the features could be collected and acted on at various points in an academic semester (e.g., Does the number of times a student login matter more early or late in the semester?). To validate measures, we used multiple 2-level hierarchical linear models (HLM), with students nested within courses. Dependent variables included a standardized post-assessment given to all Statway students. We then modeled the effect of a given feature in relation to this post-assessment, controlling for students' incoming content knowledge using a standardized pre-assessment. If a measure was correlated with the outcome, controlling for incoming knowledge, we conjectured that it might potentially be useful. However, in order to be truly useful to instructors and students, it had to be interpretable (e.g., Is this measure capturing a recognizable behavior? Does the predictability of the measure change throughout the semester?) and support directing subsequent actions (e.g., Does this measure help an instructor intervene on the recognizable behavior?)

Theory helped in developing interpretable measures. For example, we used research related to choice-based assessments where the actions that precede and follow assessment activities can be as useful for assessing learning as the outcomes of the assessment [2]. Research on the choices students make sensitized us to the various preparatory activities students engage in and what they do following a Checkpoint—importantly those that follow a student failing a Checkpoint. We then aligned these generic activities to elements of productive persistence. Measures of learning behaviors that were explicitly linked to theoretically grounded mechanisms helped in identifying the potential next steps instructors and students could take [4].

Example Practical Measures

Below, we describe two example practical measures. These measures were developed using historical data and in subsequent semesters will be integrated as automated measures within the online platform for researchers and instructors to use. Overall, we identified more than 25 features that have different predictive validity over time, which is important as instructors do not make just-in-time decisions with an entire semester's worth of data.

The two practical measures capture the type of sessions that students logged in the online platform. The first practical measure captures the percent of Checkpoint-only (CP-Only) sessions that a student logged. CP-Only sessions represent those where students take and re-take end-of-topic quizzes without engaging in reading or practice activities. The second practical measure captured the percent of sessions whereby students attempted another activity after they failed a Checkpoint (After-Fail). While many learners retook Checkpoints multiple times, others quit following a poor score.

Preliminary Results and Discussion

Students in the highest quintile group (Q5) on the post-assessment had the lowest percent of CP-Only sessions (see Table 1). Likewise, students in Q5 had a higher percent of sessions with attempts after they failed a Checkpoint. Going beyond these descriptive statistics, Tables 2 and 3 present the results of the relationship between CP-Only and After-Fail practical measures on the Statway post-assessment, controlling for the pre-assessment. Results indicate that both measures are predictive. Importantly, CP-Only represents a negative effect whereby more of these types of sessions led to lower scores on the post-assessment; appropriately, the opposite was true for After-Fail.

	CP-Only		After-Fail	
Post-Assess. Quintile Groups	**Mean**	**SD**	**Mean**	**SD**
Q1	30.3	30.4	59.0	21.2
Q2	30.0	28.1	62.4	21.9
Q3	25.1	27.7	66.7	21.9
Q4	23.8	27.5	67.7	23.4
Q5	20.9	25.3	74.6	24.0

Table 1. Descriptive statistics for CP-Only (N=1,134) and After-Fail (N=1,084) practical measures.

	B	SE	p
Constant	64.29	1.43	<.001
CP-Only	-.24	.02	.018
Pre-Assessment	.33	.02	<.001

Table 2. 2-Level HLM for CP-Only Model. Using Post-Assessment as dependent variable, controlling for Pre-Assessment, which is grand mean centered.

	B	SE	p
Constant	57.16	1.43	<.001
After-Fail	.09	.02	<.001
Pre-Assessment	.33	.02	<.001

Table 3. 2-Level HLM for After-Fail Model. Using Post-Assessment as dependent variable, controlling for Pre-Assessment, which is grand mean centered.

These preliminary results show the promise in using online learning system data to develop practical measures of productive persistence. These measures, along with others that are currently in progress, can be used by instructors to directly intervene on students' *unproductive* persistence. For example, an instructor can immediately work with students after one CP-Only session; therefore, developing measures that support immediate interventions on the part of instructors are becoming possible and represent useful goals for measurement aimed at improving learning environments at scale.

Acknowledgements

This paper is based upon work supported by the National Science Foundation (NSF) (SMA-1338487) and SRI International. Any findings or opinions expressed in this paper are those of the authors and do not necessarily reflect the views of NSF or SRI.

References

[1] Krumm, A. E., Waddington, R. J., Teasley, S. D., & Lonn, S. (2014). Using learning analytics to support academic advising in undergraduate engineering education. In J. A. Larusson & B. White (Eds.). *Learning Analytics: From Research to Practice* (pp. 103-119). New York: Springer.

[2] Schwartz, D. L., & Arena, D. (2013). *Measuring what matters most: Choice-based assessments for the digital age*. Cambridge MA: MIT Press.

[3] Silva, E. & White, T. (2013). *Pathways to improvement: Using psychological strategies to help college students master developmental math*. Carnegie Foundation for the Advancement of Teaching. Stanford, CA.

[4] Yeager, D., Bryk, A., Muhich, J., Hausman H., & Morales, L. (2013) *Practical measurement*. Carnegie Foundation for the Advancement of Teaching. Stanford, CA. http://www.carnegiefoundation.org/resources/publications/practical-measurement/.

Demographic Differences in a Growth Mindset Incentive Structure for Educational Games

Eleanor O'Rourke
University of Washington
Computer Science
Seattle, WA
eorourke@cs.washington.edu

Yvonne Chen
University of Washington
Computer Science
Seattle, WA
evechen@cs.washington.edu

Kyla Haimovitz
Stanford University
Department of Psychology
Stanford, CA
kylah@stanford.edu

Carol S. Dweck
Stanford University
Department of Psychology
Stanford, CA
dweck@stanford.edu

Zoran Popović
University of Washington
Computer Science
Seattle, WA
zoran@cs.washington.edu

L@S 2015, Mar 14-18, 2015, Vancouver, BC, Canada
ACM 978-1-4503-3411-2/15/03.
http://dx.doi.org/10.1145/2724660.2728686

Abstract
Video games have great potential to motivate students in environments for learning at scale. However, little is known about how to design in-game incentive structures to maximize learning and engagement. In this work, we expand on our previous research that introduced a new "brain points" incentive structure designed to promote the growth mindset, or the belief that intelligence is malleable. We replicate our original findings, showing that brain points increase student persistence and use of strategy. We also explore how brain points impact students from different demographic groups. We find that brain points are less engaging for low-income students, and discuss methods of improving our design in the future.

Author Keywords
Educational games; growth mindset; incentive structures

ACM Classification Keywords
H.5.0 [Information Interfaces and Presentation]: General

Introduction
Video games are widely recognized for their ability to motivate players to perform complex tasks. As a result, there is a growing interest in using games to engage students in educational settings [5]. Student motivation is especially important in the context of learning at scale.

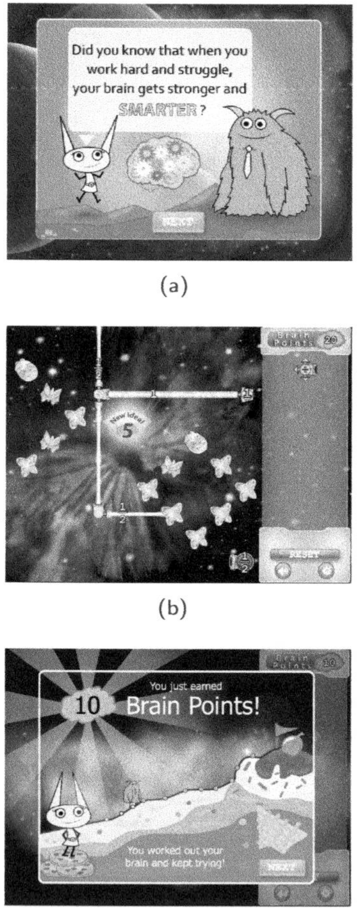

(a)

(b)

(c)

Figure 1: Screenshots of the brain points version of *Refraction*. Figure (a) shows the introductory animation, (b) shows brain points being earned, and (c) shows a brain points summary screen.

Studies show that the student-teacher relationship, and particularly the teacher's perceived physical and psychological closeness with students, can have a strong impact on motivation in the classroom [3]. In environments where there are thousands of students for every teacher, it is not possible to provide this type of interpersonal motivation. Educational games could be leveraged to help motivate students in these settings.

While educational games have potential, little is known about how to design in-game incentives to maximize learning and engagement. In previous work, we explored the impact of fundamentally changing game incentives to reward behaviors associated with the growth mindset [7]. Psychology research shows that praise can have varying effects on motivation [6]. Praising a student's inherent ability promotes the fixed mindset, or the belief that intelligence is unchangeable, while praising a student's strategies and effort promotes the growth mindset, or the belief that intelligence is malleable [6]. These mindsets can have a strong impact on students' motivation, reaction to failure, and academic achievement [2].

This research inspired us to explore whether rewarding behaviors associated with the growth mindset would increase student motivation and performance in an educational game. We created a "brain points" incentive structure for the game *Refraction* that rewards students for their effort, use of strategy, and incremental progress. Screenshots of the intervention are shown in Figure 1. In an online study of 15,000 students, we found that brain points produced higher student persistence and use of strategy compared to a standard incentive structure [7].

Encouraged by these results, we are continuing to study the impact of rewarding growth mindset behaviors in games. Our current work studies the effectiveness of the brain points version of *Refraction* in a new environment: the online schooling website K12.com. Our collaboration with K12 provides us with access to students who play for much longer than students on the casual website BrainPOP.com, where we conducted our initial study. Furthermore, K12 provides demographic data for their students. Growth mindset interventions have been shown to have a particularly strong effect on traditionally underperforming groups [1, 2], so we were interested in measuring whether our intervention has a similar effect.

Study Design

We conducted our study on the online schooling website K12.com. K12 is a for-profit company that provides curriculum content for online public schools as well as for home-schooled students. K12 was interested incorporating educational games into their curriculum, so we partnered with them to release the games developed by our research group, the Center for Game Science, through their website. Links to the game *Refraction*, designed to teach fraction concepts, were provided under an "additional activities" heading in 64 different locations within the K12 curriculum for third, fourth, and fifth grade math.

Our K12 study has an identical design to the BrainPOP study described in [7]. It has a single between-subjects factor *intervention* with two levels: experiment or control. The experimental version of the game included an introductory animation that describes the growth mindset, and used the brain points incentive structure that rewards effort, use of strategy, and incremental progress. The control version included an introductory animation that presents a neutral message, and used a "level points" incentive structure that awards points for each completed level. We chose this incentive structure for the control because progress is commonly rewarded in games.

Cond.	Time (minutes)	Strategy (per minute)
Brain	14.7	2.9
Control	10.8	2.7

Table 1: The median time played and strategies used for students in the experimental (brain points) condition and the control (level points) condition.

Gender	Time (minutes)	Strategy (per minute)
M	19.3	3.0
F	12.5	2.8

Table 2: The median time played and strategies used for students of different genders.

Grade	Time (minutes)	Strategy (per minute)
3rd	24.3	2.7
4th	19.1	2.8
5th	16.1	3.0
6th	9.5	3.1

Table 3: The median time played and strategies used for students of different grades.

Free Lunch	Time (minutes)	Strategy (per minute)
Yes	12.8	2.7
No	19.1	3.0

Table 4: The median time played and strategies used for students of who were and were not eligible for free/reduced lunch.

Preliminary Results

We collected data from 7,940 students in between October 2013 and August 2014 (3,924 students in the experimental condition and 4,016 in the control). We report an analysis of two outcome measures. The first captures student persistence by measuring the amount of time played. The second captures use of strategies that are associated with the growth mindset by combining the four metrics used to award brain points, described in detail in [7]. We use non-parametric statistics in this analysis because our data is non-normally distributed.

First, we analyzed our data to determine the impact of the *intervention* factor. We found that students in the experimental condition were significantly more persistent (Z=6.81, p<0.0001) and exhibited significantly more growth mindset behaviors (Z=4.93, p<0.0001) than students in the control condition. Median values are given in Table 1. These results confirm the findings from our original study, showing that the brain points intervention promotes students' persistence and use of strategy.

Next, we analyzed the impact of student demographics. For this analysis, we only included students who reported demographic information to K12, a total of 2,024 players in the experimental condition and 2,064 in the control. We studied three demographic factors: *gender*, *grade*, and *free/reduced lunch status*. We were particularly interested in measuring interactions between the *intervention* factor and each demographic factor, so we performed a factorial analysis. Since our data was non-normally distributed, we applied the Aligned Rank Transform [4] procedure, which aligns and ranks non-parametric data so that a standard ANOVA model can be used to perform a factorial analysis. We used the ARTool program developed by Wobbrock et al. to align and rank our data [8].

The *gender* factor has two levels: male and female. We found that male students played for significantly longer than female students (F(1,4084)=42.74, p<0.0001), and that male students used significantly more growth mindset strategies than female students (F(1,4084)=56.41, p<0.0001). The median values for each metric by gender are given in Table 2. However, the *intervention*gender* interaction did not have a significant effect on either metric, showing that the brain points intervention was equally effective for students of both genders.

The *grade* factor has four levels: 3rd, 4th, 5th, and 6th grade. We found that younger students played for significantly longer (F(1,4084)=63.61, p<0.0001), but that older students used significantly more growth mindset strategies (F(1,4084)=37.9, p<0.0001). The median values are given in Table 3. While *intervention*grade* did not have a significant effect on either outcome measure, the results for the time played measure trend towards younger students being more positively impacted by the brain points intervention than older students (F(1,4084)=2.44, p=0.06). This suggests that the intervention may be more motivating for younger students.

The *free/reduced lunch status* factor has two levels: eligible for free and/or reduced lunch, and not eligible. Lower income students in the United States are eligible for free or reduced school lunch, and as a result lunch status is often used as a proxy measure for socioeconomic status. For this analysis, we grouped all students who were eligible for free and/or reduced lunch and compared them to those who were not eligible. We excluded students with an unknown lunch status. We found that eligible students play for significantly less time (F(1,3226)=43.70, p<0.0001) and use significantly fewer growth mindset strategies (F(1,3226)=59.47, p<0.0001) than students who are not eligible. The median values are given in Table 4. More importantly, while the *intervention*lunch status* interaction did not have an effect on strategy use, it did have a statistically significant effect on time played ($F(1,3226)=4.67$, $p=0.03$). The brain points intervention was more effective at engaging students of higher income and encouraging them to play for long periods of time.

Discussion

Our preliminary results replicate the findings from our first study [7], showing that our growth mindset intervention has a positive impact on student persistence and strategy use. However, we also found that it does not benefit all students equally. The intervention may be more engaging for younger students, and is less engaging for lower income students. While we hoped that brain points would have a stronger effect on female students, as has been measured for other growth mindset interventions [2], we found that it has the same effect on students of both genders.

These results may say more about *Refraction* than about the brain points incentive structure. The game itself may be less appealing to girls and lower income students, and the cartoony style of the game characters may be more engaging for younger students. However, it is also possible that the effects are caused in part by the design of the intervention. The growth mindset messages used in the game are all presented through text in the user interface, which might be less engaging for students who are weak readers. We are currently exploring whether presenting growth mindset messages using an audio voiceover improves the effectiveness of the intervention for lower income students. We are also working on integrating brain points into other educational games to determine whether these effects are primarily driven by the design of *Refraction* or the design of the brain points intervention.

Acknowledgements

This work was supported by the Office of Naval Research grant N00014-12-C-0158, the Bill and Melinda Gates Foundation grant OPP1031488, the Hewlett Foundation grant 2012-8161, Adobe, and Microsoft.

References

[1] Aronson, J., Fried, C. B., and Good, C. Reducing the Effects of Stereotype Threat on African American College Students by Shaping Theories of Intelligence. *Journal of Experimental Social Psychology 38* (2002).

[2] Blackwell, L. S., Trzesniewski, K. H., and Dweck, C. S. Implicit Theories of Intelligence Predict Achievement Across an Adolescent Transition: A Longitudinal Study and an Intervention. *Child Development 78*, 1 (2007), 246–263.

[3] Christophel, D. M. The relationships among teacher immediacy behaviors, student motivation, and learning. *Communication education 39*, 4 (1990).

[4] Higgins, J. J., and Tashtoush, S. An aligned rank transform test for interaction. *Nonlinear World 1*, 2 (1994), 201–211.

[5] Mayo, M. J. Video Games: A Route to Large-Scale STEM Education? *Science 323* (2009), 79–82.

[6] Mueller, C. M., and Dweck, C. S. Praise for Intelligence Can Undermine Children's Motivation and Performance. *Journal of Personality and Social Psychology 75*, 1 (1998), 33–52.

[7] O'Rourke, E., Haimovitz, K., Ballweber, C., Dweck, C., and Popović, Z. Brain points: A growth mindset incentive structure boosts persistence in an educational game. In *CHI* (2014), 3339–3348.

[8] Wobbrock, J. O., Findlater, L., Gergle, D., and Higgins, J. J. The aligned rank transform for nonparametric factorial analyses using only anova procedures. In *CHI* (2011), 143–146.

Behavior Prediction in MOOCs using Higher Granularity Temporal Information

Cheng Ye
Vanderbilt University
Cheng.Ye@vanderbilt.edu

Douglas H. Fisher
Vanderbilt University
douglas.h.fisher@vanderbilt.edu

John S. Kinnebrew
Vanderbilt University
john.s.kinnebrew@vanderbilt.edu

Gayathri Narasimham
Vanderbilt University
gayathri.narasimham@vanderbilt.edu

Gautam Biswas
Vanderbilt University
gautam.biswas@vanderbilt.edu

Katherine A. Brady
Vanderbilt University
katherine.a.brady@vanderbilt.edu

Brent J. Evans
Vanderbilt University
b.evans@vanderbilt.edu

L@S 2015, Mar 14-18, 2015, Vancouver, BC, Canada
ACM 978-1-4503-3411-2/15/03.
http://dx.doi.org/10.1145/2724660.2728687

Abstract

In this paper, we present early research evaluating the predictive power of a variety of temporal features across student subpopulations with distinctive behaviors at the beginning of the course. Initial results illustrate that these features predict important differences across the subpopulations and over time in the courses. Ultimately, these results have implications for effectively targeting adaptive scaffolding tailored to the particular intentions and goals of subpopulations in MOOCs.

Author Keywords
MOOCs, Behavior Prediction, Machine Learning

Introduction

The popularity and large initial enrollments in Massive Online Open Courses (MOOCs), driven by their wide accessibility, relative openness, and the reputation of the instructors and institutions offering these courses, has created significant interest in analyzing students' learning behaviors in these systems. However, a common pattern across the spectrum of MOOCs has been the large number of no-shows, early dropouts, and the generally low completion rates [2]. However, a certificate of completion may not be the goal of many students taking a MOOC. Rather, a variety of distinct MOOC subpopulations have been identified by their behavior [1, 4].

The common trend of low completion rates and the recognition of subpopulations with different behavior trends in MOOCs suggests an overall research question that motivates the analysis and initial results presented in this paper: *What behavior features are useful for accurate early prediction of student dropout and performance in different MOOC subpopulations?* In the longer term, our hope is that early dropout predictions tailored to specific subpopulations will provide a framework for targeting adaptive scaffolding mechanisms in MOOCs that could provide individualized guidance and small group support for achieving a variety of goals.

A number of researchers have explored factors related to low completion rates and dropout prediction in MOOCs. For example, Halawa *et al.* [3] attempted to predict dropout with a variety of lecture-viewing behavior features; specifically they looked at: video-skip, assignment-skip, lag (e.g., whether the student was viewing week 1 videos after week 3 videos had been released), and assignment performance. In this paper, we use similar lecture behavior features to those in [3] (e.g., number of lecture video views for current and previous weeks) as part of a baseline feature set, but show that the introduction of finer-grained and temporal features boosts early predictive performance in certain subpopulations.

Methodology, Tools, and Data

In this paper, we present initial results from the analysis of two MOOCs offered on the Coursera platform. These courses have an overall structure common to many MOOCs, including a series of short video lectures released on a weekly basis, weekly multiple-choice quizzes that are related to the lecture materials, and larger peer-graded assignments. However, in order to provide a preliminary evaluation of the generality of our approach and analysis, we chose courses from two different domains: a course on principles in a programming domain and a course on data management and administration in the clinical research domain.

The first course, "Pattern-Oriented Software Architectures for Concurrent and Networked Software" (POSA), is a ten-week Coursera MOOC covering programming principles for networking and other software dealing with concurrent operations. The second course, "Data Management for Clinical Research" (DM), is a seven-week Coursera MOOC focused on (clinical) research data collection and management. Both courses offered certificates of completion and distinction based on weekly quizzes and peer-graded assignments.

Initial analysis of student behavior in the first week of the course suggested two distinct subpopulations among the "active" students who at least watched a lecture in week 1: (1) students who watched at least one lecture in week 1 in each MOOC but did not take the quiz, *i.e.*, the *lecture only* group; and (2) students who watched at least one lecture and took the summative multiple-choice quiz that week, *i.e.*, the *lecture and quiz* group. Analyzing students' subsequent behavior with respect to lecture-watching and quiz-taking, indicated that most students in the lecture-and-quiz group continued watching lectures and taking the weekly quizzes (unless they dropped out of the course), and most students in the lecture-only group continued watching most lectures but not taking quizzes (unless they dropped out of the course).

The specific categories of features we defined for this analysis were:
Baseline lecture quantity features provide a baseline for lecture-watching features that are defined by the combinations along 3 dimensions: (1) aggregation (total

number of lecture accesses or number of unique lectures accessed), (2) access type (viewing online or downloading), and (3) course segment (grouping lectures by whether they are designated for previous weeks, the current week, or subsequent weeks), resulting in individual features, such as "total number of lectures designated for the current week that were viewed online".

Lecture temporal features are aggregated across the current week's lectures accessed by the student: (1) average first access time of lectures (as the offset between the time the lecture became available and the time the student first accessed the lecture), (2) average first lecture-embedded quiz answer time (as the offset between the time the lecture became available and the time the student first answered an embedded quiz question in the lecture), and (3) difference between average first lecture-embedded quiz answer time for the current week versus the previous week.

Lecture-quiz quantity features describe the frequency of lecture-watching activity with respect to answering lecture-embedded quiz questions: (1) the total number of lecture-embedded quiz questions answered, (2) average number of times a lecture was accessed before the first lecture-embedded quiz question was answered, and (3) average number of times the lecture was accessed after the first lecture-embedded quiz question was answered.

In order to evaluate the predictive potential of different feature sets early in the MOOCs, we assigned one of four labels to each student in the course that indicated whether they ultimately dropped out in week 1, week 2, week 3, or not dropped out by the end of week 3 (i.e., the student dropped out in a later week or continued through the end of the course). We used a soft threshold for dropout, identifying a student as having dropped out in a given week if they accessed fewer than 10% of the remaining lectures in the course and performed no further assessment activities (i.e., summative weekly quizzes or submission of peer-graded assignments). Random forests were used for classification as they consistently performed better than, or on par with, other classifiers (logistic regression, support vector machines, and decision trees) tested in preliminary analysis.

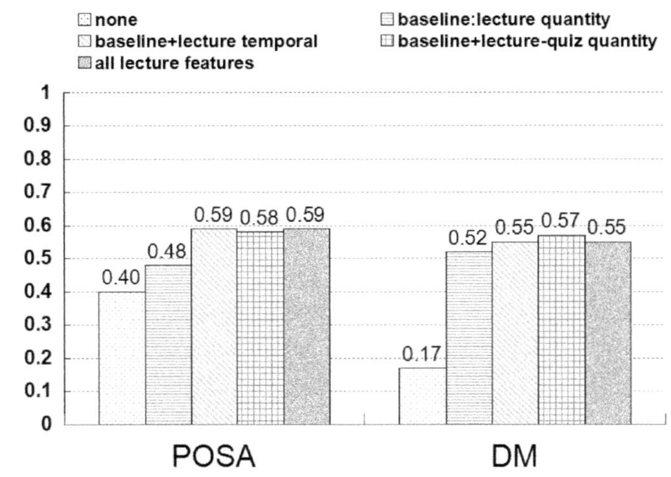

Figure 1: Dropout prediction F1 score in lecture-only group

Results

To better understand how useful these features were in early dropout prediction across different subpopulations, Figures 1 and 2 show the results of this analysis applied separately to the lecture-only and the lecture-and-quiz groups. In the lecture-only group, the addition of either *lecture temporal* or *lecture-quiz quantity* features improved predictive performance over the baseline, however, little or no additional predictive power appears to be gained by using both additional feature sets. This suggests that while temporal lecture-access patterns and lecture-quiz patterns may each be used for prediction, the underlying factors likely to result in dropout may tend to manifest in *both* the timing of lecture-watching activities and the quantity of lecture-embedded question answering.

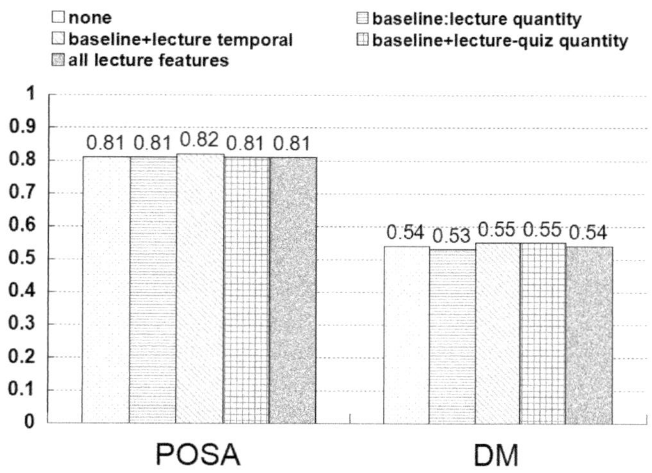

Figure 2: Dropout prediction F1 score in lecture-and-quiz group

Discussion and Conclusion

Initial results suggest that in the lecture-only subpopulation, sufficiently fine-grained lecture behavior features could be very useful in targeting immediate scaffolding for students who are dis-engaging with the course as early as the first week. However, all lecture behavior features analyzed were of little to no use in early prediction of dropout for the lecture-and-quiz subpopulation. Overall, the results illustrate the importance of identifying and analyzing different subpopulations for targeting scaffolding in the diverse populations of MOOCs.

In future work, we will extend these results by identifying specific rules based on the presented and further fine-grained behavior features to predict dropout in different subpopulations. We will improve the definition of subpopulations by running unsupervised learning methods on the extended feature sets to determine finer-grained groups that provide contextual information for developing specific scaffolds. In addition to helping us better understand which specific behaviors relate to dropout and performance, this will be vital for targeting adaptive scaffolding to support students. In the longer term, we hope to employ refined versions of these predictive models to identify students for targeted scaffolding in a variety of subpopulations to support them in achieving their individual objectives in taking a MOOC.

References

[1] Breslow, L., Pritchard, D. E., DeBoer, J., Stump, G. S., Ho, A. D., and Seaton, D. Studying learning in the worldwide classroom: Research into edxs first mooc. *Research & Practice in Assessment 8* (2013), 13–25.

[2] Clow, D. Moocs and the funnel of participation. In *Proceedings of the Third International Conference on Learning Analytics and Knowledge*, ACM (2013), 185–189.

[3] Halawa, S., Greene, D., and Mitchell, J. Dropout prediction in moocs using learner activity features. In *Proceedings of the European MOOC Summit (EMOOCs 2014)* (Lausanne, Switzerland, 2014).

[4] Kizilcec, R. F., Piech, C., and Schneider, E. Deconstructing disengagement: analyzing learner subpopulations in massive open online courses. In *Proceedings of the third international conference on learning analytics and knowledge*, ACM (2013), 170–179.

Analysis of a Large-scale Formative Writing Assessment System with Automated Feedback

Peter W. Foltz
Pearson and Univ. of Colorado
4940 Pearl East Circle,
Suite 200
Boulder, CO, 80301 USA
Peter.foltz@pearson.com

Mark Rosenstein
Pearson
4940 Pearl East Circle,
Suite 200
Boulder, CO, 80301 USA
Mark.rosenstein@pearson.com

L@S 2015, March 14–18, 2015, Vancouver, BC, Canada.
ACM 978-1-4503-3411-2/15/03.
http://dx.doi.org/10.1145/2724660.2728688.

Abstract
Formative writing systems with automated scoring provide opportunities for students to write, receive feedback, and then revise essays in a timely iterative cycle. This paper describes ongoing investigations of a formative writing tool through mining student data in order to understand how the system performs and to measure improvement in student writing. The sampled data included over 1.3M student essays written in response to approximately 200 pre-defined prompts as well as a log of all student actions and computer generated feedback. Analyses both measured and modeled changes in student performance over revisions, the effects of system responses and the amount of time students spent working on assignments. Implications are discussed for employing large-scale data analytics to improve educational outcomes, to understand the role of feedback in writing, to drive improvements in formative technology and to aid in designing better kinds of feedback and scaffolding to support students in the writing process.

Author Keywords
Data mining; student actions log analysis; automated writing evaluation; computer assisted instruction; machine learning; mixed effects models.

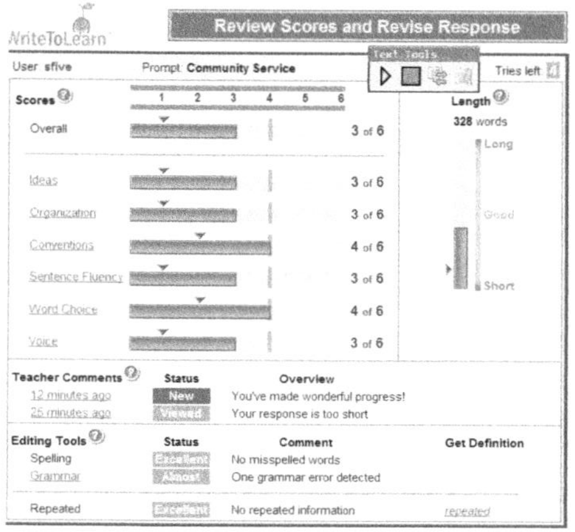

Figure 1. Student feedback screen from WritetoLearn

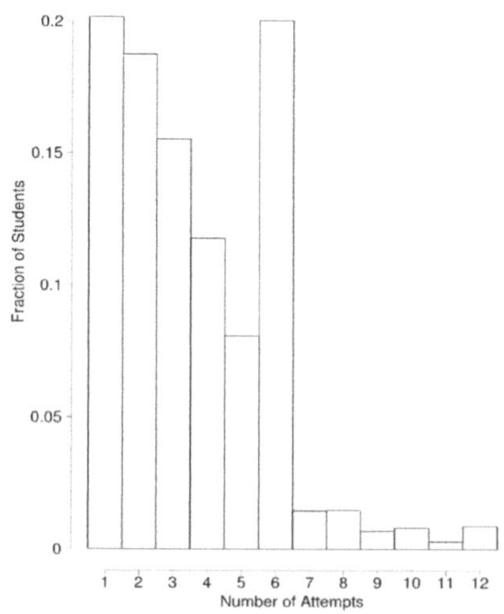

Figure 2. Number of attempts (revisions made by students)

Introduction

Automated scoring of writing, or Automated Essay Scoring (AES), provides the ability to analyze student writing and provide scores and feedback instantly. Studies of AES systems have shown that the scoring of such systems can be as accurate as human scorers (e.g., [1, 2, 3, 4]), can score on multiple traits of writing (e.g., [4]), and can provide feedback on content [3]. While much of the focus in the evaluation of AES has examined the accuracy of the scoring and the different types of essays that can be scored, AES has wide applicability to formative writing, where evaluation can focus on how it aids student learning. By providing instantaneous feedback to students, AES supports the teaching of writing strategies based on detecting the types of difficulties students encounter.

In a formative writing assessment system, all student writing is performed electronically, automatically scored and recorded. Thus, there is a record of all the student actions and all feedback they received. This archive permits continuous monitoring of performance changes in individuals as well as across larger groups of students, such as classes or schools. Teachers can analyze the progress of each student in a class and intervene when needed. In addition it now becomes possible to chart progress across the class in order to measure curricula and teaching effectiveness as reflected in student writing performance scores.

Automated formative assessment of writing provides a rich data set to examine the changes in writing performance and system features that influence that performance. The goal of the present work is to analyze how changes in student writing performance are influenced by features of the system and identify features that promote improvement. We describe instances of applying data mining to components of the formative writing process to investigate specific classes of questions about how a formative system is currently being used, its efficacy, and how understanding current use yields suggestions on ways to improve learning, both through improving the system implementation and by introducing direct interventions aimed at the student during their use of the system.

Method

The formative writing assessment system used for the analyses was WriteToLearn™, a web-based writing environment that provides students with exercises to write responses to narrative, expository, descriptive, and persuasive prompts (see Figure 1). Students use the software as an iterative writing tool in which they write, receive feedback and then revise and resubmit their improved essays. The automated feedback provides an overall score and individual trait scores for aspects of the writing such as "ideas, organization, conventions, word choice, and sentence fluency". Evaluations of WriteToLearn have shown significantly better reading comprehension and writing skill resulting from two weeks of use as well as validating the system scores being as reliable as human raters.

Data

The data comprised two large samples of student interactions with WriteToLearn collected from U.S. adoptions of the software. One set comprised approximately 1.3 million essays from 360,000 assignments written by 94,000 students collected over a 4 year period. The second set represented approximately 62,000 student sessions with nearly 900,000 actions. The data consisted of student essays

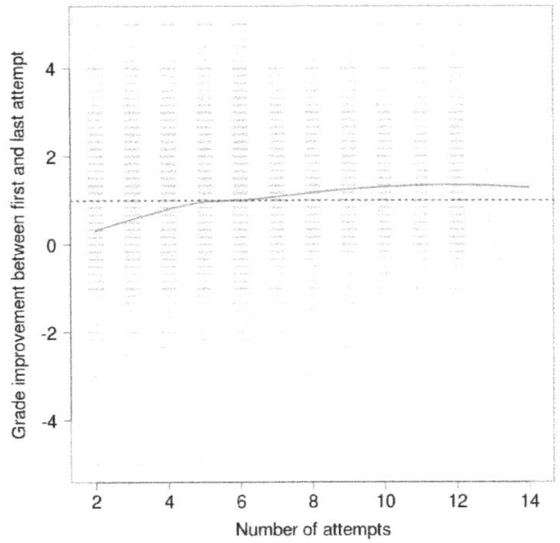

Figure 3. Change in student grade based on number of revisions

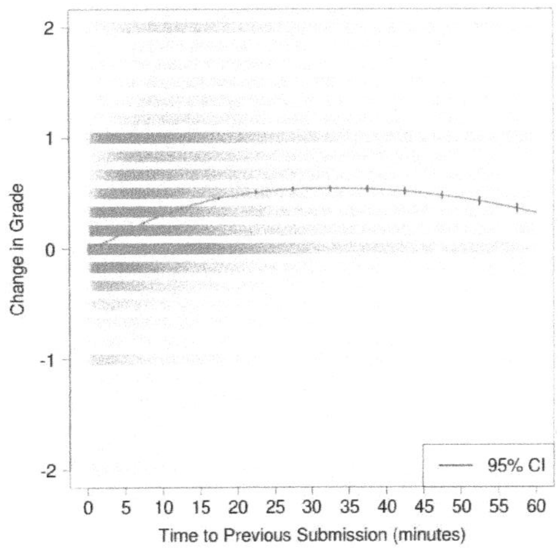

Figure 4. Change in student grade based on time spent between revisions

and a time-stamped log of all student actions, revisions and feedback given by the system. Essays were recorded each time a student submitted or saved an essay, resulting in a record of each draft submitted. The essays were written to approximately 200 pre-defined prompts. No human scoring was performed on these essays. All essay scores were generated by automated scoring, with the prediction performance of the models validated against human agreement from test sets or using a jack-knife procedure.

Results

Number of revisions made by students per prompt
WriteToLearn is designed to support a rapid cycle of write, submit, receive feedback and revise. This cycle is one of the key differentiators of automated formative writing from standard classroom writing practice, where human scoring of essays is time consuming so students can not receive immediate feedback. Thus, it is critical to determine how often students submit and revise essays and determine the factors and time paths that lead to greatest success. Figure 2 shows the distribution of submissions made by students per writing prompt. The distribution shows that nearly equal proportions of students submit a single attempt as submit the default six submissions (approximately 20%). These results indicate that students are taking advantage of revising essays and resubmitting for feedback.

While we see evidence that students are revising their essays, it is important to know whether the revisions result in improved essay quality. Thus, we examined the impact of number of attempts on student performance. In Figure 3 the gray dots show the difference in score between the last and first attempt for an individual student, with essay scores on a six point scale. The red line shows a locally weighted regression curve of the data, indicating about a one score point improvement with 5 or 6 attempts.

Time spent between revisions
We can further investigate the impact on student performance of the time spent writing before requesting feedback (the best allocation of time among the write, submit, feedback, and revise phases). The change in grade shown in Figure 4 indicates that the improvement in writing score generally increases up to about 25 minutes at which point it levels off and begins to drop. We further see that most of the negative change (essays receiving a lower score than the previous version) occurs with revisions of less than five minutes. The results suggest that there is an optimal range of time to spend revising before requesting additional feedback.

Session Analysis – Student Actions
The results above show that students do revise their essays and the time pattern of essay revision suggests that the greatest improvement in writing follows when one revision to the next occurs between 15 to 25 minutes. What the results don't indicate is which actions the students are taking between submissions, and what patterns of actions best improve their writing in those intervals. Thus, we examine performance at the level of actions taken by students within a session.

Actions in the session can include such tasks as logging in/out, submitting an essay for assessment, performing spell or grammar checks, requesting additional formative information about writing (such as examining scoring rubrics, investigating how to improve writing on

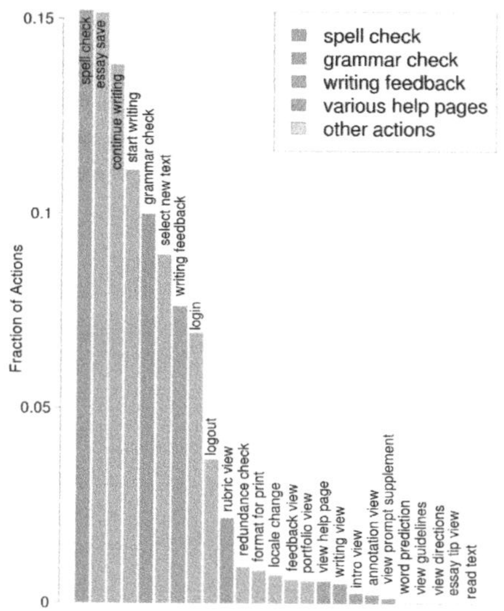

Figure 5. Proportion of student actions taken during writing sessions

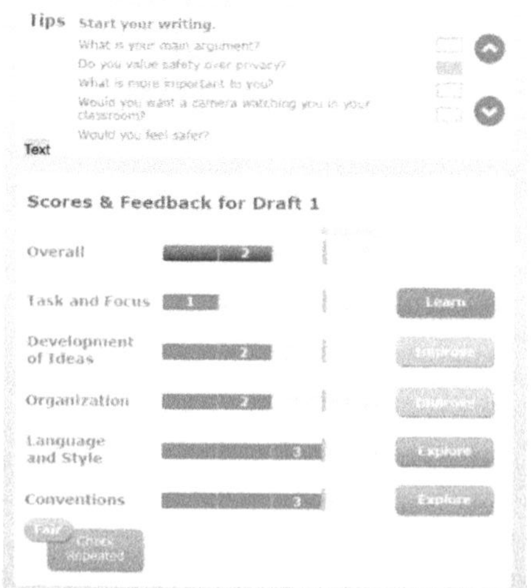

Figure 6. Revised user interface to provide more student writing guidance

different traits, etc.). While there were a median of 15 actions per session, the relative frequency of types of actions performed allows us some insight into the use of features and are shown in Figure 5.

Approximately 15% of the actions were spell check and another 15% were saving the essay (as backup). What is quite noticeable is that almost all the infrequently used actions are various types of request for guidance, such as providing information on the scoring rubric, and suggestions on ways to improve their writing on different writing traits. This suggests that these features needed to be better integrated and made more readily available or automatically provided to students when their need is detected.

Revision of the user interface

Based on the log file analysis, usability results, as well as feedback from customers, a revised user interface was developed which provides additional student feedback and guidance (see Figure 6) Ongoing research is now analyzing how the new interface changes student behavior and performance compared to the original interface.

Conclusions

Large-scale implementations of formative writing provide rich sets of data for analysis of performance and effects of feedback. Automated scoring of writing allows monitoring of student learning as students write and revise essays within these implementations. By examining the log of student actions, the amount of time taken, and the changes in the essays, one can monitor the quality of the students' writing. In assessing writing, the focus has often been put on the product (e.g., the final essay). The analysis of over 1.3M student draft submissions, makes it possible to track the process the learners take to create the product. This analysis allows interventions to be performed on the process of writing rather than just the product. This study further illustrates how data mining can provide new ways of thinking about collecting evidence of system and student performance and uncover patterns that may not be apparent from watching individual students or classrooms.

The overall findings validate a key tenet of formative writing; students improve with revisions and based on feedback from the system. The approach allows examining the changes in learning and the effects of the feedback on writing performance. The data further permits us to discover, prioritize and address concerns as they arise and determine which changes are most likely to improve the students' experience and their ability to sharpen their writing skills.

References

[1] Burstein, J., Chodorow, M., & Leacock, C. (2004). Automated essay evaluation: The Criterion Online writing service. *AI Magazine, 25*(3), 27-36.

[2] Foltz, P. W., Streeter, L. A., Lochbaum, K. E., & Landauer, T. K (2013). Implementation and applications of the Intelligent Essay Assessor. *Handbook of Automated Essay Evaluation*, M. Shermis & J. Burstein, (Eds.). Pp. 68-88. Routledge, NY. NY

[3] Landauer, T. K, Laham, D. & Foltz, P. W. (2001). Automated essay scoring. *IEEE Intelligent Systems.* September/October

[4] Shermis, M. and Hamner. B. (2012). Contrasting state-of-the-art automated scoring of essays: Analysis. In *Paper presented at Annual Meeting of the National Council on Measurement in Education*, Vancouver, Canada, April.

Designing MOOCs as Interactive Places for Collaborative Learning

Saijing Zheng
The Pennsylvania State University, University Park, PA.
suz128@ist.psu.edu

Patrick C. Shih
The Pennsylvania State University, University Park, PA.
patshih@ist.psu.edu

Mary Beth Rosson
The Pennsylvania State University, University Park, PA.
mrosson8@ist.psu.edu

John M. Carroll
The Pennsylvania State University, University Park, PA.
carroll@ist.psu.edu

Abstract
The Massive Open Online Course (MOOC) paradigm has developed rapidly and achieved significant attention from a broad range of populations. However, many people who enroll in MOOCs do not have successful learning experiences. For example, some studies suggest that the relatively weak feelings of community and meager opportunities for collaboration may be contributing to a high dropout rate in MOOCs. In light of such problems, we are exploring new design features that could support enhanced social interactions, collaborative learning and feelings of community. We present our design ideas through a set of activity design scenarios, along with an analysis of possible benefits and negative consequences of our design.

L@S 2015, Mar 14-18, 2015, Vancouver, BC, Canada
ACM 978-1-4503-3411-2/15/03.
http://dx.doi.org/10.1145/2724660.2728689

Find a Good Place to Learn
Jenny wants to register for a machine learning course on Coursera. She doesn't know anyone else taking the course but is hoping she might meet a few people who are also trying to learn this new topic. She is very curious about machine learning but also is a bit concerned about the challenges she might encounter. When she clicks "enter the course", she lands on a webpage. At the top it says: "Supplying the requested information will help us to find you a comfortable classroom for you. You can also choose a classroom by yourself". She is invited to choose a location on a map and selects her hometown "State College". When asked about language preferences, she chooses English. After that, she indicates that her learning goal is to "Get a Certificate". When she submits her information she lands in something called a "classroom." After exploring the information associated with other learners in the room, she fines that most are in her time zone with her, speak English and want to get certificates at the end of the machine learning course. Her location is East America Classroom 6.

Figure 1. Scenario 1.

Author Keywords
MOOCs; online learning; Scenario-Based Design; sub-networks; space and place; collaborative learning.

ACM Classification Keywords
H.5.3 Group and Organization Interfaces

Introduction
This Massive Open Online Courses (MOOCs) has developed rapidly and achieved extensive attention from a broad range of populations. Recent work has shown that people joining MOOCs have diverse motivations, which lead to a variety of learning behaviors and innovative uses of MOOCs [8]. Thus, the online courses should no longer be viewed simply as a means of disseminating educational materials, but rather as a *virtual organization* where people learn individually and collaboratively, make friends, exchange learning insights, and interact with people who come from different countries and disciplines.

However, current MOOCs platforms are limited to playing videos, sending announcement, and hosting a generic discussion forum; there is little support for

Find a Place to Learn with Friends
James and his friends Mike and Jake want to take a machine learning course together, and they plan to go online together as much as possible. When James clicks "enter the course", he jumps into a webpage. At the top it says: "Supplying the requested information will help us to find you a comfortable classroom for you. You can also choose a classroom by yourself". James decides to find his own classroom; he will then tell Mike and Jake where they can meet up. He first tells the system where he lives; after this he is shown a list of classrooms in his time zone. The classrooms are divided into two types: Auditing classrooms and Certificate classrooms. He chooses a classroom in the Certificate group because he and his friends want to take this course following schedules and get a certificate at the end. He is told that the classroom has 30 seats still available, more than enough for the three of them. Once he is settled in East America Classroom 6 he tells Mike and Jack to choose the same when they register. They will meet up in that room and learn together.

Figure 2. Scenario 2.

social activities. Studies in MOOCs have identified the lack of a sense of community and ineffective social interactions and collaboration contribute to the high dropout rate in MOOCs [8]. MOOC instructors and researchers also have been active in proposing ideas and design plans to better fulfill those needs [4].

In light of the increasing needs for MOOCs redesign, draw from successful applications of computer mediated communication systems (CMC) and from examples of large successful online communities (e.g., Massively Multiplayer Online Games (MMOGs)) to frame our preliminary design arguments. We present these design ideas through a set of activity design scenarios, along with an analysis of possible benefits and negative consequences of our design. Our aim is to help MOOC designers achieve the potential positive consequences in our design analysis, while alleviating or avoiding the downsides or negative tradeoffs.

Challenges in MOOCs

Based on MOOCs studies and observations, we have identified three major problems of MOOC platforms:

- Lack of community building mechanisms: it was hard to find and know their MOOC peers because there were no community awareness features (e.g., roster information, real time status update on who and how many students are online at a given time, etc.)[8].
- Lack of interpersonal communication mechanisms: MOOC forum suffers from information overload. Numerous discussions flood into forum and quickly become infeasible for anyone to navigate and find relevant information. Thus, it is hard to have meaningful and in-depth discussions in forums.
- Lack of collaborative work features: Learning with peers is an essential form of learning, and many MOOCs require students to do group projects. However, there are no built-in features to support student collaborations on projects.

Learning From CMC and Online Community

Sub-Networks

A body of research points to the significant role played by sub-networks in building community [3]. Students in MOOCs vary widely in their background, value systems, and personal objectives. If sub-grouping can be enabled, the diversity within the population might coalesce, emerge, shape and contribute to the richness and tenacity of the larger community. Subgroups offer opportunities for smaller-scale activities, such as idea sharing, brainstorming, identity formation, and in-depth discussion, which in turn benefit the larger community. Membership across groups will ultimately strengthen the overall community. Thus, we would suggest a design for MOOCs that supports social interaction and collaboration through a sub-network structure.

Space and Place

Harrison and Dourish [7] articulate the important interplay between "space" and "place" in CMC. CSCW researchers have proposed using "place-making" or a "sense of space" to foster social interaction in online places. The basic idea in these applications of spatial metaphors is that, in collaborative settings designers can exploit our familiarity with the spatial organization of our everyday physical environments [7]. We propose that a spatial metaphor can be applied to partition course-related activities, where feelings of place can be encouraged through appropriate segmentation of the students into sub-networks. Our overall idea is to apply this metaphor to construct MOOC sub-networks that

Join a Group and Get to Know Them

There is still one week before the course officially begins. James checks into the MOOC and see that their classroom has more classmates now; it's almost full with 96 learners (Maximum capacity is 100). He and his classmates introduce themselves on the classroom-level discussion board. He sees an announcement from the instructor encouraging them to form groups of 4-6 students. James posts an advertisement that his group still needs at least one more team member. Jenny sees the post and asks to join this group. James happily accepts her as a team member. Thereafter, James, his friends and Jenny are in a group that they name "State Collegiates". They find that they can chat and discuss questions in a private chat room. Jenny is delighted because she now has three other team members. She is not alone anymore.

Figure 3. Scenario 3.

can build a sense of community and further encourage and support social interactions and collaborations.

Social Interaction and Community in MMOGs

Massively Multiplayer Online Games (MMOGs) (i.e. World of War Craft), as the long and successful history of large online gaming communities, use the concepts of space and place to engage and foster a strong sense of community, social interaction, and collaboration among large groups of gamers. They are useful for thinking about MOOC design for several reasons 1) both are large in scale; 2) similar to MOOC students, MMOG players exhibit wide-ranging differences in motivations and usage patterns [6]; 3) MMOG players display different kinds of sociality as MOOCs: players may join for individual play or as a cohort with their friends [6].

After reviewing literature of MMOGs (i.e. [5]), we find several features of online games promoting effective social interaction: (1) use space and place to segment the game's large subscriber base into more manageable units; (2) define and advertise communication places where gamers can gather together; and (3) include communication tools for sharing ideas and opinions. Reasoning by analogy, we might design a similar spatially defined sub-grouping mechanism, shared places and communication tools for MOOC learners. With these lessons in mind, we turn next to a scenario-based presentation of a new MOOC design.

Scenario-Based Design of Group creation and collaboration in MOOCs

Scenarios are a helpful medium for envisioning and analyzing novel technology usages, particularly when constructed within a user experience design process [2]. Figure 1, 2, 3, and 4 present our four scenarios that convey some aspects of what learners might experience in a MOOC that enables and leverages sub-groups, as well as places and tools for collaboration.

Scenario Rationale

After presenting the design scenarios, we analyze the scenarios for the design rationale behind them, generating a systematic explanation of *why* such design features should be considered and why those features result in the consequences illustrated by the scenarios and their variants. These explanations are called "claims" including upsides (denoted as "+") and downsides (denoted as "-") associated with design features that have been embedded in a usage context. The rationale is guided by research findings in HCI as well as theories of learning and human behavior.

Using time zone as a first-order criterion to segment a large population of learners...

+ Suggests that users think of their learning activities as happening in a "space"

+ Simplifies the time-based constraints of interacting with others in real time

- But learners may be less likely to meet up with interesting peers in a different time zone

- But time zones may not map to reasonably sized sub-networks

Using a metaphorical classroom as a second-order feature in sub-group formation...

+ Can be visualized to suggest a "meeting place" for learners to meet up and interact online

+ May encourage learners to apply their pre-existing "classroom behavior", helping to cultivate a sense of shared values and norms

Engage with a Group in Course Discussion

The course has reached the third week and the material is becoming quite challenging. James and the other State Collegiates have many discussions regarding the topic. They begin a practice of setting a time to watch the lecture together so that they can raise and discuss questions as they come up. But the topic of week is quite hard, and they still have a detailed question after their team discussion. So Jenny copies their question to the classroom-level discussion board. The question quickly attracts attention from other classmates. They discuss together but are still not sure the answer. Eventually they decide to post the question to the all-course discussion forum in the hopes that someone will have suggestions.

Figure 4. Scenario 4.

- But some learners may over-apply the metaphor and expect too many details (e.g., desks, walls, doors)

Distinguishing classrooms by two types of learning motivation (audit or certificate)...

+ Classrooms will include different services for learners with different learning motivation and goals

+ Enhances coherence within classroom groups because people hold similar schedules and goals

- But some learners may not align with either "audit" or "certificate" as learning goals

Facilitating "private" interaction by small groups...

+ Encourages a significant degree of informal interaction and personal sharing

+ Enables efficient interaction over time as team members learn and appreciate their common ground

+ Construct small groups efficient and effective in a manageable sized environment—classroom

- But some small groups will be low in diversity, expertise, or some other team-building attributes

- But in a small group, it is likely that some questions will never be raised and others will never be answered

Enabling multiple levels of group discussion...

+ Suggests a natural "escalation" process for questions that are complex or important for the community

- But learners must now take on the task of choosing where to broadcast the question

- But a question that is raised at more than one level may lead to confusing or redundant partial answers that are difficult to synthesize and draw conclusions

Future Work

In future work, we will build prototypes and analyze MOOCs data in our college to explore the scenarios and tradeoffs in a more direct fashion. For instance, we will instantiate and evaluate different options for students to enroll and join a classroom, so that we can see whether the time zone and course motivations are a meaningful and sufficient sub-grouping mechanism, and how important it is for students to control their own class assignment process.

References

[1] Brinton, C. G., Chiang, M., Jain, S., Lam, H., Liu, Z., & Wong, F. M. F. (2013). Learning about social learning in moocs: From statistical analysis to generative model. arXiv preprint arXiv:1312.2159.4

[2] Carroll, J.M., 1995. Scenario-based Design: Envisioning Work and Technology in System Development. Wiley, New York.5

[3] Carroll, J.M. (2012). The Neighborhood in the Internet: Design Research Projects in Community Informatics. Rutledge.8

[4] Coetzee, D., Fox, A., Hearst, M. A., & Hartmann, B. (2014). Should your MOOC forum use a reputation system?. In Proc. CSCW 2014 (pp1176-1187).12

[5] Choi, D. and Kim.J (2004) Why People Continue to Play Online Games: In Search of Critical Design Factors to Increase Customer Loyalty to Online Contents, Cyberpsychology & Behavior Vol 7, Number 1, 2004

[6] Ducheneaut, N., & Moore, R. J. (2004). The social side of gaming: a study of interaction patterns in a massively multiplayer online game. In Proc. CSCW 2004 (pp. 360-369). 17

[7] Harrison, S. & Dourish, P. 1996. Re-Place-ing space: The roles of place and space in collaborative systems. CSCW'96, 67-76. New York: ACM.22

[8] Zheng, S., Rosson, M., Patrick, S., and Carroll, J. M., Understanding Student Motivation, Behaviors and Perceptions in MOOCs, In Proc. CSCW 2015.49

Toward the Evaluation of Educational Videos using Bayesian Knowledge Tracing and Big Data

Zachary MacHardy
UC Berkeley
354 Hearst Memorial Mining Building
Berkeley, CA 94720
zmmachar@cs.berkeley.edu

Zachary A. Pardos
UC Berkeley
4641 Tolman Hall
Berkeley, CA 94720-1670
zp@berkeley.edu

L@S 2015, March 14–18, 2015, Vancouver, BC, Canada.
ACM 978-1-4503-3411-2/15/03.
http://dx.doi.org/10.1145/2724660.2728690

Abstract
Along with the advent of MOOCs and other online learning platforms such as Khan Academy, the role of online education has continued to grow in relation to that of traditional on-campus instruction. Rather than tackle the problem of evaluating large educational units such as entire online courses, this paper approaches a smaller problem: exploring a framework for evaluating more granular educational units, in this case, short educational videos. We have chosen to leverage an adaptation of traditional Bayesian Knowledge Tracing (BKT), intended to incorporate the usage of video content in addition to assessment activity. By exploring the change in predictive error when alternately including or omitting video activity, we suggest a metric for determining the relevance of videos to associated assessments. To validate our hypothesis and demonstrate the application of our proposed methods we use data obtained from the popular Khan Academy website.

Author Keywords
knowledge tracing, educational videos, instructional technology, bayesian inference, online education

ACM Classification Keywords
K.3.1 [Computer Uses in Education]: Computer-assisted instruction (CAI).

Introduction
The design of curricular materials has been described as a process of iterative refinement[4] and, as with any design process, in order to refine curricular materials there must be metrics by which to evaluate them. Research on how best to evaluate and improve online education is not new[1, 7] but there remain many distinct approaches to accomplishing this goal [5]. In order to address the need for scalable and reproduceable evaluation, we hypothesize that by relating the use of materials and performance on subsequent assessment items, we can construct a metric to evaluate the relevance of those videos, without needing to resort to comparative studies.

In order to model student interactions with educational material and improvement over time, we have chosen to use an adaptation of Bayesian Knowledge Tracing (BKT), a technique developed and used in conjunction with Intelligent Tutoring Systems (ITS) but which has been applied outside of that domain as well (e.g. [6]). Here we seek to incorporate student behavior, such as video observation, which falls beyond the purview of attempting assessment items. We contrast this extended model with a simpler one excluding resource usage in order to discover whether videos contribute to model accuracy, and if some models benefit more than others.

Data
The data we obtained from Khan Academy contains 1,044,930 problem attempts and 3,797,676 video observation events collected over about two years, from June 2012 to February 2014. Assessment items are categorized hierarchically as part of a larger exercise representing a particular skill, and further as a member of a problem type, describing the template used to generate a specific problem. Though more complex approaches to discovering the concepts which underlie educational content have been described [3], for the sake of simplicity we have chosen to consider each exercise as a separate knowledge component (KC) for the purposes of training BKT models. After filtering out unassociated videos and exercises that were associated with fewer than 500 events, 353,202 events remained, representing work within 193 distinct exercises and 353,202 distinct student-exercise pairings. Of the 193 exercises, 176 (91%) were associated with video observations, with around 10% of all events being video viewings. Each exercise was associated on average with 1,803 events.

Methods
Bayesian Knowledge Tracing [2] is used extensively in computer-assisted instruction environments, intended to approximate mastery learning. More specifically, it is a means of predicting when a student has acquired a skill (or KC) associated with a set of assessment items, in order to ensure that a student has attained proficiency before moving on to the next subject. The model in its most basic form is defined by four parameters: $P(L_0)$, the prior probability that a student has mastered a KC; $P(S)$, the probability a student who knows a concept will get an associated question wrong, or slip; $P(G)$, the probability that a student who does not know a concept will correctly guess the correct answer; and $P(T)$ the probability that a student who does not know a particular KC will learn it after a given observation. Though this model describes the fundamentals of BKT, we employ several extensions for evaluative purposes. First, for all models, we condition $P(G)$ and $P(S)$ for each observation on which template is being observed, to model varying template difficulty. Second, we similarly condition the transition probability $P(T)$ on the observed template, generating a second distinct but still video-free Template model. Third, we

incorporate video observations, conditioning $P(T)$ either on the specific template observed or the specific video, generating the Template-Videos model. Finally, we simplify the Template-Videos into a Template-1-Video model, conditioning $P(T)$ only on the presence of either a video or a question, but not the specific identity of the resource observed.

Training and Evaluation

All models were trained and evaluated using 5-fold cross validation. For each model above, one BKT model was trained for each of the 193 exercises. For each model, for each fold, each of the 193 KC models was randomly initialized and trained using Expectation Maximization (EM) algorithm to minimize the log likelihood of the observed events 25 times, with the maximally likely resulting model chosen for that model-fold-model tuple. The metric used to compare the four models is the root mean squared error (RMSE) averaged across each fold. The error used to compute the RMSE was calculated by predicting the probability of correctness at each problem attempt, the finding the difference between the computed probability of success [0, 1] and the observed result $\{0, 1\}$.

Results and Discussion

The 'Template-Videos' and Template-1-Video models performed best, with a mean RMSE of .3810 and .3811, respectively, while the Template model showed no significant difference from the baseline distribution, at .3824 (Table 1). Not all KC models were better described given the inclusion of resources, however; 77 of the 193 models performed the same or worse than they did when no resources were included, while the remaining 116 saw some improvement.

Model	Mean RMSE	Significance
Pct. Correct	.4930	.0000*
Standard BKT	.3824	—
Template	.3824	.9448
Template-Videos	.3810	.0253*
Template-1-Video	.3811	.0061*

In order to gain an intuition for why some models were better described by the inclusion of resources and others by excluding resources altogether, we chose to consider the three models that performed best under the Template-Videos condition as compared to the baseline, and the three that performed worst.

For all three of the highest performing models, the videos associated with the exercise were highly relevant to the actual exercise itself. One of the three videos, The Fundamental Theorem of Arithmetic, involved explaining the manipulation of a bespoke tool created by Khan academy for that particular exercise (Figure 1), as well as the completion of a practice problem using that tool. Similarly, 'Measuring Segments' and Two Sided Limits from Graphs', the assessment items very closely resembled, both in content and in format, the example problems worked in their associated videos.

For the low performing models the possible sources of error somewhat mirror the effects seen in the high performing case. In the case of 'Scalar Matrix Multiplication' and 'Linear Inequalities' the assessments are presented very differently and involve customized input fields, which may introduce an additional obstacle to transfer between watching the video and applying the related concepts. The issues with 'Defined and Undefined Matrix Operations' are somewhat less clear, though an additional confound may be that the video was added partway through our data-collection period.

Intuitively, an unhelpful video does not contribute to a predictive model, simply adding additional complexity and noise. By measuring which videos do and do not contribute constructively to predictive accuracy, it may be possible to detect which videos might be most appropriately suggested as helpful for a learner, and which need revision.

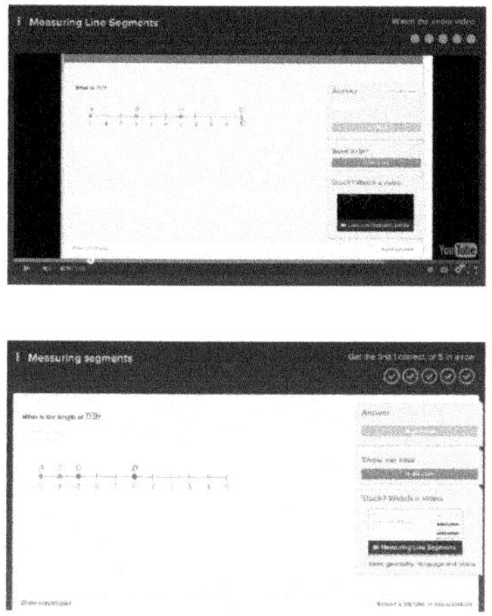

Figure 1: Videos contributing maximally to model accuracy tended to closely mirror subsequent assessments

Conclusions and Future Work

In this paper, we have demonstrated that the inclusion of video observations in a KT model can offer information relevant predicting student behavior. Further, we have begun to explore an avenue for evaluating the relevance of educational videos, by observing the relative performance of models that include or exclude observations involving those videos.

Though the effect size is small, the statistically significant decrease in error under the 'Template-1-Video' and Template-Videos conditions is an encouraging sign. It is indicative that, though relatively few resource observations were recorded and many potential video-problem associations were missed or incorrectly made, there is information to be gleaned from a learner's use of educational resources. Further, as suggested by our qualitative investigation of the best and worst performing 'Template-1-Video' models when compared to the baseline, it is possible that the delta in accuracy, coupled with the associated P(T) when including resource observations could itself be an interesting metric for evaluating video relevance.

One helpful piece of missing meta-data is a canonical association of videos to exercises. Due to the volume of unique videos we employed an automated process based on chronological distance for associating videos to exercises, but may have lost information. Another avenue worth pursuing is the possibility that, due to diversity of academic experience, some users would benefit strongly from video resources while others may not. Finally, it would be useful to apply this framework of evaluation to different sets of data, such as those from MOOC courses.

References

[1] Achtemeier, S. D., Morris, L. V., and Finnegan, C. L. Considerations for developing evaluations of online courses. *Journal of Asynchronous Learning Networks 7*, 1 (2003), 1–13.

[2] Corbett, A. T., and Anderson, J. R. Knowledge tracing: Modeling the acquisition of procedural knowledge. *User Modeling and User-Adapted Interaction 4*, 4 (Dec. 1994), 253–278.

[3] Lindsey, R. V., Khajah, M., and Mozer, M. C. Automatic discovery of cognitive skills to improve the prediction of student learning.

[4] Linn, M. C., Davis, E. A., Bell, P., and Bell, A. P. D. o. M. C. P. *Internet Environments for Science Education*. Routledge, July 2013.

[5] Oncu, S., and Cakir, H. Research in online learning environments: Priorities and methodologies. *Computers & Education 57*, 1 (Aug. 2011), 1098–1108.

[6] Pardos, Z. A., Bergner, Y., Seaton, D. T., and Pritchard, D. E. Adapting bayesian knowledge tracing to a massive open online course in edX. *Proceedings of EDM 2013* (2013), 137–144.

[7] Song, L., Singleton, E. S., Hill, J. R., and Koh, M. H. Improving online learning: Student perceptions of useful and challenging characteristics. *The internet and higher education 7*, 1 (2004), 59–70.

The Visible and Invisible in a MOOC Discussion Forum

Eni Mustafaraj
Department of Computer Science
Wellesley College
Wellesley, MA, USA
emustafaraj@wellesley.edu

Jessica Bu
Department of Computer Science
Wellesley College
Wellesley, MA, USA
jbu2@wellesley.edu

L@S 2015, Mar 14-18, 2015, Vancouver, BC, Canada
ACM 978-1-4503-3411-2/15/03.
http://dx.doi.org/10.1145/2724660.2728691

Abstract

Online discussion forums in a MOOC setting allow students to become aware of other students enrolled in the course. However, what is (usually) visible in the forums is the output of "active" students who engage in asking and answering questions. In addition to such active participants, there is (as always in online communities) a large group of "passive" users (so-called lurkers), who might find the forum useful to their learning, and read it regularly, despite remaining "invisible". Our analysis of a large MOOC online forum shows that for every active participant in the forum there are two passive ones. 30% of active participants complete the course, compared to only 6.6% of the passive participants. Vice-versa, 67% of students who complete the course are also active in the forum. However, "invisible activity" (e.g. reading or searching the forum) is something that both groups practice equally and more frequently, while only 3.3% of forum actions are visible.

Author Keywords

MOOCs, online communities, discussion forums, lurkers

ACM Classification Keywords

I.5.m [C]: omputing Methodologies, Miscellaneous

Course and Data Description

We were given access to anonymized data from the two iterations of MITx 6.00x – *Introduction to Computer Science and Programming*, offered in Fall 2012 and Spring 2013. More information on the course details can be found in [4]. Course data in the edX platform are stored in different databases: course content, discussion forums, student personal data, etc. We received the databases for the discussion forums and the event tracking.

Forums – Each entry in the forum database contains information about a single user post, such as the author id, the time of creation, the body of the message, the type of the message (a thread or a comment), the list of all user id-s who have upvoted the comment, and more.

Event Tracking – Each entry in the event tracking database corresponds to an HTTP request (a GET or POST) recorded on the edX servers. Parsing the event information allows us to recreate the complete history of a user interaction with the course content: what pages were visited and in what order, what videos were played or paused, what discussion posts were initiated, read, or upvoted, and many more.

While the forum database stores the **visible** activity of users in the forum—where visible means that a user action is visible to everyone in the platform (user started a thread or commented)—the event tracking database stores everything, most of which is **invisible** to others in the platform, such as, who is reading a thread, what keywords were used for searching posts, which thread is being followed (to be notified of future changes), etc.

Visible Activity in the Discussion Forums

The forum database allows us to identify two visible user activities: posting and voting. Posts can be of two kinds: starting a thread (commonly used to ask a question) and commenting on a existing thread (answer a question).

Counts for posting (threads+comments), threads alone, and votes are shown in the first three rows of Table 1. These are followed by the number of users engaging in every single activity, and the total number of active users on the forum (which is less than the sum for each category, since many users engage in more than one). We also report statistics about the output of the visible behavior in an aggregated form, which allows for interesting observations (e.g., the very fast response time for a question, or the total of unanswered questions).

Statistics	Fall 2012	Spring 2013
Nr. of posts	89,608	68,548
Nr. of threads	19,644	15,600
Nr. of votes	62,420	31,138
Nr. of thread starters	7,299	5,654
Nr. of comment writers	9,015	6,566
Nr. of voters	8,795	5,555
Nr. of all participants	14,080	10,327
Nr. of voted users	5,516 (49%)	3,694 (43%)
Nr. of unanswered questions	2,454 (13%)	1,991 (13%)
Median thread size	3	3
% of original posters returning	53%	56%
Median vote count per thread	1	1
% of threads with 0 votes	42%	49%
Median response time	12 minutes	22 minutes

Table 1: Statistics to characterize the visible forum activity in the two terms in which the MitX 6.00X course was taught.

We also looked at how users are distributed across the different activities: creating threads, commenting on

Term	Th	Ct	V	Th+Ct	Th+V	Ct+V	Th+Ct+V	Total
Fall 2012 (nr. of users)	1,619	1,959	2,895	1,707	551	1,927	3,422	14,080
Fall 2012 (% of users)	11%	14%	21%	12%	4%	14%	24%	100%
Spring 2013 (nr. of users)	1,550	1,726	1,817	1,496	394	1,130	2,214	10,327
Spring 2013 (% of users)	15%	17%	18%	14%	4%	11%	21%	100%

Table 2: Distribution of user participation in each of the three activities: Th - start a thread, Ct - write a comment, V - Vote, or their combination. In both semesters, the highest % is for users who performed all three activities, but still, that is less than one fourth of all active users.

existing posts, voting, or any combination of the above. This breakdown is shown in Table 2. While the biggest group of users engages in all three of these activities (24% in the Fall and 21% in the Spring), still this is less than one fourth of all active users. More interesting is that almost half of users (46% in Fall 2012 and 50% in Spring 2013) engage in one single activity.

Invisible Activity in the Discussion Forum

We will use the data from the *event tracking database* to answer some questions, whose answers depend on the **invisible** behavior of users. Because the database is missing data for three weeks of the Spring 2013 term, we will only report results for the Fall 2012 term.

Q1: What is the ratio of active users (visible activity) to passive users (invisible activity) in the course data?

Searching the database for events that contained the partial URL to the discussion forums (`/courses/MITx/6.00x/2012_Fall/discussion/`), we identified 4,550,298 events generated by 41,744 different students. Since in Table 1 we reported 14,080 active participants, the ratio of active users to passive users is 1 to 2 (thus, one third of forum visitors are active at some point in time). The total number of events also allows us to calculate the visible portion of forum activity (number of posts and votes from Table 1 is 89,608 + 62,420 = 152,028) as 3.3% of the total forum activity.

Q2: What % of active and passive users successfully completed the course?

We don't have access to personal student data to check for certificate-earners, thus, we used the event of taking the final exam as a proxy for course completion. There are 6,247 such students in the Fall 2012 database, with only 184 of them having never visited the discussion forum. We divided the data according to two dimensions: completion (took exam or not completed course) and forum activity (was active or passive in the forum), see Table 3 for the results. We discovered that 67% of exam-takers were active in the forum. However, more than 2/3 of active forum participants didn't complete the course.

	Active	Passive
Took Exam	4,212	1,851
Didn't complete	9,475	26,236

Table 3: Counts of four categories of students according the dimension of course completion and forum activity. Total number is 41,744 participants.

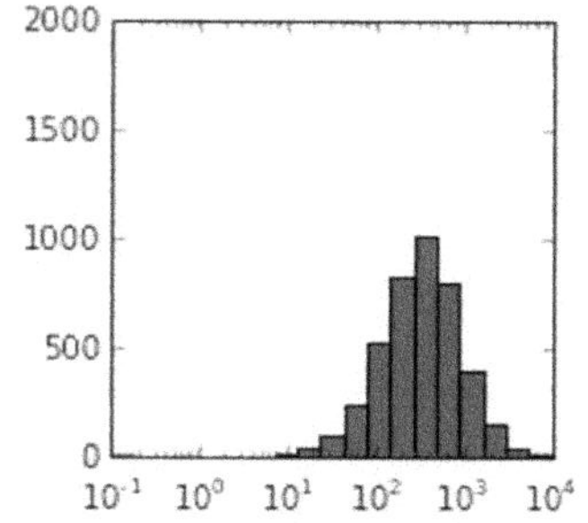

Figure 1: Distribution of event counts for the group of active participants who completed the course. N=4,212. Notice log scale for X axis.

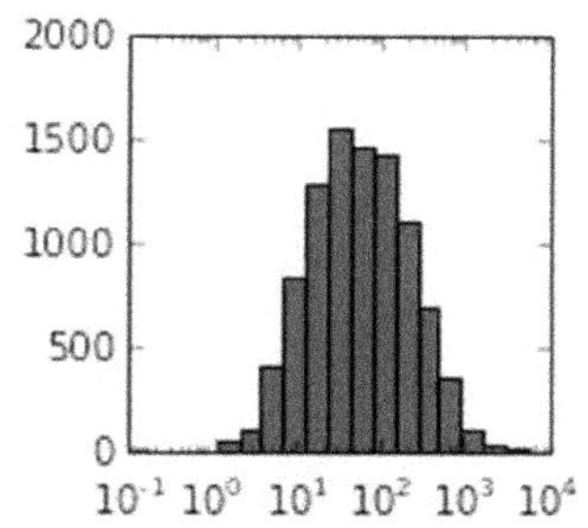

Figure 2: Distribution of event counts for the group of active participants who did not complete the course. N=9,475. Notice log scale for X axis.

Related Research

Recent research that has studied user activity in MOOCs has found that engagement in forums is different for different categories of users. For example, [3] found that students completing a course "exhibit significantly higher levels of activity on the discussion board compared to Auditing, Disengaging, and Sampling students". In [5], focusing only on the certificate-earners, the authors discovered that these students were spending about 1-1.5 hours/week in the forums, which was much more than the time spent on required components of the course, such as labs. One study that analyzed the impact of built-in (online forums and Q&A) versus external social tools (Facebook, Twitter, etc.) [1] found that students preferred the online forum and engaged in it more often than in the other venues. However, a discouraging number reported in [2] puts the number of students who actively participated in the forum of the MITx 6.002X course to 3% of all students.

Discussion

Our results confirm previous studies that students who complete the course are more active in forums than other categories of students. However, that is only one side of the story. Comparing the two distributions in Figure 1 and Figure 2 indicates that many students who didn't complete the course had activity-levels of the same range as students who completed the course, and vice-versa, many students who completed the course had very low engagement in the forum.

This suggests that we need to move away from metrics that indicate engagement with the forum as number of visits or amount of time spent towards a deeper analysis that captures the nature of these visits. By tabulating the fragments of the event URLs, we identified 43.3% of the total forum activity as being the reading of problem sets' discussion threads. For comparison, reading the question threads attached to video lectures amounts to 27% of the total activity. These numbers suggest a series of new questions. Who is reading the question/answers in the lectures and at what point in time? Who are the students who ask questions about lectures, and who reads these questions and answers? Learning more about this "invisible activity" is the focus of future research.

Acknowledgements

The authors are thankful to the MIT Office of Digital Learning for providing access to the MOOC data.

References

[1] Alario-Hoyos, C., Pérez-Sanagustín, M., Kloos, C. D., G., H. A. P., Organero, M. M., and de-las Heras, A. R. Analysing the impact of built-in and external social tools in a mooc on educational technologies. In *EC-TEL* (2013).

[2] Breslow, L., Pritchard, D. E., DeBoer, J., Stump, G. S., Ho, A. D., and Seaton, D. Studying learning in the worldwide classroom: Research into edx's first mooc. *Research & Practice in Assessment 8* (2013), 13–25.

[3] Kizilcec, R. F., Piech, C., and Schneider, E. Deconstructing disengagement: analyzing learner subpopulations in massive open online courses. In *Proc. of the 3rd LAK*, ACM (2013), 170–179.

[4] Mustafaraj, E. What does enrollment in a mooc mean? In *Proc. of the 1st ACM L@S*, ACM (2014), 203–204.

[5] Seaton, D. T., Bergner, Y., Chuang, I., Mitros, P., and Pritchard, D. E. Who does what in a massive open online course? *Communications of the ACM 57*, 4 (2014), 58–65.

Exploring Collaborative Storytelling as a Method for Creating Educational Games

Ruth Wylie
Center for Science & the Imagination
Mary Lou Fulton Teachers College
Arizona State University
ruth.wylie@asu.edu

Kiyash Monsef
1041 Alvarado Rd.
Berkeley, CA 94705
kiyash@gmail.com

Ed Finn
Center for Science & the Imagination
School of Arts, Media & Engineering
Department of English
Arizona State University
edfinn@asu.edu

Robert Hawkins
World Bank
1818 H. St. NW
Washington DC 20433
rhawkins@worldbank.org

Joseph Eschrich
Center for Science & the Imagination
Arizona State University
jpe@asu.edu

L@S 2015, March 14-18, 2015, Vancouver, BC, Canada.
ACM 978-1-4503-3411-2/15/03.
http://dx.doi.org/10.1145/2724660.2728692

Abstract
Designing educational games that meet both learning and entertainment objectives is a challenging task. Games that begin by developing specific educational goals and are later wrapped in a game or narrative context risk appearing forced, while those that begin with gaming elements to which educational elements are added may appear superficial. In this paper, we describe the methodology and results from a three-day interdisciplinary hackathon for developing game narratives designed to address both needs. We present details regarding the hackathon, the collaborative teams, and an example of the outcomes produced.

Author Keywords
Educational games; Interdisciplinary collaboration; Narratives.

ACM Classification Keywords
K.3.1. Computer uses in education; K.4. Computers in society

Introduction
When developing educational games, it is important to balance both learning and entertainment objectives. Focusing on one over the other early in the design

process can lead to games that lack authenticity and integration. Barab, et al. [1] describe the importance of framing and context when balancing learning and entertainment goals, especially since these goals may conflict [4]. Additionally, there is much research on how to embed learning principles into games (e.g, [3]) and the impact of games on increasing motivation [2,5] that suggests the power of successful educational games. We propose that one way to address the tension between education and entertainment goals is through the use of interdisciplinary collaboration during the narrative development process. In this paper, we present the results of a three-day narrative hackathon during which groups comprised of science fiction writers, graphic artists, and domain experts collaborated to build narratives for an online massive multi-player gaming platform called EVOKE, which was initially established by the World Bank in 2010. Below, we describe the EVOKE platform as well as the structure for our three-day hackathon. Finally, we present the results of the hackathon and plans for moving forward.

EVOKE

Current global challenges such as food and energy shortages and the devastating impacts of illiteracy cannot be solved without collaboration among multidisciplinary groups of experts and large scale engagment with diverse publics. EVOKE (www.urgentevoke.com) is an online educational game that aims to raise awareness and foster a sense of ownership and agency around global grand challenges, while helping players develop 21st century skills. In previous iterations, EVOKE "agents" (our term for students or players) engaged with both online and face-to-face social networks to complete missions and to develop creative solutions to pressing global problems (e.g., sustainable energy, access to clean water, food security). EVOKE employs graphic novel aesthetics to tell stories and create a vivid narrative universe wherein players collaborate with one another to generate solutions to complex global challenges. We chose to work within the EVOKE platform because of its strong focus on narrative and flexibility.

Hackathon

In an attempt to balance educational and domain needs with entertainment goals, we hosted a three-day hackathon that united top science fiction writers, artists, futurists, and subject area experts to develop narratives and visual artwork for EVOKE's fictional universe. Each team of three to five members focused on a specific global grand challenge, including nuclear disarmament, food security, environmental conservation, developing new economic models, human trafficking, and literacy. One of the challenges in conducting a three-day interdisciplinary hackathon is finding the appropriate balance between providing guidance and support and providing enough freedom to foster creative discourse and outcomes. The three days were divided into morning and afternoon sessions, with specific goals for each session. The goals for the morning of Day 1 were to set the context, via a panel discussion on "How do stories help us change the world?" and to foster team collaboration through a guided discussion on setting educational goals and developing strategic assessments. These sessions served the dual purpose of helping teams get to know each other and fostering discussion around the main educational goals for the narratives. During the guided session, teams worked together to identify agents' prior knowledge and motivations, select specific learning objectives, design in-game methods for assessment and evaluation, and outline instructional missions or quests that align with the goals and assessment. This process established an important foundation from which the narrative could grow. In the afternoon, the focus shifted towards meeting the entertainment objectives with another guided discussion on character development and establishing context and motivations. During this session, teams began developing specific character profiles, selecting the location or context for their games, and structuring the overall plot. We chose to have teams discuss the educational components of the game before beginning plot and character development in an attempt to better integrate the educational objectives with the story and ultimately the gameplay. Day 2 consisted largely of dedicated working sessions for teams to continue to develop their narratives. Each working block was followed with a session for groups to ask questions and receive feedback from the other teams. Day 3 began with a review of the goals for the narratives and reiteration of the expected deliverables before a final working session. In the afternoon of Day 3, each team presented their story ideas and visual art created during the hackathon (see Figure 1), and described how the educational missions would be integrated into the story. We concluded the hackathon with a discussion of next steps and feedback on the process and hackathon experience.

Hackathon Teams and Outcomes

Each hackathon team consisted of one science fiction writer, one graphic artist, and between one and three domain experts or futurists. None of the team members had collaborated with each other previously, but most reported experience working with interdisciplinary teams. Topics were assigned to writers based on

Figure 1. Sample artwork generated during the hackathon.

interest and availability of domain experts. Artists were assigned to groups based on a portfolio review and an attempt to align artistic style with story themes. All teams were able to complete the task and generate a narrative and art, and identify specific educational components. To illustrate, we present the ideas generated from the team focused on the issue of universal literacy. The team consisted of a science fiction author, a professional animator and three literacy experts with international development experience. The team worked to develop a narrative that highlighted the challenges and missed opportunities associated with illiteracy. Their story pitch

(Figure 2) traces the lives of Toniah and Andre and highlights the opportunities that Andre misses because he is unable to read. EVOKE agents would be led through a series of missions or quests where they first learn more about the issue on both a global and local scale and are then provided with appropriate scaffolding to help to identify how literacy affects their own community and how they might begin to address the problem through advocacy, volunteerism, research, and other active modes of engagement.

When little Toniah's toy drone fell from the sky while playing at a London park, it connected her forever to Andre. Growing up, their bond only grew stronger, even though their lives took dramatically different paths. With each passing year, door after door opened up for Toniah while Andre's dreams were slowly snuffed out because the world he lived in never taught him how to read. When he realized his young daughter, Marina, was on the brink of heading down the same path of his life, Toniah and Andre call for an EVOKE. At risk are Marina's dreams—and the future breakthrough contribution she might bring to our world. The EVOKE network is urgently recruiting agents to join the effort to ransom her dreams and contributions and those of the 250 million kids just like her, just over the population of England, Germany, Spain and Italy combined. Are you in?

Figure 2. Story teaser generated by the Literacy Team.

In addition to the story idea, the team developed a set of educational objectives that could be integrated as missions within the game. For example, towards reaching the goal of increased awareness of the prevalence of illiteracy, agents may be challenged to research literacy statistics and associated reasons (e.g., reasons girls are not in school, economic impact of schooling). This example illustrates how game narratives developed through interdisciplinary collaboration can be entertaining while providing hooks for further educational content.

Future Work

We are currently in the process of finalizing the narratives developed during the hackathon and have begun creating development and deployment plans for two of the six narratives.

Acknowledgements

This material is based upon work supported by the World Bank Group under Award No. 7171335.

References

[1] Barab, S., Thomas, M., Dodge, T., Carteaux, R., & Tuzun, H. (2005). Making learning fun: Quest Atlantis, a game without guns. *Educ Tech Rsch and Dvlp*, *53*(1), 86-107.

[2] Garris, R., Ahlers, R., & Driskell, J. E. (2002). Games, motivation, and learning: A research and practice model. *Simulation & gaming*, *33*(4), 441-467.

[3] Gee, J. P. (2007). What video games have to teach us about learning and literacy: Revised and Updated Edition. Macmillan.

[4] Kam, M., Agarwal, A., Kumar, A., Lal, S., Mathur, A., Tewari, A., & Canny, J. (2008, February). Designing e-learning games for rural children in India: a format for balancing learning with fun. In *Proc of the 7th ACM conf on designing interactive systems* (pp. 58-67). ACM.

[5] Malone, T. W. (1980, September). What makes things fun to learn? Heuristics for designing instructional computer games. In *Proc of the 3rd ACM SIGSMALL symposium and the first SIGPC symposium on Small systems* (pp. 162-169). ACM.

Do Numeric Ratings Impact Peer Reviewers?

Catherine M. Hicks
The Design Lab
UC San Diego
cmhicks@ucsd.edu

C. Ailie Fraser
The Design Lab
UC San Diego
cafraser@ucsd.edu

Purvi Desai
The Design Lab
UC San Diego
pdesai@ucsd.edu

Scott Klemmer
The Design Lab
UC San Diego
srk@ucsd.edu

L@S 2015, March 14–18, 2015, Vancouver, BC, Canada.
ACM 978-1-4503-3411-2/15/03.
http://dx.doi.org/10.1145/2724660.2728693

Abstract
Research suggests that online peer review can provide critical help to learners who would otherwise not be given individualized feedback on their work. However, little is known about how different characteristics of review systems impact *reviewers*. This extended abstract presents preliminary results from an online experiment examining how explicit numeric ratings change peer reviews. A between-subject experiment found that peer reviewers who were asked to generate a numeric rating as well as general feedback gave significantly more explanations and made more positive comments compared with reviewers who were asked to give general feedback only. These exploratory findings suggest the need to further examine how online peer review systems' affordances can impact the reviews given in these systems.

Author Keywords
peer review; peer assessment; online learning; writing

ACM Classification Keywords
K.3.1: Computer Uses in Education: Collaborative Learning.

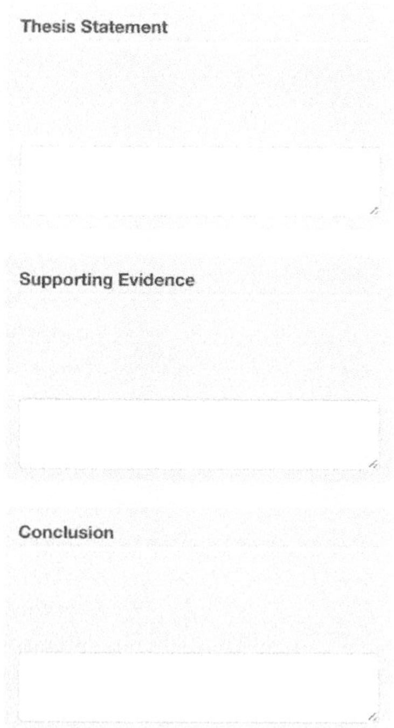

Figure 1. Non-numeric feedback condition. Peer reviewers were provided with open-ended text boxes only when giving feedback.

Introduction

Online environments provide increasing opportunities for people to interact collaboratively, creating and refining their work with feedback from peers. Different types of feedback may be formally imposed within an online system (such as voting on answers in an online forum or user-generated scores in an online course), or informally generated by group members (such as discussion between students in an online forum).

In the classroom, peer feedback has been shown to help students improve their writing as effectively as feedback from instructors [1, 3, 5, 7, 8]. It can therefore be a valuable replacement for expert feedback when the latter is not available, as in many online learning environments [e.g., 3]. Despite this increasing focus on peer review, little is known about how feedback givers are influenced by the structure of the feedback *environment*. Research on peer reviewers has primarily focused on improving reviewers' performance relative to instructors or experts; for instance, providing instructor training sessions for peer reviewers [e.g. 4]. Some recent research also finds that rubric clarity, such as providing parallel sentence structure and unambiguous wording, can improve the quality of peer reviews in online classes [3]. However, many questions about peer reviewers remain to be explored. For instance, in the absence of an explicit rubric, how are peer reviewers influenced by the affordances of an online environment?

GradStudio Study

We present preliminary results from a pilot investigation into online peer review for writing outside of a course environment.

Previous research has found that students are impacted by critical feedback, often making fewer writing revisions in response to feedback that criticizes their writing during early stages of review [2]. However, it is unknown whether reviewers generate different feedback when prompted to give more or less critical reviews. For example, would cues like a numeric scale change the content of reviews? In this paper we provide some suggestive work exploring this question. It is possible that reviewers will give more developmental feedback in the absence of critical cues, focusing less on what is wrong than on what can be changed. On the other hand, it is possible that providing peer reviewers with an explicit rating system encourages them to justify their ratings with deeper and less vague reviews.

Method

Participants

Participants were recruited through from online advertisements as well as flyers on a Southern California University campus. There were 53 participants; 70% applying to a Science program, 21% Social Science, and 9% Arts & Humanities or Other. 41% of participants were enrolled in college, and 88% of participants were native English speakers.

Materials and Procedure

Participants enrolled for the project through an online website created by the authors, where they provided their area of application, college enrollment, and whether they were native English speakers. Native and non-native English speakers were assigned in equal numbers to the two conditions in order to control for any language confounds across conditions.

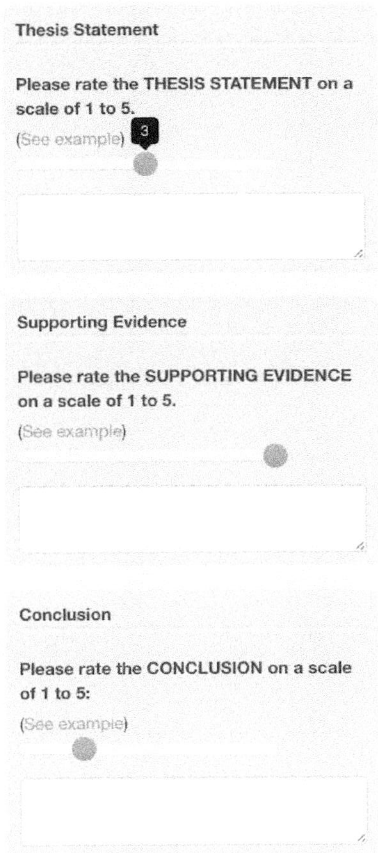

Figure 2. Numeric feedback condition. Peer reviewers were provided with numeric sliders and open-ended text boxes when giving feedback.

Participants then uploaded their graduate application essay for peer review through PeerStudio, an online peer review platform developed by Kulkarni and colleagues in the Stanford HCI group [6]. Participants were randomly assigned to one of two conditions: non-numeric or numeric. After submitting their essay, participants were required to review two other essays before receiving feedback on their own work. Based on this feedback, participants were then asked to submit their revised drafts for a second round of feedback. The study was open to enrollment and participation for one month, and participants were allowed to work at their own pace during that time.

Experimental Conditions

Participants were randomly assigned to receive and give reviews in one of two conditions: non-numeric (Figure 1) and numeric (Figure 2). Both conditions provided reviewers with open text boxes for comments on the essay's thesis statement, supporting evidence, and conclusion. In the numeric condition, reviewers were also asked to rate the thesis statement, supporting evidence and conclusion respectively with a sliding scale from 1 to 5.

Results

53 participants submitted at least one essay, and 24 went on to submit a revised essay after receiving feedback. A few participants submitted more than 2 drafts, with one submitting as many as 12.

Peer Reviews

204 reviews were submitted by peer reviewers. Because some reviewers failed to follow all the experimental instructions, the numbers of observations vary in the following analyses.

To analyze the content of the reviews, each review was assigned an "Explanation Score", representing the number of explanations given for suggested changes, and a "Positivity Score", representing the number of positive comments. One explanation point was given if a comment had a suggestion for improvement and justified it with an explicit explanation (e.g., "change the first paragraph *because it is repetitive and will be boring*"), while a half point was given if the review had a suggestion with an implied but unstated justification. No explanation point was given if a comment had no suggestions or made only vague statements (e.g., "change the conclusion"). Positivity scores were calculated by adding each positive statement in the review (e.g., "very strong intro", "fantastic writing"). Across 121 reviews, the mean Explanation score was 2.90, with a SD of 1.39, and the mean Positivity score was 1.54, with a SD of 1.31.

The presence of numeric ratings had a significant effect on the content of reviews; reviewers in the numeric condition were more likely to give explanations (M = 3.03) compared with reviewers in the non-numeric condition (M = 2.37), $F(1, 120) = 4.34$, $p = .03$. Reviewers in the numeric condition were also significantly more likely to make positive comments, $F(1, 120) = 4.55$, $p = .03$. However, Explanation scores and Positivity scores were not correlated.

Discussion

This study suggests that even small changes in the online review system, such as the presence or absence of numeric ratings, can influence the meaningful content of reviews. Peer reviewers who were given a numeric rating scale were both more positive and more detailed in their feedback, providing clearer justifications for their suggestions and more encouraging comments.

One explanation for this finding could be that numeric ratings are perceived as more critical than open-ended comments alone, and peer reviewers therefore feel compelled to justify the implied criticism in their rating. It is also possible that requiring peer reviewers to choose a numeric rating encourages them to engage more deeply with the work in the first place, making more comparisons between essays. Finally, it is possible that providing an explicit rating system simply increased the overall clarity of the reviewers' task, which has been found to prompt higher quality reviews [3]. Future research should explore these possibilities.

Because of the relatively low number of participants and the self-selected nature of their participation, caution should be used in generalizing from these results. Follow-up work will investigate questions such as how receiving numeric ratings benefits or discourages online writers. We believe that our preliminary findings suggest useful directions for further research into how peer review systems' design impacts users both inside and outside of a classroom environment.

Acknowledgements
This work was supported by the National Science Foundation. We also thank Chinmay Kulkarni and the PeerStudio team for their support.

References
[1] Cho, K., and Schunn, C. D. Scaffolded writing and rewriting in the discipline: A web-based reciprocal peer review system. *Comput. Educ. 48*, 3 (Apr. 2007), 409–426.

[2] Ferris, D. R. The influence of teacher commentary on student revision. *TESOL Quarterly 31*, 2 (July 1997), 315–339.

[3] Kulkarni, C., Wei, K. P., Le, H., Chia, D., Papadopoulos, K., Cheng, J., Koller, D., and Klemmer, S. R. Peer and self assessment in massive online classes. *ACM Trans. Comput.-Hum. Interact. 20*, 6 (Dec. 2013), 33:1– 33:31.

[4] Min, H. T. Training students to become successful peer reviewers. *System 33*, 2 (2005), 293-308.

[5] Patchan, M.M., Schunn, C.D., and Clark, R.J. Writing in natural sciences: Understanding the effects of different types of reviewers on the writing process. *Journal of Writing Research 2*, 3 (2011), 365–393.

[6] PeerStudio. http://www.peerstudio.org.

[7] Richer, D. L. The effects of two feedback systems on first year college students' writing proficiency. *College of Education University of Massachusetts-Lowell* (1992).

[8] Topping, K. Peer assessment between students in colleges and universities. *Review of Educational Research 68*, 3 (Oct. 1998), 249–276.

Learner-Sourcing in an Engineering Class at Scale

Elena L. Glassman
MIT CSAIL
32 Vassar St.
Cambridge, MA 02139 USA
elg@mit.edu

Christopher J. Terman
MIT CSAIL
32 Vassar St.
Cambridge, MA 02139 USA
cjt@mit.edu

Robert C. Miller
MIT CSAIL
32 Vassar St.
Cambridge, MA 02139 USA
rcm@mit.edu

L@S 2015, March 14–18, 2015, Vancouver, BC, Canada.
ACM 978-1-4503-3411-2/15/03.
http://dx.doi.org/10.1145/2724660.2728694

Abstract
Teaching computer architecture as a hands-on engineering course to approximately 250 MIT students per semester requires a large, dedicated teaching staff. This Spring, a shortened version of the course will be deployed on edX to a potentially far larger cohort of students, without additional teaching staff. To better support students, we have deployed developmental versions of three learner-sourcing systems to as many as 500 students. These systems harvest and organize students' collective knowledge about debugging and optimizing solutions. We plan to deploy and study the next iteration of these systems on edX this Spring.

Introduction
One-on-one tutoring has been established as a costly gold standard in education [1]. In MOOCs, the teacher-to-student ratio is drastically lower. Teaching staff cannot walk around the lab to get a sense of common success and failures. They also suffer from the "curse of knowledge": the difficulty experts have when trying to see something from a novice's point of view [2].

We are developing systems that harvest and organize students' collective knowledge about debugging and optimizing solutions. Students themselves are each becoming experts on their own bugs and solutions. The key design principle is that students write hints immediately after completing a task or fixing a bug. Later, other students can use these hints to help guide them to a correct solution or better design. While students do not have the pedagogical content knowledge to necessarily generate optimal explanations, they also do not suffer from the curse of knowledge. These systems relieve some of the pressure on the relatively small teaching staff, and give students the valuable educational experiences of reflection and generating explanations [3].

We present ongoing case studies of three systems deployed in an undergraduate computer architecture course at MIT. Around 250 students enroll each semester. The three deployed systems have distinct objectives: (1) learner-source hints for debugging, (2) learner-source hints for optimization, and (3) prompt students to reflect on other students' solutions. Learner-sourcing refers to crowd-sourcing within the community of students enrolled in a course.

These systems have already been deployed at scale to as many as five hundred students over multiple semesters. Our case studies prepare us to design, deploy, and study the next iteration of these systems on edX this Spring. Throughout the process, we continue to develop design principles that can guide future learner-sourcing systems for engineering classes.

Related Work

In order to generate hints for others, students must reflect on their bug, solution, or optimization, and then explain. We review relevant literature at the intersection of learning theory and engineering education.

Reflection

Reflection and confusion are both treated at length in learning theory literature. Piaget theorized that cognitive disequilibrium, experienced as confusion, could trigger learning: the creation or restructuring of knowledge schema [8]. However, D'Mello et al. point out that, for this learning to take place, it is important for confusion to be both appropriately injected and resolved [5]. Dewey theorized that reflection is a critical method for triggering that transformation from conflict and doubt into clarity and coherence [4]. Turning that reflection into a self-explanation also improves understanding [3]. Turns et al. [11] argue that the absence of reflection in traditional engineering education scholarship is a significant gap. In this work, we aim to design scalable automated opportunities for students to reflect in an engineering course.

Peer Instruction and Assessment

While reflection is valuable in its own right, it is also a building block of larger frameworks, like Peer Instruction [9] and Peer Assessment [10]. Reflecting on a peer's conceptual development or alternative solution may bring about cognitive conflict that prompts reevaluation of the student's own beliefs and understanding [7]. We aim to trigger productive cognitive conflict that students can attempt to resolve through written reflection.

Generating Hints for Students

With a mixture of automation and human input, helpful hints have been delivered to students in multiple problem domains. HelpMeOut [6] tracks the changes programmers make when fixing a compilation error or runtime exception. Users can write helpful messages to accompany these automatically extracted bug fixes. Our work uses a

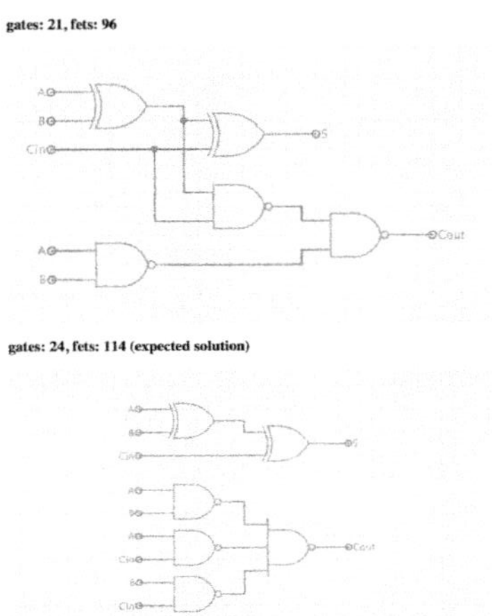

Figure 1: Two correct student solutions (Full Adders), composed of different numbers and arrangements of XOR and NAND gates. The more optimal solution has only 21 gates and 96 transistors (FETs) while the expected, less optimal solution has 24 gates and 114 transistors.

similar strategy for learner-sourcing hints for a new domain. We also learner-source optimization advice.

Debugging

In our course, students design entire simulated processors composed of logic gates. These processors can be challenging to debug even with the one-on-one help of seasoned teaching staff. Students who have recently resolved a particular bug can be in a better position than available staff members to help a fellow student with the same bug. Bugs are revealed by verification failures found by a staff-designed testbed. There are hundreds of possible unique verification failures. The course forum's generic structure does not lend itself to searching for other students' difficulties with particular verification failures.

We built *Dear Beta*, a system that serves as a central repository of debugging advice for and by students, indexed according to verification failures. As soon as a student resolves a bug, they can post an explanation of their bug on Dear Beta along with the verification failure it caused. Students can easily look up advice for their particular failure. Students upvote hints they found helpful. Initial evidence suggests it was consistently helpful. One teaching assistant said, "Whenever I went to help a student, I first asked them if they'd checked Dear Beta." We will create a Meteor or Django-backed version for edX students this Spring.

Optimization

Students optimize their own processors for additional points, which are a function of the processor's size and speed. Students also get a long list of optimization hints written by staff that students consult when choosing which optimizations to implement. Students can take hours to act on a single optimization hint, without knowing which has the greatest payoff.

We deployed a system for learner-sourcing optimization hints and results, with the aim of giving students more transparency and assistance. We indexed hints according to whether they were intended to reduce the processor's size, increase its speed, or both. We also gave students the option of submitting the magnitude of the speed and size improvement they got from acting on a hint, so that future students could gauge which optimization hints were most beneficial on average.

This system was not as successful as Dear Beta. We are, however, confident that students are ultimately capable of generating high-quality processor optimization hints, based on results shown in the next section on reflection and comparison.

Reflection

Early on in our course, students design a piece of their processor: a working Full Adder. Students create a variety of solutions that fit the behavior specification. Some are unnecessarily large, and some optimize to use as few transistors as possible. In this scenario, fewer transistors translate to better performance.

Through exploration of hundreds of previous students' solutions, we picked a representative set. Each student was then shown their own solution next to (1) a worse solution in the representative set and (2) the best solution in the representative set. Students were asked to give a hint to future students about how to improve the poorer solution in each pairing (see Figure 1). When the student's own solution is the better solution in the pair, then the student can hint at what the peer had conceptually missed. For example, *Remember DeMorgan's*

Learner-sourced Advice
"Do not try to be too clever with C_{out}—design your schematic as the expression is written. This way you will achieve the [standard] schematic."
"Mutate the boolean function for C_{out} such that all OR and AND operations are being NOT'ed. This allows you to design a circuit using only naturally inverting CMOS gates."
"I would ask: is there a way for you to use some intermediate node in one circuit to bypass a CMOS gate in the other, leading to a reduction of used mosfets?"

Table 1: Examples of learner-sourced advice for optimizing fellow students' Full Adders.

Law: you could replace the 'OR' of 'ANDs' with a 'NAND' of 'NANDs.' When the students' own solution is the poorer solution in the pair, they are challenged to first understand how the better solution uses fewer transistors and then write a hint about the insight for a peer.

This reflection and explanation process is pedagogically valuable on its own. In addition, students' explanations give a rich window into their understanding, while serving as strikingly cogent potential advice to future students (see Table 1). The online version of this course may afford us the opportunity to deliver these optimization hints back to students.

Conclusions and Future Work

This work in progress is the accumulation of several semesters of system development and deployment in a large undergraduate engineering course. Students can write high-quality optimization advice when their solution is paired with a distinct peer solution. Learner-sourced debugging hints, indexed by verification failures, are a valuable student resource. We are preparing to deploy the next iteration of these systems on edX this Spring, while considering how best to measure impact on the student learning experience.

Acknowledgments

We appreciate support from NSF GRF No. 1122374, Quanta Computer, and the Amar Bose Fellowship.

References

[1] Bloom, B. S. The 2 sigma problem: The search for methods of group instruction as effective as one-to-one tutoring. *Educational Researcher* (1984), pp. 4–16.

[2] Camerer, C., Loewenstein, G., and Weber, M. The curse of knowledge in economic settings: An experimental analysis. *Journal of Political Economy 97*, 5 (1989), pp. 1232–1254.

[3] Chi, M. T., De Leeuw, N., Chiu, M.-H., and Lavancher, C. Eliciting self-explanations improves understanding. *Cognitive Science 18*, 3 (1994), pp. 439–477.

[4] Dewey, J. *How we think: A restatement of the relation of reflective thinking to the educational process.* D.C. Heath and Company, 1933.

[5] D'Mello, S., Lehman, B., Pekrun, R., and Graesser, A. Confusion can be beneficial for learning. *Learning and Instruction 29* (2014), pp. 153–170.

[6] Hartmann, B., MacDougall, D., Brandt, J., and Klemmer, S. R. What would other programmers do: suggesting solutions to error messages. In *Proceedings of the SIGCHI Conference on Human Factors in Computing Systems*, ACM (2010), pp. 1019–1028.

[7] Kavanagh, L., and O'Moore, L. Reflecting on reflection - 10 years, engineering, and UQ. In *Proceedings of the Conf. of the Australasian Assoc. for Engineering Education: To Industry and Beyond*, Institution of Engineers, Australia (2008).

[8] Kibler, J. Cognitive disequilibrium. In *Encyclopedia of Child Behavior and Development*, S. Goldstein and J. Naglieri, Eds. Springer US, 2011, p. 380.

[9] Mazur, E. *Peer Instruction: A User's Manual.* Series in Educational Innovation. Prentice Hall, 1997.

[10] Topping, K. Peer assessment between students in colleges and universities. *Review of Educational Research 68*, 3 (1998), pp. 249–276.

[11] Turns, J., Sattler, B., Yasuhara, K., Borgford-Parnell, J., and Atman, C. Integrating reflection into engineering education. In *Proceedings of the ASEE Annual Conference and Exposition*, ACM (2014).

Clustering Student Programming Assignments to Multiply Instructor Leverage

Hezheng Yin
The Institute for Theoretical Computer Science, Institute for Interdisciplinary Information Sciences, Tsinghua University
yhz11@mails.tsinghua.edu.cn

Joseph Moghadam
UC Berkeley
jmoghadam@berkeley.edu

Armando Fox
UC Berkeley
fox@berkeley.edu

L@S 2015, March 14–18, 2015, Vancouver, BC, Canada.
ACM 978-1-4503-3411-2/15/03.
http://dx.doi.org/10.1145/2724660.2728695

Author Keywords
clustering; MOOCs; autograding

ACM Classification Keywords
K.3.2 [Computer and Information Science Education]: Computer science education.

Abstract
A challenge in introductory and intermediate programming courses is understanding how students approached solving a particular programming problem, in order to provide feedback on how they might improve. In both Massive Open Online Courses (MOOCs) and large residential courses, such feedback is difficult to provide for each student individually. To multiply the instructor's leverage, we would like to group student submissions according to the general problem-solving strategy they used, as the first stage of a "feedback pipeline". We describe ongoing explorations of a variety of clustering algorithms and similarity metrics using a corpus of over 800 student submissions to a simple programming assignment from a programming MOOC. We find that for a majority of submissions, it is possible to automatically create clusters such that an instructor "eyeballing" some representative submissions from each cluster can readily describe qualitatively what the common elements are in student submissions in that cluster. This information can

be the basis for feedback to the students or for comparing one group of students' approach with another's.

Introduction

The enormous growth in demand for computing education [8] has resulted not only in a proliferation of Massive Open Online Courses (MOOCs) about programming, but to record enrollments in campus courses: the introductory programming courses at Berkeley and Harvard are now the largest-enrollment undergraduate courses on campus in any department, serving thousands of students per year. A key challenge of helping students learn the computational thinking skills associated with programming is understanding the different problem-solving approaches students used. However, extracting such a high-level description from student source code can be time-consuming, and at large scale, it is impossible for instructors to personally sift through all the solutions.

We would like the instructor to be able to explore and get a comprehensive understanding of these variation easily. In this paper, we propose a clustering based approach which takes advantage of the observation that the diversity of algorithms and language constructs is much smaller than the total number of unique submissions for an open-ended programming assignment. By clustering against well-designed features, we group thousands of submissions into a dozen of "meaningful" clusters. Our qualitative definition of "meaningful" is that an instructor who views a few representative examples from a cluster can readily describe what strategy or elements of the problem-solving approach are exemplified by that cluster.

Clustering and Visualization

Our test corpus consists of 800 student-submitted solutions to a simple "warm-up" programming assignment in the MOOC "Engineering Software as a Service" from UC Berkeley and edX (`http://saas-class.org`): Given an array of strings, group the strings so that all strings in a group are anagrams of each other. Figure 2 shows four examples of actual student submissions, illustrating the wide range of both idiomatic mastery and problem-solving approaches.

In general, there are two different ways to cluster. One is just using feature vectors and another is using a similarity measure between items to be clustered. We did experiemnt in both clustering by features and by similarity metric, but we will focus on the latter in this paper. Since visualizing clusters formed in high-dimensional spaces is challenging, we must do some dimensionality reduction to provide an instructor-friendly visualization. So we have three design choices to make: how to compute similarity between pairs of student submissions; which clustering algorithm to use and how to evaluate the quality of clusters; and how to visualize the clustering results.

Similarity Metric

A natural representation of the syntactic structure of a block of code is its abstract syntax tree (AST), so we need metrics that capture similarity between ASTs corresponding to different student solutions. One widely used metric is the tree edit distance (TED), defined as the minimum cost sequence of node edit operations that transforms one tree into the other. However, instead of using TED directly, we propose a variant of standard TED, which we call normalized TED. Inspired by the top-down structure characteristic of programming, normalized TED emphasizes the importance of high-level

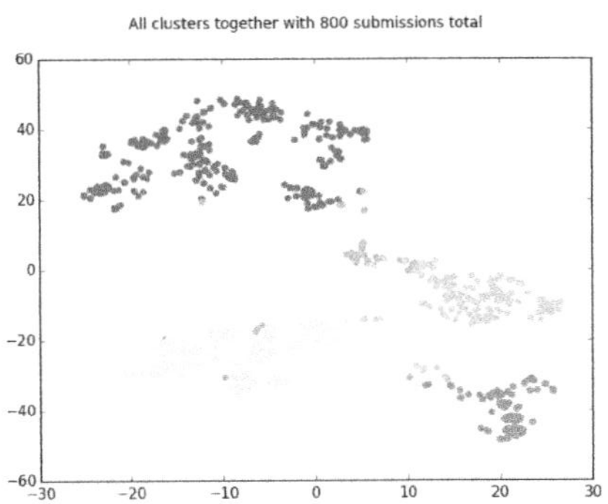

Figure 1: t-SNE visualization of running OPTICS against normalized TED of AST feature (preprocessed by spectral clustering). Each color in the picture represents a cluster. Blue represents outlier points. Silhouette score is 0.545.

program structure by assigning heavier weight to nodes higher up (closer to the root) in the AST. The idea is to prevent minor differences in syntax (that is, code at the leaves of the tree) from unduly affecting the similarity score of programs that are structurally similar but differ in low-level details. Empirically, we find that normalized TED outperforms standard TED in clustering according to the clustering quality score we describe next. A dynamic-programming algorithm by Zhang and Shasha [10] is used to compute both TED and normalized TED.

Clustering Algorithm and Quality
We experimented with several well-known clustering algorithms including k-means, weighted k-means, spectral clustering, DBSCAN and OPTICS. Our stated goal is to produce clusters such that a human instructor can readily "write down a label" describing the strategy represented by each cluster after viewing a few cluster members; empirically we found that the best results were achieved by density-based DBSCAN and OPTICS, which intuitively makes sense since clusters of common solutions are much denser than clusters containing convoluted solutions or outliers (very complex solutions that still manage to be functionally correct).

For measuring cluster quality, we chose the silhouette score (`http://en.wikipedia.org/wiki/Silhouette (clustering)`), a widely used internal clustering validation measure that validates clustering performance based on the pairwise difference of between- and within-cluster distances. Mathematically, the silhouette score s is given by

$$s = \frac{1}{n}\sum_{i=1}^{n}\frac{b(i) - a(i)}{\max\{a(i), b(i)\}}$$

where $a(i)$ is the average distance between the i'th sample and all other samples within the same cluster; $b(i)$ is the minimum average distance between the i'th sample and any other cluster in which i is not a member. From the above equation, we have $-1 \leq s(i) \leq 1$. A larger silhouette score generally indicates better clustering quality.

Visualization
To generate a two-dimensional visualization of clustering result, we used t-SNE (`http://lvdmaaten.github.io/tsne/`), a nonlinear dimensionality reduction technique that aims to preserve the local structure of data. An example of t-SNE visualization is shown in Figure 1. Each color in the figure represents a cluster. Blue points are outliers that do not have enough neighbor points to form a cluster. We built a simple interactive GUI in which the instructor can click on each datapoint to view the corresponding submission.

Example

In this section, we present example results obtained from running OPTICS algorithm against normalized TED of AST feature. The visualization of clustering result is shown in Figure 1.

After the clustering, we manually viewed a few randomly-chosen submissions from each cluster and tried to label each cluster according to what strategy or problem-solving approach is exemplifed by the submissions in that cluster. We found that all four clusters are "meaningful" in that we can easily assign such a label to every cluster. Each cluster's label and a representative submission are illustrated in Figure 2.

```
def combine_anagrams(words)
  words.group_by { |w|
    w.downcase.chars.sort.join }.values
end
```

```
def combine_anagrams(words)
  hash = Hash.new
  words.each do |w|
    key = w.downcase.chars.sort.join
    if hash.has_kay? key
      hash[key] += [w]
    else
      hash[key] = [w]
    end
  end
  hash.values
end
```

```
def combine_anagrams(words)
  hash = Hash.new
  words.each do |w|
    key = w.downcase.chars.sort.join
    if hash.has_kay? key
      hash[key] << w
    else
      hash[key] = [w]
    end
  end
  result = []
  hash.each_key do |key|
    result << hash[key]
  end
end
```

Figure 2: These four solutions are from red, purple, orange and green clusters respectively. Red: a canonical solution with average solution length of 3.7 lines; Purple: a typical but longer solution, average solution length 10.9 lines; Orange: similar to Purple, but students are unaware of the `values` method available to collect all the values in a hash table, resulting in longer average solution length of 12.5; Green: complex solutions with average length 21.3 lines.

We observed that red, purple and orange clusters have less internal variation than green (complicated solution) cluster, which intuitively make sense since there are many more ways of writing a complex solution than of writing a simpler one.

To illustrate the benefit of normalized TED, we compared it with raw TED by running OPTICS against these two features. The reachability plots obtained from OPTICS are shown in Figure 3 and Figure 4.

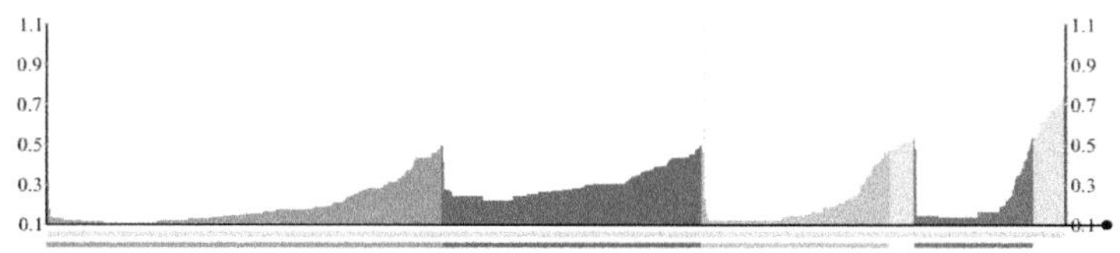

Figure 3: Reachability plot of normalized TED generated by ELKI, yellow represents outliers

Figure 4: Reachability plot of standard TED generated by ELKI, orange represents outliers

For OPTICS, the clusters show up as valleys in the reachability plot. A deeper valley usually indicates a denser cluster. From Figure 3 and Figure 4, we can see that normalized TED has more stable clusters and fewer outliers than TED.

Related Work

We are inspired by early work on feature engineering for automatic clustering of student programs [3], which proposed the use of variation theory to explain differences in student submissions. Applying variation theory to programming assignments essentially means using a hierarchical approach: first, distinguishing clusters of approaches to solving a problem, and then within each cluster identifying differences in various students' implementation of a particular approach.

This "divide and conquer" approach has many other use cases, including pairing students based on their problem-solving strategies and making it easier to illustrate to students the relateive merits of different approaches. For the moment our main focus is to multiply instructor leverage rather than fully automating the feedback process. We envision, for example, that our techniques might be used in conjunction with a system such as "Divide and Correct" for providing feedback on large groups of student submissions at once [1], or embodied in a system similar to OverCode [9], which helps visualize major groupings of variation among student submissions to a code assignment.

We use Abstract Syntax Trees (ASTs) as the basis of representing program structure and explore various metrics of similarity between ASTs. Much previous work has used ASTs to detect plagiarism [4, 6] or flag needless code duplication in a codebase by using techniques such as Latent Semantic Analysis to compare source files [5]. As in our approach, most previous work focuses on the fundamental difficulty that "raw" AST differencing captures differences at too low a level of abstraction to permit identifying higher-level patterns in the code. More recently, approaches such as Codewebs [7] compare "code phrases," or subgraphs of ASTs, to determine the probabilistic semantic equivalence of two pieces of code. An alternative approach is to provide an instructor with triples $R, C1, C2$ of solutions and ask which of $C1$ or $C2$ is more similar to R in the instructor's opinion [2], then evaluate several algorithms according to which ones show highest agreement with the instructor's opinion. This approach revealed Jaccard distance and various term-frequency based distances as promising candidates for AST differencing, but was tried only on synthetic data consisting of mutated reference solutions, not real student data.

Acknowledgments

Thanks to John Canny for valuable feedback and advice on clustering metrics and the project as a whole. This work was supported in part by the National Basic Research Program of China Grant 2011CBA00300, 2011CBA00301, the National Natural Science Foundation of China Grant 61033001, 61361136003.

References

[1] Brooks, M., Basu, S., Jacobs, C., and Vanderwende, L. Divide and correct: Using clusters to grade short answers at scale. In *Proceedings of the First ACM Conference on Learning @ Scale Conference*, L@S '14, ACM (New York, NY, USA, 2014), 89–98.

[2] Gaudencio, M., Dantas, A., and Guerrero, D. D. Can computers compare student code solutions as well as teachers? In *Proceedings of the 45th ACM Technical Symposium on Computer Science Education*, SIGCSE '14, ACM (New York, NY, USA, 2014), 21–26.

[3] Glassman, E. L., Singh, R., and Miller, R. C. Feature engineering for clustering student solutions. In *Learning At Scale (L@S)* (Atlanta, GA, Mar 2014). Work-in-progress submission.

[4] Lancaster, T., and Culwin, F. A Comparison of Source Code Plagiarism Detection Engines. *Computer Science Education 14* (June 2004), 101–112.

[5] Maletic, J., and Marcus, A. Supporting program comprehension using semantic and structural information. In *23rd Intl. Conf. on Software Engineering (ICSE)* (Toronto, Canada, May 2001).

[6] Martins, V. T., Fonte, D., Henriques, P. R., and da Cruz, D. Plagiarism detection: A tool survey and comparison. *OpenAccess Series in Informatics* (2014).

[7] Nguyen, A., Piech, C., Huang, J., and Guibas, L. Codewebs: Scalable code search for moocs. ACM (2014), 491–502.

[8] Patterson, D., and Lazowska, E. Why are English majors studying computer science? http://blogs.berkeley.edu/2013/11/26/why-are-english-majors-studying-computer-science/, Nov 2013.

[9] Scott, J., Singh, R., Guo, P. J., , and Miller, R. C. OverCode: Visualizing variation in student solutions to programming problems at scale. *ACM Transactions on Computer-Human Interaction (TOCHI)* (2014). Special issue: online learning at scale (to appear).

[10] Zhang, K., and Shasha, D. Simple fast algorithms for the editing distance between trees and related problems. *SIAM journal on computing 18*, 6 (1989), 1245–1262.

Feature Factory: Crowd-sourced feature discovery

Kalyan Veeramachaneni
CSAIL, MIT.
32 Vassar Street
Cambirdge, MA 02139 USA
kalyan@csail.mit.edu

Una-May O'Reilly
CSAIL, MIT.
32 Vassar Street
Cambirdge, MA 02139 USA
unamay@csail.mit.edu

Kiarash Adl
CSAIL, MIT.
32 Vassar Street
Cambirdge, MA 02139 USA
kiarash@csail.mit.edu

L@S 2015, Mar 14-18, 2015, Vancouver, BC, Canada
ACM 978-1-4503-3411-2/15/03.
http://dx.doi.org/10.1145/2724660.2728696

Abstract
We examine the process of engineering features for developing models that improve our understanding of learners' online behavior in MOOCs. Because feature engineering relies so heavily on human insight, we engage the crowd for feature proposals and guidance on how to operationalize them. When we examined our crowd-sourced features in the context of predicting stopout, not only were they impressively nuanced, but they also integrated more than one interaction mode between the learner and platform and described how the learner was *relatively* performing.

Introduction
We have been trying to quantitatively characterize learners' online behavior from *web logs* and *click stream* data. The raw data, after processing, curating, and storing in a database [1], enables extraction of *per-learner* time sequences of click stream events. These sequences are primitive but, if formulated into *variables* that abstract learners' behavior, via *feature engineering*, they could help gauge learners' intent, interest and motivation in the absence of verbalized or visual feedback. We are interested in:

[1]These three steps are extremely complex and challenging but are not in the scope of this paper

Figure 1: Engaging crowd to understand the data from Massive Open Online Courses.

Variables that capture per learner behavior with respect to a *resource*: For example, consider two variables such as: *total time spent of the video* and the *number of pauses while watching the video.* When these two variables are evaluated for all the learners and analyzed they can reveal patterns; if too many learners *pause* too many times, the video could be fast and/or confusing.

Per-learner longitudinal variables: For example, consider *time each student spent on the course website during the week* or, more complex, *on an average, the length of time before the deadline that the learner starts to work on an assignment.*

Humans need to help engineer features

Feature engineering learner variables should be primarily driven by humans, rather than be automated, because humans can:

Generate ideas based on their intuition: Everyone has been a student so it is possible to self reflect to invent variables. E.g, when considering prediction of *stopout*, we might each quite naturally suggest "*If the student starts to homework problems very close to the deadline, he might be very likely to fall behind and eventually drop out*". Subsequently, we might propose how to operationalize such a variable into a quantitative value by measuring, " Time difference between the deadline and the student's first attempt for the homework problem". While many other aspects of feature engineering can be automated, intuitive generation one cannot.

Offer instructor knowledge: For MOOCs, designing variables requires understanding of *context* and *content* of the course for which the variables are sought. This makes instructors or experts in the course perfectly positioned to propose variables. E.g., an instructor might be aware of an important concept whose understanding is critical for continued success in the course and may hypothesize that a variable that captures whether the learner understood the concept or not could help predict stopout.

Offer highly specialized learning science knowledge: Researchers from learning sciences are able to propose variables grounded in theory that elucidate latent constructs such as *motivation*, *intention*, and *self-efficacy*.

Help operationalize feature ideas: Moving from a feature idea to its operationalization is involved. Key decisions have to be made about definition and thresholds. For example, we might have to define what constitutes as "start" time for student working on an assignment. Since there is no mechanism where students notify when they started to work on the assignment, a human can help judge whether it should be the first time they looked at the problem, or the time of the first attempt for the problem or the time they attempted but saved the answer instead of checking for correctness.

Given that humans are NOT replaceable in feature engineering, we are exploring *how to increase the number of people who can participate in it.* Our exploratory context is predictors for *stopout.*

Naturally, we started by thinking up feature ideas ourselves then operationalizing them. Realizing this tact is vulnerable to missing some features, we have constructed activities that allow us to solicit feature ideas from others, i.e. the "crowd". This expands our feature set and eliminates our blind spots. Post-hoc, we can compare our original set to the crowd's set and discern whether it provides extra value.

Stopout prediction problem

Herein we define our notion of *stopout.* We considered defining it by the learner's last interaction in the course, regardless of the nature of the interaction [1]. However, this definition yields noisy results because it gives equal weight to a passive interaction (viewing a lecture,

Describe feature	Why is this feature useful?
pset grade over time: Difference between grade on the current pset and average grade over previous psets. Significant decreases may be likely to be correlated with dropouts.	Anecdotally it appears that users who perform poorly on the current week (especially after not performing poorly in the preceding weeks) will subsequently give up. They may also, with low probability, post on the forum explaining their issue with the task at hand.
average pre deadline submission time: average time between problem submission time and problem due date.	people who get things done early are probably not under time pressure that would make them drop out.
proportion of time spent during weekends): Fraction of observed resource time spent on each day of the week (7 variables for Mon-Sun that add up to 1). Just for previous week, and averaged over all weeks so far.	Heavy weekend users might be more likely to drop out, because they don't have spare weekday time to devote to the course.

Table 1: Three examples of features proposed by the students and instructors in the MIT class.

accessing an assignment, viewing a Wiki etc) as it does to a pro-active interaction (submitting a problem, midterm, assignment etc). A learner could stop submitting assignments in the course after week 2, but continue to access the course pages and not be considered stopped out. Instead, we define the *stopout*point as the time slice (week) a learner fails to submit any further assignments or exercise problems. A submission (or attempt) is a submission of any problem type (Homework, lab, exam etc.). Using this definition for *stopout* we extracted the week number when each learner in the cohort stopped out. To illustrate the predictive model's potential application, we will use a realistic scenario. The model user, likely an instructor or platform provider, could use the data from week 1 to week 3 (current week) to make predictions. The model will predict existing learner *stopout* during weeks $i+1$ to 14.

6.MITx Experiment

To generate ideas for features, we sought help from a class at MIT called 6.MITx. We presented the data model (what was being collected), explained what we meant by a feature and asked members of the class (professors and students) to posit features for each student/learner that could predict a student's stopout. We collected the input *via* a google form asking the users to describe each feature and describe why they think it will be useful in predicting stopout. We did not present our ideas for features to the class.

Outcomes: Out of the 30 features that the class

proposed, 7 were in common with ours. Out of the remaining 23 features, we extracted 10. The features proposed by the students and instructors in this class were *intuitive*, based on *experience* and self identification as once/or currently being a student. Participants also gave detailed reason as to why the feature is useful. We present three examples in Table 1.

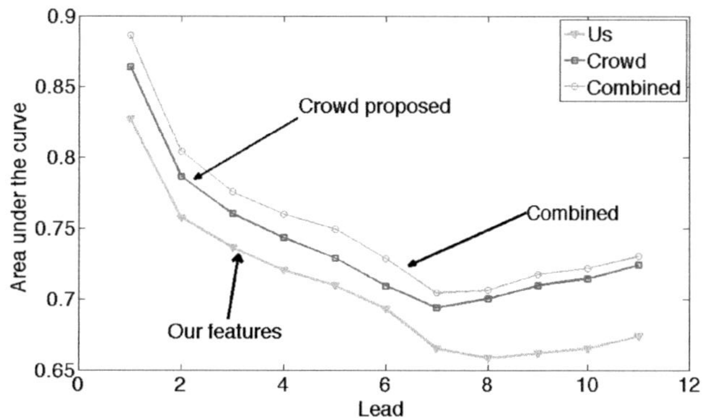

Figure 2: Performance of different sources of features in terms of prediction accuracy for stopout prediction problem at the end of week 3. We compare crowd proposed features with features proposed by and then performance when both of them are combined.

When we extracted these features and used them for stopout prediction, they consistently performed better than the features we ourselves came up with. In Figure 2 we compare the predictive accuracy (measured in AUC -higher the better) for different week-ahead prediction problems at week 3. We see that the features proposed by crowd help significantly, specially when we are trying to predict far ahead. Also note that combining the features proposed by the *crowd* and us leads to an even better performance. In general, for different learner cohorts we found that features proposed by the crowd mattered significantly more than the features we proposed ourselves.

We also found the more influential features were quite nuanced and complex. They incorporated data from multiple modes of learner activity (submissions, browsing and collaborations), required carefully linking data fields. Relational features that compared a learner to others and statistical summaries were proposed by the crowd and mattered quite a bit.

Based on this experience, we are building a web-based platform (WWW.FEATUREFACTORY.ORG) that allows many people to participate in defining features. The general public can enter a new idea, or comment on an existing one while programmers can script features.

Related work

The "more features the merrier" theme is prominent among feature engineering studies. For example, the 2010 KDD cup resulted in a paper "Feature engineering and classifier ensemble for KDD cup 2010" [2]. In the 2013 "Big data for education" MOOC offered by Prof. Ryan Baker, he suggests that, in practice, it is a process of ideation that happens by researchers brainstorming as a group with support for the free flow of ideas.

References

[1] Balakrishnan, G., and Coetzee, D. Predicting student retention in massive open online courses using hidden markov models. In *Technical Report No. UCB/EECS-2013-109*, EECS, University of California, Berkeley (2013).

[2] Yu, H.-F., Lo, H.-Y., Hsieh, H.-P., Lou, J.-K., McKenzie, T. G., Chou, J.-W., Chung, P.-H., Ho, C.-H., Chang, C.-F., Wei, Y.-H., et al. Feature engineering and classifier ensemble for kdd cup 2010.

Are You Listening? Social Roles and Perceived Value of Statements in Online Learning Communities

Ruth Shillair
Michigan State University
East Lansing, Michigan
shillia7@msu.edu

Rick Wash
Michigan State University
East Lansing, Michigan
wash@msu.edu

L@S 2015, March 14-18, 2015, Vancouver, BC, Canada.
ACM 978-1-4503-3411-2/15/03.
http://dx.doi.org/10.1145/2724660.2728697

Abstract
An important part of learning is interactions with peers, mentors, teaching assistants and the instructor. Discussions and group work allow for interactive learning and deeper understanding of class concepts. Online learning environments struggle to replicate this process. This is especially true when the scale of an online class is increased. In order to address this issue a few MOOCs solicit teaching assistants to answer questions, and through their social position, help set academic standards in discussion forums. However, little is know about how different social roles influence the attribution of value to statements in these environments. This study demonstrates that the attitudes expressed by individuals in facilitating roles influence the acceptance of information shared in a discussion board setting.

Author Keywords
Online education; MOOCs; social status in online environments; attribution of value

ACM Classification Keywords
H.5.3 asynchronous interaction, theory and models, computer-supported cooperative work

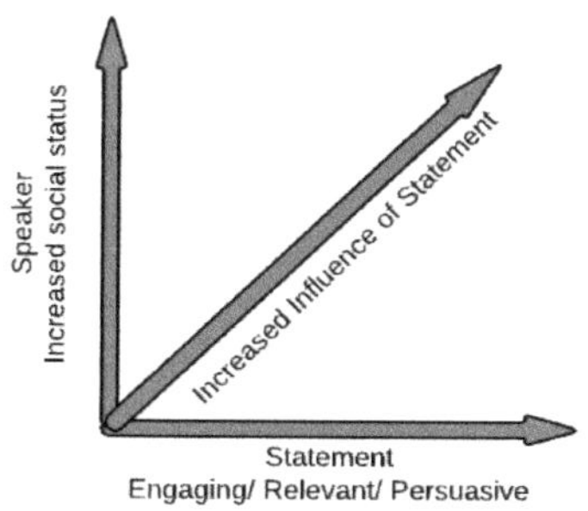

Figure 1: Expected Ratings of Statements

Introduction

In traditional educational environments, students interact with the instructor, the learning material and with each other. Each student learns not only from personal experience, but also learns vicariously by observing other students interact with those in various roles. The transition to learning in computer mediated (CM) environments brings challenges in trying to replicate strategies that have proven to enhance interactive and observational learning. There is a need for systematic, theory-based research to begin to fully comprehend the intricacies of the social relationships in these environments and how these affect CM collaborative learning, especially when scaled to larger sizes.

One consistent finding in online educational case studies is the importance of social presence and immediacy, which is traditionally established through the instructor's responses to students questions, comments, and postings [6]. This sense of immediacy not only improves student satisfaction, it has been found as a key factor in retention [5]. In Massive Open Online Courses (MOOCs), there are even greater challenges to provide students with a sense of connectedness, immediacy and spaces for meaningful interaction. Encouraging students to answer each other's questions is the norm, but without guidance, the array of disjointed discussion threads do not substantively foster learning [2]. If there is no socio-technical structure to provide direction to discussions, demonstrate norms of civil engagement, and encourage substantive quality, it is no wonder that MOOCs frequently become a spectator arena, where participants simply download learning materials or watch videos. The student struggles on, alone in the midst of thousands.

To address this issue, a few MOOCs offer a handful of trained TAs to help answer questions and guide discussion boards or peer feedback. In addition to these planned interventions, a few students are able to negotiate these amorphous forums very successfully, interacting with fellow students and providing clear and insightful comments [7]. These "superposters" add value and community to group discussions [7]. The contribution of social roles such as T.A. and "superposters" are just starting to be understood [10].

Even though these positions are generally seen as adding some value to the MOOC experience [8], they require the investment of resources to develop and support these roles. Social interaction with experienced class members or teaching assistants could provide feedback and guidance in what is frequently a complex learning environment. A further challenge is that MOOCs reach a wider age demographic than typical college classes. Older or non-traditional students might benefit from social engagement that includes hierarchical guidance [4]. Research is needed not only to justify this investment, but also to understand the potential influence these roles have.

Theoretical Framework

MOOC research, up to this point, is primarily case studies [9]. Our research is theoretically guided by learning theories (e.g., social cognitive theory, social presence, and Bloom's taxonomy), online communities engagement research, and generative collective models.

The theoretical framework that has been frequently used to understand the learning process is Social Cognitive Theory (SCT) [1]. This framework includes the constructs of the individual, the environment, and

Discussion 1 (All student condition) Mean =3.38 (N=8)		
	Teaching Assistant	Starred Student
Authority supported	3.82 (N=11)	4.00 (N=10)
Authority opposed	3.90 (N=8)	3.44 (N=9)

Table 1:
Results of a discussion with low ratings when all student condition

Discussion 3 (All student condition) Mean =3.88 (N=8)		
	Teaching Assistant	Starred Student
Authority opposed	3.18 (N=11)	3.40 (N=10)
Authority supported	4.00 (N=8)	3.56 (N=9)

Table 2:
Results of a discussion with high ratings when all student condition

behavior. All of these constructs work in a dynamically evolving and changing process. In a traditional setting, students learn by observing others ask questions and how those in authority respond to those questions. Often behavioral changes or mastery of a new skill is best developed in a small group or setting where interaction and encouragement from either the instructor or others can help in the learning process [3].

Immediacy in verbal and non-verbal behaviors by teachers in traditional, face-to-face, classrooms are significant in improving student learning[3]. Simple actions like smiling, nodding, or looking attentively at a student improves student engagement [3]. Smaller online classes rely on the instructors to be available to answer questions, interact with students and provide a sense of social presence. Giving teaching assistants, experienced students, and those who are willing to commit to being group leaders the training and status to help answer questions may help alleviate this situation.

Bloom's taxonomy is a widely adopted rubric for helping evaluate the learning process by setting measurable objectives. In this research, three elements of Bloom's taxonomy are utilized in assessing the participant's perception of class content on the learning spectrum. This would indicate levels of readiness to learn. If a student finds information understandable (clear), interesting to think about (engaging), and able to influence their attitudes (persuasive), then they are already learning from it.

Social Status in Forum Experiment

Our participants go through a pre-test to assess the mental models of the participant, comfort with learning in online spaces, and previous experiences with online learning. Then the participants are assigned to one of five conditions: the TA or a starred student who either support or oppose statements that were highly rated by the initial testing of statements without attribution. This is a 2 by 2 design with an extra condition with only fellow students as a control condition. Subjects are given the class scenario and read four short discussions. They rate if the discussion was persuasive and evaluate the persona in the role under consideration. Demographic information is also gathered to look for the influence of age, gender, or cultural background in influencing the view of a persona's social status. Ratings are done using seven point Likert-type scales.

Pretesting statements

The valance of the statements, apart from social context, was tested using a student sample (N=115) from a major Midwestern university for credit in a communications class as a convenience sample. Both individual statements and entire discussions were rated for clarity, engagement and persuasiveness. Discussions were then arranged for the experiment with social attribution added.

Experiment Population

To get a sample that would best represent MOOC participants and test for a later, larger sample, we collected an Amazon M-Turk sample of 45 individuals using only United States IP addresses and individuals who had a 90% or higher approval rating. Both attentiveness and manipulation check questions were added. Participants were told about the classroom scenario and asked to rate the discussions. Social roles were introduced and are represented using small icons rather than actual pictures which might produce a bias.

Initial results indicated that both roles examined had influence on the participants. Surprisingly, the "starred student" seemed to have the most impact. Even though the authority figure only made one statement in each discussion, it appeared to have influence.

Further research in this area may demonstrate the value of developing systems to encourage, support and reward peers who are willing to invest time and effort into enhancing group discussions. Ongoing work is to duplicate this study in a larger scale.

If having established roles within the MOOC experience brings increased engagement, deeper processing of information, and increased interaction then it is well worth the investment.

Acknowledgements

The material is based upon work supported by National Science Foundation under award No. 1350253.

References

[1] Bandura, A. Social cognitive theory : An agentic perspective. *Annual review of psychology 52*, (2001), 26.

[2] Dennen, V.P. From message posting to learning dialogues: Factors affecting learner participation in asynchronous discussion. *Distance Education 26*, 1 (2005), 127–148.

[3] Gorham, J. The relationship between verbal teacher immedicacy behaviors and student learning. *Communication Education 37*, 1 (1988), 40–53.

[4] Guo, P.J. and Reinecke, K. Demographic differences in how students navigate through MOOCs. *Proceedings of the first ACM conference on Learning @ scale conference - L@S '14*, (2014), 21–30.

[5] Hart, C. Factors Associated With Student Persistence in an Online Program of Study: A Review of the Literature. *Journal of Interactive Online Learning 11*, 1 (2012).

[6] Hill, J.R., Song, L., and West, R.E. Social Learning Theory and Web-Based Learning Environments: A Review of Research and Discussion of Implications. *American Journal of Distance Education 23*, 2 (2009), 88–103.

[7] Huang, J., Dasgupta, A., Ghosh, A., Manning, J., and Sanders, M. Superposter behavior in MOOC forums. *Proceedings of the first ACM conference on Learning @ scale conference - L@S '14*, (2014), 117–126.

[8] Lea, M., Spears, R., and de Groot, D. Knowing me , knowing you: Anonymity effects. *Personality and Social Psychology Bulletin 27*, (2001), 526–537.

[9] Liyanagunawardena, T.R., Adams, A.A., and Williams, S.A. MOOCs: A systematic study of the published literature 2008-2012. *The International Review of Research in Open and Distance Learning 14*, 2013, 202–227.

[10] Miller, K., Zyto, S., Karger, D., and Mazur, E. Improving online class forums by seeding discussions and managing section size. *Proceedings of the first ACM conference on Learning @ scale conference - L@S '14*, (2014), 173–174.

All It Takes Is One: Evidence for a Strategy for Seeding Large Scale Peer Learning Interactions

Marti A. Hearst
UC Berkeley
Berkeley, CA 94720 USA
hearst@berkeley.edu

D Coetzee
UC Berkeley
Berkeley, CA 94720 USA
dcoetzee@berkeley.edu

Armando Fox
UC Berkeley
Berkeley, CA 94720 USA
fox@berkeley.edu

Björn Hartmann
UC Berkeley
Berkeley, CA 94720 USA
bjoern@berkeley.edu

L@S 2015, Mar 14-18, 2015, Vancouver, BC, Canada
ACM 978-1-4503-3411-2/15/03.
http://dx.doi.org/10.1145/2724660.2728698

Abstract
The results of a study of online peer learning suggests that it may be advantageous to automatically assign students to small peer learning groups based on how many students initially get answers to questions correct.

ACM Classification Keywords
H.5.m [Information interfaces and presentation (HCI)]: Miscellaneous.

Introduction
We investigated [1] how to introduce synchronous interactive peer learning into an online setting appropriate for students in massive online courses. Motivated by the literature of peer learning [4, 6, 2, 5, 3] and by a goal of making the experience of online learning more social, we conducted studies in which groups of three participants are formed and answer multiple choice questions via synchronous discussions. In those studies, participants first answered a multiple choice question on their own and then saw the answers proposed by the others in the group. They were then encouraged to discuss the answers and try to help each other figure out the correct answer. They each had an opportunity to revise their response based on the discussion. Questions were selected from a set of 20 GMAT practice questions on critical reasoning.

This paper provides a more detailed analysis of the group breakdown than described in [1]. In particular, we found that more participants will change from an incorrect to a correct response if *at least one* participant in the group initially makes a correct response than if there is no such initially correct response. (Fishers test, $p < 0.05$). Figure 1 illustrates the data in detail. For the 21 peer learning chat groups in which one person started with the correct answer, in only 4 cases did the group degenerate into fewer correct answers by the end of the exercise, and in 12 cases the scores improved. Similarly, for the 26 chat groups in which two participants began with the correct answer, in only 3 cases did the results get worse, and in 12 cases the results improved with the third participant moving to the correct answer.

Num initial choice correct	Num Final Choice Correct 0	1	2	3
0	10	1	1	
1	4	5	5	7
2	2	1	11	12
3			1	13

Figure 1: Number of correct answers to a multiple choice question in a group of three participants before and after a discussion takes place. Red signifies a decrease in the number correct, green an increase in the number correct, and the neutral color signifies no change in the number correct after the discussion takes place.

Another interesting observation from this data is that when everyone in the group started with the correct answer, the group as a whole was very unlikely to move away from that correct answer. However, the converse was also true: if no one in the group had the correct answer, then the group was very likely to stay in that state of everyone remaining wrong.

A New Strategy For Assigning Peer Learning Groups

This observation suggests intriguing new strategies for large scale online learning that are not feasible in in-person classrooms or in small-scale online learning environments.

One idea is to develop a software platform that first serves a question to a set of students, and after determining their initial answers, automatically groups the students with others based on what has been determined in advance to lead to a pedagogically fruitful conversation. This can cascade still further: if a student gets the answer wrong a second time, that student could be given a hint as to why their choice is wrong, and grouped again with other students who had a similar misconception. Thus another option is to experiment whether certain prompts or hints will further improve the performance of the groups.

In our study there was no evidence that more participants will improve from an incorrect to a correct response if two students are correct, rather than only one (Fisher's test, $p > 0.5$). The parameters of how to group students may vary depending on the kind of material being learned and question being asked. Further study may show empirically that certain types of problems work better when only one of several students is well-informed, whereas for other kinds of problems it may be best to have a majority of knowledgable students.

Acknowledgements

This material is based upon work supported by a Google Social Interactions Research Award and the National Science Foundation under Grant No. IIS 1149799 and IIS

1210836.

References

[1] Coetzee, D., Lim, S., Fox, A., Hartmann, B., and Hearst, M. A. Structuring interactions for large-scale synchronous peer learning. In *CSCW: ACM Conference on Computer Supported Collaborative Work* (2015).

[2] Crouch, C. H., and Mazur, E. Peer instruction: Ten years of experience and results. *American Journal of Physics 69*, 9 (2001), 970–977.

[3] Deslauriers, L., Schelew, E., and Wieman, C. Improved learning in a large-enrollment physics class. *Science 332*, 6031 (2011), 862–864.

[4] Millis, B. *Cooperative Learning in Higher Education: Across the Disciplines, Across the Academy*. Stylus Publishing, LLC., 2012.

[5] Smith, M. K., Wood, W. B., Adams, W. K., Wieman, C., Knight, J. K., Guild, N., and Su, T. T. Why peer discussion improves student performance on in-class concept questions. *Science 323*, 5910 (2009), 122–124.

[6] Springer, L., Stanne, M. E., and Donovan, S. S. Effects of small-group learning on undergraduates in science, mathematics, engineering, and technology: A meta-analysis. *Review of Educational Research 69*, 1 (1999), 21–51.

Evaluating the Relationship Between Course Structure, Learner Activity, and Perceived Value of Online Courses

Ido Roll
The University of British Columbia
220-1961 East Mall
Vancouver, BC V6T 1Z1
ido.roll@ubc.ca

Leah P. Macfadyen
The University of British Columbia
Buchanan C110, 1866 Main Mall
Vancouver, BC V6T 1Z1
leah.macfadyen@ubc.ca

Debra Sandilands
The University of British Columbia
sandilan@mail.ubc.ca

L@S 2015, March 14–18, 2015, Vancouver, BC, Canada.
ACM 978-1-4503-3411-2/15/03.
http://dx.doi.org/10.1145/2724660.2728699

Abstract
Using aggregated Learning Management System data and course evaluation data from 26 online courses, we evaluated the relationship between measures of online activity, course and assessment structure, and student perceptions of course value. We find relationships between selected dimensions of learner engagement that reflect current constructivist theories of learning. This work demonstrates the potential value of pooled, easily accessible, and anonymous data for high-level inferences regarding design of online courses and the learner experience.

Author Keywords
Learning management system; learning analytics; student evaluation of teaching; engagement

ACM Classification Keywords
K.3.1 Computer Uses in Education - *Computer-managed instruction (CMI); Distance learning*

Introduction
All educational institutions generate and store large volumes of information about learners, learning and teaching, but few have explored the data they collect or used what they have learned [1][2]. Learning analytics

(LA) research may allow higher education to better leverage the increasing availability of sets of 'big educational data' and the analytic and interpretive affordances of fields such as educational data mining, statistics, machine learning and the learning sciences [3].

The Society for Learning Analytics Research[1] (SoLAR) defines the goals of LA as "understanding and optimizing learning and the environments in which learning occurs". To date, most LA research has focussed on individual learner performance and Learning Management System (LMS) data (c.f., [4]). In this exploratory project we seek to analyze additional kinds of 'big educational data' from our institution to advance our understanding of how learning unfolds in online courses, and to use this information to improve design and increase engagement.

Our work is underpinned by the 'Community of Inquiry' theoretical framework [5]. This model proposes that successful learning experiences occur when a virtual learning environment supports three inter-related "presences": Social, Cognitive, and Teaching. Here, we are specifically interested in using analytics to investigate *the learning environment*, with a focus on a core element of 'teaching presence': "the design of the educational experience" [5]. We are exploring available metrics of this 'course design' element, and investigating their relationships with learner activity in the course and learner perception of course value (as indicated by scores in Student Evaluations of Teaching (SEOT). SEOT scores are multi-dimensional and valid indicators of teaching performance [5] but their use for

[1] http://www.solaresearch.org

assessment of teaching performance remains contested. In this study, however, we re-direct attention to the potential value of selected SEOT scores as indicators of course design effectiveness and the student learning experience.

Research Questions

Our work seeks to evaluate whether course-level aggregate data can be used to evaluate relationship between different dimensions of course engagement: course and assessment structure, online activity, and perceived value (see Figure 1).

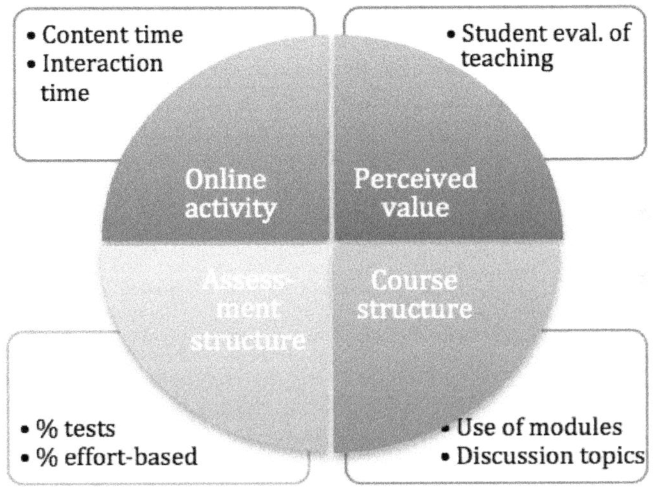

Figure 1: Dimensions and metrics of engagement.

We used aggregate course-level data, rather than individual learner data with the goal of making such approaches generalizable across higher education institutions, while avoiding use of sensitive personal information.

Method

Our analysis includes data from all undergraduate online courses offered by one faculty in a large university during a single academic term. To prevent inter-dependencies, we randomly selected single sections from multi-section courses, leaving us with N=26 courses. The average number of students per course was 35 (SD=18.3).

Next we operationalized each of the dimensions identified above. ***Online activity*** was assessed using three metrics: Overall time per student per week, in minutes (M±SD: 168±97); Time on content pages per student per week (73±49); Time on peer interaction activities per student per week (discussion forums and chats; 63±45). Notably, we only looked at data from weeks 2-12, as the first and last weeks of the term are less typical. ***Course structure*** was assessed using the following two metrics: Number of learning modules (7.5±3.1) reflects instructor choices to structure course materials into smaller, more manageable, units; Number of discussion topics (20.4±17.0) shows the number of different discussion threads established by the instructor. ***Assessment structure*** was operationalized as the weight of two components of the final grade: Tests, including final exam (37±24%); and Effort-based Activities, e.g. required participation in discussions (14±16%). Notably, we only had reliable assessment structure data from eleven courses. ***Perceived value*** was evaluated using a single item from institutional SEOT scores: "Considering everything, how would you rate this course?" Students answered this question on a 5-point Likert Scale. There are several reasons for using SEOT scores. First, unlike course grades, SEOT can be used to compare courses. Second, it is a relatively robust measure. For instance, this specific SEOT item is not associated with number of students (r =0.10) or response rate to the SEOT survey (r=0.10). Somewhat surprisingly, SEOT scores correlated significantly and negatively with average grade – that is, courses with higher grades were rated *more poorly* by students: $r(20)=-0.49$, $p=0.03$. Only 20 courses in the sample set have SEOT data.

Results

We first evaluated the relationship between engagement activity and course value. There is a positive, yet insignificant relationship between time-on-task and course value: $r(20) = 0.34$. Interestingly, this is driven mainly by peer interactions. The correlation between weekly time spent on peer interaction activities (within the course framework, almost exclusively on the discussion board) and perceived value is $r(20)=0.42$, $p=0.06$. While only marginally significant, this correlation reveals that 18% of the variation in SEOT scores is explained by variations in average weekly time in the discussion forum.

As expected, the course structure, as determined by the instructor, has an effect on students' choices with regard to engagement and perceived value. Courses with more built-in discussion topics also tend to have more interaction in them: $r(26)=0.51$, $p<0.01$. However, there is no direct relationship between number of discussion topics and perceived value, $r=0.0$. That is, while instructor-initiated discussion threads were associated with increased volume of interaction, this was not the interaction that was associated with perceived value. On the other hand, organizing course materials into sequential learning modules is associated with increased perceived value, albeit insignificantly: $r(20)=0.35$.

Last, the assessment structure offers additional insights into student engagement. There is a strong association between the weight of effort-based grades and perceived course value: $r(9)=0.38$[2]. Notably, these effort-based grades require higher overall time on task: $r(11)=0.76$. There is no association between the weight of tests and perceived value, $r(9)=0.0$.

Discussion

This study offers preliminary results describing the association of different aspects of learner engagement in online courses, namely, perceived value, online activity, and structure. Courses in which students spend more time on peer interaction activities (mainly the discussion forum) receive higher evaluation scores, while the relationship between time spent on content pages and perceived value is not as clear. Although the number of discussion threads is associated with increased interaction, it does not necessarily promote valued interaction. Having an emphasis on effort-based assessments, on the other hand, is associated with valued interactions. Results also show that organizing the course in modules is associated with higher perceived value.

It is important to emphasize that correlation is not causation. For example, it is unclear whether students value more courses with much interaction, or interact more in courses that they value. Moreover, our study has several limitations: results were determined using a small number of courses, and we did not correct for multiple comparisons. Overall, however, this study demonstrates the promise of using different dimensions of learner engagement, even in aggregate format.

[2] Due to the small N, no significance values are calculated.

Specifically, our analysis suggests that courses whose activities and assessments are more demanding of learner time are, in fact, associated with increased perceived value, especially when students use their time in the course to interact with peers. Results also show that course structure can contribute to productive interactions, but not as simply as one would think.

References

[1] Macfadyen, L. P., & Dawson, S. Numbers are not enough. Why e-learning analytics failed to inform an institutional strategic plan. *Educational Technology & Society*, 15(3) (2012), 149–163.

[2] Manyika, J., Chui, M., Brown, B., Bughin, J., Dobbs, R., Roxburgh, C., & Byers, A. H. *Big data: The next frontier for innovation, competition and productivity*. McKinsey Global Institute (2011). http://www.mckinsey.com/insights/business_technology/big_data_the_next_frontier_for_innovation

[3] Ferguson, R. Learning analytics: Drivers, developments and challenges. *International Journal of Technology Enhanced Learning, 4,* 5/6 (2012), 304–317.

[4] Macfadyen, L.P. & Dawson, S. (2010) Mining LMS data to develop an 'early warning system' for educators: A proof of concept, Computers & Education, 54, 2, (2010), 588-599.

[5] Garrison, D. R., Anderson, T., & Archer, W. Critical inquiry in a text-based environment: Computer conferencing in higher education model. *The Internet and Higher Education*, 2, 2-3 (2000), 87-105.

[6] Marsh, H. W. Students' Evaluations of University Teaching: Dimensionality, Reliability, Validity, Potential Biases and Usefulness. In *The Scholarship of Teaching and Learning in Higher Education: An Evidence-Based Perspective* edited by R. P. Perry and J. C. Smart. Springer (2007), 319-383.

Cultural Relevance in MOOCs: Asking About Socioeconomic Context

Anna Kasunic
Carnegie Mellon University
5000 Forbes Avenue
Pittsburgh, PA, 15213 USA
akasunic@andrew.cmu.edu

Jessica Hammer
Carnegie Mellon University
5000 Forbes Avenue
Pittsburgh, PA, 15213 USA
hammerj@cs.cmu.edu

Amy Ogan
Carnegie Mellon University
5000 Forbes Avenue
Pittsburgh, PA, 15213 USA
aeo@andrew.cmu.edu

L@S 2015, Mar 14-18, 2015, Vancouver, BC, Canada
ACM 978-1-4503-3411-2/15/03
http://dx.doi.org/10.1145/2724660.2728700

Abstract
Existing datasets tell us only a partial story about the contextual factors that impact learners in Massive Online Open Courses (MOOCs). Information about race/ethnicity, education, and income helps us understand socioeconomic status, but such data is notoriously difficult to collect in an international context. Extant MOOC studies have not paid due attention to socioeconomic variables; they have either taken a U.S.-centric approach, ignored important country-specific dimensions of variables, or failed to ask about certain variables altogether, such as race/ethnicity. During a qualitative study of 24 self-regulated learners from population groups underrepresented in MOOCs, we piloted a short U.S.-centric demographic questionnaire. Preliminary results suggest that a large-scale survey designed for both cross-national and country-specific analyses would provide valuable information to MOOC researchers.

Author Keywords
MOOCs; survey design; international; demographics; socioeconomic status

ACM Classification Keywords
H.5.m. Information interfaces and presentation: Misc.

Introduction

Although it is well established that cross-national demographic survey design is difficult, the issue has been largely absent in discussions of MOOC survey design. Despite intentions to make the courses "education borderless, gender-blind, race-blind, class-blind and bank account-blind" [1], survey data indicates that MOOCs disproportionately benefit learners who already have a bachelor's degree or higher and reside in developed countries [2], [3]. In the U.S., income and race/ethnicity are highly correlated with socioeconomic status and education level [4]–[6]. Such issues carry U.S.-specific history and context, but the concept of educational inequities intersecting with income and race/ethnicity factors is by no means unique to this country [7]–[9]. Nonetheless, existing MOOC survey instruments typically ignore race/ethnicity and income altogether. Meanwhile, HarvardX and MITx ask learners about their education level using broad categories, but are lacking in that they do not allow for country-specific responses or analyses. Other widely cited surveys, e.g. the U Penn 2013 Coursera survey [2], have used U.S.-centric education categories.

It is worth noting that some studies have explored income in the MOOC space through non-survey means. By supplementing HarvardX data with U.S. Census data, Hansen and Reich demonstrated that U.S. HarvardX learners live in more affluent neighborhoods [10]. However, such a method may not reflect true income levels, and may not be feasible in some countries where income data by postal code is not readily available. In another study, Dillahunt et al. sought to explore course behavior of those unable to afford higher education using Coursera entrance survey data [11]. However, given that the notion of affordability may vary widely by individual, this data, too, may misrepresent true economic status.

Method

We recruited 24 adults that identified as self-regulated learners; twelve participants had enrolled in at least one MOOC, and the other 12 had engaged in other forms of self-regulated learning. Because we were interested in understanding learners that are currently underrepresented in MOOCs, all participants either were from the U.S. and did not have a college degree (n=11), or were of a non-U.S. cultural and educational background (n=13). We administered a brief questionnaire, either in person (n=14) or online (n=10) prior to an interview lasting roughly 35-60 minutes.

We designed the questionnaire 1) to pilot test demographic questions for a large-scale survey, and 2) to elicit additional context that might not emerge in the interviews. For the socioeconomic survey questions, we decided to gauge responses to U.S.-centric categories, such as those used in the U Penn 2013 Coursera survey [2]. We encouraged participants to write in their own responses if any categories did not fit them, and to ask questions of the researcher.

Results

Education. Three participants stated that due to differences in national education systems, they felt unable to specify either their own or their parents' education level with the categories provided. One non-U.S. respondent[1] chose GED for a parent's education

[1] We use "U.S. respondent" to refer to those born and raised in the U.S., and "non-U.S." to refer to those of international

Education [2]
Less than High School or Secondary School
High School or Secondary School
GED
Some college
2 year college degree (such as Associate's degree) or equivalent
Technical degree or certification
University degree (such as BA, BS) or equivalent
Master's degree (such as MA) or equivalent
Professional degree (such as JD, MD, MBA) or equivalent
Doctoral degree (PhD)
Other: (Write in)
Race/Ethnicity [14]
Yes, Hispanic or Latino
No, not Hispanic or Latino
American Indian or Alaska Native
Asian
Black or African American
Native Hawaiian or Other Pacific Islander
White
Other: (Write in)
Income [15]
Less than $5,000
$5,000 through $11,999
$12,000 through $15,999
$16,000 through $24,999
$25,000 through $34,999
$35,000 through $49,999
$50,000 through $74,999
$75,000 through $99,999
$100,000 and greater
Don't know
Other: (Write in)

Table 1: Three question categories from the questionnaire.

level; it is unclear whether this designation carried the meaning of high school equivalency for this participant.

Race/Ethnicity. Two non-U.S. respondents did not use the provided categories; one wrote in "Mestizo," and another left the questions blank. A third non-U.S. participant sought assistance for the race/ethnicity question, as she was of an ethnic minority in her country. In the end, she decided to choose one of the existing categories instead of "Other." In addition, two U.S. respondents chose other options; one left the question blank, and another wrote in "Adopted." In this way, we see that questions about race/ethnicity can be grey and sensitive areas even when categories purportedly fit a given national context.

Income. Six non-U.S. participants chose "Don't Know." Several of these participants were current students and explained they were unsure of their parents' earnings; another participant didn't know if his spouse's scholarship stipend would be considered income. In this way, the "don't knows" may stem from factors that are not country-specific. The accuracy of other responses to the U.S.-dollar based question is unclear.

Survey Design Implications and Future Work

Challenges in cross-national demographic survey design are nothing new, but they have received insufficient attention in the MOOC space. Preliminary results from this study suggest the need for survey design that better accommodates both cross-national and country-specific analyses.

Existing survey models for international comparisons such as the International Standard Classification of Education (ISCED) [12] and cross-national ethnicity surveys that focus on minority status [13] can serve as guides for MOOC research. For example, ISCED surveys typically start with country-specific questions about education, and then later map these responses onto international standard categories, rather than starting with the broad categories, as do HarvardX and MITx surveys. MOOC students should have the option to respond to questions specific to their national contexts, which would provide valuable country-specific data. Researchers could later map the data onto standardized categories to allow for cross-national comparisons.

Future surveys could also provide a link or tool to help respondents convert U.S. dollars into an equivalent income in their local currency, adjusted for Purchasing Power Parity. However, as we saw, regardless of national specificity, answers to income-related questions are not always readily known or comfortable to share. In this way, Hansen and Reich's method of supplementing through postal code data [10] deserves further attention in international contexts. Although such a method may be reasonably reliable in a U.S. context, data sets may not be publicly available for other countries. Researchers may need to directly collaborate with international statistical agencies.

Future work related to this pilot study will include a large-scale survey based on findings from the pilot questionnaires and in-depth interviews. Later, we will design and test new tools for enhancing MOOCs. As these preliminary results have demonstrated, designing culturally relevant tools—from software programs down to survey instruments— will be a trying but important area of future MOOC research.

origin and non-English primary language, regardless of current country of residence

Acknowledgements

We thank all the study participants that shared their time, learning experiences, and other feedback. We also thank Google for their support in this and related research through a Google Focus Award.

References

[1] A. Agarwal, "Online universities: it's time for teachers to join the revolution | Education | The Observer," The Guardian, p. 1, 2013.

[2] G. Christensen, A. Steinmetz, B. Alcorn, A. Bennett, D. Woods, and E. J. Emanuel, "The MOOC Phenomenon: Who Takes Massive Open Online Courses and Why?," SSRN Electron. J., Nov. 2013.

[3] M. Weber. "Thoughts on Digital Equity: Justin Reich." Harvard Graduate School of Education. 14 November 2011. Accessed 11 November 2013.

[4] S. F. Reardon, "The Widening Academic Achievement Gap Between the Rich and the Poor: New Evidence and Possible Explanations Sean F. Reardon," no. July, 2011.

[5] National Center for Education Statistics. (2013). The Nation's Report Card: Trends in Academic Progress 2012. New Directions for Youth Development (Vol. 2013, pp. 1–57). Washington, D.C. doi:10.1002/yd.20075

[6] S. Helme and S. Lamb, "Closing the gap clearinghouse Closing the school completion gap for," no. 6, pp. 1–15, 2011.

[7] M. Zhou, "Language Policy and Illiteracy in Ethnic Minority Communities in China," J. Multiling. Multicult. Dev., vol. 21, no. 2, pp. 129–148, Mar. 2000.

[8] M. Luciak, "Minority schooling and intercultural education: a comparison of recent developments in the old and new EU member states," Intercult. Educ., vol. 17, no. 1, pp. 73–80, Mar. 2006.

[9] B. S. Okun and D. Friedlander, "Educational stratification among Arabs and Jews in Israel: historical disadvantage, discrimination, and opportunity.," Popul. Stud. (NY)., vol. 59, no. 2, pp. 163–80, Jul. 2005.

[10] Hansen, J., & Reich, J. (2014). Socioeconomic Status and MOOC Enrollment: Enriching Demographic Information with External Datasets. In Learning Analytics and Knowledge Conference (pp. 1–10).

[11] T. Dillahunt, B. Chen, and S. Teasley, "Model Thinking": Demographics and Performance of MOOC Students Unable to Afford a Formal Education," in Learning @ Scale, 2014, pp. 145–146.

[12] B. R. J. Barro and J. Lee, "International data on educational attainment": updates and implications," vol. 3, pp. 541–563, 2001.

[13] Hoffmeyer-Zlotnik, J. H. P., & Eds, J. A. H. (2005). Methodological Aspects in Cross-National Research (pp. 1–305). Manheim, Germany: Zuma.

[14] "The Integrated Postsecondary Education Data System." [Online]. Available: http://nces.ed.gov/ipeds/reic/definitions.asp [Accessed: 08-Jan-2015].

[15] "MacArthur SES & Health Network | Research." [Online]. Available: http://www.macses.ucsf.edu/research/socialenviron/economic.php. [Accessed: 08-Jan-2015].

Does Online Q&A Activity Vary Based on Topic: A Comparison of Technical and Non-technical Stack Exchange Forums

Saif Ahmed
George Mason University
5400 Nguyen Engineering Building, MS 1G8
Fairfax, VA 22030 USA
sahmed36@gmu.edu

Seungwon Yang
George Mason University
5400 Nguyen Engineering Building, MS 1G8
Fairfax, VA 22030 USA
syang20@gmu.edu

Aditya Johri
George Mason University
5400 Nguyen Engineering Building, MS 1G8
Fairfax, VA 22030 USA
ajohri3@gmu.edu

L@S 2015, Mar 14-18, 2015, Vancouver, BC, Canada
ACM 978-1-4503-3411-2/15/03.
http://dx.doi.org/10.1145/2724660.2728701

Abstract

With the increasing demand on knowledge sharing and problem solving, there is a growing participation on online Question & Answer (Q&A) forums in the recent past. We classify the online community participation on Stack Exchange into two different genres, one is technical and another is non-technical. Though several studies have measured community activity, studies that compare activity across forums within different topic areas are limited. In this work we examine the effect of incentives on contributions by exploring the differences between technical and non-technical communities in terms of user's participation. Given the increased attention on discussion forums as part of online learning, especially MOOCs, we believe that our findings can assist with providing better support for learners across different content areas.

Author Keywords

Technical, Non-technical, online community, activity, Stack Exchange, Q&A forum

ACM Classification Keywords

H.3.5. Online Information Services: *Web-based services*.

Introduction

Over the past decade, there has been an emergence of online Q&A forums – a place where people talk about their problem and interest, pose questions and receive answers or comments from others. Networks like Yahoo-Answers, Stack Exchange, Quora are the popular sites for this purpose. Among all of the current networks with diversified question and answer archive, Stack Exchange (SE) is one of the most widely used platforms for both experts and newcomers. Initially, it was only a computer programming Q&A network which is Stack Overflow (SO), started in 2008, later it expanded additional sites following the SO model on various topics and become even larger and spontaneous. In SE there are few categorical classifications like *technology, culture/recreation, life/arts, and science* etc., which cover around 130 different topics. These forums can be categorized into technical (largely professional or problem based) and non-technical (largely hobbyists or interest based), depending on the discussion topic and user participation [6]. Studies of user motivation and activity within the community demonstrate that a few highly active users are responsible for the majority of participation and overall users can be characterized as lurkers, help-seekers (askers) and givers (responders) [4]. In a recent study [2], authors studied the user activity of SE network, particularly from content creation perspective. They studied around 36 SE forums to analyze the user activity in terms of Q&A, user longevity, and impact of reputation award process. They report that, in this sort of community most of the questions and answers are done by a small number of people. Also, some other works like [1, 3] studied the quantitative and qualitative analysis of user interaction and behavior on participating any topic discussion in SO - the largest technical community of SE. In [1], authors found that, the probability of a response being chosen as the best one, depends on temporal characteristics of its arrivals, like response speed which could be applicable to predict long-term value of a post. Besides, the other work [3] shows that, successfully of being answered about expert topic is not only because of the technical design, but also the regular involvement of design team of that community.

In our work we wish to study these two types of forums to understand the activity across topics to understand any variations. We want to investigate the effectiveness of one-size-fits-all discussion forums versus diverse support. This work, we believe, has implications for online learning particular through platforms such as MOOCs.

Method and Preliminary Results

To perform our study, we used SE public dataset which contains the updated data for the entire network. Almost each of the forum under SE has a different starting time, and we have data from that specific time to July-August 2014, for those corresponding forums. We started our experiment on two instances of the categories that we assume, code-review forum (CR) [5] as technical instance and bicycle forum (BC) [5] as non-technical one. We chose these two for our experiment as both these community has similar site age, almost 4 years. BC started in August 2010, and CR started in January 2011. In order to match the time frame for analysis in Figures 1 and 2, we did not include the first five months of data from BC. We further cleaned the data by removing records with missing values and inconsistencies. Our final dataset included 46,656 posts from CR and 18,798 posts from

BC. Since we were interested primarily in user participation, after removing users who never posted we had 14,551 users from CR and 4,047 users from BC.

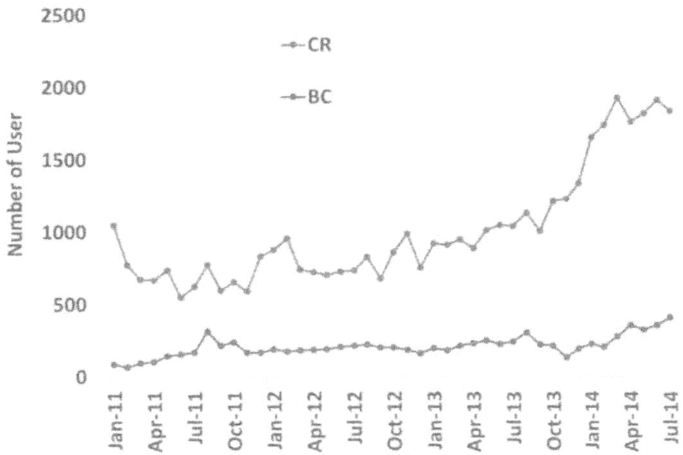

Figure 1. User registration trajectories of CR and BC forums.

Initially we analyzed some basic statistics such as a total number of posts (Q&A) by time, number of users registered and its trajectory, user who ever posted a question or answer, user activity against number of posts etc. In Figure 1 and 2 we see how number of users increases over the time, distribution of user activity and how these users contribute in terms of asking, responding and editing, throughout the site age, respectively.

Though CR started later than BC, in the registration trajectory it shows the increasing number of user registration. Also this tendency matches the increase in the user activities in Figure 2.

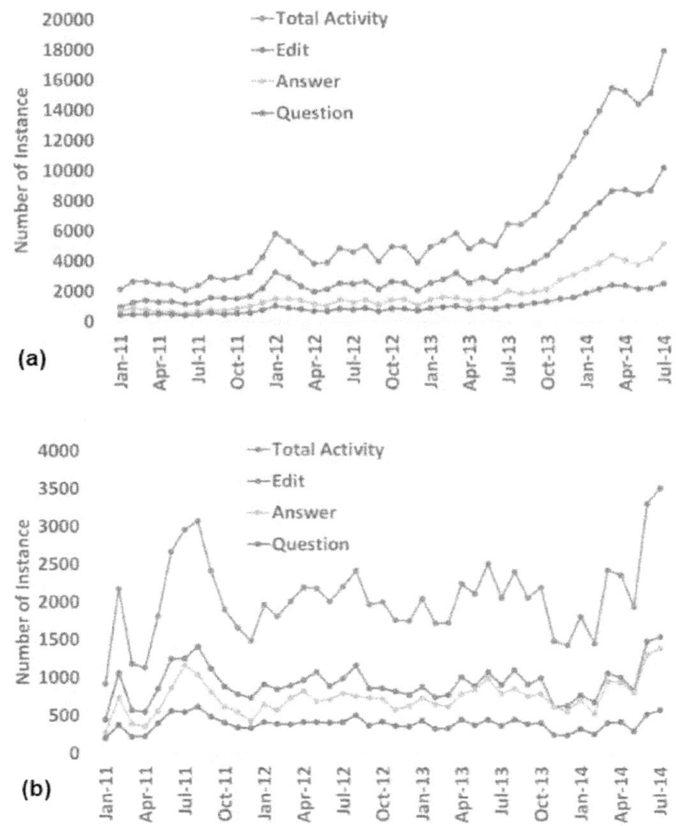

Figure 2. Distribution of user activity of (a) CR and (b) BC forum

We considered the entire dataset and grouped by asker and responder for each forum, aimed to see the percentage of user based on their questioning and answering activity. For that we calculated the both percentages of users ever posted a question and an answer for each forum with respect to the number of users who ever posted either a question or an answer. For those, who posted at least one question we got 66.74% and 55.56%; on the other hand, 44.45% and 60.17% of users answered at least once, respectively, for CR and BC. Figure 3 shows the number of asker and responder percentage by their post activity.

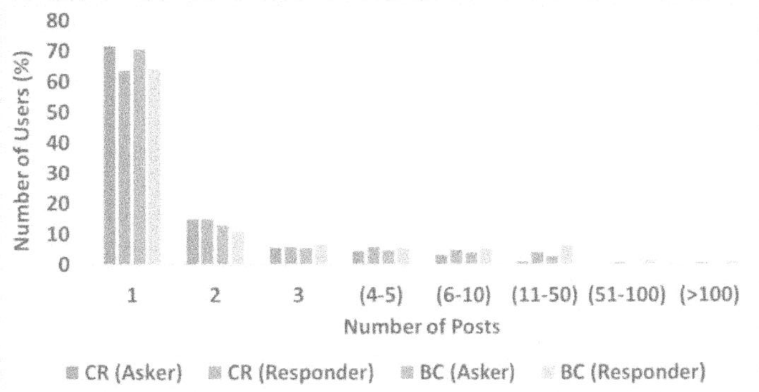

Figure 3. The percentage of the number of user posts (both questions and answers).

In both forums, more than 60% of users only posted a single question or answer. To be able to take a deep look we decided to set a post threshold for our further analysis. We filtered our data for each forum by selecting users who posted (question or answer) more than once. Considering responder as *source* and asker as *target* node, we created a node and an edge list and afterwards, a directed edged graph for each forum where an edge is directed from a responder node to the asker node.

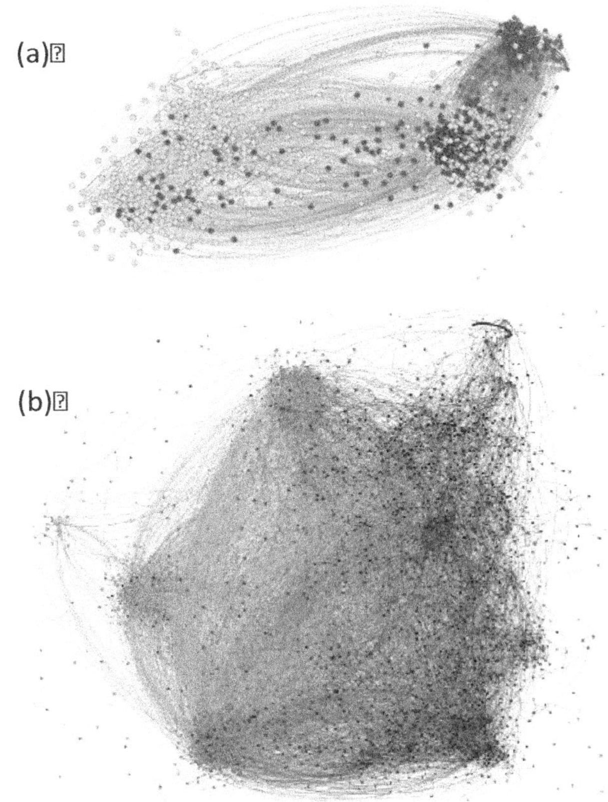

Figure 4. OpenOrd layout for (a) BC and (b) CR forum.

We used Gephi visualization toolkit [8] to develop such an asker-responder based graph using OpenOrd [7] layout which is a multi-level, force-directed layout and uses average-link clustering based on both edge weights and distance between nodes which is determined using a force-directed algorithm [7]. In the

	CR	BC
Modularity	0.523	0.367
Number of sub-communities	306	50
Number of tags	1,317	809
Correlation (#answer, reputation)	0.971	0.965
Correlation (#answer, #question)	0.160	0.319

Table 1. Comparison between CR and BC

cluster that emerges the intra-cluster distance and inter-cluster distance might vary community to community based on the number of edges associated with a specific node. This layout aims to highlight clusters of strongly connected nodes.

Applying OpenOrd in asker-responder network we got the layouts illustrated in Figure 4(a) and 4(b) for BC and CR respectively. After this, we computed the modularity – a metric to measure how well a network decomposes into sub-networks and the number of sub-networks (or communities) in each of CR and BC (See Table 1). It is to be noted that, a community with high modularity has dense connection between the nodes within sub-community and sparse connection between nodes in different sub-community [9]. In Figures 4(a) and 4(b) we see more sub-communities in CR than BC. Visually, nodes within the sub-communities in BC do not appear to be connected strongly compared to CR.

To motivate users to voluntarily contribute, SE uses a reputation system which roughly measures how much the community trusts any of its users. Basically, a user can gain reputation by posting useful questions and answers. We found strong correlation between number of answers given and reputation score achieved by a user which is quite similar for both the forums (See Table 1). There was a small correlation between the number of answers and questions given by a user, it was smaller in CR than BC.

Discussion and Limitations

Though BC started before CR, we observe an increasing rate of registration in CR lately; whereas the registration rate in BC is rather stable. The recent increase of activities in CR is due to the increase of users registered for CR (Figure 1). In Figure 2, the rate of edits and answers are similar with each other in BC. However, the rate of edits is higher than that of answers in CR. A possible reason for this difference in CR may originate from the fact that the CR forum is curated more frequently by the community members considering that the questions and answers in CR require much higher accuracy.

Moreover, for further interpretation on Figure 4, we observe that CR has more number of sub-communities than BC (Table 1). This is probably because the number of topics discussed in CR is higher than those in BC. The fact that the number of tags in BC is only 61.5% of that in CR further supports our assumption (Table 1).

Since the modularity score of CR is higher than that of BC, the members in the sub-communities of CR are more tightly connected with each other than those in the sub-communities of BC. We assume that the users in CR are rather interested in specific topics and thus forming tight sub-communities; however, those in BC are interested in more diverse topics in various aspects of bicycles in general.

The work has several limitations at this time. In order to match the time frame of analysis for both forums in Figures 1 and 2, we did not include the initial 5 months of the data from BC. Therefore, we could not illustrate the activities when BC was started. Regarding the activities in the forum, we did not consider 'edit' behaviors so far even though edit activities contributed in the reputation score of users. We will consider edit activities in our follow-up study.

Conclusion and Future Work

In this study we examined the different characteristics of two forums, CR and BC, from Stack Exchange. CR can be considered as technical, and BC as non-technical. We found several differences in the characteristics of the two forums. The first is that the number of registered users in CR has increased almost exponentially in the latest months, and it may have led to the recent increase in the activities in CR. In the case of BC, both the registration rate and the number of activities are rather stable. Another difference is that CR might be curated more frequently than BC. The number of topics in each forum may also have contributed to the different number of sub-communities. In addition, the users in CR seem to be interested in specific topics (tighter sub-communities); whereas those in BC might have diverse topical interest (looser sub-communities).

The distinct characteristics of users in technical and non-technical forums found from this study may be transferred to other online communities and MOOCs. It is our hope that this study may provide insights to the authorities of online Q&A communities and MOOCs to improve their services that might make these communities flourish and be more useful.

As our future study, we plan to continue this work in a deep approach by applying K-means clustering method to the activity data on the entire Stack Exchange forums to examine their similarities and differences in the user activities and in the social network dynamics.

Acknowledgements

This work is partly based upon research supported by U.S. National Science Foundation (NSF) Award#DUE-1444277 & EEC-1408674. Any opinions, recommendations, findings, or conclusions expressed in this material are those of the author(s) and do not necessarily reflect the views of NSF.

References

[1] Anderson, A., Huttenlocher, D. P., Kleinberg, J. M., and Leskovec, J. Discovering value from community activity on focused question answering sites: a case study of Stack Overflow. In *Proc. KDD 2012*, ACM press, 850–858.

[2] Sinha, V. S., Mani, S., and Gupta, M. Exploring activeness of users in QA forums. In *Proceedings of the Tenth International Workshop on Mining Software Repositories 2013*, IEEE Press, 77-80.

[3] Mamykina, L. and Manoim, B. and Mittal, M. and Hripcsak, G. and Hartmann, B. Design Lessons from the Fastest Q&A Site in the West. *CHI 2011*. ACM Press.

[4] Teo, H. J. and Johri, A. Fast, functional, and fitting: expert response dynamics and response quality in an online newcomer help forum. In *Proc. CSCW 2014*, ACM press, 332-341.

[5] Stack Exchange sites. http://stackexchange.com/sites#traffic

[6] Lampe, C., Wash, R., Velasquez, A., and Ozkaya, E. Motivations to Participate in Online Communities. In *Proc. CHI 2010*. ACM Press, 1927-1936.

[7] Martin, S., Brown, W.M., Klavans, R., & Boyack, K.W. OpenOrd: An open-source toolbox for large graph layout. Paper *presented at the Conference on Visualization and Data Analysis, 2011.*

[8] Gephi - The Open Graph Viz Platform http://gephi.github.io/

[9] Modularity (networks) http://en.wikipedia.org/wiki/Modularity_(networks)

Clustering-Based Active Learning for CPSGrader

Garvit Juniwal
UC Berkeley
garvitjuniwal@eecs.berkeley.edu

Alexandre Donzé
UC Berkeley
donze@eecs.berkeley.edu

Sakshi Jain
UC Berkeley
sakshi.jain@eecs.berkeley.edu

Sanjit A. Seshia
UC Berkeley
sseshia@eecs.berkeley.edu

L@S 2015, Mar 14-18, 2015, Vancouver, BC, Canada
ACM 978-1-4503-3411-2/15/03
http://dx.doi.org/10.1145/2724660.2728702

Abstract
In this work, we propose and evaluate an active learning algorithm in context of CPSGrader, an automatic grading and feedback generation tool for laboratory-based courses in the area of cyber-physical systems. CPSGrader detects the presence of certain classes of mistakes using *test benches* that are generated in part via machine learning from solutions that have the fault and those that do not (positive and negative examples). We develop a clustering-based active learning technique that selects from a large database of unlabeled solutions, a small number of reference solutions for the expert to label that will be used as training data. The goal is to achieve better accuracy of fault identification with fewer reference solutions as compared to random selection. We demonstrate the effectiveness of our algorithm using data obtained from an on-campus laboratory-based course at UC Berkeley.

Author Keywords
Auto-Grading; MOOC; Embedded/Cyber-Physical Systems; Active Learning; Dynamic Time Warping; Density-Based Spatial Clustering of Applications with Noise

Figure 1: Cal Climber laboratory platform.

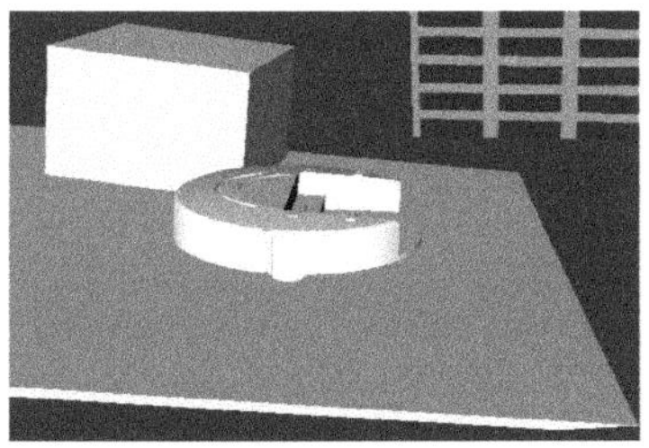

Figure 2: Cal Climber in the LabVIEW Robotics Environment Simulator.

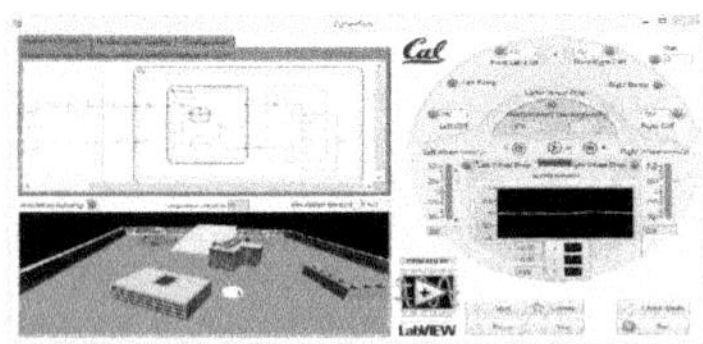

Figure 3: Simulator with auto-grading functionality used in EECS 149.1x.

ACM Classification Keywords
K.3.2 [Computers and Education]: Computer and Information Science Education; I.2.6 [Artificial Intelligence]: Learning.

Introduction and Background
CPSGrader [4, 1] is a virtual lab automatic grading system designed for courses in cyber-physical systems and robotics. An example of such a course is the *Introduction to Embedded Systems* at UC Berkeley and its online counterpart on edX [5], in which students program the Cal Climber (Fig. 1) robot to perform certain navigation tasks like obstacle avoidance and hill climbing. Students can prototype their controller to work within a simulated environment based on the LabVIEW Robotics Environment Simulator by National Instruments (Fig. 2, Fig. 3.) The dynamical model for the virtual lab is complex and CPSGrader employs simulation-based verification, the only scalable approach. Correctness and the presence of certain classes of mistakes are both checked using *test benches* formalized in *Signal Temporal Logic* (STL) [6], and these test benches are generated in part via machine learning from solutions that have the fault (positive examples) and those that do not (negative examples). In machine learning terminology, this can be thought of as the *training* phase. The resulting test bench then becomes the *classifier* that determines whether a student solution is correct, and, if not, which fault is present. CPSGrader was used successfully in the edX course EECS149.1x offered in 2014.

An issue with this approach is the availability of "positive" and "negative" reference controllers. An instructor has to manually look at the simulation video to decide whether a particular controller is good or bad and then it can be used for training the test bench. In essence, labeling of controllers is an expensive manual process. In this work, we formulate the problem of obtaining labeled data as an active learning problem. We give a clustering-based active learning methodology that takes as input a large set of unlabeled controllers and chooses the controllers that an instructor should label. We believe clustering is useful because amongst many student solutions, the total number solution strategies are still few. We show that selection of training examples based on clustering leads to higher accuracy of classification as compared to random selection of the same number of training examples, and therefore it can lead to reduced overhead for instructors in providing labeled data.

Approach
Test benches in CPSGrader are generated by machine learning from positive and negative labeled reference solutions (*training data*) [4]. We use this as a black box *training* module TRAIN. A synthesized test bench then is used by a *classification* module CLASSIFY that can label new solutions as being faulty or not.

Active Learning [10] is a form of machine learning where the learning algorithm is able to interactively query the user to get the correct labels for new data points. Our active learning technique is described in Algorithm 1. The algorithm works iteratively by using clustering to select the controllers to be added to the training data and using the training module TRAIN at each step. TRAIN first generates a classifier based on some sets of training controllers. Depending on the results of the classifier, the controllers labeled as 0 and 1 are separately clustered by a clustering module CLUSTER. Using the clusters formed, the selection module SELECT chooses new controllers to get correct labels for. Balance of the number of positive and negative examples is important for TRAIN to work well, hence, SELECT attempts to choose few representatives from each cluster accounting for the balance at the same time. All the selected controllers that were incorrectly labeled by the classifier are now added to the training set and the classifier is trained again. This continues until no fresh training data is added.

We use *dynamic time warping* (DTW) distance [2] as a measure of dissimilarity between controller behavior and density-based spatial clustering for applications with noise (DBSCAN) [9] as the clustering technique. We choose multi-dimensional DTW distance as a measure of dissimilarity between controller behavior since DTW can capture similarities in timed sequence even if matching patterns occur at shifted/scaled positions in time. We use DBSCAN as the clustering technique since it can work with pair-wise distances between data points (instead of requiring full knowledge of feature vectors) and also does not require the number of clusters to the specified in advance. More details of this approach can be found in [3].

Preliminary Results

The experimental evaluation is done using a collection of solutions implemented by 50 groups of students in the Fall 2013 instance of EECS 149 at UC Berkeley. We evaluate the iterative synthesis algorithm (referred to as ISYN in the rest of the section) by comparing it against the technique RANDOM where we randomly choose the training set and show that ISYN can obtain higher overall accuracy, with a smaller size of training set used.

Algorithm 1: ITERATIVESYNTHESIS

Input: A dataset of student solutions $\mathcal{D}$, a true labeling oracle $\mathcal{O}$, and a test template γ with untuned parameters corresponding to some fault

Output: A classifier Γ for $\mathcal{D}$

```
C+, C- ← ∅
repeat
    Γ ← TRAIN(γ, C+, C-)
    D0, D1 ← CLASSIFY(Γ, D)
    θ0, θ1 ← CLUSTER(D0), CLUSTER(D1)
    R0, R1 ← SELECT(θ0), SELECT(θ1)
    C+_Δ = {C s.t. (C ∈ R0 ∧ O(C) = with_fault)}
    C+ = C+ ∪ C+_Δ
    C-_Δ = {C s.t. (C ∈ R1 ∧ O(C) = without_fault)}
    C- = C- ∪ C-_Δ
until C+_Δ or C-_Δ is empty
return (Γ(p), ρ)
```

For each fault, we train the test bench using both ISYN and RANDOM and then test the accuracy of the obtained test bench on a disjoint set of solutions. To simplify the comparison, we set the upper bound on the number of training instances used in both techniques as 30. In some cases, ISYN may terminate with less than 30 examples in the training set if the clustering algorithm is not able to find enough number of clusters. To compare accuracy we note the True Positive Rate (TPR), True Negative Rate (TNR), and F-score for both techniques in Table 1. The F-score is individually higher in case of ISYN than RANDOM for all the faults except avoid_left, thus leading to the conclusion that ISYN leads to better accuracy of classification than RANDOM for equal or lesser size of training set. For the fault avoid_right, we see that ISYN performs significantly better than RANDOM for positive examples but worse for negative examples. The reason is that ISYN ends up selecting only 13 (30 being the upper bound) training examples because CLUSTER cannot find enough number of clusters.

Related Work DTW has been previously used for classification of temporal sequences of video, audio, and graphics data [8], using an algorithm similar to k-nearest neighbours [7]. Active learning is a popular methodology for cases where obtaining training data is expensive [10]. We have not seen past work that applies clustering based strategies for active learning.

References

[1] Donzé, A., Juniwal, G., Jensen, J. C., and Seshia, S. A. CPSGrader website. http://www.cpsgrader.org.

[2] Giorgino, T. Computing and visualizing dynamic time warping alignments in R: The DTW package. *Journal of Statistical Software 31*, 7 (8 2009), 1–24.

[3] Juniwal, G. CPSGrader: Auto-grading and feedback generation for cyber-physical systems education. Master's thesis, EECS Department, University of California, Berkeley, Dec 2014.

[4] Juniwal, G., Donzé, A., Jensen, J. C., and Seshia, S. A. CPSGrader: Synthesizing temporal logic testers for auto-grading an embedded systems laboratory. In *Proceedings of the 14th International Conference on Embedded Software (EMSOFT)* (October 2014).

[5] Lee, E. A., Seshia, S. A., and Jensen, J. C. Eecs149.1x cyber-physical systems. https://www.edx.org/course/uc-berkeleyx/uc-berkeleyx-eecs149-1x-cyber-physical-1629.

[6] Maler, O., and Nickovic, D. Monitoring temporal properties of continuous signals. In *FORMATS/FTRTFT* (2004), 152–166.

[7] Mitsa, T. *Temporal Data Mining (Chapter 3)*, 1st ed. Chapman & Hall/CRC, 2010.

[8] Ratanamahatana, C. A., and Keogh, E. Making time-series classification more accurate using learned constraints. SIAM (2004).

[9] Sander, J., Ester, M., Kriegel, H.-P., and Xu, X. Density-based clustering in spatial databases: The algorithm gdbscan and its applications. *Data Mining and Knowledge Discovery 2*, 2 (1998), 169–194.

[10] Settles, B. Active learning literature survey. *University of Wisconsin, Madison 52* (2010), 55–66.

Test Bench	Training Set Size		TPR		TNR		F-score	
	RANDOM	ISYN	RANDOM	ISYN	RANDOM	ISYN	RANDOM	ISYN
avoid_front	23/133 + 7/74	15/133 + 15/74	133/133	133/133	67/74	70/74	0.97	0.99
avoid_left	23/164 + 7/45	15/164 + 15/45	164/164	164/164	42/45	39/45	0.99	0.98
circle	1/7 + 29/200	3/7 + 11/200	0/7	6/7	200/200	193/200	0.00	0.60
hill_climb($\beta = B$)	26/427 + 4/63	14/427 + 16/63	427/427	427/427	55/63	60/63	0.99	1.00
hill_climb($\beta = M$)	28/442 + 2/48	29/442 + 1/48	442/442	442/442	11/48	18/48	0.96	0.97
avoid_right	24/169 + 6/40	10/169 + 3/40	70/169	169/169	40/40	26/40	0.59	0.96

Table 1: Comparison of ISYN and RANDOM. Training Set Size denotes the (number of positive examples selected in the training set)/(total number of positive examples in data set) + (number of negative examples selected in the training set)/(total number of negative examples in the data set). TPR is the true positive rate of the trained classifier. TNR is the true negative rate.

Learning Experiments Using AB Testing at Scale

Christopher Chudzicki
Department of Physics
Massachusetts Institute of Technology
77 Massachusetts Avenue.
Cambridge, MA 54321 USA
chudzick@mit.edu

Zhongzhou Chen
Department of Physics
Massachusetts Institute of Technology
77 Massachusetts Avenue.
Cambridge, MA 54321 USA
zchen22@mit.edu

David E. Pritchard
Department of Physics
Massachusetts Institute of Technology
77 Massachusetts Avenue.
Cambridge, MA 54321 USA
dpritch@mit.edu

L@S 2015, March 14–18, 2015, Vancouver, BC, Canada.
ACM 978-1-4503-3411-2/15/03.
http://dx.doi.org/10.1145/2724660.2728703

Abstract

We report the one of the first applications of treatment/control group learning experiments in MOOCs. We have compared the efficacy of deliberate practice—practicing a key procedure repetitively—with traditional practice on "whole problems". Evaluating the learning using traditional whole problems we find that traditional practice outperforms drag and drop, which in turn outperforms multiple choice. In addition, we measured the amount of learning that occurs during a pretest administered in a MOOC environment that transfers to the same question if placed on the posttest. We place a limit on the amount of such transfer, which suggests that this type of learning effect is very weak compared to the learning observed throughout the entire course.

Introduction

The most trustworthy inferences in a complex domain like medicine or education are drawn from experiments comparing outcomes in treatment and control groups that are randomly selected from the same population. Reliability is then largely dependent on statistical uncertainty implying that large samples can support conclusions with greater certainty and/or on smaller effects. Thus treatment/control experiments (A/B experiments) in MOOCs (Massive Open Online Courses) can leverage the large number of students to study small effects such as learning from particular

The 8.MReVx MOOC is designed for those with existing knowledge of Newtonian mechanics. It concentrates on problem-solving and uses a pedagogy called Modeling Applied to Problem Solving [5].

The 2014 iteration of 8.MReVx contains 12 weeks of material, generally a single unit that contains instruction material, homework, and weekly quiz. There is a pre-test given on the first week of the course, and a post-test given at the end of the course. Most graded problems in the course allow multiple attempts, open response homework problems typically allowed 10 attempts, except only ~3 on tests. Multiple choice problems had appropriately fewer attempts also. We had ~11,000 participants in the course, with just over 500 receiving certificates.

interventions. We will discuss preliminary analysis of two of the seven A/B experiments we've done.

AB Experiments in MOOCs

The edX platform has the ability to implement A/B experiments [1] in which the user population is partitioned into two or more groups and each group is given a different version of course material. Some important aspects of edX AB experiments are:

- All students who elect to take the MOOC are randomly assigned to two or more groups that receive different instructional resources for a given experiment.
- The outcomes are evaluated by giving the same questions to both groups after the instruction is completed.

We report here the preliminary results on two of our seven experiments.

Experiment 1: Deliberate Practice and Interactive Problem Format

Introduction:

The goal of this study is to see if we could design new types of online homework problems that are more effective in developing problem solving abilities. Our design is based on two related ideas: deliberate practice and cognitive load theory. Work by Ericsson in the 1990s [2] showed that deliberate practice—characterized by a singular focus on elementary skills (procedures), repetition, immediate feedback, and self-reflection—was especially important for the development of expertise. In addition, cognitive load theory [3], [4] suggests that enhanced learning is achieved by reducing extraneous cognitive load, freeing the learner's working memory to focus on the most salient aspects of the activities. The edX platform provides a chance to design new, more intuitive problem formats with rapid feedback that follow those principles much better than traditional homework.

This experiment uses three groups to answer two separate but related questions. First, we investigate whether deliberate practice activities can build physics expertise more efficiently than traditional practice involving traditional whole problems. Second, we vary the problem format of the deliberate practice activities, comparing the common multiple-choice problems with informationally equivalent "drag-and-drop" problems that minimizes the extraneous cognitive load of multiple-choice incurred by having to match each choice item with the problem body.

Methods:

Students are randomly assigned to three groups (A, B, or C) which receive one of three different treatments during each of three successive graded units (10, 11, and 12) of our MOOC (8.MReVx on the edX.org platform). The control treatment is traditional (TRD) "whole problem" homework problems; the two variations of the deliberate practice activities differ only in format (multiple choice, MC, vs drag-and-drop, DD). In order to treat all participants in our study equally, the treatment assigned to each group rotates between units. For example, Group C received the TRD problems in Unit 10, deliberate practice problems in the DD format during Unit 11, and deliberate practice problems in the MC format during Unit 12.

A common quiz is given to all three groups together with the homework. The quiz consists of traditional problems only (mostly numeric/symbolic response).

The Traditional Problems
are a mix of conceptual and symbolic problems that mirrohomework in a standard physics course.

The Deliberate Practice
problems consisted of short problems targeting specific skills used in solving whole problems. Because each deliberate practice problem takes a shorter amount of time, we are able to include 4 times as many problems, while taking roughly the same total time for students to complete.

Multiple Choice vs. Drag-and-Drop
We created two versions of the deliberate practice treatment. One version (MC) uses the standard multiple-choice (MC) problem formats while The second version (DD) uses edX's drag-and-drop (DD) problem format which is much more interactive and should reduce extraneous cognitive load.

	Unit 10				Unit 11				Unit 12				Total		Differences			
Treatment	Group	N	mean	sd	Group	N	mean	sd	Group	N	mean	sd	mean	se	mean	sd	Z-score	*p*-value
DD	A	78	61%	23%	C	72	47%	22%	A	87	59%	22%	55.7%	1.5%				
MC	B	71	56%	24%	B	64	43%	24%	C	103	61%	20%	53.3%	1.5%	2.3%	2.1%	1.106	0.27
TRD	C	70	62%	23%	A	69	47%	23%	B	90	65%	18%	58.0%	1.4%	−4.7%	2.1%	−2.219	0.026
															2.3%	2.1%	1.137	0.26

Table 1. First attempt correct rates for each treatment group on the problems they attempted are shown in the "mean" columns for each unit; rates averaged over all three units are shown in the "Total" section. The "Differences" section shows the difference between each row and the one above it, except for the last row, which shows the difference between the DD and the TRD treatment.

Analysis:
In order to guarantee that the users we consider interacted with the treatment homework to a significant extent, we restrict our attention to only those who completed at least 70% of the treatment homework and at least 70% of the common quiz. Because the vast majority of users completed either very little or almost all of the activities in these units, our results are relatively insensitive to the particular cut-off used. This cut-off leaves a total of 219 students for Unit 10, 205 students for Unit 11, and 280 students for Unit 12.

The average percentage correct for each group on each week is shown in Table 1.

The data suggest that TRD instruction was more effective than deliberate practice in the MC format ($p=0.026$). No conclusive statement can be made based on these data about the relative efficacy of deliberate practice in the DD format vs. the other instructional methods.

Experiment 2: Pre-Post Test Transfer
Introduction:
The most straightforward method to evaluate overall learning in a course is to administer the same test to students before and after instruction (generally at the beginning and end of the course, as in this study.) This study is designed to answer the question of whether exposure to the problems in the pre-test will enhance students' performance on those same problems on the post test. This is a particularly germane question in a MOOC, because unlike in an on-campus paper test, students are informed whether their answer is correct and given multiple attempts to get it right, hence most (>90%) answer correctly and benefit from the positive feedback.

Study Setup:
Figure 1 shows the balanced design for the pre/post-test transfer experiment. The idea is that the two randomly selected groups, A and B, receive identical post-tests, but each receives a pretest with a different subset of post-test problems. If students do learn and transfer from the problems they did on the pre-test, then we should observe that user group A would have an advantage on the set of items unique to pre-test version A and vice versa.

The post-test contained fifteen problems with 23 separate questions. Post-test problems can be grouped into four item categories according to which group saw the items on the pre-test: Two problems (3 edX items, Q1–Q3) appeared only on pre-test version A. Two problems (4 edX items, Q4–Q7) appeared only on pre-test version B Nine problems (12 edX input fields, Q8–Q19) appeared on both pre-test versions A and B. Two problems (4 edX input fields, Q20–Q23) were unique to the post-test.

Users were allowed multiple attempts (usually 2–4, each with right/wrong feedback) on the pre/post-test questions and were not penalized for using multiple attempts. The pre-test was permanently hidden from students after the second week of instruction.

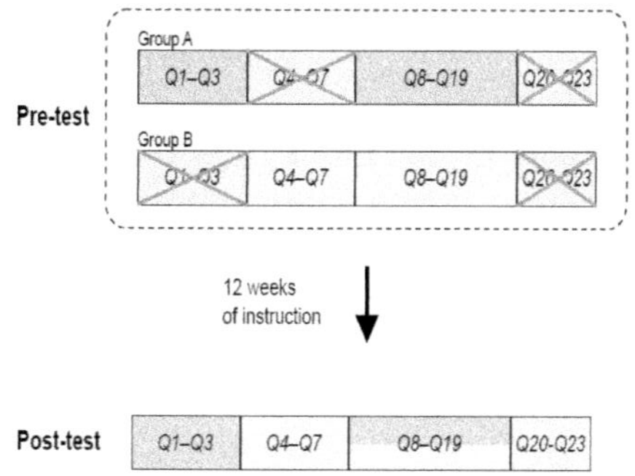

Figure 1. Setup for the pre/post-test memory experiment.

Analysis and Discussion:

A total of 516 users attempted the post-test. On average, users attempted 85% of problems on the post-test. Each user was assigned to either version A or version B of the pre-test, but not all of these 516 users completed the pre-test. Analysis is complicated by the fact that the A group scores higher than the B group even on the problems that only the B group saw on their pre-test. Correcting for this reduces the apparent superiority of the A group over the B group on the problems that only the A group saw on their pretest to statistical insignificance - except on the second problem where the B groups scores significantly lower than the A group, and lower than the significantly less skillful N-group (that didn't take the prettest). This suggests that the low score of the B group on the second item is a statistical anomaly. Thus it appears that there is no significant evidence for a memory effect on the post test.

Therefore our experiment shows no significant enhancement of post-test scores due to the fact that students were given multiple attempts to obtain the correct answer to the same questions on the pretest. This is good news for those who administer pre-post testing in a MOOC environment and wish to argue that this procedure achieves comparable results to in-class on-paper testing in which the answer is not divulged on either pre or post test.

This is a work in progress, with more in depth data-analysis being performed for these experiments as well as five other experiments. Additional A/B experiments are currently being conducted in our other MOOC.

Acknowledgements:

We are grateful to Google, MIT, and NSF for supporting our research (but not our conclusions).

References

[1] "edX Documentation: Creating Content Experiments." [Online]. Available: http://edx.readthedocs.org/projects/edx-partner-course-staff/en/latest/content_experiments/index.html.

[2] K. A. Ericsson, R. T. Krampe, C. Tesch-romer, C. Ashworth, G. Carey, J. Grassia, R. Hastie, S. Heizmann, R. Kellogg, R. Levin, C. Lewis, W. Oliver, P. Poison, R. Rehder, K. Schlesinger, and V. Schneider, "The Role of Deliberate Practice in the Acquisition of Expert Performance," *Psychol. Rev.*, vol. 100, no. 3, pp. 363–406, 1993.

[3] J. Sweller, "Cognitive load during problem solving: Effects on learning," *Cogn. Sci.*, vol. 12, no. 2, pp. 257–285, Jun. 1988.

[4] J. Sweller, P. Ayres, and S. Kalyuga, *Cognitive Load Theory*. New York, NY: Springer New York, 2011.

[5] A. Pawl, A. Barrantes, D. E. Pritchard, M. Sabella, C. Henderson, and C. Singh, "Modeling Applied to Problem Solving," 2009, pp. 51–54.

Using and Designing Platforms for In Vivo Educational Experiments

Joseph Jay Williams
HarvardX, Harvard University
Joseph_jay_williams@harvard.edu

Korinn Ostrow
Worcester Polytechnic Institute
kostrow@wpi.edu

Xiaolu Xiong
Worcester Polytechnic Institute
xxiong@wpi.edu

Elena Glassman
MIT
eglassman@mit.edu

Juho Kim
MIT
juhokim@mit.edu

Samuel G. Maldonado
San Jose State University
Samuel.g.maldonado@gmail.com

Na Li
Harvard University
nali01@fas.harvard.edu

Justin Reich
HarvardX, Harvard University
Justin_reich@harvard.edu

Neil Heffernan
Worcester Polytechnic Intstitute
nth@wpi.edu

L@S 2015, March 14-18, 2015, Vancouver, BC, Canada.
ACM 978-1-4503-3411-2/15/03.
http://dx.doi.org/10.1145/2724660.2728704

Abstract
In contrast to typical laboratory experiments, the everyday use of online educational resources by large populations and the prevalence of software infrastructure for A/B testing leads us to consider how platforms can embed *in vivo* experiments that do not merely support research, but ensure practical improvements to their educational components. Examples are presented of randomized experimental comparisons conducted by subsets of the authors in three widely used online educational platforms – Khan Academy, edX, and ASSISTments. We suggest design principles for platform technology to support randomized experiments that lead to practical improvements – enabling *Iterative Improvement* and *Collaborative Work* – and explain the benefit of their implementation by WPI co-authors in the ASSISTments platform.

Author Keywords
Intelligent tutoring system; MOOC; randomized controlled trial; A/B testing; crowdsourcing; collaborative work

ACM Classification Keywords
H.4 Information Systems Applications; H.5 Information interfaces and presentation; K.3.1 Computer Uses in Education; J.4 Social and Behavioral Sciences

Introduction

Although the concept of A/B testing is widely known [Kohavi et al, 2009], using A/B testing to improve the content and interaction dynamics of educational resources like lessons and exercises is a relatively recent development in MOOCs. edX only released A/B testing of educational content this year, while it is still under development for Coursera.

EXAMPLES OF A/B EXPERIMENTS IN KHAN ACADEMY, EDX, AND ASSISTMENTS

Examples are presented of how to conduct experiments in the platforms Khan Academy, EdX, and ASSISTments. These have been actually implemented by one or more of the co-authors. These provide context about the platform as well as insight into what kinds of variables can be manipulated and how randomization is implemented.

We then use this cross-platform comparison to elucidate two design principles that we propose platforms should support, and explain the benefits of designing ASSISTments to achieve these. These are *Iterative Improvement* and *Collaborative Work*. *Iterative Improvement* means the educational content can be repeatedly improved using the results of experiments and affordances of the technology. *Collaborative Work* refers to whether there is support for remote, asynchronous collaboration from diverse people looking at same resource, sharing insights and providing feedback on what any individual produces.

1. Khan Academy

Khan Academy makes available a documented open source framework for copying and creating new versions of math exercises. Any exercise at www.khanacademy.org/exercisedashboard can be downloaded as a single HTML file and then modified – to change the statement of the problem, the hints provided. An A/B test can then be performed that randomly assigns students to any version of the exercise with a weighted probability.

One example of a study conducted in collaboration with Khan Academy involved adding reflective question prompts above mathematics exercises which prompted students to explain while solving problems. The text was "clickable" so that when students clicked on it, new questions would appear. The original HTML file for the interactive exercise was simply copied, and then additional text and HTML code added into the copy. Four different versions of the exercise (with different questions) were created. These four files were then provided to Khan Academy, which used a weighted function to randomly assign participants to each kind of exercise whenever they visited it.

2. EdX

www.EdX.org is a platform for Massive Open Online Courses (MOOCs). A/B Testing or Content experiments in EdX involves declaring groups of participants (which must all be equal sized) and then inserting a component that can assign participants in different groups to different components.

The experiment conducted presented three different versions of an introductory motivational video to a MOOC. The first was spoken by the instructor for the course and emphasized specific steps students could take to keep themselves engaged and successful. The second was spoken by the instructor and was very positive and encouraging about their likely success, but did not provide specifics. The third had the exact same script from the first video - with specific steps students could take – but was spoken by *another* instructor. This allowed for measuring the effect of these different videos on subsequent behavior in the course.

3. ASSISTments

Any problem set or problem available on the ASSISTments platform can be copied via a button click into any user's own folder of exercises. It can then be modified using a WYSIWYG interface – changing not only hint text, but also what kind of targeted feedback is given for incorrect answers, and what problems are provided in subsequent attempts.

Any problem set can be copied and revised to create multiple versions, which are then nested within a Choose Condition problem set that randomly assigns participants to either version with equal probability. Because problem sets can be nested within problem sets, A/B testing can take place at several levels. However, it is less straightforward to link user information from one point in time to determine assigned condition at another point.

The ease with which A/B testing can be implemented within ASSISTments is highlighted by a study that was performed in only three weeks, from conception to data analysis and paper submission. Ostrow & Heffernan [2014] established an experimental design in which tutoring feedback on errors in a problem was provided as a video or as text. The benefits of this feedback on the subsequent problems of the same kind were assessed.

ITERATIVE IMPROVEMENT

One of the key strengths of online resources is that they can be constantly updated and changed. Yet many platforms do not leverage this capacity to its full potential, or make it easy for continual editing and improvement of existing resources. For example, a large proportion of MOOCs are only slightly modified once produced, yet resources like Wikipedia are repeatedly edited and improved by an impressive crowd. Figure 1 shows the extent to which each of the three platforms support the design goal of Iterative Improvement.

ASSISTments supports Iterative Improvement because it provides a large library of existing exercises, and any lesson or interactive exercise within ASSISTments (shared via URL or ID) can be copied and modified using a WYSIWYG editor from a browser.

One way in which this has supported successive improvements was having a group of teachers look at 50 exercises from the library and create new hints and feedback them, just using their web browser and with no programming experience. These are now being tested in an ongoing experiment, and if shown to be effective, will be directly incorporated simply by clicking a button.

COLLABORATIVE WORK

As extensive practical and research development in the field of crowdsourcing has revealed, one of the most powerful features of the Internet is that by collapsing typical spatial, temporal, and social barriers and distances between people, it leverages large and

Iterative Improvement			
	Khan Academy	EdX	ASSISTments
Library of Existing Reusable & Modifiable Components	Yes	- Not accessible prior to course launch without instructor provision. - Reuse of materials with permission of original instructor (and possibly institution)	Yes
Ease of Copying & Modifying	- Must download & initiate open source exercise framework - Must know HTML	- Must first be invited as staff of target course - WYSIWYG editor in EdX Studio	- Online WYSIWYG editor, regularly used by teachers with no programming knowledge
Mechanism for Replacing Existing Content	- Must first request pull from platform team for code review - Then a straightforward change to A/B test	- Must first be granted role as staff for course - Then a straightforward change to A/B test	- Straightforward change to A/B test made by user - Must then email platform for data collection
Availability of Participants & Data for Repeated Iterations	Yes - Each component is in continual use by new participants	No - Each component can be used once in MOOC offering; cycle delays until MOOC is offered again	Yes - Each component is used by teachers who assign it to their classes
Collaborative Development			
	Khan Academy	EdX	ASSISTments
Availability of Authoring Functionality	- Open Source exercise framework downloaded locally and used with knowledge of HTML	- Must be invited as staff of target course by institution in Consortium or approved for edge.edx.org. - Cloud-based WYSIWYG functionality.	- Instant cloud-based WYSIWYG authoring tool
Affordances for Sharing Modifications & Eliciting Feedback	- Share hyperlinks to real demos via Internet server, and request feedback through typical channels (email, phone, in person)	- Cloud-based sharing of hyperlinks to real demos provided to those added as course beta users; request typical feedback. - Solicit direct duplication or modifications using WYSIWYG authoring tool from those added as course staff.	- Cloud-based sharing of hyperlinks to real demos provided to anyone. - Solicit direct duplication or modifications using WYSIWYG authoring tool from anyone with ASSISTments account. - "Public Shared Folder" for all ASSISTments users
Proposals for A/B Tests & Access to Data	- Through central platform team - External collaborations uncommon, but competition was held in April	- Cooperation of instructor required for both access & implementation	- Via platform team; submission process funded by NSF grant
Freedom to Run A/B Tests with Personal User Group	No - Only exercise authoring	Yes - Direct user group to MOOC, or re-implement course on edge.edx.org	Yes - All content copied to one's folder can then be assigned to all student users.

diverse minds interacting through technology to make substantive improvements. Figure 1 shows how the platforms bring such strengths to bear, by supporting collaborative work on randomized experiments.

ASSISTments is designed so any user to share an exercise with any other user - not just a live demo, but the actual ability to copy and then modify an exercise.

This has facilitated over 10 external collaborations using ASSISTments directly between WPI and external researchers, bringing together diverse expertise in the studies conducted and resources created. In a Graduate course, 16 students were also able to form into teams of 4 and work collaboratively in person and asynchronously on designing experiments. They used the platform to receive direct feedback in the form of actual edits from the course instructor, a teaching assistant, and an actual math teacher.

An NSF Cyberlearning grant was awarded to WPI to support external researchers from multiple disciplines in proposing experiments to be run on the platform. In the period October through December, 2 complete studies were conducted and 4 are in progress, without any face-to-face meetings.

References

[1] Kohavi, R., Longbotham, R., Sommerfield, D., & Henne, R. M. (2009). Controlled experiments on the web: survey and practical guide. *Data Mining and Knowledge Discovery*, *18*(1), 140-181.

[2] Heffernan, N. & Heffernan, C. The ASSISTments Ecosystem: Building a platform that brings scientists and teachers together for minimally invasive research on human learning and teaching. *International Journal of Artificial Intelligence in Education*. (2014).

Supporting Instructors in Collaborating with Researchers using MOOClets

Joseph Jay Williams
Harvard University, HarvardX
125 Mt. Auburn St Rm. 422
Cambridge, MA 02138 USA
Joseph_jay_williams@harvard.edu

Juho Kim
MIT CSAIL
32 Vassar Street, 32-G707
Cambridge, MA, 02139
juhokim@mit.edu

Brian C. Keegan
Harvard University
430 Morgan Hall, Soldier's Field Rd.
Harvard, MA, 02138 USA
bkeegan@gmail.com

L@S 2015, Mar 14-18, 2015, Vancouver, BC, Canada
ACM 978-1-4503-3411-2/15/03.
http://dx.doi.org/10.1145/2724660.2728705

Abstract
Most education and workplace learning takes place in classroom contexts far removed from laboratories or field sites with special arrangements for scientific research. But digital online resources provide a novel opportunity for large-scale efforts to bridge the real-world and laboratory settings which support data collection and randomized A/B experiments comparing different versions of content or interactions [2]. However, there are substantial technological and practical barriers in aligning instructors and researchers to use learning technologies like blended lessons/exercises & MOOCs as both a service for students and a realistic context to conduct research. This paper explains how the concept of a "MOOClet" can facilitate research-practitioner collaborations. MOOClets [3] are defined as modular components of a digital resource that can be implemented in technology to: (1) allow modification to create multiple versions, (2) allow experimental comparison and personalization of different versions, (3) reliably specify what data are collected. We suggest a framework in which instructors specify what kinds of changes to lessons, exercises, and emails they would be willing to adopt, and what data they will collect and make available. Researchers can then: (1) specify or design experiments that compare the effects of different versions on quantifiable outcomes. (2) Explore algorithms for maximizing

Author Keywords
Collaborative work; experiment; MOOClet; education

ACM Classification Keywords
H.4 Information Systems Applications; H.5 Information interfaces and presentation; K.3.1 Computer Uses in Education; J.4 Social and Behavioral Sciences

particular outcomes by choosing alternative versions of a MOOClet based on the input variables available. We present a prototype survey tool for instructors intended to facilitate practitioner-researcher matches and successful collaborations.

Introduction
Whether in MOOCs or classrooms, many of the key affordances of digital resources have yet to be exploited in a way that simultaneously benefits instructors and researchers. This omission is striking since even the simple switch from an "offline" resource like pen-and-paper assignments and spoken lectures to online interactive exercises and webpages has the potential to change how practitioners and researchers in education interact. When implemented appropriately, detailed behavioral and user data can be collected from randomized experiments that compare the quantifiable educational benefits of different versions [3].

Digital resources can be further used to solicit feedback from diverse experts on concrete products (just by emailing a URL), and multiple versions rapidly created for comparison, personalization, and perpetual improvement. Researchers and teaching teams could mutually benefit from collaboration [4], via integration of research more directly into the development and modification of course materials.

Barriers to Instructor-Researcher Collaboration
Unfortunately, both instructors and researchers note that existing technology does not surmount many barriers to mutually beneficial collaboration. Several are listed below. These are synthesized from: A series of cross-disciplinary academic symposia and workshops; Discussions and structured interviews with MOOC instructional teams at Berkeley, Stanford, and Harvard; and our own work implementing research within the platforms EdX, Coursera, NovoEd, Khan Academy, Moodle, and ASSISTments.

1. Insufficient shared context to collaborate on aligning practical and scientific goals in concrete terms.
2. Difficulty in specifying and visualizing a vast set of potential modifications to educational materials.
3. Technical opacity in the affordances of platforms and development requirements for changes, exacerbated by risk averseness to bugs/glitches and high-pressure deadlines.
4. The challenge of scoping collaborative development rather than relinquishing editorial control over an entire course, or requiring substantial time to meetings.
4. Limited short-term payoffs for students in courses versus long-term benefit to research.
6. Difficulty understanding what data is collected and when it is available for analysis by scientists, and correspondingly instructors are uncertain about what personal participant data is shared and how to judge its ethicalness.

Focusing collaboration around Experimental Comparisons within 'MOOClets'
Drawing on our previously mentioned collaborative work, we explain the formal definition of a 'MOOClet' [2] as a user-facing modular sub-component of an online or blended educational platform (e.g. a video, lesson, exercise, assignment, email, interactive study tool [1]) that can be authored, personalized, instrumented and experimentally varied, without requiring integration with underlying website architecture. The concept of a MOOClet is accompanied

by a software design pattern for implementation across many platforms [2], a workflow for deciding details of a collaborative study, and a prototype interactive online rubric that instructors and researchers can use together to productively focus their discussion.

Modularity. Instead of discussions as the course level, discussions are targeted at potential modifications and data collection from modular components of educational experiences that are present in most courses regardless of goal and topic. Examples considered in past work [1] are exercises, quizzes, motivational videos, email reminders and suggestions, and lessons and interactive tools for practicing better study strategies.

Flexible yet abstract technical implementation. The design pattern for a MOOClet's definition and implementation in [2] provides guarantees to both researchers and instructors. Any component of a resource implemented as a MOOClet can have multiple versions created, and these can be experimentally compared yet dynamically adjusted by instructors to present preferred versions. The data collected in a MOOClet is pushed in real-time to a User Variable Store with differential privacy access, anonymity, but transparency about which variables are there and what their values are. Researchers therefore know what outcome variables and covariates are being collected, and can verify this information student-by-student as MOOClets are used.

We have shown [2] that most components of an online course or MOOC can be 'MOOCletized'. For example, any lesson, video, exercise, or email in EdX and Moodle. Researchers can conduct experimental comparisons of whatever different versions of a MOOClet they can creatively design, covering a broad range of potential levers for behavior, like adding or changing text, restructuring a lesson, including additional reflective questions [1].

Align Experimentation & Personalization. Moreover, MOOClets provide a mathematically formalization of how A/B experiments are equivalent to personalized delivery of different versions of a resource. The different versions of a MOOClet can be personalized based on any variables in the User Variable Store that come from outside sources of other MOOClets. This aligns a key behavioral science methodology of experimentation with work on intelligent tutoring systems and machine learning and artificial intelligence algorithms for adaptive presentation and recommendation of content, and application of classifiers or predictors to structured data. In addition, it aligns research efforts with a core instructional goal for digital technologies – providing individualized instruction. This approach has been taken in embedding experiments in K-12 math exercises on Khan Academy, videos on EdX, and teacher and medical professional development on NovoEd and Moodle [1].

Experimental comparisons support practical evaluation of alternative designs *and* test alternative hypotheses. Researcher-practitioner alignment and collaboration is enabled by collaboratively designing experimental comparisons of different versions of MOOClets. These versions contain both practical design alternatives of instructional interest [3] *and* experimental contrasts designed to test alternative hypotheses about how people learn and interact with technology.

Scoping modifiable course components.
By focusing on just a few modular components of a course, instructors can be confident about will and won't be changed. They can know what data is being collected about students.

Components of the Tool

The tool and examples of questions can be seen at http://tiny.cc/moocletcollaboration.

The questions in the tool are designed to elicit instructors and researchers respective beliefs about: (1) What quantifiable measures they want to improve, what kind of behaviors students engage in, and what data will be collected. (2) What modular components of the course instructors are interested in or opening to having modified and multiple versions experimented with or personalized, and so what experimental conditions researchers can design. E.g., homework exercises, text documents.

An example of a question included is "What components of the course would you like to improve? Or are you open to having modified?". All questions have both a free response open field – to get rich qualitative feedback and personal responses – as well as a list of options which is dynamically updated using responses of instructors.

To imagine one use case: Designers of an online course may care about a specific outcome, such as increasing retention. Findings from the psychology literature may point to appropriate metrics for measuring engagement as well as potential interventions to adopt [1]. The set of interventions might include additional advice videos from the instructor on the landing page or dashboard, messages embedded above exercises, or email reminders [3]. Measures of engagement might include self-reported mind-wandering, time spent on a page, and number of attempts made on a difficult problem.

References

[1] Williams, J. J., Maldonado, S., Williams, B. A., Rutherford-Quach, S., & Heffernan, N. (2015). How can digital online educational resources be used to bridge experimental research and practical applications? Embedding In Vivo Experiments in "MOOClets". *Paper to be presented at the Spring 2015 Conference of the Society for Research on Educational Effectiveness, Washington, D. C.*

[2] Williams, J. J., Li, N, Kim, J., Whitehill, J., Maldonado, S., Pechenizkiy, M., Chu, L., & Heffernan, N. (under review). *The MOOClet Framework: Improving Online Education through Experimentation and Personalization of Modules*. Tiny.cc/moocletframework

[3] Williams, J.J. & Williams, B. A. (2013). Using Randomized Experiments as a Methodological and Conceptual Tool for improving the Design of Online Learning Environments. *Paper presented at the Data Driven Education Workshop at the Conference on Neural Information Processing Systems.*

Wuchty, S., Jones, B. F., & Uzzi, B. (2007). The increasing dominance of teams in production of knowledge. *Science, 316*(5827), 1036-1039.

Viz-R: Using Recency to Improve Student and Domain Models

Ilya Goldin
Center for Digital Data,
Analytics & Adaptive Learning
Pearson
ilya.goldin@pearson.com

April Galyardt
University of Georgia
Dept. of Ed. Psych.
Athens, GA 30605
galyardt@uga.edu

L@S 2015, March 14–18, 2015, Vancouver, BC, Canada.
ACM 978-1-4503-3411-2/15/03.
http://dx.doi.org/10.1145/2724660.2728706

Abstract
We describe a new method to troubleshoot and improve domain and student models from interactive learning environments. The method is a visualization of model predictions, categorized using a metric of recent performance. It is a general method that applies to any model which generates binary predictions. We describe the method, its application in prior work to student models, and a proposed extension to domain models.

Introduction
Adaptive and intelligent learning environments include models of the domain and of student performance[5]. The purpose of a domain model is to represent what students should learn. The purpose of a student model is to characterize past student behavior and predict future behavior. Traditionally a concern of intelligent tutoring systems, refinement of student and domain models will become more salient to MOOCs as they adopt adaptivity and personalization. The refinement of the domain and student models are ever-present issues in any such learning environment. As an example, in the Assistments tutoring system for mathematics in grades K-12[3], the domain model includes a tagging of math problems by the skills that they require for successful practice. The Skill Builder feature of Assistments, which is designed for mastery learning, uses the predictive student model that a

NOTATION

j	KC index
i	student index
t	practice opportunity index
X_{ijt}	$= \begin{cases} 0 & \text{if incorrect} \\ 1 & \text{if correct} \end{cases}$
p_{ijt}	$= Pr(X_{ijt} = 1)$

$$R_{ijt} = \frac{\sum_{p=-2}^{t-1} d^{(t-p)} X_{ijp}}{\sum_{p=-2}^{t-1} d^{(t-p)}} \quad (1)$$

When $d = 0.7$:
$R \in [0, 0.3]$ indicates few successes in recent history.
$R \in (0.3, 0.5]$ indicates 2 correct answers in the last 3-4 attempts.
$R \in (0.5, 0.7]$ implies that the most recent 2 answers were correct.
$R \in (0.7, 1]$ means that at least the last 3 answers were correct.

continuous "streak" of problems solved correctly implies the student will also answer subsequent items correctly, i.e., that the student has mastered the skill.

Our work in progress is a new method to diagnose and refine domain and student models based on data from regular student usage. This technique applies to any domain and student model that makes predictions of student behavior. The more student data, the more robust the expectation of improvement. We first describe the technique in general, and second, illustrate how we used it in prior work to compare two student models. Third, we propose a new application of the method to compare domain models.

The Viz-R Method

This work leverages our prior work on R-PFA, a predictive model of student performance [2]. First, we have developed a metric that has an appealing, psychologically sound interpretation, is simple to compute mathematically, and that contains a great deal of information for predicting future performance. This metric is R, a recency-weighted proportion of successes by a student on a skill. Second, we found that the metric is useful not only as a predictor in the R-PFA model, but also as a lens for comparing R-PFA to an alternative model in a visualization. We propose that R and this visualization can be used to diagnose any predictive student and domain model. We call this the Viz-R method.

Viz-R illustrates the relationship between two models' predictions of whether or not a student will correctly respond on their next opportunity, $\hat{p}_{ijt}$ and $\hat{p}'_{ijt}$. However, it adds information that a contingency table alone would not reveal, not just what proportion of the time do the two models agree or disagree, but when do they agree and disagree? Does one model have more false positives, and the other more false negatives? Does the probability of a correct response increase as R increases?

False positive and false negative errors may have differential significance in different contexts. For example, a false prediction that a student has not mastered a skill may lead to requiring the student to practice the skill more than necessary. This is undesirable, but it may be even worse to make a false prediction that a student has mastered a skill, because this may prevent the student from having an opportunity to master the skill.

Using Viz-R to Understand a Student Model

Applying Viz-R to R-PFA and the comparison model PFA [4] showed two main differences between the models[2]. First, R-PFA outperformed PFA at predicting an incorrect response when the student had had few recent successes. Second, R-PFA outperformed PFA at predicting a correct response after multiple recent successes (i.e., at discounting evidence from irrelevant old failures).

Using Viz-R to Understand a Domain Model

We expect that the same approach can be used for domain models. There are two reasons to believe this should be successful.

First, because a domain model can be incorporated in a predictive student model, we expect an improvement in the fidelity of a domain representation to correspond to an improvement in predictive accuracy. This is the intuition behind methods such as Learning Factors Analysis (LFA) [1], which seeks out problem sequences that are tagged with a single skill but may entail multiple underlying skills. It uses the heuristic that when increased practice on a skill is not associated with an increase in subsequent successful outcomes, the skill tagging may be wrong. The intuition is not perfect, because valid distinctions in a domain model may be obscured by instruction and assessment. However, if predictive accuracy does improve, it is sensible to expect that the change in a domain model captures an important aspect of learning in the domain.

Second, Viz-R allows us to constrain the search for domain model problems with greater specificity. Thus R and its visualization may shed light on a domain model, beyond LFAs heuristic of looking for flat slopes.

For example, suppose that R is high, i.e., most of a students recent answers were correct, and that the predictive student model (incorporating the domain model) yields a false positive, i.e., wrongly predicts that the student will answer a subsequent question correctly. One cause for the false positive may be a slip, i.e., answering incorrectly even when the skill is mastered. However, another cause may be that mastery of previous questions does not entail a correct answer to the current one, i.e., a skill tagging that should be split. If multiple students have such a false-positive prediction for this question when their R is high, incorrect skill tagging is a highly plausible explanation.

Reasoning in this vein, there may be multiple opportunities to detect domain model issues. For instance, a false negative when R is low and the skill is relatively difficult may also indicate a question that has an inappropriate skill tagging.

Once we modify the skill tagging, we can retrain the predictive model, obtain a new set of predictions, and compare the predictions in a comparative visualization (fig 1). We can then examine the predictive "wins" and "losses" to make sure that these are sensible.

Conclusion

We have found the Viz-R method to be a powerful tool to investigate pros and cons of a student model and to compare one model to another. We expect that the method will apply to domain models as well. Nonetheless, even though the method enjoys strong face validity and one successful application, we have not yet evaluated how well the method generalizes to multiple datasets from varied data-generating learning environments. At the same time, the method might even apply generally to model diagnostics beyond the educational setting, and to multiple categorical outcomes. This is especially important for use cases where the predictors and model structure must interpretable. In future work, we plan to expand the Viz-R suite of visualizations to facilitate scalable and actionable model diagnostics.

References

[1] Cen, H., Koedinger, K., and Junker, B. Learning factors analysis – a general method for cognitive model evaluation and improvement. In *Proc of 8th ITS Conf of 8th ITS Conference* (2006), 164–175.

[2] Galyardt, A., and Goldin, I. M. Recent-performance factors analysis, Under Review.

[3] Heffernan, N. T., and Heffernan, C. L. The ASSISTments ecosystem. *IJAIE 24*, 4 (Dec. 2014), 470–497.

[4] Pavlik, P. I., Cen, H., and Koedinger, K. Performance factors analysis –a new alternative to knowledge tracing. In *Proceedings of AIED*, IOS Press (2009), 531–538.

[5] Woolf, B. P. *Building Intelligent Interactive Tutors: Student-centered strategies for revolutionizing e-learning*, 1 edition ed. Morgan Kaufmann, July 2010.

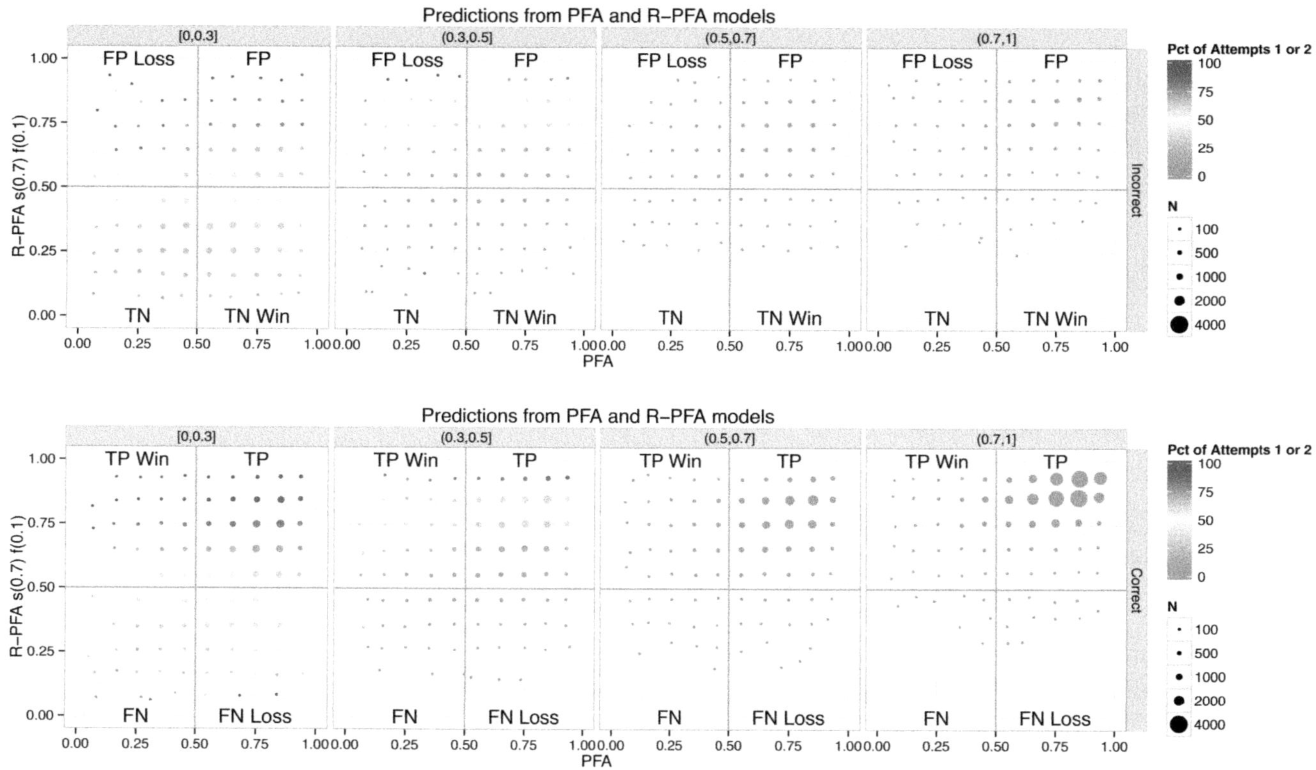

Figure 1. PFA vs. R-PFA predictions in terms of the $\hat{p} = \hat{P}(X_{ij} = 1)$ value from the logistic model. The bubbles display $\hat{p}$ values from the two logistic models; the more data points there are near that (x, y) position, the bigger the bubble. The color of the bubble indicates the percentage attempts in that position that are 1st or 2nd attempts by a student on a particular skill. The two rows of the figure correspond to actually incorrect (top) and actually correct (bottom) outcomes. Each row is divided into 4 facets according to the value of the R predictor. The closer $\hat{p}$ is to the boundary values of 1.0 or 0.0, the more confident the model is in the prediction. The abbreviations are: TP - true positive, FP - false positive, TN - true negative, FN - false negative. Win and loss are for R-PFA relative to PFA. A $\hat{p} > 0.5$ is a prediction of a correct outcome, and $\hat{p} < 0.5$ is a prediction of an incorrect outcome.

Learning the Features Used To Decide How to Teach

Min Hyung Lee
Carnegie Mellon University
5000 Forbes Ave
Pittsburgh PA 15213 USA
minhyunl@andrew.cmu.edu

Zhuoying Wang
Carnegie Mellon University
5000 Forbes Ave
Pittsburgh PA 15213 USA
zhuoyinw@andrew.cmu.edu

Joe Runde
Carnegie Mellon University
5000 Forbes Ave
Pittsburgh PA 15213 USA
jrunde@andrew.cmu.edu

Emma Brunskill
Carnegie Mellon University
5000 Forbes Ave
Pittsburgh PA 15213 USA
ebrun@cs.cmu.edu

Warfa Jibril
Carnegie Mellon University
5000 Forbes Ave
Pittsburgh PA 15213 USA
wjibril@andrew.cmu.edu

L@S 2015, Mar 14-18, 2015, Vancouver, BC, Canada
ACM 978-1-4503-3411-2/15/03.
http://dx.doi.org/10.1145/2724660.2728707

Abstract
As a step towards scaling personalized instruction, we seek to automatically identify the key features of the interactive learning process teachers use to select the next activity when teaching a single student. Such features could both inform computational student models designed to facilitate instructional decisions, and help enable automated self-improving teaching systems that leverage this identified feature set. We present preliminary results that a very small set of features is almost as good as a much larger set of features at predicting human tutor decisions when teaching students about histograms.

Introduction
Massive open online classes (MOOCs) are transforming access to education, enabling 1 or a few teaching staff to teach hundreds of thousands. However, as small teacher-to-students ratios can lead to substantial learning benefits (see e.g. Bloom [1]), scalable methods for providing students with more personalized instruction are of significant interest. Though peers and alumni are important resources (and provide an often important social component), both groups may have fewer insights into how to effectively teach the material. Therefore it would also be welcome to provide automated assistance of quality similar or exceeding an expert teacher. As a step towards this, we consider how to identify which dynamic

student features can be used to automatically predict the pedagogical activities selected by teachers.

Understanding the features used by experts to make instructional decisions is important for multiple reasons. First, the vast majority of computational student models focus on predicting the performance of a student. With few exceptions (e.g. [5]) little attention has been paid to creating student models explicitly designed to consider their impact on instruction. Indeed, that is the second key potential benefit: that armed with the knowledge of what features are used by expert teachers to select among pedagogical activities for a student, we could create automated methods to find highly effective instructional policies. Here we use the word policy to indicate a mapping from features about the student learning process to which next activity to give to the student. Reinforcement learning algorithms could help learn such policies from data, but to learn good policies typically requires an amount of data that scales prohibitively (from polynomially to exponentially) with the number of features used to describe the current state of the process. If expert teachers use only a small set of features, considering policies that only depend on such features could substantially reduce the amount of data required to find policies that meet or exceed human teacher performance.

One natural approach would be to directly ask teachers both what features they use when teaching. Unfortunately research from cognitive task analysis [2] suggests that experts may frequently fail to verbally specify all of the information they are using to make task decisions. To get at such information often requires additional effort beyond the interactions a teacher would normally have with students. Therefore it remains of use to directly infer features from existing data. A second issue is that the available data may be from good but imperfect teachers. Therefore we may not wish to be restricted to the specific policy provided by the teachers, and may wish to consider other policies that condition on the same feature set used by teachers.

Approach and Preliminary Results

Our approach follows recent exciting work on abstraction from demonstration [3]. The key idea of is to take demonstrations of a human user doing a task, infer the features of the task used by the human to make his or her decisions, and then perform reinforcement learning given those features in the task. Cobo et al. [3] demonstrated a small number of trajectories of humans playing simple video games was sufficient to identify a small set of features used by the players to make their decisions. The authors then used reinforcement learning with those features to efficiently learn a policy that well surpassed human performance.

We tried this approach in an education context, for a module about histograms. Our materials were developed as extensions of the Statway curriculum that was itself designed to help community college remedial math students.We selected this area given the enormous audience for remedial math, the rising workplace demand for statistics, and the documented challenge many students find when learning about histograms [4]. Our activities and assessments were designed to address some of the core learning objectives about histograms that are also often commonly misunderstood [4].

In our initial experiment we got data from 6 students. The student interacted directly with the computer for the test and activities. Each student took a pretest, then a human tutor hand selected an activity for the student, the student completed that activity, and then the human tutor selected a next activity based on what he or she observed about the student's performance on the tutor. This interaction was repeated until the human tutor thought the student had mastered the material (or no more practice activities were available) and then the student completed a post test. There was no additional assistance given by the human tutor to the student beyond specifying the next activity (or post test) to do, in order to best mimic the type of interaction a student would have with an automated (computerized) tutor.

Following the abstraction from demonstration approach, we then built a decision tree classifier to predict which activity type the human tutor would select for the student. The activities were classified into different learning objectives about histograms, as well as taking the post test. The classifier was provided with a large set of possibly relevant features about the teaching interaction, including the number of items completed about each learning objective, the type of the last done item, the amount of time spent so far, the amount of time spent on the last item, the student's pretest score, if the last item was completed correctly on the first try, and a number of other features. We then tried removing each feature and re-estimated the cross-validated accuracy at predicting the activity type selected by the teacher. We removed the feature that had the smallest negative cost on the overall accuracy, and then again tried removing each of the remaining features. We repeated this procedure until removing any further features resulted in a cross-validated performance accuracy of less than 95% of the maximal accuracy obtained during this removal process: we observed overfitting occurred when using the full feature set, and so the highest performance occurred with a subset of the features.

Though we started with over 50 features, we found that just four features were sufficient to achieve 64.5% accuracy student cross-validated accuracy (e.g. hold data from one student out as a test set and use the other students data to train, and repeat), which was within 95% of the best observed accuracy of 67%. The 4 features selected were: total time spent so far, the learning objective type of the activity the student just finished, how long of a time gap the student had between practicing the previous previous learning objective, and how many total times the student has practiced an activity about defining the center, spread and shape of a histogram.

Though this analysis is preliminary, it still reveals some interesting potential findings. One, the selected features do not depend on the student's performance (in terms of correctness or number of attempts). Indeed, prior work suggests that some teachers may mostly follow a fixed curriculum rather than adapting to a particular student (see summary in [6]). Second, a very small number of features could predict almost as well as the full set which is encouraging, since finding a good policy over this smaller set will generally require many less additional samples. This is important because each "sample" is a real student and may impact their learning.

Discussion

Our work on this is still in early stages and many open issues remain. One is that our classifier accuracy rates suggest that our human tutors may also be leveraging other features to make their instructional decisions (which would imply we should create a larger set of features to try to better capture human decisions) and/or that the different human tutors are either using different strategies or changing their strategies as they interact with more students. To better understand this, we may try to directly elicit feedback from teachers as to the features they consider when making pedagogical choices, as a way to augment features automatically identified.

Looking further, it could be interesting to see if other features beyond those used by human tutors are important to consider when selecting activities: indeed Van Lehn also suggests in his survey [6] that there is evidence that human teachers may be much less effective at building nuanced models of a student's state of knowledge and misconceptions, and such information may be relevant to producing the best policy. However, figuring out which features are important may again open up a much wider feature space which has implications for the speed of identifying a good policy. In our next steps we intend to first explore what instructional policies we can automatically learn using the limited features identified and how their performance compares to our human tutors.

Our proposed approach may be relevant to other domains and situations where a teacher is selecting among a relatively small amount of choices to best aid a student. However, if there are an enormous or unbounded space of options (such as if a teacher might ask a student to write a new essay on a completely new topic based on the student's previous essay) then it may be impossible or require an enormous amount of data to accurately predict a teacher's choices, and to infer the features relevant to those predictions.

To conclude, this is a step towards enabling human MOOC instructors demonstrate how to teach a few students directly, and use this data to identify features and learn a good policy that could be used to automatically provide personalized pathways to thousands of future students.

Acknowledgements

We thank Google for a focused research award and the study participants.

References

[1] Bloom, B. The 2 sigma problem: The search for methods of group instruction as effective as one-to-one tutoring. *Educational Researcher 13*, 6 (1984), 4–16.

[2] Clark, R. E., and Estes, F. Cognitive task analysis for training. *International Journal of Educational Research 25*, 5 (1996), 403–417.

[3] Cobo, L. C., Zang, P., Isbell Jr, C. L., and Thomaz, A. L. Automatic state abstraction from demonstration. In *IJCAI*, vol. 22 (2011).

[4] Kaplan, J. J., Gabrosek, J. G., Curtiss, P., and Malone, C. Investigating student understanding of histograms. *Journal of Statistics Education 22*, 2 (2014).

[5] Lee, J. I., and Brunskill, E. The impact on individualizing student models on necessary practice opportunities. In *EDM* (2012), 118–125.

[6] VanLehn, K. The relative effectiveness of human tutoring, intelligent tutoring systems, and other tutoring systems. *Educational Psychologist 46*, 4 (2011), 197–221.

Author Index

www.ingramcontent.com/pod-product-compliance
Ingram Content Group UK Ltd.
Pitfield, Milton Keynes, MK11 3LW, UK
UKHW051412290926
15471UKWH00009B/1559

9 781450 33513